Craig Claiborne's
The New York Times
FOOD
ENCYCLOPEDIA

Craig Claiborne's
The New York Times
FOOD
ENCYCLOPEDIA

WINGS BOOKS
New York • Avenel, New Jersey

This 1994 edition is published by Wings Books,
distributed by Random House Value Publishing, Inc.,
40 Engelhard Avenue, Avenel, New Jersey 07001,
by arrangement with Times Books, a division of Random House, Inc.

Random House
New York • Toronto • London • Sydney • Auckland

Printed and bound in the United States of America

Library of Congress Cataloging-in-Publication Data

Claiborne, Craig.
    [New York Times food encyclopedia]
    Craig Claiborne's The New York Times food encyclopedia / compiled by Joan Whitman.
        p. cm.
    Reprint. Originally published: New York : Times Books, c1985.
    Includes bibliographical references.
    ISBN 0-517-11906-4
    1. Food—Dictionaries. 2. Cookery—Dictionaries. I. Whitman,
Joan. II. Title. III. Title: New York Times food encyclopedia.
    TX349.C54 1994
    641'.03—dc20   94-10846
                                                                            CIP

8 7 6 5 4 3 2 1

*Dedicated to aristology, otherwise known as
the fine art of dining*

The primary requisite for writing well about food is a good appetite.

A. J. Liebling

Introduction

I cannot recall a time when I was not intrigued and infatuated with a study of words and their origins. I can trace that interest to my infancy when I was taught in kindergarten that the word "Monday" was related to the moon, "Thursday" to Thor, the god of thunder, "Saturday" to Saturn, "Sunday" to sun, and so on.

It was quite a case of serendipity, then, that I entered a profession in which, more than any other, I believe, words have a romantic association with the countless components with which I had to deal. Those components are the names of dishes served in restaurants and the ingredients used in the kitchen. Early in my career, I became closely associated with menu terminology, much of which is related to the names of composers, painters, writers, theater folk, royalty, operas, generals, admirals, battles, rogues, monks, nuns, and other assorted saints and sinners.

I learned that a piece of beef (specifically a tournedos or fillet) garnished with foie gras and truffles was named for the great composer Rossini. I learned that dishes containing cauliflower were quite often named du Barry, *crème du Barry*, for example, or cream of cauliflower soup (precisely why that vegetable was linked to the name of the courtesan who was the last mistress of Louis XV has never been made quite clear to me).

The names of many dishes on a menu are quite obvious. Those labeled *indienne*, for example, contain curry; those labeled *fines herbes* undoubtedly contain prized herbs including parsley, tarragon, chervil, and chives; while those marked *hongroise*, or Hungarian-style, almost always contain the national spice, paprika.

The history of certain names of one dish or another may be fairly well established or they may be obscure. Both Melba toast and pêches Melba were so christened because the great Australian coloratura stayed often at the Savoy Hotel in London and at that time Escoffier presided over the hotel's kitchen. He created the dishes in her honor.

One of my favorite foods is chicken or veal cutlets (salmon is also sometimes used) Pojarksi. It is made of ground meat with bread crumbs and cream, which is then shaped by hand to resemble chops. These are cooked in butter until golden brown. The name is said to derive from a tavern located, long before the Russian Revolution, in the small but prosperous town of Torjok on an old post road between Moscow and St. Petersburg. Travelers making the long journey would rest at the tavern while their carriage horses were changed. The veal cutlets were the masterpiece of the establishment and the chef's name was Pojarksi.

Many dishes bear place names and one can only speculate about their origins. The word Lyonnais indicates the presence of a great deal of onions in a dish; Florentine, spinach; and Argenteuil, asparagus. It is established that some of the finest asparagus in the world grows in Argenteuil, a town several kilometers northwest of Paris. It is not at all certain, however, that the city of Florence was ever noted for its spinach fields.

There is no denying that many chefs had a sense of humor when they named certain dishes. Thus, no one knows how many years ago lentil soup was christened—what else?—potage Esau. And as any French chef worth his salt knows, a macédoine of vegetables refers to the Macedonian empire. A literate schoolboy can tell you that the Macedonian empire consisted of many people of varied nations and races. And, thus, a putting together of numerous cubed vegetables, such as carrots and potatoes, string beans and peas, would be Macedonian-like. A macédoine. One of the most interesting legends about food—and many historians take it for absolute truth—relates to dishes named Marengo, the original of which was made with chicken. History has it that they were named for the battleground near the town of Marengo in Italy where Napoleon won a victory over the Austrians on June 14, 1800. The dishes called Marengo were so named for a dish created hastily shortly after the battle by Napoleon's chef. Legend has it that Napoleon was uncommonly hungry after that battle but rarely stayed more than a few minutes to consume any meal. The chef quickly scoured the countryside and came up with a chicken, tomatoes, olive oil, parsley, garlic, white wine, eggs, crayfish, and truffles. The chef sautéed the chicken, which was cut up, again according to legend, with a saber, in olive oil, cooked it in a tomato and garlic sauce, and garnished it with a fried egg, crayfish, and truffles.

Speaking of menu nomenclature, it is interesting to me how one bit of terminology can undergo a sea change. In France, the phrase *à la reine* has for more than a century indicated many dishes that are made with chicken. A cream of chicken soup is known as a *potage à la reine;* eggs *à la reine* would indicate that the eggs, poached or otherwise, are served on a bed of creamed chicken. And yet in America, we very often refer to creamed chicken dishes as such-and-such à la king!

I consider a cream of mussel soup, the one that is christened Billi Bi, to be one of the world's greatest. And I have no reason to doubt the authenticity of its naming. It is said that the president of the American Tin Plate Company, William Bateman

Leeds, Sr., during the late 1800s, favored Maxim's restaurant above all others in Paris. He dined there daily and almost invariably began his meal with a bowl of cream of mussel soup. Eventually the soup was listed on the menu with the tin tycoon's nickname.

The origins of the name of another dish, wholly American, is maddeningly unestablished. This is eggs Benedict. It may, according to some sources, have originated at Delmonico's restaurant, a legendary part of the New York scene in the Guilded Age. It was reputedly named for two of the establishment's regular customers, one Mr. and Mrs. Le Grand Benedict. Other sources have it that it was named for a Wall Street broker, Lemuel Benedict. I seriously doubt that posterity will ever know the truth.

During the course of the past quarter century as food editor of *The New York Times,* a host of other trivia about food has come my way that I have chosen to incorporate in this book. For example, I was delighted to learn a decade or so ago— thanks to the *Guinness Book of World Records*—that the longest word ever to occur in a literary work has to do with food, specifically a fricassee with seventeen sweet and sour ingredients. These include brains, honey, vinegar, a fish, pickles, and that anise-flavored drink known in Greek as ouzo. The word appeared in *The Ecclesiazusae,* a comedy written by Aristophanes in Greek more than two thousand years ago. In Greek the word is 170 letters long, but it transliterates in English into 182 letters. According to the book of world records the word is lopadotemachoselachogaleokranioleipsanodrimhypotrimmatosilphioparaomelitokatakechymenokichlepikossyphophattoperisteralektryonoptekephalliokigklopeleiolagoiosiraiobaphetraganopterygon.

One of the pleasures of writing about food over the years is having a forum to express not only one's special pleasures but also one's prejudices. In my columns I have been pleased to vent my prejudices against many things, including airline food (it has improved to a degree since I last wrote a column, many years ago, stating that I would prefer to bring my own aboard whether it were a simple sandwich or a tin of caviar); the garlic press, which I consider an abomination and a device of cooks who are just plain lazy; and guests who "help" with the dishes. The latter, I find, invariably put dishes in the dishwasher improperly and the breakage is phenomenal. Either that or they place one utensil or another in an unaccustomed place and I spend the following day in search of a favorite spatula, wire whisk, salad dryer, or whatever.

Many things I have written about have amused me over the years and the tiniest fraction of these would be "dishwasher cooking," which had been seriously recommended to me for cooking fish ("you wrap the fish in foil, put the package on the upper rack of the dishwasher and put it through a complete cycle"). It is one of the few recipes ever printed in my columns that has never been tested in my kitchen.

And certain columns have brought forth amusing replies.

Once, after an item appeared about apple pan dowdy, Mike Nichols, the producer, regaled me with the following:

> Shoo-fly pie
> And apple pan dowdy
> Make your eyes light up
> And your stomach say "howdy."
>
> Shoo-fly pie
> And apple pan dowdy
> I never get enough
> Of that wonderful stuff.
>
> *Et pour vous, Monsieur?*

This book, then, is the result of the columns I have written during my career as food editor of *The New York Times*. It ranges from Abruzzi (the finest Italian chefs are said to have been born there, just as the finest French chefs are said to hail from Lyons) to Zwieback (did you know that the name stems from "twice-baked"?).

—Craig Claiborne

August 1985

Craig Claiborne's
The New York Times
FOOD
ENCYCLOPEDIA

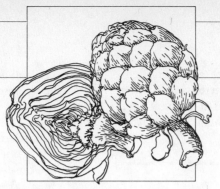

Abruzzi

The chefs of Italy are as chauvinistic about distinguishing the places of their birth as gastronomic spawning places as are the French. Just as French chefs claim that the gastronomic center of France (if not the universe) is Lyons, so do many Italian chefs claim that the mountainous Abruzzi region of Italy has produced the preponderance of great Italian chefs.

Poor regions, according to Luigi Nanni, tend to produce fine cooks, who must exercise the greatest skill with such bounty as they have.

"Where I come from is a very poor country," the chef and restaurant owner said. "We cultivate only sheep, the best baby lamb, cheeses like pecorino and caciotta and wine."

Mr. Nanni informed me that the cooking of Abruzzi is much more refined than that of the south.

Achar

See Pickled lemons.

Achiote

Achiote seeds are small, reddish, irregularly shaped seeds from the annatto tree and are widely used in Caribbean cooking, principally that of Puerto Rico and Cuba. The most common way to extract the yellow color for cooking is to fry the seeds briefly in lard or oil.

I have seen perfectly respectable recipes for paella, however, that simply call for adding the seeds—in lieu of saffron, for which they seem to be a sort of substitute—to the rice and seafood dish as it cooks.

Ackee

Ackee, also spelled akee or achee, is the fruit of a West African tree and the scientific name is *Blighia sapida*. That name comes from Captain Bligh, who introduced the tree to Jamaica, according to Elisabeth Lambert Ortiz in *The Complete Book of Caribbean Cooking*. The edible part of the ackee plant is sometimes called vegetable brains, for it does resemble brains when cooked with scrambled eggs. The best-known Jamaican dish using ackee is saltfish and ackee.

While imported canned ackee once enjoyed a reasonable distribution in this country, at the moment it is no longer available because of import restrictions.

Acorns

As a child I was given to testing almost everything that wasn't nailed down. I distinctly remember sampling the yellow kernel of young acorns newly fallen from the oak trees in the backyard. It was not a pleasant experience. The meat was somewhat sweet but somewhat caustic, with a quince-like bitterness that made the mouth pucker.

I was, therefore, surprised to learn that acorns are by no means unknown as food for human consumption.

The *Wise Encyclopedia of Food* informs us, "The sweet acorn *(Quercus esculus)* is still widely eaten in southern Europe and is prepared in the same way as chestnuts."

In Turkey, the text continues, the acorns are buried in the ground for some time to remove their bitterness. "They are then dried, washed, and ground with sugar, spices, and aromatics" to produce a product that is known as palamonte and a "food

named racahout, which is much esteemed."

In her interesting book, *American Indian Food and Lore,* Carolyn Niethammer states that acorns have long been a staple on the native Indian table. "Acorn stew," she writes, "has not faded in popularity. Many Apache housewives will keep a store of acorn meal on hand to make this . . . dish.

"According to Grace Mitchell, leader of the Yavapai tribe," the author continues, "Yavapai cowboys who work on the desert carry only a pocketful of acorns and some water for lunch."

Miss Niethammer explains how the bitterness is removed by the Indians.

"The Indians of central, northern, and coastal California used acorns to a much greater extent than did the desert Indians. To the California Indians, acorns were the staple and most important food. The type of acorn that grows in that area of California is much larger than the desert variety and also more bitter, owing to a greater amount of tannin. The tannin had to be leached out with water before the seeds were palatable."

But a Massachusetts woman who had read another technique for leaching and roasting acorns written by a highly respected nature authority wrote to me:

"Encouraged by his description, I once collected acorns with a very small boy. We shelled them, discarded the wormy ones (of which there were a good number), and then boiled and boiled them as Ewell Gibbons recommended. We roasted them and ground them in an old coffee mill. After all this work we had a scant cup of meal to give away for Christmas. The muffins we made, using only a tablespoon or so of the meal, tasted musty and old; most emphatically not 'already buttered' as Mr. Gibbons said.

"From this experience I can say that no

one in his right mind would try to eat an unleached acorn, and only people with very small boys should undertake the shelling-leaching-roasting process. So maybe our acorns weren't the eating kind. What I suspect is that acorns really don't make very good eating unless you're far from home and terribly hungry."

On the other hand, I have it from another authority on wild food cookery that acorns have multiple, delicious uses as food. He is Gary Lincoff, who teaches wild food cookery in Manhattan and demonstrates such dishes as wild mushroom soup, beach plum bread, and sassafras tea.

"I gather about fifty pounds of acorns a year from Central Park, or less than one quarter of the acorns from a single tree. I gather mostly those from the turkey oak, *Quercus cerris,* dozens of which front the southern end of the reservoir. From fifty pounds of these especially large nuts I derive nine to twelve pounds of processed acorn meal.

"There are several urban methods of leaching these acorns of their tannic acid—and all acorns, if eaten in quantity, should be leached first, even those, like the white oak, *Quercus alba,* that are more or less sweet. One leaching method is to place them in a punctured coffee can suspended beneath a running faucet for a day; but this is wasteful. Another method is to leach them with kitchen lye, but this can be dangerous if one is careless. A third method involves boiling the acorns, and this is what I chose to do.

"I gather the acorns in September, let them sit a day or two (to let the meats contract from the shells), crack the shells, and boil the nutmeats for about two and one-half hours, changing the water every fifteen minutes or so. I use a spaghetti pot (the double pot, the inner one with holes), lift out the acorns en masse, and then pour out the water, which has turned rust-colored from the tannin. (This is actually very little work compared to first growing wheat or corn or rice, then processing.)

"After boiling, I place the drained acorns on baking sheets and dry them in the oven, at 100 to 150 degrees, with the door left ajar. When dry, I grind them in a meat grinder. I get two qualities of meal, one coarse and one fine.

"The fine meal is used to make muffins and breads, and no Thanksgiving Day dinner is complete without acorn muffins."

Agar-Agar

Agar-agar is a thickening agent available in many health food stores. Vegetarians often use it in place of gelatin. The usual procedure is to use one teaspoon of powdered agar for each cup of broth or other liquid. Soften the agar first in one-quarter cup of cold broth. Add this to three quarters of a cup of very hot broth and proceed from there.

Agoursi

Larousse Gastronomique defines agoursi as a "ridge-cucumber," and it is frequently called for in rassolnik, the Russian soup. Incidentally, *Le Répertoire de la Cuisine,* a book for which I have high regard, misspells agoursi in both the English and French editions, calling it argousis.

Airline Food

I was amused when airlines introduced "no frills" flights to Europe in the 1970s. The wonder is why the airlines, both foreign and domestic, imposed all those terrible (where food is concerned) frills on passengers in the first place.

I recall the early days when traveling by air was a job. In that antediluvian age they handed you a neat cardboard box filled with a tasty sandwich, a pickle or two, a decent piece of cheese, and half a bottle of wine. Once you were up, up, and away, your own appetite and free will dictated when it was time to dine.

Then came all those elaborate frills—the Swiss steak, the rather unreasonably perfumed baked fish dishes served, all too often, with broccoli in one form or another, but generally topped with cheese. Oh, my, how those airline chefs—the majority of them raised and trained in cafeterias—loved to pile embarrassment on embarrassment. And those awful overcooked chicken dishes with canned "baby" carrots, cold mashed potatoes, and the abominable salads with their pale, insipid tomato wedges. Tinned asparagus spears and Russian salad with canned peas. Soggy apple tarts and too-sweet champagne.

Some of the most decent flights one can recall are those when platters of sandwiches were passed around. Of course, the cheese was pasteurized and domestic and the ham was just plain boiled and the mustard, if any, was of the ballpark variety and the pickles were saccharine sweet, but at least the food was honest and not overly handled.

The fact is that dining can be fun aboard the airlines, provided you carry your own.

One of the absolute triumphs of a few decades of flying involved shopping at Peck's, a fine food establishment in Milan.

At the meat counter I purchased two small roast quail, each stuffed with prosciutto and rosemary. And a few slices of Italian salamis, a bit of "eating" Parmesan, a little Gorgonzola cheese, one marvelous pear, and two individual fruit tarts made with pastry cream. These were neatly packed by the management. I used the airline's silver and napkins, purchased a small bottle of wine on the plane, and the flight was bliss.

My second grand indulgence was a flight to Paris before which I had provided myself and a companion with fresh caviar, smoked salmon, smoked sturgeon, sour cream, onions, bagels, various kinds of herrings, and so on.

If you plan to follow my example, here is a list of dos and don'ts.

Avoid things that are sticky, drippy, and likely to melt easily, things like ice cream.

Be considerate of your fellow passengers. Do not take things that reek of odors, like sardines, Liederkranz cheese, and scallions, or things with an excess of garlic.

Buy foods that are easily sliced or already sliced and can be carried compactly. Buy according to your purse and conscience. Purchase a hamper accordingly. If you delight in caviar and foie gras and smoked salmon and smoked sturgeon, consider them. These luxuries can serve as an appetizer or main course, depending on quantity and assortment and your laudable extravagance and wholesome enthusiasm.

There are few things out of any kitchen to surpass roast quail in excellence and they are ideal for air travel. So are other small roast birds, such as squab or one-pound chickens or Cornish hens. On a slightly lesser scale, cold roast pork, cold roast veal, and cold leftover meat loaf can be delectable.

There are dozens of exceptional cheeses available and, perhaps, cheese with fresh fruit would suffice for your expedition. But fine salamis and cooked sausages are something to take delight in. That plus a superior loaf of crusty French or Italian bread.

Of course, you can also indulge in many kinds of irresistible cold sliced meats—pâtés, terrines, crocked meats, prosciuttos, and so on.

How about very lean pastrami or corned beef from a top-flight delicatessen? One word of caution. Do not make your sandwiches before you board. The bread becomes soggy whether they are made with mayonnaise, mustard, or whatever. For pastrami or corned beef, choose your bread accordingly, rye or the like.

Take small, appetizing frills for the flight basket. Things like black olives imported from Greece or Italy, cornichons (real, imported-from-France cornichons), radishes, and cherry tomatoes. Forget those childish, unsophisticated additions such as carrot and celery sticks. Carry small, individually wrapped pats of butter if such is your hunger.

Pay strict account to the necessities of dining aboard. You will need plates. China or plastics? And napkins. Linen or paper? And glasses. Crystal or plastic? Don't laugh. It's an adventure.

You will need eating utensils—forks, knives, and spoons—and you will probably settle for plastic because metal may be forbidden for security reasons. If you want hot coffee or tea, a Thermos with cups. You will need salt, pepper, mustard, and mayonnaise, perhaps, all neatly packed in small plastic containers.

I must warn you, however, that flight attendants are generally not amused at such proceedings.

Fellow passengers aren't either. You are regarded either with hostility because you are going against the swim, or with jealousy for the most transparent reasons.

Thus, you will feast with more comfort if you board with your package labeled: "Gift. Do not open before boarding." Then, when the moment of opening arrives, unveil the salmon and say something like "Wouldn't you just know Aunt Mary would do something extravagant like this." Or say something like, "Oooh-la-la, sturgeon, too!"

If you plan such a gastronomic revel, it is best to go to the airport early. Rush to the reserved seat counter and ask for aisle seats for two.

Failing this, cast your eye about the plane before takeoff to discover if there is a long row of seats more than half unoccupied. Casually wander over and place one bag on each of two seats. Or, the moment before takeoff, quickly grab your bags and run to the more isolated seats. After all, who wants to eat caviar or a fat smoked salmon, sturgeon, and cream cheese hero with total strangers casting sideways glances as they tear into whatever it is on their tray that looks like yesterday's Swiss steak.

Be considerate and supertidy. Don't burden the flight attendant with your random brought-on leftovers. Gather the items as compactly as possible and put them in the plastic bags you have brought for this purpose.

One more word about things I take aboard airlines, particularly for midday flights. I loathe those canned Bloody Mary mixes and so I travel with a small insulated bag containing Tabasco sauce and Worcestershire plus one or two fresh limes. If I wish a Bloody Mary, I order plain tomato juice over ice and a miniature bottle of vodka and concoct my own.

Incidentally, the consumption of brought-on alcohol is against the law. A Federal aviation regulation, part 121.575 states as follows:

"No person may drink any alcoholic beverage aboard an aircraft unless the certificate-holder operating the aircraft has served that beverage to him." Or her, one presumes. That statement appears on tickets for domestic and international flights.

À La

There is no difference between dishes listed as à la provençale and provençale, à la niçoise and niçoise. French menu writers drop the "à la" because it is implied; if it is repeated it becomes monotonous.

Thus we find boeuf bourguignonne, "boeuf" being masculine while "bourguignonne" is feminine, with "à la mode" omitted.

À la Diable

À la diable means deviled or in the devil's style. In French cookery it means a dish generally breaded and baked and seasoned with mustard and/or other condiments. The condiments may include such things as Worcestershire sauce and/or vinegar in various combinations. The term is used in the same sense that one says "devilishly hot," the hot used in a spiced sense. Many dishes can be cooked à la diable, including chicken

wings, whole squab split as for broiling, pigs' feet, and short ribs of beef.

À la Grecque

Almost every national cuisine embraces specific flavors that are endlessly repeated in various combinations. Chinese cookery, for example, relies heavily on soy sauce, shao hsing (a wine that resembles dry sherry), fresh ginger, garlic, and monosodium glutamate. French cooking would seem impoverished without dry red and white wines, shallots, thyme, bay leaves, and heavy cream. Two of the staples of Greek cookery are lemons and olive oil. French chefs put these to good use in an assortment of inspired vegetable appetizers and call them à la grecque or Greek-style.

À la Nage

One of the great categories of French food is that called à la nage. This curious culinary expression literally means "in the swim" and refers to the fact that a fish or some kind of seafood is "swimming" in a flavorful, rich, buttery broth. This liquid is really a court bouillon with a good number of aromatics to its credit.

À l'Anglaise

It has always seemed to me that French chefs, in naming dishes, went out of their way to put down English cooking. When they speak of some food à l'anglaise, it more often than not means "breaded," and when it doesn't, it means "boiled."

One notable exception is roast quail à l'anglaise, which involves a series of dishes, including quail, croutons spread with liver paste, a delicate brown sauce, plus an English bread sauce. They all add up to a genuine regale.

Albany Beef

Sturgeon was once marketed in this country under the name Albany beef.

In *Caviar! Caviar! Caviar!* Gerald M. Stein says that sturgeon were once so commonplace they were "bumping into each other all over the world." He adds: "At the turn of the century, strollers along New York's Hudson River were used to seeing barges loaded with a couple of hundred large sturgeon on their way to Albany, where the meat was sold for as little as a penny a pound. Sturgeon meat was sold then as 'Albany beef.' "

Indeed, sturgeon were so plentiful at the time that fishermen generally used them as bait to catch more marketable fish.

Albondiga

Albondiga is the Mexican name for meatball, although the flavorings used in Mexico are generally quite different from those made, for example, in Manhattan or Milan. As Diana Kennedy points out in *The Cuisines of Mexico,* every region in Mexico "has its albondiga recipe, but I think it really comes into its own in the northwest of Mexico—Sonora, Sinaloa, and farther south in Jalisco." Her book lists what are perhaps the best albondiga recipes. Both contain finely diced zucchini and are flavored with cumin and oregano. The Jalisco version is served in a sauce made with those delightful, smoky-flavored chilies.

Alec

The word "alec" is often encountered in crossword puzzles, with the clue being "fish sauce." It is certainly not a common sauce in America nor, I believe, in Britain. Theodora FitzGibbon, in her book *The Food of the Western World,* says the word is Old Latin of Greek origin and means herring in brine.

She also quotes Lawerens Andrewe in Furnivall's *Early English Meals and Manners:* "Alex, the Heringe, is a Fisshe of the See and very many be taken betweene Bretayne and Germania and also in Denmarke about a place named Schonen. And he is best from the beginning of August to December, and when he is fresh taken he is very delicious to be eten. And also whan he has ben salted he is specyall fod unto man."

The chances are against your finding this sauce at your local store.

Ali-Bab

One of the most extraordinary books on food ever published is a forty-seven-year-old, seven-pound, 1,281-page volume on classic and regional French cookery called *Gastronomie Pratique*. It is remarkable in many respects, not the least of which is that it was written not by a chef but by a mining engineer who either through eccentricity or modesty did not even put his name on the book. The author was Henri Babinski, but the name with which he chose to sign the work was Ali-Bab.

I have owned a copy of the work for many years and have wondered endlessly about the author's identity. I came by his background in a most circuitous fashion. I found the facts of his life in a back issue of *MD* magazine, one of the most literate publications directed to doctors and their kin. It turns out that Henri Babinski's brother is even more famous than Ali-Bab. *That* Babinski was Joseph, who cut a wide swath in medical circles through his exploration of neurological symptoms.

In any event, Henri was born on July 2, 1855, and *Gastronomie Pratique* was published in 1907 when he was fifty-five years old. It was, apparently, an immediate success. The author was born in Paris, studied at the École des Mines in France, and on graduation found himself responsible financially for his father, who had Parkinson's disease, his mother, who was also unwell, and the education of his younger brother. He states in the preface to his monumental book that he started to travel widely when he was twenty-five years old but knew little enough about cooking. In his role as an engineer in foreign countries he dined with natives in outpost locations, mostly on the products of the chase and fish, these grilled or broiled without other artifice. And then he became passionately curious about French cooking.

Henri spent the last years of his life as companion to his brother, and both were confirmed bachelors. They entertained little, mostly at dinner. Henri insisted on strict punctuality and preferred "respectful silence" during a meal. The brothers traveled throughout Europe and the Americas. He had no high regard for any table *except* the French. He states in *Gastronomie Pratique* that German cooking lacks finesse and that it would not agree with anyone who was not a great beer drinker. English cooking, he observed, has been backward from the beginning and, although the kitchens in the United States are the biggest and best equipped in the world, "What is there to say for American cooking?" He also noted that kangaroo tastes like rabbit and a single ostrich egg is sufficient to produce a single omelet for eight men. He learned from cannibals that "white man's flesh is flat and tasteless but black man's tastes like pork."

In addition to the scholarly and frequently humorous nature of his volume, M. Babinski—or Ali-Bab—had the soul of a poet. Here, for example, is a rather free translation of his discourse on "How to Eat an Oyster."

Some people swallow them without chewing as if they were downing medicine tablets of dubious taste and texture. Others condescend to chew them, but only after dousing them with incendiary sauces guaranteed to disguise their taste, a culinary exercise I could only understand if I were condemned to eat, let us say, Portuguese oysters. Still other oyster "fanciers" add lemon juice and eat them with buttered black bread or caviar sandwiches. And each conceives his conceit to be best.

And yet there are the genuine amateurs—and the word is used in its original sense derived from "to love"—who know that a good oyster should be enjoyed for its basic, God-given, and inherent goodness. Here is how to go about eating an oyster.

When you are ready to dine, and not a moment earlier, open your favorite oysters and make sure that each one is still alive by exploring its reflexes. This is quite simple—simply touch the edge of the lamella; if it does not retract, the oyster has expired. Remove the living creature from its shell—in the most delicate manner possible—and bring it immediately into your mouth with no extraneous trimmings whatsoever and, in a trice, with your teeth, perforate its liver. If it is an oyster of proper freshness and quality, the whole of your gums will soak in it, your mouth will be filled with its juices, the true criterion of an oyster that has reached its peak.

You should rest for a moment in that state, then slowly swallow the juices and finish off the mastication and deglutition of the mollusk. After that, invigorate yourself with a mouthful of good, dry white wine, munch a piece of black or white bread, buttered or not, this solely to neutralize the tongue in order to savor to the fullest the oyster to follow . . .

Alkermes

Alkermes, which is sometimes called for in Italian recipes, is a rarity in this country. Dictionaries of wines and spirits point out that it is a cordial, red in color, once made from an insect known as kermes. It is of the cochineal genus and cochineal is most used in the preparation of a red dye.

I have never heard of the drink being sold in wine and spirit shops in this country. The only time I have seen alkermes was years ago when an Italian pastry chef used it for some special sweet whose name now escapes me.

Alligator Pears

See Avocado.

Allspice

Allspice, despite the name, is a single spice, a coffee-colored, brownish, round berry that varies from the size of a peppercorn to a quarter of an inch or slightly larger. To most people the aroma is akin to that of cinnamon, nutmeg, and cloves. It has many uses, principally in fruit and spice cakes, and is also important in many pickling combinations.

Almonds

The almond is considered by many gastronomes to be the world's finest nutmeat. It is believed to be of Mediterranean origin although it is mentioned in the Bible ("The almond tree shall flourish . . .": Ecclesiastes). There are bitter almonds and sweet almonds. The flesh of the bitter almond, improperly used, may be toxic, but it is used in almond extract, in the flavoring of certain confections, and in almond-flavored liqueurs. Sweet almonds are those that are sold in cans in the United States.

One of the most famous almond confections is the macaroon, the small crunchy cookie that originated in Italy, but was introduced into France about four centuries ago.

The vast majority of recipes for macaroons call for almond paste or almonds ground to a paste, sugar, and egg whites, blended and spooned or piped onto a baking sheet.

I seriously doubt that there is a standard recipe for macaroons, so a manufacturer may use whatever ingredients he desires, presuming, of course, that he comes up with texture and flavor associated with macaroons. A sourcebook informs me of a cookie known as amarettini, a variety in which apricot kernels are an ingredient. Apricot kernels give a more concentrated almond flavor.

Whether to toast almonds before grinding depends solely on what you are using them for. If you are using them for macaroons, for example, and want to start with a homemade almond paste (which is also available in cans), you should not toast the almonds. It would give a different flavor.

Quite often, however, there are desserts that may require a sprinkling of ground toasted almonds on top. My advice is to follow the recipe instructions. If it says toast, do so; if it says blanched almonds, it probably means untoasted unless otherwise specified. *See also* Marzipan, Snow almonds.

Ananas

See Pineapple.

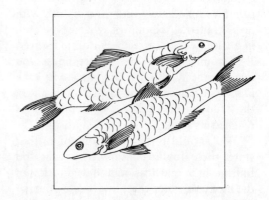

Anchovies

I've long been amused by a bit of intelligence about anchovies I found in the *Wise Encyclopedia of Cookery*. "Anchovies," I learned, "are caught in the spring and summer during dark, moonless nights by means of artificial light which attracts and completely blinds them." Howsoever caught, anchovies are a palatal delight.

Andouillettes

Add to my list of personal cravings a famed French sausage known on home territory as andouillettes. Although they are widely available in French markets, I have never found a commercial source for them in this country. Andouillettes are sausages stuffed with chitterlings, the much publicized "soul food" of American blacks. Chitterlings, the small intestine of swine, are available in many pork stores in America, and if you know of a good and conscientious butcher, he should be able to order them for you. You would also need thick pork casings to be stuffed and these are known as hog punk end, available in pork stores. I hasten to add that while I dote on andouillettes, they are, like chitterlings, not for all palates.

Angelica

Angelica derives from a plant with a thick, hollow stem and it is said to be a member of the parsley family. It has long been used

in the preparation of medicines, largely as a digestive.

It is used mostly in a candied form (only the tender young stems are used for this purpose), although some sources state that all parts of the plant may be eaten. The leaves are cooked as a vegetable, and the first young, tender shoots of the plant are used in salads.

Angelica is fairly common in fruitcakes and is also used, cut, to decorate some desserts. It is often found in candied fruit mixtures.

Angels on Horseback

"Angels on horseback" are shucked oysters that have been wrapped in bacon, put on skewers, and broiled. They are served on buttered toast.

This is one type of a classic food known in England as a savoury. Savouries, or savories, are generally salty or "savory" and are served after the dessert. The purpose is to "clear the palate" before the service of sweet fortified wines, such as port or Madeira.

Angler Fish

See Monkfish.

Angostura

According to that fine reference work, Tom Stobart's *Herbs, Spices and Flavorings,* Angostura is "the old name for the Venezuelan town on the Orinoco River now called Ciudad Bolivar." It gave its name to the bitters, "which was originally a medicine for fever invented by a Doctor Siegert during the last century." The bitters, he adds, are made with cinnamon, cloves, mace, nutmeg, orange and lemon peels, plus prunes crushed with their pits.

Anise

Anise seeds and star anise do not come from the same plant, although their licorice-like flavors are quite similar. Anise seeds have a tiny lobed base and are pointed at the top. Star anise, on the other hand, is, as the name implies, star-shaped and has the color of brownish bark, with its seeds contained in the points of the star.

The seeds of star anise, oval-shaped, smooth-skinned, and about a quarter of an inch long, are more pungent and bitter than plain anise. The whole star is used in cooking, principally in Chinese cuisine. Plain anise is sometimes referred to as sweet cumin.

Annatto

See Achiote.

Antiboise

The name antiboise derives, of course, from the resort town of Antibes on the southern coast of France. Dishes bearing the name are similar to those bearing South of France-related names such as niçoise, provençale, and so on. They invariably contain tomatoes and, generally, other ingredients characteristic of the region, such as garlic, olives, and olive oil.

Antipasto

The word antipasto does not, as many people believe, mean "before the pasta." The word pasto comes from the Latin *pastus,* meaning "food." Antipasto means "before the food"—or main course—whatever that might be. *See also* Appetizers.

Antojitos

See Appetizers.

Appetizers

Generally speaking, I find nothing more barbarous and unconvivial than dining buffet-style when that implies eating off one's lap, one's plate balanced precariously on both knees and the napkin tucked in some unseemly place to prevent its falling. There are two occasions when I find a buffet to have a redeeming virtue—a picnic and when an hors d'oeuvre table is at the heart of it.

The French, of course, have no monopoly on appetizers. When it comes to such food, there is, in fact, no civilized society on earth that does not accord a special place to that assortment of dishes known as appetizers or hors d'oeuvres. What would the Italian table be without its antipasti, the Greeks without mezedaki, the Spanish without their entremeses, the Russians without zakuska tables, and the Germans without vorspeise? Or the Swedes without cocktail tilltugg and the Mexicans without antojitos?

The nationality is notably unimportant where well-made appetizers are concerned; the late Princess Alexandra Kropotkin noted in *The Best of Russian Cooking* that "where the table is concerned, politics don't count."

Apple Butter

Apple butter, which the Dutch brought to America, is made by cooking apples, quartered or halved, in water or cider (and at times cider vinegar) to cover. When tender, they are put through a food mill or strainer and sweetened to taste.

You add spices of your own liking, such things as ground allspice, cloves, and cinnamon. You continue cooking this until it is quite stiff or until it "sheets" from a spoon. Or spoon some onto a plate; if it remains stiff and intact (no liquid oozes from it), it is ready.

Applejack

See Cider.

Apple Pan Dowdy

I have consulted many books on American dishes and not one of them can explain the origin of apple pan dowdy. The dessert, of course, is a deep-dish pie made with sliced apples and spices, covered with a thick, short crust, and baked. It is served with the crust placed on a plate, the apples scooped on top, and heavy cream poured over.

I rather doubt that my educated guess would be correct, but the dessert has a rather dowdy look when baked and an even more dowdy look when served. That is to say, it is lacking in neatness and stylishness.

A favorite correspondent proposes that the word "dowdy" may come to us from Britain. Perhaps, he says, it may be a cross between "dowler" and "crowdie."

A "dowler," according to his *English Dialect Dictionary,* is "a cake or dumpling made in a hurry." A "crowdie is a kind of porridge or oatmeal gruel made with water, milk, etc."

Another gentleman states that "dowdy" has been convincingly explained as from the Somerset dialect, "douldy, meaning a custard or pudding-like dish."

In *The Dictionary of American Food and Drink,* John F. Mariani says the dish was first mentioned in print in 1805 and is sometimes referred to as apple Jonathan in the Northeast.

Apple Pie

The one dessert that best distinguishes the differences between the cuisines of France and America is apple pie. The most obvious difference has to do with the presentation. An American apple pie is almost invariably a two-crust affair, one on top and one on the bottom. A French apple tart is just as invariably an open, single-crust creation. And, whereas the American dough for a pastry crust may be made with white shortening or lard or butter—and often a combination of two—a French pastry crust is almost always made with butter.

When I wrote that the phrase "apple pie à la mode" made absolutely no sense to me, a woman from Manhattan volunteered that

if I wanted to be precise, it would be "à la mode de Cambridge, New York." She added, "The Cambridge Hotel claims to have originated pie à la mode (pie with a scoop of ice cream on top) in an earlier day when the Washington County Fair was held in Cambridge and when it was a resort area in the horse-farm country east of Saratoga Springs."

Apricot Sheets

Apricot sheets, also known as apricot leather and apricot rolls, are a specialty of Middle Eastern confectionery outlets and are made, I believe, by cooking down apricot purée with sugar until it can be rolled out into sheets.

There are similar products with such flavors as strawberry, raspberry, cherry, plum, grape, and apple.

Arancine

Arancine means "little oranges" in Sicily. To prepare them, rice is cooked with saffron to give it a gold-yellow tint. The cooked rice is blended with egg yolks and cheese and shaped into balls whose centers are filled with a cooked mixture of ground beef and green peas. The balls are coated with egg whites and bread crumbs and deep-fried. The result is a delectable creation with a crisp crust and a fine combination of internal flavors and textures.

Argenteuil

Argenteuil on a menu invariably indicates a dish made primarily of asparagus, or one that uses asparagus as a principal garnish. The name derives from a town in the canton of Seine-et-Oise that is only 18 kilometers from St.-Germain-en-Laye, a charming village historically important as the birthplace of pommes soufflés, sauce béarnaise, and Louis XIV, but not necessarily in that order. In any event, the town of Argenteuil is noted for its fine asparagus, some of the most celebrated in the world. As a matter of record, let it be noted that the area close by Argenteuil also produces small amounts of both red and white table wines, but the fact is not even recorded in some well-known wine

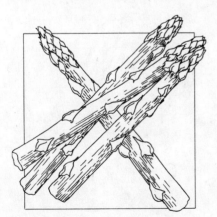

encyclopedias. It also is one of the many areas in France that produces that fiery spirit, *marc*, made from the lees of the grape.

Aristology

Aristology is the science of dining or the art of eating well. The word was coined in 1835 by a London magistrate named Thomas Walker. He published a weekly periodical called *The Original,* and his first essay about aristology appeared there. The number of guests at a meal, he believed, should not exceed eight and, ideally, there should be only six so that conversation may be general. The guests should be selected for their interests and experiences, said Mr. Walker, as well as for the exuberance of their appetites. At the table, salt and vinegar, pepper and wine should be within easy reach of every guest.

Armer Ritter

See French toast.

Arrowroot

Arrowroot in many professional chefs' minds gives a more delicate and refined look to sauces than does cornstarch. And a far clearer and more refined look than regular flour. The thickening power of arrowroot and cornstarch is more intense than that of regular flour. For each tablespoon of flour called for to thicken sauces, use half as much (one and a half teaspoons) arrowroot or cornstarch.

Most sauces with flour are made by blending the flour with fat, then adding liquid while stirring. To thicken a sauce with arrowroot or cornstarch you would add it at the end.

There are differences of authoritative opinion as to the origin of the name arrowroot. Most dictionaries state that the name derives from the use of the root (its scientific name is *Maranta arundinaces*) by American Indians to withdraw poison from arrow wounds. Other sources state that it comes from an American Indian word for flour, *araruta*.

Arroz con Pollo

Arroz con pollo, or rice with chicken, is a specialty of many Caribbean nations, including Cuba, Puerto Rico, and the Dominican Republic. It is basically of Spanish origin and includes, in addition to chicken and rice and pimientos, capers, sweet peppers, tomatoes, and green peas.

Artichokes

The origins of the name artichoke are obscure. It is pure gallows humor, but one source vows that in merry old England when a thief was hanged it was known as a vegetable dinner. Get it? A hearty choke. No, no, no.

Actually the name is derived from the Italian *articiocco* and *archiciocco*. Many of the European names for the globe artichoke are similarly derived. The current Italian name is *carciofi;* the Spanish, *alcachofas;* the

French, *artichaut;* and the Polish, *karzochy*. The name of the vegetable, in turn, is said to be traced to its cone-like shape. A Ligurian word for pine cone is *cocal* and there is, of course, a strong resemblance involved.

Most of the artichokes that grace our tables come from a town in California called Castroville, which is a few miles off the Pacific, south of San Francisco and just north of Monterey. It is especially suited to the growing of artichokes because the farmlands around Castroville are frequently shrouded in fog, a condition that artichoke plants thrive on.

Unlike most vegetables, artichokes cause an interesting chemical reaction in the mouth when eaten. They have a nutty flavor and cause any subsequent food or drink to taste sweet. Thus there are certain wine fanciers who declare that wine should never be poured at any point during a meal when artichokes are served. To my own taste, it's a trivial point.

Most recipes concerning artichokes specify that you should cut off and discard the stem. But the stem, which is merely an extension of the heart, is wholly edible. The reason it is cut off and discarded is largely

a matter of aesthetics. The artichoke bottom or heart or the whole artichoke without the stem is a bit more elegant.

If I were to use the stems for soups or salads, I would simply drop them in water, peeled or unpeeled, and cook until tender. They may then be sliced thin and used in salads or puréed and used in soups. If cooking them unpeeled, I would peel them before using.

Arugula

Arugula is a pungent and excellent salad green much used in Italian kitchens and increasingly popular in America. It can be used alone, but to some tastes it is a bit too assertive and thus can be combined with other greens, such as Boston lettuce and Belgian endive. Arugula tends to be sandy and should be rinsed in several changes of cold water.

An authoritative Italian dictionary states that the name of the herb is *eruca* and it is vulgarly known in Italy as *rucola* and *ruccetta.* (In French it is *roquette,* in English rocket, and in Spanish *eruga.*) As far as can

be determined, arugula is the American vulgarization of the herb's name.

An important note of caution: If ordering seeds for the garden, do not confuse rocket (arugula) with sweet rocket, which is a garden flower.

Asafetida

Asafetida is a spice made from the stems of foul-smelling plants that grow from eight to twelve feet high. The spice comes in the form of a powder made from the milky juice of those plants.

Asafetida is fairly common in Indian cooking, but many Westerners find it unpalatable. I have Indian friends, excellent cooks, who tell me that asafetida, when cooked, provides a flavor that is somewhat onion-like. I know one British herbalist who declares that the spice has a "quite ghastly stink" when used in bulk, "a little like bad garlic."

I have a box of powdered asafetida on my spice shelf but rarely use it other than when it is called for in Indian cookery. In small amounts, it has an undeniable appeal.

Ashtrays

It is my opinion that you should never place unrinsed ashtrays in dishwashers. The odor of cigarettes—or worse, cigars—can give an offensive odor to dishes that are subsequently washed in the machine. Ashtrays should be rinsed or let stand with ammonia to remove odors after use. Then they may be placed in the dishwasher without ill effect.

Aspic

There is a belief that aspic, which is a cold gelatin dessert, does derive from the word "asp." The story goes that at some point back in time a chef determined that his savory gelatin concoction should be chilled until it was *froid comme un asp,* or cold as a snake. That is undoubtedly a false premise in that the word "asp" does not exist in French.

A more serious work on food states that the name of the dish does, however, derive from the Latin word *aspis,* which is the name of a venomous serpent. This version suggests that the round mold of the first aspics resembled—in the eye of some learned, etymologically trained chef—the shape of a snake.

Some years ago a group of us, mostly French chefs and their wives, staged an incredible picnic on Gardiners Island across from where I live. It was an extraordinary occasion. The likes of Roger Fessaguet, the chef of La Caravelle restaurant; René Verdon, then chef to the Kennedys in the White House; Pierre Franey; and Jacques Pepin, the chef, consultant, and cookbook author, spent days in my kitchen conjuring up aspics with veal and chicken bones, and the food was a visual extravaganza. The day was cool and clear and there was dancing on the sand to traditional French tunes played on an accordion.

The next year an effort was made to duplicate the occasion. The food was splendid, the aspic clear and firm. The moment it was taken from the refrigerator, that is. An hour later the boat arrived at the beach. The day was blisteringly hot, one of the hottest, the meteorologist said, of the past decade. The chicken, the veal, the fish, everything we made was awash in a sea of melted aspic.

Take heed. Be mindful of your gelatin, ye who would decorate food to rival the rainbow. Take the day into account and act accordingly.

Atholl Brose

The Scots have an appealing, smooth but deceptively strong drink called Atholl brose.

Brose comes in many forms. Its most basic form is simply oats, to which boiling water or milk has been added. A basic brose is most commonly served with butter and sugar. Atholl brose, on the other hand, is a wicked and appealing variation of that. It consists of straining the liquid from raw oats that have been soaked in cold water. This is combined with Scotch whiskey, honey, and, if desired, a little heavy cream. The drink is named for one of the dukes of Atholl. Some say the drink dates from the year 1475 or earlier, and it is mentioned in Sir Walter Scott's *The Heart of Midlothian* and Robert Louis Stevenson's *Kidnapped.*

Avocado

I have an uneasy feeling that trying to select the perfect avocado—the one with the nutty, buttery taste, light green flesh, and whipped-cream smooth texture—is as futile as trying to determine the exact nature of a wine by squeezing the bottle. There is no predictable formula.

The trouble is that there is a bewildering variety of avocados available to the public, both from California and Florida. In the fertile valley of Santa Paula, California, you will find the ugly, dark, and pebbly-skinned Hass, which many growers claim to be the finest. Then there is the Fuerte, also rough textured but with a greener skin. This is said to be the first commercially produced avocado in California. It was brought to these parts in 1911 and survived the great freeze of 1913. Thus the name Fuerte, which means strong in Spanish. Then the small, round avocado referred to as Bacon. And the Rincon, and so on.

And if all this isn't confusing enough, consider that Florida also produces such varieties as Lula and Booth, Simmonds, Walden, and Choquette. All told, the state produces more than fifty varieties, many of which appear on the commercial market.

Prior to going to Santa Paula, it had been my notion that the fruit plucked and sampled directly from the branch would be infinitely more glorious and tasty than the product off the supermarket shelves in the cold, far Northeast. That fruit, I had told myself, had been picked in an unripe condition and shipped so as to mature on its long journey across country.

It was part of my culture shock to be told that avocados are not often eaten directly from the tree.

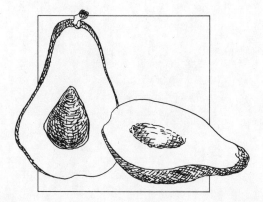

To reaffirm the answer, I asked John Bianchin, a spokesman for the California avocado industry, a hypothetical question:

"Let us suppose you were not an avocado producer and you had one tall avocado plant growing in your backyard. You wanted the best of all avocados from that tree. Wouldn't you wait until a precise moment of ripeness and then pluck the avocado?"

"Probably not," said Mr. Bianchin. "If you let the fruit fully ripen on the tree, it falls to the ground and bruises." He added that the fruit is equally palatable if—as is done by the industry—the pulp is allowed to mature after plucking.

A greengrocer long ago taught me that if the avocado you have on hand is too hard and green to be edible, you can hasten the ripening process by placing the fruit in a brown paper bag and letting it stand overnight or perhaps longer. The fruit will ripen at a much more rapid rate than if stored open in a cold place. In Santa Paula, they say that the preferred method to hasten ripening is to place the fruit in a plastic bag with a few strips of banana peel. The peel gives off a natural gas that is said to speed the ripening.

The largest producer and shipper of avocados is Mexico; the United States is second. South America and Africa both produce large quantities, but Israel is the largest supplier of avocados to Europe. Incidentally, it has taken a good many years to educate the French palate to avocados, but today *les avocats* are less and less a novelty on the French table.

The history of the avocado in the New World is traced to Hernando Cortés, who, in 1519, found the avocado flourishing in or around what is now Mexico City.

The name, which dates from that time, derives from a Nahuatl (a group of Mexican and Central American tribes that include the Aztecs) word *ahuacatl.* The Spanish transliterated that into *aguacate,* which does not mean, as many suppose, "lawyer." Later on, when the French borrowed the name of the fruit, they did name it *avocat,* which is French for lawyer.

The legend about the arrival of avocados in the United States has it that the Spanish padres used to sit under the avocado trees in Mexico, eating the ripe fruit. As they dined, they tossed the seeds in one direction or another, and as the holy fathers traveled north, so did the resulting orchards.

For many years (during my Mississippi childhood, for example), avocados were referred to as alligator pears. No one is certain how the name came about, perhaps a rural and humorous distortion of "av-o-kay-do" or because some avocados have a rough skin that resembles alligator skin. In any event, the term is, happily, disappearing.

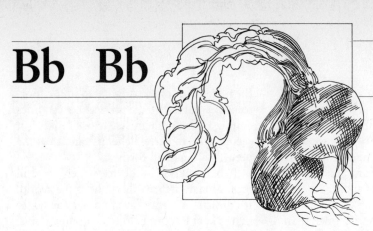

Bb Bb Bb Bb

Babinski, Henri

See Ali-Bab.

Bagel

One of the most interesting breads known to man is the bagel. Curiously in America, bagels have their greatest appeal in the Northeast and they are generally considered "Jewish food." I am told, however, that many years ago they were eaten in many European countries by the populace at large. In *The Joys of Yiddish,* Leo Rosten notes that "The first printed mention of bagels . . . is to be found in the Community Regulations of Kracow, Poland, for the year 1610—which stated that bagels would be given as a gift to any woman in childbirth." He adds that the word is derived from the German word *beugel,* meaning "a round loaf of bread." There are those who dispute this and claim that it derives from the middle High German word *bügel,* which means a twisted or curved bracelet or ring.

To prepare a bagel, you make a dough with flour, yeast, water, and oil or other fat. You knead the dough and let it rise until it is double in bulk. After shaping the bagels into a circle, drop them into a basin of boiling water and let them "cook" 2 or 3 minutes to a side, turning once. When drained, they are generally brushed with egg and baked until golden brown.

It, therefore, seemed logical to me that any properly made bagel could be referred to as a water bagel. But I was chastised by a New Yorker.

"Though it is true," she wrote, "that 'any properly made bagel' is boiled before being baked, the term water bagel refers not to this process but to the content of the dough. Any bagel eater or baker will tell you that there is a world of difference between the classic water bagel and the modern (infamous, to purists) egg bagel. I wouldn't want to sound unduly harsh as regards the egg bagel—which is actually very good, albeit a little rich—but the true and traditional bagel, the water bagel, is absolutely eggless, both inside and out."

Bagna Caôda

The Italian bagna caôda is one of the most savory, delectable, and unlikely appetizers in the world. It is a sort of fondue (in the original and proper sense of the word, meaning melted) containing anchovies that melt in a bath of olive oil and butter and in keen liaison with twenty thinly sliced garlic cloves. Twenty is an arbitrary number. Frequently there are more. I had always assumed that bagna caôda meant "hot bath." But I have learned that it has another meaning entirely.

Teresa Candler, an authority on Italian cooking, tells me that bagna is a dialectical Piedmont word for gravy or a thickened sauce. Today it is becoming more and more fashionable to dine on bagna caôda, but it started out as a peasant dish eaten by farmers during harvest time. The point was that it could be cooked at home in an earthenware casserole, then taken to the vineyard, where it could be kept over an open fire.

Bain-Marie

The name bain-marie is often associated in a farfetched manner with the Virgin Mary. One speaks of "the gentle voice of Mary," and thus some learned tomes relate the gentle heat of the water to the gentle quality of her voice. On the other hand, the *Dictionnaire Etymologique de la Langue Française* by Bloch and von Wartburg states that the name bain-marie originated in the fourteenth century. The utensil was for centuries employed by alchemists. Moses' sister, it seems, was an early alchemist and thus the utensil was named for her.

A bain-marie is a device widely used in professional kitchens throughout the world. It consists of a tray or container for water that is kept hot but below the boiling point. Saucepans containing sauces are placed in this water to be kept anywhere from warm to hot. These are sauces like hollandaise and béarnaise that, if subjected to a more intense heat, would risk curdling. A double boiler is a variation of the bain-marie, although the top of a standard double boiler fits quite snugly inside the bottom, which is not always the case with a bain-marie.

Custards are also placed in a bain-marie so that they cook evenly and do not curdle.

A gentleman wrote to suggest an admirable improvement over the simple water bath.

"The foolproof way to make perfect custards is to bake them in a pan in which two layers of paper towels have been placed and then water added to come perhaps halfway up the ramekins. The presence of the towels prevents boiling of the water and overheating of the custards when baked at 350 degrees."

And cheesecake is usually cooked in a water bath, but at least one person doesn't bother with it. She uses a springform pan and the results are delicious, she states. Her solution? She lines a springform pan with aluminum foil before pouring in the batter.

Baked Alaska

See Omelette norvégienne.

Baking Soda and Baking Powder

There are real differences between baking soda and baking powder. Baking soda is the more elementary of the two. It is sodium bicarbonate and in its most basic form does not have a leavening effect. The leavening quality is achieved when combined with an acid, such as sour milk, sour cream, buttermilk, or molasses.

Baking powder uses baking soda as a base. The soda is combined with other things to leaven food. The most basic of these is cream of tartar.

To make your own, blend one teaspoon of baking soda with two teaspoons of cream of tartar (an acid). That is sufficient for each cup of flour called for in a recipe.

The substitutes for the cream of tartar in commercially prepared baking powder may be many things, including calcium acid phosphate and sodium aluminum sulfate or a combination of both.

The best baking powder for home use and the one most widely available is the double-acting. Double-acting powder consists of sodium bicarbonate, sodium aluminum sulfate, and calcium acid phosphate, with cornstarch, the largest ingredient, as a filler and drying agent.

It is referred to as double-acting because it has two rising actions—the first when the liquid is added during the mixing process and the second when the batter or dough is exposed to heat. The double action makes it possible to mix the ingredients in advance and bake when convenient.

A Manhattan woman stoutly disagrees that double-acting baking powder is as satisfactory as single-acting, which is no longer available.

"My tongue tells me the baking results do not taste the same," she writes. "I quote from Helen Charley's *Food Science:* 'The type of baking powder makes a difference . . . the more acidic the cake batter (i.e., use of single-acting baking powder), up to a point, the finer the grain, the more velvety the crumb, and the whiter and sweeter is the cake.'

"When I telephoned Royal," she writes, "they said the cost of cream of tartar (imported from Italy) had become prohibitive, so they were no longer making their single-acting baking powder (you will note that double-acting baking powder contains no cream of tartar); so I bought out the extant supply of Royal baking powder at my neighborhood grocery store. I have the 'formula' supplied by Royal over the phone: ½ teaspoon cream of tartar, ¼ teaspoon baking soda, ¼ teaspoon cornstarch equals 1 teaspoon single-acting baking powder. But how long will my present supply (1½-ounce can) of cream of tartar last, and if the price is prohibitive for the Royal Baking Powder Company, won't it be for me, too?"

One of the most fascinating responses to the question of single- versus double-acting baking powder was received from Lorraine A. Bertan, a ninth-grade science teacher in the Bellmore-Merrick Central High School District on Long Island. Dear Miss Bertan! What I would give to have had a chemistry teacher like you when I was in the ninth grade. With what clarity you express yourself:

"I believe you might be interested in the results of experiments I have done with my science classes.

"Baking soda (sodium bicarbonate) gives off carbon dioxide when it reacts with an acid. Lemon juice, vinegar, buttermilk, and vanilla are acidic enough to release carbon dioxide from baking soda. The carbon dioxide causes the cake to rise. Baking powder contains baking soda, dry forms of acid (single-acting baking powder) or acid-producing salts (double-acting baking powder) which become acids when water is added. Cornstarch is added to the mixture to keep it dry until it is used.

"Single-acting baking powders contain dry acid or acid anhydride. Cream of tartar (an acid anhydride) is a derivative of grapes and closely related to tartaric acid. Tartaric acid may be used to produce a single-acting baking powder. It can be purchased from pharmaceutical supply firms.

"I have found that experiments dealing with the chemistry of cooking reactions have always been popular with my students."

Baking Stones

The finest pizzas and many of the finest breads are baked on baking stones or quarry tiles. These stones follow the technique used in many professional kitchens, the ovens of which have stone floors on which the pizza or bread is baked.

Most baking stones for home use are square or round and very heavy. You place them on the floor of the oven until they are very hot. Transfer your pizza or bread to the top of the stone and bake until done. I have used baking stones and recommend them for round loaves. I have also made French bread on them, but I prefer to use tin or aluminum molds designed for French bread.

Baking tiles are usually less expensive than the stones. The finest are one inch thick and are unglazed quarry tiles. They may be eight inches square or, preferably, twelve inches. They should be high-fired tiles rather than low-fired, which crack more easily.

Ball Blue Book

The definitive work, the bible of canning and preserving for home kitchens, is *The Ball Blue Book, the Guide to Home Canning and Freezing.*

The book is relatively unknown—that is, not spoken of with the same familiarity that one might employ in speaking of Irma Rombauer or Fannie Farmer and *The Settlement Cookbook.* It has never made a best-seller list, and it is not distributed by a book club. And it has sold in the millions.

It consists of ninety-six pages. There are nearly 400 recipes or formulas, and the cost is relatively modest because the book is a promotion effort by its creator, The Ball Corporation of Muncie, Indiana, one of the leading producers of canning equipment in the United States—mason jars and lids.

The Ball Blue Book would figure high, in fact, on any list of typically American cookbooks. There are recipes for such home-preserved foods as crystal pickles, watermelon-rind pickles, chow-chow relish, Dixie relish, and piccalilli or green tomato relish. But pickles are only a small part of the book's scope. There are also detailed instructions with photographs, in steps, showing how to prepare and preserve peaches, and others showing how to put up tomatoes.

There are detailed instructions for making jelly without pectin and others for making jelly with pectin added. It may come as a surprise to many people how simple and easy it is to prepare foods for months and even years to come.

Though the bulk of the recipes and canning instructions may be for pickles, jams, jellies, marmalades, and the like, there are many recipes for main courses with instructions for packing such things as meat sauce, bean soup, chili con carne, and Boston baked beans.

Elizabeth Ball, daughter of one of the founders, recalled some time ago that *The Ball Blue Book* had its origin in 1905. The Ball Company was founded in Buffalo, New York, in 1885 and in the beginning its primary interest was production of glass cans for kerosene. Canning jars developed less as a desired diversification than as a productive method for using the excess capacity of the kerosene-can machines.

In those days, of course, there were no home freezers, and almost every family in farming communities spent hours preserving the fruits and vegetables of summer.

The first book was wholly a family enterprise, Miss Ball reminisced. "Father wrote the directions for canning," she said, "and mother gathered the recipes from her own files, from those of family and friends. She knew that all of them had been tried many times over the years and were satisfactory. If there was any doubt, the recipes were tested in our home kitchen.

"My father, George, wanted to be absolutely sure that everything worked. Later on, my father found there were so many requests for recipes that weren't in the book that he turned it over to a professional cook. He insisted on a thorough testing of recipes and procedures and that continues today."

The first edition of the book, incidentally, was called *The Correct Method for Preserving Fruit*.

The basic audience for *The Ball Blue Book* is very much the home cook. There is a heap of valuable technical information included that will not be vital for, let us say, putting up a year's supply of green beans, but the data offer an excellent background to those who care to know about the chemistry of preserving.

Would you believe that some people resort to aspirin for processing foods? The book explains in some detail why this is hazardous. There are explanations why—with some rare exceptions—dishwashers should not be used for processing and neither should microwave ovens: Oven canning is dangerous. For those who need it, there is a chart for preserving at high altitudes.

This is also one of the first cookbooks to employ both the United States customary measure as well as the international metric system. Thus, recipes list both centigrade and Fahrenheit. Measures of weight and volume are listed both in liters and grams as well as in gallons (down to quarts, pints, cups, and so on) and pounds.

Balsamic Vinegar

Balsamic vinegar, which is known in Italy as *aceto balsamico di Modena,* has recently become fairly widely available in food specialty shops.

One of the great advocates of this vinegar is Marcella Hazan, who notes in her book *More Classic Italian Cooking* that "it is made from the boiled-down must of white Trebbiano grapes and aged in a series of barrels of different woods, of gradually diminishing size." Its production is quite similar to that of sherry.

The vinegar has a dark color and a somewhat pungent, sweetish taste and should be used sparingly. Add it, if you wish, to your favorite salad dressing, according to taste, or about ½ teaspoon for a dressing to serve four.

Bananas

I do not know the chemistry involved, but bananas when kept in the refrigerator tend to become unsightly both inside and out. The refrigeration seems to hasten their ripening.

You may use a very simple test in your own home. Buy two bananas of exactly the same ripeness, put one in the refrigerator and leave the other at room temperature. The one at room temperature will keep in good condition for several days. To my taste bananas improve on aging. They are more flavorful when they are still firm but just starting to soften.

Barbary Figs

See Prickly pears.

Barbecue

In certain sections of this country, the word "barbecue" is used to imply almost any meat, poultry, game, or fish that is cooked over charcoal or on a spit.

For what it is worth, in my view, foods that are cooked on a spit without basting should be referred to as spit-turned foods, while foods that are cooked on a grill without a basting sauce are properly referred to as grilled foods. This is true whether or not they are coated or served after cooking with a barbecue sauce.

A genuine, unadulterated barbecue is food that has cooked over a period of time while being basted with a sauce, the numbers, kinds, and flavors of which are countless.

It saddens me to think that the word barbecue is one of the most abused and misused words in the United States. The finest barbecues are to be found in the South (the famed and fabled foods of the late Arthur Bryant's Barbecue in Kansas City, Missouri, notwithstanding) and barbecues were a focal point of my early nourishment. In the days of my earliest youth, hundreds of guests would arrive on special occasions for barbecues that consisted of long trenches specially dug on my father's property. Wire was laid over these trenches to hold hundreds of pounds of chicken and ribs of pork, which were then basted for hours until the meat shredded at a touch. That was more than half a century ago in the Mississippi Delta.

Although I care a great deal about semantics where food names are concerned, I had never been notably interested in the origins of the word barbecue until it occurred to me to see if, by any chance, such a thoroughly American word existed in the *Oxford English Dictionary*. To my utter amazement, it does. The first definition notes that a barbecue is "a rude wooden framework, used in America for sleeping on, and for supporting above a fire, meat that is to be smoked or dried." Sleeping on? The *Oxford* adds that the name derives from the Spanish *barbacòa,* adopted from the Haitian *barbacòa*—"a framework of sticks set upon posts." The dictionary firmly denies that widely circulated fiction that the name was originally from the French *barbe à queue,* which literally means beard to tail.

Both barbecued foods and simply grilled dishes require a good deal of sensitivity to be done properly. It is not simply a question of throwing a hunk of beef, a chop, or a chicken half on the grill. Techniques vary a good deal, depending on what is being cooked.

One of the first considerations is the grill itself. The metal should be scrubbed after each use and ideally it should be washed and drained and wiped. Foods to be cooked should be brushed or marinated with oil or butter or in a sauce containing one or the other to prevent sticking when they are placed on the grill.

A charcoal fire should be started well in advance of the time for grilling, and the factors to be considered where the fire is concerned are as follows:

Some foods demand intense heat and quick cooking. Such foods include very thin slices of meat, such as a paillard of beef or veal. These are tossed on a very hot grill situated close to the firebed and the food might cook in 1 minute or less to the side.

Some foods demand moderate heat and are destined to be cooked for a reasonable length of time. These are foods such as a chicken split for broiling or a whole, cleaned, modest-size fish.

Some foods demand slow heat and prolonged cooking, frequently covered at times by the hood of the grill. These are foods such as spareribs and large portions of meat such as a loin of pork or a rump of beef. Long cooking is necessary to make them tender and well done.

Grilling, which includes charcoal grilling, of course, calls for more practical judgment than almost any other form of cookery, and a manual can give only a broad outline of the factors involved. Charcoal should be heated until a white ash forms. Generally speaking, the charcoal should be one or two layers. The coals must be checked to make certain that heat is emanating from them at all times.

It is an obvious conjecture, of course, to say that grilled foods (not barbecued dishes—they came later with sophistication) were one of the earliest known forms of cooking, ranking in time just after foods cooked directly over flame or coals. Grilled dishes are universal and one of the earliest recorded is in Oriental cookery, a Mongolian grill in which meat and vegetables are cooked on a rounded brazier. Legend has it that the first braziers were Mongol helmets heated over a fire with the food cooked on their rounded crowns. *See also* Yakitori.

Barbe de Capucin

Barbe de capucin, or the beard of a Capuchin or Franciscan monk, is wild chicory, a thin-stemmed green that resembles dandelion in appearance and is excellent but slightly bitter to the taste. I do not know where one can purchase wild chicory, but I am told it does grow wild in American soil.

Barley

It is astonishing to me how many Americans seem unfamiliar with what I consider to be one of the finest of all cereal grains: barley. It is easy to cook, enormously versatile, and its taste and texture, whether used in a soup or hearty casserole, are wholly admirable. Barley is derived from the barley plant, which is a grass. In its natural state, the grains of barley are enclosed in a husk. The majority of packaged barley to be found on the supermarket shelf is marked "pearl" and "medium." Pearl barley is that which has been husked and then polished. The grains are a grayish pale brown color. Medium has nothing to do with size, but refers to the cooking time, as opposed to the quick-cooking grains that have been presteamed at the processing plant before drying and packaging.

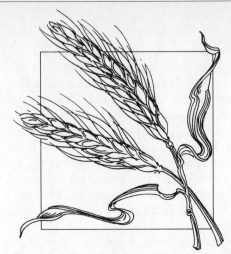

For what it is worth, there is an unpolished version of barley that is brown in color and a bit chewy once cooked; it is sometimes referred to as brown barley or barley groats.

Where barley soups are concerned, the best-known of all is probably Scotch broth, which is made with the neck bones of lamb, vegetables, and barley. Lamb (or mutton) and barley seem to have a particularly flavorful affinity for each other, and barley combined with lamb, paprika, and sour cream makes an excellent Hungarian-style goulash.

Barley Water

I have never sampled barley water but have long known about it as a restorative. The following recipe is from *Mrs. Beeton's Book of Household Management,* which was published in a bound edition in 1861:

"Rinse two ounces of pearl barley and put it in a saucepan with two cups of cold water. Bring to a boil and let simmer 15 minutes. Drain. Add eight cups of boiling water and cook until reduced by half. Strain this liquid. You may sweeten it to taste and flavor it with lemon peel.

"When the invalid may take it," Mrs. Beeton's recipe says, "a little lemon juice gives this pleasant drink in illness a very nice flavor."

A Californian, who had lived in London for several years and drank barley water frequently, wrote to say that it "has a very, very slight syrupy quality to it and feels extremely soothing to tortured throat tissues and upset stomachs. The slipperiness of the liquid helps it go down easily and feels better in the stomach than plain ordinary water, particularly if you are afflicted with an illness that has a fever involved."

Baron

A baron can be of beef or lamb, depending on the country in which you are dining. In England, one speaks of a baron of beef, which, according to Theodora FitzGibbon in her *The Food of the Western World,* is "the most magnificent of all English joints of beef.

"It consists of both the sirloins, cooked and carved as a single joint and not divided at the backbone," she writes. "It is usually roasted upon a spit and is used only for banquets, being too large for any other occasion."

In France and America, one speaks ordinarily of a baron of lamb or of mutton. This consists of the saddle or double loin of lamb or mutton plus the two legs or gigots. The baron is roasted in one piece.

Romance has it that the name was bestowed on the meat by Henry VIII of England. A great gastronome, he was so impressed by the cut of meat as it came from the spit, he knighted it "sir loin, baron of beef."

Barquito

See Sand crabs.

Basil

Some Italian authorities say you can preserve basil leaves in oil and some say no. Marcella Hazan in *More Classic Italian Cooking* says that basil should always be fresh and that it can be grown indoors in winter. Margaret and G. Franco Romagnoli in *The New Italian Cooking* say that "fresh basil may be home packed in olive oil to retain its flavor over the winter."

Giuliano Bugialli in *The Fine Art of Italian Cooking* says that basil can be preserved covered in olive oil, but he seems to prefer to conserve the leaves in salt. Put a layer of kosher salt in a jar with a tight lid; cover with leaves, add more salt, and so on until the jar is filled, ending with a layer of salt. Seal tightly and keep in the refrigerator.

As for me, when fresh basil is not available I use a good deal of dried basil. If I have leftover pesto sauce, I keep it in a jar covered with oil and with a tight lid. As it

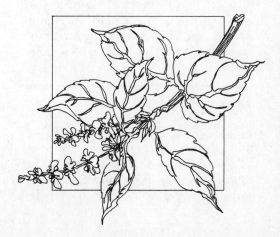

is used, add more oil to cover the pesto.

Pesto has made fresh basil almost a staple in American homes, and the American Spice Trade Association acknowledges that we are in the midst of a basil boom.

"As recently as 1964, we were importing only about forty thousand pounds of dried basil a year," according to the association. "Currently, the annual imports average more than a million pounds, and now, mostly in California, we are producing another three quarters of a million pounds, dried weight. Considering that a pound of dried basil will season enough chicken cacciatore to feed over three thousand people, the increases in poundage are nothing short of spectacular."

Basmati

Basmati is a form of rice that is much prized in India. According to my friend Madhur Jaffrey, author of *An Invitation to Indian Cooking,* basmati grows in the foothills of the Himalayas.

"It has a narrow, long grain and a very special flavor and smell," she says. "The best basmati is aged before it is cooked—and it is cooked only by the rich because it is also very expensive." Because of foreign exchanges, she adds, it is often easier to buy basmati in New York than in New Delhi.

Bay Leaf

Adding a bay leaf to a dish is more than just a "gourmet" flourish. Just as Chinese chefs almost invariably link chopped ginger and garlic in recipes, so do French chefs link

thyme and bay leaf. If you swipe a French chef's supply of bay leaves, it would be tantamount to stealing a pastry chef's vanilla. Bay leaf, except on rare occasions, should be used with discretion, but it most certainly adds a good, positive flavor to savory dishes such as soups, stews, and sauces.

Always remove it before serving the dish. If swallowed whole, the splinter-like stem could damage the intestinal tract.

Once in a while recipes call for ground bay leaf and why it is not generally available I do not know. What I have was produced and packaged in Turkey. I have bought ground or powdered bay leaf on the island of St.-Barthélemy in the Caribbean; I believe it was of French origin. However, if I am out of it and a recipe calls for ground bay leaf, I break up a whole dried leaf and pulverize it in an electric spice grinder.

Béarnaise

I have a friend and neighbor, a marvelous cook named Claudia Ferguson, who turns out her omelets, soufflés, elegant sauces, and the like in kitchens in both East Hampton and Montreal. Claudia is also a scientist, and she sent me a tear sheet from *Nature* magazine. The article was titled "Interparticle Forces in Multiphase Colloid Systems" and described all a scientist would ever want to know about the sauce known as béarnaise. The authors were C. M. Perram, C. Nicolau, and J. W. Perram.

A béarnaise sauce, they tell us, is nothing more than "colloidal particles [which] are micelles consisting of a mixture of phospholipids, fats, proteins, cholesterol, and various long-chain unsaturated fatty acids. The aqueous phase contains mainly acetic acid and sodium chloride at ionic strengths determined by the initial conditions."

So now you know what to tell your guests in case they wonder what you're serving with that artichoke heart.

Beaten Biscuits

My mother, a dyed-in-the-wool southern belle, ranked beaten biscuits among things southern, right up there with quail on toast, Jefferson Davis, and Robert E. Lee. She had them made for all her fancy gatherings, which took place mostly in the afternoon.

I say "had them made" because she

was fortunate enough to have help in the house, and the help took turns beating the dough.

Northerners, of course, are not aware of the technique of beaten biscuit-making. Beaten biscuits, the sound of them being made, was something you woke up to on a sleepy Sunday morning.

You would blend some flour with lard and salt and water. You would mix this mass a while, then take a stick or an ax handle or some other firm, heavy, elongated object, and beat the dough until blisters formed, sometimes for as much as half an hour or longer. You would then roll it out, cut it into small rounds, prick the tops with the tines of a fork, and bake them. The trick was to bake the biscuits so that they would not only be cooked, but also be as white as possible top to bottom. Another test of doneness was when they split easily.

In my earliest childhood, there was the stump of a sawed-down walnut tree outside the kitchen window. It was clean and solid and that was the surface on which the biscuits were whacked until blistered. You could hear the sound of the blisters popping to indicate that the dough was almost ready for rolling out.

My mother never had baking powder put in beaten biscuit dough, although some people did, and those homes that used baking powder were beneath my mother's regard. And according to her recipe, you always pricked the tops with the tines of a silver fork.

People who didn't know what they were about would sometimes serve beaten biscuits with jellies and jams, but the genuine articles to eat with beaten biscuits were thin, small slices of aged country ham.

Some people don't understand beaten biscuits. For example, Miss Eliza Leslie of

Philadelphia wrote in her *New Cookery Book,* published in 1857, that a beaten biscuit "is the most laborious of cakes." Miss Leslie added, "And also the most unwholesome, even when made in the best manner. We do not recommend it; but there is no accounting for tastes. Children should not eat these biscuits—nor grown persons either, if they can get any other sort of bread. Believe nobody that says they are not unwholesome. Better to live on Indian cakes."

As kitchen help became scarcer, some cooks resorted to "biscuit brakes," a contrivance with two metal rollers that operated by turning a handle. The dough was fed through the rollers many times to approximate the two hundred whacks that were normally used for beating the dough. Sometimes the rollers were powered by electricity to simplify the task.

Beefsteak Leopold

See Steak au poivre.

Beef Tea

Years ago someone gave me a recipe for beef tea but I've never tried it. As well as I can reconstruct it, you take a batch of twice-ground beef and put it in a container with a tight-fitting lid. You add cold water barely to cover and salt and pepper to taste. Seal this mixture tightly and set the container on a rack in a basin of cold water.

Bring the water to the boil and let the mixture cook about 1 hour. Remove the container and let the beef cool. Line a sieve with a double thickness of cheesecloth and strain the "tea" through it. Refrigerate. Bring to the boil before serving.

It sounds like an awfully expensive cup of tea to me, but several people assured me I didn't know what I was missing.

"When I was a child," one wrote, "thin, frail, with no appetite, my mother (who was born in Poland near Austria) made beef tea 'to build me.'

"It was always made of neck meat cut into chunks, simmered in the top of a double boiler, with just a little water around the meat. I was supposed to drink the juice. I also ate the chunks of meat. It was delicious; not dried out at all. You can't imagine how good it was. There was absolutely no fat on the meat.

"I have no idea whether it was, indeed, a cure-all, but it made me feel loved and cared for—which may be the same thing."

Another sent her mother's recipe for the tea:

"Have the butcher cut a thick slice (about one inch) of top of the round. It should weigh two pounds or more. Trim off all the fat and discard. Cut the beef into cubes, put it in a bowl, cover with cold water and let stand about two hours.

"Put the soaking water and the beef into a pot. Cover tightly and simmer for an hour or longer, depending on how concentrated you want the tea.

"Strain the liquid and discard the meat. Add salt to taste."

Beef Wellington

I am persuaded that beef Wellington is of Irish origin. In *Irish Traditional Food,* Theodora FitzGibbon offers a recipe for

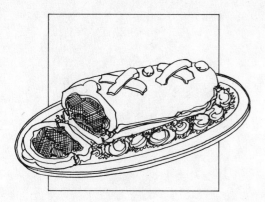

consisting of a light beer thickened with potato flour. Flavored with lemon peel and various spices, including cinnamon, it is sweetened with sugar and served hot with pieces of fried bread.

Steig Wellington, using the Irish spelling for steak. She prefaces the recipe with the statement that "this was said to be a favorite of the Duke of Wellington, who was born in Ireland, and it is sometimes also known as beef Wellington." The recipe calls for fillet of beef wrapped with cooked mushrooms in flaky pastry and baked.

Beer

Beer is often called for as a liquid in recipes, and it does, of course, contribute a slightly different flavor, although the difference is not a matter of pronounced bitterness.

I prefer to cook shrimp in beer if I want a platter of boiled shrimp. I would be hard put to tell you precisely why I feel the shrimp taste better when cooked in beer.

Beer is also used in a batter for deep-frying. In this case the beer substitutes for yeast as a mild leavening agent. The best-known main course prepared with beer is the carbonnade flamande of Belgian cuisine.

There is also a beer soup, but the samples that I have tasted are nothing I would recommend. It is said to be a German specialty

Bee's Knees

With the repeal of Prohibition in this country and even before that in such well-known watering places as the bar of the Savoy in London, bartenders were much given to the creation of new drinks, most of which were christened with fanciful, if not to say coy, names.

I tracked down the Bee's Knees cocktail in David A. Embury's *Fine Art of Mixing Drinks*, to my mind the finest American bar book, although I find it of more interest as a historical reflection of certain aspects of the Charleston and 23 Skiddoo age, than as a guide to cocktail mixing.

In any event, I learned from Mr. Embury that a Bee's Knees cocktail is made with one-half ounce of honey, one ounce of lemon juice, and four ounces of gin. These are shaken with cracked ice, strained, and served to two thirsty parties.

A friend from Washington, D.C., wrote:

"When I was young, our family lived in the summer on a farm near Mexico, Indiana. Every Fourth of July we had an absolutely smashing party of family and friends. Besides knockout fireworks we had two unchanging traditions. One was a case of twenty-four bottles of pop for the six of us children. The other was Bee's Knees for the adults.

"The Bee's Knees were made of equal parts of freshly squeezed orange and lemon juices, honey, and gin, garnished with fresh mint spears. When we children grew up and were allowed the Bee's Knees, we always figured our falling about so was due to the honey."

The definitive comment on the subject seems to have come from a cerebral and resourceful acquaintance, also from Washington, D.C., who notes, "Besides being the name of a cocktail invented at the Savoy Hotel in London, 'the bee's knees' was a slang expression of the twenties meaning something like 'super' or 'smashing.' According to H. L. Mencken's *The American Language,* the expression was coined by Tad Dorgan, the cartoonist, who also originated 'the cat's pajamas,' 'the snake's hips,' and similar absurd superlatives."

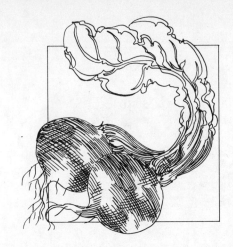

Beets

Beets—or beetroots, as they are known in the British Isles—seem to occupy a curious place in gastronomy. They are much appreciated by many people and looked on with disdain as mere animal food by others.

In the latter category, one finds that well-known and widely admired British food writer Jane Grigson. In her well-researched work *Jane Grigson's Vegetable Book,* she states that the lack of esteem in which beets are held by her fellow countrymen may be partly "the beetroot's fault. It is not an inspiring vegetable, unless you have a medieval passion for highly colored food. . . . I have not heard anyone claim it as their favorite."

Perhaps not in England. But here in America it seems duly more appreciated. It is the basis, of course, for that all-American (and appropriately crimson) dish Harvard beets; it is the heart and soul of a well-made borscht, and there is rarely a salad bar, from Bangor to Berkeley, that does not boast its bowl of pickled beets.

Pierre Franey and I even conceived the notion of a beet pie, which has been well received by neighbors and friends. We combined puréed beets with a little corn syrup, eggs, raisins, and nuts, and the result, to judge by the appetites of our guests, was admirable. Curiously enough, the flavor of the pie filling is such that there was a good deal of second-guessing among our friends to determine the major ingredient of the filling. Few could guess that it was the humble beet. *See also* Harvard beets.

Beggar's Chicken

There is a well-known legend about the centuries-old Chinese dish called beggar's chicken, involving a thief or beggar or both who stole a chicken and went down by the riverside to roast it. He had built a fire, and when the coals and ashes were almost ready to receive the bird, he looked up the hill and saw strangers advancing toward him. He hastily dug a pit next to the fire and buried the unplucked chicken, feathers and all, in the clay. After an hour or so the strangers departed and he unearthed his booty. The clay was hot and hardened, and after it cooled he cracked it. Off it came and the feathers came with it. And lo and behold the chicken was cooked from the heat. It was, the story goes, finger-lickin' good.

Belgian Endive

Among the handful of vegetables and salad greens that most appeal to my palate is one of the most difficult to cultivate, Belgian

endive. Endive is cultivated by hand, as it has been for the past 125 years, on the Flemish flatlands that surround Brussels. The vegetable defies harvesting by machine. The seeds are sown by hand and, when they produce roots at the end of six weeks, the roots must be dug up and replanted in a blend of sand and soil that offers both heat and humidity, plus total darkness. It is this combination of factors that produces a premature, straight, smooth, and fragile-crisp endive.

As if this were not labor enough, the endive is then harvested, replanted, and covered with deep-layered mounds of loamy earth. Weeks later, the ready-to-market endive is again brought to the surface by hand, washed, spin-dried, and packaged to be sold at home or shipped overseas.

An average harvest is estimated at about 80,000 tons a year; of this, more than 550 tons are exported to the United States for the delectation of those who cherish the finer things of the table.

In my own kitchen, I generally cut it, rinse, and pat or spin dry it before using, but not necessarily for reasons of hygiene. After cutting it into bite-size pieces or thin julienne strips a good rinse in cold water will prevent the cut pieces from discoloring. If left to stand after cutting, the cut edges tend to darken.

Though I am assured that the endive as it is packaged is wholly clean, rinsing only takes seconds and doesn't damage the product. Still, there have been times when, in considerable haste, I have simply cut the endive into a salad bowl without further ado.

And, to my mind, braised endive (cooked with a touch of sugar and lemon juice until brown and tender) is one of the finest vegetable dishes.

Bellyfish

See Monkfish.

Berberé

Berberé is a blended spice mixture used in Ethiopian cooking, frequently added to stews. It includes ginger, cardamom, coriander, fenugreek seeds, nutmeg, cloves, and allspice, plus a good helping of ground hot red pepper.

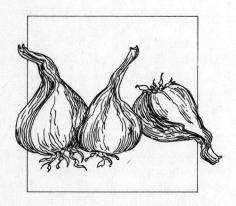

Bercy

Bercy is a ward, borough, or *quartier* of Paris that was a marketplace for wines, now the site of warehouses. Most of the dishes that bear the name Bercy generally have white wine as an ingredient. Bercy butter is made of a blend of butter, occasionally poached beef marrow, chopped shallots simmered down in dry white wine, a sprinkling of parsley, and a bit of lemon juice.

Sauce bercy is a blend of shallots cooked down in dry white wine with the addition of cream.

Beurre Blanc

Although beurre blanc has been around for generations, it has come into prominence with nouvelle cuisine, which eschews all sauces that "burden" other foods. Without question a more delicate sauce than hollandaise, beurre blanc is a very light butter sauce (the term literally means "white butter") made quickly and easily with reduced white wine and shallots, with bits of butter beaten in. It is irresistible with simply cooked fish or seafood, such as steamed shrimp or grilled salmon. Its counterpart—somewhat less frequently found on the new menus—is beurre rouge, which is the same as beurre blanc except that the "rouge" is made with red wine instead of white, and it is served with dark meats, such as grilled or broiled steaks.

There is one pitfall to be avoided in making the sauce. Basically, it is prepared by beating butter into the reduced wine while stirring vigorously with a whisk, but special caution must be taken so that the butter does not reach the point just below boiling when it could separate and become clear. It should, however, be hot.

Beurre Manié

A beurre manié is a blend of flour and butter that is added to thicken soups or sauces.

For one chemical reason or another, when a beurre manié is added to a soup or sauce, the raw taste of the flour is not apparent. If you add flour blended with water, the raw taste of the flour is going to be apparent in whatever you are cooking. Also, a beurre manié will give you a smoother or silkier result.

Bialy

A bialy is an onion roll five to seven inches in diameter, made with yeast and with a depression in the center. The onions with which it is garnished are chopped fine, browned lightly, and baked on top. The name derives from Bialystok, a Polish city.

Bible Leaf

See Costmary.

Bigos

A bigos is a hunter's stew, a winter holiday dish in Poland. It is one of those rare dishes that is best made a few days in advance, because by tradition it must be reheated three or more times before serving.

There is an interesting legend attached to the origin of the stew. It seems that back when aristocracy was in flower and servants were a commonplace, it was customary for hunters to go into the forests or mountains with porters or kettle-bearers along in what were occasionally quests, several days long, for furred and feathered animals.

At the start of the kill, fires were built and the kettles put over the coals. Cabbage and sauerkraut were added and allowed to simmer at intervals for several days. As the hunting progressed, depending on the hunter's skill, various wild meats were added to the kettle. The hunters feasted on the contents day by day and, according to the legend, the dish reached the peak of flavor on the last day of the hunt.

Billi Bi

Billi Bi is to my mind conceivably the greatest soup ever created. I have always ascribed the name of this soup to a tin tycoon named William B. Leeds (Billy B.). The gentleman dined often at Maxim's in Paris and his favorite soup was a cream of mussel that the restaurant eventually listed on the menu as Billi Bi.

A friend alleges that the soup was named not for the tin tycoon but for his son, who bore the same name. The son inherited $7 million on his father's death in 1908 and became a famous playboy and philanthropist.

In his obituary in *The New York Times* January 3, 1972, it was noted that he was "an ardent yachtsman, speedboat racer, and airplane pilot" and "spent much of his time on his 254-foot yacht *Moana,* which had been built at a cost of $1.5 million."

Seriously ill, he committed suicide at the age of sixty-nine.

Birchermuesli

See Muesli.

Birds

Among my favorite foods are almost all stuffed and rolled meats, and I am equally fascinated by the names that they bear. In English, they are called veal birds, lamb rolls, and beef bundles. They are also known as "birds" in France and Italy. French chefs speak not only of *paupiettes* but also of *oiseaux sans tête,* or birds without a head. Stuffed veal rolls in Italy are sometimes referred to as *quagliette di vitello,* or little veal quails. Italian cooks also refer to *gli uccelli scappati,* or birds that have escaped.

Bird's Nest Soup

A proper, classically made bird's nest soup is indeed made of birds' nests. It is one of the most expensive and sought-after dishes in Chinese cuisine. One explanation of how the nests are created appears in Tom Stobart's *The Cook's Encyclopedia.* The birds are similar to swifts and nest in colonies in Southeast Asia, fastening their nests to the rocky walls and ceilings of caverns with a gelatinous spit rather than mud.

The nests are collected in semidarkness, and it is dangerous work. There are two main categories of nests used, the black and the white. The white nests are of first quality; the black are cheaper and must be cleaned of debris to make them edible, a tedious process.

Another explanation came from a Manhattan woman, who attributed much of her information to *Golden Earth—Travels in Burma* by Norman Lewis.

"The white nests," she wrote, "are made by the gray-rumped swift. This bird breeds in caves on the islands of the Mergui Archipelago, once belonging to Siam, now a part of Burma. Its nest is transparent and takes three months to make from the fine web-like threads of saliva secreted by the bird. These white nests are exported to China, where they have long been prized as a delicacy and restorer of life. A related species of bird produces 'black' nests containing feathers and flies, difficult to clean, and are sold to less exacting Chinese."

Birds' nests, by the way, are available in specialty shops in America.

Biscaïenne

Biscaïenne refers to the Bay of Biscay, an inlet of the Atlantic Ocean bordered by Spain and France. The ingredients that characterize Biscayan dishes include those commonly associated with Spain and the South of France—tomatoes, peppers, pimientos, and garlic.

Biscuit

See Zwieback.

Bishop

The drink called bishop bears a strong resemblance to mulled wine, which is to say a heated spiced wine. Basically a bishop, sometimes spelled bischof, consists of wine that is heated and spiced with such seasonings as allspice, cloves, ginger, nutmeg, cinnamon, and mace. It is also flavored with the peel of oranges or lemon or sometimes with whole baked or roasted oranges. The wines used in preparing a bishop range from a table wine, such as a Rhine or Alsatian wine or a Bordeaux, to fortified wines, such as Madeira, sherry, and port.

The drink has been especially popular in northern European countries and has never had a widespread appeal in America.

The following is from Dickens' *A Christmas Carol* and occurs at the end of that fable:

"A merry Christmas, Bob!" said Scrooge, with an earnestness that could not be mistaken, as he clapped him on the back. "A merrier Christmas, Bob, my good fellow, than I have given you for many a year! I'll raise your salary, and endeavor to assist your struggling family, and we will discuss your affairs this very afternoon, over a Christmas bowl of smoking bishop, Bob! Make up the fires, and buy another coalscuttle before you dot another i, Bob Cratchit!"

Blackbirds

Blackbirds—or *merles* as they are called in French—are one of the great Corsican specialties. The birds are simply plucked without clearing away the inner parts and roasted entire. This is by no means uncommon throughout Europe. Whole woodcocks, ortolans, and rice birds are great delicacies when cooked without eviscerating. To clean them before cooking would—to many fine palates—be considered a sacrilege. The flesh of blackbirds is tender and dark and not at all dry.

Black Pudding

See Sailor's duff.

Black Radishes

Black radishes are most widely admired in Jewish cuisine. They should be peeled and sliced or shredded. One of the most popular

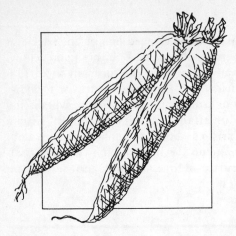

uses for them is in a "conserve" of radish and chicken fat.

The best version of this is one I dined on years ago in the home of the late Paula Peck. In her notable book *The Art of Good Cooking,* she recommends that you scrape the radishes and shred them on a coarse grater. You sprinkle with salt and let them stand in the refrigerator, covered, for about two hours.

Rinse the radishes well first in cold water, then in ice water and squeeze out as much of the water as possible until they are quite dry. Put them in a bowl, add about ⅓ cup of rendered chicken fat for each 2 cups of radishes, 1 small chopped onion, and ½ teaspoon of black pepper.

Blend well and pack into clean jars, tightly covered. Store in the refrigerator.

Blanc Légume

A blanc légume is a "whitener" made of flour and water that is added to the liquid in which vegetables are cooked to keep them white. A blanc légume is used chiefly for cooking artichokes, which darken rapidly on oxidation. It is sometimes used in cook-ing cauliflower, for the same reason.

The technique for adding it is generally to place a sieve over the cooking utensil containing the vegetable, which is covered by cold water. Flour is added to the sieve and water is poured over it so that it is added slowly and evenly to prevent lumping. A similar solution is sometimes—but by no means invariably—used for cooking calves' heads, sweetbreads, and brains.

Blanquette

There are two outstanding dishes in French cookery that are strongly similar but cooked by two distinct methods. One is blanquette, the other a navarin. Both are generally made with veal or lamb or chicken and both are enriched with cream and egg yolks. In the navarin, the meat is browned before the stew is made. In a blanquette, the meat is cooked for a brief period, but browning must be carefully avoided. The name blanquette comes from the French word blanc, meaning white.

Blawn

This dish is or was a specialty of the Orkney Islands of Scotland. Blawn reputedly means windblown and refers to a manner of preparing codfish or whiting. The fish is cleaned and rubbed inside and out with salt. A length of string is passed through the eye sockets and the fish is suspended outdoors for a day or so to be dried in the wind. It is then sprinkled all over with flour and cooked over an open fire with a little melted butter poured on it.

Blind Broth

In many broths there are droplets of fat on the surface that the French often refer to as "eyes." *Bouillon aveugle,* or blind broth, is an ordinary broth without these droplets.

Blood Oranges

See Maltaise sauce.

Bloody Mary

To my taste, the greatest preprandial, mid-day drink ever created in America is a Bloody Mary. I have no earthly idea where the cocktail originated, although I have heard numerous claims in that direction, all of them open to question.

As far as I can date the drink, it came about shortly after the end of the Second World War. Before that—and this may be difficult for anyone under the age of thirty to believe—vodka was virtually unknown in this country and Tabasco was something that, in those days of yore, Southerners added to soups and stews and sprinkled on breakfast eggs.

Hughes Rudd of *CBS News* offered his thoughts on the origin of the Bloody Mary.

"I had my first Bloody Mary at Felix's Blue Bar on the Croisette in Cannes in 1944," he said. "It was called a Blood and Guts, and Felix told me he'd named it for General George Patton. It was made exactly as are most Bloody Marys today: vodka, tomato juice, Worcestershire sauce, and hot pepper sauce (I doubt that Felix had any genuine Tabasco sauce squirreled away).

"In 1948 I went back to Felix's, this time as a newspaperman, and he was still serving the Blood and Guts but by then had changed the name to Bloody Mary."

An article by Jill Newman in *Gentleman's Quarterly* mentioned that determining the origin of the drink was "almost as difficult as determining who first cooked a beef patty and named it a hamburger.

"Leonard Lyons proclaimed in his column that George Jessel was the inventor," she wrote, "while his rival, Walter Winchell, countered that it was novelist Ernest Hemingway who came up with it sometime during the twenties. A more likely prospect is Fernand L. Petiot, who began experimenting with vodka drinks in 1920 while dispensing libations at Harry's New York bar in Paris." She added, "The drink never caught on in France, but Petiot brought it with him to the States in 1934 when he went to work for Vincent Astor, who then owned New York's St. Regis Hotel."

Petiot's drink was not called a Bloody Mary. George Jessel, Miss Newman wrote, says that he not only created the drink but named it as well. He was, she says, a sort of toastmaster and roving ambassador for a leading vodka maker.

And no one, I firmly believe, will ever know the truth.

Blue Cornmeal

Blue cornmeal, which is referred to in Mexican or Tex-Mex kitchens as blue cornmeal masa, is a delectable oddity. I have dined on tortillas made with blue cornmeal, and

have seen the cornmeal packaged, but I have never seen blue corn.

I am told that the corn kernels are indeed a pale purplish blue and that they are roasted before they are milled. Experts in the field find that blue cornmeal masa has a deeper, richer, more nut-like flavor. I do not know why the cultivation of the corn and the production of the masa seem largely limited to New Mexico.

Blue-Plate Special

The term "blue-plate special" used to be found frequently on menus, and you still see it occasionally.

Webster's New World Dictionary, Second College Edition, says the term refers to "an inexpensive restaurant meal served at a fixed price on a large plate, originally blue, with compartments." The *Wise Encyclopedia of Cookery* says, "Originally the plates were made in a blue-patterned ware, which explains the name, but they may now be bought in a variety of makes and patterns in china and glass." It adds, "The compartments prevent sauces from running into

each other, and such vegetables as stewed tomatoes may be served on the same plate as the rest of the dinner, thus saving dish-washing."

Boiled Dressing

A staple in my home as a child, boiled dressing is something I have not tasted in years. It consists of mustard, sugar, red pepper, flour, eggs, butter, milk, and vinegar, which are cooked over low heat until thickened and served on mixed fruit. My mother also churned all the ingredients, including the fruit, to produce a frozen fruit salad; I disliked it intensely.

Bombay Duck

Bombay duck is a fairly traditional accompaniment for curried foods. It has nothing to do with poultry, however, but is dried salted fish. A package that I have on my pantry shelf (purchased at a local supermarket in the specialty food section) notes that the name of the fish is bommaloe. My research tells me that the name derives from bombil, a regional name for certain fish.

The curry accompaniment is a bit distasteful to many Western palates; it reminds some people of asafetida. There are several ways in which the "ducks" are prepared. They may be baked until crisp, broken into small bits and sprinkled over the curry, or they may be deep fried or grilled before crushing.

Bombe

I do not know precisely when the name bombe came to be used for a dessert, but I have been told that it was after the First World War. I have also been told that the original bombes were in the shape of large shells and that, perhaps, actual empty shells were used for packing ice cream before unmolding. As time went on, bombes took on an endless number of less-than-lethal designs.

Bonne Femme

The term "bonne femme," literally translated as good wife, is applied to numerous foods including chicken, small birds, meats, soups, and apples. The most famous dish called bonne femme is made with fish, more often than not sole, in which the poached fish is served in a white wine sauce made with fish stock, shallots, butter, and mushrooms.

Booya

According to Karin Winegar, food editor of the *Minneapolis Star and Tribune,* booya is Bohemian in origin and appears frequently on the table of large gatherings in Minnesota. She says there are many versions of the dish, which is, essentially, chicken and beef cooked together with assorted vegetables, such as navy beans, carrots, celery, onions, string beans, and mushrooms. More elaborate versions call for oxtails, corn, and cabbage, plus pickling spices.

Borscht

The best-known soup in the Russian repertory is, of course, borscht, which most people think of as a simple beet and cabbage potage served at table with a dollop of sour cream. Actually, a borscht, made to the tsar's taste, resembles a rather fancy and elaborate beet-colored pot-au-feu. The finest borscht is made with an assortment of vegetables, sausages, and, if you really want the feast to be sumptuous, roast duck and roast meat.

As far as can be ascertained, beets or beetroots are an absolute essential for any kind of borscht, of which there are many. In *The Food of the Western World,* Theodora FitzGibbon defines borscht (there are numerous spellings, including borsch, bortch and bartch) as "a traditional beetroot and cabbage soup eaten in Russia, the Ukraine, and also Poland. It is made with pieces of beef, bacon, game, or poultry, with the meat stock, onions, caraway seed, cabbage, and beetroot and half the beetroot stock."

She also notes that borscht flotsky adds to the basic recipe a quantity of diced vegetables. Borscht kholodny, she adds, is a cold borscht with the addition of pickled cucumber, scallions, hard-boiled eggs, sour cream, and kvass, a fermented beverage made with barley or rye. Borscht polsky is Polish borscht containing roast duck, and borscht skobelev contains, in addition to the basics, diced salt pork, potatoes, fried sausages, and meatballs.

Then came a letter from a Queens woman:

"Borscht does not have to be made with beets. Theodora FitzGibbon was referring to 'summer' and 'winter' borscht. 'Spring' or 'green' borscht, which has been in my husband's family (the Russian half) for many years, is a great soup if you have a jaded palate and don't know what you want to eat. And a good way to use up hard-boiled eggs after Easter." *See also* Chlodnik, Rossel borscht.

Boston Baked Beans

Boston baked beans are a blend of navy beans, salt pork, and molasses, cooked for hours until the beans are tender. In *The Dictionary of American Food and Drink*, John F. Mariani says that it is sometimes maintained that the dish was introduced to the American colonists by the Indians.

But, he adds, the novelist Kenneth Roberts, in an essay on "The Forgotten Marrowbones," printed in Marjorie Mosser's *Foods of Old New England*, argued that baked beans had long been a traditional Sabbath dish among the North African and Spanish Jews, who called it *skanah*.

Mr. Roberts also cites "Riley's Narrative" (1816) by James Riley, as a source and supposes that New England sea captains carried the idea home with them from Africa.

Mr. Mariani adds that the dish became associated with Boston. The Puritan women baked their beans on Saturday and served them the same evening. On Sunday they served the leftovers with cod cakes and Boston brown bread for breakfast. Because cooking was forbidden on Sunday, they often served beans again for lunch.

Boston Coffee

Boston coffee is made simply by mixing cream and sugar in a cup and pouring in freshly percolated coffee.

Curiously enough, coffee does seem to have a smoother taste if the ingredients are blended in this fashion, although I cannot explain the chemistry. Why coffee thus made is dubbed Boston I do not know, but presumably the recipe must have been popular at some time in the home of the bean and the cod.

Boston Cream Pie

There is a recipe in Fannie Farmer's *Boston Cooking School Cook Book*, dated 1896, called Boston favorite cake. It is made with butter, sugar, eggs, milk, flour, and baking powder and is essentially the same as the layer cake used in making a Boston cream pie, which is really not a pie at all but a cake that is layered with a filling of pastry cream in the center. It can be supposed, of

course, that some cook used that "favorite cake," filled the center with pastry cream, and dubbed the creation Boston cream pie.

Boudins Blancs

Boudins blancs are white sausages, literally white puddings. Technically, if you go by Escoffier in the preparation of your boudins blancs, they may be made with pork (boudin blanc ordinaire) or chicken breast (boudin blanc de volaille).

The ordinary sausages, made with finely minced or ground pork, plus pork fat, are blended with eggs, onion cooked in butter, cream, salt, pepper, and nutmeg. The chicken sausages are made with finely ground or minced chicken breast, pork fat, onion cooked in butter, thyme, bay leaf, salt, pepper, egg whites, and a touch of nutmeg. Either of these preparations is stuffed into sausage casings before cooking.

Weisswurst, the great white sausage specialty of Munich, is generally made with veal, pork, bread crumbs, nutmeg, salt, pepper, and, sometimes, lemon peel or parsley. It is also stuffed into casings before cooking.

Bouillabaisse

One of the most engrossing and best-known (in food circles) treatises on a single dish ever written is contained in Waverley Root's scholarly and invaluable *The Food of France*. It is that section of the book that deals with bouillabaisse. There are nine pages dedicated to that famous Mediterranean stew, and only the most self-denying ascetic could peruse those pages without surges of hunger pangs and nostalgia for the French Riviera in general and Marseilles in particular (although the author avers that the finest bowls of bouillabaisse he's encountered were not in Marseilles but elsewhere).

Mr. Root rather strictly outlines the definition of a genuine bouillabaisse, which he terms "a sort of fish chowder." He declares that there is one fish imperative to a proper bouillabaisse and that is *rascasse* or devil fish, and the remainder of the catch may be somewhat free-wheeling but bearing such names as conger (conger eel) and grondin (sea robin). The bases of the liquid and seasonings include olive oil, tomatoes, and saffron. A true bouillabaisse, he concludes,

must be made exclusively with fish from the Mediterranean. I do not dispute Mr. Root and his conclusions, but I feel strongly that by using local fish from the Atlantic and Pacific shores of the United States you can produce a *soupe de poissons* that would be a peer of the finest bouillabaisse. *See also* Bourride.

Bouillon

See Broth.

Bouillon de Noce

Bouillon de noce, or wedding broth, is a specialty of the Périgord region and is a hearty soup that could serve as a meal in itself. It is made by cooking four kinds of meat—veal knuckle, beef, a stuffed chicken, and turkey—as well as carrots, celery, and Swiss chard in a well-seasoned broth. Thin strands of pasta, such as vermicelli, are added to the soup before serving.

Boula-Boula

In my childhood, boula-boula was a soup to be served on fancy occasions. It was made with a blend of two canned soups, a cream of green pea and a green turtle. As a finishing touch my mother always added a dollop of whipped cream, and the dishes were run briefly under the broiler until the cream was lightly browned.

I have never found the definitive volume that points out the exact origin of the soup.

One source says that it is an American soup, but adds, oddly enough, that it "originally came from the Seychelles." At least one reason for the diminished popularity of the soup is that in many parts of the world it is forbidden by law to trap green turtles.

Boulangère

Boulangère means in the style of the baker's wife, thus named because any dish so-called is baked. The other characteristic of a dish boulangère is that it contains potatoes and onions.

Bouquet Garni

In its broadest sense, a bouquet garni is any small bunch of herbs and seasonings tied together, often in cheesecloth, and added to a soup, stew, liquid for cooking fish (a court bouillon), and so on. The most basic and traditional bouquet garni consists of parsley, thyme sprigs, and bay leaf tied with string into a small bundle. When fresh thyme sprigs are not available, a little dried thyme can be substituted for the fresh. The bouquet garni is removed, of course, once a dish is cooked.

Bourride

Bouillabaisse is, of course, the most famous of all Mediterranean fish dishes, but there is a related soup that I consider even more interesting. It is called bourride, and the fine points that distinguish the two have been argued for years. Some say that essentially bouillabaisse contains saffron and that bourride does not. I dispute that and can find sound sources to prove it. I feel that the difference lies in other more basic ingredients. Bouillabaisse contains shellfish, bourride does not. Bourride is blended with aïoli, a sort of garlic mayonnaise, bouillabaisse is not.

Boxty

Boxty is a blend of grated raw potatoes and cooked mashed potatoes; some recipes call for a small amount of baking soda blended with a little flour, which is blended into the mixture to make a dough. The dough is shaped into a round and cut into quarters or scones. It is cooked on a greased griddle until both sides are well browned.

The food is sometimes referred to as boxty bread. One source notes that the bread dates from the Irish famine, "when it was made to eke out the limited supplies of flour and make the best use of poor potatoes."

Braciola

Braciola is the Italian word for chop or cutlet, and in this country it applies to beef or veal. In Italy you will find braciola dishes made of lamb chops or pork chops.

A specialty of Sicily consists of "cutlets" of swordfish, skinless, boneless pieces of fillet that are stuffed with more fish, bread crumbs, and cheese, rolled and baked.

The word "braciolette," a derivative, often refers to meat rolls, sometimes cooked in a tomato sauce.

Braising

A couple of decades of observing the cooking and dining patterns of Americans have led me to the conclusion that cooks have one need that, if met, would put them in a state of absolute nirvana in the kitchen. Particularly those cooks with a desire to entertain guests. The need is for a dish, subtly seasoned and tempting, that could be made hours or even days in advance, or, for that matter, frozen and defrosted on schedule.

There is in the cooking lexicon a six-letter word that, as much as any other, would be the answer or solution to this need, and it is b-r-a-i-s-e. In its broadest sense, braising consists of cooking foods, large or small, in a small quantity of water.

In the strictest sense, too, it is not essential to brown foods in fat to braise them. The fact is, however, that foods that have been browned—sometimes floured before cooking—before braising generally look and taste more appealing.

In France, the word "braise" means active cinders or live charcoal, and braising, no doubt, originally meant cooking in a casserole or other vessel over live embers. Boeuf à la braise, for example, is braised beef.

Almost all foods can be braised but not all braised foods keep or fare equally well the second time around. Meats such as beef, pork, lamb, and veal fare best. Braised shellfish dishes, such as those made with shrimp, lobster, and crab, can be reheated, but they lose something in both texture and flavor. Chicken, turkey, and duck tend to take on second-day or refrigerator flavors when left overnight.

Branch

Branch refers to branch water, which is, at a New York bar, only a figure of speech. Water from a branch, in the mind of some bourbon drinkers, is the purest form of water. I am much taken with the poetic definition of a branch found in the second edition of *Webster's New International Dictionary*: "A brook, run or rivulet, smaller than a creek and ranging in size down to the tiniest rill. Such branches often come from springs or seeps."

Brandade

A brandade de morue, often poorly translated as a salt cod paste or a mousse of salt cod, is to many a Western food connoisseur the quintessential food from Provence. It is made with the ultimate ingredients of that region—pure olive oil and an abundance of garlic. Plus the salt cod. It is to my taste one of the finest of all appetizers or first courses and is inevitably served in my home as part of a New Year's Eve buffet.

The dish is made with boiled potatoes and cooked salt cod that are beaten to a paste, along with a good quantity of chopped garlic, oil, and hot milk and cream. The finest brandade is garnished with chopped black truffles. Ideally, it is served with thin triangles of bread that have been brushed with melted butter or olive oil and baked until crisp and golden brown.

Brawn

See Headcheese.

Bread-and-Butter Pickles

I have been told that the term bread-and-butter pickles came about because some home chef made a preparation of sliced cucumbers with vinegar, turmeric, mustard seeds, sliced onion, and sugar and sold the bottled pickle slices at a roadside stand.

The income they produced was pro-

other food writer, stale bread in my mind indicates bread that is becoming moldy, both in taste and appearance. That, obviously, would never do. Bread that is a day or two old is also loose terminology. If it has been kept closely wrapped in plastic, it is still soft throughout.

Ideally, the crumbs should be made from bread that is not too fresh but by no means stale. It should be a trifle dried out, otherwise the crumbs may be a bit gummy.

nounced "bread and butter"—the earnings for the summer. In the dictionaries bread-and-butter means basic or commonplace as opposed to fancy; the term has a long history in the meaning "taken as a type of everyday food."

Bread Crumbs

Dried bread crumbs refer to commercially sold bread crumbs. Fresh bread crumbs are those prepared by putting bread slices trimmed of crust in a blender or food processor and blending until the crumbs come out fine. Freshly made bread crumbs, by the way, can be spooned into glass jars with a tight seal and stored for a week or longer in the refrigerator. They can be frozen indefinitely. Dried bread crumbs and fresh bread crumbs cannot be used interchangeably. In fact, the occasions on which I have used dried bread crumbs are exceedingly rare. Fresh bread crumbs give a better texture to breaded dishes and to such things as meat loaf.

Although I have been as guilty of calling for "stale" bread for bread crumbs as any

Breading

There are some basic cooking techniques that cannot be repeated too often for the sake of inexperienced cooks, and breading is one of them. Put a quantity of flour, enough to coat your food generously, in one dish. In a second dish put beaten raw egg to which you may add a spoonful of water or oil or both. In a third, place fresh bread crumbs, and by that I mean trimmed white bread that has been converted into crumbs by an electric blender or a food processor.

Dip your food first into the flour to coat it well; shake off the excess. Then dip the food into the beaten egg, coating it well. Then dip the food into the bread crumbs until thoroughly coated. To make the crumbs adhere, place your food on a flat surface and tap it lightly with the flat side of a large-bladed kitchen knife.

If you wish, you may then arrange the coated pieces on a rack to dry for a brief period. Heat your oil or butter or a blend of both in a skillet large enough to hold the pieces in one layer without crowding, and cook, turning once or twice, until nicely browned on both sides and cooked through.

Brek

This deep-fried pastry, a specialty of North Africa, is generally served as an appetizer and is spelled both brek and brik. Although ground meat is sometimes used as a filling, it may be made with many things, including tuna and anchovies. It is usually accompanied by a spicy sauce called harissa as a dip. It is one of the most interesting dishes in the world, and I have dined on it in Tunisia and Morocco as well as in Paris. The name is probably related to the Turkish word *boerek,* which is also a stuffed, deep-fried pastry.

Brisling

Brisling is the Danish and Norwegian name of a sprat—a small sardine-like fish that swims from the north of Norway down to the Mediterranean. These sprats are, perhaps, best known when they are seasoned and canned with oil added. They are then labeled brisling, although in Sweden they are referred to as Swedish anchovies. In America, they are sometimes referred to as brisling sardines.

Broccoli

The word "broccoli," sometimes called Italian asparagus, is derived from the Italian word *brocco,* meaning sprout or shoot. This in turn derives from the Latin word *brachium,* which means arm or branch.

Broccoli is one of the most versatile, delicious, and nutritious members of the bras-

sica family, which includes cauliflower. It is excellent steamed and served simply as a vegetable; it blends extremely well with pasta when cut into small pieces and cooked; it makes a fine soup for summer or winter, hot or cold. The tough stems may be peeled and used along with the "flowers."

Brose

See Atholl brose.

Broth

The terms broth and stock are used interchangeably. Bouillon is the French name for a stock or broth. They are the liquid that results from cooking chicken, meat, or fish bones in a liquid, generally water, and frequently with seasonings added, such as herbs and spices or vegetables. Most canned versions are labeled broth rather than stock.

I frequently freeze broths in glass jars, and it is imperative, of course, to leave enough head space between the cap and the broth so that when the broth expands on freezing it does not break the jar.

If the glass does break, my own technique for saving that broth is to line a mixing bowl with several layers of cheesecloth. I put the jar with the broth inside the cheesecloth and let it melt. I simply strain the broth and bring it to the boil. I then either use it or refreeze it in another freezer container. *See also* Consommé.

Brown Eggs

According to poultry experts, the nutritional value of brown and white eggs is identical. I asked Sal Iacono, my knowledgeable poultry grower in East Hampton, and he states that many people come to his farm asking for brown eggs. It is his opinion that many of his local customers grew up on farms where they produced Rhode Island reds, which lay brown eggs. For them, the preference is a matter of what they're accustomed to. Summer and weekend residents and other city folk seem to prefer brown eggs on the ground that most of the

eggs sold them in town are white. Therefore, a brown egg seems more "countrified."

I received two interesting suggestions for using brown eggs:

"In England one always buys brown eggs for boiling at breakfast, in that their shells are much thicker than white ones and less apt to crack. Try it."

I did. You're right.

And the other:

"If white and brown eggs are bought alternately, one can always tell which of the last few left are the oldest in the refrigerator."

Browning

Foods are browned before stewing, braising, and so on for two reasons: Foods as they brown take on a welcome depth of flavor. The browning process also adds an appetizing color to the finished dish.

One most important factor in browning food is not to crowd the pieces of food when they are added to a skillet. Particularly in the case of cubed meat, if the pieces touch they start to give up their juices and this prevents browning.

One way to achieve this is to brown a few pieces at a time and then transfer them to a casserole for further cooking.

Generally speaking, you should cook the meat in a heavy skillet, over moderate to very high heat. You should let the fat become very hot before the foods are added.

There is no rule of thumb as to when you should or should not use flour in browned meat dishes, but meat that has been coated with flour generally browns faster.

Butter and oil are usually recommended for browning foods because the temperature at which butter starts to "burn" is quite low. The temperature at which oil starts to "burn" is quite high. By combining the two you obviously moderate the temperature.

The combination of butter and oil for this use is found mostly in Western cuisine. Butter is rarely if ever used in traditional Chinese cookery. The oil used in Chinese cookery is generally a vegetable oil.

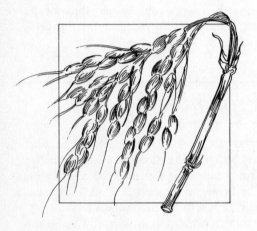

Brown Rice

Brown rice and white rice are derived from an annual grass, *Oryza sativa*. They are identical except that the brown rice retains its outer coating and is, therefore, considered to be superior in nutrients. The flavor is more nutty than that of white rice.

A spokesman for River Brand brown rice informed me that if brown rice costs more than white rice, it is because it is more difficult to process, that there are more steps involved. It is necessary to keep the rice as uniform in color as possible; it has to go through several steps in order to ensure that the darker, broken grains of rice are discarded.

To cook brown rice, use one and three-quarter times as much liquid as rice. Bring the mixture to the boil, cover, lower the heat, and cook for approximately 40 minutes.

Brown Sugar

The production of various grades or types of sugar—granulated white, light brown, and dark brown—is, to a nonprofessional, a very complicated procedure. Briefly, white sugar, light brown sugar, and dark brown sugar can be produced from the same harvest of sugarcane. The color you find is derived from the sugarcane as it comes from the field. After the white sugar is made, the syrup used to make it is reboiled in a very high vacuum to produce a light brown or dark brown sugar.

The number of molasses constituents in the original sugarcane will determine the concentration of color in the light or dark brown sugars. To put it another way, natural plant pigments in the sugarcane account for the color.

Dark brown sugar has a stronger flavor. You would probably use it when a heavy flavor is desired, such as in molasses cookies. Perhaps you would use a light brown sugar for, say, butterscotch cookies. In my kitchen, I have used them interchangeably when out of one or the other.

I have spoken to several sugar manufacturers about the problem of brown sugar becoming hard and have been unable to come up with a wholly satisfactory solution. One of them proposes putting the box of sugar in a cold, not too dry place, such as a refrigerator, and letting the sugar stand until it softens.

I am of the opinion that if you pour the sugar into a glass jar with a tight lid and keep it in a fairly cool place, you will avoid the problem.

If you have a food processor with a strong steel blade and a powerful motor, you might try to pulverize the hardened brown sugar in that.

Other solutions have been sent to me:

"Add just a slice of apple, close the jar, and wait a day or so and the sugar will regain its softness and graininess. However, if you put in much more than one slice, you will end up with a brown liquid."

"A slice (or chunk) of slightly stale bread put into that same jar with the lid tight will keep brown sugar soft indefinitely. The bread, by the way, and for reasons beyond my apprehension of mycology, does not become moldy. When the bread itself is finally as hard as a rock, simply substitute another piece. This always works."

The solution may lie in the use of liquid brown sugar, which has recently come onto the market. Use half as much of the liquid as called for in recipes listing regular brown sugar.

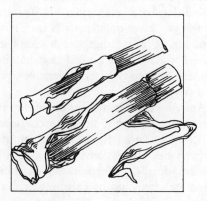

Brunch

Although the word "brunch" has a distinctly American ring to it, it is, like smog and chortle, according to H. L. Mencken, of British origin. "Brunch, designating a combination of breakfast and lunch, eaten about noon, appeared in England about 1900," Mencken wrote, "but it was thirty years later before it began to make any headway on this side of the water." The author added the following footnote: "On April 10, 1941, the Fifth Avenue Hotel in New York was advertising a 'Sunday strollers' brunch, $1 per person, served from 11 A.M. to 3 P.M.' "

In 1896, according to the 1972 Supplement to the *Oxford English Dictionary*, the word appeared in *Punch*. "To be fashionable nowadays," the magazine noted, "we must 'brunch.' Truly an excellent portmanteau word, introduced, by the way, last year, by Mr. Guy Beringer, in the now defunct *Hunter's Weekly,* and indicating a combined breakfast and lunch." In both the 1933 and 1972 Supplements, the dictionary styles the word as originally university slang.

Patterns of dining in Western culture are as mindlessly entrenched in our mores and style of living as the use of knives and forks.

We take our three meals a day at more or less regular and established intervals, which is certainly monotonous in its reflexive sort of way. It also explains why meals, when taken out of that humdrum and predictable routine, seem stimulating and appetite whetting: Dinner taken at 11 in the evening in Spain; cress sandwiches, crumpets with marmalade, and tea on a late afternoon in England; and, for backpackers and fishermen, fried trout cooked over an open fire at sunup beside a mountain stream.

High on that list of breakaway routines are late breakfasts or brunches served at home or in the home of friends on weekends, preferably Sunday at midday or thereafter.

There may be no other meal in which amateur (or even professional, for that matter) menu planners can let their imagination run so freely. Plain bacon and eggs are transformed to crisp bacon atop grilled calf's liver or kidney, for example; the eggs scrambled with cream, perhaps, and a touch of fresh-chopped tarragon added. Or served on toast with anchovies in the form of Scotch woodcock; or in a happy liaison with broiled kippers and grilled tomatoes.

A Sunday brunch doesn't need fancy trappings. Serve it Louisiana-style with that classic southern combination of veal grillades and grits casserole. Or splurge with that wondrous New York fantasy, a brunch of smoked salmon and smoked sturgeon and cream cheese and onion slices and bagels.

Which reminds me of the Myron Cohen story about two gentlemen from Texas who visited Miami Beach for the first time. The first morning they went to breakfast and, seeing lox and bagels on the menu, ordered same. Delicious! The next day more lox and bagels, and the third day, and the fourth. At the end of their stay one of them turned to the waitress and asked in his deep southern drawl, "Tell me, miss, which are the lox and which are the bagels?"

It is difficult to define precisely what dishes are eminently suited to a fine brunch and which are not. The food should definitely be on the light side—no porterhouse steaks, although grilled lamb chops are ideal. Almost all specialty cuts—liver, kidneys,

sweetbreads, and so on—in almost any preparation, grilled, creamed, and so on, are excellent. Broiled tomatoes go with a variety of main courses.

Preprandial drinks may be spirituous or not (for some guests they'd better be or acts of aggression might ensue). Fruit juices, grapefruit or orange, for example, should be freshly squeezed. These may be served with vodka (the orange juice for a screwdriver; the grapefruit with a dash of salt for a salty dog). Plain spiced tomato juice over ice (salt, pepper, fresh lemon or lime juice, plus generous dashes of Worcestershire and Tabasco sauce) or a Bloody Mary (same ingredients plus vodka) is in order.

The same juices unspiked go well as a first course at table. As, of course, do chilled melon wedges or melon balls (honeydew, Spanish, cantaloupe, cranshaw, watermelon); berries (strawberries, Bing cherries, raspberries, blueberries, etc.); and grapefruit halves, garnished, please, with mint sprigs or rosemary sprigs. Maraschino cherries are vulgar and OUT!

A few minor snobbish, if not to say precious, technicalities where taste is concerned:

It is theory only to say that grapefruit or orange marmalade should not be served at a meal that has been prefaced by grapefruit or orange halves or juice. It is tantamount to saying, of course, that you shouldn't serve grilled tomatoes at a meal that has been prefaced by Bloody Marys. Everybody to his own trivia.

Any or a combination of breads are suitable for an elegant brunch: croissants, brioches, buttered toast, English muffins, biscuits depending on the occasion, hot homemade rolls. Needless to say, homemade breads would be flattering and complimentary to guests. An assortment of marmalades, jams, jellies, and preserves is also fitting.

A choice of beverages is highly subjective. The ultimate drink would be dry champagne, although there are some foods that go best with other beverages. Grilled kippered herrings are infinitely compatible with hot tea. Both coffee and tea should be offered to guests who have an adventurous appetite.

Other than a fine champagne, I prefer still white wines to red. A dry white wine is excellent, but I prefer for the occasion the somewhat more fruity wines of Alsace, the Rhine, the Mosel, and Austria.

The end of a brunch might include an assortment of fine cheese, such as Brie, Camembert, Gorgonzola, and so on, and then a fine Burgundy would not be at all amiss.

Brunoise

A brunoise is a combination of diced or shredded root vegetables—carrots, onions, leeks, turnips, and so on—used for an endless number of French soups and sauces. I have never seen a French encyclopedia that mentioned the origin of the name. I have one English encyclopedia that attributes the name to Brunoy, a district of France that is well known for its vegetables.

Brussels Sprouts

Authorities seem to disagree on the origins of Brussels sprouts. One says they were first grown in Brussels in the thirteenth century,

thus the name. Another says they originated in the Low Countries (Belgium, the Netherlands, and Luxembourg) and were introduced to America in about 1800. The latter source states that they have been produced commercially in this country only since the beginning of this century. They are grown predominantly in California and New York State. The total annual production of Brussels sprouts in America is about sixty-nine million pounds.

B'steeya

B'steeya, or pastilla, one of the great main courses of this world, is a buttery, fragile-crusted pigeon pie that comes out of Morocco. It is a curious dish but infinitely gratifying. Curious because it contains, in addition to shredded cooked flesh of pigeons (Cornish game hens make an admirable substitute), ground almonds, confectioners' sugar, and cinnamon. I first sampled it and became enamored of it about thirty years ago in Morocco and, in the ensuing period, on a brief visit to Casablanca.

Bubble and Squeak

No nation on earth has a more amusing set of names for a vast assortment of native dishes than England. You hear of pork oaties, priddy oggies, rabbit in the dairy, toad in the hole, and, of course, bubble and squeak. The last dish is, I am told, almost two hundred years old. The origin of the name is said to be derived either from the bubble and squeak in the stomach once you have tasted it, or from the noise given off in the skillet as the ingredients cook.

I have received much correspondence over the years about bubble and squeak, all of which has given me amusement and pleasure. One such letter was from Manhattan:

"I ate bubble and squeak every Monday of my life when I lived in England but have never been able to duplicate it here, only because its prerequisite is an English Sunday dinner—a joint (of beef, mutton, or pork) with potatoes roasted around it in the pan, Yorkshire pudding, mashed potatoes, cabbage (boiled), and/or Brussels sprouts, parsnips, turnips, green beans, peas—in other words, what my father would call a blowout.

"The fat from the joint was poured into an earthenware basin and used for that week's cooking—thus our Monday's bubble and squeak took on the flavor of Sunday's joint."

And I received the following, taken from Louis P. De Gouy's *The Gold Cook Book*, which may be the definitive recipe for the dish:

BUBBLE AND SQUEAK OR FRIED BEEF AND CABBAGE

"This popular English dish, which has gone by the name of 'Bubble and Squeak' for well over a century, was enjoyed as far back as the 16th century and in an old cookery book of that period we find a recipe for 'long wortes'—vegetables, but especially cabbage—and 'powdred beef'—meat salted or sprinkled with salt.

"Following is the traditional recipe, as written by Dr. Kitchiner in the *Cook's Oracle,* published in 1823, in London.

"For this, as for a hash, select those parts of the joint that have been least done; it is generally made with slices of cold boiled salted beef, sprinkled with a little pepper, and just slightly browned with a bit of butter in a frying pan. If it is fried too much it will be hard.

"Boil a cabbage, squeeze it quite dry, and chop it small. Take the beef out of the frying pan, and lay the cabbage in it. Sprinkle with a little pepper and salt over it; keep the pan moving over the fire for a few minutes; lay the cabbage in the middle of a dish, and the meat round it.

"As for the sauce given by Dr. Kitchiner, who recommends it as an accompaniment to Bubble and Squeak—it goes by the delightful name of 'Wow Wow Sauce,' the exact meaning of which nobody can trace. Dr. Kitchiner had probably never heard of that expressive American slang word, 'a wow.' This is how the sauce is made:

"Wow Wow Sauce. Chop some parsley leaves very fine, quarter two or three pickled cucumbers or walnuts, divide them into small squares, and set them by ready; put into a saucepan a bit of butter as big as an egg; when it is melted, stir to it a tablespoon of fine flour and about one-half pint of the broth in which the beef was boiled; add a tablespoon of vinegar, the like quantity of mushroom catsup, or port wine, or both, and a teaspoonful of prepared mustard; let it simmer together till it is as thick as you wish it, put in the parsley and pickles to get warm, and pour it over the beef, or rather send it up in a sauce-tureen."

Buckwheat

Buckwheat is actually a fruit with seeds that derives from a plant that bears fragrant flowers. The seeds are vaguely triangular and are said to resemble beechnuts. The

prefix buck stems from the Dutch word *boek,* which means beech.

When ground, buckwheat produces a variety of products, including buckwheat flour (light and dark), buckwheat groats, and kasha. Regular wheat comes from a variety of grasses that, when ground, produce an endless number of flours used in pasta and bread-making and so on.

Bulgur

Bulgur is the Turkish word for cracked wheat. Burghul is the same thing in Arabic. In the Middle East, it is served as a side dish like rice. It is also the base for tabbouleh, a Lebanese salad or appetizer made with cracked wheat, chopped parsley, tomatoes, lemon juice, green onions, and olive oil, among other things.

Bulgur, or burghul, figures prominently in kibbee, which is made with raw or cooked lamb and is sometimes referred to as the national dish of Lebanon and Syria.

A gentleman from Massachusetts wrote that the Turkish word *burghul* literally means "bruised grains." He added, "A fa-miliar American derivative is the word bur-goo, undoubtedly well known to you."

I am still puzzling that one. Just how that regional Kentucky dish made with beef and chicken (originally squirrel and wild duck) and a gardenful of southern vegetables is related to "bruised grains" eludes me, unless it has to do with the corn kernels essential to a genuine burgoo.

Bündnerfleisch

See Cornichons.

Burgoo

See Bulgur.

Butter

Because I am on a low-sodium diet, I use unsalted or sweet butter exclusively. It is my opinion the reason butter is salted is that salt is something of a preservative and was originally added for this reason.

Basically, sweet butter is always preferable to the salted version, but this is more apparent when the butter is used as a table spread. In actual fact, the difference between the two when used for cooking is minimal and one may be substituted for the other with fractional differences in the end result.

To make your own sweet butter, pour 1 cup of heavy cream into the container of the electric blender. Blend on high speed for about 15 seconds, or until the cream is whipped, at which point the cream will start to thicken around the blades. Add ½ cup of cold water and a couple of ice cubes. Blend on high speed for 2 minutes.

The ice serves to solidify the butter as it rises to the top of the liquid. Spoon the fresh butter from the top of the liquid into a cup to drain. Knead the butter with a cold wooden spoon to extract the liquid trapped in the butter. This produces about 6 ounces of sweet butter.

Speaking of ice, many restaurants, including some of the best, have the irritating habit of placing chilled butter and sometimes butter on ice on the table, rather than serving the butter at room temperature. It is probably a practice that dates back to the days when most dining rooms weren't air-conditioned. And there are a surprising number of people who are not aware of the fact that very few dining rooms could boast air-conditioning until several years after the Second World War. In midsummer, the butter would melt on the bread-and-butter plate. While I can condone the service of chilled butter, I deplore butter served in chipped or shaved ice. It is a tacky and an unreasoned practice on the part of management.

Butter Pecan Ice Cream

Although butter is not normally used in ice cream, it is indeed an ingredient in butter pecan ice cream. To make it, you prepare a hot syrup of brown sugar and water. Beat in eggs and add a little butter. When this is chilled, you add milk. Fold in whipped cream and broken pecans. This mixture is then frozen like any other ice cream.

Buttermilk

One of my favorite beverages as a between-meal drink or as a basis for soup has the misleading name of buttermilk. As a child in the South, I grew up on it; back then, pardon the expression, the name was more richly deserved. The milk was made from clabbered milk, which is to say milk that had been left to stand and become slightly sour overnight (thanks to the action of harmless bacteria). The fat from the milk would rise to the top, and the milk would be churned up and down with a paddle. The top fat would become sweet butter, and there would be flecks of this throughout the snow-white and, to my taste, delectable liquid that remained.

The buttermilk that is found in supermarkets and grocery stores today generally has not a trace of those golden-fat particles. Although excellent, it is mass-produced by adding a culture to sweet milk—either whole or skimmed. It is for the most part low in calories and can be obtained with no salt added.

There are many ways—most of them not so well known—for using buttermilk. In the South, it is a standard ingredient for that staple of the breakfast table, hot biscuits. One may also use buttermilk for cakes, soups, and various breads other than biscuits. The taste of buttermilk, by the way, is quite similar to that of yogurt, and I prefer it when it is well chilled.

In that buttermilk seems invariably available at my local supermarket, I have never felt called upon to use a substitute. But for those who have difficulty finding it, yogurt may be used. You substitute it volume for volume, that is to say, cup for cup or tablespoon for tablespoon.

There is a buttermilk powder commercially available that has a fairly long shelf life if kept properly, preferably stored in the refrigerator. I have never tried it.

Buttery

Originally the word "buttery" meant a storeroom for alcoholic beverages in butts or casks; it has come to mean a pantry and, hence, a place where provisions are sold. The derivation, through the French, is from the Latin word *botaria,* wine vessel. In origin, at least, the word has nothing to do with butter.

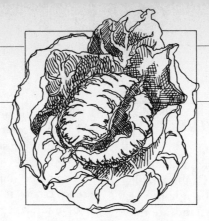

Cc Cc Cc Cc

Cabbage

That I have a small passion for cabbage—whether in coleslaw or stuffed or prepared some other way—may be why I have always found legends and literary references to it particularly appealing. The most obvious, of course, is the contrast of cabbages and kings. And who could not be amused by the French essayist Montaigne, who mused that he wanted "death to find me planting my cabbages."

One of the most dramatic of all cabbage legends is Greek, according to the late Waverley Root in his estimable book *Food*. It seems that Dionysus, the god of wine who was also known as "the raging god," caught Lycurgus, the king of the Thracian Edonians, pulling up grapevines.

Dionysus, in his fury, had the king roped to a grape stalk, then blinded him and tore him limb from limb. Lycurgus wept, and his tears, falling to the ground, "engendered cabbages."

The word "cabbage" has ranged from the endearing to the insulting: *mon petit chou* to "stupid fool and cabbage-head, thou art!"

At one point in American letters, cabbage was used to demonstrate the absurdity of some men's thinking. An idealist, H. L. Mencken observed, "is one who, on noticing that a rose smells better than a cabbage, concludes that it will also make better soup."

Cabinet Pudding

Two puddings bear the name cabinet, one French and one English. The *pouding de cabinet* of the French kitchen is made with ladyfingers soaked in a liqueur, such as kirsch or maraschino. They are layered with chopped crystallized fruits, such as cherries and angelica that have also been marinated in a liqueur.

The layers are spread with apricot jam and the mold is filled with a vanilla-flavored custard. It is baked, unmolded, and served with an English custard or sabayon sauce.

The English version is made with bread crumbs and a vanilla-flavored custard and currants. It is baked and can be served with a vanilla-flavored sauce. I am told that it is rarely made today.

Café Filtre

See Espresso.

63

Cajun and Creole

Although a good many of the meals of my Mississippi childhood were Cajun, Creole, or soul food, I would have been hard put, until recently, to make an elaborate distinction between what is Cajun and what is Creole. But my solution was simple: Go to the undisputed pontiff and grand panjandrum of the Cajun and Creole cookstove, that genial genius of massive girth, Paul Prudhomme. Through his restaurant, K-Paul's Louisiana Kitchen, and a book published in 1984, *Chef Paul Prudhomme's Louisiana Kitchen,* he has become recognized as a world authority on the two cuisines.

Paul Prudhomme was born the youngest of thirteen children in the heart of Cajun country, just outside the southern Louisiana town of Opelousas, which is down-to-earth crawfish territory (crayfish are called crawfish in the South). His well-honed knowledge of cooking developed from a lifelong interest in food preparation, and he attributes his culinary ability to his mother, who was, he says, one of the best cooks in Louisiana.

One morning I drove with him in his pickup to a small town near his birthplace. There his sister-in-law Odelia Mae would prepare in her home kitchen a meal consisting of typical Cajun foods, including roast pork backbone, roast Muscovy duck, corn maque choux, a corn casserole thickened with eggs, dirty rice—so-called because it is slightly darkened with chopped chicken giblets—and a lemon-meringue icebox pie. The beverage was sweetened iced tea.

During the meal we discussed the differences between Cajun and Creole food preparation.

"Cajun cooking," Paul reminded me, "is old French cooking as it was transformed into a southern style when the settlers came from Acadia."

The name Cajun derives from Acadia, a French colony in eastern Canada more than two hundred years ago. Shortly after 1755, a group of exiles from the colony made their way to Louisiana. The parish where they established themselves is still called Acadia. They were, for the most part, poor, servantless people who lived a hardscrabble existence, foraging what they could from the fields, forests, bayous, rivers, and streams, and combining these foods with their basic French ingenuity to create whatever inspired them. It was from the very beginning a make-do cuisine that relied little on imported spices or any other luxuries common to the French table. It is today a far spicier style of cooking, employing many kinds of peppers unknown to those forebears who settled in the South. This improvisational character is one of the major differences between Cajun and Creole cooking.

In the most basic manner, you might say that Cajun cooking is *country* cooking, nowhere nearly as sophisticated and elegant as Creole. The basis of most Cajun cooking—as opposed to Creole—is oil, principally rendered pork fat.

"Creole cooking uses butter as a basic fat and in its own way is much more refined," Chef Prudhomme explained. "You could call Creole *city* cooking. It is a combination of French, Spanish, and Italian and other ethnic groups who came to Louisiana all those years ago.

"One of the main reasons that it came about is the black influence. Many wealthy settlers had black servants, and it was they who formulated the Creole cuisine. They would work in the kitchens of those European settlers and borrow and blend ideas. They borrowed the recipes and adapted them, using their own techniques. For that reason a good deal of Creole cooking is also based on soul food."

Both Cajun and Creole kitchens employ one ingredient that is a borrowing from the American Indians. It is filé (pronounced fee-lay) powder, which many cooks consider essential to an authentic gumbo. It was a contribution of the Choctaw Indians, who made it by drying and crushing the young, tender leaves of the sassafras plant.

In both Cajun and Creole cookery, finely chopped onion, celery, and green peppers are the "holy trinity" of the kitchen. Tomatoes, according to Prudhomme, do not play as important a role in Cajun cookery as they do in Creole, where a great many creations would be impossible without them. The numerous ingredients native to both cuisines include cornmeal, okra, grits, and, of course, crawfish.

Later, Paul told me he would prepare a basic gumbo that would be unarguably Cajun, and would explain how to convert it into a Creole dish.

It may be said that the heart and soul of both Cajun and Creole cooking is the roux. A roux is also used in traditional French cooking, but there is a difference. Basically, a roux in all three cuisines is made by combining flour with a fat such as butter, lard, or oil, to which you add a liquid.

A roux in Cajun and Creole cooking is made, more often than not, by browning the flour to some degree, but if it is to be used for a light cream sauce it is not browned at all, Prudhomme explained.

Roux that are light or medium-brown in color form the bases of sauces that envelop dark meats, such as beef or game or dark-meat fowl, including duck, goose, and blackbird. These brown roux, he explained, give a toasted, nutty flavor to sauces.

On the other hand, he continued, roux that are dark, reddish-brown, or almost black go with meats of lighter color, such as veal, pork, rabbit, fish, or shellfish. Black roux, he added, are best for gumbos because, curious as it may seem, the darkest roux yield the thinnest, best-tasting gumbos.

"But," he added, "it takes practice and talent to make a black roux without ending up with a burned flavor."

It is his theory that browned roux began in the Cajun kitchen and was borrowed some years later by Creole cooks.

"The gumbo I'll cook starts off with a very dark roux; the flour is cooked and stirred until it has the color of dark chocolate. You then add stock and, to make it genuinely Cajun, a good amount of chopped, heavily smoked sausage, the one known hereabouts as *tasso*."

Ham, he added, is a characteristic, basic ingredient in a good deal of Cajun cooking. He said the use of ham points up a basic difference between Cajun and Creole cookery:

"If you take the same gumbo and add that ham, plus crawfish, your dish will be Cajun. Crawfish have always been plentiful

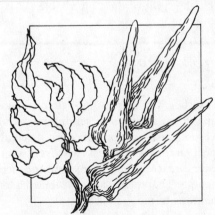

and cheap in this area. If, on the other hand, you substitute fancy and costly seafoods like shrimp, crab meat, or oysters, or if you replace the ham with a lightly smoked ham like you buy in any supermarket, it then becomes Creole."

Genuine Cajun cooking, as opposed to Creole, uses game, such as rabbit, turtle, squirrel, and alligator, as well as a great deal more freshwater fish. The Creole cook has available a larger supply of luxury saltwater fish and shellfish, such as shrimp, flounder, oysters, crabs, and soft-shell crabs.

It is pure conjecture, but I am convinced that many of those early settlers in Louisiana must have hailed from the Mediterranean region of France. The most popular Creole sauce of all is made of ingredients that smack of that sunlit area—tomatoes, onions, green pepper, and garlic, plus celery, bay leaf, and thyme. And absinthe—the strongly alcoholic beverage once so popular in New Orleans—was the equivalent of anisette or pastis—two of the favorite drinks in southern France.

On the other hand, there are dishes in the French kitchen described as *grandmère* or *bonne maman,* names that imply foods cooked with human warmth and care and homespun inspiration. That, it seems to me, reflects the spirit of the Cajun table.

Cake Break

My mother had something called a cake break, which she used in serving pieces of angel food cake. A cake break is a specially shaped, sterling silver fork with very long tines and resembles a large, long-toothed hair comb. That utensil always seemed a bit pretentious to me.

I frankly prefer angel food cake cut with a knife, although I am familiar with the two-fork technique, which is similar to the cake break.

Calamari

See Squid.

Caldo Verde

Caldo verde might well be the national soup of Portugal. It is made by shredding fresh kale and, separately, cooking Portuguese sausages named linguica or chorizos. You cook sliced potatoes in broth until tender, mash them, return them to the broth along with your kale, plus olive oil, and cook for 5 minutes or so, until the kale is tender. Add the sliced sausages and serve piping hot.

Calvados

See Cider.

Calzone

Calzone is an Italian pastry from Naples or the Apulian region of Italy. It is a kind of stuffed pizza in which dough is filled with any of several savory fillings—cheese and ham or anchovies, cooked onions, capers, and olives. The dough is folded over to make an envelope. It is then either deep-fried or brushed with oil and baked until golden.

Cancoillotte

Cancoillotte is a specialty of the Franche-Comté province of France, and a liking for the dish, which is genuinely aromatic, is, indeed, cultivated. It is a kind of fondue generally made from September to June. In his invaluable book on cheese, *The Complete Encyclopedia of French Cheese,* Pierre Androuet states that cancoillotte is made with a cheese of the Franche-Comté province called Metton. According to his "recipe," you "put some well 'rotted' (golden ripe) Metton in a cast iron pot with 3 percent of its weight of salt water (3 percent solution or 2 tablespoons of salt to a quart of water). Warm over low heat or in a double boiler, stirring to blend. Then add an amount of fresh butter equivalent to 30 percent of the weight of the cheese. Stir again to blend. When the mixture is smooth and uniform, pour into serving dishes."

He adds that the fondue is eaten warm at any time of the day on toast or in sandwiches. Sometimes, depending on the family, garlic and white wine are added to it. The author adds, "It does not keep well and must be remelted periodically."

Candied Violets

Candied violets are used in my home to decorate custard desserts, such as an English custard, white and yellow ice creams, yellow puddings, and so on. They are my favorite conceit where dessert garnishes are concerned.

They are prepared in many ways. The simplest is to dip them into beaten egg whites and then into very fine granulated

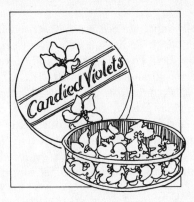

sugar. You can also dip them into a syrup that has been cooked until it spins a thread, then into granulated sugar.

I suspect that this simpler method, done on a large scale, is more like the commercial method. The syrup and sugar into which they are dipped or with which the violets are coated are generally tinted a purple or violet color to enhance the presentation.

Canned Tomatoes

For those who complain about the acid flavor in tomato sauces, it is possible that it is the brand of tomatoes that they buy. Some canned tomatoes have citric acid added to them as a preservative. This is clearly stated on the label. I would never buy or use these tomatoes because, while the additive is not harmful, it does affect the flavor.

Read the labels on canned tomatoes carefully and select those that contain nothing but pure tomatoes, plus, perhaps, basil. Incidentally, you cannot rely on the brand name alone because some packagers produce canned tomatoes with citric acid as well as without it.

If you use canned tomatoes as often as I do and are concerned about salt, this is especially important because they vary greatly.

I have three brands at present on my pantry shelf: Pope, Progresso, and Montini. The Pope brand does not list salt. A large can of Progresso tomatoes with tomato paste added lists "trace of calcium salt, citric acid, and bay leaf." On the other hand, an 8-ounce Progresso can's label lists only peeled tomatoes and tomato juice. The Montini brand lists salt and calcium chloride.

To the best of my knowledge, the most popular brands of tomato paste do not contain salt, but always check the labels.

As to the differences in canned tomato products, it is quite simple. Tomato purée is made by cooking tomatoes just until they are soft and can be put through a sieve or food mill. This purée is seasoned and cooked briefly, and it is a fairly thin but dense liquid.

Tomato paste is made by cooking tomatoes with or without seasonings for about one hour. The tomatoes are then put through a sieve or food mill and cooked for about two hours or longer, until a thick paste is formed. Tomato paste is far more concentrated than purée, gives more instant body to sauces, and has a thickening effect on sauces to which it is added.

As to what to do with the can of tomato paste after you've removed the tablespoon needed for a recipe, I have compiled a host of interesting ideas.

Smooth out the paste remaining in the can with the back of the spoon, then overlay its surface with a small amount of vegetable oil. This keeps the air away. To use, just tip the can, exposing fresh tomato paste, and spoon out.

You clean the rim of the can carefully, seal it with plastic wrap (or find a plastic cap that just fits, a quest in itself), and freeze it. When next you need a tablespoon, you remove it from the freezer and open the bottom of the can with a can opener (the around-the-rim type). Within a few minutes you will be able to push the bottom up, forcing the frozen paste over the top. About three-quarters inch or so equals a tablespoon, which you slice off. Refreeze immediately and use in that manner until done.

Lay a sheet of wax paper on a baking sheet and measure out the tomato paste in teaspoon and tablespoon quantities, in whatever proportion you find is most useful, leaving about two inches between dollops. Freeze the paste on the wax paper on the baking sheet. Once it's frozen, roll up the paper, with the paste blobs on it, as closely as possible. Fold it in half and store in a tightly closed plastic bag in the freezer.

Capers

Although many herbs and spices normally play what might be called a grace-note role in a dish, there are occasions when one of these so-called minor or minimally used flavorings is given a starring part, or at least becomes integral to the "classic" composition of a dish.

One of the grace notes I am most often asked about—its origin, primarily—is a Mediterranean staple called the caper. Capers have been used as a condiment for several thousand years and they grow wild all around the Mediterranean basin.

A caper bush is a small, brown shrub with small, oval leaves. Bottled capers are the pickled buds of the bush.

One of the greatest of caper dishes is raie au beurre noir, or skate fish with black butter, in which the delectable fish, rarely found in American fish markets, is poached lightly and served with a black-butter sauce in which capers play an essential role. Capers go well in many sauces.

One of the most curious and interesting of appetizers containing capers (capers also figure in Liptauer cheese) is known as a tapenade. This is a fairly pungent Provençal specialty made with ground black olives and anchovies.

And one of the most famous German dishes, Königsberger Klopse, consists of meatballs in a caper sauce.

Cappellacci con la Zucca

Cappellacci con la zucca means "little hats with pumpkin." To prepare them roll out a fresh egg pasta and cut it into circles, place small quantities of freshly cooked puréed pumpkin seasoned with a little nutmeg on the circles, and form them into small ravioli-shaped "hats." They are cooked like ravioli and served with melted butter and Parmesan cheese.

Caraway Seeds

I have long been fascinated with the mistaken notions that some people have about one flavor or another. Caraway seeds, for instance, are a common ingredient in rye breads and there are those who suppose that the caraway flavor is that of rye, which is untrue.

Caraway is a common spice used in many recipes for sauerkraut, in various goulashes and in the German liqueur *kümmel*. Legend has it that caraway will prevent infidelity in love, and that it also aids in digestion.

Oddly enough, caraway seeds do not figure to an impressive extent in French cookery. As a matter of fact, there are many French chefs who do not know the French term for caraway, which is *karvi*.

Cardoons

It is puzzling that cardoons have never become popular in this country. They are a choice vegetable with a choice flavor and are best, to my taste, when eaten raw, as

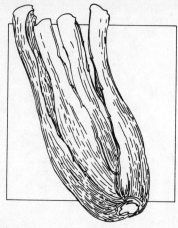

the Italians do, as part of a bagna caôda, a sauce of heated olive oil, garlic, and anchovies.

In the United States, cardoons, thistle-like plants, can sometimes be found in open-air markets in the country. They are related to the artichoke but look more like celery.

To cook cardoons you use the stalks, cut into small pieces, and the heart. They discolor quickly, so you must rub the cut portions with lemon juice. You cook them in water to which vinegar or flour has been added to prevent further discoloration.

You may serve them with a sauce, such as cheese or hollandaise.

Carimañolas

See Yucca.

Carnations

I have never used carnations in my kitchen, but in her book *The Forgotten Art of Flower Cookery,* Leona Woodring Smith proposes several uses of carnations in edible creations.

There is a carnation and strawberry jam, pickled carnations, and a carnation dessert omelet. The author states that garden-grown carnations, as opposed to the hothouse variety, are best for eating. The home-grown variety, she adds, are more tender and have more flavor.

Carob

Carob powder is obtained from a tree of the locust family. The carob bean is about the size of a very large lima bean, about four inches long. When it dries on the trees, it falls to the ground and is picked up and harvested. It is dried further, the seeds are removed and used to produce locust gum, which is used in the food industry as a thickener.

There is a pulpy material inside the pod and around the seed. This is dried and ground, and that is carob powder. This powder is roasted like cocoa beans and used as a substitute for cocoa or chocolate. The advantage is that it does not contain caffeine. And it does not have the allergy-causing factors contained in chocolate to which some people are susceptible.

Carolina Rice

It seems that in the latter part of the seventeenth century, the year 1694 to be precise, a captain of an ailing sailing vessel put into what is now Charleston, South Carolina. He was en route from Madagascar to Europe, and he paid for his stay and repairs with several pounds of rice that was in the ship's hold. Thus, rice was introduced to

America. The colonists planted the cereal, it flourished, and the strain was thenceforth known as Carolina.

Carpetbag Steak

I have, over the years, received more requests for carpetbag steak than almost any other dish, and I suspect much of its appeal has to do with the name, which has a fascinating ring. I own few Australian cookbooks and cannot find the recipe in any of them. The most logical recipe I have ever found appeared thirty years ago in the late Helen Evans Brown's *The West Coast Cook Book*.

To prepare the dish, she recommends that you have fillet of beef cut into rounds about 2½ inches thick. Partly split each round through the center to make a sizable pocket with as small an opening as possible. Sprinkle with a generous grinding of black pepper and salt to taste, if desired.

For each serving cook 4 medium-size oysters in a little butter until the edges curl and they are heated through. Put them in the pocket and truss the opening. Brush each steak on both sides with butter, and grill or broil to the desired degree of doneness.

An Australian who now lives in Manhattan subsequently wrote, quoting a passage from *The Captain Cook Book: Two Hundred Years of Australian Cooking,* by Babette Hayes:

"The carpetbag steak is now a truly Australian dish although it came to us from the U.S. of A. A thick chunk of tender sirloin, rump or fillet steak, which has a pocket cut in the middle, is stuffed with oysters and then fried to the required degree of doneness.

"That's the basic recipe. There are many variations: add chopped mushrooms, onions, herbs, or lemon juice."

She says that the name probably derives from the term for a one-pound note in Australia, which is "carpet," and "bag" from the term "in the bag," meaning a winner.

And finally, from a New Yorker: "It is not necessary for us to go all the way to Australia to enjoy a steak stuffed with fresh oysters. We recently tasted this delectable dish at the King's Arms Tavern in Colonial Williamsburg, Virginia.

Cassis

One of the most delectable cordials ever created is cassis (pronounced *ka-cease),* a rich black-purple syrup, a Burgundian specialty, made from black currants. Not everyone shares my enthusiasm for cassis, including my longtime friend, Frank Schoonmaker. In his estimable *Encyclopedia of Wine* he states, "Only the deplorable but now diminishing French preference for sweet apéritifs . . . can conceivably explain its popularity." I am not keen on cassis as something to sip, perish the thought, but it has admirable other uses, such as something to pour over vanilla ice cream. It is also fine as an ingredient in a fruit ice.

There is both a syrup and a cream of cassis, which are similar but not the same. Both are a dark purple dense liquid. The syrup, however, does not contain alcohol, whereas the crème de cassis, a liqueur, does. The syrup is made by blending a concentrate of cassis with a sugar syrup. The liqueur is made by macerating cassis berries in an eau de vie. Either of the two may be used in preparing fruit ices. *See also* Kir.

Cassoulet

It is one of the great mysteries of gastronomy why the greatest wine and food regions on earth happened to be allotted to France. It is as though nature, untold centuries ago, played some gigantic dice game that bestowed on Burgundy and Bordeaux the most fertile soil for wine. Strasbourg got geese and the Périgord truffles. Normandy was awarded apples and cream. Provence got the olive groves, garlic fields, and the fruits of the Mediterranean for the express purpose of contriving a dish called bouillabaisse.

In the southwest area of France there is a small arc defined by three towns that fell heir to a peculiar endowment. These towns in the region called Languedoc are Toulouse, Castelnaudary, and Carcassonne. Together they are responsible and celebrated for the cassoulet, one of the three greatest winter dishes known to man (the other two are onion soup and sauerkraut).

Over the years, cassoulet has sparked more controversy and produced more heat than a pyromaniacal maître d'hôtel flaming his crêpes. The contretemps in this casserole includes the kinds of beans to be used. To prepare a true cassoulet, must the beans come from Pamiers or Sazères, as some connoisseurs aver? Are the white haricots of Soissons acceptable?

The three main meats for a cassoulet (pork, lamb or mutton, and goose) vary from Castelnaudary to Toulouse to Carcassonne. Could you combine all three? Can you add partridge? Must or may you add preserved goose, duck, pork, and so on?

These are arguments that will, happily, never be concluded, and there will always be a body of fortunate jurists sitting at table and sampling them all with knife, fork, or spoon in hand and that blissful grin that can derive only from dining well.

Caster

A caster, or castor, is a small metal container with perforated holes in the top. It is used for sprinkling sugar on the top of cakes, pancakes, and so on. It is also called a muffineer. Caster or castor sugar is granulated table sugar that is slightly finer than ordinary sugar and is called verifine or superfine in the United States. It is not confectioners' sugar.

Catchup

See Ketchup.

Catfish

Like most Southerners, I admire catfish. Eating deep-fried catfish on Sunday outings was a ritual in my childhood and the menu was always the same: the cornmeal-coated catfish with its golden brown crusty exterior and moist white inner flesh; deep-fried hush puppies; deep-fried potatoes, and coleslaw. And tomato ketchup. Deep-fried catfish without ketchup is like a hot dog without mustard. Now that catfish are being raised in freshwater ponds, they are available frozen all over the country and can be used in any recipe calling for a white nonoily fish. Even after freezing and defrosting, catfish remain snow white and as firm as when taken from the water.

It is generally agreed within and outside the industry that catfish is a somewhat unfortunate name for such a highly edible delicacy. A gentleman from Memphis told me that his family was always careful to refer to it, properly, as tenderloin trout.

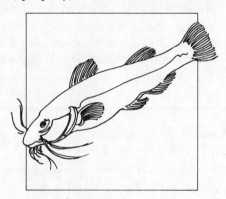

Catherine de Médicis

Catherine de Médicis was only fourteen years old when she married the duc d'Orléans of France in 1533. When her husband became King Henry II fourteen years later, Catherine reputedly altered the manners and style of the nation. It is recorded that her chefs introduced to the French table such things as truffles, tournedos, artichoke bottoms, grated Parmesan cheese, macaroons, and frangipane tarts.

But a student of the history of cooking questions whether Catherine's cooks were all that influential. She writes from Cambridge, Massachusetts: "In the course of work here and in France on the history of fine European cooking, I have been trying, without success, to track down these cooks for a dozen years. I have found no references to them before the second half of the eighteenth century.

"It is very probable that Catherine did bring cooks with her when she came to France in 1533, because important people traveled then with large suites that always included cooks. But no sixteenth-century account of them or of their influence has come to my attention. Observers of the French court of the period, such as Brantôme and Pierre de L'Estoile, tell us a lot about Catherine, but her table does not seem to have been of any importance in their eyes.

"During her first fourteen childless, isolated years at the French court, she was in no position to lead fashionable taste; her husband's mistress, Diane de Poitiers, did that. Of the many ingredients and recipes which Catherine is said to have introduced into France, most were already known there.

"Only in the case of crème frangipane have I been able to find an Italian recipe which antedates any French one, and it was entitled crema Francese—French cream.

"There is, however, evidence of earlier Italian influence. Two editions of an Italian cookbook, Platina's *De honeste Voluptate*, had already been published in France in translation, one before Catherine was born, and the second while she was still an infant. Undoubtedly Italian cooks were employed in France; the culture of Italy was admired, and workmen in many crafts came to France throughout the century.

"This process had begun long before Catherine was born, when the French kings and nobility, fighting a series of wars in Italy, fell under the influence of its Renaissance culture.

"Apparently we owe the germ of the legend of Catherine's cooks to the Chevalier de Jaucourt, a prolific contributor to Diderot's *Encyclopédie*. Here he wrote contemptuously that France inherited its knowledge of 'la bonne chère' [good cooking], 'to the transalpine cooks [who] settled in France, and it is one of the least obligations we owe to that crowd of corrupt Italians who served at the court of Catherine de Medici.'

"To this slender beginning subsequent writers have added many other supposed items to the cargo with Catherine's train: fireworks, syphilis, parsley, sherbets, perfume, and various embroidery stitches.

"Nevertheless, the legend of Catherine de Medici's cooks is well established in French gastronomic literature. [Skeptics] may read about them in many authoritative works, including the *Larousse Gastronomique*, Dr. Gottschalk's *Histoire de l'Alimentation* and the writings of Raymond Oliver."

Caul

See Crépinette.

Cauliflower

Although cauliflower is a bit odorous as it cooks, it is one of the most elegant of vegetables. It is a descendant of the common

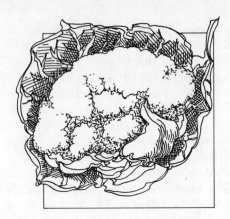

cabbage and is related to broccoli, arriving in Europe from Asia by way of Italy. Its uses are many, both raw in salads and eaten with a dip, cooked in soups, as a main-course accompaniment, and in casseroles.

Many people have told me over the years that their cauliflower tends to darken as it cooks and I've found a remedy for that. Cook it in water to which half a cup of milk has been added.

Caviar

Over the years it has been my good fortune to observe the harvesting of a number of culinary delicacies. I have been on a truffle hunt in Italy, watched vineyard snails go from vine leaf to snail pot in Burgundy, and, near Strasbourg, witnessed the transfer of foie gras from a fattened goose to the table of a great French chef.

But until recently I had never seen how that most luxurious of all luxury foods, fresh caviar, is processed. And when I finally did, it wasn't in Russia or Iran but on the Tennessee River, just outside Chattanooga.

That is one of the spots where Mario

Garbarino, who was among the first producers of caviar in this country, sets his nets for the long-billed sturgeon that are known locally as shovelnose cats (and sometimes, more simply, paddle fish). From the highly prized eggs of these ugly creatures, Mr. Garbarino, a forty-year-old native of Genoa who learned his trade from an Iranian refugee in this country, processes some of the finest American caviar.

"You can find the sturgeon over a vast territory of this country, principally in the Mississippi-Missouri River system," Mr. Garbarino, whose New York-based company is called Aquamar Gourmet Inc., said. "It extends as far north as Minneapolis and St. Paul, as far east as Pittsburgh and as far south as New Orleans."

Mr. Garbarino employs thirty-five to forty fishermen who work the waters of Kentucky, Tennessee, Alabama, Mississippi, Oklahoma, Arkansas, and Louisiana. When ready to produce caviar, the fish they are after measure six feet or longer and weigh anywhere from seventy-five to one hundred fifty pounds. The season for them varies, depending on water temperatures, but generally it runs from October through June.

On the day of my visit, the morning's

catch from the Tennessee River was two good-size shovelnose sturgeon, which were hauled into a small, spotless building with gleaming stainless-steel worktables. After the fish were washed down with clear water, a couple of fishermen proceeded to extract the eggs and to press them by hand through a rectangular stainless-steel mesh with ¼-inch holes. The eggs were then repeatedly blended by hand with noniodized salt.

"The eggs get a firmer texture as they stand," Marion Tipton, one of the fishermen, explained. It takes an expert touch to know precisely how much salt is necessary. When properly blended and firm, the eggs were poured into a fine-meshed sieve and allowed to drain for 10 to 15 minutes, or until they were drier—not overly dry but far from soupy.

At this point, the caviar was ready to be shipped in tightly sealed 3½-gallon plastic drums to New York for a final "aging" and to be put into tins for the market.

Once there, it is stored in refrigerated rooms (at a temperature of 26 to 28 degrees Fahrenheit) for at least a week, but no longer than three months. During this time, Mr. Garbarino explained, the salty flavor dissipates. Just before it is packed in 7- or 14-ounce tins, it is transferred to a second refrigerated room with a temperature of 38 degrees to "defrost" and thus become more manageable for handling (though at no time during the processing is it frozen).

"If you pack caviar when it is too cold," he said, "you ruin it."

Mr. Garbarino estimates that seven years ago the total caviar production in the United States probably did not exceed five thousand pounds. Today it is forty to fifty thousand pounds a year.

His own entry into the American caviar

business was something of an accident, he said. After working for several years on Italian ocean liners, first as a cabin boy, and eventually as a busboy in the dining rooms ("where I had my first taste of caviar, which I had sneaked from the galley," he said), he came to this country in the early 1960s. For a while he waited on tables at Orsini's restaurant in Manhattan and eventually, through friends in shipping, found a European source for Russian caviar and decided to set up a small import company.

"And then," Mr. Garbarino added, "a funny thing happened because of my American wife."

He explained: "She's part American Indian, and one spring we visited her relatives in Gore, Oklahoma, on the Arkansas River. We went to a local fish market, and they were selling the fillets of a fish that was known as a shovelnose cat. I took one look and said to myself, 'That's a sturgeon.'

"I asked the owner if I could see a whole fish, and he took me into the back. I had him cut open the fish and out came the eggs. One look and I knew. He was about to throw them away.

"I offered him three times the value of the fish as he sold it," Mr. Garbarino said, "and he thought I was crazy."

His wife told him that the rivers nearby were full of shovelnose cats. "I did a lot of research with the fishermen and with the fish and game divisions of several states," he said. "One of my sources told me that they used to harvest the fish before the First World War and that they sold up to 100,000 pounds of eggs to Europe each year."

Mr. Garbarino found a couple of local fishermen who were still making small homemade batches of the salted eggs. "That was in 1979," he recalled. "I brought a few pounds back to New York and sold it to some of my customers without telling them it was made in this country. They liked it, so I decided to market it as American.

"In the beginning," he continued, "I knew the production was crudely made, but at least it was fresh. Then I found the Iranian caviar specialist in this country who had recently left his homeland. His name was Petros Azarian and he taught me how to refine the techniques, which are very important for a good product—how to extract the eggs without breaking, the amount and kind of salt to use, how long to age the caviar, the proper temperatures for keeping it."

He taught Mr. Garbarino that the caviar must be produced within minutes or less than an hour after the fish is hauled in and that you must work fast—and in immaculate surroundings—to prevent spoilage.

Given the expense of caviar (the American version is considerably less expensive, but it is still a luxury item), it should be treated with great care at home, too.

According to Mr. Garbarino, the qualities to look for are "a sparkle and glitter, a shiny texture with proper moisture—not too dry—and grains that are clearly separated with no broken eggs. And not sticky."

Once a container is opened, air should be kept out as much as possible. "Air is the enemy of caviar," he says. When resealing a container, compress the remaining caviar as compactly as you can and cover very closely with clear plastic wrap. Better still, transfer it to a smaller container just large enough to be completely filled. Properly stored, it will keep at least a week. The best temperature for storing leftover caviar is 28 degrees Fahrenheit. It will not freeze at that temperature because of its salt content. Small-grain caviar can be frozen at 0 degrees without ill effect. But when beluga or other large-grain caviar is frozen the grains may burst.

Caviar should be served on chilled plates, and the accompanying beverage, usually vodka, in chilled glasses. Place the vodka in the freezer at least one hour before pouring (vodka may be kept in the freezer indefinitely).

Incidentally, according to that reliable publication *Sea Secrets,* published by the International Oceanographic Foundation in Miami, the eggs of numerous fish, including whitefish, lumpfish, and carp, are dyed black and sold as caviar. Originally the dye used on these eggs was carbon black, but the Food and Drug Administration banned this as cancer-causing. Vegetable dye is now most commonly used.

The Food and Drug Administration has defined caviar as eggs that derive from the sturgeon only. Other eggs sold as caviar must state clearly the fish of origin on the label.

No sourcebook on words indicates precisely how the name caviar came about. It is believed to be mainly of Turkish origin, deriving from a word transliterated as khavyar. In the sixteenth century, this may have been adopted by the Italians as caviale. Some sources note simply that it is Turkish-Italian.

Cavour

Camillo Benso Cavour was an Italian count who lived from 1810 to 1861. It was largely through his efforts that Italy became a free and united state.

The name on French menus represents a garnish of cutouts of polenta (a cornmeal mush) that is a popular regional dish in the Piedmont area of Italy, where Cavour was born.

In addition to polenta, a Cavour garnish includes mushrooms stuffed with a purée of chicken livers and slices of black truffles.

Cayenne Pepper

Cayenne pepper more often than not is used to describe almost any finely ground hot red pepper, but it originally came from Cayenne in French Guiana. You will find cayenne in abundance on the spice shelves of many supermarkets, but, according to a spokesman for the American Spice Trade Association, "The spice industry is phasing out 'cayenne' as a labeling term, and using the simpler designation 'red pepper' to signify all hot, ground red *(capsicum)* pepper. Tradition years ago dictated that the hottest ground red pepper product was called 'cayenne.' But, in trade practice, this did not refer to any particular variety and there never was a heat standard for it. So, the new move becomes more realistic labeling from the consumer's standpoint. It's all simply 'red pepper' and that means very hot (as a frame of reference, this is the ground version of 'crushed red pepper'—the fiery product that is frequently seen on the tables of pizzerias and other Italian-style restaurants)."

Cebiche

See Seviche.

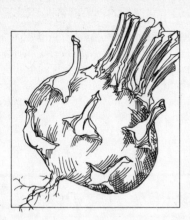

Celery Root

American taste has, without question, become infinitely more sophisticated within even a limited memory span. It was but the briefest while ago that the audience for celery root was by and large limited to those who dined in French restaurants, either in metropolitan cities in this country or abroad. Happily, it is finding its due favor even in supermarkets in some of the outer lands like East Hampton, more than a hundred miles from New York City. Celery root, sometimes called knob celery or celeriac (a clumsy word) in English and *céleri rave* in French, is a diamond in the rough. It is related to the stalk celery family and tastes like celery, but has a totally different texture and is a bit more flavorful. Stalk celery is no substitute. Celery root is somewhat turnip-shaped and has a brownish, mottled exterior that must be peeled away. A well-made purée of celery root is a delight, surpassing in excellence even a well-made purée of potatoes.

In its most popular form, it is cut into very fine slivers and blended with a rémoulade sauce to prepare céleri rémoulade.

Celery Victor

Celery Victor was originated many years ago by Victor Hirtzler, then chef of the St. Francis Hotel in San Francisco. He gave the recipe to Helen Evans Brown, who interpreted his directions for householders in *The West Coast Cook Book.*

"Halve celery hearts, trim root end and remove all but the most tender leaves. Cook celery, lying flat, in chicken broth till barely tender. Cool in broth.

"Drain thoroughly; press broth from celery. Arrange in serving dish. Sprinkle with coarsely ground pepper and chopped parsley. Cover with two parts of oil and one part of tarragon vinegar. Chill.

"Garnish with alternate slices of hard-cooked eggs and tomato or with crossed anchovy fillets or with pimiento strips."

Chafing Dish

Although the most common meaning of the word "chafe" is to vex or annoy, it also means to warm by rubbing, from the French *chauffer,* meaning to heat. Thus, a chafing dish is a warming or heating dish.

Cha Gio

I first sampled cha gio, considered by many to be the national dish of Vietnam, in a few of the flourishing Vietnamese restaurants of Paris and on a subsequent visit to that endlessly troubled land.

Cha gio is a bit curious, perhaps a trifle

exotic, by Western standards. It consists basically of morsels of ground meat, sometimes with chopped crab, shrimp, or chicken, wrapped in pastry, and deep-fried. These morsels, cooked to a golden brown, crisp without, tender within, are served hot at table with an assortment of fresh herbs, including mint, basil, and coriander, cold (Boston) lettuce leaves, and that ubiquitous Vietnamese sauce, nuoc mam. The pastries, glorified with fresh herbs, are wrapped in lettuce, dipped in the sauce, and eaten. Cha gio is as irresistible, in sum, as peanuts, popcorn, new radishes, fresh cider, and caviar. And cha gio is but one small savory fragment from the Vietnamese kitchen, which is among the most outstanding on earth.

Champagne Sauce

I am frequently amused when I see the term "champagne sauce" on a menu. I am a born skeptic and strongly suspect that most of the champagne sauces on most menus are really made with a still, dry white wine, rather than with champagne itself. Though I hasten to add that a first-rate still, dry white wine is a perfectly acceptable substitute for champagne as an ingredient, it seems a bit fraudulent to label a sauce "champagne" unless the real beverage has been used. In fact, the average palate would not know the difference. I know I would not use a costly bottle of champagne to make such a sauce. Better to reserve it for enjoying with a meal.

Chapon

The word *chapon* is French for capon. It is also a piece of bread, generally a slice that has been rubbed with garlic. To make this, you would need a loaf of bread with a fairly firm crust and center. You simply slice the bread, cut a clove of garlic in half, and rub it gently but firmly all over the surface of the slice.

Sometimes toast is also used. At times also, the bread is sprinkled with oil and/or vinegar. The chapon is added to a salad bowl and tossed with the greens.

Chapon is a family-type joke in France. It means a large piece of bread added to a very watery soup. You serve the bread, previously dipped in poultry fat, as a stand-in for a big fat capon.

Char

Char is a member of the salmon family and has a red understomach. The fish is sometimes cut into fillets, cooked in a vegetable broth, and cooled. It is then drained, covered with melted butter, and cooked further in small earthenware crocks. It is served cold with buttered toast.

Charcuterie

Charcuterie is one of the chief, delectable arts of the French kitchen. The word derives from *chair cuit,* meaning cooked meat, principally, if not exclusively, of the pig.

In *The Art of Charcuterie,* Jane Grigson writes that the trade of the charcutier goes back "at least as far as the time of classical Rome, where a variety of sausages could be bought, as well as the famous hams from Gaul." The world of charcuterie embraces, in addition to hams, such delicacies as terrines and pâtés, white sausages, blood sausages, and, of course, andouilles and andouillettes.

Charlotte

The "bible" of classic French cooking, *Dictionnaire de l'Académie des Gastronomes,* ascribes the dessert, charlotte, "probably" to Queen Charlotte of England, the wife of George III.

The best-known and most popular charlotte over the past decades is the one known as charlotte russe. It is made with a custard

or Bavarian cream filling to which gelatin has been added. This custard is poured into a mold lined with ladyfingers before it is allowed to set.

My much-favored dictionary states that this was not the original creation. It was, in fact, a filled, cooked apple dish baked in a crust—top, bottom, and sides—of sliced, buttered bread.

Although I am keenly fond of both versions, there seems little to relate the two other than the mold and, therefore, the shape in which they are baked.

The dictionary continues that the charlotte russe, as we know it, was first created by that great and illustrious chef of the French kitchen Antonïn Carême, who lived from 1784 to 1833. He created it when he was the chef in the kitchens of the French diplomat and statesman Talleyrand.

Carême dubbed his creation charlotte à la parisienne. The name was later changed to charlotte russe during the era of the Second Empire when table service à la russe (a greatly simplified form in which dishes were presented to the assembled guests, each of whom helped him or herself) replaced the highly ornamental service à la française (in which the food was displayed as an elaborate and elegant buffet).

Chayote

Over the years I'd heard of the vegetable chayote, a member of the squash family. And I knew that it is to be found almost all year long in the markets along Ninth Avenue in Manhattan. But through some curious circumstance, I never sampled it until a visit to the Caribbean island of St.-Barthélemy.

Chayote enjoys a considerable popularity on the tables of Louisiana in general and New Orleans specifically. It is listed on menus and in cookbooks there as mirliton.

On St. Bart's I was served chayote stuffed, potato fashion, with its own pulp, plus langouste, in a light cream sauce. I was astonished at its goodness and the overall delicate nature of the dish. When I returned home I visited Ninth Avenue to load a shopping bag with the vegetable so that Pierre Franey and I could experiment with it.

What we discovered was that the chayote—it is known as *christophene* in French—is infinitely variable in its uses. It is tender yet crisp when briefly cooked and used in salads and can be filled with any of a number of savory fillings and baked. It can be fried, stewed, or simply baked after being split like an acorn squash and seasoned with butter, herbs, or spices.

The chayote resembles a pale green quince, although some people think it looks more like an avocado or a pear. It is available everywhere there are markets that sell South American or West Indian foods.

The chayote is said to have originated in Mexico and is today much enjoyed in the southwest of the United States as well as in Australia and South America. According to Elisabeth Lambert Ortiz, an authority on Mexican, Caribbean, and South American cookery, it goes by many names, including chocho, choko, and chuchu.

Diana Kennedy in her book *The Cuisines of Mexico* refers to it as vegetable pear as well as chayote and says that there are three common cooking varieties: small, light green ones; creamy white ones, and those that are large and dark green "with long thin spines like a porcupine."

I was surprised to note her observation that "The ones available in New York, at least in Spanish-American and West Indian markets, are rather tasteless and watery; they are pale green or whitish in color." She does add that they need a rather heavy hand in seasoning and the ones we experimented with were given that treatment.

Some we stuffed with a grated cheese filling (Muenster is one of the best), others with a curry of beef, and still others with shrimp in imitation of that langouste dish I had first sampled. The salad was made with a standard dressing plus garlic, hot pepper flakes, and a touch of anchovy.

In its natural state the chayote is low in calories. It has a pleasant, crunchy texture like that of a not-too-ripe unsweet melon. Its flavor makes it a natural for almost any assertive flavors you wish to employ. A properly filled chayote half will serve as a luncheon dish. It will also serve as a fairly substantial first course at dinner or as a vegetable accompaniment.

Cheddar

Cheddar cheese is one of the most basic of cheeses and also one of the most versatile.

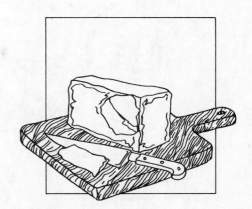

It is made from cow's milk and may be used in almost any recipe that calls for cheese, although it would be a sacrilege to use it, rather than Gruyère, in a cheese fondue. It is excellent in cheese sauces, as a topping for broiled dishes, in casseroles, and so on.

Cheddar cheese is known to have been produced in Cheddar, England, since the latter part of the sixteenth century. Cheddar is now so widely produced in this country it is sometimes referred to as American cheese.

Cheese

See Cheddar, Cottage cheese, Feta, Fromage blanc, Gloucester cheese, Gruyère, Mascarpone, Rat cheese, Stilton.

Cheese Rind

Eating the rind of a cheese is a matter of taste and judgment. Whether I eat the rind of Brie or discard it has a lot to do with how I feel at the moment. There are rinds I would not eat under any circumstances,

including those of most Camembert, those heavily imprinted, and those of oiled and paraffined cheeses.

The rind occurs in various ways: In soft cheeses it forms by the accumulation of certain ferments and mold over time. In some cooked and uncooked pressed cheeses it results from the natural hardening of the outer caseous layers. I know of some Italian chefs who save the rinds of their Parmesan wheels, cut them into small pieces, and add them to soups shortly before serving.

Chef

I am often asked to distinguish between the words "chef" and "cook." The word "chef" means chief in French. *Chef de gare* is a station master. *Chef des pompiers* is a fire chief, and so on.

The word "cook" refers to an amateur who prepares food with whatever degree of skill. It also refers to a person in the kitchen who has not mastered all the cooking techniques of a professional.

In America one speaks of an executive chef, a man or woman who is in overall charge of a kitchen and presumably has the skills to substitute for any member of the staff. In French, the executive chef is known as the *chef de cuisine*.

There is, in a classic French kitchen, a man who is designated *sous-chef*, or underchef, who is second in command. And under them both are various *chefs de partie*. These are chef specialists who have a marked expertise in one branch of cookery. The roast cook is *chef rôtisseur;* the fish cook is the *chef poissonnier;* the sauce cook is the *chef saucier;* the pastry cook is the *chef pâtissier,* and so on.

Cherrystones

See Clams.

Chess Pie

I have been asked many times over the years if I knew the origin of the name chess pie. On a recent visit to Kentucky, it was explained to me as follows: A visitor to the South went to a dining establishment. At the time for dessert, the waitress told him that pie was included. He said he would like apple pie and she replied that it was not served. "Then I'll take peach," he said. No peach either. "What kind of pie do you serve?" he asked. "Jes' pie," she told him. Chess pie is jes' pie with a filling of sugar, cream, and eggs baked in a crust.

Chestnuts

Chestnuts are commonly used in Europe— in stewed red cabbage and in hundreds of desserts from a sweetened purée to nesselrode pudding. They are most frequently found in America in poultry stuffings.

I am often asked the best method for peeling chestnuts and the one I recommend is as follows:

Insert the tip of a sharp paring knife into one side of the thick, oval crown of the chestnut. Bring the tip around the chestnut, circular fashion, to the other side of the crown. Continue until all the chestnuts are carved.

Put the chestnuts in a skillet with water to cover and salt to taste. Bring to a boil

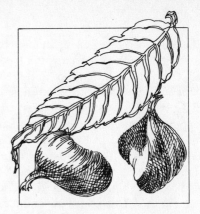

and simmer 15 to 20 minutes, or until the shells can easily be removed with the fingers. Drain. When cool enough to handle, peel the chestnuts. Remove both the outer shell and the inner peel.

A friend has another technique: After making the circular gash from one part of the crown to the other, he puts the chestnuts in a flat pan, places them under the broiler, and toasts them for 2 minutes. "Voilà," he says, "the tops and bottoms come off like hats, leaving the chestnuts raw and unscorched to do with as you may."

Chewing Gum

Without question, the single most gratifying piece of mail to be anchored in my mailbox within recent memory was from the Arlington Confection Company of Arlington, Texas. The letter, which forwarded a do-it-yourself chewing gum kit, is as follows:

"We are enclosing a sample of our product so that you, too, may enjoy the difference between freshly prepared and commercially available chewing gum.

"As you will note, our product will make about 16 feet of chewing gum approximately one-half inch in diameter, and/or may be portioned for chewing in numerous ways. POW! can be prepared with no color added, cut with cookie cutters, and the figures then painted with food color and a small artist's brush for an absolutely great eye-appealing, unique, after-dinner treat.

"Also, we would like to point out that never before has the opportunity been available for Mr. (or Mrs.) Person Who Loves To Cook to prepare their own chewing gum, in the kitchen, with minimum ease, in a manner that best suits their individual preference. Finally, many people will no doubt find ways to flavor their gum which are now unknown to ourselves and other manufacturers.

"Thank you for your time," etc.

Chicken

Chicken has traditionally succored the poor in years that are lean. By contrast, it has for centuries delighted the palates of the royally robed as well, in the form of such dishes as *suprêmes de volaille Polignac* (chicken breasts with mushrooms and truffles in cream sauce) and *poulet reine sauté à l'archiduc* (sautéed chicken in a Madeira-flavored cream sauce).

As chicken broth it has, for countless generations, been nourishment and balm for mind and body and made those who imbibe feel whole again. If proof were needed as to the appeal of chicken for the masses, consider Colonel Sanders.

It is true in ages past in certain cultures—particularly primitive tribes—the consumption of both chickens and eggs was a greater taboo than sin. Even in Athens and Rome. But both the Greeks and Romans learned early to replace superstition with super-

suppers. It is recorded, in fact, that nearly two thousand years ago Quintus Horatius Flaccus, the Roman poet better known as Horace, considered a fat roast fowl all the more tasty if the bird had first been drowned in a vat of wine.

The definitive book on chicken lore is a seemingly exhaustive work titled *The Chicken Book, Being an Inquiry into the Rise and Fall, Use and Abuse, Triumph and Tragedy of Gallus Domesticus,* by Page Smith and Charles Daniel.

If there is an aspect of chicken culture that has not come under their scrutiny I have yet to find it. It embraces sexual topics, ancient history, origins, and, lastly, recipes. There you will find the origins of such words as "cockalorum" (a "kind of bantam man, small and self-important, a strutter"), and "cockatrice" ("a fabulous creature, hatched, it was thought, from a cock's egg by a serpent whose glance would kill"). There, too, you will find the explanation that chicken, used as a prefix, usually means small, as in chicken lobster.

Chicken à la King

Over the years I have speculated several times about the origin of the dish called chicken à la king. Curiosity about the source has to do with a possible sea change that may have occurred when the dish arrived here, as I supposed, from France.

Numerous classic dishes in the French kitchen are listed on menus as *à la reine* or in the queen's style. Thus you find *omelette à la reine,* or an omelet filled with creamed chicken, *potage à la reine,* a cream of chicken soup, and so on.

James N. Keen, a professional photographer in Louisville, Kentucky, has a brochure that purports to tell the genesis of the name chicken à la king. Mr. Keen states that a brochure was given to him forty years ago by one E. Clark King 3d, whose father was a restaurateur.

"It was in the early 1900s that chicken à la King was first served to the public," the brochure says. "My father was the proprietor of the Brighton Beach Hotel, a fashionable summer resort outside Manhattan.

"One night his head chef, George Greenwald, sent word he had concocted a dish he would like to serve my parents. It was enjoyed immensely and they asked for seconds, but only enough had been prepared for two individual portions. The next morning, the chef asked permission to place it on the menu. After learning of the various ingredients used, my father remarked that 'a fair price must be asked.'

"The next day the bill of fare carried the following:

" 'Chicken à la King—$1.25 a portion.' "

If that was indeed the origin of the name, then here is the original recipe as detailed in the brochure:

"Melt 2 tablespoonfuls of butter and then add ½ of a green pepper shredded and 1 cup of mushrooms sliced thin. Stir and cook 5 minutes and then add 2 level tablespoonfuls of flour and ½ teaspoonful of salt. Cook until frothy and then add 1 pint of cream and stir until sauce thickens. Put this all in a double boiler, add 3 cups of chicken cut in pieces and let stand to get very hot. In the meantime, take ¼ cup of butter and beat into it the yolks of 3 eggs, 1 teaspoonful of onion juice, 1 tablespoonful of lemon juice and ½ teaspoonful of paprika. Stir this mixture until the eggs thicken a little. Combine the two, add a little sherry and finally shredded pimiento before serving on toast."

Chicken Breasts

One of the greatest bargains where meat is concerned are chicken breasts. They may be purchased with the bone left in, with the bone removed, and with the skin left on or not. Chicken breasts adapt well to almost any flavors from curry powder to cheese, and to dishes from soups and casseroles to salads. The breasts may, in most cases, be substituted in recipes that call for veal. They both have a fine texture and a fairly neutral flavor.

Chicken Claws

See Perche-pierres.

Chicken Feet

I have recently started tossing a few chicken feet into the kettle when I make chicken broth, and it does, indeed, give a nice body to the stock. It also congeals when chilled. You do, however, have to peel off the thin yellow coating of the feet before putting them in the broth. My supplier gave me the following instructions: Heat a kettle of water to the boil on top of the stove to a temperature of 150 degrees. Drop in the chicken feet, and bring the water back to the 150-degree temperature as quickly as possible. Let the feet stand in the water at that temperature for about one minute, no longer.

Drain and chill the feet. At this point it should be relatively easy, with the fingers and fingernails, to pull, scrape, and skin off that yellow integument. It does, for me at any rate, require some patience, but it is worth it.

Other cooks have their own ways of removing the skin: "Simply singe them over an open gas flame until the skin 'bubbles' and chars slightly. It takes only a minute, and the skin peels off without trouble."

"You will probably hear from a million Jewish mothers about your silly way to struggle to skin chicken feet. With patience and fingernails, indeed! Just plunge them into boiling water for a couple of seconds and peel the hot skin off with a paring knife. It comes off like a glove. Chilling would cause the skin to stick on."

Incidentally, chicken feet are hard to come by in many areas. The law says they may be unsanitary and therefore bans them. My poultryman is forbidden to sell the feet, but he offers them free to those customers who ask for them.

Chicken Fillets

If you remove the entire breast of a chicken, you will note a long strip of meat attached to the main part of the breast meat. That is the fillet, also called the mignon filet.

I have only once been served a dish made with the fillets. That was in the home of a friend, Marcel Gosselin, who in those days was the proprietor of the now defunct L'Armorique Restaurant on East Fifty-fourth Street. He prepared the fillets in a rich cream sauce, and it was one of the great dishes of my time. He had, he told me, accumulated the fillets over a period of months and had kept them frozen for a special occasion.

Chicken-Fried Steaks

I have never seen a recipe for chicken-fried steaks. It is my conjecture that the name came about years ago when it was impossible to get beefsteaks of good quality in the rural South.

Most steaks were cut thin and pounded with the side of a heavy plate to tenderize them. They were then coated in a mixture of flour, salt, and a generous amount of black pepper. They were fried like chicken, either in lard or solid white shortening.

After frying, the steaks were removed. The fat was poured off and milk was added to the brown particles in the pan. This made a "cream gravy," which was served over the steaks.

I believe Swiss steaks had more or less the same origin. After the steaks were fried they were covered with a sauce of tomatoes, carrots, celery, and peas and baked until fork-tender.

Chicken Pot Pie

Although French is generally accepted in the Western world as the language of classic menus, there are some dishes so typically un-french the names are rarely translated from the country of origin. One of these is chicken pot pie, which can be, in truth, one of the great dishes of the world. I do not speak of the basic and hearty pie of New England and Pennsylvania Dutch territory made with boiled birds. No offense intended, but that is wine from a lesser bottle. What I do speak of is the elegant, when perfectly made, chicken pot pie of England. It contains pieces of sautéed chicken, mushrooms, carrots, small white onions, hard-boiled eggs, and strips of bacon in a well seasoned wine and cream sauce.

Chick-Peas

I have on very rare occasions dined on soups or stews that my host or hostess told me were made from fresh, nondried chick-peas, but I have never seen a direct-from-the-garden chick-pea.

I use chick-peas fairly often in my kitchen as an ingredient for couscous or hummus. I use the dried peas that must be soaked overnight, or, if in a rush, I use the canned version, which is drained, sometimes rinsed, and added to a dish toward the end of the cooking time. *See also* Hummus.

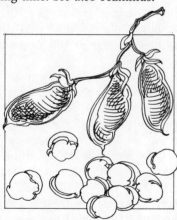

Chicory

Two kinds of chicory are found in this country and both are basically salad ingredients. One of them is best known as endive or white Belgian endive. The other is a green

with large, open, green-and-white leaves, large roots, and a slightly bitter flavor. It is sometimes called escarole.

It is the roots of the latter that are roasted and ground. As far as I know, the roasted chicory is never used as the sole ingredient for brewing coffee. To the best of my knowledge, it is always blended with roasted ground coffee.

Chili con Carne

That Americans love to argue about food there can be no question. New Englanders can expound for hours on the virtues or vices of a well-made or poorly made clam chowder or pot of Boston baked beans. Arguments as to the merits or demerits of using lard, Crisco, or butter as the proper fat for frying chicken are sufficient unto themselves to render asunder close ties in the South. In Pennsylvania Dutch country, one man's Schnitz un Gneppe may very well be anathema.

But these are regional arguments. On the national scene, there is one dish that has, within the last decade, inspired more controversy than any other in the United States: chili con carne.

And what is to account for this national preoccupation with a dish whose origins are so obscure, a dish that varies from kitchen to kitchen yet whose appeal is almost universal? What inspires such extraordinary enthusiasm for a dish so thoroughly basic, unsophisticated, and down to earth? I think I have arrived at an answer.

Instinctively, one knows that chili originated in the Southwest, was of Mexican inspiration, and that it moved eastward to the southern states in the early part of this century.

Although American Indians used for one dish or another such chilies as could be found in various parts of America, chili con carne was not an Indian invention. Carolyn Niethammer, in her book *American Indian Food and Lore,* states that the tiny round chili called chillipiquin was known in New Mexico and Arizona, but the Indians did not know the large, domesticated chilies such as those used in chili con carne "until the Spaniards brought them [here] after passing through Mexico."

The late Frank X. Tolbert, perhaps the nation's leading historian on the subject of chili, indicates in his book, *A Bowl of Red,* his assurance that chili originated in San Antonio, Texas. Incidentally, a bowl of red, for the enlightenment of nonchiliheads, is a Texas term for a bowl of chili.

The initial, large-scale hoisting of chili con carne into the national consciousness came about through the efforts, no matter how unwittingly, of three men. The first of these was H. Allen Smith, the humorist and author best known for his book *Low Man on a Totem Pole.* He ignited the fires beneath the chili pot in 1966 with an article in *Holiday* magazine titled, "Nobody Knows More About Chili Than I Do."

The impact was devastating. "No living man," he wrote, "can put together a pot of chili as ambrosial, as delicately and zestfully flavored as the chili I make. This is a fact so stern, so granitic that it belongs in the encyclopedias as well as in all the standard histories of civilization."

Although Mr. Smith was a native of Illinois, by the time the article was published he had long been a New Yorker, and this bit of Eastern bombast and self-praise was more than a couple of Texans—namely Frank Tolbert and one Wickford (Wick) Fowler, a newspaperman and celebrated, locally at least, as the grand Texas aficionado of chili-making—could tolerate.

Mr. Tolbert termed Mr. Smith's chili a "chili-flavored, low-torque, beef and vegetable soup." The recipe did call for tomatoes, onions, green pepper, and—sacrilege of sacrileges—canned pinto beans. The addition of beans to a genuine Texas chili is grounds in some camps for a nice little western auto-da-fé.

With Mr. Tolbert's encouragement, Mr. Fowler pitted his talents against Mr. Smith's. The event took place in 1967 and attracted only a thousand spectators, but it made a few hundred headlines around the country. The contest ended in a draw, but Texas chili cook-offs became an annual event.

By far the most famous chili recipe throughout the land is for Pedernales River chili, favored by Lyndon Baines Johnson and much publicized during his stint in the White House. The end product of that recipe is a somewhat standard, run-of-the-mill item guaranteed not to offend anyone but dyed-in-the-wool chiliheads.

The most famous bowl of restaurant chili in the world comes from the kitchen of

Chasen's dining spot in Los Angeles. It achieved worldwide notoriety due to the enthusiasm for it shared by Elizabeth Taylor and Richard Burton. When in Rome they did as the Texans do: They dispatched a cable to Chasen's and ordered ten quarts, frozen, to be sent to their address on the Via Appia Pignatelli.

Chasen's chili isn't bad, but then again I esteem no chili to be bad provided it is honestly made with decent ingredients. Which brings me back to my original thought of why such a basic and unsophisticated dish as chili can have such universal appeal. It is quite simple. It is a dish that almost anyone, including a reasonably intelligent six year old, can make with pride and pleasure and the thought that his or hers is the best darn chili in the land.

Chili Peppers

See Peppers.

Chili Powder

Chili powder is not, as a few hundred thousand people seem to think (if they think about it at all), made of ground-up dried chilies, only that and nothing more. Almost all the chili powder bottled commercially today is composed of pulverized chilies plus dried garlic, cumin, oregano, cloves, coriander, and flaked or powdered dried onion. The chili itself lends heat plus a subtle flavor. What most people think of as the chili flavor is actually that of powdered cumin.

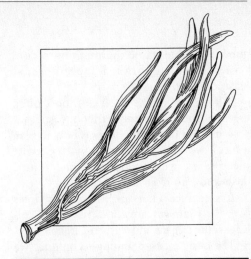

Chinese Chives

Chinese chives are, like ordinary chives, a long-stemmed herb. They are, however, somewhat flatter in shape, and their flavor is far more pronounced than run-of-the-garden chives. The flavor is quite pungent and assertive. They have many uses in Chinese cookery and they are sometimes used in abundance in spring rolls.

In Western cookery, scallions would be the best substitute for ordinary chives and either chives or scallions could be substituted in recipes that call for Chinese chives. The flavor will, however, be much milder.

Chinese Menu Planning

It is as basic as chopsticks to say that the greatest obstacle in the preparation of a Chinese dinner is the ability to organize dishes to be served of an evening in a manner that permits the home cook to join guests at table while maintaining a cool presence and an outward appearance, at least, of calm.

In fact, one of the questions most often asked of those with more than a casual involvement in Chinese cookery is how to plan a menu without panic and how to execute the cooking without repeated and frantic dashes to and from a hot wok.

It is a subject I have explored many times over the years with my late friend and colleague, the elegant and learned Virginia Lee.

The basic menu-planning techniques we agreed on are these: Make the menu in a family-style pattern. This consists generally of four to six dishes, when there are to be four to six people at table. Add an additional dish for each two additional persons.

Prepare several dishes in advance. For example, a few cold appetizers, a hot soup, and one or two casseroles or long-simmered dishes. Keep the stir-fried dishes or dishes that must be made at the last moment to one or two, and have all the ingredients for these dishes sliced, chopped, ground, and assembled, ready to toss into the wok on a second's notice.

Chinese New Year

What you eat at Chinese New Year feasts can bring you health, wealth, happiness, or an untroubled carefree life, according to Chinese tradition and most of the Chinese cooks I know.

If you eat large bean sprouts, for example, "no matter how rough the road, your path will be smoothed." Should you choose braised duck, "all money will come to you." And how about a bite of casserole pork bel-

ly? That would provide "all happiness." Or, perhaps, a personal favorite both from the standpoint of flavor and prophecy: Whole fish with hot bean sauce means that "everything you have is more than you have, or in other words, everything we do is head and tail, there is no halfway."

I once asked a Shanghai-born scholar and friend how it came about that each year of the Chinese calendar bears the name of an animal.

"First," he said, "you must understand that the Oriental calendar like your own is divided into twelve cycles. But whereas your calendar cycle consists of twelve units known as months, ours consists of twelve cycles known as years. Each year has a name starting with 'mouse' and ending with 'pig,' or 'boar' if your prefer.

"When the year of the pig is ended, so is the cycle, then it starts all over again.

"Okay, you ask, how did the animal names come about. No one knows, but the most commonly repeated legend attributes it to the first Buddha, an itinerant preacher born in India about five hundred years before Christ.

"The legend says that Buddha entreated all the animals in the forest to come into his presence and only twelve came. The first was the mouse, the last was the pig. To honor them all, he named each cycle or year of the calendar for the order in which the animals came before him." They are the mouse, cow, tiger, rabbit, dragon, snake, horse, lamb or sheep, monkey, chicken, dog, and pig.

Chinese Parsley

See Coriander.

Chinois

A typical chinois, or French sieve, is cone shaped, has a rounded or slightly flat bottom, and is made with closely woven, fine metal strands. It is probably the most finely meshed sieve used in the home. Its purpose is to strain sauces. When the sauce is poured into the chinois, the liquid passes through as in most sieves. With a chinois, however, the solids are pressed firmly inside the utensil, so that most of the liquid essence of the solids can be extracted, usually using a heavy metal spoon to press them. If the same sauce is prepared using a regular sieve, the sauce will not be as fine in texture. The name, incidentally, derives from the fact that the shape of the sieve resembles, to some chefs' minds, a coolie hat turned upside down.

Chipped Beef

Chipped beef, frequently sold commercially as sliced dried beef, is basically prepared like corned beef. It is, however, smoked and dried until most of the meat's moisture disappears. The beef is then sliced wafer thin and packaged, frequently in small jars.

The saltiness of chipped beef varies from processor to processor. The salt flavor can be reduced by separating the slices, putting them in a sieve, and pouring boiling water over them.

To prepare creamed chipped beef, blend 1½ tablespoons of butter with an equal amount of flour in a saucepan, stirring with a wire whisk. When blended and smooth, add about ¾ cup of milk and ¼ cup of cream. Do not add salt at this time. Add freshly ground pepper, nutmeg, and the beef from a two-and-a-half ounce jar. Stir and bring to the boil. If desired, add salt to taste and a touch of Worcestershire sauce. You may add a little grated Cheddar or Swiss cheese if that is your taste. Serve on toast.

Chitterlings

See Andouillettes.

Chlodnik

One of my favorite cold soups for summer is borscht, which is of Russian origin and one of the tastiest liquids associated with hot-weather dining. But there is another beet soup—of Polish origin, although it is also Russian by adoption—that is rarely found in cookbooks. It is called chlodnik.

In my view, it is one of the most appetizing and gratifying soups ever created. What makes this soup so remarkable are the ingredients that are added to the beets and broth to give it its flair, substance, and goodness. These things include chopped cucumbers and scallions, a touch of vinegar, sugar, sour cream, and shrimp. That plus veal and, perhaps, hard-boiled eggs.

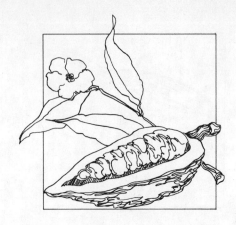

Chocolate

It seems that since man first discovered the uses to which the cocoa bean (from which chocolate derives) could be put, chocolate has been thought of as celestial manna. The botanical generic title of the cocoa tree is *theobroma,* which translates into the hyperbolic "food for the gods."

And heaven knows, once the Spaniards got wind of the bean, its influence was immediate.

History has it that the first Spaniard to taste the stuff was an officer on the staff of Cortez who noticed Montezuma in 1519 drinking a foamy concoction made with cocoa, vanilla, and sugar from a golden vessel.

According to *Ward's Encyclopedia of Foods,* "as early as 1550 chocolate factories of considerable size existed in the south of Europe—in Lisbon, Genoa, Turin, Bayonne, and Marseilles.

"The industry within the original thirteen United States was only ten years old at the commencement of the American Revolution, the first factory having been located in Dorchester, Massachusetts, in 1765."

Modern chocolate making was explained to me by Thomas Kron, the Hungarian chocolatier now living in Manhattan.

"Cocoa trees grow in many countries, like Brazil, Mexico, Venezuela, Ghana, and Nicaragua," he said. "The trees flourish best in regions that lie ten degrees above or be-

low the equator. The trees have to be grown on plantations and they must not have any other kind of tree next to them. They spoil the roots.

"It takes ten years, a long time, for a cocoa tree to develop a crop that is ready to harvest, that is to say for a new tree to produce a bean. A mature cocoa bean is about the size of a pineapple and one tree produces about twenty cocoa beans.

"Within each of these beans are about two hundred small pods. What happens is the large, ripe cocoa beans are removed from the tree and placed in the sun. After they dry they're cracked open and the pods spill out. The pods, in turn, are placed in the sun and allowed to dry. After they are dehydrated, they're put in burlap bags and shipped to the United States or Switzerland. They're the only two countries with the technology for making cocoa butter.

"To process the pods, they have to be ground and pressed. What is pressed out of the pods is the valuable cocoa butter. The pods are then ground and they become cocoa powder.

"Most people," he continued, "haven't the slightest notion of how chocolate candy comes about. Actually, it is very, very simple. The finest chocolate is made from three—four in the case of milk chocolate—ingredients. These are cocoa butter, which is a very hard and expensive substance and comes in various sizes, cocoa powder, and sugar.

"The important thing is the amount of cocoa butter you use. It has to be 33 percent of the whole. The amount of cocoa powder and sugar can be varied, but the 33 percent cocoa butter must remain constant. The more cocoa used the more bitter the chocolate; the more sugar, the sweeter.

"Milk chocolate, by the way, varies from dark chocolate in one respect. Instead of using all cocoa, you substitute part dry milk solids."

White chocolate, according to a spokesman for the Hershey Chocolate Company in Hershey, Pennsylvania, is a wholly different product from dark chocolate.

To make white chocolate, whole milk and sugar are cooked until condensed to an almost solid state. Cocoa butter is added to produce white chocolate.

Cholent

Cholent is a traditional food of the Jewish Sabbath, with many variations. The usual ingredients are dried beans, such as lima beans or navy beans, which are cooked with onions, potatoes, and beef short ribs or chuck. Barley is generally added, as well as such seasonings as finely minced garlic and paprika.

Cholent is prepared before the Sabbath eve and, since cooking is forbidden on the Sabbath, it is simmered at the lowest heat possible so that it can be the hot dish for the Sabbath afternoon meal.

Chopsticks

I am an avid wielder of chopsticks, convinced that Chinese food tastes the poorer when taken to the mouth with a fork. The *Peninsula Magazine,* a publication of the Peninsula Hotel in Hong Kong, once carried a fascinating article by Derek Maitland, described as a "Hong Kong-based author and journalist" who writes about Asia "and uses chopsticks admirably."

He, in turn, had been spurred to write the piece because he had read an essay-article in a Hong Kong newspaper titled "Easy When You Know How." The gist of the article was instruction of a group of children at a Kowloon (across from Hong Kong) kindergarten on how to master the tools. The children, it was noted, had reached the age when "the days of sticky fingers and plastic spoons are quickly drawing to an end."

Mr. Maitland admitted that learning that Chinese children had to "learn" to use chopsticks was a little like "reading that the Russians can't really hold their vodka and Swiss trains don't always run on time."

In any event, he mused on: "Why did the Chinese invent chopsticks in the first place?

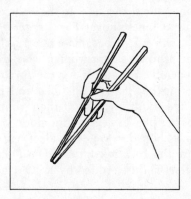

Why didn't they choose to slice and spear their food as we do with our knives and forks? With all the problems they've had to face throughout their long and illustrious history, why did they have to compound it all by turning the simple process of eating into something almost as difficult as juggling?

"It all goes back to China's perennial problem—feeding its monumental millions. Not only has food always been scarce, but fuel for cooking, too. In answer to this dilemma, the Chinese developed a cuisine that was not only widely diversified in ingredients but also relatively simple to cook.

"Small, chopped or sliced portions of meat and vegetables are stir-fried in the wok over a charcoal brazier, requiring minimal cooking time and thus conserving expensive fuel. And since almost everything reaches the table in collective tidbits, it is easier—and certainly more refined—to delicately pluck at the morsels with two precisely choreographed sticks than to adapt the Western style.

"The earliest chopsticks were made of bamboo, then various hardwoods, then ivory and jade and finally silver and gold—the latter of which were for Chinese nobility and wealthier classes. To sit at their tables you needed fingers that were not only nimble but quite strong, too. In the eighteenth-century Chinese novel *The Dream of the Red Chamber,* it became embarrassingly apparent to a peasant woman who, eating in upper-class company for the first time, takes up her gold chopsticks and is so shocked by the weight of them that she drops her pigeon's egg on the floor."

That chopsticks were prevalent centuries before the fork is confirmed in *Food in Chinese Culture,* edited by K. C. Chang.

Chopsticks, the book notes, were available from at least the eighteenth century B.C.

They were "used during the Shang and Chou periods, although hands were probably used more often than chopsticks," according to Mr. Chang.

Whenever the merits of chopsticks as opposed to forks enters a discussion, I am reminded of the Chinese who, when asked why his countrymen employ chopsticks rather than knife and fork, replied: "We Chinese prefer not to butcher at table."

Choron

A sauce Choron is essentially a béarnaise sauce to which tomato has been added. The name Choron has been attributed to a French composer, Alexandre Etienne Choron, a native of Caen (famous for its tripe ragout perfumed with Calvados) who lived from 1771 to 1834. I prefer the theory, however, that it is the creation of Choron, the French chef of a once celebrated restaurant called Voisin in Paris.

Chowder

Although the chowders of America's East Coast seem as distinctly Yankee as flapjacks and brown bread, the name is of French origin. It is said to have been brought to this country by fishermen who came from the coastal regions of France. The name derives from *chaudière,* or cauldron, in which the fishermen had made their fish soups and stews on native soil.

Christmas Goose

The most famous legendary dinner in the world had nothing whatsoever to do with Belshazzar, Trimalchio, Henry VIII, or Tom Jones. It is a feast about which one—meaning me—may have two minds, and it is the Christmas dinner indulged in by the Cratchit family in Dickens' *A Christmas Carol*.

It was Dickens, of course, who in the course of that tale made roast goose the bird so ineradicably linked to the glad and festive Yuletide season. But it really doesn't pay to examine all the details of the Cratchits' feast with a Scrooge-like and microscopic eye.

For example, after making the gravy "hissing hot" and after grace is said, Mrs. Cratchit looked "slowly all along the carving knife, prepared to plunge it in the breast; but when she did, and when the long expected gush of stuffing issued forth. . . ."

Now, that strains my credulity, never having seen a stuffing issue forth from the breastworks of any fowl.

And what about that pudding to be served after those assembled were "steeped in sage and onions to the eyebrows." Such a to-do, old Dickens describes.

"Suppose it should not be done enough!"

Exclamation point. Exclamation point, indeed.

But read on to the moment when the pudding is readied for dessert.

"Hallo! A great deal of steam! The pudding was out of the copper. A smell like washing-day! That was the cloth. A smell like an eating-house, and a pastry cook's next-door to each other, with a laundress's next-door to that! That was the pudding."

Thanks, Charles, but no thanks.

One of the reasons those Cratchits wound up "steeped in sage and onions to the eyebrows" after their meal is the pre-prandial brew that old Bob Cratchit concocted before the meal. According to Dickens, "Bob . . . compounded some hot mixture in a jug with gin and lemons and stirred it round and round and put it on the hob to simmer."

Churrasco

One of the grandest ritual feasts in the world is of agrarian origins and comes from Brazil. This is the churrasco à gaucha, the traditional feast of southern Brazil, specifically from the state of Rio Grande do Sul, the center of the nation's cattle country.

I was involved in a highly sophisticated version of the churrasco à gaucha assembled under the expert guidance of Dorotea Elman, a redoubtable, enthusiastic cook, an old friend, and a native of Rio de Janeiro.

"Although the churrasco had basically humble origins—in the beginning it was nothing more than a cattleman's lunch or dinner made of freshly killed beef cooked over an open fire—the meal is tremendously popular in Rio and Sao Pãolo," she said.

The meal she was to prepare during the day was to be cooked and consumed late in the afternoon, at long tables situated next to a charcoal pit where the assorted meats—beef ribs, chicken, pork, lamb, and sausages—would be grilled over hot ashes.

The time in which the meat would be grilled would be sufficient to unleash the hounds of hunger, the enraged appetite only partly assuaged by morsels of spicy Brazilian sausages wrapped in foil and buried in the hot coals. These are taken with a seemingly innocent, superficially innocuous and irresistible but potent Brazilian elixir known as caipirinha, made with the clear distillate of sugarcane, lime, and sugar over ice.

The meats, still amber and still sizzling, would be removed from the long skewer and cut, sliced, or carved, then served with an ingeniously, seductively seasoned salad of mixed vegetables—bits of broccoli, cauliflower, green beans, zucchini, green peas, carrots, and so on blended in a tangy mayonnaise. That plus a platter of buttery farofa, a splendid dry cereal dish cooked with banana. And to bind the meal together, to give it an exceptional and uncommon fillip, a spicy onion sauce, made with oil and vinegar, chopped parsley, and coriander.

Before the meal began, the long tables

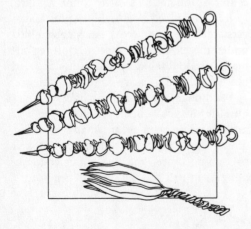

were covered with sheets of heavy brown wrapping paper as is done in Brazil.

Forks and knives were provided, plus linen napkins, although the churrasqueira (that's the female name of the person who cooks the meal; the male is churrasqueiro) explained that these were civilized conceits; the gauchos use their fingers.

Mrs. Elman went about her business of preparing foods and cooking them as well with cool, assured dedication and determination awesome to behold. The meats were threaded or simply impaled on long iron skewers, and when the coals in the pit were properly ashen, she shoved the metal bottoms into the earth with a powerful, educated thrust, taking care that the foods on the rods were neatly centered directly over the heat. The skewers were inserted into the earth at a ten- or fourteen-degree angle, centering the foods about twelve to fourteen inches from the heat.

As the meats were seared on one side, the skewers were deftly turned so that the other side would roast. The moment the meats were turned, she would dip a neatly tied and sizable bundle of leaves together to use as a basting "mop." She would swish the mop inside a vessel containing a basting brine made of water, garlic, and salt, then onto the meats.

"You wait until the meats are seared on one side before basting with the brine. After that you must brush them often. And if flames start in the pit and under the meat, you must extinguish them at all times with a dash of brine from the mop.

"Take care," she added, "that the meats don't burn. Just let them get nice and crisp on the outside and cooked inside."

As the meats were ready for eating, the skewers were removed and the tips wiped off with a clean damp rag. The meats were removed, transferred to a cutting board, and sliced or carved and served piping hot.

"There's one thing to remember," Mrs. Elman advised. "If you plan to cook at one of these, don't ever plan to sit with the guests until the end of the meal. That's why the table should be close to the pit. So you can cook and talk at the same time."

Chutney

Concerning chutney, which is so often served with Indian food, I have received many requests to print "the origin of Major Grey's chutney pickle and tell us who Major Grey was." I have done some casual research over the years and have not come any closer to the identity of the gentleman, if indeed he ever did exist, than when I first began my quest.

I asked one major producer of Major Grey's chutney for information, and an hour later they returned my call with a very dull script. Major Grey, I was informed, was a British army officer (what else?) stationed in India (but, of course), during the late 1800s (give or take a few years). He had a passion for curries (hear, hear!), and he liked to cook, so he concocted a chutney to go with his curry.

And he sold it to our scriptwriter's firm, which did not have the good sense to go out and copyright the name. Since that time every cheating Tom, Dick, and Harry food producer within a thousand miles of Bombay has been stealing his firm's original recipe and calling their chutney Major Grey.

Before hanging up, my man told me that unfortunately in his research he had not unearthed the major's first name.

I hasten to add a footnote to this. Chutney in India is not considered "a pickle." Chutneys are relishes, although in India they are sometimes used as a sauce for hot and cold dishes. Some of them are also served in India as a vegetable.

Chutneys come in hundreds of varieties. They may be salty, sweet or sour, spicy or mild, or a blend of several of these qualities. They are made with an endless list of ingredients, including mangoes, ginger, tamarind, bananas, fresh coriander leaves, mint, yogurt, onions, garlic, and coconut.

Cider

Apple cider comes in two different varieties. Sweet apple cider is simply pure, freshly made apple juice. Hard cider is fermented apple juice. Applejack is a distilled spirit that is made from hard cider. In Normandy, this is called Calvados.

Cigars

Since my first encounter with cigars (it was at a "smoker" when I was a freshman in college) I have held them in vilest esteem and regard as an ultimate paradox that anyone with pretensions to a sensitive palate could follow, let us say, sole in champagne sauce, a royal dish of squab, an elegant dessert, or similar fare with the foul stench and taste of a cigar. But come to think of it, I don't think they would be any more appropriate after oatmeal, but I do know people who smoke them after breakfast. I've even heard of people who can smoke them on an empty stomach.

I agree that there is a place for everything—including cigars—and some of the places that come to mind are the open road, a canoe for one, an unpopulated golf course, and, naturally, the Augean stables.

When I dine in a restaurant, I regard people who smoke cigars (even ten, forty, fifty feet away) with the same passion normally reserved for screaming waiters with those loud and abusive voices.

Cilantro

See Coriander, Culantro.

Cioppino

Cioppino, the excellent California fish stew, rarely appears in any standard English dictionary and I have never been able to trace the origin of the name elsewhere, although some sources speculate it may have to do with an Italian dialect word meaning "chopped fine."

One story of its origins appears in Morrison Wood's *More Recipes with a Jug of Wine.* Mr. Wood attributes his information about the soup to Mrs. Winfield G. Wag-

ener of Palo Alto, California, and an interesting history it is.

"Cioppino," Mrs. Wagener wrote, "was a familiar dish" in San Francisco, particularly on Meigg's Wharf, as Fisherman's Wharf was called prior to World War I. It seems that the practice in those days was for friendly natives to make the rounds of small boats moored in the bay in an effort to coax the fishermen to toss in, gratis, one or two small fish or any other edible oddment for a stew. "One fisherman," she added, "would toss into the . . . bucket a nice, fat fish, another would drop in a crab," and so on.

"The cry that instigated this wonderful stuff was 'Chip in! Chip in!' " To make the soup sound more Italian—most of the fishermen were of Italian descent—an "o" was added to the cry, thus "cioppino."

Most often I tend to discredit these homespun legends of word origins, but somehow the above sounds as logical to my ears as it is amusing.

Cipolline

Cipolline is applied to several members of the onion family, including chives, scallions, very small onions, and shallots.

In his *The Food of Italy,* Waverley Root refers to two preparations made with cipolline—*cipolline in agrodolce,* "tiny new spring onions in a thin tomato sauce" containing sugar and vinegar, and *cipolline sott'aceto,* very small onions "steeped for at least a week in vinegar perfumed with bay leaf, thyme, cloves, cinnamon, pepper, and garlic."

My research on cipolline, a specialty of southern Italy, led me to believe that the flavor resembled shallots or chives. Not so, according to a Long Island correspondent.

"In the Bari area where my family came from, the local word for cipolline is 'lampasciuni,' " she wrote, and enclosed a quotation translated from *The True Cuisine of Bari and the Puglie:*

"Lampasciuni are wild onions, agreeable for their bitter flavor. Pugliese gastronomy makes wide use of them, as it does of many other types of wild plants usually neglected by the cuisines of other regions."

"Despite their appearance," she continued, "cipolline or lampasciuni in their taste do not resemble shallots, onions or chives, in the least. They are lacking in characteristic oniony taste and are prized only for their bitterness, which pleases some. It should be pointed out that a great many people find them extremely indigestible."

Citron

Citron is a kind of lemon whose best-known use is, outside the Jewish religion, in its preserved or candied form, chopped as an ingredient for fruitcake. I have never seen citron in any other form.

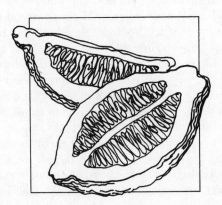

But I had a visit from Joshua David Kreindler, a rabbinical student at Mesivtha Tifereth Jerusalem, who elaborated on citron to my great enlightenment.

"Citron," Mr. Kreindler said, "grows in the Holy Land, in Morocco, Italy, and other Mediterranean countries. It is used primarily for the Jewish celebration of Succoth. At that time citron can be obtained in Lower East Side markets in New York City—from late August through early October.

"The fruit is known as esrog, or ethrog, and it is true that some of them weigh up to five pounds," he said. In fact, it is noted in the Talmud that one esrog in biblical days required two men to carry it down from the orchard. When esrog, or ethrog, is chosen for ceremonial uses, there are several things to look for. "One is whether it has a pitum, which is the stem with the crown on top," Mr. Kreindler said. "That is desirable but not essential. The fruit should be as clean as possible and the color is important; it should range from very light to bright yellow.

"The Succoth custom of having a citron—palm branch—three myrtles and two river willows is taken from the Bible," he added. "There it says, 'Thou shall take unto thyself a choice fruit, a palm branch, myrtle and river willow.' We wave these together in six directions—the four cardinal points of the compass and up and down to signify that God is in all directions and in Heaven as he is on earth."

Civet

A civet is a stew or ragout of game, such as venison, hare, or rabbit. It is made with red wine, pieces of salt pork, small onions, and mushrooms. In a classic sense, the fresh blood of the animal is used to thicken the sauce rather than flour, cornstarch, or other thickener.

Today, quite often on menus of French chefs who practice the so-called nouvelle cuisine of France, you will find civets of langouste, or lobster. These are old preparations that have recently come back into vogue. A civet of lobster is more or less the same as lobster américaine. Like the américaine, it is made with white wine, not red. One difference is that the civet has a more pronounced flavor of garlic. It is a dish of the Languedoc region of France.

Clabber

Clabber with sugar (and sometimes with black pepper and cream instead of sugar) was a common dish in my southern childhood. My father raised and milked cows. The milk was allowed to stand in churns and more often than not became clabber, a semifirm, very white liquid on the bottom and a semifirm layer of yellow cream on top. The clabber was a pure product, the result of a natural bacterial action. Clabber tends to "break apart" when dipped into. It is quite sour but of a different texture and flavor than yogurt. When you churned the clabber, you wound up with butter (from the top cream layer) and buttermilk.

Clamart

There is no absolute certainty why dishes made with green peas bear the name Clamart, although over the years there has been

much speculation about it. Some authorities aver that the name derives from a misspelling of Clermont, in which case it could issue from French town names (Clermont-Ferrand, Clermont-l'Herault) or the names of people such as Louis de Bourbon, Comte de Clermont. The likeliest possibility, however, is that it derives from a small French town called Clamart, which is or was locally famous for its sweet green peas. There are many dishes named Clamart, including eggs Clamart in which poached eggs are served on toast covered with a purée of green peas; artichokes Clamart in which the artichokes are filled with green peas or a purée thereof. Crème Clamart is one of the most elegant of cream soups. It is perfection when made with new, freshly shelled peas direct from the vine.

Clambake

One of the most dramatic, ceremonious, and—in its own way—gratifying of American feasts is the jolly institution known as a clambake.

Not that pot-boiler type thing, that easy-way-out, top-of-the-stove steamed dinner with its mess of seafood and corn cooked with a potato on top until the spud is tender. I mean that aching-back, blockbuster affair that may require three days from start to finish. One that begins with collecting driftwood, anything from twigs to tree trunks, plus any other burnables that may be lying loose on the beach, to make an immense six-hour fire to heat up the rocks.

I mean the ceremony that involves digging a 6-by-6-foot (or even larger) trench, hand-dug by spading through rock and sand. A routine that encompasses gathering six hundred pounds of wet seaweed to be bedded on the fired-up rocks. A procedure that includes wrapping an assortment of foods in cheesecloth, including clams, corn on the cob, and chicken, the latter paprikaed and lightly grilled, and topping the whole with lobsters, all to be cooked on top of the steam now billowing from the wet seaweed.

The food, placed on sheets to protect it from sand, is covered with live lobsters, then covered with another sheet, a tarpaulin, and a layer of sand to make it leakproof. And then the long wait for the glorious moment when all is cooked, the sand swept away, and the tarp and sheet removed to reveal a magnificent, multicolored display—gray clams, yellow corn, lobsters the red of Chinese lacquer—all the food too hot to handle but soon to be eaten with butter dribbling down the cheeks and downed with ice-cold beer.

The only trouble—other than the aching backs—is that there is no other feast so subject to the vicissitudes of the weather.

The man who first showed me the technique of a genuine beachside clambake told me once that one of the saddest occasions of his life came on the day when he made a clambake starting beneath skies brilliantly clear and under a dazzling sun. As the top tarpaulin was placed on the food and the sand shoveled over, the heavens clouded over. Within minutes a drenching rain came and everyone scattered for shelter.

It rained and rained and rained. Four hours later, the sopping-wet sand was swept away and the tarpaulin was removed. The rain had seeped into the trench and dampened the rocks, and a dozen or more lobsters groggily climbed out of the pit and moved oceanward.

A few years ago my colleague Pierre Franey and I volunteered a clambake for one charity or another (the charity agreed to supply the manpower for digging) and a television crew came down from Canada to photograph the event. Once more all went swimmingly for the preparation. The trench was a masterpiece with a veritable mountain of seaweed on the side, ready to be shoveled. The lobsters arrived in wet potato sacks. The corn was ready to be wrapped. Fortunately, the rains came early that day.

There was only one solution, of course. Steamed lobsters with clams on the half-shell and corn on the cob, all of it prepared in my kitchen in whatever large kettles we could muster from the storeroom and neighbors. Everyone had a good, if anticlimactic, time.

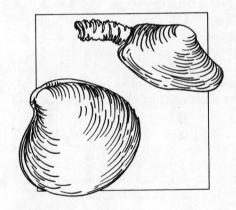

Clams

Eastern waters yield two kinds of clams: the soft shell, also known as "steamers" or long clams, and the hard shell, known as quahogs, which generally fall into three categories. These are: littlenecks, the smallest; cherrystones, which are medium in size; and chowder clams. They are all the same clam at various stages of development, and there is no precise guide that states at which moment a littleneck becomes a cherrystone and a cherrystone becomes a chowder clam. Littlenecks measure approximately two inches in width at the widest point; cherrystones are about two to three inches across. Chowder clams are anything larger. Littlenecks, to my taste, are best for eating on the half shell. Littlenecks and cherrystones go well in soups, sauces, and for stuffed clams. Chowders, sometimes specifically referred to as quahogs, are best used in chowders and clam pies.

It is not a problem to rid hard-shell clams of sand; simply give them a good rinsing under cold running water.

Soft-shell clams are another matter.

I have one great peeve about soft-shell clams and that is that they are, under the best of circumstances, devilishly sandy, even after numerous rinses in changes of water. I know the old-fashioned techniques for getting rid of the sand—adding cornmeal to the water on the theory that the clams will eat the cornmeal while simultaneously disgorging the sand within; adding flour to the water, and so on. To my mind, the clams still come out sandy. The best technique I learned was from my Chinese cooking teacher Virginia Lee. She rinsed the clams many times in very cold water and then put them in a bowl with more cold water to cover. She then added a few spoonfuls of salad oil to the bowl and let it sit for a while at room temperature. After a few hours, the clams start spuming and spurting (to prevent suffocation, I suppose) and, in this manner, rid themselves of a maximum amount of sand. Some cooks add vinegar to the cold water instead of salad oil, but I have never tried this method.

Because I loathe the feeling of even a single grain of sand between my teeth, I propose an even further refinement: if the clams are to be served cold, I rinse them once more after they are taken out of their shells.

For the nonexpert and would-be clam shucker there are two things to remember that enormously facilitate opening the bivalves. Clams are closed tightly because of the powerful (but delicious and tender) muscle that joins the two shells and keeps the shells well-seated. If the clams are well-chilled before they are to be opened, the muscle tends to relax. The clams can be chilled for several hours in the refrigerator or briefly (without freezing) in the freezer. It is also imperative that the clam knife be sharp to facilitate its insertion between the "jaws" of the clam. Avoid those guillotine-like clam-shucking gadgets. They mangle clams and are quite frankly an abomination.

Some correspondents have disputed my suggestions, one quite forcefully:

"Oh, my God!! Holy ¶& $⅝!!," a gentleman from East Rockaway, New York, wrote. "Chills go up my spine when I think of all those readers sharpening up their clam knives and gouging their fingers and hands. I have found that an old butter knife, thin edge and thin blade, does a great job. Treating the clams gently before opening also helps."

Another said: "The imperative that 'the clam knife be sharp' is an invitation to ruined paring knives at best and at worst can result in the severance of an extremely useful and versatile thumb.

"I've found a dull clam knife to be far the superior utensil in terms of speed and effectiveness. They are sold at hardware and fishing supply shops in clam-digging neighborhoods for under two dollars.

"Your error is forgiven only because you haven't recommended one of those silly 'clam shucking machines' that certain of my in-laws insist on bestowing on festive holidays." *See also* Geoduck, Razor clams.

Clarified Butter

Clarified butter can be heated to a higher temperature and, therefore, foods cooked in it brown better than in ordinary butter. The milky liquid discarded when you clarify butter is a protein that scorches when subjected to high heat. Clarified butter can also be stored longer than ordinary butter.

To clarify butter, melt it slowly and skim off any foam. Then carefully pour off the clear golden liquid in the center. This is clarified butter. Any milky liquid on the bottom should be discarded. *See also* Drawn butter, Ghee.

Clotted Cream

Clotted cream is a specialty of Devonshire, although it can be found at times in other parts of England. It is made with unpasteurized rich milk (unpasteurized milk is very hard to find in America), which is left to stand about twelve hours in warm weather, twice as long in winter.

The milk is heated, without boiling, until a semisolid circle appears on the surface. The milk is removed from the heat and allowed to become quite cool. A fairly thick yellow crust forms on top while the material beneath becomes creamy.

I am told that there is a similar Cornish cream made in much the same way, but it is rough rather than creamy in texture.

A recipe for clotted cream, made from homogenized milk, can be found in *The Best of Baghdad Cooking* by Daisy Iny.

"Heat oven to 300 degrees for 2 minutes, then shut it off. Combine 1 cup homogenized milk and 2 cups heavy cream in a baking pan 14 by 9 inches, and bring to a boil over medium heat. Reduce heat to very low and simmer for about 10 minutes.

"Remove from heat, and place in the oven, which should now be lukewarm. Leave in oven for about 3 hours, or until the oven is almost cool. Remove pan carefully so as not to break the top crust. Cover with aluminum foil and refrigerate overnight.

"The next morning, cut around the edges to make sure the gaimar [chunky cream or clotted cream] is not sticking to the pan, then cut it into 3-inch strips. Lift out each strip with a spatula, and place on a serving dish. Refrigerate. Serve for breakfast or afternoon tea.

"At breakfast it is usually served with date syrup or honey, with hot Arabic bread; corn syrup or any sweet jam may be substituted. Dates are also a good accompaniment. This cream will keep well for three or four days."

Cloudberries

I have dined many times on cloudberries in Scandinavia but have never seen or heard of them cultivated or harvested wild in this country. It is a yellow berry not unlike the raspberry and it has a similar texture and seeds. I have been told that it grows in mountain regions of Britain and some food dictionaries state that it does grow in North

America in peat bogs. In Canada, the berries are known as yellow berries. The name derives from the obscure English word "clud," which means rock or hill.

Club Sandwich

I believe the club sandwich is probably an American creation, and yet a prestigious dictionary and an encyclopedia of American foods ignore it entirely. A third volume offers a recipe but no conjecture as to the origin. My belief is supported by *New York, a Guide to the Empire State,* which states: "In 1894 Richard Canfield (1865–1914), debonair patron of art, purchased the Saratoga Club to make it a casino. Canfield Solitaire was originated in the casino's gambling rooms and the club sandwich in its kitchens."

The perfect club sandwich is made with a slice of bread, freshly toasted and spread lightly with homemade mayonnaise, a layer of crisp lettuce (in this case iceberg because of the texture), and thin slices of freshly cooked chicken or turkey breast; another slice of toast with mayonnaise, crisp strips of bacon, if your diet allows, thin slices of ripe tomato, and a final slice of toast with mayonnaise. I trim the edges of the sandwich before serving.

Another view comes from James Villas, food editor and restaurant critic for *Town & Country* magazine, and author of *American Taste:*

"I consider this sandwich one of the most luscious of American creations. I agree with James Beard, who has noted that the original was not a triple-decker.

"Second, a genuine club sandwich must be made only with chicken, never turkey. Third, I'm convinced the name stems not from a bar or restaurant or country club but from the elegant old club cars on the streamliner trains. Lucius Beebe once agreed with me about the great clubs on the Twentieth Century—two-deckers, mind you. And I distinctly remember always ordering a club on the Crescent Limited back in the forties and fifties. I could eat a club for lunch every single day."

Club Soda

See Seltzer.

Cockaigne

See Salmon.

Cock-a-Leekie

In Ena Baxter's *Scottish Cookbook,* she notes that cock-a-leekie is Scotland's national soup "and one that has been popular in royal palaces and humbler dwellings in

Scotland since the sixteenth century." One of the characters in Sir Walter Scott's *The Fortunes of Nigel* says, "Come, my lords and lieges, let us all to dinner for the cock-a-leekie is a-cooling."

Coconut

The two best indications of a good coconut are its weight and the amount of coconut milk inside. You can judge the weight by feel. You should also shake the coconut, to ensure that there is a good supply of liquid in the center. Shaking first one coconut and then another will give you a comparative notion of how much liquid to expect.

These are not the sole criteria for a first-rate coconut. No matter how much liquid is there, the meat of the coconut may be very old, in which case the liquid and flesh may take on a moldy taste. The only recommendation I can offer is that you choose one with a very vibrant brown exterior, one in which there is a brightness about the "eyes," the three soft spots in the shell. As coconuts age they do take on a lighter, less intense look.

To open a coconut, crack it sharply with

a hammer at four or five points to produce large pieces. Rest one piece at a time, shell side down, over a gas or electric burner for about one minute. Using a towel to protect the fingers, lift the coconut, and lift the fleshy part from the shell. It should come off easily.

Cod

Although Boston is celebrated as the home of the cod, that most delectable of winter fish is generally available up and down the eastern seaboard.

Gastronomically, cod belongs to that interesting group of foods distinguished by a more or less neutral flavor that complements naturally and to a fine degree a host of other flavors. Just as a perfectly cooked potato can give unexpected luster to sour cream and chives (or sour cream and fresh caviar, for that matter), so does poached cod seem to bring out the finest nuances of flavor in an assortment of sauces including mayonnaise, hollandaise, Mornay, and their derivatives. Cod has that splendid virtue of nonassertiveness that makes the palate revel in the things with which it is bedded or topped.

Some of the finest codfishing grounds in America are in the vicinity of Block Island and Montauk, off the eastern tip of Long Island, where most of the cod in the New York area originates. The bulk of the harvest comes from draggers—commercial fishing vessels whose nets drag on or close to the ocean bottom—although those small boats with trawls are sometimes used.

A trawl—sometimes called a tub-o'-gear—consists of a round or square tub or bucket-shaped apparatus generally made of metal and containing a mass of coiled fishing line outfitted with approximately one thousand hooks. The hooks are furnished with clams or other bait and are generally set early in the morning for four or five hours.

The lines are retrieved late in the evening and—with luck on good days—with a few four- to seven-pound cod in tow. Scrod, by the way, are nothing more than small cod, those weighing three pounds and under.

Although most of the cod sold today weighs from about four to seven pounds, the fish can actually grow to mammoth size. While the largest cod on record is said to have weighed more than two hundred pounds, cod weighing more than one hundred pounds are rare. *McClane's New Standard Fishing Encyclopedia* observes that the cod is noted for the mass of eggs it can produce and adds that at least one seventy-five-pound fish is known to have contained nine million eggs. *See also* Scrod.

Coddled Eggs

See Eggs mollet.

Coffee

It is utterly impossible to explain the perfect method for preparing a cup of coffee. There are too many techniques available, too many excellent coffee makers on the market, and a good deal of it depends on personal taste. I am often asked if I buy coffee already ground and in tins and the answer is yes. To my taste there are first-rate brands of canned coffee on the market, both of the breakfast and after-dinner variety.

I am often asked how to keep canned coffee fresh once the can has been opened and my answer is to keep it tightly covered in the refrigerator, where it keeps quite nicely for long periods. If you do grind your own, coffee beans, too, can be kept for long periods in the refrigerator or freezer. *See also* Boston coffee, Espresso, Demitasse.

Comfrey

Comfrey is better known as a healing herb than as a culinary herb. It has been used for years in folk medicine for wounds, broken

bones, and sore chests. The name is derived from a Latin verb meaning "to heal or to grow together." It is an edible plant and can be used—sparingly—in salads, and it can also be cooked and served like spinach.

Common Crackers

One manufacturer says that common crackers were invented by a baker named Charles Cross in Montpelier, Vermont, and that they date from the early 1830s. A cookbook says they were invented by Artemus Kennedy of Massachusetts in the 1700s.

I have not seen a recipe for these hard crackers, which are made of whole wheat flour. However, I have seen recipes calling for their use: A few old recipes call for breaking common crackers into chowder before eating, and, in Imogene Wolcott's *The New England Yankee Cook Book,* a recipe for cracker pudding lists common crackers as an ingredient.

I learned, via scores of letters, that common crackers are readily available. The crackers seem to have vast appeal, especially among New Englanders. The most frequently mentioned mail-order source for

them was the Vermont Country Store, P.O. Box 3000, Manchester Center, VT 05255-3000.

I received boxes, bags, and tins of them. People wrote that "they are better with Cheddar and other cheese than even the best of English crackers"; that "they are best in a bowl with milk and also with Vermont melted Cheddar cheese on top."

Literature sent with the crackers suggested many uses, including adding them to soups, chowders, and stews; as a stuffing base for turkey or baked lobsters; for miniature pizzas; for meat loaves, scalloped toppings, and cracker pudding; and for grinding into crumbs to use on top of casseroles. One much-recommended recipe called for soaking them briefly in ice water, then splitting them and broiling them lightly with butter. Some people said that on Long Island, where they are found in a thicker and harder variety, they are sometimes called pilot biscuits. They have also been called "naval ship's biscuits" or "ship's bread."

The packages from the Vermont Country Store listed the ingredients as "wheat flour, water, lard, salt, potato flakes, yeast, and baking soda." A no-salt version is also available.

The biscuits are on the dry side, hard and crumbly. To my mind, they are the Yankee counterpart of the southern beaten biscuit.

Conch

There are many kinds of edible snails in the world, but escargots, the snails of Burgundy, spring principally to mind. These are land snails that reach a fine, plump maturity after feasting their brief lifetimes on grape leaves.

Perhaps the second best-known edible

snails are the sea snails known as conch or scungilli. These are widely admired in this hemisphere in the waters around the Bahamas and other parts of the Caribbean. Divers jump off boats and bring them up from the depths. They are cracked open and cleaned (a messy and tedious proposition for the unskilled) and pounded to make the raw, rubbery muscle tender. Then, uncooked, they are turned into a tasty salad, preferably with lime juice, chopped onion, tomatoes, and hot pepper among the ingredients.

As scungilli they are much admired in two styles, both of Italian origin. They are cooked, sliced, and tossed with oil and lemon or lime juice, plus garlic, salt, pepper, chopped parsley, and hot red pepper flakes. Or they are turned into a sauce for spaghetti or other pasta, or a soaked hard piece of bread, by cooking the slices with tomatoes and hot red pepper.

Conch in one form or another have an important role in the cooking of many parts of the world, including Japan and China. Land snails are popular in North Africa.

Condensed Milk

See Evaporated milk.

Confit d'Oie

One of the fabled—but genuine—glories of the French table is a dish or ingredient that has received little notice in America. Except for some rare and special occasions, it is almost nonexistent in the nation's French restaurants.

The French name of the dish is confit d'oie, which in English is preserved goose, and it is a delicacy of consummate goodness that is easily, if a trifle expensively, made.

Like most other preserved foods, including ham and sausages, the desirable flavor and texture of confit d'oie undoubtedly came about more as a conservation measure than as an end in themselves. The idea was to cook the goose and maintain it in natural fat throughout an extended period, long after the last goose of the season was killed.

The preparation of the goose is simplicity itself. The goose is cut into large pieces and seasoned. It is marinated overnight, and the following morning it is cooked in a boiling bath of goose fat and lard for about two hours. The goose is then put in a terrine or casserole and the fat is poured over it. When cooled, it must be stored in a cold place. It is then ready to be used, whenever desired, up to a year or longer.

Preserved goose is a specialty of the southwest of France, although it is known and admired, if not to say coveted, throughout the nation. Those Americans who may be conversant with the dish know it best as a classic ingredient for some of the traditional cassoulets of France, principally those of Castelnaudary and Toulouse. While cassoulets are fairly well known in America, that one essential taste is missing in all but the tiniest fraction of them in this country.

To the purist with only a miser's share of preserved goose in his larder, the mélange of the food with the likes of beans in a cassoulet may be quixotic. That is for those who can employ the ingredient with abandon. Ultimately preserved goose, cooked simply until it is crisp and golden brown and served with crisp, thin-sliced potatoes cooked in hot goose fat, is paradise enough. It is a sublime, ethereal creation.

There are numerous other ways in which the goose is served in the provinces of France. The *Dictionnaire de l'Académie des*

Gastronomes includes Basque-style, with cèpes (fleshy wild mushrooms), garlic, and parsley; béarnaise, with the potatoes replacing the mushrooms; sarladaise, with potatoes and truffles; landaise, with a small onion, ham cut into small cubes, and petits pois.

Consommé

A consommé refers to a stock or broth that has been cooked down to make it more concentrated in flavor. To be a genuine consommé, it should also be clarified. This is done by cooking the broth with raw meat and/or egg whites, plus eggshells. For what it is worth, a double consommé is a consommé that has been cooked down to the point where it has, in theory, twice the flavor of a single consommé.

Consommé has been an honorable, indispensable foundation of great dinners since the dawn of the sophisticated kitchen in France. A fine, well-tended, rich, and amber-colored consommé can be compared to a rare vintage wine in its elegance and breeding.

The importance of a consommé for great feasts is obvious. It offers a clean, clear, hot, appetite-whetting introduction to a meal, particularly one that will include rich foods laced with cream, be they main courses, accompaniments, or desserts. And the kinds of consommés are almost without number. Nearly two hundred consommés with different garnishes are listed among the *consommés clairs* in Louis Saulnier's *Le Répertoire de la Cuisine*.

The consommés there range from a *consommé ailerons* (a chicken consommé garnished with boned, stuffed, braised chicken wings) to *consommé Windsor* (consommé with calf's foot and flavored with turtle herbs, garnished with julienne of calf's foot-and-chicken quenelles with chopped yolk of egg).

As with many dish names in the French repertory, there's a good deal of romance and history in the names of the various consommés. Carmen has the flavor of Spain in the form of tomatoes and a touch of finely shredded chilies. *Consommé chasseur,* or hunter-style, is, but of course, a game consommé. And then there are those with standard classic garnishes: Doria with cucumbers; Du Barry with cauliflower; and Crécy with carrot. Perhaps the best-known consommé (chiefly, no doubt, because it is available in cans) is *consommé madrilène,* which is to say, "in the style of Madrid."

Continental Cuisine

Continental cuisine consists, among other things, of great undecisiveness and unknowingness on the part of the restaurant owners. It indicates, in my mind, that there is a chef in the kitchen who has absolutely no sense of direction and is totally lacking in professional security. It is an evasive term that doesn't indicate anything other than what I have specified.

I was once on a panel with Calvin Trillin, the *New Yorker* writer, who stated that he used to wonder which continent the owners had in mind when they specified continental cuisine. Australia, perhaps. Then he decided it meant the chef of the establishment had once worked for the Continental Trailways bus company. He then decided that the continent was Antarctica because most of the food had been prepared from a frozen state.

Cooking Wine

Any wine that is drinkable can be used to cook with. The products sold on supermarket shelves and called "cooking wine" are abominations. They are ordinary wines or worse, doctored with salt, something for wildly unsophisticated cooks who wouldn't recognize being duped if they stumbled over it.

The finer the wine you use in a sauce, the finer the sauce will be. Ideally, you should use the same wine to make your sauce as you will drink with the dish. This is not always feasible, however. If you have one single bottle of a rare vintage Burgundy, for example, you probably wouldn't want to use it in your red wine sauce. Thus, you should use some good, substantial bottle within your means.

Coquilles St.-Jacques

There is a good deal of poetry in the names the French have chosen for their foods—Du Barry, Richelieu, ravigote, Rachel. One of the most interesting names, coquilles St.-Jacques, is applied both to a food—scallops—and to a dish made up of that food. Many people, even among the French, don't know that the name in its beginnings had religious connotations. The word *coquille,* of course, means shell in French. Starting in the Middle Ages, it was commonly believed that St. James (in French, St. Jacques) was buried in the province of Galicia in northwest Spain. The place of his burial is said to be in Compostela, now indicated on maps as Santiago (St. James) de Compostela.

Pilgrims who visited the burial site in

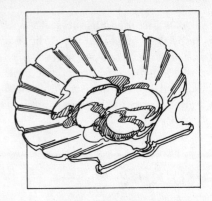

Spain traveled with the scallop shell as their badge of reverence and identification. Interestingly enough, the dainty scallop-shaped cakes known as madeleines (most celebrated because of Marcel Proust's remembrances) are also associated with those pilgrimages to the grave of St. James. One historian has noted that the town of Illiers, where Proust lived as a child, was a common halting place for medieval pilgrims on the way from Paris to Spain.

The name of that elegant, delectable preparation known as coquilles St.-Jacques, with its fine blend of scallops in a cream and butter sauce, simply echoes the name of the principal ingredient.

Cordon Bleu

The name cordon bleu is one of the most incorrectly placed appellations in French gastronomy. It is a title of distinction and properly applies to women only. Some sources state that Louis XV started the tradition by presenting the cook (name unknown) of the Countess du Barry with a cordon bleu medal. However, the *Dictionnaire de l'Academie des Gastronomes,* which I consider the highest authority, says the name came from an order of Saint-Esprit, created by Henri III, and the order's insignia was a blue ribbon. It also says the term means "a female cook or chef of great class."

In any event, the name is also applied to meat dishes—veal or chicken—when stuffed with cheese and ham before sautéing. On many Swiss menus, incidentally, the cordon bleu dishes are listed as Princess Margaret.

Coriander

Fresh coriander leaves, long a staple flavor in international cookery, were until quite recently a rare ingredient in American kitchens. In the kitchens of India, China, and Mexico—to choose a few random nations—the fresh leaf of the coriander plant is as common as parsley (which I presume to be this country's commonest herb) is here.

In his excellent book, *Herbs, Spices and Flavorings,* Tom Stobart observes as follows: "Green coriander," which is to say the fresh leaf, "is not much used in Europe, and in England it is usual to dismiss it as 'unpleasant' or 'not a kitchen herb.' This is nonsense."

What really impresses me is the author's statement that fresh coriander "is probably the most commonly used flavoring herb of any in the world." It is, he continues, found in almost every market from Beirut to China and "loved, not only in the whole of southern Asia, but also in the Americas in Mexico and South America."

Although the coriander leaf and the dried coriander seed—which is widely used in American kitchens—come from the same plant, their flavors are wholly different and, thus, so are their uses. Fresh coriander is one of those flavors you do or don't become addicted to. It is not one of those ordinary, predictable flavors like parsley and chives.

There are, in fact, those for whom the perfume of the coriander leaf is anathema. The scent is undeniably droll, and I have mused at times that it smells musty, and relate it to an old trunk in a damp and little-used attic. The origin of the name is also droll. It stems from the Greek word *koris,* which means a bug, and it is said that those who coined the name a few thousand years ago related the scent of the coriander leaf to that of bedbugs.

Since I am enthusiastic in depth for the cooking of China, Mexico, India, and so on, I find fresh coriander absolutely essential to my peace of mind. In midsummer I have two sources for it: the groceries and the supermarkets in Chinatown and the *bodegas* in Hispanic communities, and my own small herb garden in East Hampton. Fresh coriander (also known as Chinese parsley, cilantro, and culantro) is purchasable by the bunch, and it will keep fresh and in excellent condition in the refrigerator if treated as follows: Place the coriander bunch in a jar and add enough water to immerse the stems at least halfway up. Cover the leaves with clear plastic and refrigerate, snipping off as many leaves as necessary, then recover.

Coriander is as easy as any other herb to grow, and the coriander seeds are widely available. *See also* Culantro.

Corkscrew

Inasmuch as a fine corkscrew will last for years, it is best to take considerable care in selecting one. It should be sturdy and with a spiral, sometimes referred to as a bore, worm, or screw, approximately two inches long. For my own personal use, the finest corkscrew I have ever encountered is called The Screwpull Cork Puller. It is manufactured by the Hallen Company, Houston, Texas 77001.

Corn

It is not a freshly coined thought, the observation that, given a purse that's large enough and a few hours' notice, there is almost no food out of season that can't be whisked to the kitchen and thence to the dinner table. If you have an old-fashioned turn of mind, you may resent such a reality. There is something infinitely desirable about having things arrive according to a natural pattern: things that staunchly preserve their own season and their own times. I have a small personal catalogue of such things and await their arrival throughout the year with almost child-like delight and unabashed pleasure. One is the fresh corn of summer, and there is no sweeter corn produced anywhere in this country (and, therefore, the world) than in Long Island's green fields.

Corn is not the most sophisticated food on earth, nor does it have such pretensions. Fresh corn is the basis for such comforting, homespun, delicious, down-to-earth fare as corn pudding, corn chowder, and just plain corn on the cob.

There are few, very few, uses of fresh corn in classic French cooking. One of these is suprême de volaille Washington, named for George, of course. It consists of chicken breasts in a cream sauce lightly flavored with bourbon whiskey. The chicken doesn't necessarily include corn, but the essential garnish, corn fritters, does. This dish, by the way, is sometimes confused with suprêmes de volaille Maryland (breaded chicken breasts), but they are not the same. The Maryland dish (also classic French) is served with crêpes made with cornmeal rather than the fritters, which contain fresh corn kernels.

It was inevitable that corn would become a descriptive word in the English language, thus "pure corn" and "corny." Like onions, however, one suspects that if corn weren't quite so abundant, if it did not flourish in proper soil, if it were scarce like diamonds, it would doubtless have an admirable snob appeal like truffles and foie gras. Incidentally, I would place one by-product of corn

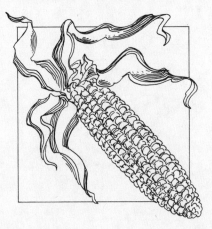

in that elevated and much-sought-after category. This is the huitlacoche or cuitlacoche, a black corn fungus found on ears of corn during the rainy season in some parts of Mexico. It is sensually delicious.

There are hundreds of hybrids of corn, but basically corn falls into two categories: The indentata, which is high in starch and is used to produce, among other things, cornstarch; and the saccharata, which is table corn or the common sweet corn.

When I detailed what I consider the finest method for cooking fresh corn on the cob (drop the shucked corn into boiling water and cover; return the kettle to the boil, and immediately remove from the heat; let stand for five to ten minutes), I added that if the corn stood longer it would toughen.

This prompted a letter that I quote without further comment:

"I tried your method last evening, but after putting the lid back on the pot and letting it stand for ten minutes, I found that the lid had become sealed so tightly that it could not be removed. I tried in vain for more than two hours to remove the lid, but to no avail. Today I put the pot back on the stove, reheated it until the lid was able to be removed. Much to my amazement, the corn appeared to be in very good condition and thoroughly edible. I, therefore, wish to take issue with your statement that the corn will toughen if left for more than ten minutes, since mine remained for over seventeen hours and still retained its freshness and flavor."

One technique that I use to facilitate (or expedite) the eating of corn on the cob is to prepare a kind of seasoned butter to be smeared on the corn. This eliminates the need of serving salt and pepper separately. To prepare the butter, simply soften it and beat in any given quantity of freshly ground

black pepper plus salt. The butter keeps indefinitely in the refrigerator and may be served melted or as a spread. *See also* Popcorn.

Corned Beef

Corned beef and pastrami are cured in very different ways. Corned beef, often the brisket, is cured in a brine flavored with such things as garlic, cloves, peppercorns, and thyme for a week or longer. It is then cooked in water flavored with various seasonings until tender.

Pastrami is either flanken or brisket cured in a nonliquid mixture that includes sugar, crushed peppercorns, chopped garlic, and coriander seeds. It is left to stand in a refrigerator for a week or longer, then dried and smoked for several hours. Finally, it is cooked in fresh water or steamed until tender.

Cornell Formula

The Cornell formula for bread making was developed many years ago by Dr. Clive MaCay of Cornell University, long before the natural foods craze swept this country. Its purpose is the enrichment of white flour for bread making.

A spokesman at Cornell states that the formula is as follows:

For each cup of formula combine in a measuring cup 1 tablespoon of dry milk solids, 1 tablespoon of soya flour, and 1 teaspoon of wheat germ. Fill the cup with exactly enough white flour to make 1 cup. Use for breads.

Cornichons

I first encountered cornichons while acting as a student-waiter in a hotel in the mountains above Zurich. It was a mountain-climbing station approachable only by a cable car, but there were hordes of tourists each day, mostly Swiss, who came to picnic on the terrace of the hotel where I worked.

It was my first taste of table service in public and I relished it. The waiters were dressed in white jackets, black ties, and formal trousers and, oddly, one of the things I recall most were the platters of bündner-fleisch, the dried beef of the Grisons, and also known as viande sechée in French. The meat was cut into the thinnest shavings possible and still retained a flat shape. The slices were arranged, the edges slightly overlapping, and the tiny bright green gherkins were quite carefully cut into and pressed to make a fan shape. That was the only garnish, and it was enough.

Cornichons derives from *corne,* which means horn, and the small pickles have a tiny horn shape (a horn in this case meaning like the horns of an animal).

They are made from the very young of a special variety of cucumber that are available for only a short period each year.

There are numerous ways to pickle them, including one in which they are cooked in a vinegar bath. That is the principal method and the one most widely used for cornichons sold commercially and used for platters of charcuterie. There is a cold method in which the small cucumbers are cured in a brine, quite similar to the new or "fresh" sour pickles so widely available in America.

Cornish Pasties

See Turnovers.

Corn Oil

I am frequently taken to task for the redundancy in specifying "corn or vegetable oil." I do it because some jars of oil are labeled corn and others vegetable. It is to simplify things for readers, to reassure them, in other words, that the oils marked corn or vegetable are interchangeable.

But I received an interesting note from a Manhattan gentleman:

"Have you read the label on vegetable oils in supermarkets?" he wanted to know. "Vegetable oils are, in fact, all of them, soybean oils. And soybean oil has a definite taste, very different from corn. Personally, I am not too keen on that taste and, therefore, avoid vegetable oils."

Corn Salad

See Mâche.

Cornstarch

Cornstarch, or corn flour as it is known in Britain, is one of the most valuable thickening agents in the kitchen, and it gives a clearer end result than regular flour.

Cornstarch has twice the thickening power of flour. Which is to say that one tablespoon of cornstarch will give the same thickness to sauces, soups, and so on as two tablespoons of flour. To use cornstarch as a thickener, you blend it thoroughly with cold water and add it to soups, sauces, and so on while stirring vigorously with a whisk. *See also* Arrowroot.

Corn Syrup

The commonest use for corn syrup (with the possible exception, perhaps, of southern pecan pies) is in candy making. The purpose of corn syrup is to prevent the developing of large crystals of sugar as the candy is cooked and otherwise handled. In this it serves a purpose similar to that of cream of tartar or lemon juice. Most expert candy makers feel that corn syrup is preferable.

Corn syrup in the preparation of fudge, for example, generally gives a smoother texture and provides a desirable, moist texture for a longer period of time after the candy is made. Corn syrup is used in the preparation of many other candies, including white taffy and pulled mints.

As a general rule, you should not substitute dark corn syrup for light corn syrup. Dark corn syrup has a heavier flavor and the color is not suited to many recipes.

Costmary

I am familiar with costmary in name only. It is an herb that is very much of a rarity in American kitchens, but I am told that in Britain it is occasionally used to season poultry and veal dishes, soups, salads, and even certain cakes. I have also read that it often grows wild in this country and has been called bible leaf because the long leaves were used as Bible markers by early settlers.

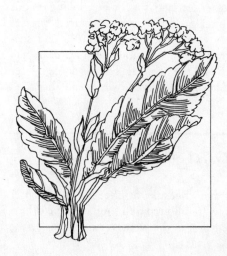

Coteaux

In the seventeenth century, coteaux was frequently used to describe people of good if not exquisite taste, people whose palates and noses were so refined they could sample a wine and tell you not only which commune it came from but also which hillside. Coteaux means hillsides. At one point, it was applied in contempt to those who presumed theirs was the ultimate taste in food and wine. The word is seldom used today.

Cotechini

See Garlic sausage.

Cotriade

Cotriade is sometimes known as the Brittany equivalent of bouillabaisse. It is made with various fish from the waters of that region of France, but it is notable for its use of potatoes. A cotriade is made by cooking onions in butter or lard in a kettle placed, preferably, over a wood fire. Potatoes and seasonings are added, along with water or fish broth and the fish. The soup is cooked over high heat. It is served over bread slices.

Cottage Cheese

Cottage cheese, pot cheese, and farmer cheese are all prepared similarly, the difference being in the wetness or dryness of the

cheeses. Cottage cheese is made by using milk that has naturally soured.

When this happens, the milk becomes a fragile solid, and this is called clabbered milk. The clabber is put into cloth or another material to drain. The curds—cheese—result when the thin liquid known as whey drips out. Rennet hastens the clabbering process.

Cottage cheese is one of the first stages, when the curd turns into a fairly firm but still wet mass. Pot cheese is left to drain for a longer period. More whey drains away and it becomes drier. Farmer cheese and pot cheese are practically identical, except that farmer cheese is generally molded.

Ricotta cheese is quite different in that it is made from the whey that separates from the curd. See also Quark.

Coulibiac

It is not easy to explain to the uninitiated precisely what a coulibiac de saumon is. The easiest way out would be to define it, as it frequently is in dictionaries of gastronomy, as a "pâté of salmon." Such a definition is woefully inapt. It is no mere trifle, no ordinary pâté, something to be dabbled with while awaiting a second course or third or fourth. A coulibiac is a celestial creation, manna for the culinary gods and a main course unto itself. I'm not at all convinced that anything should precede such a sublime invention, except perhaps a spoonful or two of caviar. And I am less convinced that anything should follow it. Who can improve on paradisiacal bliss?

A coulibiac admittedly demands patience, time, talent, and enthusiasm, and if you are possessed of these, what a magnificent offering to those invited to your table. Blessed be the table graced with coulibiac. And blessed be any cook who can master it. And almost any cook can; any cook who is skilled enough to prepare a brioche dough, a standard French crêpe, and a cream sauce.

One of the bonuses of a coulibiac is that almost all the components can be made the day or night before. The brioche and crêpe are the externals, the outer trappings of the dish. The filling is a well-seasoned but easily made compendium of textures and flavors that include fresh salmon, hard-boiled eggs, rice, dill, mushrooms, and shallots. And, classically but by no means essential, vesiga, the spinal marrow of sturgeon.

One of the greatest and most celebrated titans of French cooking shared in his day an unabashed enthusiasm for the dish.

Edouard Nignon by name, who lived around the turn of the century, wrote quite lyrically about food and dining well. In his book, *Eloges de la Cuisine Française,* a compilation of essays and recipes, he relates quite rhapsodically the fact that he served a coulibiac (made with perch; salmon is better) to Tsar Nicholas at the Kremlin Palace and the tsar was equally unstinting in his praise for the chef's sorcery and, one presumes, his coulibiac.

Although the name coulibiac, or koulibiak, is of Russian origin, one French food dictionary states that it derives from a German word, *kohlgebäck,* a dish brought to Russia many years ago by German immigrants. Kohlgebäck, apparently, was a pastry filled with chopped cooked cabbage, a pastry similar, one suspects, to a pirog.

Coup du Milieu

The literal translation of coup du milieu is "a whack at the midpoint"; what it means is an ice or a glass of eau-de-vie, which is a white spirit like kirsch—something that stimulates the appetite. It is also called a trou du milieu, that is, a gap in the middle of a meal during which the appetite is recovered.

Originally, it was usually brandy or liqueur drunk between courses; today it is often a small serving of an ice or sherbet, sometimes with a bit of spirits poured on it. To be authentic a trou normand must be Calvados, the apple brandy for which Normandy is known.

Court Bouillon

A court bouillon is a well-seasoned liquid in which foods, generally fish, are destined to be cooked. Vegetables to be cooked *à la grecque* may also be said to be cooked in a court bouillon but the use of the term in English is rare. A court bouillon for fish generally consists of water, wine and/or vinegar, and herbs and spices, such as bay leaf, parsley, onion, carrots, salt, and peppercorns. Lemon juice is sometimes substituted for the vinegar.

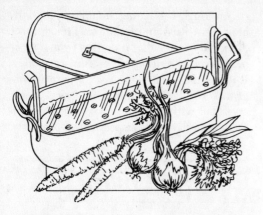

I am often asked if a court bouillon may be used more than once for cooking fish. You will probably not find a dictum in the writing of Escoffier and other authorities against using a court bouillon a second or even a third time around. On the other hand, the chef would be rare who would make a practice of reusing the liquid. The fresher and purer a court bouillon in which a fish is cooked, the better the fish will taste. And if you were to freeze a once-used court bouillon, think of the space you'd waste.

The French term *court bouillon* is derived from the Latin word *curtus,* meaning cut short or, in this case, to put together hastily, and bouillon, which comes from the French verb *bouillir,* to boil.

Couscous

Sentimental reasons aside, the North African dish known as couscous is, to my mind, the most intriguing of all "foreign" foods. It is also true that it was the first alien, which is to say, non-American, dish that ever passed my lips, an experience that occurred more than four decades ago when I was stationed in Morocco during the Second World War. I decided then, with a limited basis for comparison, that it was one of the world's grandest creations. Nothing has changed my mind.

For anyone not yet aware of the ins and outs of couscous, I must explain that the name refers to two things: a basic grain-like cereal that might be compared to rice, and that cereal when it is served as a main course accompanied by a stew or ragout made of meat, poultry, or fish and whose principal flavor is that of ground cumin. At times, sweetened couscous is also served with fruits and becomes a highly enjoyable dessert.

Couscous is like a fine-grained pasta that is made with ground semolina, a sort of white flour, and water. The flour and water are blended and rolled by hand or machine until tiny pellets are formed.

Many years ago, this product required hours of steaming. Today's more popular packaged product, available in fine-food specialty shops, is "precooked" and the package directions indicate that it may be cooked in a saucepan by adding boiling water before cooking or heating briefly. But it is much more authentic to steam it in the top of a utensil called a couscoussière. One may substitute a colander that fits inside a kettle for the couscoussière.

Larousse Gastronomique, in its discourse on couscous, quotes an author named Léon Isnard in reference to its origin: "It seems that the word couscous is a Gallic version of *rac keskes,* which means *crushed small.*"

Cownose Ray

See Skate.

Crab

The small, sun-baked town of Crisfield, Maryland—it is said to be built on millions of tons of shucked oyster shells—sets the stage each year for one of the oldest seafood festivals in the United States. Crisfield, celebrated as the cradle of the nation's blue-crab industry, crowns Miss Crustacean, sponsors a crab-picking contest, a crab-cooking contest, and a crab-crawling—call it racing, if you will—competition.

The grand marshal of Crisfield's Crab Parade one year was James A. Michener, the author, whose willingness to participate was, by his own estimate, based on his understandably unabashed enthusiasm for crab meat, which is, indeed, one of the world's foremost seafood delicacies. It ranks in some minds above lobster, shrimp, squid, conch, octopus, and the theroas of New Zealand. Even—to some palates—caviar.

In his acknowledgment Mr. Michener stated, "Although I know absolutely nothing about crabbing, nor about crabbers, nor about crabs themselves, I shall accept your invitation to be Grand Marshal of your National Hard Crab Derby parade on Saturday, September 3, at high noon.

"I accept this honor because, although I may be deficient in my knowledge of crabs and crabbing, I am one of the world's great authorities on the consumption of crabs, and if everyone ate as much as I, all crab men would be millionaires.

"Crab imperial, crab salad, crab soup, and crab cakes are my specialties, with an added expertise in crab Norfolk. My wife makes one of the best crab salads, Japanese-style, in the business and shares my enthusiasm."

On arrival in Crisfield one brilliantly clear day, I might have known even less about "crabs and crabbing" than the author had I not previously equipped myself with William W. Warner's *Beautiful Swimmers: Watermen, Crabs and the Chesapeake Bay,* which won the 1977 Pulitzer Prize for general nonfiction.

It was in a roundabout way, through that book, that I had made the acquaintance of Alex Kellam, a rugged, soft-spoken, weather-marked waterman who told me that he was a native of nearby Smith Island and that he was "born with a crab net in my hand."

A waterman, if you don't know it, is, he explained, "any man here who makes his living off the water—a commercial fisherman. Before I retired I spent my entire life crabbing in summer, oystering in winter."

Mr. Kellam quit school at the age of fourteen and went on his father's shipjack, the *Ruby G Ford.* That was in the days of the sailing boats, before the motor age."

Mr. Kellam welcomed me aboard a sizable motorboat outfitted with a metal-and-net crab scrape, a piece of equipment with two metal triangles joined together at one end that is dragged over one side of the small boat to trap the crabs—and, for better or worse, other sea creatures.

After fifteen minutes out, he threw the

scrape overboard and within five minutes hauled it back aboard. He emptied the contents, which included, in addition to four hard-shell crabs, three oysters, four trash fish (fish not commonly used for eating), and a batch of seaweed. One of the crabs was a jimmy crab, the large male of the species and one of the most assiduous lotharios of the sea.

Back went the scrape into the shallows, and this time it was retrieved with an even larger haul. After half an hour, the bushel basket aboard was nearly half full. Mr. Kellam veered the boat around the harbor to a buoy marker. He was demonstrating another method of crab trapping. He hauled aboard a crab pot in which two crabs were trapped in the process of mating.

Mr. Kellam pointed out that most visitors to Crisfield believe that soft-shell crabs and hard-shell crabs derive from different stock. Not so.

After he had taken aboard about three dozen hard-shell crabs (they must measure 5½ inches from one tip of the top hard-shell to the other to be legal) Mr. Kellam took me to visit the "floats" or pens of a neighboring crab man. The floats are fairly large, shallow, rectangular wooden boxes filled with constantly running bay water where "peelers" are dumped just before they pass from the hard-shell stage to the coveted and highly marketable soft-shell stage. Peelers, called green crabs, are those crabs within a day or two of shedding or "peeling" off their hard shell. The average crab— male or female—molts or sheds three times a year.

Within a half-hour period, I saw three pairs go from the hard- to the soft-shell stage, one of the most curious of nature's phenomenons. All of a sudden, the body of a hard-shell crab will start to expand and

slowly, like a small, oddly shaped balloon, a bulbous dark form starts to emerge from the rear opening of the crab. There is an apparently painful pushing and puffing and panting as the new body casts off its old shell. And the moment the soft-shell crab emerges from its former outer prison it is half an inch or so larger than its former self.

"My wife cooked dinner for a well-known politician recently," Mr. Kellam told me proudly. "He told her that her soft-shell crabs were sweeter and better than any Maine lobster he ever ate."

Shortly thereafter I was led to a crab-packing plant where workers were in the process of picking the meat from the bodies and claws of thousands of hard-shell crabs and where the soft-shell crabs were being frozen and shipped, uncooked, all over the country.

The hard-shell crabs are first cooked in steam and then cooled, and cracked, and the delicate snow-white meat is removed for packing in one-pound tins. The choicest crab meat is lump and backfin. Essentially they are the same—both are taken from identical "chambers" of the crab's body. Lump crab meat is simply the choice or select large pieces; backfin are broken or small pieces of the lump.

The claw meat is extracted and packaged either with or without the claw tips.

The fourth category of crab meat used in cooking is the "regular," which are bits and pieces of body or claw meat. It has a shredded appearance and is generally used for stuffed crab dishes. One of the principal reasons for the elevated price of crab meat is that it is almost without exception picked or extracted by hand.

Because the entire body of soft-shell crabs, including the main portion and the claws, are edible, they are much easier to prepare and package for market. The soft "apron" of the crab is cut off; the tips of the top soft "shell" are lifted up and the lungs on either side are easily removed and discarded. Then the mouth and eyes are cut away with scissors. That's all there is to it.

Soft-shell crabs are shipped frozen all over the country. The reason for the elevated cost of soft-shell crabs is the personal care that must be given them while they are in captivity in the floats or pens. They must be carefully tended and removed within minutes after they shed their shell.

Crab meat from hard-shell crabs and the delicate, wholly edible nature of the soft-shell crabs are among the most elegantly blessed foods on earth. When asked which I prefer, I am once more reminded of the anecdote related by Frederick S. Wildman in his *A Wine Tour of France*. It has to do with the age-old argument of which is the finer wine, Burgundy or Bordeaux.

"Which is the winner?" he asked. "The classic Bordeaux or the grand vin de Bourgogne? It would be virtually impossible to decide. One can only agree with the jurist of the *ancien régime* who, when asked by a marquise at supper one evening which he preferred, answered, 'Madame, in this sort of trial I get so much pleasure examining the evidence that I postpone giving my verdict from week to week.' " *See also* Horseshoe crabs, Sand crabs, She-crab soup.

Crab Cakes

Alone and together with Pierre Franey, my colleague and one of America's best French chefs, we had on numerous occasions prepared crab cakes, but never with the same results as those sampled in Baltimore.

Many variations were tried. Béchamel sauce as a binder, a few bread crumbs, many bread crumbs, whole eggs, egg yolks, and so on. We had even heard of recipes that called for mayonnaise. *Quelle horreur!*

On one particular occasion I was dining with Mr. Franey in a then well-known Baltimore restaurant. As we were leaving, we met, by chance encounter, the restaurant's chef, Bernard Pfanner, a native of Alsace.

As French chefs do, he and Mr. Franey rattled on about the glories of French cooking, mutual friends on both sides of the Atlantic . . . and then, in his best confidential French, Pierre asked: "Tell me, how do you make your crab cakes?"

Mr. Pfanner was only too willing to offer his secrets.

"Would you believe," he said, "when I first came to Baltimore they told me to make crab cakes with the local formula?" He gasped, Gallic-style. "They combined the crab meat, this beautiful, white, lump crab meat with mayonnaise. Of course, you add a little egg white to the mixture and a few crumbs and that's all there is to it."

It is true. Mayonnaise produces superior crab cakes and, on reflection, why not? After all, it is a blend of egg and oil and mustard.

Crab Imperial

Crab imperial is one of the classic American creations. Generally, it is made by blending crab meat with mayonnaise that is then packed into crab shells and baked. Some cooks prepare it by combining crab meat and a white sauce.

Crab Louis

No one seems to know precisely who "Louis" was. But crab Louis is said to have originated at one of two San Francisco restaurants, either Solari's or the dining room of the St. Francis Hotel.

To prepare a Louis sauce, you simply combine a cup of mayonnaise (the quantity is arbitrary) with one-quarter cup each of heavy cream and chili sauce. To this you add a few spoonfuls of chopped scallions, chopped green olives, and chopped green pepper. Add salt, pepper, and lemon juice to taste. You might also improve this with a dash of Cognac, although it would not be traditional. The sauce is simply a West Coast version of the French sauce rémoulade.

Crab Norfolk

Crab Norfolk is a dish that I recall, with a good deal of pleasure, from visits to Virginia. I might point out that there are many recipes for the dish, but basically it consists of lump crab meat sprinkled with vinegar, a little Worcestershire and Tabasco sauces, and butter. It is baked in a very hot oven.

The name originates from the small oval aluminum pan in which the crab must be baked to be authentic. That pan originated in Norfolk and is known as a Norfolk aluminum pan. I have been told that the dish was created by W. O. Snowden at the Snowden and Mason Restaurant in Norfolk, which was opened in 1924 and closed in 1975.

Cracklings

Cracklings, pronounced "cracklin's" in the South, are made from pork rind that is cooked until it is almost wholly rendered of its fat, when the rind becomes crisp and brittle and crackles when bitten into.

Ideally, the cracklings are nicely browned when ready to eat. Crackling bread is corn bread (generally made with buttermilk) to which the cracklings are added before baking.

The cookbook of my hometown, Indianola, Mississippi, is titled *Bayou Cuisine,* and after the recipe for crackling bread is this admonition: "Serve at dinner with vegetables, or dunk in buttermilk to enjoy as a noontime snack, or serve with turnip greens and garden relish."

Incidentally, cracklings are also used in other cuisines. There is an Italian yeast bread made with them, a German version, and so on.

Crapaud

The word *crapaud* means toad (or, as some people would have it, frog) in French. Squab or pigeon crapaudine refers to a whole

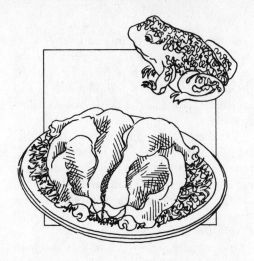

squab that is arranged before cooking to resemble a toad. This is done by splitting the squabs down the center and opening them up as for broiling. They are flattened with a mallet. The birds are grilled and oftentimes decorated with cutouts or hard-boiled eggs, which are situated on the "toad" to resemble eyes. The squab is then served with a piquant mustard and vinegar sauce.

Crayfish

One of the most curious things about the American kitchen is how it seems to ignore—except regionally—various indigenous foods that are uncommonly good, foods that are in great and understandable demand on the tables of Europe.

Among these are crayfish, better known in the South as crawfish. These freshwater delicacies are a national passion in Finland and Sweden, and the major part of that institution known as a krebfest in which the small crustaceans are brought hot to the table, opened with the fingers, and enthusi-

astically downed with numerous glasses of aquavit and well-chilled beer. The only region of this country that holds crayfish in equal esteem is Louisiana, where they are the rock-solid basis for the Creole or Cajun crawfish boil.

There are many species and subspecies of crayfish in this world, and there are more than thirty, I am told, to be found in Louisiana waters alone.

The crustacean has infinite uses, from the *étouffée* of crayfish of Louisiana to the *écrevisse à la bordelaise* of France. They are not, as many people presume, difficult to clean. There is a simple technique widely used in France to eliminate the small intestinal tract: You simply pull and twist one of the center segments at the fan-shaped tail-end of the crayfish. Or even this step may be eliminated, as it is at those krebfests in Scandinavia and the crawfish boils in Louisiana.

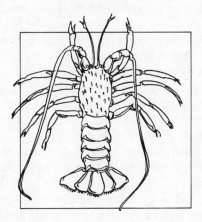

Crayfish are produced in almost every region of America, principally in Louisiana, Mississippi, Wisconsin, and California. They are literally harvested by the ton, though finding them at the local fish market outside the South might be another matter.

Small shrimp may be substituted in almost any recipe calling for crayfish. The size of crayfish varies, but, on the average, ten live crayfish in the shell will weigh about one pound. One pound of average-size crayfish, when shelled, will yield about three-quarter cup of meat.

Crazy Oats

See Wild rice.

Cream

Quite honestly, I have no argument with heavy cream labeled "ultrapasteurized," and find it can be whipped with just as much facility as the cream that was not ultrapasteurized.

But there is considerable disagreement over this. A Manhattan man has written me that "ultrapasteurized dairy products virtually dominate the markets in Europe nowadays. It takes some doing to find any dairy products in France not labeled 'long-conserve,' surely a disgrace in the land of Escoffier. This product, whether milk or cream, always has the characteristic boiled taste.

"And so it has been with great dread that I have noticed that this same ersatz product has taken over the dairy stores in America. The reasons for this are obvious: The ultrapasteurized products keep for many weeks, and, therefore, merchants never have to worry about keeping their stock fresh.

"Once again, in a way that is becoming all too familiar in food merchandising, the consumer gets the short end of the stick. And it saddens me that you do not take the side of the consumer here. We all must resist the continuing efforts of food merchants to sacrifice quality in the name of cost effectiveness."

Another Manhattanite writes, "I find that the ultrapasteurized variety has a 'boiled' taste and does not whip as well. Also, I have never had the regular pasteurized kind turn sour, so unless the store or producer dates the cream incorrectly, there is no practical reason for ultrapasteurization."

Incidentally, heavy cream that is left in the refrigerator too long will spoil, rather than turn into sour cream or crème fraîche. This is because it has been pasteurized and the pasteurization process kills not only the harmful bacteria but the lactic acid bacteria that would allow the cream to become naturally sour (or, to phrase it another way, to sour sweetly).

Crécy

On menus around the world the name Crécy pertains to dishes prepared or garnished with carrots. Some sources date the use of the word to a famous battle that occurred between the French and the English near the village of Crécy, France, on August 26, 1346. It is said that the British troops were fed carrot soup on the battlefield. Crécy, which is north-northwest of the champagne country, produced what are probably the most famous carrots in the world. Among the many dishes labled Crécy one finds *purée Crécy* or puréed carrots; *consommé Crécy,* a rich beef broth garnished with julienne of carrots; *omelette Crécy,* and so on. *The Wall Street Journal* did a lengthy feature on carrots and stated that Craig Claiborne hates carrots, and that is patently untrue. He is convinced that carrots are good for eyesight as well as the complexion, and a *crème Crècy,* or cream of carrot soup, is one of the most elegant on earth.

Crème Fraîche

The standard recipe for crème fraîche calls for combining in a saucepan 1 cup of heavy cream with 1 teaspoon of buttermilk. Heat this gently to a temperature not to exceed 85 degrees. Remove the saucepan from the heat and let stand at a temperature of between 65 and 85 degrees until thickened. Stir with a wooden spoon and refrigerate.

A woman from Brooklyn who didn't like my formula sent the following suggestion:

"Try the following on fruit: ½ pint heavy cream and 1 tablespoon yogurt. Shake the mixture in a tightly closed jar and wrap in a dish towel. Leave in a warm but not too hot place overnight. Yes, yogurt. Try it on cherries. The best sour cream you ever tasted!"

Creole

See Cajun and Creole.

Crêpes

Crêpe, the French "pancake" that has become so much a part of the American dining scene, derives from the Latin *crispus,* meaning "in trembling motion." Its first use in French had to do with a cloth or fabric that is light, soft, and thin with a wrinkled surface. I suspect that the chef who first created a crêpe may have produced a round edible object that possessed those characteristics. A wrinkled surface is certainly not what a practiced chef would hope for today.

Crêpes are, without question, one of the finest creations of Western cuisine, admirable on many counts. Primary among these is the contrast between their texture and flavor and whatever they are allied with—sweet crêpes with the likes of a Grand Marnier sauce or savory crêpes to be filled with countless foods in cream and other sauces.

There is one major difference in crêpes

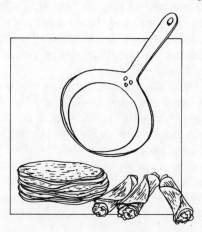

destined for desserts and those prepared for first or main courses. Dessert crêpes almost invariably contain sugar and vanilla; savory crêpes do not contain either.

There are many ways to fold crêpes. They may be folded in quarters to make a fan shape. They may be rolled cigar shape with the filling in the center. And they may be folded into a lily shape like that of an Easter lily with the top "open" slightly and a pointed bottom.

Incidentally, crêpe or crêpes, singular or plural, should be pronounced to rhyme with step. The word does not rhyme with drape. In the plural, the "s" is silent in French, pronounced in English.

Crêpes Suzette

Some of the legends in the world of food are amusingly apocryphal. Some of the legends are irritatingly apocryphal and that is how I react to that tedious, naive, and much repeated anecdote about the origins of crêpes Suzette. It is a ridiculous and foolishly romanticized tale that would give Georges Auguste Escoffier acute indigestion if not a full-size case of crise de foie. It is suitable for a TV script and, to tell the truth, it was dramatized, with Walter Slezak flaming the crêpes as the alleged creator of the dessert. The legend goes like this:

Henri Charpentier, who became one of the best-known restaurateurs on America's West Coast, was at one time an assistant waiter at the Café de Paris in Monte Carlo. Edward, then Prince of Wales, arrived with a sweet young thing in tow named Suzette. Some say that Suzette was a child, others that she was a demimondaine—to use a word appropriate to the age. In any event,

at the end of the meal, Charpentier started to prepare a crêpe dessert at tableside when all of a sudden, zut alors, the spirits in the dish burst into flame and voila, succès fou. Merde alors!

When Charpentier died in 1961, Joseph Donon, who had maintained a discreet silence until Charpentier's death, lit a match under the legend and wrote what might be presumed to be the true gospel. For credentials, incidentally, M. Donon was one of the last great private chefs in America in the service of Mrs. Kate Twombly of the Vanderbilt family.

On M. Charpentier's death he wrote—and I translate—in France-Amerique:

Many American newspapers have attributed to him the origin of crêpes Suzette and the matter takes looking into. In the first place, Charpentier was never a chef as many people supposed and it was, of course, an image that M. Charpentier took no pains to dispel. He did own the restaurant Henri on Long Island during Prohibition and later was on the staff of the Louis XIV at Rockefeller Plaza. Of M. Charpentier's talents there could be no doubt. He came to America when he was twenty-five years old and joined a pléiade of maîtres d'hôtel who knew how to talk cooking to their customers. But, the author adds, no one could seriously pretend that Charpentier invented these crêpes.

M. Donon then quotes M. Raymond Bodet, a member of the Académie Culinaire de France and author of Toques Blanches et Habits Noirs, published in 1939.

Crêpes Suzette, that authority adds, were created by M. Joseph, director of the Restaurant Marivaux in honor of the actress Suzanne Reichenberg, who was known professionally by the simple name of Suzette. The crêpes named in her honor were served to her as part of the action on stage. M. Joseph was subsequently director of the Paillard Restaurant in Paris and was later with the Savoy Hotel in London.

Crépinette

A crépinette is a flat, round, hamburger-shaped sausage wrapped in a caul and grilled or sautéed in a skillet. If you can ignore the calories, it is delectable, particularly when accompanied by a potato purée. The caul, from the omentum, a peritoneal sac, is a lacy membrane heavily laden with fat.

The word crépinette derives from crépine, meaning caul. A basic recipe for one filling for crépinettes would be 1½ pounds of freshly ground pork blended with 2 eggs, salt if desired, and freshly ground pepper to taste. You wrap this in the caul (available in pork stores in metropolitan areas) and grill it or cook it in a skillet.

Other less common fillings are made with chicken hash, lamb hash, or prepared sausage meat. Chopped truffles or chopped pistachios can be added to make the dish fancier.

Crespelle

The Italian pancakes known as crespelle can be treated in numerous fashions. They can be served opened out in a stack with various fillings between each layer. Or they may be filled and rolled. They are also sometimes filled with the edges folded over to make a square "dumpling." They are, in short, used very much as crêpes are used in the French kitchen.

Cretons

I have sampled the pâté known as cretons and have seen only one recipe for it, in a Canadian cookbook. It is simply made. You preheat your oven to 300 degrees. Combine 1 pound of ground not-too-lean pork with 1 cup of fine fresh bread crumbs, a chopped onion, salt, pepper, chopped garlic, and a touch of cinnamon and nutmeg.

You moisten this with milk, spoon it into a casserole, and bake about 1 hour, stirring occasionally. Spoon it into small molds and chill. Serve as an appetizer with crusty French bread.

Croque Monsieur

Although sandwiches are British in origin, they seem quintessentially American and, with two exceptions, curiously un-French. The exceptions are the croque monsieur and the croque madame. There is no literal translation for the name, but it pertains to *croquer,* which means to "crackle when bitten into" as well as to "eat hastily."

The origins of both sandwiches are obscure, and I am indebted to the French-chefs-in-America publication, *Toque Blanche,* for what I do know about their beginnings.

They first appeared in the brasseries of *les grands boulevards* in Paris between the last two wars. It is possible, the historian claims, that they first appeared on the menu of the now defunct Brasserie Weber on the rue Royale. "In Paris," the article continues, "all brasseries soon copied this as well as restaurants that enjoyed a night trade."

The croque monsieur is a ham and cheese

sandwich; the croque madame, a sliced chicken and cheese sandwich.

However, several people have told me that when they ordered croque madame in France they were served a grilled ham and cheese sandwich topped with a fried egg, sunny side up. One person said there is also a grilled sandwich made with sliced chicken, pineapple, and melted cheese called a croque Hawaienne.

Crow

I have never eaten crow, other than when it was used for humble pie. On the other hand, Theodora FitzGibbon, in her often-quoted book *The Food of the Western World,* states that "the crow, a member of the family Corvidae, is a large blue-back bird which is edible when very young. It is best skinned, filleted, and made into a pie, although it can be used to flavor a soup which has other good ingredients."

Miss FitzGibbon is British, and I suspect that crow pie is more of a specialty in England than it is in this country.

A Manhattan gentleman sent me the following explanation of the term "eat crow":

"When Napoleon's army was in disorganized retreat, freezing and starving, in the winter of its debacle in Russia, the countryside was devastated and bare.

"For survival, his soldiers shot the crows over the carnage and boiled them over open fires. Thus came the association of eating crow as a signal of humiliation."

I have also been made aware of an account of what it is like, literally, to eat crow from a book by William Manly titled *Death Valley in '49.*

Mr. Manly and his companion were at-tempting to find a passage out of Death Valley. In their hunger, the two men killed three birds, a quail, a hawk, and a crow. The meal was described as follows:

"As to those birds, the quail was as superb a morsel as ever a man did eat. The hawk was pretty fair and quite good eating. But that abominable crow! His flesh was about as black as his feathers and full of tough and bony sinews."

Crown Roast of Lamb

I have never felt that the basic flavor and goodness of a dish should be sacrificed for dramatic flair. There is one theatrical dish, however, that I cordially recommend for home cooks, and that is a crown roast of lamb. It is not only dramatic to the eye, but it is easy to prepare.

Curiously, as far as I can tell, this dish was created in American kitchens; it is rarely, if ever, found on French tables.

Crumpet Rings

Crumpet rings are available in good kitchenware stores, but you can substitute the metal rings of wide-mouth canning jars. The inside band of the rings should be lightly oiled before adding your crumpet batter.

I have also been advised that a very serviceable substitute for crumpet rings are the bands left by removing the tops and bottoms of tuna and cat food cans.

"These," my informant says, "are especially nice for the occasional crumpet baker, as they can be accumulated for an occasion and then thrown away. In the same spirit we use [sterilized] hair curlers for cannoli forms."

Culantro

As a matter of routine, I specify in recipes "fresh coriander leaves, sometimes referred to as Chinese parsley, culantro, or cilantro."

In Puerto Rico, cooks will tell you that there is a decided difference. Fresh coriander leaves or Chinese parsley, known in Spanish as *cilantrillo,* resemble parsley leaves.

Culantro, on the other hand, is blade-like, about five or six inches long, and has a serrated edge. The flavor and aroma of the fresh coriander leaf and a blade of culantro are similar, but the latter is stronger, more pungent in flavor.

An enlightening report on the herbs came to me from a Connecticut man.

"I would like to try to add a bit," he wrote, "to what you learned about cilantro/culantro.

"First, you said fresh coriander is known in Spanish as *cilantrillo.* This is not quite

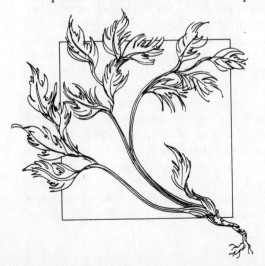

accurate, because, as far as I know, that term is used in Spanish only in Puerto Rico and the Dominican Republic. In Mexico, for example, where I lived for fifteen years, it is unheard of and the word used, exclusively, is *cilantro.* The Latin name for the latter, by the way, is *coriandum sativum.* The leaves are widely used in Mexico in fish dishes (especially when prepared 'a la Vera-cruzana') in salsa cruda, in guacamole, and always in seviche.

"Another interesting sidelight on cilantro is that, it is said, it could very well be the first spice to be used by mankind and, supposedly, was known as early as 5000 B.C. Reportedly, it was growing in the Hanging Gardens of Babylon; was in the medicinal plants mentioned in the Medical Papyrus of Thebes (1522 B.C.); and was placed in Egyptian tombs some three thousand years ago. *See also* Coriander.

Culls

See Lobster.

Curdled Sauces

Whether you can restore a curdled sauce depends on whether your sauce has curdled because of improper technique or excessive temperature.

If it is caused by overheating, the eggs have in effect "scrambled" and you are out of luck. If, however, the failure has been the addition of oil or butter too quickly, you still have an option.

To restore a mayonnaise (which does not require cooking at all), you start over with a fresh egg yolk; begin beating and gradually add the curdled mixture. Another way is to put a tablespoon of very cold water into a small mixing bowl and gradually add the curdled mixture while beating vigorously with a whisk. Or put a tablespoon or so of ready-made (fresh or commercial) mayonnaise into the bowl and add the curdled mixture while beating vigorously.

To restore hollandaise that has curdled (but not because of overcooking) while being made, remove it from the heat. Add 1 tablespoon of cold water to a mixing bowl and, using a wire whisk, gradually beat in the curdled mixture, stirring vigorously.

To restore a hollandaise that has been allowed to cool and curdled while standing, place a small but heavy mixing bowl in a saucepan or skillet of barely simmering water (do not let the bowl become too hot). Add a tablespoon of hot water and, using a wire whisk, gradually beat in the curdled hollandaise. Take care that it heats but does not cook or the eggs will scramble.

Cured

The word "cured" when it refers to food simply means that the food is treated in such a manner as to preserve it from spoilage and decomposition. It may be fish, fowl, meat, or any other edible. Smoked hams, pickled herring, confit d'oie (or preserved goose, boiled in its own fat)—all these are cured foods. So are corned tongue, pickled tongue, and smoked tongue.

Corned products are generally prepared by soaking for several days in a brine (water and salt) solution with seasonings, such as herbs and spices. After the food is corned, it is rinsed and cooked.

Pickled foods are those that have been cooked or soaked for any given length of time in acid solution, generally made with vinegar.

Smoked foods are those that, as the name denotes, are smoked generally by one or two methods. The food may be treated by cold smoking, in which the foods are smoked and subjected to a temperature of about 90 degrees while being treated. This can take as long as a month. As opposed to this, the food may be treated to hot smoking, in which foods are smoked and subjected to a temperature from about 100 degrees to 190 degrees. By this method the food may be totally or partly cooked.

These are traditional methods and do not take into account the fact that some commercial producers resort to artificial methods to produce and preserve their smoked foods.

Curry

I have been fascinated over the years by letters received after I have printed recipes for curries that do not contain curry powder. The final word on the subject appears in the work of a friend, Madhur Jaffrey. It is an explication found in the introduction to her book, *An Invitation to Indian Cooking,* perhaps the best Indian cookbook available in English.

"To me the word 'curry' is as degrading to India's great cuisine as the term 'chop suey' was to China's," she states. "But just as Americans have learned in the last few years to distinguish between the different styles of Chinese cooking . . . I fervently hope they will soon do the same with Indian food instead of lumping it all under the dubious catchall title of 'curry.' 'Curry' is just a vague, inaccurate word which the world has picked up from the British, who, in turn, got it mistakenly from us. It seems to mean different things to different people.

"Sometimes it is used synonymously with all Indian food. In America it can mean either Indian food or curry powder. To add to this confusion, Indians writing or speaking in English use the word themselves to distinguish dishes with a sauce, i.e., stew-like dishes. Of course, when Indians speak in their own languages, they never use the word at all, instead identifying each dish by its own name.

"If 'curry' is an oversimplified name for an ancient cuisine, then 'curry powder' attempts to oversimplify (and destroy) the cuisine itself. Curry powders are standard blends of several spices, including cumin, coriander, fenugreek, red peppers, and turmeric—standard blends which Indians themselves never use. Here again I am sure the British are responsible for its creation. This is how I imagine it happened:

"*A British officer in full uniform (possibly a young David Niven) is standing under a palm tree looking fondly at his bungalow as Indian servants go back and forth carrying heavy trunks from the house into a waiting carriage. When the carriage is loaded, the servants line up on the veranda with tears in their eyes. The officer himself, overcome with emotion, turns to khansamah (cook):*

"Officer: 'How I shall miss your delicious cooking. My good man, why don't you mix me a box of those wonderful spices that you have been using. I will carry it back with me to Surrey, and there, whenever I feel nostalgic about India, I will take out this box and sprinkle some of your aromatic spice mixture into my bubbling pot.'

"Khansamah: 'Yes, sa'ab, as you say, sa'ab.' *(Runs off into kitchen).*

"*Scene shifts to kitchen, where cook is seen hastily throwing spices into the box. He runs back with it to officer.*

"Khansamah: 'Here is the box, sa'ab. Sa'ab, if your friends also like, for a sum of two rupees each, I can make more boxes for them as well. . . .'

"*Several years later: Former cook is now successful exporter. He is seen filling boxes marked 'Best curry powder.' When boxes are filled, he puts them in a large crate and stamps it in black: 'FOR EXPORT ONLY.'* "

Curry Leaf

I must confess that until quite late in my career I was ignorant of the fact that there is a single spice or flavor that is called a curry leaf. I recanted in detail with proper contrition when I conceded that this was true. It is also true that many, and I suspect most, formulas for curry powder (or garam masala, which is similar) do not contain powdered curry leaves.

Again from Madhur Jaffrey: "The 'curry leaf' does, indeed, exist! It is not, and is not meant to be, a substitute for commercially packaged curry powders. It is an herb, rather like the bay leaf, but smaller and more aromatic. Its aroma, like that of basil, is strong and distinctive. I refer you to my cookbook, page 5, the second line of the last paragraph. I have spelled the Indian word phonetically—*kari*—but the English version is 'curry leaf.' The *Oxford English Dictionary* says, 'Curry-leaf tree, a name for bergera konigii, the aromatic leaves of which are used to flavour curries.' Needless to say, not all Indian dishes are flavored with the curry leaf. In northern and north-western India it is hardly used at all. But along India's coastal states and in the south it is extremely popular—for flavoring certain dishes. While it adds an unusually delicious aroma to foods when added in its fresh form, it seems to lose both aroma and flavor when the leaf is dried.

"I once dried a large bunch of leaves, freshly plucked from a tree in our Delhi garden, in order to bring it to New York. But all my effort seemed wasted. By the time I opened my precious plastic bag in New York, the leaves had lost about 95 percent of their character. Perhaps some enterprising American will begin growing the trees and then selling the fresh leaves."

Curry Powder

To preserve curry powder, keep it tightly sealed in an airproof bag or jar and let it stand in a cool place until you use it. Store it as compactly as possible, so that most of the air in the bag or jar is at a minimum. It is my opinion that freezing tends to diminish the flavors of spices and dried herbs.

Custard

The best way to tell if a custard mixture is done is to heat it until it coats the sides of a wooden spoon. Lift the spoon and run your finger through the coating. If it leaves a clear track from your finger marking, the custard is ready. Incidentally, when the mixture is thick enough you should pour the custard immediately into a cold bowl; otherwise it might continue cooking in the saucepan because of retained heat, in which case it might curdle.

Dd Dd Dd Dd

Dandelions

Can you conceive of a town where the mayor boastfully declares that his is the dandelion capital of the world? Well, those gardeners and lawnkeepers who curse and hack away at the roots of those plants may be depriving themselves of one of the most toothsome delicacies of the season, according to the mayor of Vineland, New Jersey, which also boasts that it is New Jersey's largest city—sixty-nine square miles.

The town is one of the principal farm communities that give that state its nickname, the Garden State, providing fresh produce to such diverse points as Canada, Florida, Chicago, and St. Louis. "Dandelion," the mayor asserts, "is a seventy-thousand-dollar-a-year cultivated crop." And cultivated dandelions, he adds, are exactly the same as those that grow wild on your front lawn.

I recently received from the mayor's office a dandelion "cookbook" with recipes featuring dandelions as an important ingredient in such dishes as veal and dandelion sauté, dandelion soup, dandelion wine, an Italian dandelion casserole, and dandelion salad with eggs.

Incidentally, to speak of dandelions as toothsome is not too far off the mark. The name dandelion derives from the French *dent de lion,* or lion's tooth.

"The best cuttings of dandelion," the book says, "are the first three or four cuttings in springtime. These new leaves are tender and tasty.

"The older leaves that grow all through the summer may be used in any of the cooked dishes that are described in this booklet. The young tender leaves that are cut in the spring are suitable to make a delicious salad.

"If you are cutting dandelions from your lawn or a field, be sure that they have not been sprayed with a chemical such as a weed killer or fertilizer."

Dariole

A dariole is both a small, cylindrical mold, and it is also the food cooked in it. The original dessert was make by lining a mold with puff pastry, then filling it with almond cream and baking it. The mold then took on the name.

The word "dariole" no longer refers exclusively to desserts. Vegetable custards made in the molds are also called darioles.

Dash

A dash is a judicious amount and it is, in my mind, a perfectly reasonable measure of volume for certain recipes. Tastes vary greatly, but in this case the taste is left up to the individual cook. I, for example, like very spicy foods and would probably add a touch more of a peppery spice. A dash of Tabasco sauce would, in most cases, imply from one to three drops; of Cognac, from a teaspoonful to a tablespoon. Start with a very small, if not to say tiny, amount and keep adding until the flavor of the dish suits your sensibility or palate.

Decanting

The most basic reason for decanting a wine is to separate the pure wine from any deposits lying on the side or bottom of the bottle. These deposits are normally found only in bottles of a certain age and generally only in red wines. I have been known to decant very young California wines to serve guests who declare they never touch anything but French or other imported wines.

On occasion I have bought wines by the gallon (don't smirk) and these I have decanted because a gallon bottle looks ungainly.

To decant an old bottle of wine, handle the bottle with the greatest care so as not to shake up the deposit. Hold the flame of a candle behind the bottle to illuminate the clear liquid and the deposit. As carefully as possible tilt the bottle so that the clear liquid flows into the decanter, leaving the deposit where it lies.

Deglaze

During my college days I was told that French is the most concise language on earth. "The French," my professor said, "use a minimum of verbal space to express an idea."

This thought came back full force recently when someone asked if I would tell them precisely what the word "deglaze" implies when used in a recipe. It is, of course, a direct translation from the French word *déglacer*.

When foods are roasted or browned in butter or other fat, a "glaze" forms in the skillet or other cooking utensil. This glaze is caused by the liquids that emanate from the meat, poultry, or fish that is being cooked. The glaze obviously has a desirable flavor provided it isn't burned. Thus, when the fat in which the food was browned is poured off, wine or broth is added to the skillet to loosen the glaze and cause it to melt to provide a basic sauce for the dish. Often, of course, wine is used to deglaze and then a broth or cream is added to make the sauce even more palatable.

Now consider the wordy, awkward English equivalent to explain this same action. If you do not borrow the French term, a recipe writer must spell out the procedure as follows:

"Add wine or broth to the skillet and, using a whisk or wooden spoon, stir to dissolve the brown particles that cling to the bottom and sides of the pan."

Delicatessen

Delicatessen derives from the German word *delikatesse,* a delicacy; delikatessen is the plural form. Delicatessens are said to date in America from the 1800s. According to the *Oxford English Dictionary* supplement, one of the first mentions of the word appeared in 1889. A news account in Kansas City reported that "burglars broke into Blake's delicatessen store and made an awful mess of the juicy stuff, canned and bottled."

In a book called *Meat and Meat Foods,* published about thirty years ago by a bacteriologist named Dr. Lloyd B. Jensen, he states that as early as 1183 there were cook shops along the Thames where one could bring meat for roasting or buy already cooked dishes. Meat had to be sold by daylight, never by candlelight, in case a dealer was "up to tricks to sell a piece of old cow for a chop or a young oxe."

Demerara Sugar

Demerara sugar is a soft sugar with fairly large, light amber crystals, the equivalent of light brown sugar. Demerara is the name of the principal river of Guyana and flows into the Atlantic. Presumably demerara sugar was first refined along the banks of that river.

Demerara sugar may be used in any recipes that call for light brown sugar, whether they be desserts, barbecue sauces, and so on.

Demiglace

A demiglace is literally a half-glaze. It is often used in small quantities in the preparation of many classic French sauces, primarily in professional kitchens rather than in home cookery because it is time consuming to prepare.

A demiglace is prepared by roasting meat bones, almost always veal bones, with vegetables and spices. These are put in a large kettle with water and cooked down for several hours to a small quantity.

When strained and cooled, the sauce is quite thick. If you continue cooking that sauce down, it becomes a glace de viande. When this is cooled it is much thicker and paste-like. A little goes a long way.

You can, of course, buy acceptable demiglaces and glaces de viande in certain specialty shops, but they are quite expensive.

Demitasse

In the United States, a demitasse almost invariably implies very strong, dark roast "after dinner" coffee served in a small cup. In France, it simply means coffee served in a very small cup. Although the demitasse in France usually is a dark brew, it could mean any coffee served in a small cup no matter what time of day.

However, you will rarely, if ever, hear a

Frenchman ask for a demitasse. A café, yes, or a café noir.

It has come to my attention that the word is classified by the French as *franglais,* or American French. I do not have the Académie Française manual of usage, but I do have the 1938 edition of *Larousse Gastronomique* in French. It states quite clearly that a demitasse is one of two things: a small coffee cup, or a small cup of black coffee.

Dem Sum

On a brief trip to China, I heard a good deal of quiet but unstinting praise for a restaurant called the Pan Hsi. Most of the praise was focused on the dem sum, those varied Chinese appetizers. They were supposed to be not only superior in flavor but also enchanting to the eye. They were, I was told, fashioned in the shape of small animals, including a rabbit.

The trouble was that I had a language problem with my guide. We had been scheduled to visit a restaurant noted for its lacquered suckling pig, but I told my guide that I wanted to go to the dem sum house for dumplings instead. He smiled and nod-

ded agreeably. He took me—with a party of four—to the restaurant famous for its suckling pig. Not a dem sum to be had.

For twenty months I dreamed of that meal of rabbit dumplings that I had missed. And then it was announced that a group of Chinese chefs from China was coming to this country to give a series of banquets. It was also disclosed that they were from the Pan Hsi in Canton.

In my elation, I invited them to come into my kitchen to demonstrate their cookery, my main thought being that I would not only dine on those fantasies but that I could also watch them being made.

The chefs arrived, a joyous, enthusiastic lot. There were two women, Liu Wan Yi and Liu Hui Duan, and three men, Luo Kun, the master chef, Fan Han Hong, and Ye Zao.

The better part of a morning was spent in preparation of a complex presentation dear to the hearts of most Chinese, a cold, intricately arranged platter of food known as a phoenix bird. The closest approximation of this in Western culture is Art Deco. There is an elaborately designed combination of items like sliced thousand-year eggs, steamed mandolin eggs, sliced aromatic

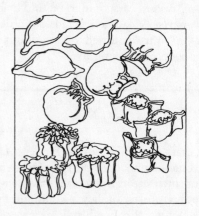

beef, sliced lacquered duck with skin, and assorted carved vegetables and cutouts of gelatin-like agar-agar, all arranged to resemble a bird of gorgeous plumage.

During their stay they prepared marvelously inventive "beehive" dumplings stuffed with a stir-fried blend of pork, shrimp, and black mushrooms as well as Chinese crêpes stuffed with chopped shrimp, salted duck eggs, and seaweed, rolled and deep-fried.

As they prepared these flavorful morsels, they were impressed with several things in a Western kitchen. The Chinese crêpes tended to stick in my own not-too-well-seasoned wok with its slightly scratched surface. They were handed a Teflon skillet and the crêpes turned out splendidly.

They marveled at the pilot lights on the gas stove. They asked if they might use monosodium glutamate in their cooking. I said no. It was explained that in China the monosodium glutamate is made, unlike in the Western world, of organic materials, notably rice and wheat. In America, it is made with, among other things, coal products.

Eventually they got around to those rabbit dumplings. They were, indeed, enchanting to the beholder. What's more, they were easy to make.

Start with a blend of wheat starch (it resembles cornstarch), widely obtainable in Chinese groceries and supermarkets. To this add boiling water and stir rapidly. Shape this dough into small circles, add a small amount of shrimp filling, and bring up the edges of the dough, twirling between the fingers to seal.

Twirl the excess dough from the gathered edges into a point. Clip this point lengthwise in half and bend the two parts back to make the rabbit "ears." Pinch the dumpling on either side to make the rabbit's nose and nostrils. Add a couple of dots of chopped ham to make the pink eyes, and the rabbit dumpling is ready for steaming.

Dende Oil

Dende oil is an oil of palm nut used primarily in Brazil in the kitchens of Bahia, a state on the eastern coast. It is available in specialty food shops in the United States.

Derma

The word *derma* refers to a beef casing, a sausage casing in which various ingredients are stuffed. The basic ingredients for the filling are assorted cereals, flour, onions, and chicken fat or beef breast fat. Modern recipes for this dish include cracker crumbs or bread crumbs. Some recipes call for oats and grits. At least one recipe calls for corn flakes. After the casings are filled, they are boiled until the stuffing sets. They are then generally baked until brown.

Deviled Bones

Deviling was quite popular in eighteenth- and nineteenth-century Britain. James Boswell, Samuel Johnson's biographer, often referred to partaking of deviled bones for supper.

The bones were generally those of cold poultry, game, or beef. The pieces of meat were covered with one of three kinds of devil sauces: a brown, slightly thickened devil sauce made of mustard, chutney, and Worcestershire; a wet devil sauce made of cream, curry powder, and mustard; or a white devil sauce made with cream, mustard, mushroom ketchup, and Worcestershire.

These sauces were poured or brushed onto the bones, which were then grilled until brown on top.

Deviled Ham

I am convinced that almost all recipes that call for deviled ham have the canned product in mind, but Evan Jones, in *American Food: The Gastronomic Story,* notes that "deviled ham may come in cans, but it is better . . . when produced at home."

"The process," he goes on, "is a variation of the old English method of making potted ham, and it is simple. Combine 2 cups of finely minced or ground country ham with a sauce composed of 1 cup of cream, 4 tablespoons of butter, 1 tablespoon of flour, a dash of red pepper, ½ tablespoon of dry mustard."

He adds that you should cook the sauce about 10 minutes and then add the ham. Pack the mixture into a mold and chill. "An even simpler version," he continues, "is a mixture of the same amount of ground ham with 2 teaspoons each of Dijon mustard and mayonnaise to serve as a binder."

Dindonneau en Demi-Deuil

See Turkey.

Dinnerette

Having an infatuation with words—an obsession may be more like it—I was interested while thumbing through the 1897 edition of the *Oxford New English Dictionary on Historical Principles* to discover there is such a word as "dinnerette."

A dinnerette, you will be happy to know, is "A little dinner; a dinner on a small scale, or for a small party." The authority illustrated the word's use as follows:

"1872 M. Collins, Pr. Clarice II. v. 74 He has a luxurious bachelor's first floor in Piccadilly . . . where he sometimes gives excellent dinnerettes."

Diplomat

The term "diplomat," implying something a bit ornate and elegant, is used in French cuisine for both the pudding, made with a Bavarian cream and apricot preserves, and a sauce that consists of sauce normande, the basic white-wine sauce, plus lobster butter, Cognac, chopped truffles, and lobster cubes.

Dirty Rice

Dirty rice is an excellent, uncommonly tasty dish of Cajun and/or Creole origin. It is called dirty because it is a bit dark once it is cooked. The ingredients are chicken livers and gizzards that are chopped, but not so finely chopped as to lose their identity.

Some people add ground pork and cubed eggplant. You cook these in oil along with green pepper, onion, and celery, then the rice and chicken broth. Toss in some chopped scallions (in Louisiana these are referred to as shallots) and cook until tender.

Dishwasher Cooking

"Cooking" in a dishwasher came to my attention while on vacation in the Caribbean. I overheard a conversation in which a woman said her hairdresser had told her that you could cook a chicken by wrapping it in aluminum foil and putting it through the complete dishwasher cycle.

I paid little heed until I found that a publication known as *Saltwater Sportsman* had reviewed *Bluefish Cookbook* by Greta Jacobs and Jane Alexander Sherin. The review offered a sample recipe and said: "For 'different' bluefish, she suggests wrapping bluefish fillets separately and tightly in foil, placing on the upper rack of the dishwasher (no soap!), and running wash through complete cycle. For big fish it may take two cycles. Serve with tartar sauce and lemon wedges."

Dividing Recipes

One of the questions most often asked of me is how to divide recipes. And the answer is that almost any recipe can be divided in half or thirds, although you will certainly have to exercise some imagination in making conversions. If a recipe to serve eight calls for a ten-inch-long oval dish, you will, naturally, have to use a smaller dish to prepare the same recipe for two or four.

When dividing a recipe containing eggs, and the results indicate half an egg, go ahead and use a whole egg. In the vast majority of cases, the end product will be comparable, whereas if you dropped the half an egg, the custard or whatever might conceivably not thicken properly.

Dollop

On those rare occasions when I would use the word "dollop" in a recipe, I would indicate that the quantity was not all that important, that the amount would be left up to the appetite and taste of the cook. There is, of course, no specific amount to be indicated when the word is used. It is a vague term and of the same general nature as saying a dash of nutmeg or Tabasco, a pinch of pepper, and so on. According to *Webster's New World Dictionary*, a dollop is a blob, a lump, or a small quantity.

Doner Kebabs

Doner kebabs, a Turkish dish, are pieces of lamb or mutton that are seasoned and ar-

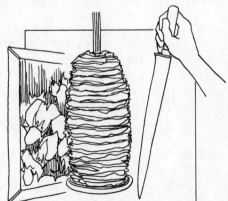

ranged in layers on an upright revolving spit that turns in front of a vertical charcoal fire. As the spit turns and the meat is cooked from the outside toward the center, a long, lethal-looking knife is used to carve the meat into thin slices. These are often eaten sandwich fashion.

Drawn Butter

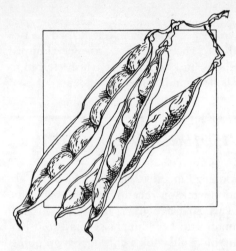

Drawn butter and clarified butter are the same. They refer to butter that has been melted and the clear golden liquid poured or drawn away from the liquid sediment or milk solids that settle on the bottom.

For what it is worth, there is a recipe for a drawn butter sauce in the earliest edition of *The Boston Cooking School Cook Book* by Fannie Merritt Farmer, prepared like a white sauce with flour and butter, using water with a touch of lemon juice as a liquid. However, it is not a sauce of much consequence and does not appear in later editions.

Dried Beans

As far as I can determine, there are no standards among dried bean producers for the time required for soaking beans and it is a bit maddening. Some beans come with a notation on the sacks in which they are packed, "No soaking necessary." I have even seen beans with two recipes on the back, one of which advises the reader to soak the beans overnight, the other requiring no presoaking.

When I use dried beans I look for clues on the packaging. If it says "No soaking

necessary," I do not soak them. If there is a single recipe on the back that indicates that the beans need not be soaked, I do not soak them.

In my own kitchen, I find it virtually impossible to tell at the moment I start a dried bean dish whether it will require an hour or two to cook them to the desired degree of tenderness. I add water to about one inch above the top of the beans and let them simmer as slowly as possible, testing them often to determine if they are properly tender.

There is a "quick-soak" method for beans. If you determine that beans should be soaked and want to hasten the process, put the beans in a kettle and add water to cover to a depth of about two inches above the top of the beans. Bring to the boil and let simmer for two minutes. Cover and let stand for an hour before continuing with the recipe.

In any event, you should test the beans often to prevent them from overcooking.

As to cooking dried beans that have been used as weights in baking a pie crust, I would not recommend it. On the other hand, they are most certainly reusable in pastry shells.

Dried Red Pepper Flakes

See Peppers.

Drying Lettuce

See Salad greens.

Du Barry

It is by no means surprising that a chef in the course of French history decided to name a dish after Countess du Barry, born Marie Jeanne Bécu. She was reputedly, of course, a lady of interesting virtue and the favorite of Louis XV. On a menu the name du Barry almost invariably denotes the use of cauliflower in one form or another—as the base for a dish or a garnish. One of the principal and best-known of such dishes is *crème du Barry,* or cream of cauliflower soup.

Duck

See Long Island duck, Muscovy duck.

Duck Bigarade

Unlike duck à l'orange, which can be made with any orange whatsoever, duck bigarade technically must be made with the orange called bigarade. This orange in France is known as an *orange amère,* or bitter orange. It is referred to in French-English dictionaries as a bitter orange or Seville orange, which is not commonly found in America. It is the finest orange for making marmalade. The sauce for duck bigarade consists of cooking the duck juices with a brown veal sauce and adding to this finely shredded orange skin, a touch of vinegar, and, in some rare cases, bitter orange marmalade.

Dumaine

In countless corners here and there I have a few thousand scribbled notes pertaining to cooking and dining that never saw the light of print. I recently found several pages in a steno pad labeled "Alexandre Dumaine—Hôtel de la Côte d'Or, Saulieu" and, turning the pages, I recalled one of the pleasantest interviews of my days. M. Dumaine was one of the kitchen titans of his time until his retirement in 1963, and he was known with the utmost fondness as "Alexandre le Grand." Those who had graced his table embraced many of the titled heads of Europe, the world's most civilized gastronomes, artists, writers, the rich and poor alike. There were scores of Americans (and Europeans) who hoarded their savings for weeks or months to dine on the great chef's pike quenelles, baron of lamb, or, perhaps, what might have been his most celebrated creation, *poularde à la vapeur,* a truffled perfection that had to be ordered twenty-four hours in advance. If any guest ordered *poularde à la vapeur* and failed to appear precisely at the appointed hour, the chef refused him service. His philosophy went something like this: If a dish is to be honored with the care and preparation required of twenty-four hours' time, it is worth the guest's punctuality. Or the guest is not worthy of the dish.

"My guiding motto for fifty years," he once told me, "is simplicity. The French peasant cuisine is at the basis of the culinary art. By this I mean it is composed of honest elements that *la grande cuisine* only embellishes.

"In great cooking there are no tricks, no attempts to disguise the true taste by overuse of wines or condiments. What it requires is patience. One must avoid the temptation to hurry, to use substitutes."

During his working years, M. Dumaine was an amiable host, but he deplored being disturbed as he worked in the kitchen. And understandably. He did not supervise a large and highly skilled staff as many might have supposed. Quite atypically, he did his own cooking. His *équipe*, or team, consisted of four assistants in a kitchen that measured approximately twenty-seven feet long and fourteen feet wide, a room dominated by a vast coal range. In this setting, he was regarded by his colleagues as "a tempestuous man and a perfectionist" as he went about sampling his sauces, pressing a thumb into a tournedos to test for doneness, choosing a wine, or selecting the plumpest of quail and pheasant for this guest or that.

M. Dumaine believed that book learning is of limited value where the preparation of fine foods is concerned. "You are born with the genius of the stove or you are not."

"It's all in knowing how," he once said. "You won't find the essential ingredients—imagination and devotion—in cookbooks.

"To be a chef you have to have the soul for it and work at it every day. It is not a business . . . one must start early in life and learn the real traditions. And use only the best ingredients: the best butter; the best

chickens; the best hams; the best wines."

The good chef found flaming dishes in a dining room contemptible—cheap showmanship—and felt that far too many cooks used Cognac, an essential at times, to excess.

Like most chefs of great rank, he felt that la grande cuisine is not to be eaten—could not be eaten—as a steady diet, and he added, "When you taste all the time you are rarely hungry. It is a sacrifice chefs must make."

Dumaine did not believe, as many so-called gourmets are prone to, that smoking is abhorrent for the palate. He considered it proper to smoke during dinner, "but not," he cautioned, "until the main course has been finished."

P.S.: I add the last paragraph simply to share M. Dumaine's point of view. I do not smoke nor do I encourage it at table. On the other hand, I certainly consider cigarette smoking the privilege of any guest who may join me.

Dumplings

The stuffed dumpling, humble as it may seem, is a dish with a fascinating history, going back many centuries and interwoven into the cuisines of a number of countries.

The story has often been told of Marco Polo arriving in China during the thirteenth century and discovering with delight that the Chinese were producing a variety of stuffed noodles that included won ton. So impressed was he that he brought the secrets back to Italy. That tale is considered apocryphal by both the Chinese and Italians, but wouldn't it be fascinating to know how the two cuisines are related?

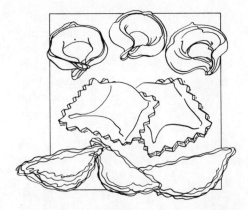

Similarly, what about the pelmeni of Russia? These are delectable Siberian dumplings filled with meat or mushrooms or potatoes or cabbage. What cook traveled the roads from Canton, or wherever, to the Irtysh River in the cold plateaus of Siberia, bringing with him the goodness of filled pasta?

Or consider the kreplach, the filled dumpling held in such high esteem in the Jewish kitchen. The migrations of the Jews, carrying with them a culinary heritage from various parts of the world, are well known, as is the fact that many Jewish specialties are borrowings from the Russian. At what point did the pelmeni turn into kreplach, with its economical use of ground cooked beef as the filling?

That use of cooked meat, probably from a soup or stew, is also characteristic of dumplings. The lack of kosher meat in medieval ghettos dictated that there be ways to stretch a meager supply from one meal to another.

The uses to which dumplings are put are intriguing as well. They are probably most often used in soups, and yet a wide array of sauces may also be served with them.

Won tons, for example, go deliciously with a blend of soy sauce, garlic, vinegar, grated ginger, hot chilies, and the like, a combination that would seem odd to an Italian chef thinking of ravioli. For ravioli there is nothing like a tomato sauce with freshly grated cheese or alla panna—a reduction of heavy cream and cheese. Or (as they do in Rapallo when they serve pansotti, a form of ravioli) a salsa di noce made with walnuts and a form of ricotta cheese.

Curiously, however, the Siberians and those who prepare pelmeni are not averse to serving them with a sauce somewhat akin to the Chinese soy sauce, vinegar, and herb combination.

Pelmeni are often served with a mustard sauce, sour cream, and chopped dill. Kreplach, like the Chinese dumplings, are often fried in chicken fat, rather than served in soup. *See also* Dem sum, Knedlicky, Pansotti, Quenelle, Spaetzle.

Dutch Treat

Dutch treat is of English coinage, I am told, and came about during the seventeenth century when there was a good deal of rivalry between Britain and the Netherlands in international trade and for control of the seas. At first it was probably derogatory, but it is so commonly used today that I do not feel it implies any disrespect. Another term came about at that time: Dutch courage, which is to say, the courage that arises after a few drinks.

Earl Grey Tea

It would seem that a volume could be written about the origins and flavor of Earl Grey tea. The best explanation I know comes from *The Tea Lover's Treasury* by James Norwood Pratt.

According to the author, the tea is named for Charles Grey, the second member of his family to bear the title of earl. He was a prime minister during the reign of William IV, who ruled from 1830 to 1837. There are various legends about the origin of the tea, one being that Earl Grey obtained the formula as a diplomat in China.

There are several producers of Earl Grey tea, all of them contending that they possess the original formula. In any event, according to Mr. Pratt, the flavor is derived from oil of bergamot, a pear-shaped citrus grown around the Mediterranean.

Eating Styles

A good deal has been written about the proper styles of holding a knife and fork and the placing of the food in the mouth. I seriously doubt that today's behaviorists could offer an explanation for the American style of eating versus the European, although I personally favor the European style. This is snobbism, but the European technique—holding the fork in the left hand for spearing and putting morsels in the mouth, the knife in the right for cutting—seems to be more natural and efficient than the American method of cutting meat with the right hand, resting the knife on the plate rim, transferring the fork to the right, then negotiating the fork-speared food to the mouth. Wasted motion!

One could further complicate such speculation by asking why Moroccans, Indians, and Pakistanis take their food from plate to mouth with their fingers, while the Chinese, Japanese, and other Asians use chopsticks.

Eccles Cake

One history of British food, *British Cookery,* edited by Lizzie Boyd, says Eccles cake was first made in the eighteenth century by a well-known cook named Mrs. Raffald, who gave the recipe to a servant girl as a wedding present. The servant moved to Eccles, where she baked and sold the cakes.

I have always noted that they were made with a short—meaning buttery—pastry. But

145

several people, many of them British, have written me to "set the record straight."

One commented, "I lived for a long time in the Manchester area and ate hundreds of them. There they are made with flaky or rough puff pastry—usually cutoffs of puff pastry that has been rolled and cut so that it won't 'puff' properly. The cake is filled with a mixture of butter, currants, mixed candied fruit peel, sugar, nutmeg, and mixed spices."

He noted that the Eccles cake has a special shape, resembling "a slightly expanded powder compact."

Edinburgh Fog

Edinburgh fog is a dessert made with sweetened whipped cream flavored with vanilla. You fold crushed ratafia biscuits—macaroons about the size of a quarter—and chopped almonds into the mixture and chill it. The biscuits are made with ratafia essence, which is oil of almond. Ratafia is also an almond-flavored cordial.

Eel

In America eels are something of a gastronomic curiosity and, with the exception of smoked eels, are rarely found on menus in Manhattan, a regrettable truth, for eels can be a delicacy of excelling goodness. Eels are a commonplace in Japan, where they are grilled and served with a somewhat sweet, dark brown, lacquer-like sauce. The Greeks eat them with gusto stewed or fried or in other olympic preparations. Escoffier lists more than twenty preparations for *anguilles,*

or eels, and one of the most delectable and praised of the "new" appetizers served in the great luxury restaurants of France are pâtés of eel.

One of the most sublime dishes of the Western world is *anguilles au vert,* or eels in a green sauce made with a purée of sorrel and other greens.

Eels are caught commercially and by amateur fishermen near my home in eastern Long Island.

"You don't need much equipment to go eeling," according to Bill Lusty, a neighbor and eeling enthusiast. "You need a bucket or something to put the eels in and you need a spear." An eel spear resembles a small lyre attached to the end of a sixteen- or seventeen-foot pole made of spruce or white pine. The lyre-like business end consists of a center, rounded blade. On either side of it are two sets of hooks, three to each side. The spear is shoved into the mud or sand and, with luck, an eel is trapped within the hooks. When the spear is lifted, the eel, of course, is hooked. On his expeditions, Mr. Lusty carries two spears in case one breaks.

In winter, eels may be caught either by ice fishing or by going out in a boat. Mr. Lusty, who, like his father before him, has been eeling since he was an infant, prefers the ice. He finds boating in winter a bit too raw and brutal.

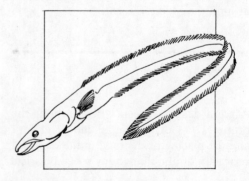

"When you go out on the ice, it's got to be firm enough to support a man's weight. Three inches of ice is enough, but the last freeze we had the ice was eight inches deep." In the wintertime the basic equipment includes, in addition to the spear and bucket, an ax of the standard sort found in many households.

"You use the ax to break the ice. You make a hole in the ice about eighteen inches across. You fish there for a while, and, if there's no luck, you move on. Sometimes you fish eight or nine holes with no success, and on the tenth you can pull up eight to ten good eels. The last three holes I cracked I got about thirty pounds of eels."

Mr. Lusty formerly worked in New Jersey as a detail man for the Eli Lilly Pharmaceuticals Company. He retired in 1969, and he eels primarily as a hobby.

In summer, when he goes out in a boat, it is generally with one other companion, and they take turns eeling and propelling the boat. "At night in summer we go firelighting, as they say. We take the headlight of a car attached by wires to a storage battery. The headlight is submersible and lights up the bottom of the harbor." In winter when you drop the spear through the ice, it is pretty much a hit-or-miss proposition. "When you go firelighting in summer, you can see the eels squirming around on the bottom."

Mr. Lusty generally throws back into the water any eels that are eight inches or less in length. The eels range from a few inches to sixteen inches, and he prefers those ten to twelve inches long. These, he claims, are more tender and less fatty.

Mr. Lusty's favorite dish is his wife's barbecued eels. "I cook them," she stated recently, "according to an old Girl Scout recipe for barbecue sauce. It's made with ketchup, brown sugar, lemon, bay leaf, dry mustard, mixed spices, vinegar, and water." The eels are grilled over charcoal for about thirty minutes and basted often with the sauce.

Eggnog

I grew up in a home where alcohol was permitted only once a year and that was at Christmastime. Mother was famous for her eggnog and no wonder—it was heavily spiked with bourbon. For such a dedicated Southerner, no other whiskey or anything as alien as rum or Cognac would do. I remember Christmas as a very special time when everyone in the house, including children, got giddy.

I, frankly, find eggnog a bit too much to serve as a preface to any meal. It is best served in midafternoon or after dinner. I prefer it frozen.

Because of its intensely sweet richness, eggnog does not team well with any appetizers unless you consider salted nuts appetizers. It does not go well, for example, with such seafood as shrimp, lobsters, clams, crabs, or anchovies. It certainly does not go well with anything containing mayonnaise. And so on. The ideal accompaniment for eggnog, if you insist on teaming it with something, is fruitcake.

Eggplant

I once offered an opinion on how to tell whether an eggplant has few or many seeds. It was my educated guess that the younger the eggplant, the fewer the seeds.

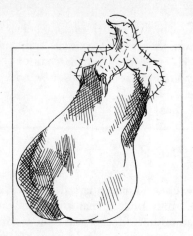

Therefore, I advised, look for eggplants that have the freshest looking and greenest stem ends. The thought was that the greener the stems, the younger the vegetable.

Shortly thereafter I received a notably enlightening message from a woman telling me that I knew less than beans about aubergines.

"Years ago," she advised, "a friend told me how her mother's family in Italy picked the eggplants with the fewest seeds."

It depends—would you believe?—on the sex of the product.

"Check the large blossom end," she continued, meaning the end opposite the stem end. "You will note in the center at the base there is a 'scar' or 'indentation.' If this scar is round, the eggplant is male. If it is oval, it is female. And the female is loaded with seeds.

"I am not," she adds in closing, "trying to be funny. And there are more males than females among eggplants."

I subsequently made a brief investigation into the matter, hauling home four eggplants, two with round scars, two with oval scars. Sure enough, when cut into, those with the round scar had the fewest seeds.

But the preponderance of those in the vegetable bin had oval scars.

A woman from Brooklyn has written: "Our family is Romanian in origin and, of course, we know the difference between the male and female and there *are* more seeds in the female." But, she added, "We preferred the female because it was sweeter and when baked it took less time and was generally more tender."

A botanist with the University of Massachusetts Cooperative Extension Service has written:

"Actually, the flowers of eggplant are perfect, that is, they possess male parts, stamens, with pollen, and a female part called the pistil. The flowers are self-pollinating and upon fertilization develop into the fruit we all love. Eggplant is not dioecious, having male and female flowers on separate plants like asparagus and hollies.

"The large scar on the blossom end is the result of poor pollination, causing a condition known as 'catfacing,' which is more severe on tomatoes. This condition is usually caused by cold weather or drought at the time of pollination. Some eggplant varieties are more susceptible than others. When poor pollination occurs, all the ovaries in the fruit are not fertilized and do not develop into seeds. Fertilized ovaries produce hormones that promote normal fruit growth, hence a small scar on the blossom end. Poorly pollinated and fertilized fruits have less seeds and less hormones. Here, the fruit cannot develop normally, leaving a large scar on the blossom end."

Finally, a letter from a produce handler. "Let me convey to you the way to determine the sex of an eggplant—that is, if the vegetable is wholly fresh and not previously handled too much. You can determine the sex by the 'sheen' on the outer skin. If the sheen is notably bright it is female, if notably dull it is male. I will add that the female is the better as to texture and flavor and has less fiber."

One last comment: There is a creditable theory that the original eggplants on this earth were of the porcelain variety. The white color, in fact, is said to be the reason the vegetable was known as an eggplant in the first place. The size of the white eggplants varies and some are as large as an ostrich egg. White eggplants and purple eggplants can be used interchangeably.

As to salting eggplant before cooking, it is absolutely not essential. When I used salt, I did, on occasion, follow such advice, but I could never figure out why. It's true that when salt is sprinkled on eggplant slices, they will exude a certain amount of liquid, but I never thought that salt improved either flavor or texture. *See also* Poor man's caviar.

Eggs

In the world of food, there may be nothing more versatile than the egg. The yolk provides the emulsion of the world's most basic and elegant sauces—mayonnaise and hollandaise. The white is the essence of a multitude of meringues, and gives lightness to soufflés. Almost all foods that are breaded are dipped in beaten egg before they are crumbed. The thickening power of the egg for soups and sauces and stuffings and custards is universal. And the uses of hard-boiled egg are varied and delicious.

Because of their constant use, eggs seem to elicit more questions than almost any other food. Here are some of my answers.

Assuming that they are reasonably fresh when you buy them even at the neighborhood supermarket, eggs will last from thirty

to forty days if properly refrigerated. There is no way to tell if an egg is over the hill without cracking it. If spoiled, an egg's yolk will be discolored and, of course, the egg will not smell or taste fresh.

■ ■ ■

A highly informative booklet titled *Eggcyclopedia,* published by the American Egg Board in Chicago, says that the rare egg with a blood spot in the yolk is fit to eat both chemically and nutritionally. The spots do not, as many people believe, indicate fertility. According to the booklet, they are "caused by the rupture of a blood vessel on the yolk surface during formation of the egg or by a similar accident in the wall of the oviduct."

Fewer than 1 percent of eggs contain the spots, the booklet reports.

■ ■ ■

It is true that the older an egg is, the easier it is to peel once it is hard-boiled. The theory is that an air layer develops between the membranes of the shell as the egg stands.

If you know approximately how fresh your eggs are, it may be wise to refrigerate them and let them stand a week or two before hard-boiling them. Once peeled, the outer surface of the egg will then be smoother. Egg specialists also say that if you

pierce the large end of an egg—you can buy a device that neatly performs this task—before cooking, this will also aid in peeling.

In any event, once you have cooked an egg you should run it under cold water to chill the shell before starting to peel it, then keep it under the water while you peel. It makes the shell come off more easily and prevents a greenish tinge from forming around the yolk.

■ ■ ■

Howard Hillman, the food expert and author, sent me an excerpt from his book, *Kitchen Science,* about green-tinged egg yolks.

He had noted that one may eliminate the problem by following three rules: First, use only very fresh eggs (the green tinge is a ferrous sulfide that develops more readily in older eggs). Second, never cook the eggs longer than fifteen minutes. Third, once they are cooked, halt further cooking by quickly cooling them in cold water.

He added his recommended technique for preventing the eggs from cracking as they cook in boiling or simmering water. Remove the eggs from the refrigerator, pierce them carefully with the fine point of a standard pushpin, available in stationery stores, and ease the eggs gently into a pot of boiling or simmering water.

■ ■ ■

As to beating eggs, it is a generalization to say that the eggs added to a dish need not be beaten unless there is an express reason for doing so. More often than not I beat eggs before adding them to the other ingredients of a meat loaf (to choose one example) simply because I feel that they will blend more evenly. This is a very minor point, however, and not always necessary.

I also often beat eggs with other liquids

if the liquids are to be added, again to achieve even distribution.

In some recipes for cakes, however, whole eggs are added alternately with the other ingredients. This is designed to save beating the eggs before adding since they are going to be well beaten into the batter. You could beat the eggs in advance, but it would be unnecessary.

■ ■ ■

Some recipes call for adding eggs one at a time and there is a good reason for this. One of the most obvious recipes that calls for this technique is a basic cream puff paste. You blend flour and water and cook, stirring rapidly, until the mixture comes away neatly from the sides of the saucepan. Then you beat in the eggs, one at a time, generally with a wooden spoon. If you add them in this fashion, the mixture homogenizes or comes together quite nicely. Gradually, logically, and step by step. If, on the other hand, you tried to add the eggs all at once, it would require considerable expertise, beating, and time to get them to homogenize using either a spoon or machine. *See also* Fried eggs, Eggs Benedict, Eggs mollet, Brown eggs.

Eggs Benedict

There are several legends as to the origin of the name eggs Benedict. One states that the dish originated at the old Delmonico's Restaurant in Manhattan. It is said that two regular customers were a Mr. and Mrs. LeGrand Benedict. Mrs. Benedict, the legend has it, complained that the menu was always the same and the maître d'hôtel asked what she would recommend. Out of this dialogue

in hard-boiled eggs. Cooking time depends on the size of the eggs and how cold they are.

Generally speaking, they may cook from five to six minutes. Or they may be brought to the boil and removed from the heat. Let them stand covered for ten minutes and then peel them.

Egg Whites

Most French chefs strongly recommend using copper bowls for beating egg whites.

To beat properly, whites must be free of all fat of any nature. That is why they should not be beaten in a plastic container; the plastic tends to absorb and retain fat once it has been added. Nor should they be beaten in an aluminum bowl, which will, because of a chemical reaction, give a grayish cast to the whites.

Some recipes for beating egg whites, particularly in American cookbooks, recommend the addition of a little cream of tartar. This is an acid and it is said to give a stability and a more tender foam to egg whites.

If the cream of tartar is used, the whites should not be beaten in a copper bowl; the copper, combined with the acid of cream of tartar, will give a greenish cast to the whites.

Also, room temperature egg whites foam up much more quickly than those just out of the refrigerator, though whites and yolks should be separated while the eggs are still cold.

Both egg whites and egg yolks freeze exceedingly well. Put either one in a plastic container, covering tightly with the lid, and freeze. Or put them in ice trays and freeze. Unmold and refreeze in plastic containers.

came the eggs on toasted bread, plus ham and hollandaise sauce.

Many people who like to serve eggs Benedict for brunch dread the thought of poaching all those eggs at the last minute.

The solution is to do as many restaurants do, that is to say, poach the eggs in advance and drain them. Just before you are ready to serve the eggs, bring another batch of water to the boil, enough to cover the eggs when added. Turn off the heat. Add the eggs and heat them as briefly as possible. They can then be drained and served. Take special care, however, that the eggs are only heated and do not cook the second time around.

Eggs Mollet

Eggs mollet, known as coddled eggs in English, are somewhere in between soft-boiled and hard-boiled eggs.

The eggs are cooked until the whites become slightly firm while the yolks remain moist. Unlike soft-boiled eggs, eggs mollet can be shelled and retain their egg shape as

Egg Yolks

Sauces thickened with egg yolks are among the trickiest to prepare. Skilled cooks can add egg yolks directly to a hot, even boiling, sauce, but this is certainly not recommended for novices or those who are unsteady of hand or faint of heart. The moment the yolks are added, you must stir the sauce as rapidly as possible and withdraw the sauce from the heat. A more certain method of adding the yolks is to beat them in a mixing bowl. Add a little of the hot sauce and blend quickly. Then add this mixture to the saucepan, stirring as rapidly as possible with a whisk.

Eighty-Six

The term "86" is used widely by bartenders and others to indicate that a customer is in his cups and must not be served another drink. Similarly, in restaurants it indicates that the kitchen has run out of one dish or another.

The *American Thesaurus of Slang* states that numbers were once used as codes in soda fountains across the land to indicate various beverages and other preparations to be found on menus. Fifty-five, according to this authority, meant root beer and nineteen indicated a banana split. Eighty-six signaled that one soda spigot or a certain dish was kaput.

Several people wrote to dispute this notion. One interpretation that I particularly admired came from a Manhattan woman.

The term "86," she wrote, derives from the fact "that the Second Avenue El

stopped—completely—at 86th Street, so everyone had to get out. Bars picked up the conductor's call '86' to throw out drunks."

Another interpretation is that the term originated in California "by bartenders who derived the expression from the California beverage code—Section 86—which prohibited serving alcoholic beverages to persons in an intoxicated state."

At P.J. Clarke's on Fifty-fifth Street in New York City, the explanation is this: "In the early days of this country, when much of the distilled liquor was served 100 proof, a bartender would cut off an offensive or intoxicated customer by '86ing him.' That is, by cutting the proof of the liquor to 86."

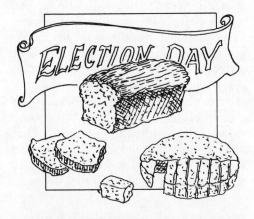

Election Cake

Perhaps the oddest American romp to be celebrated with a food is our national election. Yes, Horace, there is an election cake, and I have it on the best authority that it was created in the eighteenth century, but there is some disagreement over which election the cook had in mind.

When a recipe for this cake first appeared

in *The New York Times* many years ago, it was noted that the cake originated in Hartford. Some said that the cake was created to celebrate the inauguration of the governor of Connecticut, when the communities got together for parades, speeches, dinners, and drinking.

But another authority maintained that the cake was more likely associated with voting in November. Casting one's ballot was a privilege that had been fought for at the time of the cake's creation and, therefore, demanded special foods and festivities.

When this cake was first tested in *The Times'* test kitchen, according to an original formula, it was so exceedingly rich that the surface sank in the center, the cake itself hardly held together, and the grain was coarse.

An old New Englander who was asked to sample and comment on the loaf stated that it was "quite within the framework of tastes of the early times."

Elephant

For reasons that are wholly transparent to anyone other than a pachyderm, there are numerous food jokes and anecdotes about elephants.

One of the earliest I recall was told to me years ago by a man who was then a restaurateur, Ralph Daniels of Miami Beach.

It concerned a man who walked into a restaurant and, glancing over the menu, noted a listing for elephant omelets.

The waitress approached and asked, "May I take your order?"

Man: "Yes, I'd like to sample the elephant omelets."

Waitress: "How many, sir?"

Man: "Only one, of course."

Waitress: "I hope you don't think the chef is going out and kill an elephant just to make you one omelet."

There was a time during the Siege of Paris when numerous animals that we do not ordinarily find in the kitchen found themselves in stews, ragouts, and a host of other preparations, elephant among them.

In *The Art of French Cooking* there is a menu reproduced verbatim from a Paris restaurant and dated December 25, 1870, the ninety-ninth day of the siege, which occurred during the Franco-Prussian War. Among the other delectables there is stuffed donkey's head, elelphant consommé, roast camel English-style, jugged kangaroo, roast bear chops with poivrade sauce, haunch of wolf with venison sauce, and cat flanked by rats. The restaurant was the Café Voison on the rue Saint-Honoré.

In any event, I was given a recipe for elephant stew by the late Paul Steindler, proprietor of several restaurants in Manhattan. Here is the recipe.

ELEPHANT STEW

1 large elephant
Brown gravy
Salt and pepper to taste
2 rabbits, optional

1. Cut the elephant into bite-size pieces. This should take about 2 months.

2. Add brown gravy to cover and salt and pepper to taste. Cook over a kerosene fire for about 4 weeks at 465 degrees. This is sufficient to serve 3,800 people.

3. If more guests are expected, 2 rabbits may be added, but do this only if necessary, as most people do not like to find hare in their stew.

Yield: 3,800 and more servings.

Empanadas

See Turnovers.

Endive

See Belgian endive.

English Breakfast Tea

The best explanation I have found for the term "English breakfast tea" is in an excellent book titled *The Tea Lover's Treasury* by James Norwood Pratt:

"Over a hundred years ago in Scotland, a man named Drysdale went into the specialty tea business within sight of the castle of Edinburgh and offered a tea called Breakfast. The firm is still there and still so Scottish they sell refills for their tins. And they still sell the only tea on the market called simply Breakfast and nothing more, probably reasoning that Scots have little need of English or Irish breakfast, after all, and at that time of day want to be told nothing more than which blend of teas makes a good eye-opener."

Enriched

The word "enriched" means that flour or bread has had vitamins and iron added to it. It does not mean that it has been made more rich with the addition of fats. Bread that has been enriched does not have a higher calorie count.

Entremeses

See Appetizers.

Entremets

Larousse Gastronomique points out that the word *entremets* actually means "between dishes" or "between foods." From the fourteenth through the seventeenth century in France, an entremet also meant an entertainment staged between courses by minstrels, troubadours, and so on.

"Nowadays," *Larousse* continues, "the word entremets means sweets and these are served in France after the cheese."

Epazote

Diana Kennedy, one of the foremost authorities on Mexican cooking in this country, first introduced me to epazote, a much-used herb in Mexico. She found it growing wild near her apartment when she lived in Manhattan—to her great delight, in that she could not find it in any local market.

It is a tall, greenish plant with flat, pointed leaves and gives a distinctive pungent flavor to tortilla fillings, soups, and so forth.

Epicure

A very young man with a considerable enthusiasm for food, wine, and the other good things of life recently asked me whether I, as a professional food writer, would prefer to be referred to as a gourmet, an epicure, a gastronome, or a connoisseur. I quickly assured him that I dislike labels and would rather be referred to as someone with a professional interest in cooking and the good life.

In any event, the subject aroused enough enthusiasm in me to go back and reread an essay by the late A. J. A. Symons, an Englishman who with André Simon founded the Wine and Food Society and edited its quarterly journal.

In that essay, in a work entitled *The Epicure's Anthology,* he points out that Dr. Johnson included the word "gourmand" in his dictionary. He defined an epicure as "a man given wholly to luxury." Mr. Symons finds omens in the fact that Dr. Johnson did not include the word "gourmet" in his tract.

The author has what I consider the most thoughtful of all definitions of an epicure. It is as follows:

"The epicure is most frequently a man of affairs, who has distinguished himself by talent, or played some prominent part in the world's administration, to whom care in eating and drinking is a relaxation, a hobby, or an inspiration. The modern definition 'one who cultivates a refined taste for the pleasures of the table' is explicit and sufficient; and no qualification should be added to it.

"The epicure is not a man who thinks of, and lives for, his belly alone; he is not a sensualist for whom dinner is merely an elaborate prelude to sexual passion; he is not a hedonist who sees life as a succession of pleasurable sensations to be obtained by hook, crook or levitation; he is not a table-bore who rams his one subject down your throat; he is not a pride-starved victim of insufficiency striving to assert a false superiority by making undue fuss over wine and food. He is simply 'one who cultivates a refined taste for the pleasures of the table.' No more. He may profess any of a dozen religions (though not those of Mahomet or Confucius, which forbid wine), he may be a carpenter in Surrey or a Burgundy cooper, a colonel of infantry or a private detective; all that we can predict or expect of him is that, as an epicure, he conforms to the definition already quoted."

Epigrammes

One of my favorite anecdotes relating to food also has to do with a lamb dish known in the French kitchen as *épigrammes d'agneau,* or lamb epigrams. It supposedly came about a couple of hundred years ago when a nouveau riche and upwardly mobile French woman listened to the conversation around the table in her home, and someone remarked that she had dined the evening before in the home of royalty. What's more, her guest recalled, they had enjoyed the epigrams of the host more than anything else.

When the meal in her home ended, the lady of the house called in her chef and demanded that for the next dining occasion he produce a dish of epigrams. The chef's creation consisted of lamb chops, plus braised breast of lamb, breaded and served together. (The breast of lamb is classically cut into the shape of a heart; don't ask me why.)

Ersatz Food

I have only once, by choice, found an occasion to try "bacon" made of processed, textured vegetable protein foods, and let the moment slip by without recording my impressions.

I was, therefore, delighted to receive in the mail a communication from a highly lucid and knowledgeable gentleman who was executive director of the Coatings Research Group in Cleveland, Ohio. His reaction to the product so neatly dovetailed with my own that I offer it:

"I thought you might be interested in one person's comments on a first encounter with one of the widely advertised processed, textured vegetable protein foods simulating a meat product, in this case bacon.

"As a chemist who has specialized in paints and plastics, I have a natural curiosity about what my fellow chemists are accomplishing in their own fields of specialization. Thus, I recently yielded to an impulse to try the textured vegetable protein product referred to as 'breakfast strips.'

"My first reaction was one of amusement as I observed how techniques which have long been used for 'marbleization' of plastics had, in this case, been cleverly applied to simulation of the familiar fat and lean

structure of bacon strips. In this case, the 'fat' and 'lean' portions were the same material, differing only in color.

"I fried a few strips in cooking oil, as directed (since there is none of the natural animal fat that supplies its own browning medium in real bacon). The odor, during cooking, was somewhat reminiscent of the smoky aroma of frying bacon, but with an unmistakably synthetic, musky, and slightly unpleasant undertone.

"Then came the tasting. The 'bacon' taste was not quite as realistic as the fruit flavor in a Life Saver; the texture suggested thin strips of compressed sawdust.

"Wholesome? The contents listed on the package label indicate the absence of any unwholesome ingredients. Nutritious? Undoubtedly; after all, soya protein is protein. But as an experience in eating, my own conclusion is that these strips are to bacon as Masonite is to solid walnut, or as marbleized linoleum is to marble."

Escabeche

If the summer hath his joys, to borrow a phrase from the poet Thomas Campion, it also hath his dishes. Not the least of these is a category of foods, basically related to one another, that includes the escabeches of Spain and Latin America, the soused dishes of England, and certain marinated or vinaigrette dishes of France and Italy.

All are served cold and all have a combination of ingredients in common: a discreet amount of vinegar judiciously blended with herbs and spices and, often, with slices of lemon, lime, and onion and garlic.

I explored these foods recently when a

friend showed up at my doorstep with a pail of fresh-caught mackerel. My first impulse was to prepare these fish marinated in the French manner. But their abundance led me instead to recipes for soused mackerel. And etymological curiosity made me delve into the origins and techniques for preparing the similar escabeches, not only with fish and seafood, but also with chicken. The foods, all of which can be, indeed should be, made in advance, are ideal for picnics and summer buffets or as cold appetizers.

The word *escabeche* is Spanish, derived from the Arabic *sakbay,* which means a mixture or stew of meat with vinegar. As near as I can trace the history of escabeches, they are, like many dishes popular in Spain, of Arab origin.

One of the best and most famous escabeches is known as *perdices escabechadas,* partridges in escabeche. To prepare it, the partridges (I recently substituted squab chickens and Cornish game hens) are browned in olive oil and cooked with a preparation of dry white wine, garlic, and herbs.

English soused foods are almost identical to escabeches. Part of that pail of mackerel was soused using a traditional English recipe that called for arranging mackerel fillets in a baking dish, pouring over them a diluted vinegar mixture containing onions, herbs, and spices and baking until done. This was refrigerated overnight before serving.

The best-known French version of a soused food is probably marinated mackerel, to be found in cookbooks as *maquereaux marinés.*

There is to be found in Italian kitchens a preparation similar to these others, but far less well known. This consists of sardines in a savory sauce made with vinegar, onions, pine nuts, and raisins.

Escargots

See Conch.

Escarole

See Chicory.

Espresso

Although espresso coffee and café filtre are similar in character and, properly made, serve similar ends as a rich, dark brew, their method of preparation is different. Café filtre is made by the drip method with boiling water filtering slowly through dark roast grounds enclosed in the center section of a two-chamber coffeepot.

Espresso is made by machine with a steaming liquid forced through the instant coffee grounds, and this action gives the coffee its name, according to one of my correspondents:

"While, strictly speaking, the word in Italian means both 'very quick,' and 'pressed out,' the naming of the coffee was derived from the latter meaning. On the Italian espresso machines used in restaurants and other public places (of which we see regretfully few on these shores) a batch of ground coffee is placed into a holder that is then inserted tightly under a steam nozzle. Steam is injected into the coffee by lowering the lever handle of the valve, such as in the simple orange juice press. This downward pressing motion creates the impression of 'pressing' the juice out of the coffee into the cup. Hence 'espresso.' "

I have long held a special regard for Medaglia d'Oro and Bustelo, which I think produce the finest after-dinner brew packaged in a tin. Over the years I've never taken precise note of the quantities I use for an after-dinner brew, simply spooning it into a coffee maker by guess and by eye and adding water accordingly.

I felt constrained recently to read the instructions for making coffee on the Medaglia d'Oro can and find that they err in much the same direction that macaroni manufacturers err in their instructions for cooking pasta.

Almost invariably noodle makers tell you to cook their product from nine to twelve minutes (or some other range equally absurd), guaranteeing that the pasta will be hopelessly cooked to an unpalatable, too-limp state. The Medaglia d'Oro people recommended one tablespoon of their product for each demitasse cup.

In the first place, the capacity of demitasse cups varies greatly; in my own cabinet a set from Denmark contains ⅓ cup; another from England ½ cup, and that is a considerable difference when dealing with such small volumes of liquid.

To my mind, a ration of 1 tablespoon of dark roast coffee for each ¼ cup of water—about 2 tablespoons for each demitasse cup—will result in a good, substantial after-dinner brew. And if it isn't a substantial brew you're after, why dawdle with a dark roast, so-called after-dinner coffee brand?

Incidentally, I asked Sirio Maccioni of the esteemed Le Cirque restaurant in Manhattan, about the custom of serving espresso coffee with a twist of lemon peel. He assured me that lemon peel in after-dinner coffee is by no means a tradition nor a commonplace of any sort in his native land.

"It seems very much an American custom and it probably came about in this country many years ago when returning tourists had drunk an after-dinner coffee 'punch' in some sidewalk café in Italy," he said. "Such a punch—or *ponce,* as we call it—is generally made with coffee plus anisette or grappa or a mandarin liqueur. That plus lemon peel. In the South, they use rum and lemon peel. That punch is also called a 'caffè corretto,' or coffee with a correction."

Esrog

See Citron.

Etouffée

Etouffée, which means "smothered," is applied to dishes that are cooked in a tightly closed utensil with little or no liquid. The most famous crayfish recipe in Creole cookery is also called étouffée, and it consists of cooking vegetables such as chopped green pepper, onion, and celery in a roux, a blend of fat and flour cooked to the brown stage. You then add crayfish, including the crayfish "fat," plus a little liquid. This is cooked, generally uncovered, until the crayfish are tender.

Evaporated Milk

Evaporated milk is unsweetened whole milk that has been evaporated to half its volume.

In his book, *Kitchen Science,* Howard Hillman explains that evaporated milk is heated in the can to a temperature above 200 degrees to sterilize the milk. He adds that condensed milk does not have to be sterilized because it has a high sugar content that serves as a preservative and hinders bacterial growth.

One example of the differences in the cooking properties of the two milks: Sweetened condensed milk is the traditional base for Key lime pies. Add lime juice and egg yolks, plus sugar to the condensed milk and it will thicken without cooking. Do not substitute evaporated milk because the filling will not thicken.

Ff Ff

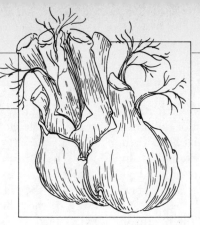

Fabada

The origin of the soup called fabada is the Asturias region of northern Spain. The soup is made like any bean soup with white beans, salt pork, smoked bacon, ham hocks, beef, onions, green pepper, cloves, tomatoes, potatoes, and the Spanish sausage known as *morcillas*. The sausages, for a genuine fabada, are essential. They are available in Hispanic markets.

Faisandé

See Game.

Falernum

Although I have never seen it in a recipe, falernum is a flavoring syrup made, I am told, of a simple sugar syrup to which is added lime, ginger, almonds, and spices.

It is made in Bermuda but originated more than two hundred years ago in Barbados. The name is said to derive from a wine that dates from Roman times. It is used primarily as a flavoring for drinks made of rum, but I know of no reason it could not be used as a flavoring for cakes and cookies. The alcohol content is about 6 percent.

Fallow Deer

Fallow deer, according to one book on game, are known scientifically as *Dama dama* or *Dama mesopotamica*. They have a yellow coat spotted with white in the summer. The male of the species has broad, flattened antlers. In another book on game cookery, I read that the best deer for eating purposes is the roe deer, followed in order of preference by the fallow deer.

Farmer Cheese

See Cottage cheese.

Fat

The professional way to remove fat from the surface of broths and stews is to use a ladle and skim the fat off frequently as the broth or stew cooks. This is particularly important for the first half-hour of cooking.

Another method, and one that I use when preparing chili con carne, for example, is to blot the surface of the stew with several layers of absorbent paper toweling as the stew cooks.

Another method is to let the broth or stew cool and then refrigerate it. The fat will solidify on top and can be spooned and scraped off. There are, of course, cups with spouts especially designed for ridding a broth of fat.

Feijoada

King John VI of Portugal, who lived from 1779 to 1826, fled to Brazil with the royal family during the first decade of the nineteenth century and there set up his court. He probably died unaware that he was, in a sense, father of one of the great dishes of the world, Brazil's famed feijoada.

His presence, at least, is credited with the beginnings of the dish in the mind of Dorotea Elman, who makes without question the best and most ambitious feijoada (pronounced fay-joe-ahda) I've ever been privileged to dine on, and I've dined on several, including one for which composer Heitor Villa-Lobos scribbled a small, unfinished fugue in the cook's notebook.

"Beans have always been a staple in my country," explained the Brazilian-born Mrs. Elman, "the constant diet of the poor. The everyday bean dish is called feijao [pronounced, vaguely, fay-jaw], which may be simply a dish of beans flavored and cooked with a bay leaf and a pig's tail."

According to Mrs. Elman, it was King John who imported slaves from Africa into Brazil, and it was the African influence that raised the feijao to its ultimate glory as feijoada.

"The African influence is very much apparent in the extraordinary use of various parts of the pig that had never made their way to the white man's table—pig's ears, pig's feet—as well as collard greens and, perhaps, even mandioca [manioc] flour, which is made with ground cassava root."

A feijoada completa is one of the most festive dishes known to man, and I wholeheartedly agree with Mrs. Elman's long considered appraisal that it is also one of the most sensual.

"There is this extraordinary blending of textures—the coarseness of the manioc flour, the seductive flavor of the beans cooked with meats, the crunchiness of onion and collard greens—the marvelous combination of flavors—tomato and oranges and hot peppers and, of course, the substantial but tender variety of sausages and meats. There's a good bit of voodoo involved in all of this."

I have yet to meet the person, including myself, who on being introduced to the dish, did not start rhapsodizing in a similar vein.

Although there are more than a score of components to the best feijoada, including the basic bean dish with its meats and the cold garnishes, there are an infinite number of conceivable and acceptable mutations. The dish calls, for example, for two kinds of Portuguese sausages, which are available at special sources. For these, Polish or other sausages commonly found in supermarkets could be substituted. Fresh pork hocks could be substituted for the odd parts of the pig, such as the tail, ears, and foot. The ears could be eliminated altogether, and so on.

The workings of a proper feijoada are as follows: The meats, including the sausages, are thinly sliced and arranged neatly on platters. The meats with the beans, which have somewhat disintegrated into a fantastic dark sauce, are served hot in a separate dish. So is the rice.

The garnishes, all of which are served separately, include a cold onion sauce, the hot shredded collard greens, a tomato and heart of palm vinaigrette, a cold orange salad, the manioc flour plus hot peppers. The flour is always browned when Mrs. Elman makes a feijoada and blended with olives and eggs. In many homes it is simply served raw.

Fennel

Fennel is a crisp, aromatic vegetable or herb that, for one reason or another, is more closely identified with the Italian table than any other. It is established that it was known in England, however, long before the Norman Conquest and that for centuries it has been traditional throughout Europe for use with both fresh and salted fish.

Fennel is most commonly served in America as a cold appetizer, like radishes, celery ribs, and scallions.

Its association with fish is, however, undeniable, and one of the most felicitous dishes of the French kitchen is *loup de mer au fenouil,* which is to say, a kind of sea bass, grilled and flamed with dried fennel leaves and stalks.

Legend has it that at one point in history, fennel was inalterably associated with fish in Europe, and on fast days the very wealthy dined on fish with fennel. The poor on those days dined, it is related, on fennel alone, the fish in absentia.

Fennel is known as *fenouil* in French,

fenchel in German, *finocchio* in Italian, and *hinojo* in Spanish. Although it is delicious eaten out of hand, it is an enormously versatile vegetable when cooked. It is excellent in salads; it makes a fine hot soup; it complements baked fish dishes; it is fine braised and served with a meat sauce; and it excels when cooked au gratin with grated Parmesan cheese.

Fenugreek

Fenugreek seeds are widely used in Indian cooking. In *An Invitation to Indian Cookery,* Madhur Jaffrey says that the seeds are yellow in color and rather flat and adds: "Since their taste borders on bitterness, very few are used at a time. They are excellent with eggplant and potatoes."

Fermière

In classic French cooking, the garnish known as fermière consists of vegetables—notably carrots, turnips, onions, and celery—cooked as slowly as possible in butter until they almost fall apart.

The result is served as a garnish for large cuts of meat that have been roasted or braised. The vegetable mixture is often served inside artichoke bottoms and with braised lettuce as an accompaniment.

Chances are that you will find such an accompaniment in kitchens that turn out nouvelle cuisine.

Feta

Feta cheese is usually produced by shepherds in the mountain regions near Athens. Traditionally it is made from ewe's milk, but frequently it is made from goat's milk.

One difference between the Greek feta—whether it is made from ewe's milk or goat's milk—and the French chèvre is that feta is invariably contained in a brine solution. There are mild, medium, and sharp feta cheeses depending on the strength of flavor. They are generally sold directly from the brine solution, which may be made with milk and salt or water and salt.

Feta has a curious and delectable affinity for anchovies, black olives, and tomatoes.

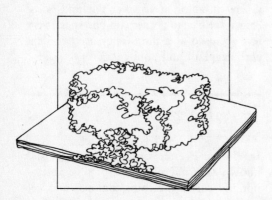

Fettuccine

Both fettuccine and fettuccelle stem from the word *fettuccia* in Italian. Fettuccia means ribbon. As nearly as I can determine, fettuccine means small ribbons, and is one of the most widely used and widely available of noodles. Fettuccelle also means little ribbons, but is slightly narrower than fettuccine. It is my opinion that they could be used interchangeably.

Fiddleheads

Fiddleheads, or crosiers, are the coiled young fronds of ostrich ferns or bracken ferns that are plucked when they are four to eight inches tall. The name comes from the curved shape of the head of the frond, which is not unlike the tuning end of a violin. They are popular on Canadian tables and in the northern parts of the United States. When they are freshly picked, they are especially delicious; I find them only acceptable when canned or frozen.

Some authorities describe fiddleheads as

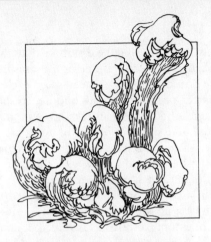

resembling asparagus, but I do not find this to be true in either taste or texture; I find them more like tender string beans. They may be treated like asparagus in cooking; however, buttered or served with a hollandaise or vinaigrette sauce. They should be cooked only briefly, just until they lose their raw taste.

Fig Newton

A spokesman for Nabisco, manufacturer of Fig Newtons, is an honest man if ever there was one. He states that the company has no certain knowledge of the origin of the name. It is presumed by many, he added, that the product was produced by a bakery in Newton, Massachusetts, but this is pure conjecture.

I have since been given many explanations for the name. A Connecticut gentleman wrote to state that he had an older brother who served in the First World War, and "he bought me some Fig Newtons and told me they were developed with the encouragement of the government to meet a need for a high-energy, small-sized food item. It was named after Newton Baker, who was Secretary of the Army at that time."

A columnist on *The Albuquerque Tribune* claims to have known the original "Newton."

"We heard this story," she states, "from Newton himself. The 'Newton' is the late J. Newton Rumble, who lived in Albuquerque for many years and died in 1976. He was born in Clinton, Iowa, and grew up in Tipton, Iowa.

"When he was about nine years old, the owner of the Iden Biscuit Company in either Clinton or Tipton created two cookies. One was a square ginger cookie named for Helen Iden, daughter of the owner, and the other was a fig-and-batter cookie named Newton for her school friend. That was about 1907. Rumble worked for the company for a while after graduating from the University of Iowa. The Iden Biscuit Company later was sold to Nabisco, which marketed the now-famous cookie with the original name."

Finally, a spokesman for the Gramercy Cook Shop in Manhattan contributed the following information taken from *Out of the Cracker Barrel, the Nabisco Story from Animal Crackers to Zuzus,* by William Cahn.

Just before the introduction of the Fig Newton, "Cookies and crackers had been named Brighton, Boston Family, Cambridge Salts, Beacon Hill, Shrewsbury, Melrose. The exciting new product . . . needed some such name. Later an assistant to James Hazen, manager of the Cambridgeport bakery, recalled, 'The name was taken from the name of the town of Newton—a suburb of Boston.' When this name was selected, it reflected a practice—by Mr. Hazen, who was manager of this plant—of using the names of towns and cities in the vicinity of Boston."

Filé Powder

Filé powder is a traditional seasoning and thickening agent used in the preparation of gumbos in the South and is usually added after the gumbo is cooked and just before serving. The powder is made from the dried leaves of the sassafras plant.

I was fascinated by one cook's technique for making the filé in the home.

"I have here at my home two acres of woodlands in which, beneath a tall canopy of oaks, the main growth of underbrush is young sassafras. Each spring some of the leaves have been removed to be dried for making filé.

"Drying has in the past required special conditions and several weeks' time. This year I have a microwave oven which makes drying a cinch. Hence, my filé supply is unlimited in quantity.

"My method is this: I pick the young leaves and dry them immediately in the micro oven until crisp but still quite green in color. I place the dried leaves and tender stems in the blender at moderately high speed until a coarse or fine powder obtains."

See also Gumbo.

Filo

See Phyllo pastry.

Finnan Haddie

Since I first encountered finnan haddie on a breakfast menu at the Connaught Hotel in London more than twenty-five years ago,

it has been my long-held notion that this smoked-fish delicacy is one of the consummate breakfast foods of the world. Give me a platter of choice finnan haddie, freshly cooked in its bath of water and milk, add melted butter, a slice or two of hot toast, a pot of steaming Darjeeling tea, and you may tell the butler to dispense with the caviar, truffles, and nightingales' tongues.

On a trip to Spain, I was enchanted to learn of a possibility—however remote—that one of my ancestors "invented" finnan haddie (the name derives from haddock smoked on the seaside banks of Findon, Scotland), and, in my books, that is something to celebrate. My mother, a Craig by birth, always claimed that she was descended from Scottish nobility. I forget which king or queen it was. I was not impressed. But, ah! to think that the sweet smell of smoke under haddock is part of my ancestry; that is something else.

In crossing the street in Barcelona, I stepped off a curb and broke two small bones in my foot. A young man, a merchant captain named James Buckett, saw my body crumple to the ground and rushed to my side. He aided me back to the hotel, fed me aspirins, and, as I waited a doctor's decision, we talked.

The talk, of course, veered to food, and I told him of my great fondness for finnan haddie. Jim told me that he was from Aberdeen, Scotland, only six miles from Findon. He laughed.

"Did you know it is entirely possible that finnan haddie was first 'created' a long, long time ago by one of your ancestors on your mother's side of the family?"

I told him, no, of course not.

"Like you," he said, "my mother was a Craig. All the Craigs have been fishing people and lived up and down the Scottish coast

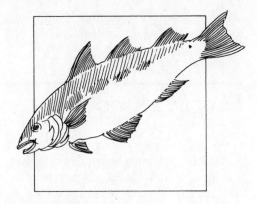

around Aberdeen.

"The 'discovery' of finnan haddie was accidental and had to do with a house fire. I can't fill you in on the details, but I have an uncle named James Lees in Aberdeen who can. Drop him a note. He's the family historian. As for me, I must run now. My plane leaves in an hour and I've a boat to catch." He gave me Mr. Lees's address and departed.

When I returned to New York, I wrote James Lees and explained the circumstances of my writing. I received the following in response:

"My grandmother, Helen Wood, was born in 1812 in a small fishing village called Findon, known locally as Finnan, situated about seven miles south of Aberdeen.

"Helen grew up in this village, whose livelihood depended on the menfolk going to sea in small boats called yawls. In those boats they pitted their wits, skills, and energy against the sea to reap its harvest.

"These yawls were without decks, compass, or engine and were propelled by sail or oar, but the fishermen, nevertheless, ventured thirty-eight or forty miles off shore to cast or 'shed' their fishing lines.

"It isn't surprising that disaster was forever close at hand, and personal tragedies—

lost limbs and frequently death—were something the community lived with.

"The women had an important role to play because, in addition to caring for large families, they also assumed the arduous tasks of baiting the lines with mussels, gutting and cleaning the fish, then processing the fish by tying the tails of a few fish firmly together with dry grass and eventually hanging these bunches over rods known as tinters.

"These tinters hung overnight in the fish sheds or 'hoosies.' The following day the fish were packed into vast wicker baskets called creels. In the absence of an available market, the fisherwomen strung the creels around their necks and shoulders with ropes and off they went to 'hawk' or sell their fish at farms, crofts, and villages ten or fifteen miles inland.

"In 1835, my grandmother married her true love, a fisherman called James Craig, and in time brought up her family, baited the lines, cleaned, prepared, and hawked the fish.

"Everything seemed to go according to predestined plan until one summer morning some 128 years ago, when my grandmother woke to discover wisps of smoke seeping from the fish shed. It appeared that sawdust strewn on the floor to absorb the moisture dripping from the fish had caught fire.

"The family speculated later that the fire was started by the refraction of light from the sun as it passed through the primitive, handcrafted glass of the windowpanes. A spark of heat had ignited a fragment of sawdust in the afternoon and that had gone unnoticed when the hoosie was closed shortly before dusk."

Whatever the cause, Mrs. Craig discovered, "to her great mortification, that half the precious catch of fish had been 'damaged' by smoke and they were now golden yellow in color.

"She decided they were still edible, however, and as she set out on her journey, her creel was filled with fresh white fish. But on her arm she carried a basketful of the smoke-damaged haddocks. As she walked along the country roads, she offered each of her customers a gift of the smoked fish. In those days of hardship, there were few to refuse such bounty.

"To her astonishment, when she returned to these customers a few days later, she was repeatedly beseeched for fresh supplies of the 'smoked yellow haddocks.'

"In that brief period, according to family records, finnan haddie came about. From that day on, the sawdust in the hoosie was deliberately set alight and allowed to smolder. The fish drying houses became kilns, and another cottage industry was born.

"You come to Scotland and I can assure you of, one, a warm welcome, and two, a plate of 'yellow smoked haddock' poached in milk or fried with bacon and eggs, and you will come to understand that Northeast folks over here know what's good for them."

The proper way to poach finnan haddie for breakfast or brunch is to place it (defrosted, if frozen) in a skillet with water barely to cover. Add about ½ cup of milk and, if desired, 1 bay leaf, 2 cloves, and 2 slices of onion. Bring to the boil but do not boil. Let the haddock gently simmer about 2 minutes, or until the fish is piping hot. Do not cook long or it will toughen and become fibrous. Drain the fish, spoon it onto hot plates, and pour hot melted butter over it. Serve immediately with lemon halves on the side and a pepper mill for those who wish it. After a first course of freshly squeezed orange juice, serve the fish with buttered, boiled potatoes, buttered toast, marmalade, and tea or champagne. Breakfast coffee is not a suitable drink with smoked fish.

Fireplace Cookery

In this age of energy consciousness, fireplace cookery is suddenly a better idea than ever. It is an interesting challenge, and a watched pot (one has to watch the pot and tend the fire) can create an exceptional appetite.

Clean out the fireplace, removing the grate if there is one. Place four fire or flue bricks toward the rear of the fireplace flat side down, domino fashion. (Do not use ordinary red bricks for this. Fire bricks can be bought at builders' supply companies for about forty cents each.) Place them parallel left to right with five or six inches of space between each brick. Arrange two or three more bricks in front of these on which a fireproof casserole can be placed. Leave space between the bricks for hot coals. Construct the fire on and behind the rear bricks. Use long-burning hardwood such as oak or apple. Do not use an oily wood (like pine) that may impart flavor. Use as little

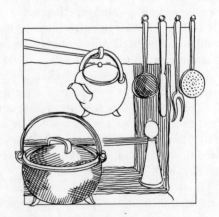

paper as possible in lighting the fire. Let the wood fire burn until most of the flames subside and the wood is fiery hot. Shovel some of the hot natural charcoal beneath the casserole and keep the hot wood situated close around the casserole. Replenish the wood as necessary to ensure constant cooking.

Fish

I am passionately fond of fish and care not a fig if the fish comes from rivers, lakes, oceans, or streams. The essential thing, however, is that the fish be fresh and clean to the taste. I've been asked frequently over the years for the simple formula of determining if a fish has been newly taken and this is it. The fish should above all have a clear, piercing brilliance in its eyes. The opposite is a dull, glazed opacity. The gills located within the head should have a lively red hue. The opposite is a tired and wasted look. And then there is the flesh to be accounted for. A fresh fish will have a stiffness, the equivalent of muscle tone. If the flesh is flabby and limp, it may be best to shop elsewhere or alter the menu.

Fisherman's Joke

There is an Italian dish called *scherzo del pescatore*, which means "a fisherman's joke." It refers to a platter of cooked (fried, I presume) small squid or calamaretti, customarily eaten by popping them whole into the mouth. Planted somewhere in the platter of seafood is one squid, the sac of which has been filled with hot red pepper.

Fish Gills

In instructions for fish broth, I generally say, "Use fish bones and preferably the head with gills removed."

The note about the gills is stressed for the cooks of the world who are not fortunate enough to live by the ocean. If you have a fish freshly caught, there is no reason to remove the gills. If you are working with a fish a day or so old, the gills are the first part to take on an off-odor and an off-taste because of the blood that is naturally inherent in them.

Five-Spice Powder

Five-spice powder is a blend of powdered star anise, fennel, cinnamon, cloves, and peppercorns. Sometimes referred to as five-fragrance powder and five-flavor powder, it is used primarily, I believe, for poultry and meats. It is available in many stores that specialize in Oriental products, and you can find limitless quantities in good grocery stores and supermarkets that sell Chinese foods.

One blend I know calls for 60 pepper-corns, 4 whole star anise, 2 teaspoons fennel seeds, 4 one-inch pieces stick cinnamon, and 12 whole cloves. Using an electric blender, blend this to a powder to produce about 1½ to 2 tablespoons. Store in a small, tightly sealed screw-top jar or plastic bag.

Flageolets

I have frequently spoken of perfect harmonies in food, and one of the celestial combinations is lamb and flageolets. Flageolets are small green kidney beans available both dried and tinned in this country. Most of them are imported from France, and the boxes are frequently labeled haricots secs.

Flaming Dishes

As any novice in the dining room can tell you, theatrics can play an interesting role in creating appetite or, to put it another way, in stimulating the sale of food. That's why Americans went through that silly fad of flaming dishes for a couple of decades. It was pure razzmatazz and razzle-dazzle. In most cases, the flames never so much as licked the top of the shish kebab, or whatever.

There are times, of course, when flames can serve a useful if not vital purpose. Flaming crêpes suzette are nice, and the flame does help burn off the alcohol. But the alcohol will evaporate in any event, as the sauce for the crêpes simmers. A very wise old maître d'hôtel told his students many years ago that the principal thing about flaming dishes in the dining room was that

you could add twenty-five cents to the cost of the dish, and if you did it with enough panache, it would increase the amount of the tip.

Flank Steak

Keenly observant students of Chinese cook-books printed in English may note that a dominant number of recipes calling for beef specify flank steak. Similarly, a vast majority of the recipes calling for stir-fried dishes made with beef, pork, chicken, shrimp, or whatever call for the addition of one or more egg whites.

I was, therefore, vastly amused when someone asked me, "What, in the name of heaven, happens to the rest of the beef and the yolks of the eggs?"

It was a thought I had not previously pondered; and it took the occasion of a visit to the kitchen of one of New York's finest Chinese chefs to find out.

The chef is Wen Dah Tai, better known as Uncle Tai. He is Peking-born, fifty-six years old, and is known as uncle because uncle is a title of respect in his native land. Hunan is, of course, the Chinese province whose food is, like that of Szechuan, characteristically fiery-hot to the palate. Proprietors of Hunanese restaurants tend to claim it is even more so. Uncle Tai, who is sober-minded and portly, told me over a cup of tea that flank steak in America most closely resembles in flavor and texture the hip steak that is most commonly used in China and Formosa. He hastened to add—through an interpreter, he does not speak English—that the remainder of the cow was in no sense wasted or ignored in the Chinese kitchen.

"The fillet, which is the most expensive, is always cut into neat cubes and used in high-class banquet dishes; the shin of beef, the juiciest part of the beef, goes into a cold appetizer, five-flavored beef; and the rest of the animal goes into casserole dishes." Beef, he added, is expensive in China, which is one reason for the number of pork and chicken dishes on the menus.

As for those egg yolks, they are directed toward fried rice, a few tons of which are consumed in Chinese restaurants throughout America each day.

Florentine

The commonest usage of the name florentine in French cookery has to do with dishes containing spinach. Thus there is a soufflé florentine; eggs or fish florentine, in which poached eggs or poached fish are served on a bed of spinach and glazed with a Mornay sauce; and *crème florentine,* or cream of spinach soup.

Flour

Although there are many kinds of flour in this world, including cornstarch, made from corn and also known as corn flour, and rice flour, made from rice, the most common flours are made with wheat.

The characteristics of wheat vary. Most flours are made from "soft" wheat, "hard" wheat, or a combination. All-purpose flour is a blend of hard and soft wheat flour. Cake flour is, by and large, made primarily from soft wheat.

You can substitute all-purpose flour for cake flour by measuring 2 tablespoons

cornstarch into a 1-cup container and then sifting all-purpose flour over the cornstarch until the container is full when leveled at the top.

Semolina is a flour made from a hardy wheat called durum. "Whole" wheat flour is made by grinding the entire kernel of wheat into flour. Semolina is made from the center kernel of wheat known as the endosperm. This kernel is broken up and sifted, or bolted.

The largest particles of the endosperm are the semolina, which produces a hard or "strong" flour used in bread and pasta making.

Self-rising flour is a flour that contains a leavening, such as baking powder and salt. It is not an uncommon ingredient in America and was often used in my family kitchen when I was a child in the South, but I have never understood the need for it when it is so easy to add your own leavenings.

The flour is used to make self-rising biscuits and other breads. Some cooks are opposed to it, for after a certain amount of time on the shelf, the effectiveness of the leavening is dissipated. I am advised that if you do use it you should not add more salt to the basic ingredients.

As to the necessity for sifting flour, it is

my belief that years ago it was the better part of wisdom to do so for the simple reason that small insects were fairly common in most flour barrels. That was in the days when most of the flour consumed in America was sold in bulk form. But today it is not essential.

On the other hand, if you have a reliable source that specifies sifting the flour, by all means do it. That would indicate that the recipe had been tested with sifted flour and, therefore, it should be sifted. Quite logically, sifted flour is lighter than that which is taken directly from the bag, and, thus, it weighs less than unsifted flour. And it is the weight of the flour rather than the volume that has a direct bearing on the end results of a dish.

If I do need to sift flour, I shake out the flour from my sifter after each use. When, on those rare occasions, I find it necessary to give the sifter a thorough cleaning, I entrust that job to my handy electric dishwasher. On the other hand, my sifter is an all-metal utensil (specifically, a Foley five-cup sifter) purchased several years ago. It has had many a bath without damage. Some sifters, particularly those with wooden parts, may not take kindly to the dishwasher treatment. In that case, simply soak the sieve portion in hot water with detergent and then clean it by hand.

Flummery

Considering the origins of this nation, it seems curious that the cuisines of America are not more solidly based on the cooking of Britain. There are several well-known "borrowed" dishes that do exist—Yorkshire pudding, finnan haddie, Cheddar cheese, Scotch woodcock, fish and chips, lemon curd, and trifles—but there are not many.

It came as something of a surprise to learn that many people considered flummery an American creation, most of them having dined on it throughout their childhoods. The most popular of these Yankee versions of flummery is one made with fresh blackberries stewed with sugar and thickened with cornstarch.

But flummeries as known in Britain, where they originated, are sometimes made with oatmeal cooked until gelatinous, sometimes with granular or sheet gelatin, and sometimes like an English custard with flour, milk, and eggs.

Foie Gras

Saying a few words in praise of the finest pâté de foie gras is tantamount to saying a few nice things about the pyramids, the Taj Mahal, the Rheims cathedral, the soil of Burgundy, or the cream and butter of Normandy. Where man-made foods are concerned, foie gras is purely and simply the ultimate creation.

Larousse Gastronomique, the authoritative dictionary of gastronomy, quotes C.

Gerard, the author of *L'Ancienne Alsace à table,* as follows: "The goose is nothing, but man has made of it an instrument for the output of a marvelous product, a kind of living hothouse in which grows the supreme fruit of gastronomy." That "fruit," the product of force-fed geese, is, of course, foie gras.

There is to my mind one consummate liaison in the world of food, and that is fresh foie gras, black truffles, and Sauternes, preferably Château d'Yquem or Château Sigalas-Rabaud. The colors of the three together are classic: the burnished golden yellow of the wine, the stygian blackness of the truffles, and the admirably rosy look of the foie gras. The color is roseate, mottled, and blended with a delicate beige. Genuine foie gras, when sliced, is like a free-form mosaic, although its markings may seem a trifle blurred. Also, the best foie gras has a vibrant look, although this, too, is by nature muted. The texture of foie gras is silken and velvety. It is as rich as butter but, gloriously, will not so quickly melt in your mouth.

There are a multitude of foods that for better or for worse are labeled foie gras, which literally means "fat liver." There is a foie gras of duck that is excellent and a foie gras of goose that is infinitely superior.

The zenith in foie gras is the whole goose liver, deveined, macerated, and gently simmered in a broth seasoned with herbs and spices. It is a luxury and it is costly. At the other end of the scale both in flavor and price is the most common form of foie gras—actually a pâté that may contain such diverse elements as pork meat, pork livers, eggs, onions, flour, or cornstarch.

Next there is a mousse and a purée of foie gras that consists of puréed duck or goose liver and may contain such other elements as pork, pork liver, eggs, and so on.

This is more delicate, less compact in texture than a pâté or whole foie gras.

And finally there is a cream of foie gras that is puréed even more finely than a mousse or cream and has a smoother texture. But the texture of a pâté, a mousse, or a cream is no guide to quality. And any or all products labeled foie gras may or may not contain truffles.

Further complicating the world of goose liver, the various preparations are packed in a plethora of tins with varying shapes. There are tunnels (trapezoidal tins), lingots (oblong tins), blocs that may be tunnel-shaped, round, or oval, and a *boîte rouleau,* which is cylindrical. Foie gras comes in *bocaux,* hermetically sealed glass jars, or in fancy terrines, round porcelain crocks, fancily decorated and more expensive because of the packaging.

Before buying foie gras, the first thing to do is check the label for contents. Many foie gras products, some of the best-known brands, in fact, contain preservatives in the form of sodium nitrite and ascorbic acid. Several of the pâtés, mousses, and so on contain either flour or cornstarch that is no credit to the finished product.

Such rules as do govern the foie gras industry in France are these: The blocs (which also include parfait-blocs and baby blocs), tunnels, pâtés, and terrines must contain a minimum of 75 percent pure foie gras—whole, chopped, puréed, or otherwise—plus truffles and lard, which is used as a liner. That is wholly acceptable.

The tins or whatever contain foie gras that is puréed, made into a mousse or a cream, must have "a minimum content of 75 percent genuine foie gras. The remaining 25 percent is composed of truffles, eggs, and filler," the French government says. That is playing it loose. A teaspoon of genuine foie gras and a slice of truffle would easily meet those demands.

When he was visiting my home, Jacques Grimaud, one of the leading producers of foie gras in France, told me that he raises ten thousand specially fattened geese each year and twenty thousand ducks, which are also fattened. The livers from both birds are processed as foie gras and the meat is turned into a confit, or preserved dish, also canned.

Foie gras begins with the fattening of the poultry and this requires from four to five months. The geese or ducks are fed for a short while on bran. The diet is then changed to nettles and cabbage with lots of water. For three months they dine on grass; after four months, on wheat and oats. During the final two weeks they are fed corn that has been cooked in water or milk.

When the geese or ducks have been killed, the livers are soaked in milk and then drained. Before cooking, the livers are marinated with salt, a touch of nutmeg, pepper, Armagnac, and port wine. The livers are then either pressure-cooked or baked.

I was fascinated to learn that although more than two million pounds of foie gras are processed in France each year, less than half the livers are from domestic geese. French foie gras producers must necessarily rely on imports, chiefly from Poland, Hungary, Czechoslovakia, and Israel. Israel, Mr. Grimaud said, produces and exports to France enormous quantities of the raw livers. Israeli foie gras, he adds, is some of the finest in the world.

A word or two about serving foie gras, fresh or tinned:

It is best served with fresh, hot buttered toast on chilled plates and, for my taste at least, it should be served while the guests are at the table. It is not "lap food."

Foie gras should be kept refrigerated until about ten minutes before serving. It is best cut with a knife (or a spoon from an earthenware crock) that has been dipped in piping hot water. It may be served with a small leaf of lettuce and, if desired, chopped aspic.

If you want to splurge with a bottle of Sauternes, it should be fully iced before serving.

Fork

The first fork, I am told, was two-pronged. Gradually, the fork took on a third prong, and finally a fourth one.

Larousse Gastronomique says that the fork is at least two thousand years old and is mentioned in the Old Testament. But the Book of Samuel notes that it was used in those days to spear pieces of meat that were used sacrificially.

The Italians, it seems, were the first to accept the use of forks on anything like a wide scale instead of merely as a means of serving food. The common folk used forks made of iron; the nobility used forks of silver.

An eleventh-century scholar named Damiani observed that forks were introduced to the society of Venice by a Byzantine princess. Toward the end of the fourteenth century, they were listed in the inventory of King Charles V of France, and during the reign of Edward II of England, from 1307 to 1327, mention is made of the use of a fork by one Piers Gaveston while eating a pear.

But an English traveler named Thomas Coryate is credited with bringing the fork from Italy to England in 1608. Coryate was quick to adapt to using a fork, although he subjected himself to the scorn and ridicule of his fellows at table. A particularly nasty type once labeled him "furciferous," a term meaning, in zoology, "having a forked appendage," or, more casually, "rascally."

But these isolated cases, *Larousse* explains, "do not mean that forks were in general use. In fact, eating with forks did not become all that fashionable until the seventeenth century." The work cites a French treatise on manners and customs dated 1545 in which the author dictates how a well-educated person should behave at table: "Take the meat with three fingers and do not fill your mouth with too big pieces. Do not keep your hands for long on the dish."

Another arbiter wrote in 1530 that "it is a great breach of etiquette when your fingers are dirty and greasy, to bring them to your mouth in order to lick them, or to clean them on your jacket. It would be more decent to use the tablecloth."

Fortified Wine

A fortified wine is one to which a degree of brandy is added during the fermentation of the wine to stop the fermenting process. This causes the wine to be sweeter than a table wine and to have a higher alcoholic content.

Unlike the dry still wines, fortified or apéritif wines are generally added shortly before a sauce is ready to serve. These wines lack acidity for the most part and are used as a direct, unreduced flavoring: lobster in sherry wine sauce, for example, consommé with a glass of port, kidneys in a Madeira sauce, and so on. Even when these wines are used at the beginning of sauce making,

it is generally customary to add another dash before serving.

Fortnum & Mason

There is probably not a food anthology in or out of print that doesn't refer to the Christmas dinner served in the Cratchits' home in Dickens' *Christmas Carol*.

Rarely mentioned and little known, however, is another Dickens gem, a marvelously descriptive passage about food and celebration in an essay on the derby at Epsom Downs. Specifically, the passage deals with the early years and influence of that grand food emporium, Fortnum & Mason.

I discovered it while delving into the life of Isabella Beeton, who wrote the classic *Mrs. Beeton's Book of Household Management,* first published in 1861.

On the great day of the derby, Dickens wrote, all the roads leading to the track were "so thronged and blocked by every description of carriage that it is marvelous to consider how, when, and where they were all made—out of what possible wealth they are all maintained—and by what laws the supply of horses is kept equal to the demand . . . barouches, phaetons, broughams, gigs, four-wheeled chaises, four-in-hands, hansom cabs, cabs of lesser note, chaise-carts, donkey-carts, tilted vans made arborescent with green boughs and carrying no end of people, and a cask of beer . . . equestrians, pedestrians, horse-dealers, gentlemen, notabilities, and swindlers, by tens of thousands."

"Never, to be sure," Dickens wrote, "were there so many carriages, so many fours, so many twos, so many ones, so many horsemen, so many people who have come down by 'rail,' so many fine ladies in so many broughams, so many of Fortnum & Mason's hampers, so much ice and champagne! If I were on the turf, and had a horse to enter for the Derby, I would call that horse Fortnum & Mason, convinced that with that name he would beat the field. Public opinion would bring him in somehow. Look where I will—in connection with the carriages—made fast upon the top, or occupying the box, or tied up behind, or dangling below, or peeping out of a window—I see Fortnum & Mason. And now, Heavens! all the hampers fly wide open, and the green Downs burst into a blossom of lobster-salad."

On the Monday before the race, the author continues, he made a tour of the "Grand Stand," and was lured into the basement by the smell of cooking, where he found:

"Wine-cellars, beer-cellars, larders, sculleries, and kitchens, all as gigantically appointed, and as copiously furnished as if they formed part of an Ogre's castle. To furnish the refreshment saloon, the Grand Stand has in store two thousand four hundred tumblers, one thousand two hundred wine-glasses, three thousand plates and dishes . . . a whole flock of sixty-five lambs have to be roasted, and dished, and garnished, by the Derby Day. Twenty rounds of beef, four hundred lobsters, one hundred and fifty tongues, twenty fillets of veal, one hundred sirloins of beef, five hundred spring chickens, three hundred and fifty pigeon pies; a countless number of quartern loaves, and an incredible quantity of ham have to be cut up into sandwiches; eight hundred eggs have got to be boiled for the pigeon pies and salads. The forest of lettuces, the acres of cress, and beds of rad-

ishes, which will have to be chopped up; the gallons of 'dressing' that will have to be poured out and converted into salads for the insatiable Derby Day, will be best understood by a memorandum from the chief of that department to the chef-de-cuisine, which happened, incidentally, to fall under our notice: 'Pray don't forget a large tub and a birchbroom for mixing the salad!' "

Fortune Cookies

The only history of "Chinese" fortune cookies that I have ever seen came from a source in the San Joaquin Valley in California. A librarian there once wrote that the cookies originated in the bakery of a man named David Tsung. The date of their invention is given as 1818 or 1819.

The story goes that Mr. Tsung first prepared them with an egg roll casing and that the fortunes were first written as messages of goodwill prepared by a Presbyterian minister. As time passed he experimented with different types of batter to be used as casings until the standard casing used today was developed. It was 1922 or 1923 that the whimsical "fortunes" now used came into being.

One researcher disputes this. He writes: "According to Ray Clary, historian of San Francisco's Golden Gate Park, 'Chinese' fortune cookies as we know them today were invented not by a Chinese at all but by Makota Hagiwara, longtime caretaker of the Japanese tea garden in the park. The practice was begun by Mr. Hagiwara in 1907 upon his return to the tea garden as caretaker after having been thrown out by

anti-Oriental Mayor James Phelan at about the turn of the century. Thus they were a kind of 'thank you' to those who had helped him make the comeback to his former position.

"Incidentally, I find your report of a Chinese in the San Joaquin Valley in 1818 or 1819 rather incredible in that there were no Americans in the area at the time, much less Chinese. California was still Spanish territory."

He adds that "George Hagiwara, grandson of the fortune cookie's inventor, is still alive and well and living in San Francisco."

In Grace Chu's book, *Madame Chu's Cooking School,* she says that in China "birth announcements have been known to be sent wrapped in sweet dough. In one ancient Chinese parlor game, players were instructed to compose wise or witty sayings and write them on a scrap of paper inside a twisted cake."

She adds: "However, the fortune cookie, as we Americans know it, was invented in the United States. George Jung, who immigrated to Los Angeles in 1911 and founded the Hong Kong Noodle Company in 1916, is credited with the invention."

Fortune cookies are made of flour, sugar, water, and eggs. The batter is dropped onto a hot griddle and stamped into a cookie shape. After quick cooking the batter is lifted from the griddle, a paper fortune is put in the center, and the still-warm cookie is folded, either by hand or by machine, into its customary shape.

Fraise de Veau

Fraise de veau is the mesentery of the calf (mesentery, if you must know, is "peritoneal folds that join the intestines to the back abdominal wall"). Anatomy aside, fraise de veau has nothing to do with strawberries. The uses to which it is put include, according to Escoffier, deep-frying, cooking with onions like tripe, in blanquettes, in fricassee, and with sauce rémoulade. But it is not all that common in French kitchens.

Frankfurter

The ingredients for frankfurters vary greatly from one manufacturer to another.

One recipe source states that the meats used in preparing frankfurters range from lean bull or cow trimmings to regular pork trimmings, beef cheeks, skinned pork jowls, trimmed pork cheeks, fat pork trimmings, fat beef trimmings, and pork fat.

The best hot dogs are made from first-quality meat, whether that includes trimmings or not. Those of lowest quality are made from less desirable trimmings.

It is said that the term "hot dog" first came into use in 1900, but no one apparently knows the precise origin or first use of the term.

French Fries

One source says that French fries were first cooked in America in the late 1800s and were known as French fried potatoes until the 1930s, when they began being referred to as French fries. Clearly their lineage can be traced to France, where they are called *pommes frites*.

French fried potatoes are cut into strips two inches or so long and almost one-half inch wide. They are deep-fried until crisp and brown. Ideally, they should be fried twice, once without browning and then drained, and a second time just before serving to yield a crisper, more golden product.

French Toast

French toast is a dish we have borrowed from the French, who call it *pain perdu*, or lost bread. Because French bread dries out so quickly, it is frequently thrown out, or lost. But it is this "lost" bread that is soaked in a batter of beaten egg and milk, then fried in butter to create what we call French toast.

It is known in England as poor knights of Windsor, which is the same phrase used in many countries: *fattiga riddare* in Sweden; *arme ridder* in Danish; and *armer ritter* in German.

One theory about how the latter name came about goes as follows:

In olden times, one of the symbols of distinction between the gentry and the common herd was that the former were expected to serve dessert at dinner. Knights, of course, were gentry. But not all of them were rich. Those who were not, in order to maintain their status, made do with armer ritter, often served with jam.

Fried Eggs

It is my curious conceit that fried eggs with bacon, ham, sausages, and so on are a distinctly American invention. There are, of course, numerous ways of conveying an order for fried eggs to a waiter or waitress. One may order them sunny side up, straight up, or simply "up," and the notion of what you have in mind registers immediately. Similarly, one orders eggs over light, over easy, or simply "over," and no further discussion is necessary.

In Europe, further amplification may be necessary. Europeans, by and large, simply don't comprehend what is meant by the likes of "eggs, with bacon, sunny side up" or "eggs over easy with ham."

Although in this respect I have suffered on numerous visits to Paris, Madrid, and Geneva, my most memorable encounter came with a non-English-speaking waiter in Lisbon some years ago.

Seated in the spacious dining room of the

Ritz, I ordered "eggs, sunny side up with ham," and what he brought me from the kitchen was a dish I had encountered many, many times before in many, many European dining rooms.

He placed before me a sizzling round metal dish with a bottom layer of a slice of ham topped with an egg that had been dotted with butter and baked in the oven. Okay, that's the European version.

The next morning, I sat at the same table and was approached by the same waiter. With body English that involved hands and facial expressions, I tried to communicate the idea that I wanted my egg cooked with the eye up and with the ham languishing on the side and not baked in the oven. Did he understand? Si, si. Si, si, si.

A few moments later he emerged from the kitchen, with a beaming smile, eyes aglow, and with great ceremony placed before me one perfectly fried egg accompanied by one large, oval platter of thinly sliced, cold, boiled ham, sides overlapping and garnished with a border of pickles of the sort the French call cornichons.

This reminded one Manhattan correspondent "of a French friend who, after arriving in the States for the first time, blissfully conjured up what feats of culinary

delight might emerge from coffee shop kitchens across the land if 'Eggs Louis Quatorze' or 'Eggs Directoire' or 'Eggs Art Nouveau' were ordered at the counter. The sign above the counter, of course, said EGGS ANY STYLE."

Fromage Blanc

Fromage blanc means, of course, "white cheese," and it is probably the most basic of cheeses. Cottage cheese is a salted variation. When fresh, unpasteurized milk is left to stand it takes on harmless bacteria from the air.

The development of the bacteria causes the milk to form into whey, a thin liquid, and curds, which are semisolid. When the mixture is drained, generally in cheesecloth (hence the derivation of the material's name), the curds become fromage blanc.

Sometimes rennet, a curdling agent, is used to expedite the process. Typically the fromage blanc is not salted, although it is often seasoned before eating.

Frosting vs. Icing

Some of the most reputable books on cake decorating use the terms "frosting" and "icing" interchangeably.

I prefer to believe that there is a difference. To my mind the word "frosting" is best applied to cake coatings that are sticky to the touch. Icings are those coatings that are fairly firm glazes, such as hardened fondants. Icings are what you often find as colorful, nonsticky coatings on petits fours.

Fruitcake

The nicest Christmas presents of all, it seems to me, are those that bear a personal touch. One in particular that is recalled fondly is a marvelous ten-year-old fruitcake, given to me years ago by a friend's mother who was aware of my interest in cooking. Black with currants and raisins and mellow and satiny in texture, it was perfumed with the aged Cognac with which she had carefully doused it over the years.

My inordinate liking for fruitcakes stems from childhood, when my mother was inclined to make them weeks in advance. The advantages of fruitcakes are numerous: They come in many varieties; they keep well and may be preserved for a long time, improving as they go. Of course, they may be eaten soon after their removal from the oven.

Fruitcakes seem to be distinctly British in origin. *Mrs. Beeton's Book of Household Management,* the be-all and end-all of British cookery published in 1861, refers to the fruitcake as a "good holiday cake." The recipe specifies flour, butter, currants, "stoned and cut raisins," candied peel, and "moist sugar." "To ascertain when it is done, plunge a clean knife into the middle of it, and if, on withdrawing it, the knife looks clean, and not sticky, the cake is done," wrote Mrs. Beeton—an admonition that still serves cooks well.

As to storing fruitcake, my friendly informant from the Reynolds Wrap people in Richmond, Virginia, strongly recommends that you first enclose your fruitcake in cheesecloth after adding the Cognac. Then wrap the cake in foil to prevent its drying out.

Alcohol, acids, and salt can cause foil to "pit," because of chemical or electrolytic action. I am told that this pitting is not toxic or harmful and that foods wrapped in foil that has pitted are perfectly safe to eat if the pitting is scraped away. The most adverse thing about the pitting is aesthetic.

Fruitcakes can be kept almost indefinitely. Many years ago, I took one of the many fruitcakes that my mother baked each year and packed it in an airtight metal box. Every so often I would open the box and add a touch of brandy. A year later, I served the cake. It was one of the best fruitcakes I have ever eaten.

The most amusing piece on fruitcake I have ever read was written by Russell Baker and appeared in *The Times* on Christmas day 1983.

"Thirty-four years ago, I inherited the family fruitcake. Fruitcake is the only food durable enough to become a family heirloom. It had been in my grandmother's possession since 1880, and she passed it to a niece in 1933.

"Surprisingly, the niece, who had always seemed to detest me, left it to me in her will. There was the usual family backbiting when the will was read. Relatives grumbled that

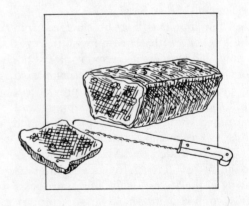

I had no right to the family fruitcake. Some whispered that I had 'got to' the dying woman when she was *in extremis* and guided her hand while she altered her will.

"Nothing could be more absurd, since my dislike of fruitcake is notorious thoughout the family. This distaste dates from a Christmas dinner when, at the age of 15, I dropped a small piece of fruitcake and shattered every bone in my right foot.

"I would have renounced my inheritance except for the sentiment of the thing, for the family fruitcake was the symbol of our family's roots. When my grandmother inherited it, it was already 86 years old, having been baked by her great-grandfather in 1794 as a Christmas gift for President George Washington.

"Washington, with his high-flown view of ethical standards for Government workers, sent it back with thanks, explaining that he thought it unseemly for Presidents to accept gifts weighing more than 80 pounds, even though they were only eight inches in diameter. This, at any rate, is the family story, and you can take it for what it's worth, which probably isn't much.

"There is not doubt, though, about the fruitcake's great age. Sawing into it six Christmases ago, I came across a fragment of a 1794 newspaper with an account of the lynching of a real-estate speculator in New York City.

"Thinking the thing was a valuable antique, I rented bank storage space and hired Brink's guards every Christmas to bring it out, carry it to the table, and return it to the vault after dinner. The whole family, of course, now felt entitled to come for Christmas dinner.

"People who have never eaten fruitcake may think that after 34 years of being gnawed at by assemblages of 25 to 30 diners my inheritance would have vanished. People who have eaten fruitcake will realize that it was still almost as intact as on the day George Washington first saw it. While an eon, as someone has observed, may be two people and a ham, a fruitcake is forever.

"It was an antiques dealer who revealed this truth to me. The children had reached college age, the age of parental bankruptcy, and I decided to put the family fruitcake on the antique market.

" 'Over 200 years old?' The dealer sneered. 'I've got one at home that's over 300,' he said. 'If you come across a fruitcake that Julius Caesar brought back from Gaul, look me up; I'll give you $10 for it.'

"To cut expenses, I took it out of the bank. Still, there was that backbreaking cost of feeding 25 to 30 relatives each Christmas when they felt entitled to visit the family fruitcake. An idea was born.

"Before leaving town for a weekend, I placed it on the television set. When burglars came for the TV, they were bound to think the antique fruitcake worth a fortune and have it in some faraway pawnshop before discovering the truth.

"By Monday morning the television set was gone, all right, but the fruitcake was still with us. 'I should have wired it,' I told Uncle Jimmy. 'Burglars won't take anything that isn't electronic these days.'

"Uncle Jimmy was not amused. 'You're a lucky man,' he said.

"Lucky? Bankrupted by an idiotic faith in higher education was what I was.

" 'Lucky!' he shouted. 'Don't you know there's a curse on the family fruitcake? It is said that a dreadful fate will fall upon anyone who lets the family fruitcake pass out of the possession of the family.'

"That didn't really scare me. Still, it couldn't hurt to play safe. After that, I kept the fruitcake locked in the crawl space under the kitchen. This afternoon, I shall bring it out again when 25 to 30 relatives come to dinner, and afterward we will all groan as people always groan when their interiors feel clogged with cement.

"I now suspect Uncle Jimmy of lying about the curse. I suspect the dreadful fate carried by the family fruitcake is visited upon the one who inherits it. I wish I had a relative in the higher-education business so I could will it to him."

Frumenty

Curiously, I have read in an English encyclopedia of food that there is a dish called frumenty served to children in America. But I can find no reference to it in any American food encyclopedias. I do know (from research rather than personal experience) that there is a well-known old-fashioned English pudding or custard called frumenty and sometimes spelled furmity. It is made by steeping wheat kernels in barely simmering water for twenty-four hours or longer. The liquid is strained and cooked with milk, spices, and sugar.

The dish, which dates from medieval days, is said to be the one from which flummery originated. Flummery is an old-fashioned, sweet, gelatinous pudding of English and Irish origin made with oatmeal.

An amusing note about frumenty, or furmity, came from a Manhattan gentleman.

"Furmity," he wrote, "plays a key role in Thomas Hardy's novel *The Mayor of Casterbridge,* published in 1886 and dealing with events in the first half of that century.

The furmity, described by Hardy as a 'mixture of corn in the grain, flour, milk, raisins, currants and what-not,' composing an 'antiquated slop,' is sold in a tent at a fair in the south of England. A man buys some for himself, his wife and his daughter, slyly arranging that his own be heavily laced with rum. He becomes drunk and auctions off his wife, thus getting the novel off to a rousing start."

Frying

There are definitely nuances of language in the kitchen. While fry is an all-embracing term meaning to cook something in fat, there are subcategories of the term. There is deep-frying, meaning to cook something in a great quantity of fat; shallow-frying, which is done in a skillet with fat that does not cover the food to be fried, and then comes sautéing. In my mind sautéing more often than not means to cook in as little fat as possible. Stir-frying is similar to sautéing, in that the foods are quickly cooked in a small amount of oil.

Fumet

Fumet, one of the commonest terms in French kitchen terminology, has to do with flavor, bouquet, and aroma. The most widely called for fumet is a fish fumet, or fumet de poisson, an aromatic liquid that is nothing more than fish stock made with fish bones and/or fish flesh, plus water and seasonings. On the other hand, there are other fumets including a fumet of mushrooms, of game, and of truffles.

Funeral Pie

I have an amusing small book on pies published by Pacific Intermountain Express, or P.I.E., a large trucking company. The book is not available to the public but, in any event, it offers a recipe for funeral pie, which is a raisin pie (it also contains nuts and spices).

"Raisin pies," the book explains, "became known as funeral pies by the Pennsylvania Dutch because they were often served to mourners. Not being fragile, they had the advantage of traveling well, so were a common sight at the gatherings of family and friends that followed funerals."

A funeral pie is also referred to as a rosina, from the German word for raisins, *rosine*. The Welsh also have a funeral cake that is a fruitcake made with brown sugar, nuts, raisins, currants, candied fruit peel, and spices. It too is a traditional offering to a family that has had a death.

Fungus

I am always a bit loath to use the word "fungus" in terms of cookery, in that the word has a negative connotation in the public mind.

Nonetheless, both in this country and throughout the world fungus of some sort is consumed by the ton each year.

All mushrooms, cultivated or wild, are a form of fungi and, as a matter of fact, one of the great delicacies of the Mexican table is the marvelous dish called *huitlacoche para quesadilles*. Huitlacoche is a corn fungus that Diana Kennedy calls "ambrosia of the Aztec gods." It is available in Mexican res-

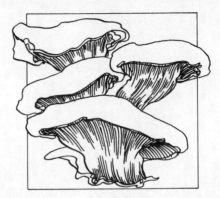

taurants in Mexico—and even there only for a brief period in summer.

Tree ears, so common in Chinese dishes, are also mushroom-like fungi. They are sometimes called cloud ears and black fungus and are widely available, in a dried state, generally in plastic bags, in almost every Chinese grocery store. They have a brownish black color and expand greatly when soaked in warm water for twenty minutes or so. If you find then that the stems are too tough for your liking, cut them away and discard them. Years ago when I wrote a Chinese cookbook with Virginia Lee, she almost invariably cut away the stems of the dried black mushrooms that she used, even the black tree ears. I personally am not opposed to the slightly chewy texture of some soaked black dried mushroom stems.

Gg Gg

Gg Gg

Galantine

See Turkey.

Galingale

See Laos.

Gallimaufry

Gallimaufry generally means a hodgepodge. Originally it came from the French and is spelled *galimafrée*, which meant a ragout or stew of one meat or another, generally chicken.

Supposedly, the dish originated in medieval times, and consisted of roasting a chicken, frying it, and then cooking it in a sauce of wine, sour wine, ginger, salt, and mustard. For obvious reasons, it is not a dish you're likely to find on any of today's menus.

Game

There is a bit of hypocrisy in my attitude toward game. On the one hand, I am quite uncomfortable around shotguns, rods, and reels, but, on the other, I yield without hesitation to well-made venison dishes, pâtés of quail, roast pheasant, roast quail, quail in vine leaves, or with grapes. Offer me a platter of *venaison bourguignonne* with a rich old bottle of Chambertin and it will turn any cold winter day's feast into a sumptuous occasion. It occurs to me, however, that no aspect of cookery is more intimidating to home cooks than turning a piece of game into a triumph for the table. One of my earliest frustrations in trying to do so was nearly forty years ago, when my sister gave me a brace of pheasants as a Christmas present.

I carried them back to Chicago and my one-room flat with the intention of hanging them—a procedure, I had read, required for game birds before cooking. I arrived with the pheasants in midweek and invited friends to join me for dinner on the weekend. I then suspended each pheasant with string from the water faucets in my tiny, overheated kitchen. My intention was to let them "rest" for a proper period. In a day or so, of course, they became unbearable and I had to throw them out.

It is true that some game tastes best if it is allowed to do what the French call getting *faisandé* (from *faisan,* the word for pheasant), or "high." French and English epicures, in particular, like to hang game until it takes on an unmistakably gamy taste.

Unlike me, Pierre Franey is a skilled hunter and he has also had many years' experience in preparing game for the table. It is his theory that the hanging and aging of any game is not absolutely essential but is preferable (very small birds, such as doves and quails, do not demand hanging). The length of time varies from overnight for birds such as partridge to seven days or longer for a deer. Needless to say, a cool or somewhat cold place is essential—not a warm kitchen in Chicago. The temperature should be 40 degrees or less but not sufficient to cause freezing.

One does not have to marinate all game before cooking either. Indeed, one of the finest meals I have had was served on a cold winter weekend when Pierre and I were invited to a hunting party on Gardiners Island,

off the eastern end of Long Island. About 10 P.M. Pierre shot a young deer (the island is at times so overrun with deer that some must be eliminated so those that remain will have enough food) and a wild turkey. The morning after, we ate some of the finest deer liver I have ever tasted and that evening we dined extremely well on the turkey, which had not been marinated.

When game is marinated, the length of time will depend on the type of game and the size of the cut. A leg of venison may marinate for as long as a week in the refrigerator, being turned frequently in the marinade, which might consist of wine, generally red, a touch of vinegar, herbs and spices such as bay leaf, thyme, parsley, peppercorns, and rosemary, plus such chopped vegetables as carrots, onions, and celery.

The ingredients and proportions for the marinade will vary according to taste and to what you have on hand. The better the wine in the marinade, the better the game will be, but any wine suitable for drinking will be suitable for the marinade.

It is almost always recommended that you marinate meat that is going into a stew—a ragout of venison or rabbit, for example. You needn't marinate all foods that are to be roasted, such as pheasant, quail, or woodcock, or the most tender cuts of game, such as venison chops and ribs.

American books on game cookery rarely specify how to hang game, but they certainly do not lack for adventurousness in their recipes. Glancing through the indexes of a few of them one can find the likes of elk stroganoff, elk sukiyaki, venison enchiladas, squirrel mulligan, barbecued beaver, sweet-and-sour raccoon, armadillo ragout, roast possum, and woodchuck in sauce. Not to mention snipe in the bag and goulash of teal.

Ganache

Ganache is an incredibly rich chocolate "filling" that has numerous uses in pastry making. It takes considerable skill to make, because the chocolate mixture must be cooled to a critical temperature before whipping.

Garam Masala

Garam masala is a basic blend of Indian spices and varies from Indian cook to Indian cook. One mixture is made with ground cardamom pods, cinnamon, cloves, peppercorns, cumin, and coriander seeds. It is available in bottles and tins from specialty food shops.

In her excellent book, *Classic Indian Cooking,* Julie Sahni points out that the word sometimes "refers to a 'wet' blend of spices"—that is to say, a spice paste. Garam means warm or hot. Most of the fine Indian cooks I have known generally express disdain for commercially prepared curry powder, saying they are too uniform and lack the special characteristics of a blend that is made according to taste. To me, a garam masala is most certainly one form of curry powder.

Garlic

It was Marcel Boulestin, a French chef and cookbook author who spent most of his life in London, who observed about Provence, "It is not really an exaggeration to say that peace and happiness begin, geographically, where garlic is used in cooking." But apparently not everyone would agree. One detractor suggested that in deference to alliumphobes I should say in recipes that garlic may be added "if desired," just as I now do with salt.

It is not a question of deference. I have never considered my recipes to be unalterable. Minor flavors should be altered according to taste. Although I am quite fond of garlic, I consider it in most uses as a minor ingredient. For those who are allergic to garlic, finely minced shallots could be substituted.

I add "if desired" to recipes calling for salt because it has been established that for some persons salt is deleterious to health. I add it as a cautionary matter because the vast majority of home cooks consider salt a basic ingredient to foods. I have learned, to my pleasure and vastly improved health, that it is not.

I should add that there are some dishes in which garlic is absolutely essential. These include garlic soup, garlic sausages, aïoli, that Italian garlic "bath" for vegetables known as bagna caôda, and skordalia, the Greek garlic mayonnaise.

When a dish is made with whole, unpeeled garlic cloves as opposed to chopped or minced garlic the taste of the garlic will be much more subtle. The cloves are usually removed before the dish is served. If you peel the garlic and if the dish cooks for long, the cloves might disintegrate.

Many dishes call for whole, unpeeled garlic that is roasted, so it does not leave an aftertaste but is slightly sweet and buttery.

The easiest way to peel garlic is to place each garlic clove on a flat surface and to smack it lightly with a mallet or the flat blade of a chef's knife. The blow must be strong enough to crack the garlic skin. The skin pulls off quite easily if you cut into it with a small paring knife.

If the cloves are large, you can chop them the way you do an onion. And if the recipe calls for a lot of garlic, you can chop it in a blender or food processor.

You may also add a little oil to the garlic as it is processed. Chopped garlic in oil will keep well briefly, if tightly sealed and refrigerated.

To my mind, the purchase of chopped garlic in oil is a highly expensive indulgence. It is much too easy to chop garlic with a good knife, and you can add your own oil. I also would not recommend storing garlic in oil longer than overnight. After a while the garlic starts to taste "old."

I have met a few chefs who insist that the center part that you may find in some garlic cloves is distasteful. It may be that my palate is not as sensitive as theirs, but I don't find it necessary to remove and discard that portion.

As far as I can tell, it is nothing more than a new shoot that, if planted, would produce more garlic. And the tender green shoots of garlic, which are chive-like when sprouted, are much coveted in Chinese cookery.

Garlic Press

To my taste, garlic put through a press takes on a smell and taste reminiscent of acetylene gas. There are also some schools of cookery where the texture of not-too-finely chopped garlic is a desirable characteristic in certain dishes. The spicy dishes of the Chinese kitchen are complemented by coarsely chopped garlic. My feeling is that cooks who use a garlic press are lazy.

Garlic Sausage

Garlic sausage is what the Italian sausage-makers call cotechini and what the French call saucisson à l'ail.

These sausages are used in cassoulets and numerous bean dishes. In New York, they are most often served as a first course wrapped in pastry and baked. As an appetizer, they are often served with a warm potato salad vinaigrette and mustard.

A typical recipe for garlic sausage is made with the lean and fat of pork ground with salt, pepper, quatre épices, cayenne, saltpeter, brandy, and garlic.

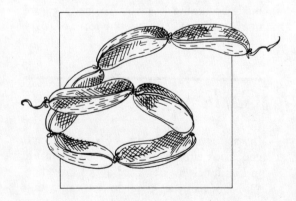

Garum

Garum is a highly flavored fish sauce that is made by placing ungutted whole fish in a heavy brine solution in a container and exposing the mixture to the sun. When fermentation results, the liquid is extracted.

A. J. McClane, in his *Encyclopedia of Fish Cookery,* writes that the much-prized fish sauce of Vietnam called nuoc mam, and that of Thailand called nam pla, are today's counterparts of garum.

Gastrique

Gastrique is a sweet-sour preparation added to dishes that may be overly rich or fatty, such as duck. You combine sugar and vinegar and cook down over relatively high heat until the sugar caramelizes and becomes a dark amber color.

You must take care that the caramel does not burn and become bitter. It is added to the orange or lemon sauce to be served with the duck. Since the skin of domestic duck has a high fat content, the gastrique tempers the fatty taste.

Gastronomade

If I am not mistaken, the word "gastronomade" was coined by the man considered in France to be the foremost epicure of his generation, Curnonsky. Curnonsky, who died several decades ago, was the pseudonym of Maurice-Edmond Sailland. He was dubbed the *prince élu des gastronomes,* or the elected prince of gastronomes. Gastron-

omade was a blend of gastronome and nomad. Curnonsky defined a gastronomade as "one who visits a country in search of good hotels, good restaurants, and good inns."

Gazpacho

For anyone with more than a passing interest in the etymology and origins of food, it was more fun than a "snare Andalusian," Franklin P. Adams's interpretation of a snare and delusion.

One evening I was sipping gazpacho with Dr. Luis Casas, a Spanish physician, and his American-born wife, Penelope.

Now, the gazpacho of Spain, like the quiche of Lorraine, long ago became a borrowed but integral part of America's kitchen culture. But the gazpacho that most Americans know, a zesty blend of tomatoes, chopped peppers, cucumbers, garlic, and oil, hails from Seville. What few people in this country seem aware of is that in various parts of Spain there are also two more gazpachos with neither a speck nor a smidgen of tomatoes. These are the white gazpachos.

In Malagá, for example, there is a gazpacho made with almonds and grapes. The soup on which I dined in the Casas home was a sieved, palate-beguiling, milk-white broth made from a clear vegetable broth and seasoned with such aromatics as green pepper, cucumber, vinegar, oil, eggs, and bread.

There are, according to Luis Casas, many theories about the name gazpacho. "Bread," he explained, "is in one form or another essential to gazpacho of no matter what nature." It may be in the form of croutons served with the soup, or the bread might be soaked in the soup before it is sieved or put

through a food mill.

It is surmised in some quarters that the "pacho" of the word derives from the Latin *pasti,* meaning bread or dough or paste.

"There is a Basque word, *gazpachoa,*" Dr. Casas said, "which means a paste that is crushed or mashed. *Empachar,* by the way, means to get sick of food from eating too much. It means to be stuffed."

Mrs. Casas offered another version of the name's origin. "Some say," she volunteered, "that it comes from the Spanish word *caspa,* which means a fragment or morsel. This would relate to the pieces of bread used in the soup."

Mrs. Casas, has, incidentally, become one of the best known authorities where Spanish cooking is concerned. She is the author of the widely acclaimed *The Foods and Wines of Spain.*

Génoise

One of the greatest desserts in all of French pastry making is quite conceivably of Italian origin. Or perhaps the pastry chef who created it was an Italophile. In any event, it is génoise, a delicate, cake-like affair named after the city of Genoa. It is excellent served with a sprinkling of various spirits, such as rum or kirsch, but it has multiple other uses as a "layer" for other desserts.

Geoduck

The late Helen Evans Brown in her book, *The West Coast Cook Book,* states that geoduck clams are called "gooeyduck" by those who dig them and "gweduck" in most dictionaries.

The geoduck, she adds, "is a clam that must have been a favorite of the Brobdingnagians, who lived, according to Swift, where the Olympic Peninsula is actually situated." *Geoduck,* according to the author, means "dig deep" in an Indian language. The clams can be seven inches across the shell and have a siphon six times that long.

They are prepared by scalding in hot water, at which point the shells will open. They are skinned and the stomach is discarded. The neck may be ground for chowder and the body cut into steaks that must be tenderized by pounding before being breaded and fried in butter.

Oddly, I have never sampled a geoduck, which came as a surprise to many correspondents:

One wrote to say that you might dine on these clams at any fine Japanese restaurant in Manhattan and beyond.

"Ask for mirugai (pronounced me-roo-guy)," she wrote, "either in sushi form or as sashimi." The Japanese use only the neck, I was told, and discard the body.

Joseph Alsop, the columnist, said that in his opinion, "Gooeyduck cutlets are far superior to abalone, and you ought to go out of your way to try them. The reason gooey-ducks are all but unknown in the United States, although one of the real American delicacies, is that these clams, despite their enormous size, are capable of propelling themselves under the sand at close to the speed of light. They make quite conspicuous breathing holes, but locating a breathing hole is only the beginning of the battle. You have to have the knack of foretelling which way the gooeyduck will go, and the strength to dig down for them with utmost rapidity. Otherwise they escape."

Ghee

I was once the happy recipient of a smart-looking ceramic glass jar containing a pint or so of solidified, clarified butter.

The friend who gave it to me stated that it was homemade ghee and advised me to use it whenever I cooked Indian style. I discussed ghee recently with another acquaintance, who also stated categorically that ghee was the fat always used in Indian kitchens.

I pursued the subject through the index of the book on Indian cookery to which I most often make reference, Madhur Jaffrey's *An Invitation to Indian Cooking,* and I quote from it as follows:

"There is a slight misconception even among knowledgeable Americans, which is that most Indian food is cooked in ghee, and that ghee is clarified butter. Actually, there are two kinds of ghee. The usli ghee or 'real ghee' is indeed clarified butter, but if you consider India as a whole, it is very rarely used.

"In a nation where milk and butter are luxuries, cooking in usli ghee for the masses is unthinkable. Most people keep a small jar of usli ghee in their kitchen and use it occasionally on chappatis or dal, for cooking special dishes, or for religious and medicinal purposes.

"The other ghee, the one that is most commonly used, is made of various oils and is what is called vegetable shortening in America. It is sold under various brand names—Dalda and Rath being the most popular—and can be purchased in large cans. In my own family we always used this vegetable ghee because my father insisted that usli ghee was too rich for a daily diet."

Ghiveci

I am told that ghiveci is the national dish of Rumania, and is simply a provincial stew made with almost any vegetable you can find in the garden: eggplants, onions, leeks, potatoes, celery, peas, beans, and so on.

The vegetables are first cooked in a large quantity of oil with herbs, and meat or fish is added at some point during the cooking. My information tells me that the name means "flower pot," which is the shape of the utensil in which it is cooked.

Ginger

Twenty years ago, fresh ginger was a rare commodity in America; it was almost imperative that you travel to Chinatown to procure it. Happily, all that has changed. It is widely available today in supermarkets and at farm stands.

To store fresh ginger, I keep it in a plastic bag in the refrigerator. On the other hand, I use it in such quantities it rarely remains there for more than a week or two.

Some Chinese cooks recommend peeling it and pouring dry sherry or the Chinese wine called hsao-hsing over it. An acquaintance from India showed me a bottle of her "freshly grated" ginger, which she keeps in a storage bottle in her refrigerator. She adds a blend of equal parts of white vinegar and water, just enough to moisten well, and it will keep fresh for months. She cautioned that the grated ginger should not be overly wet or the preserving liquid (vinegar and water) will extract too much flavor from the ginger.

Other methods suggested to me for keeping ginger fresh:

Wrap it in plastic and put it in the freezer. When it is to be used, a wash in hot water will enable you to peel the skin off easily and the ginger is ready to be sliced or chopped.

Keep it in a plastic bag, freeze, and grate as needed.

You can have a supply of really fresh ginger on hand by simply planting a piece in a flower pot in ordinary potting soil. The ginger grows down and after a few weeks you will have a cluster of tender, fresh roots.

When a recipe calls for grated ginger, I recommend that you peel and chop it unless you have a specially designed ginger grater.

The one in my kitchen is made in China. It resembles a miniature wash board, consisting of several notched parallel strips of wood on which you grate the ginger. I believe this product is available in many specialty shops that deal in cooking utensils.

And ginger juice is also made from grated fresh ginger. To make the juice, break off a small piece of ginger and peel and grate it. Squeeze through cheesecloth.

Gingko Nuts

Gingko nuts are widely used in Asian cookery in appetizers, soups, and desserts. They are defined by Grace Chu in her book, *Madam Chu's Cooking School,* as follows: "The nut of a large ornamental tree native to eastern China. Gingko nuts are oval, about one-half inch in diameter, with light brown shells and ivory-colored meat. They are sold in Chinese grocery stores, either already shelled and canned, or in dried form. Dried gingko nuts must be shelled and blanched before using. Widely used in vegetarian dishes and in stuffings."

I learned from a nursery man in Lewisburg, Pennsylvania, that the gingko is a "unique" tree that has been growing on this earth at least ten million years. Today it exists as an extremely tolerant tree for growing in today's environment. Apparently, most of the trees planted in recent years in metropolitan areas are male. Otherwise you might run into the problems of a lady from New Rochelle, who sent me an amusing letter:

"An ancient and noble 150-foot high fe-

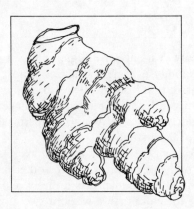

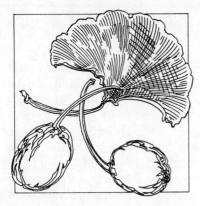

male gingko tree adorns my front lawn—a corner lot—spreading its graceful fan-shaped leafy branches over my entrance way and public sidewalk as well.

"When my spreading gingko tree is in heat, it takes more than 'grit' to approach it. Soon my front lawn and surrounding territory will be covered with beautiful plum-colored velvety fallen 'fruit' concealing the nut within. Then the frost will come and at a given time there will be a shower of golden leaves not one by one—but the whole tree, usually within an hour or so.

"So far, so good, but then the olive-shaped plum begins to ripen and eventually rot away from the nut. . . . By now the air is polluted with something akin to a barn-yard stench, only worse. If all the dogs in New Rochelle were led to my corner for their necessary routines, the resulting odor-iferous air quality could not equal that already created by my little sleeping gingko nuts.

"Pedestrians take to the streets. Friends are warned and before a dinner party I sweep the walk every fifteen minutes. Each year my gardener threatens to cut the tree down as the nuts mangle his leaf blower, thus releasing more 'fumes.'

"He must then shovel the nuts into bags, for the city refuses to dispose of them otherwise. Apparently leaf sweepers are not designed to include gingko nuts.

"We tried giving the tree 'the pill' one year in the form of a series of expensive sprays. It worked for one year, but subsequent sprayings did not, and we have more than ever before. So we have given up on that."

Girasole

See Jerusalem artichoke.

Glasswort

See Perche-pierres.

Gloucester Cheese

Both single and double Gloucester are made from cow's milk in Gloucester County, England. Single Gloucester is, I am informed, about half as thick as the double version. Both have the round shape of mill-stones. Double Gloucester almost invariably has a clear yellow color, whereas single Gloucester, a mild, undistinguished cheese, has a pale natural-milk color.

An interesting note about the coloration appears in *The Cheese Book* by Vivienne Marquis and Patricia Haskell:

"At one time the exteriors of all double

Gloucesters were painted red, a practice which developed in the mid-eighteenth century when many dairywomen were already coloring the curd with carrot juice, in the hope of deceiving customers into thinking that their cheeses were made from richer milk than the uncolored cheeses of their competitors.

"By the time double Gloucesters came into favor all hard cheeses were colored, and so the distinctions were lost. Then, at the urging of cheese merchants bent on finding a 'characteristic' that would set the [double] Gloucester apart from other cheeses, dairy-women took to painting it—they stained the Gloucester's surface with a mixture of Spanish brown and Indian red, and then rubbed its perimeters until the carroty yellow of the cheese showed through."

Most of the double Gloucester produced today is colored, I am told, with seeds of the annatto tree, a coloring and flavoring widely used in Caribbean cookery, particularly that of Puerto Rico.

In his book *The World of Cheese,* Evan Jones avers that the names of the cheeses derive from the fact that single Gloucester "requires only half the milk and much less aging than double Gloucester."

Goette

Goette, or ghetta, is another version of scrapple or, as it is frequently referred to, Philadelphia scrapple. The difference is that scrapple is made with pork trimmings and cornmeal mush. To prepare goette, a certain amount of oatmeal is substituted for the cornmeal. The town best known for goette is Cincinnati. As far as I know, goette is, like scrapple, of Pennsylvania Dutch origin.

Golden Syrup

Golden syrup, which is a common ingredient in England, is sold at times in specialty shops that deal in fine imported foods. Theodora FitzGibbon, in *The Food of the Western World,* defines golden syrup as "an English golden treacle (which resembles corn syrup in texture and color) made from refined sugars." By that I presume she means corn syrup that has a dark caramel or mahogany color. Light corn syrup is practically colorless.

Goose Fat

After roasting a goose, you will end up with a large quantity of fat, which can be poured into glass jars with tight-fitting lids. It will keep indefinitely and can be used as a substitute for oil or lard. Many people feel that the finest French fried potatoes in the world are those cooked in pure goose fat. They are delicious, but they are certainly not low in calories. Goose fat is also often the base for that famed regional specialty of French gastronomy (notably Gascon) called confits, as in confit d'oie (preserved goose).

Götterspeise

One simple recipe that I have seen for götterspeise, the German dessert, calls for combining whipped cream with grated pumpernickel crumbs and grated chocolate. Another is a steamed pudding made with grated, toasted, buttered pumpernickel crumbs, beaten egg yolks, beaten egg whites, grated almonds, and grated bittersweet chocolate. The pudding is steamed in a mold and served with whipped cream.

Goulash

There are probably more recipes for Hungarian goulash throughout the world than there are for sauerkraut, coq au vin, and bouillabaisse—not to mention baked beans—put together. Actually, both a soup and a meat stew go by the name goulash.

George Lang explains in his immensely edifying book, *The Cuisine of Hungary,* that originally a gulyas was a shepherd's dish made with meat cooked with onions until all the liquid disappeared. The dish was then put in a bag made of sheep's stomach and placed in the sun to dry. When the shepherds got hungry, they simply added a little water to make a meat stew (gulyashus), a lot of water to make a soup (gulyasleves).

Gourmet

Gourmet is, of course, the ultimate praise to describe an individual of extraordinary sensitivity, one of whose ruling passions is food and wine. To my mind, however, the definition must be far broader. That is why out of the endless stream of men and women I've known with a strong and educated interest in food and wine, there are only one or two who might conceivably merit the name—and even in these instances, I have doubts. To tell the truth, by my own standards I don't know any. Certainly I would not lay claim to the title.

What, then, would a gourmet be? It would be, first of all, someone of impeccable taste who would know, blindfolded and with only a sip, the vineyard and vintage of the wine he samples. It would be someone of scrupulous taste who could detect the least trace of any herb, spice, or spirit in a sauce; someone who could relate instantly a precise choice of wine to any given food. This admirable figure would never drink strong spirits and an excess of alcohol would be unthinkable.

It would be a raconteur of elegant manners and speech—one who never repeated a choice anecdote twice in the same manner—a person without pretense or self-praise; a person from whose lips a harsh phrase would be rare; a word of profanity unthinkable. It would be an individual who could discourse with authority on all of the world's great dishes and most of the lesser ones. It would also be someone who could discuss with equal enlightenment the humanities and art.

But, by Bacchus, give my source of idolatry one human trait. Let him or her indulge—in private life—in a few wicked sins. Oh, I'd encourage that. There's spice there, too. *See also* Epicure.

Graham Crackers

I wonder if the man for whom Graham crackers are named could possibly have foreseen how many billions of crackers would be baked and bear his name. What he really did was produce a flour made from whole kernels of wheat and it was the flour to which his name was first given.

Sylvester Graham, who lived from 1794 to 1851, was an American physician and a reformer in the field of nutrition. About ten years before his death he perfected a fine ground whole wheat flour that today bears his name. As a point of interest, in Finland certain rusks are known as grahamkorputs and in England, Graham flour is known as Grant flour.

I have never seen Graham flour, but a spokesman for a local health food store states that Graham flour and whole wheat pastry flour are the same. Both Graham and the pastry flour are made from soft wheat.

Granité

See Ices.

Grapefruit

Grapefruits are so named because they grow in clusters like grapes.

If you can find a grapefruit that seems to have a vibrant, shiny skin that is tight and resilient when pressed lightly, the chances are that you will not find those sprouted seeds, which produce, to my palate, an "earthy" taste.

You will also find that the heavier a grapefruit is in relation to its size, the juicier it will be.

Grasshopper Pie

A grasshopper pie is made with green crème de menthe, white crème de cacao, and cream. The filling comes out a delicate green color, which gives it its name. The word derives from the cocktail that bears the name grasshopper. It is made with those ingredients, which are shaken with ice and strained.

Gratin

Much has been written on the various types of gratins, but basically it boils down to putting food in a small baking dish, sprinkling it with more sauce, and lightly covering it with melted butter and bread crumbs. It is then run under the broiler until a nice brown glaze is achieved.

At times the bread crumbs are combined with grated cheese before sprinkling. And at times—and this is the quickest method of all—only the cheese and melted butter are used.

Gravy

See Sauce.

Greek Easter

There is conceivably no religious festival on earth that is not in some way related to the eating of food and the drinking of wine. Historians are generally agreed that until a few centuries ago, most such celebrations were seasonally inspired and sacred. We learned as children that the earliest of these ceremonies originated when pagan man tilled the soil, yet found himself helpless in the face of flood and drought and other caprices of nature. It was then that he appealed

to and attempted to appease whatever gods might be out there.

One Easter season, in Athens, I found myself a most willing participant in a celebration of the holiday, Greek Orthodox fashion. It was Holy Saturday and a night of brilliant stars and moonlight, and as midnight approached we strolled through otherwise darkened streets to a tiny church. Hundreds of other "pilgrims" had preceded us to the small plaza in front of the church, to await the tolling of the bells that would signify the arrival of Easter morning. In the darkness someone handed us candles and, as bells were tolled, the priest emerged bearing a candle with which he kindled the candle of the closest member of those assembled.

"*Christos anesti,*" he declared. "Christ is risen." The second candle illuminated a third, the third a fourth, individual to individual, chain-reaction fashion, until moments later that entire square was awash with light.

The second event of that evening remains equally vivid in memory. I was a guest at a traditional Greek Easter feast. It consisted merely of soup and bread, but it was an incredibly delicious spread, including one dish of which I had had no prior knowledge.

Of course, in years past, I had dined on avgolemono soup, that typical Hellenic specialty made of an abundantly rich broth thickened and flavored with lemon and eggs. But on this occasion I was told that the soup was named mayeritsa avgolemono, and that at that moment in thousands and thousands of households throughout Greece, celebrants would be dining on this particular soup made with the head of lamb and assorted other parts of the animal, including the neck, knuckles, and liver, all bones removed and the meat chopped fine. Like an avgolemono, this, too, was flavored with egg and lemon.

The Easter bread was made with a lightly sweetened egg and yeast dough of surpassing flavor and texture. Red-dyed Easter eggs were offered the guests and these, too, are traditional, representing both the rebirth of the season and the resurrection of Christ. And those three elements were the sum and substance of that meal.

Earlier, when asked why the mayeritsa soup was so traditional in Greek homes at the beginning of Easter, it was explained that roast baby lamb is the almost inevitable main dish for the principal feast of Easter day. The soup uses all the parts of the lamb that are not commonly served with the roast.

Green Onions

Green onions and scallions are one and the same. In some sections of the United States, however, notably the South, some regional cookbooks specify shallots when they actually mean scallions or green onions. Shallots are similar to scallions only in that they

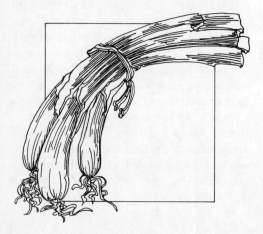

both have an onion flavor and belong to the onion family.

Green Peppercorns

See Peppercorns.

Green Sauce

Almost every cuisine of the Western world has a green sauce to be served with grilled poultry, boiled beef, and so on. They are invariably made with a basic vinaigrette sauce (one part vinegar or lemon juice to three parts oil), blended with chopped green herbs and perhaps other ingredients that might include chopped hard-boiled eggs and even bread.

I am very fond of an Italian salsa verde that contains, in addition to a mustard and green herb vinaigrette, chopped capers and anchovies. One German green sauce uses chopped chives, parsley, sage, watercress, borage, sorrel, tarragon, and dill, plus chopped hard-boiled eggs.

Green Tea

The leaves used in the preparation of green tea or black tea are the same. The leaves are green when harvested.

Black teas are put through a fermentation or oxidation process, which accounts for their color. Green tea leaves are put through a withering or panning process, and their color when dried is much more like the original color.

Green tea is a staple in Japanese homes. It is also used in the preparation of green tea ice cream, to which, I suspect, a touch of green color is added for visual effect. *See also* Gunpowder tea.

Green Tomatoes

Mexican green tomatoes, according to Diana Kennedy in *The Cuisines of Mexico,* are not related to the ordinary tomato but are a member of the Cape gooseberry and goose-cherry family. Mexican green tomatoes are known in Mexico as tomates verdes, tomates de cascara, or fresadillas. In the United States they go by the names tomatillos enteros and tomatitos verdes. To cook them, put the green tomatoes in a saucepan with water to cover and bring to a boil. Let simmer about ten minutes and drain.

Grenadine

Grenadine syrup is a nonalcoholic fruit syrup made with sugar and the juice of pome-granates. A bottle that I have (and rarely use) notes that the ingredients are "sugar syrup, citric acid, natural flavors, certified color, 0.1 percent sodium benzoate as a preservative."

If the bottle does not specify the word "pomegranate" on the label, there is the possibility that those "natural flavors" are the juice of other fruits.

Grenadine is used for bar drinks, and I believe it was a far more fashionable ingredient shortly after the repeal of Prohibition than it is today. No one has asked for a Jack Rose or a pink lady in *my* home.

Those were the days when such drinks as the pink lady (made with grenadine, lemon or lime juice, apple brandy, gin, and egg white) or something called the sheik (grenadine, Cointreau, Grand Marnier, lime juice, rum, and gin) were popular.

I have seen recipes in which grenadine is used as a minor cooking ingredient, but I have not tried them.

Grilling

See Barbecue, Marinade, Mixed grill, Mongolian grill, Satays, Yakitori.

Grimod de la Reynière

Grimod de la Reynière was a French gastronome, eccentric, and barrister who is remembered historically in just about that order. He was born in Paris in 1758 and died in 1838. He was the son of a butcher, had webbed fingers, and on the death of his father he must have fallen into a sizable inheritance, for he moved into a splendid hotel at No. 1 rue des Champs-Elysées, now the site of the American Embassy. He entertained on an elaborately expansive scale, and his guests included financiers, theater people, and "people of thought."

His dinners were sumptuous but are today largely remembered for the bizarre goings-on that attended them. He was among other things a rather serious practical joker and at dinner, closets would open mysteriously by themselves; framed portraits of his ancestors would leer and stick out their tongues; and here and there skeletons danced on frames.

He was celebrated in his day as one of the greatest of gastronomes and wrote two books for which he is still remembered (it is said that Brillat-Savarin "borrowed" from the works). These were *Manual des Amphytrions* published in 1808 and *Almanach des Gourmands, ou Calendrier Nutritif*. They included helpful hints for nouveaux riches, thoughts, reflections, and anecdotes. One of the dishes invented in his honor is filets mignons Grimod de la Reynière, made with rounds of sautéed polenta, topped with a filet, then an artichoke bottom and truffle slice.

Grits

Grits, the cereal that swept into the public consciousness when President Carter was elected, are no joke, despite that unfortunate name. The name, incidentally, is not the lackluster invention of a dimwitted backwoodsman. It stems, rather, according to scholarly sources, from a Middle English word *gryt,* meaning bran, and from the Old English *grytt*. Ditto groats.

Although grits are thought of mostly as a deep-South breakfast specialty, they are sold in supermarkets nationwide. Heaven knows, one box of grits goes a long way. The cooking directions on the box sitting just aft of this typewriter state that 1 serving can be made by cooking 3 tablespoons of the fine white grain in 1 cup of water.

A liking for any food may be highly subjective. I know people who can't abide caviar. I like both caviar and grits and can speculate that the two together would be quite compatible in the same way that fresh caviar and a hot buttered baked potato is a marriage made in heaven.

Grits are, after all, like snails, noodles, and potatoes, a somewhat neutral food whose character depends on what you serve with them or on them. A pat of butter is the most elementary and universal addition to hot grits. One of the glories of this world—to a southern palate, that is—is a slice of fried, country-cured ham, served with grits and red-eye gravy.

Other foods notably suited to grits are sautéed chicken livers or calf's liver; braised wild birds and other game; and a Louisiana specialty known as grillades, a savory, braised meat dish.

One of the most championed of all grits dishes in the deep South is one that became a regional rage two or three decades ago. This is freshly cooked grits combined with a commercially made six-ounce roll of garlic cheese, a soft, yellow processed cheese with garlic flavor, but grated Cheddar, plus a touch of garlic is an admirable substitute. Cheese and grits, incidentally, have a remarkable affinity for each other.

Grits are, to put it as briefly and mercifully as possible, made from white or yellow corn kernels. Dried corn with 14 percent moisture, for some reason or other, brings the best price. I know, because a producer of an excellent product, Honey Suckle Quick Cooking Grits from Memphis, told me when I contacted him by telephone. He said that the dried kernels are shelled in the field and sent to a milling company. The kernels are put through a cleaning process and are ground through mill rolls six times. The heart of the corn is taken out and the hull of the kernels are removed. What's left is ground into cornmeal or grits. Grains of grits are larger than grains of cornmeal.

The largest producer of grits in this country and the brand most commonly found in America is Quaker Oats. That's the brand I grew up on as a child. The person I spoke to at Quaker told me that one hundred forty million pounds of grits are sold each year in America. That's a silo-full.

As a child of the South (and one who has not infrequently been described as having cornmeal mush in his mouth) I felt notably secure in stating that grits constituted a plural noun. I staunchly defend this opinion, but do feel moved to give the opposition a moment of self-defense. I heard from a fellow-Mississippian as follows:

"I wonder whether you have quietly fallen victim of a Yankee malaise, one which causes even editors of dictionaries, alas, to refer to grits as a plural noun. Never mind what these Yankee dictionaries say, come back home where grits is IT, not them. Do Yankees refer to those oatmeal? Does one eat one grit or many? Isn't it supposed, at least by tradition, to be a singularly singular noun? Please say it's so.

"I remember, growing up on the Mississippi Gulf Coast, laughing with smirking pleasure over Yankee references to grits as 'them' and 'those.' I do not recall whether any of them referred to the finer-ground cousin of grits, cornmeal, as 'them' or 'those' cornmeal, but maybe I was not listening.

"Until I hear better, I am going to assume that you remain well, and the dictionary usage for grits was insinuated (or were insinuated) into your otherwise impeccable article by some scurrilous (Yankee) copy editor.

"P.S.: Now, repeat after me: 'I like grits. It is good. I eat it (not them) whenever possible.' "

Gruyère

One of the best indexes of the increased sophistication of the public palate is the discovery that one doesn't have to travel to a specialty food shop for an item generally considered arcane.

I was pleased—if not a bit surprised—recently to discover numerous packages of Gruyère cheese at the local supermarket, one that is not necessarily patronized exclusively by the well-heeled and well-traveled.

For several decades, Gruyère has been my preferred choice for most recipes that call

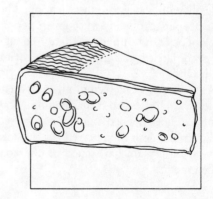

for cheese. It has a nuttiness, a deep mellowness in flavor that is not found in run-of-the-mill Swiss cheese. It is indeed a cheese from Switzerland, but it is creamier, firmer, more pungent and agreeably assertive than the cheese called Swiss, the one with the holes.

The name derives from the fact that it is made in an Alpine village called Gruyères and the valley surrounding the Gruyère River. The cheese is made from cow's milk.

The virtues of Gruyère are limitless, although its chief uses are in a fondue and for gratinéed onion soup (for these dishes it is infinitely more respectable than ordinary Swiss). Gruyère is a marvelous addition to cheese sauces (any calling for Swiss), as a topping for many casseroles, and at its best makes an excellent "dessert" cheese to be served on the platter right alongside Brie and Camembert.

Guasacaca

Guasacaca is an absolutely delectable sauce of Venezuela, very much like some versions of guacamole. To prepare it, chop a ripe, unblemished, seeded, and peeled avocado. Add to it a small, diced red ripe tomato, a little olive oil, vinegar to taste, chopped hot chili pepper, chopped sweet green pepper, salt, pepper, chopped hard-boiled egg, chopped parsley, and chopped fresh coriander leaves.

That is the basic recipe, all ingredients added more or less to taste. You may vary this by adding chopped onion and/or minced garlic, even a dash of imported hot mustard. Serve it with plain barbecued or charcoal-grilled meats.

Guests

A considerable number of words have appeared in print about manners in America during the last few decades. I was recently asked if guests in my home did anything in my dining area or kitchen that might be called an annoyance, and the answer was "One."

I do not object to elbows on the table. I don't even mind off-color jokes. And life is too brief to be irked by those individuals who hold a wineglass by the bowl instead of the stem.

What I really find bothersome are those who try to "help" with the dishes between courses or at the end of a meal. It leads to nothing but chaos and disaster.

If one unappointed individual stands to help remove the dishes, the other guests rise almost in unison. And those who don't are generally guilt-ridden. Thus, what would otherwise be a fairly civilized occasion takes on the air of Mulberry Street during the Feast of San Gennaro, a track meet, or a church supper.

There are times when I have stood by helplessly while perfectly well-meaning guests (God deliver me from well-meaning guests) stack my dishwasher until it resembles the New York subway at rush hour. Over the years I could have paid a butler what it has cost to replace wineglasses that were broken, repairs to the machine caused by waywardly stacked salad forks, or by the refuse that went partway down the drain because the dishes were improperly rinsed before "stacking."

Equally debilitating to my spirits are those well-meaning souls who attempt to "put away" the dishes after they are washed and dried. Have you ever searched for the bottom of the drip coffee maker in its accustomed storage place, only to discover after a frenzied search that it is tucked away in the oven, the very spot, no doubt, where it is invariably to be found in their own home?

So much for the dining and kitchen area. There is an even greater annoyance when guests are assembled before or after a meal and drinks, such as cocktails or coffee and liqueurs, are served.

I feel a certain reverence for some books in this world, several of which are to be found at almost any time scattered around the living area—on the cocktail table, assorted end tables, and storage chests that double as book rests. I do not mind stains on the wood of the cocktail table or the end tables. I cringe, however, at the sight of a stain on the dust jackets of my favorite books, including the massive *The Times Atlas of the World* or various works on food that I treasure. End of sermon.

Gumbo

The word "gumbo" derives from an African word meaning okra. In the strictest sense, okra is an essential ingredient in gumbo. However, it is frequently omitted in Louisiana gumbos and as a substitute filé powder is added. The powder, when used, should be stirred in after the gumbo is cooked and ready to be served. There are recipes extant that call for both okra and filé powder, but the use of both is unreasonable and unnecessary. *See also* Filé powder.

Gunpowder Tea

The best explanation I know for the origin of gunpowder tea can be found in an excellent book titled *The Tea Lover's Treasury* by James Norwood Pratt.

"Gunpowder tea," the author notes, "is so called because that's what some long-gone John Company agent in China thought it looked like, though whether on account of its granular appearance or grayish-green complexion I cannot say. It is for these reasons, at any rate, that the Chinese themselves have always called it pearl tea. Gunpowder is a special style of green tea, in which each leaf has been rolled into a tiny, compact pellet."

Hh Hh Hh Hh

Haggis

One of the most curious dishes in the world is the one to which Robert Burns gave immortality when he wrote "To a Haggis."

Be assured, haggis is no weird and ludicrous creation conceived in the Highlands by some balmy Scottish cook. When well made, it can be delectable, the kind of dish that would inevitably appeal to anyone (and their number is legion in so-called gourmet circles) who dotes on tripe and other innards, such as liver and kidneys.

The tripe—the sheep's stomach—acts as a bag for the "pudding," which is made with oatmeal, liver, and kidneys, plus seasonings. It is boiled for about three hours, until the oatmeal is nicely puffed.

Incidentally, haggis is a meat pudding and, in all probability, would be relegated to the nether regions of Scots' kitchens if Burns had not celebrated it in verse. In his much-quoted poem, dear to the hearts of Scotsmen everywhere, he calls the dish the "great chieftain o' the puddin' race!"

Many years ago, in a class in English literature, the teacher asked each of us to explain what that meant. One young classmate explained that haggis was a favorite dish of a race of people who liked puddings. What Burns intended, of course, is that haggis is the greatest of all puddings.

Halab

See Mahleb.

Half-and-Half

Half-and-half, which is a combination of milk and light cream, can be used as a substitute for both milk and heavy cream, but the results of the dish will be different. If you substitute half-and-half for milk, the end result will be far richer than called for. You could diminish this richness by diluting the mixture with a little water, but I prefer diluting it with a chicken, beef, or vegetable broth.

If you substitute half-and-half for heavy cream, the result will be less rich. Also, heavy cream when cooked down, as it is in many French recipes, tends to thicken and become sauce-like in its consistency. You will not get the same sauce-like consistency if you substitute half-and-half.

Half-Stoned

It is an educated guess that half-stoned refers to a jelly that includes some of the pits of the plums from which the jelly was made. Pits are on occasion referred to as stones. Come to think of it, I can't think of a single logical reason why anyone would want the pits in jelly unless it is to show the authenticity of the product. It is like the cook I know who always throws a little birdshot into his pheasant dishes to establish the fact that they are game birds and not cultivated.

I received a letter that threw some small light on the subject. A Connecticut woman wrote:

"I once commented to the owner of a shop where I purchase the Tiptree brand of preserves that I avoided the morello (a dark red, black sour cherry) because of the 'half-stoned' or 'part-stoned' legend. She laughed and told me that they do not contain pits or stones but assumed that the producer protected himself from lawsuits in the event that one slipped through."

Hallacas

Hallacas are tamale-like appetizers or main-course foods that are found in several South American countries including Venezuela.

They are generally stuffed with ground or chopped beef and pork, but they may also contain chicken.

The seasonings vary widely. They may include, in addition to cheese and olives, capers and raisins. They may be made with cornmeal or ground corn or hominy. And they may be wrapped in banana leaves or parchment paper rather than corn husks. They are delectable served hot and steaming.

Halvah

Halvah, also spelled halva, is a candy that is often made from ground sesame seeds and sometimes contains pistachio nuts. I have only seen one printed recipe, and it suggested using a lemon-flavored sugar syrup, plus rice flour that had been browned in butter.

In her book *The Complete Middle East Cookbook,* Tess Mallos says the candy's preparation "requires cooking under pressure and the skill of a professional confectioner." She adds that "it is not possible to duplicate the process in the home."

Ham

It is far easier to limn the pagan origins of Easter than divine why ham is so thoroughly accepted in America as the holiday dish.

In an estimable work titled *Easter Garland,* by Priscilla Sawyer Lord and Daniel J. Foley, the authors point out that the name Easter refers to the "season of the rising sun," or the dawn. This meaning long antedates the Christian era and was adopted as appropriate for the Resurrection, the

"Feast of the New Life." They add that the Venerable Bede, a medieval monk and writer, volunteered that the name Easter derived from Eostre, the name of an Anglo-Saxon goddess, although "present-day scholars claim that no such person was known in German mythology."

The curious thing about the Easter feast in this country is that we did not adopt the European custom of serving lamb as the principal course. In Italy, France, Greece, and almost any European country you can name, spring lamb is the focal point of the family meal.

I have my own theories about how ham came to be associated with the day. In the first place, lamb strikes many Americans as an "exotic" flavor and as such to be avoided. Lamb has also never been cultivated in this country on anything like as vast a scale as beef, poultry, and pork.

Many of our customs stem from the wilderness days of the Pilgrims and the curing of meats is very much a part of that tradition. The custom was, and is in rural areas, to slaughter pork in late fall. The hams are "laid down" either in salt or in smokehouses and many reach the peak of maturity and flavor five or six months later, at approximately Easter.

What choicer morsel for the Easter feast than a ham, patiently and painstakingly cured by hand!

Speaking of ham, I have read more than one supposedly serious tract on dining in which the author maintained that a ham made with the left hind leg of the pig will be more tender than one made with the right hind leg because the right hind leg gets more exercise as it's the leg that the pig scratches himself with. Tell that to your butcher and see how far you get!

If you want less than a whole ham, you can tell your butcher to cut the ham in half, and you come up with the butt end and the shank end. The shank end is the smaller of the two and slightly tapered at the bottom where the bone starts to emerge. It obviously has less meat.

The butt end is the bulkier, meatier half. If you wish, you may cut away center slices from the butt end to make ham steaks. The remainder may be used for baking.

Ham is one of those rare foods that all but defies any marriage with wine to perfect its harmony. The wine most commonly recommended for ham is a rather well-chilled rosé, preferably a rosé of Anjou, of Provence, or Portugal. Although there are very few who would dispute the pairing of ham with rosé, it doesn't show a great deal of imagination. If you are serving ham with a cream sauce, a Médoc would be appropriate, as would a red Graves or a California Cabernet Sauvignon. You could never go wrong with champagne, of course, provided it is very dry. *See also* Jambon persillé, Parma ham.

Hamburger

There is a moment in Noel Coward's play *Private Lives* in which a couple, divorced, meet by chance on a terrace in the south of France. It is a moment charged with old-fashioned sentiment, heightened abruptly by the sound of a piano off-stage playing "I'll See You Again." Amanda, the lady in the case, remarks, "Extraordinary how potent cheap music is."

That's the way I feel about hamburgers, if you happen to think that hamburgers are trashy and banal, if not to say vulgar—to use the word in its meaning of "popular." To put it one way, I infinitely prefer a well-made hamburger to an overcooked filet mignon or an ill-seasoned porterhouse.

Although the name is of German extraction, a hamburger is as quintessentially American as pasta is Italian or paprika dishes Hungarian. It would seem, after a considerable amount of random research that has spanned a couple of decades, that there is no concretely documented evidence of the precise moment the first hamburger came into evidence.

Evan Jones, in his *American Food,* offers a most reasonable explanation for the name. The patty itself was originally "a nineteenth-century import from Germany, a meat dish of chopped beef," first known in this country "as a Hamburg steak after the . . . port on the Elbe River." Rombauer-Becker's well-known *Joy of Cooking* reprints the most commonly accepted conjecture as to the hamburger's origin. It was, the book notes, at "the St. Louis World's Fair in 1904 that broiled, bunned beef was introduced to the rest of the world by the Germans of South St. Louis."

It is not the patty itself that makes the hamburger so typically American. It is, rather, the patty-cum-bun or sandwich factor that puts it in league with apple pie (only more so; it has been estimated that Americans consume more than forty billion hamburgers a year, and if there is any other dish that exceeds that figure, I'll eat those words). Ground meat in various shapes, patties and otherwise, occurred in the world's cuisines years, perhaps centuries, before the St. Louis exposition. There are polpette di carne of Italy; the frikadeller of Sweden; the boulettes de viande of France; the albondigas of Mexico, and the koftas of India, to offer

a brief sample of cooked, shaped ground-meat dishes. But a broiled or grilled meat patty in a bun you can waltz around with smacks of the Stars and Stripes forever.

I have long held a theory that the simplest dishes in the world are frequently the most difficult to cook. It is, in truth, I feel, more difficult to scramble an egg than make a good soufflé; it is far more difficult to make a succulent and splendid roast chicken than a platter of coq au vin. The same is true of hamburgers. It takes talent to turn out a hamburger with class.

To do so, shape ground beef, preferably round steak or sirloin (the ground tail of porterhouse or T-bone makes excellent hamburgers), into flat round patties.

There are two recommended methods for cooking hamburgers in a skillet. In the first, sprinkle a light layer of salt in the bottom of a heavy skillet, such as a black iron skillet. Heat the skillet thoroughly and add the hamburgers. If the heat is hot enough under the skillet, they will not stick. When cooked on one side, use a pancake turner and, with a quick motion, scoop under the hamburgers, turning them in the skillet. Reduce the heat and continue cooking to the desired degree of doneness. Add a touch of butter and salt and pepper to taste.

The more conventional method of skillet cookery is to melt for each hamburger half a teaspoon of butter in a heavy skillet, and when it is hot but not browning, add the hamburger or hamburgers. Cook until browned on one side, turn and continue cooking to the desired degree of doneness. Sprinkle with salt and pepper and serve with the pan juices.

The preferred method for cooking hamburgers is on a grill fired with charcoal or gas-fired coals. The grill should be very hot when the hamburgers are added. Cook until nicely grilled on one side, turn and cook to the desired degree of doneness. Add a touch of butter and salt and pepper to taste.

Hangtown Fry

Although many Americans tend to view the names of certain British foods with wry amusement, this nation has its own share of odd appellations in the kitchen. Consider, if you will, things like hoppin' John, blueberry grunt, and apple pan dowdy. The Indians gave us succotash and the South contributed corn dodgers, corn pone, and hush puppies. New England provided us with that oddment among breads called anadama, so named because the husband of a lazy wife named Anna created a bread in anger and desperation, all the time muttering "Anna, damn'er."

One of the most memorable of food names is the West Coast specialty called Hangtown fry. The genesis of that name can be found in the late Helen Evans Brown's *The West Coast Cook Book*.

Mrs. Brown states that it doubtless has to do with a town named Hangtown that later was renamed Placerville "to appease some of its more fastidious citizens."

"One story is that a man about to be hanged asked that his last meal be 'fried oysters with scrambled eggs on top and bacon on the side.' "

There is another version, she notes, of the dish's origin—that it "was named after Nick 'Hangtown,' whose nickname was acquired when he cooked for Mr. Studebaker, the wheelbarrow king in Hangtown."

Hardtack

Hardtack is a hard, brittle bread or biscuit made with flour and water; it is also called sea biscuit, sea bread, or pilot bread. If hardtack is properly kept, its lasting qualities are almost limitless, which is why it is appropriate for long sea voyages and for soldiers' rations.

"Tack" is a contemptuous term for food; the *Oxford English Dictionary* describes tack as "foodstuff; chiefly in hard-tack, ship's biscuit; soft-tack." I have never encountered soft-tack.

Harissa

Harissa, served with couscous, is a very hot sauce, recipes for which vary. It is made with dried hot chili peppers plus garlic, caraway seeds, cumin, coriander, salt, and olive oil. You may buy harissa in cans at stores that specialize in Middle Eastern foods. There is, I am told, an Armenian appetizer also known as harissa. This is made with pearl barley, water, cubed meat, salt, pepper, butter, cinnamon, and cumin.

Harvard Beets

The origin of Harvard beets has been explained to me as follows:

The color of the beets is the same as that of Harvard's banners and football jerseys.

It's a fascinating thought, perhaps trustworthy. But there are, of course, other theories. I have a letter from a man who explains that "actually, what is now called Harvard beets were concocted in an English tavern in the early seventeenth century, when vegetables were the staple diet of most working-class Englishmen. The name of the tavern was Harwood's and a Russian émigré to America, who paused in England on his journey to the New World, opened a restaurant in Boston in 1846. Because of his accent, the name Harwood sounded to the Boston customers of his restaurant like Harvood and was quickly changed to Harvard because of the proximity of the university."

Likely or not, it's a good story.

Headcheese

Headcheese is made of pig's head and frequently pig's feet, and seasonings, including bay leaf and mace, the whole cooked down in water until the meats are tender. The meats are removed from the stock, the broth is reduced, and when blended and cooled, the headcheese jells. It is served cold and iced, often with chopped onion, oil, and vinegar. In Ireland, where it is called brawn, a grated beet is sometimes added to the ingredients to give the headcheese a red color.

It is pure conjecture, but it is probably called cheese because of the texture of the jelled meat.

Hearts of Palm

The palm that contributes its heart to the dinner table is known as *Sabal palmetto,* the best-known sources for which are Florida

and Brazil. The palm is often referred to in Florida and other parts of the South as swamp cabbage. To arrive at the heart of palm you cut down a tree, strip off the fronds that surround it, cut away a good bit of other tough sheathing, and arrive at the tender heart. It is a tedious, time-consuming process, particularly for the unskilled. I am told that the palm proliferates so easily and is available in such abundance that its use should not alarm conservationists.

Henri IV

The most aptly named dish in the world may be *poule au pot Henry IV.* At the time of his coronation he said, "*Je veux que le dimanche chaque paysan ait sa poule au pot,*" or "I wish that every peasant have a chicken in his pot on Sundays." A noble desire, indeed.

Herbes de Provence

I first noticed packages of dried herbs bearing the name herbes de Provence about a dozen years ago at Fauchon's on the Place

Madeleine in Paris. Within recent years, of course, numerous food specialty shops in Manhattan and across America have been selling what is labeled "herbes de Provence," and I'm sure the packagers and purveyors have made a good deal of money by using that lure. Whether any of this has been to the greater glory of the American kitchen, I cannot say. I suspect one would do better by adding one's own "herbes de Provence" depending on the recipe.

To get down to facts, there are many herbs, wild and cultivated, growing in Provence. The most prominent of them—and it is almost surely an assortment of these herbs in one combination or another that is known commercially as "herbes de Provence"—include bay leaf, thyme, fennel, and rosemary. Garlic, "the truffle of Provence," is used in abundance, but it would not figure in a packaged assortment of dried herbs.

A recipe for herbes de Provence appears in R. J. Courtine's *Feasts of a Militant Gastronome*.

PROVENÇAL HERBS
(For flavoring Niçoise-type dishes)
1 tablespoon each dried thyme, chervil, tarragon, marjoram
1 teaspoon each dried oregano, rosemary, summer savory
½ teaspoon dried mint

2 Mediterranean bay leaves, well crumbled
Mix well; store in a tightly covered glass jar. Use sparingly. It is very fragrant.

Herbs

Because of the large volume of herbs and spices that I use each year, I rarely put them up, preferring to buy them fresh at my local grocery or supermarket. I recently received an interesting letter from a cook who strongly advocates the use of a microwave oven for drying herbs (she adds that she has few uses for her machine other than cooking bacon and reheating leftovers).

I followed her directions in drying a bunch of fresh coriander leaves with what I consider adequate results. I tried the coriander, which in commercially dried form has no flavor at all. The flavor of coriander dried in my own microwave oven was an improvement, although there was definite flavor loss.

Basically, the method involves rinsing fresh herbs, patting them dry with paper towels, and placing them between fresh paper towels on paper plates. Using the lowest cooking level, heat the herbs for one-minute intervals, checking after each interval. Continue until the herbs are dried and somewhat brittle. Store in tightly sealed containers.

I have tried drying herbs at room temperature and in the oven, and this technique seems to be as satisfactory as any, and more so than most. As I have noted, there was a noticeable decrease in pungency in the herbs I dried.

You can make herb vinegar with fresh or dried herbs at the end of the season. Some useful herbs are tarragon, basil, parsley, rosemary, and marjoram. Time for the infusion will depend on the herb and whether it is fresh or dried.

If fresh herbs are used, simply insert them in a bottle of white or red vinegar.

If dried herbs are used, here is the procedure:

Crush ½ teaspoon dried basil, tarragon, rosemary, or other herb with the flat side of a knife. Put the herb in a sterilized glass jar with a tight-fitting lid. Heat 2 cups of vinegar to the boiling point and add it. Cover and let stand for 10 days at room temperature. Shake the vinegar on occasion. At the end of 10 days, strain the vinegar through cheesecloth, rebottle, and cover.

Hero Sandwich

Over a glass of white wine at an end-of-the-season picnic, one of the guests wondered about the origin of the hero sandwich. I averred that although the hero sandwich was probably relatively new, which is to say less than half a century old, I doubted that anyone could pinpoint when the first such oversized sandwich was served.

Later, I happened to glance through a column that appeared in *The New York Times* nearly twenty-five years ago in which Manganaro's, the famed food establishment at 492 Ninth Avenue in Manhattan, staked claim to the original hero. That may be open to debate, but I was interested in that store's beginnings, which I had never read before.

"In 1905," the account read, "James Manganaro, who had been making whale-sized sandwiches of prosciutto and French bread to nourish himself on all-day fishing trips, came from Italy to New York to join his cousin in the grocery business. The store was at the same address even then.

"It was James Manganaro who branched into the sandwich business, making them the same way that he liked a sandwich—big." At the time of that article in 1957 (when the store had branched out into a special sandwich shop next door), the management was turning out two thousand "heroboys" a day.

One well-known food writer noted in the 1930s that a person would have to be a hero to down such a hefty sandwich, which may have prompted the name. Heros are also known as submarines, grinders, and hoagies.

Herring

See Matjes herring.

Hoe Cake

See Johnny cake.

Hogmanay

Hogmanay must be the most oddly named feast day in the world. It is Scotland's name for a New Year's celebration and derives, according to the *Oxford English Dictionary*, from the old French word *aiguillanneuf*, meaning "the last day of the year at which New Year's gifts were given." Don't ask me how the two words are related for, frankly, I can't figure it out.

On one occasion when I sampled a traditional feast, the foods included a haggis, the most Scottish of all foods, steamed in a sheep's stomach.

There was also a cloutie dumpling (a black fruit pudding, so named because it is traditionally steamed in cloutie or cloth); stoved chicken or chicken stovies, a remarkably simple and delectable chicken stew with potatoes and onions and herbs; crumpets leavened with baking powder; cranachan, a rich, irresistible, and easily made sauce of whipped cream, powdered sugar, and Drambuie and, oddly, toasted, fine-cut oats to be served as is or with fresh berries or over tarts.

Hoisin Sauce

Hoisin sauce is widely used in Chinese cookery. It gives a slightly sweet flavor and thickening to dishes to which it is added. Its commonest use is probably as a table condiment to be smeared on Chinese pancakes to which bits of Peking duck and scallions are added, before the pancakes are rolled and eaten.

I have never seen a recipe for hoisin sauce. It is, of course, widely available commercially, and I have never had a need to make it in my own kitchen. The basic ingredients, which I am certain vary at least slightly from manufacturer to manufacturer, are soybeans, fermented rice, garlic, sugar, vinegar, flour, and assorted spices. The commercial product, once opened, should be transferred to a glass jar with a tight lid. It will then keep indefinitely in the refrigerator.

Hominy

It is an irritating fact of life that Yankees do not comprehend that hominy connotes whole hominy in the minds of those who would use it in the first place.

Hominy grits are, to my mind—or, perhaps I should say, to my taste—redundant. Grits are made from hominy. Similarly you wouldn't say corn hominy for the simple reason that hominy is made from corn kernels that have been dried and then soaked in lye. However, many recipes calling for hominy undoubtedly mean grits as the principal ingredient and not whole hominy.

The word "hominy" derives from an Algonkian Indian word, *tackhummin,* which means to grind corn. Don't labor the point and tell me that whole hominy isn't ground. I know it.

When I was a child we often dined on whole lye hominy. To make it, whole kernels of dried corn are soaked in wood-ash lye. The kernels become snow white and one end opens up like a flower. The hominy can be cooked and served several ways—in butter, in milk or cream, or in a cheese casserole.

There is a technique for preparing whole hominy in Diana Kennedy's *The Cuisines of Mexico*. She uses unslaked lime for her process. *See also* Samp.

Honey

A keen appetite for honeys of various sorts is totally comprehensible. Having a perverse taste, however, I am not an avid honey fancier. To my palate, it is too devastatingly sweet, and, therefore, a little goes a long way on my slice of buttered toast.

Aside from taste, one problem with honey is that, if left to stand, it becomes sugary and develops crystals.

This is not harmful, and if the honey has been tightly capped, it is still usable. If you want to make it liquid once more, place the bottle in a bowl of lukewarm water and the crystals will disappear.

Corn syrup is a perfectly good substitute for honey in most recipes, and I would use the substitution volume for volume. You might also make a sugar syrup using 1¼ cups of granulated sugar for each cup of honey, plus ¼ cup of water. Combine the sugar and water in a small saucepan, bring to a boil, and stir until sugar is dissolved. The reason for the increased volume of sugar is that honey is sweeter than sugar.

Hoppel-Poppel

Although I have heard the name hoppel-poppel for many years and have scanned numerous traditional or "classic" encyclopedias of American cookery, I have not found a clue as to the origin of the dish.

In fact, the only recipe I have ever found for the dish is in Jan Mitchell's *Lüchow's German Cook Book*. It consists of cooking cubed boiled beef, chopped onion, and chopped bacon in butter until the bacon is done. You then add beaten eggs, which are stirred over the meat. The eggs are allowed to set as in a flat omelet. It is folded and served.

Hop Shoots

Although we know of hops primarily in making beer, you can also cook with hop shoots, although I have never seen them on the market in the United States. I have eaten them in Switzerland and they are delicious. In *Le Guide Culinaire* by Escoffier, he mentions that the edible part of the hop is broken off like asparagus. The shoot is washed in several changes of cold water and cooked in boiling salted water with a touch of lemon juice to prevent discoloration. They may be served with melted butter, in a cream sauce, or other ways. "When served as a vegetable it is traditional," the text states, "to make a circle of poached eggs, alternating them with cockscomb-shaped croutons of bread that have been fried in butter. This is either placed on top or around the hop shoots."

Hors d'Oeuvres

See Appetizers.

Horse Meat

Years ago I dined on horse meat and, as I recall, it was lean, tender, and suitably tasty. *Larousse Gastronomique* notes that it is consumed in many civilized countries and that "for centuries it has been the principal food of the Gaucho Indians of South America." The encyclopedia adds that "the people of Paris have always eaten horse meat."

Horseradish

Fresh horseradish is delectable and easily prepared. You peel the horseradish root, which is generally a bit gnarled and carrot-shaped. It is an off-white color. You simply grate or finely shred it.

Some people prefer fine grating, others rather coarse grating. I enjoy both depending on the use. I may grate the root coarsely and serve it on the side with a dish like boiled beef.

If I intend to make a light cream sauce, which I also enjoy with boiled beef and roast beef, I grate the horseradish fine and add it according to taste. It is my experience that the strength of a horseradish root varies

from the extremely mild and uninteresting to the teardrop-making.

You may use a hand grater, blender, or food processor to do your grating. If you want to duplicate the bottled horseradish that you can find commercially, you simply use finely grated horseradish and add a little white vinegar to moisten it properly and salt, if desired.

If you make a large batch of horseradish with vinegar and salt, make sure that you keep it in a glass jar compactly filled so that there is as little air space as possible. Keep it tightly sealed and refrigerated so that it retains its pungent flavor. Horseradish is also delicious when grated and blended with cooled, finely grated beets.

One of the dishes the patrons liked best at New York's old Colony Restaurant was the applesauce served with roast fowl. It was made by combining a cup or so of applesauce with a tablespoon or more of horseradish, preferably freshly grated, and a teaspoon or less of imported Hungarian paprika.

For the cold, skinned, smoked trout fillets, for which the restaurant was famous, there was always a horseradish sauce. It was made by folding freshly grated horserad-

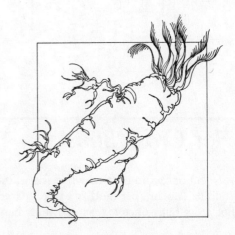

ish—a tablespoon more or less, according to taste—into a cup or so of whipped cream. Lemon juice and salt were added to taste before serving.

Horseshoe Crabs

Esthetically, horseshoe crabs may leave something to be desired. You might like to know that they have, however, been around for something like 200 million years and are often referred to as a living fossil. According to Alan Davidson's *North Atlantic Seafood,* "The proportion of meat to shell is small, but what meat there is is edible and has sometimes been eaten in the Middle Atlantic states. The crab itself should be detached from the huge carapace before being prepared."

Hot Cross Buns

A friend once told me that when she was a child in London, her mother had prepared hot cross buns once a year and that there

was a spice that to this day pervades her memory. Her children told her that she was romanticizing the whole thing and that the spice she had in mind was no doubt cinnamon.

I once expressed surprise that I could find no recipe for hot cross buns in *Mrs. Beeton's Book of Household Management,* but that another volume on English breads indicated that the commonest spices for the buns are allspice, nutmeg, cinnamon, and cloves.

I subsequently discovered that while Mrs. Beeton did not include hot cross buns in her index, they were detailed in the book under buns. I returned to the volume and found at the end of her recipe for plain buns the note stating that "the above mixture answers for hot cross buns, by putting in a little ground allspice; and by pressing a tin mold in the form of a cross in the center of the bun."

Hot Dog

See Frankfurter.

Hot Plates

I have an absolute idée fixe when it comes to serving hot food on hot plates. Not just warm plates. Hot plates. The following letter from Pleasantville, New York, went far to warm my heart's cockles:

"Since moving to the U.S. a few years ago, I have become aware that my preoccupation with serving hot food on hot plates and serving dishes is not generally shared. I probably inherited this bias from my Canadian mother, who virtually baked the plates before putting them on the table—the quality of the cooking was another matter, which is best to overlook, but everything *sizzled*. Platters of meat and vegetables were whisked back to the 'warming oven' to await a second round. Maids (who still existed in the remotest recesses of my childhood memories) rushed back and forth, scarcely avoiding scorched fingers, with layers of napkins folded between their hands and the plates. Now, I find that my dinner guests seem baffled or amused, or simply think I've made a blunder when I warn them that the plates are hot. One young guest, helping me serve, actually suggested that I run cold water over the plates in order to make them easier to handle!

"Many, even most, of these friends care about good food, and both men and women can spend hours preparing a superlative meal, then plop it casually onto chilly plates. Now this is not even strictly American, as many of my friends are of Italian or French origin. Do they suffer a sea-change, or did mama/maman also feel that getting the food onto the table was the important thing, and heating plates a bother or even affectation? I know that I have never been aware of cold plates in European restaurants of any category; hot plates are as normal as hot food, indeed the Swiss are most fanatical in this respect and every restaurant has elaborate plate-warming machines.

"I do remember one French couple, though, who spent hours preparing delectable sauces and served it all on cold plates. But I considered this a personal tic, as they also tossed the salad several hours in advance; the wife explained to me once that 'my husband likes his salad *bien cuit!*'

"On this side of the Atlantic, though, what am I to make of the Roman friend who cooks a succulent *abacchio al forno*, plops it onto a cold platter and proceeds to slice the entire roast with an electric knife, leaving it to congeal in its own fat while we work through the pasta course? And the French hostess who recently cooked a glorious couscous dinner, once again served from, and onto, cold plates?

"Have I stumbled onto a sort of gastronomic amnesia on the part of people of otherwise impeccable taste, unlikely to patronize any restaurant which served them as they serve themselves at home? Personally, I find that there is no extra work involved in putting plates and serving dishes into the bottom of my oven as I prepare a meal. Admittedly, it is a double oven and the space under the broiling tray is just the right temperature to heat, without cracking, good china.

"But my dishwasher also has a 'dry' cycle which is perfect for heating plates, and, in a pinch, hot water can always be poured over them in the sink at the last minute. A friend has confirmed to me that her Canadian mother was also deeply concerned with plate-warming, and thinks this may be an inherited English custom."

Hot-Ta-Meat Pies

See Turnovers.

Howtowdie

Howtowdie is a perfectly respectable and quite delicious stuffed chicken specialty found in Scotland. The chicken is stuffed with bread crumbs and, according to one recipe I know, browned in a casserole. It is sprinkled with spices and a little chicken broth and cooked closely covered until tender. It is served with a sauce of the chicken's liver and cream, and on a bed of spinach.

Huitlacoche

See Fungus.

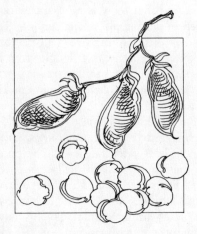

Hummus

Hummus is the Middle Eastern name for chick-peas. Most Americans who dine in Middle Eastern restaurants know it best in the preparation known as hummus bi tahini, or chick-peas blended with lemon juice, garlic, salt, olive oil, and tahini, which is a paste of sesame seeds.

Hummus is most often used as a dip for bits of pita bread. It may also be used as a dip for raw vegetables and as a sauce for fish and meats.

Humorous Story

It would be impossible to name the single most humorous true food story I have ever read. Here, however, is an account that I have kept for several years in my file of miscellany. It is a report from United Press International:

SLIDELL, LA.—Duck hunter Warren Stovall, relaxing at home after bagging a pair of mallards he intended to have mounted, went to his freezer to get ice for a drink.

When he opened the freezer door, a half-frozen duck with buckshot wounds in the neck and wing flapped out of the refrigerator and flew around the room.

"He started screaming," his wife, Charlotte, who was in another room watching television, said. "I think he thought the dead bird had come back to get him.

"He came running in with the duck, and it was alive. It had worked its way out of the foil and was sitting in the freezer when he opened it, and it flew out."

Stovall had shot the drake and a hen about dawn Saturday, and a busy taxidermist told him to freeze the birds and he would stuff them.

Stovall wrapped each duck separately in tin foil, sealing them with tape, and popped them in the freezer at 10 A.M. Saturday. It was 10 that night when the duck flew out of the freezer.

"The duck had worked his way out of the foil and must have been out a long time," said Mrs. Stovall. "There was bird mess all inside the freezer."

A weeping Mrs. Stovall wrapped the bird in a blanket and rocked it like a baby. She nursed it through the weekend and took it to the veterinarian. The vet said the stunned bird survived in the freezer because of its natural insulation.

The Stovalls decided to give the drake to a man who raises ducks.

Hundred-Year Eggs

The Chinese delicacy called hundred-year eggs, which are highly aromatic, have a very special taste, and resemble discolored hard-boiled eggs, go by several names, including thousand-year eggs and, simply, preserved eggs.

The eggs, only from ducks, are coated with a "muddy" blend of lime, ashes, and salt and are left to stand for forty-five days or longer. The lime causes the whites to become firm and the yolks partly firm and a trifle liquid in the center. The yolks take on a greenish cast and the whites are yellowish green. Their taste is slightly sulfuric.

Hush Puppies

One specialty dear to Southerners is hush puppies, those deep-fried cornmeal patties that were said to come about during the Civil War when a group of Southerners were cooking over an open fire. When a platoon of Yankee soldiers came nearby, the Southerners would fry up a few patties and toss them to their yelping dogs with the admonition, "Hush, puppies."

Hush puppies are made with, among other things, cornmeal, flour, eggs, baking powder, and buttermilk. An essential ingredient is chopped onion or scallions. This mixture is dropped by spoonfuls into deep fat.

Iceberg Lettuce

Iceberg lettuce is mundane and very low on the scale of salad greens. Watercress, Belgian endive, escarole, Boston lettuce, romaine, and others are simply more sophisticated and have more class. To put it another way, iceberg is to other lettuces as peanuts are to almonds, hazelnuts, and walnuts.

However, there are numerous dishes in this world that are complemented by iceberg lettuce, when, indeed it would be first choice. Such dishes include shredded iceberg lettuce for fare such as tacos and enchiladas. It is ideal as a wrapping for the Chinese dish sometimes called lettuce packages or chicken soong in which cubed chicken is stir-fried with chopped water chestnuts, bamboo shoots, black mushrooms, and so on. A chiffonade of iceberg lettuce can be quite acceptable as a base for some cold seafood dishes.

Someday there will probably come into being an organization called "The Society of Iceberg Lettuce Fanciers," "Friends of Iceberg Lettuce," or somesuch. I believe in giving equal space to those who admire iceberg lettuce, thus the following comment I received in its defense:

"I feel I must come to a half-hearted defense of the iceberg.

"Botanically, iceberg is in a class. True, it may be nutritionally low on the scale of salad greens, but to say that it is not sophisticated is being very elitist.

"How can iceberg become classy, sophisticated? Is there any hope of raising its social status? Maybe at the Restaurant Troisgros a masterpiece could be created utilizing iceberg. Or, maybe some country gentleman of fading gentility might be coaxed into raising iceberg and lending his name. It is possible that iceberg might achieve elevation to position through a farmer. After all, didn't peanuts soar above almonds, hazelnuts, and walnuts right into the Washington Social Register?

"Iceberg lettuce has become the *lares et penates* of the traditional American household and even the warmth of that American hearth cannot warm the frostiness of your remarks."

Ice Cream

It would seem that nothing could be less Chinese than ice cream. And yet there are legends that Marco Polo returned to Italy from his travels in the fourteenth century with "tales of Orientals reclining on embroidered cushions, dabbing at dishes of ice brought from the mountains on camel back, and flavored with exotic fruits." Frozen desserts in the form of water ices were thus—according to that exotic account—established in Italy. The idea was spread to France through the Medicis, according to the same source, and French chefs took their usual giant step forward and replaced water ices with ice cream. Thence the idea traveled as a "court secret" to England and eventually, in colonial times, to America.

Food lore is nothing if not romantic. Another account has it that the Aztec emperor Montezuma engaged servants to pour liquid chocolate into the snows of distant mountains. The chocolate, when frozen, was rushed to the emperor for his delight.

There are literally thousands of recipes for ice creams. The most famous and basic regional American ice cream is Philadelphia ice cream, made with a combination of cream and sugar that may or may not be cooked. To this is added one flavoring or another before freezing.

Perhaps the most basic and universally made ice cream in the Western world is that prepared with an English or vanilla custard. Puréed fruits may be added to the custard before freezing. *See also* Ices.

Iced Tea

To prevent iced tea from clouding, I have my own simplistic version. I simply make a strong brew and let it stand at room temperature until it is used up. I never put it in the refrigerator, for I have found that refrigeration tends to cloud the tea.

This technique, it turns out, is by no means universal. Many people, it seems, use

a solar technique when they make their tea.

"I have been making 'sun' tea for years and found it does not cloud, even if refrigerated for two or three days," one said. "My method is this: Put 2 tea bags in a half-gallon, clear-glass jug with cold water. Place this in the sun for 6 to 8 hours. When the tea is dark, remove the tea bags and refrigerate. This type of tea will cloud if lemon or sugar are added."

Another, who uses a similar method for tea preparation, adds that the tea "tastes especially bright and is never bitter."

Others wrote to state that even if your tea does cloud when poured over ice, there is nothing lost. A spokesperson for The Tea Council in New York recommends that you do not refrigerate iced tea that is made the traditional way with boiling water.

But if it does cloud, "you can generally restore its crystal clarity by adding a little boiling water."

Furthermore, "there is a way of making perfectly beautiful cloudless iced tea using cold water. For this, you simply put eight to ten tea bags in a pitcher or container containing a quart of cold water. Let it stand at room temperature or in the refrigerator for at least 6 hours or overnight. Then remove the tea bags and pour over ice to serve.

This cold-water method is guaranteed never to cloud."

Years ago I wrote an essay that appeared in a popular food magazine in which a man named Richard Blechynden was credited with inventing iced tea.

Mr. Blechynden came to America in 1904 to promote the sale of Ceylon and India black teas at the St. Louis international exhibition of that year. The trouble was, the summer in St. Louis that year was stiflingly hot and nobody was interested in a cup of piping hot tea. Thus he resorted to a revolutionary and hitherto unknown technique: pouring the tea over ice. The drink was an instantaneous success.

A travel agent from Forest Hills disagrees:

"It is a fact, though perhaps not too well known, that the travel industry has its roots in the temperance movement. In fact, the original Thomas Cook was a temperance leader who hardly ever thought of himself as the father of the package tour. If he did organize tours mostly for his teetotaler groups, it was to make sure the delegates would not be exposed to the distressing spectacle of public indulgence.

"When he toured the U.S. West by train one hot summer in the 1880s, he was greatly disturbed to find that at every station his traveling companions kept heading for the refreshment room, there to partake of a brown beverage served in glasses and looking suspiciously like sherry. After further investigation he was much relieved to discover that the beverage was nothing more than tea that these funny Americans drank . . . cold. After having tried it himself, however, he found that 'nothing ever quenched thirst or ever satisfied thirsty appetite as well as cold tea.'

"With all due respect to St. Louis, I fear that they will have to abandon their claim to iced tea. Thomas Cook's visit to the United States took place many years before the 1904 World's Fair."

And yet another version of the origins of iced tea:

"Iced tea appeared in the United States, the creation of some anonymous individual, prior to the Civil War. In 1860 a writer for Horace Greeley's *Tribune,* Solon Robinson, published a small volume, *How to Live.* In this appeared the sentence, 'Last summer we got in the habit of taking the tea iced, and really thought it better than when hot.'

"By 1871 the new beverage competed with iced milk and iced water on hot summer days at the Fifth Avenue Hotel in New York. In the same year a writer in New Orleans noted that 'in these hot climates, cold tea lemonade, iced, is declared by the few who have tried it to be more fragrant and refreshing than the most liberal libations of soda-water or other effervescing liquids.'

"By 1878, travelers found iced tea for sale on the Rock Island Railroad and a 'popular' beverage in Sidney, Nebraska. Cookbooks began to offer recipes for iced tea and in 1886 Senators in their Washington offices were said to have had 'large coolers' of it 'to mitigate the force of the weather.' "

Ices

I am addicted to well-made ices, sherbets, and ice creams. I am not one to race to the icebox for a midnight snack, I do not get the midnight munchies. But I am almost invariably tempted to visit the freezer after a meal at least once of an evening (and even twice if the craving gets too fierce) if I know there is homemade raspberry, grape-fruit, strawberry, or lemon ice waiting there. Or a fruit sherbet. And I am not above making that journey if the ice is not home-made, provided it is a good commercial product (the boysenberry sherbet of Häagen-Dazs falls into this category, to mention but one).

I am only a hair less passionate for ice cream, particularly vanilla. But I can happily settle for other ice creams, provided they have a vanilla or "white" base, things like peach or banana or coconut.

Although I love both sherbets and ices, if given a single choice I would order the ice. I have often been asked the difference between the two, and the answer should be simpler than it is. Technically, an ice, known as granité in French, is a frozen dessert made with pure fruit juice or purée plus sugar or fruit juice plus a simple syrup made with sugar and water. A sherbet is a fruit ice to which has been added either a meringue (of the sort you use to frost cakes) or beaten egg whites. This "pure" difference is some-times corrupted by manufacturers who add milk or cream to their fruit sherbets rather than the meringue or whites.

The word fruit is used loosely here, for on a recent occasion I happily sampled one of the most unusual and delectable ices I've ever encountered, this one made with dried rosemary and a simple syrup. It was the creation of Josef (Seppi) Renggli, the in-spired chef of The Four Seasons restaurant in New York City, who offered it at a special banquet. Dried rosemary was steeped in a hot syrup overnight. It was then strained, blended with a bit of white wine and lemon juice, and frozen. It was given a final garnish with sprigs of fresh rosemary that had also been sugared and frozen.

Icing

See Frosting.

Illusion

Illusion in food is important in dining. Farcical though it may sound, I know of a man who is both excellent hunter and ex-cellent cook. He has what they used to call a fine, upstanding character.

Otherwise honest, he told me that he re-sorts to one bit of trickery when, out of sea-son, he buys domestic game from a butcher. He tosses a birdshot or two into each serv-ing. Makes the birds taste better, he main-tains.

Of course, you could carry this to endless limits. Add a fresh pea pod to your frozen peas, add a seed of a lemon to your store-bought mayonnaise. But for heaven's sake, add a touch of fresh lemon juice, too!

Imam Bayeldi

The genesis of the name *imam bayeldi,* which means "the priest fainted," has to do with the oil-soaking properties of eggplant. The story goes that there once was an elderly priest—or *imam* as the Mohammedans call him—who married a wealthy olive oil mer-chant's daughter, the finest cook in the land. On her wedding day she received a dozen stone barrels of olive oil as a dowry. The day after the marriage she prepared a wholly irresistible dish of eggplant with tomatoes and the *imam* ate it with relish. It was so much to his taste, in fact, he asked her to prepare it every day.

On the thirteenth day she served a quite different dish. When the *imam* asked her why, she replied that her dowry was depleted. There wasn't a drop left. He fainted.

Indian Nuts

See Pine nuts.

Indian Pears

See Prickly pears.

Indian Pudding

If Americans by and large cannot be called ardent epicures, there are, apparently, a dozen or so dishes about which they care passionately enough to take up their chef's knives and do battle.

These ire-arousing preparations include clam chowders, white and red; chili con carne; Boston baked beans; mint juleps; and, on the eastern tip of Long Island, at least, clam pies.

I would have ranked Indian pudding relatively low on that list and I would have been mistaken, for rarely has any column elicited such a heated response as did one where I offered a recipe for what I presumed to be an authentic version, with brown sugar, raisins, and eggs.

"An emotional reaction seized me upon reading—and incredulously re-reading—the recipe for Indian pudding," wrote a New Jersey woman. It is "drastically twentieth century" and has "suffered more fanciful accretions over the years than the legends of some saints."

The basic recipe, she added, was "cornmeal, milk, molasses, with fresh-grated nutmeg, and a touch of ginger" in a buttered crockery bowl or deep granite pan.

"When Indian-meal was first combined with Barbados molasses and plentiful skimmed milk, white sugar was very expensive; it came in a loaf, was used for tea (lumps) and delicate recipes and would never have been wasted on an already sweet pudding."

In addition to which, the reader notes, "Possibly our not using raisins was an economy measure; the seeded black sultanas were expensive. Wasn't it about 1918 that the Thompson seedless came along? The milk and cornmeal cured (not curdled) together with the molasses. . . . Baking powder was unheard of, and unnecessary to boot." And so on.

Another not only chastised me for that "ridiculous travesty," but added that Indian pudding was "invented" by poor country people who had cornmeal and molasses as staples of their diet.

One of the most fascinating pudding recipes came from Mrs. Ivy Dodd of Rockland, Maine. Mrs. Dodd is with the book division of Rockland's *Courier-Gazette,* which has published such books as *Maine Cookery— Then and Now* and *All-Maine Cooking.*

"Traditionally," Mrs. Dodd told me, "Indian pudding was composed solely of cornmeal, molasses, milk, and spices with no eggs, raisins or anything else added. Made according to tradition, the pudding when taken from the oven will quiver and be of a jelly-like consistency. The old way that has never been improved upon was to bring a quart of milk to a boil in an iron kettle, and then to add to it about one scant cup of fine cornmeal with the left hand, holding the meal high and sifting it slowly through the fingers, stirring it constantly meanwhile with the right hand.

"When this has thickened and cooled a little, add ½ teaspoon of cinnamon and ½ pint of cold milk. Beat the whole mixture until smooth, then pour into a deep, well-buttered pudding dish.

"When it has baked nearly an hour (modern cooks might need to know about 300 degrees) pour over it a half pint of cold milk which must not be stirred but allowed to soak in gradually. Bake in a steady oven 3 to 4 hours, the longer the better. The New England housewife, in the days of the brick oven, baked hers in a stone pudding dish all night.

"In baking, if it was desired to have the pudding extra rich, our forebears added 1 cupful of currants or raisins after the pudding had baked a few minutes. In this case, an additional ½ pint of milk was added. I have also added 2 well-beaten eggs, but oldtimers used no eggs.

"Note: When sweetening agents such as molasses and especially sugar were expensive and hard to come by, sweetener was added to taste after the pudding was cooked. Molasses could be poured over or sugar sprinkled on as might be available, if any. One-half cup of molasses could be added to this pudding with the cinnamon, if desired."

As a postscript, I was offered "Further Notes on the Great Indian Pudding Controversy," in the words of an instructor in anthropology and sociology at Hartwick College in Oneonta, New York.

"If you can stand it," he added. Rather perceptively, I thought.

" 'Indian,' " he continued, "is such a vague term it is meaningless when applied to a supposed specific recipe, so any recipe for anything can be called 'Indian'—especially given the fact that there are millions of Indian cooks alive today who are as inventive as any other ethnic group. Also, the heretical tapioca recipe is certainly 'Indian' since Indians 'invented' tapioca—the first domesticated manioc, the source of tapioca, six thousand or more years ago in South America, where it is still the staple food in many areas."

So much for the Great Indian Pudding Controversy.

Indian Spices

I have noted (confessed may be a better word) that to my palate the flavors, the ingredients of Indian cooking are, in any given dish, the most difficult to analyze. The ingredients and techniques for preparing French, Italian, Spanish, Viennese, almost all Western cookery, are a relative cinch to detail in terms of taste. Even the Chinese is simpler; so much of it based on ginger, garlic, star anise, various forms of sesame, soy sauce, hot chili peppers, and so on.

By comparison, the battery of Indian spices is extraordinary, and many of the spices are unknown in the Western kitchen—fenugreek, amchoor, asafetida, and tamarind.

It is due, in part no doubt, to this broad spectrum of flavors—all of which can be used in countless combinations—that Indian cooking is a natural base for a wholly palatable diet. The clue to such a diet is to avoid monotony. A variety of flavors is a key element in the preparation of food with that goal in mind. The other elements are contrasts in textures and flavors—sweet versus sour, spicy-hot versus bland, and so on.

Inky Pinky

Although I have never had the pleasure of sampling it, I am told inky pinky is a hash made with cold leftover roast beef that is thinly sliced and cooked with beef broth, finely chopped carrots, and onions. Before serving, a touch of vinegar is added and the sauce is thickened with cornstarch. The dish is Scottish and might stem from a similar dish of French origin called a *miroton,* which is made with thinly sliced leftover boiled beef rather than roast beef. The dish is lightly thickened with flour.

Isinglass

Isinglass was commonly used as the gelatin in preparing desserts in Europe many years ago. There are still European chefs who prefer the isinglass version of gelatin.

The gelatin most often used today is, of course, the powdered kind available universally in supermarkets. Isinglass is a totally transparent gelatin that comes in sheets. It is made from fish bladders, including those of sturgeon.

I have a box of it in my kitchen pantry that was made in Germany and was brought into my kitchen by Gaston Lenôtre, the celebrated French pastry man.

I used isinglass years ago while attending a hotel school in Switzerland but have never seen reference to it in cookbooks written in English.

A Queens gentleman wrote: "One must be not only British but probably well over sixty to have used isinglass.

"My recollections go back more than sixty-five years, when my father had two grocery and provision shops in Kensington—where the rich were.

"But you didn't have to be rich to buy isinglass. There just wasn't any other product for thickening jellies.

"Isinglass also was used, you may know, for windshields on early-century roadsters. No doubt it melted in hot weather.

"But, then, when is the weather hot in England?

"You say that you have never seen mention of isinglass in any English cookbook. I would refer you to *Mrs. Beeton's Book of Household Management,* self-titled 'The World's Greatest Cookery Book.' I have an early edition, probably published some fifty-five years ago. In it are given two recipes using isinglass. One is called 'Isinglass jelly.' However, the old sheet-type product must have been on its way out even in 1924 since in both recipes 'Patent Isinglass' is called for—meaning a trademarked product, undoubtedly in powder form."

On perusal, I noted in Mrs. Beeton's book that she offers the following explanation of isinglass:

"Isinglass is the purest variety of gelatine, and is prepared from the sounds or swimming-bladders of certain fish, chiefly the sturgeon. From its whiteness, it is mostly used for making blanc-mange and similar dishes."

Jambon Persillé

One of the glories of the Burgundian table is a cold, mosaic-like dish called jambon persillé or, more flatly to my ears, parsleyed ham. It is made with a whole boned fresh ham, preferably home cured, and all the parsley that conscience will allow—actually about two quarts, well washed and loosely packed. When the meat is cured and ready to be cooked, it is put in a kettle with a good dry white Burgundy wine, vegetables, and seasonings and simmered until quite tender, about five hours. The ham is cut into strips or large cubes and molded along with the parsley in a deep dish, preferably one with a round bottom. When the ham is cut, the slices have a colorful, mosaic-like pattern that is a delight to the eye and the taste.

Jansson's Temptation

Jansson's temptation, or Jansson's *frestelse*, I have been told, was not created in Sweden but in this country. The splendid dish is made with potatoes that have been cut into julienne strips and blended with anchovy fillets or sprats, plus cream and onions.

As the story goes, it was named after a nineteenth-century Swedish religious leader, Erik Jansson, who brought his followers from Sweden to America and founded a community called Bishop Hill in Illinois. Jansson preached staunchly against the pleasures of the flesh and appetite but had a weakness—a particular potato-and-anchovy dish. He was discovered devouring the dish so ravenously that it ruined his reputation.

Jeff Davis Pie

If a Southerner were to admit that he or she was not familiar with a Jeff Davis or Jefferson Davis pie, it would be tantamount to treason. There are many versions; basically it is a vanilla custard pie baked in a pastry shell.

It generally contains spices such as allspice and/or cinnamon. It may contain raisins and nuts, such as pecans, and it may or may not be topped with meringue.

Jefferson

Is connoisseurship in the world of fine food intuitive, or is it learned? Or both? How does it come about that two men, each endowed with uncommon sensibilities, can be exposed for an extended period to the great dining salons of France and return to native soil, one to be immortalized as perhaps America's greatest gastronome, the other far better remembered for going out and flying a kite?

The palates in question are, of course, those of Thomas Jefferson and Benjamin Franklin. Franklin, although gout-ridden late in life, was an advocate of vegetarianism (he also, according to the *Encyclopedia Britannica,* eleventh edition, took "a cold air bath regularly in the morning, when he sat naked in his bedroom beguiling himself with a book. . . .").

When it came to the pleasures of the table, Jefferson possessed extraordinary, undisputed taste. Oddly, however, this aspect of his nature is mentioned only tangentially by his biographers, if at all. (Pedagogues, I have noted over the years, seem, by and large, to care very little for their stomachs.) They do go on at some length about the ingenious and sometimes highly amusing devices that he invented or created for his dining room, kitchen, and cellar, and many of these are remarkable.

To one man's mind, however, the most fascinating aspect of Jefferson, epicure, is the handwritten recipes or "receipts" for dishes he had tasted in France. Some of them are written in a compelling mixture of English and French. His recipe for making meringues, for example, calls for "12 blancs d'oeuf, les fouettes bien fermes, 12 cueillères de sucre en poudre, put them by little and little into the whites of eggs, fouetter le tout ensemble, dresser les sur un papier avec un cueiller de bouche, metter les dans un four bien doux, that is to say, an oven after the bread is drawn out. You may leave them

there for as long as you please," he wrote.

When Jefferson arrived in France in 1784 as Minister Plenipotentiary to the court of Louis XVI (succeeding Benjamin Franklin), the haute cuisine of that nation was long out of its cradle. Cafés and restaurants were flourishing in Paris. Interestingly enough to food historians, he arrived in Paris to serve the year that Antonin Carême, the supreme chef of the eighteenth century and known as the Moses of classic French cooking, was born. Jefferson doubtlessly supped on hundreds of the dishes that Carême was later to record for posterity.

The most comprehensive work yet compiled on Jefferson's gastronomic adventures is Marie Kimball's *Thomas Jefferson's Cook Book.* The volume makes note of hundreds of dishes, recipes for which Jefferson had culled from his own servants, chefs, and the mistresses of various stately homes in the French capital. The dishes include grilled pork cutlets with a piquant sauce Robert; civet de lapin, or rabbit in a red wine sauce with bacon and small onions; vol au vents, or puff pastry shells filled with any of many creamed or otherwise sauced dishes; and one of the most elegant dishes of all, a galantine of turkey, the skin of the bird stuffed with various meats, pistachios, and truffles before poaching, cooling, and serving with an aspic coating.

At rural Monticello, there was much game to be had for his home table, and there are numerous French recipes for venison, including one for venison, marinated and roasted and served with a sauce piquante, sometimes called a sauce poivrade.

In addition to meringues, his detailed connoisseurship extended to blanc-manges, ladyfingers, and macaroons. One guest at a dinner given by Jefferson at the White House noted that "the ice cream was brought to the table in the form of small balls, enclosed in cases of warm pastry, a feat." It is reasonable to surmise that this dish was that marvelous and easily made confection, profiteroles—cream puffs—filled with ice cream and served with a hot chocolate sauce.

It is more than conjecture to say that until his sojourn in France the basis of the great man's diet had been soul food, that distinct form of cookery evolved from the hearts and minds of slaves. Without question throughout his lifetime, his table was supplied with such southern staples as fried chicken, country ham, numerous kinds of foods based on corn, including corn bread made in a black skillet, grits, and whole hominy. The staple greens on the Jefferson table were undoubtedly mustard, turnips, and collards plus a variety of peas and beans, including cow peas, crowder peas, and snap beans. Plus watermelon, hot biscuits, and pecans and sweet potato pies.

Jefferson was once denounced—spitefully and politically motivated, no doubt—by Patrick Henry as a man who "abjured his native victuals."

Whatever his association with the southern table, the Jefferson garden grew an exceptional number of vegetables of great sophistication: broccoli, asparagus, cauliflower, artichokes, and endive. Mushrooms were also cultivated at Monticello.

Jefferson is credited with being the first to import many foreign gadgets and delicacies for his kitchen at Monticello, among them a waffle iron from Holland and a pasta-making machine from Italy. He also imported packaged spaghetti from Europe. Jefferson owned an ice cream freezer, a contrivance also owned by George Washington, who spent, according to the recipe, 1 pound, 13 shillings and four pence for "a cream machine for ice." Again to quote Mrs. Kimball, Martha Washington left numerous recipes for posterity but none for ice cream. Jefferson discovered his recipe for the dish and wrote it down. "Thus it happens that our first American recipe for ice cream, then no vulgar commonplace, is in the writing of a President of the United States."

Jefferson in Europe developed a lusty appetite for the likes of Parmesan cheese, almonds, fine mustards, tarragon vinegar, oil, and anchovies, and these he had shipped to Virginia throughout his lifetime. I have before me the receipt of Jefferson's hotel in Amsterdam dated 10 to 28 March 1788. It details many of his room service requests and shows that he was long in the tooth for oysters. Fortunately these he could find in abundance in the waters of Virginia.

Jefferson traveled extensively through the vineyards of France and Germany, making a painstaking study of grape-growing and wine-making, and he had an enthusiastic respect for the wines of both countries. Records show that he imported hundreds of cases of European wines for his home cellar. He seems to have had a special regard for the wines of Bordeaux as well as Sauternes. He seems not to have held the sparkling wines of Champagne in high esteem, preferring the still wines of that region. "The mousseux or sparkling champagne is never brought to a good table in France. The still, or non-mousseux, is alone drunk by connoisseurs," he is said to have written.

Jefferson went to considerable lengths to obviate the need for servants in the dining room. He was not so much concerned that these "mute but not inattentive listeners" would repeat what they had heard but rather that they would repeat it incorrectly.

Thus, he devised an ingenious silent butler, a one-panel door that turned on a central vertical swivel. One side of the door was a series of shelves where food might be placed. When the door was turned to the dining room, a single waiter or perhaps two would take the food from the shelves and take it to the various tables where guests were seated. There were tiered stands at each table and, presumably, the food was placed on these so that the guests would serve themselves.

Jefferson, when he entertained, also preferred to have several small tables spaced in the dining room rather than one large one. This, he felt, provided a greater intimacy and made conversation more personal.

Jefferson's wine cellar was and is situated directly below a mantelpiece in the dining room. On either side of the mantel two more "dumbwaiters" were installed. The person in charge of the cellar would position the bottles from below as they were required above and hoist them up by an "endless" conveyor belt. Open the door and, voilà! Le vin. It was thought for many years that this was a Jefferson original, but it now appears that he visited, on occasion, a place called the Café Mécanique in Paris and this same conveyor belt system was used there.

In Paris, Jefferson's first staff consisted of a cuisinière. Later he acquired a valet de chambre named Adrien Petit and there was James Hastings, a black slave who had followed him from Monticello. Hastings received extensive training in the art of French cookery and Jefferson signed a document on September 15, 1793, witnessed by Petit, in which he offered Hastings freedom if he agreed to return to Monticello and teach "such person as I shall place under him to be a good cook . . ."

During his tenure as president, the White House staff consisted of Joseph Rapin, a French maître d'hôtel, who was succeeded by Etienne Lemaire (at $20 a month). There was a French chef named Julien, and an assistant to the chef named Noel. Jefferson brought two slaves from Monticello, known simply as Edy and Fanny, to be trained under Julien and it was they who staffed Jefferson's kitchen when he retired to Monticello. Jefferson's wife had died early on in their marriage and his household on retirement was presided over by his daughter, Martha Jefferson Randolph.

Throughout his lifetime, Jefferson was unstinting in his hospitality, and he died on July 4, 1826, impoverished.

Jerky

Jerky, which is traditionally made of strips of beef that have been salted and cured either by drying in the sun or smoking, is said to derive from *charqui*. Dictionaries state that the word *charqui* is Spanish or, more specifically, a word of the Quechua language spoken by about four million people including many Peruvians. There is also an English transitive verb jerk. This means to cut meat into strips and dry it in the sun or smoke it. The word "jerk" in this sense entered the English language after jerky.

Jerusalem Artichoke

One of the most abundant, curiously neglected, and oddly named foods in America is the Jerusalem artichoke. Since its inception the name has involved a comedy of errors not only in this country but also in France.

The vegetable's English name has nothing really to do with the capital of Israel, but that requires explanation. The Jerusalem artichoke is not an artichoke at all, as we know the more sophisticated globe artichoke. The Jerusalem version is actually related to the sunflower. The sunflower is called *girasole* in Italian, which means gyrating or turning to the sun. And, at least according to folk etymology, girasole through some slip of nomenclature turned into Jerusalem.

That is even more fascinating historically considering that the vegetable is native to North America. It was indigenous to the central United States and Canada and was first taken to France by Samuel de Champlain in 1616, where it began to flourish. The French called the rapidly proliferating root vegetable *poires de terre* (earth pears) or *artichauts de Canada* (Canadian artichokes).

In today's French kitchens, it is known as a *topinambour,* again for an unusual reason: At approximately the same time that it was introduced into that country, there was an exhibition featuring a tribe from Brazil known as topinambours. The vegetable was thus christened.

One of the first artichoke dishes was a purée known in traditional French kitchens as purée Palestine, probably because the chef who created it had heard that the vegetable was imported from Jerusalem. There is a recipe for that purée in Auguste Escoffier's *Le Guide Culinaire,* on page 144, and it calls for eight hundred grams of topinambours.

Obviously in the course of the tuber's history, some cook decided that it tasted somewhat like the heart of that much more aristocratic food known as a globe artichoke, and upgraded its name accordingly. Most recently, it goes by the name of sunchoke.

Jewfish

There are two species of fish known as jewfish that are caught off the Florida coast. I have no idea where the name comes from, but the two species are the grouper and the giant sea bass. Groupers have a fine, firm texture and make a fine fish stock. Also, they are said to be one of the finest fish you may choose for chowders.

I have been told that the name is a corruption of the Italian term *giupesce,* which means bottom fish. But I received a highly

informative letter that strongly refuted that idea.

" 'Jewfish' cannot be 'a corruption of the Italian term *giupesce* because *giupesce* is not an Italian term, and it doesn't even mean 'bottom fish,' as was stated. The combination of *giu,* meaning 'down' (not 'bottom'), and *pesce,* meaning fish, does not occur in Italian or in any of its dialects, because it doesn't make any sense.

"*Giupesce* sounds like the command a fish-trainer might give to his pupil, if such were possible: 'Down, fish!' "

Jicama

Jicama is a pale brown, thin-skinned root vegetable that varies in size from that of a beet to that of a rutabaga. It is quite crisp and is best when slightly chilled. Its texture is not unlike a tender radish's and is similar to a brittle-fleshed apple's. The flavor of a jicama is slightly sweet and a bit wild. It is pronounced HICK-a-mah.

Johnny Cake

The original name for johnny cake, which is made of cornmeal, was journey cake, according to some sources. It was a bread carried by itinerant preachers in their travels because it had long-keeping qualities. Other sources say that the original name was Shawnee cake, from the Shawnee Indians who first made it.

Similarly, a hoe cake was supposedly a bread taken into the fields by the workers who did the hoeing. Others say it was so named because the metal end of the hoe was used to keep the bread in place on the griddle as it cooked.

Jugged

Many dishes are described as jugged in English cookery. There is jugged hare, probably the most famous, jugged steak, and jugged celery. All, if prepared according to tradition, must be cooked in a "jug" of some sort, I believe.

Some recipes call for a tall fireproof jar, others for a deep crock, a deep stoneware jug, and so on. To choose one example, to prepare jugged hare you fry pieces of the disjointed animal in hot fat and transfer it to the jug (or casserole, if you must make a substitute). You add onions, herbs, and spices, plus stock, and cover. You bake the dish several hours and garnish it with the animal's cooked liver.

The sauce is sometimes thickened with the reserved blood of the hare and flavored with red currant jelly.

Julep

The word "julep" has been traced to Middle English, Old French, Arabic, and, finally, to a Persian word, *gulab,* meaning rose water. Originally it was a sweet, syrupy liquid, and time was when it might be added to certain medicines to improve their flavor. The drink made with mint, sugar, and bourbon is an American invention. An English quotation dated 1659 says, "Whose heat, not all the jewleps of their tears [could quench]."

Julienne

The name julienne is presumed to have originated during the latter part of the seventeenth century, and it is further conjectured that the chef who introduced that use of foods finely cut into strips was named Julien. Julienne is, of course, the feminine version for Julien, but no one would give credence to the thought that the originator of that style of cutting was a woman. Not back in the seventeenth century.

Juniper Berries

Juniper berries are used in recipes for sauerkraut, pâtés, gin, and so on. But the flavor of juniper berries varies tremendously from climate to climate. I understand, for example, that the juniper berries from the mountains of Italy are several times stronger than those grown in Scandinavia.

I have used homegrown juniper berries in my own kitchen, but I fear that they, too, lack the flavor of the store-bought variety.

Apparently it is the degree of essential oils contained in the berries that determine their strength or lack of it.

The flavor of a perfect juniper berry is somewhat sweet, is neatly perfumed, and smacks of pine. To dry them, I harvest them and let them stand in the open air until dried. I then put them in bottles and secure tightly.

A spokesman for the American Spice Trade Association wrote that "the domestic product can be used, but American berries are not ordinarily found in commerce because they tend to have a higher terpene content."

He did not imply that terpene is injurious (it is widely used commercially in essential oils), but he added that this factor is important to the gin industry, which is the largest user of the berries.

Terpene, he adds, "can give the water bluish streaks (and very few people favor blue martinis)." The finest berries, he said, are the giant Italian berries from the southern slopes of the Alps.

If juniper berries are not in your market, simply add a dash of gin as a substitute in the recipe.

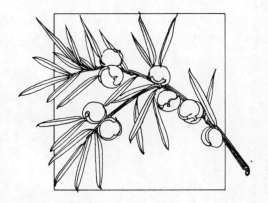

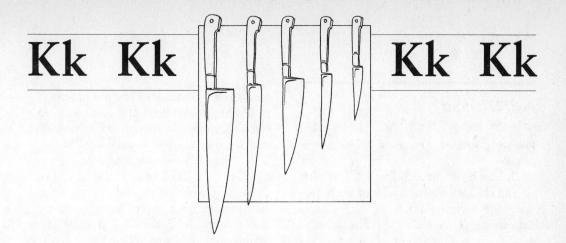

Kk Kk Kk Kk

Kecap

Kecap *(ketjap)* is the Indonesian name for soy sauce in its basic form. It is logically believed that the American condiment called ketchup, which more often than not is made with tomatoes, derives from the Indonesian sauce. Kecap, with its broad uses in Indonesia, became simply "table sauce" to English-speaking foreigners. By extension, ketchup became the national table sauce in America. *See also* Ketchup.

Kedgeree

Kedgeree, sometimes spelled kegeree, is said to have been, during the era when the sun never set on the British Empire, an English variation of an Indian dish. It was much like a curry and contained fish and rice as principal ingredients. It also contained onions and lentils and ghee. Eventually the dish was modified to contain only cooked fish that was flaked, cooked rice, butter, hard-boiled eggs, and cream.

Kefir

Kefir, according to *Larousse Gastronomique,* is a fermented drink made of milk and is of Caucasian origin. The book adds that it is authentically made of camel's milk, but more often than not it is made from cow's milk. Bacteria is added and the product is bottled.

After it has fermented for three days it becomes slightly intoxicating and contains about 2.5 percent alcohol. It is frothy and has a rather sour taste.

"Kefir," *Larousse* notes, "is easily digestible and is often recommended for invalids."

Kefir is widely available in the United States, primarily in health food stores. The drink is sold in small cartons such as those used for milk and heavy cream and must be kept refrigerated. It is apparently prepared in a variety of flavors, including strawberry. I recently purchased a small carton in a piña colada flavor. I thought it resembled liquid yogurt; the taste was fairly pleasant but slightly astringent. The carton indicated that there were 150 calories in 1 cup.

Kermesse

The word *kermesse* means a village fair in Belgian.

The *kermesse aux boudins* actually takes place in restaurants. The owner of the restaurant invites his favored customers in for a special evening of dining. An entire carcass of meat—veal, lamb, pork, or whatever—is cut up and special dishes are made with all the components of the animal including the innards, the liver, heart, brains, and so on. One presumes that boudins, or white sausages, of one sort or another figure in the menu.

Ketchup

The New York Times prefers to spell it ketchup, but catchup and catsup are generally accepted. The name is ascribed by various authorities to various origins.

Theodora FitzGibbon, in her book *The Food of the Western World,* states that the word may come from the Chinese *koe-chiap* or *ke-tsiap,* "which means the brine of pickled fish."

The late Tom Stobart, in his *The Cook's Encyclopedia,* says that the word came into English "from the Orient, perhaps from the Malay or Chinese."

"You find ketjap benteng or ketjap manis in Indonesian recipes and that is a form of sweet soy sauce," he wrote. "Cookbooks of the last century abound with recipes–oyster ketchup (oysters with white wine, brandy, sherry, shallots and spices), mussel ketchup (mussels and cider), pontac or pontack ketchup (elderberries), Windermere ketchup (mushrooms and horseradish), wolfram ketchup (beer, anchovies and mushrooms)."

There are also ketchups made with walnuts, cucumbers, and many other items that caught some cook's imagination.

A New Jersey man wrote to me that "catchup is a Chinese invention and is still called in Cantonese *fan-kei cheop. Fan-kei* is the name for tomato, literally 'foreign vine-vegetable' and *cheop* is juice as in *chang-cheop* (orange juice). The truncated word *kei-cheop* or catchup is obtained by dropping *fan.*"

Incidentally, the standard way to get the last of the ketchup out of the bottle is to stand it on end long enough for the ketchup to drain to the capped end, or to add a small amount of water and then shake the bottle. My solution is to add lemon juice or Worcestershire sauce. This is because when I use ketchup it is almost invariably in a combination with one or more liquids, such as the two mentioned.

Key Lime

See Limes.

Kibbee

See Bulgur.

Kickshaw

A kickshaw is either a fancy food or dish, delicacy, or tidbit, or a trinket, trifle, or geegaw, depending on how you interpret the dictionary. I tend to think of it as a trivial appetizer. I would not refer to foie gras or caviar as a kickshaw, but I might in a loose moment use the term to refer to peanuts or cheese straws. It derives from the French *quelque chose,* which means "something."

Kimchee

Kimchee, that staple item in all Korean homes, is considered by many to be the most inspired of all pickle dishes. It does not contain vinegar, but ferments of its own accord and develops a slightly sour taste. One in particular that I have enjoyed is made with Chinese cabbage, which is today often found in American gardens. The seasonings include garlic and ginger and a sizable amount of dried hot chili peppers that are finely crumbled or ground.

Kir

If memory serves, the vogue for a drink called kir was first taking hold in New York at approximately the time I arrived on the "food scene" almost thirty years ago. It was the kind of drink that, in today's parlance, would make people know you knew where it's at.

A kir, well chilled and at its best, is an excellent drink. It is made with a very dry white Burgundy wine and a judicious amount of crème de cassis, a dark red syrup made from the juice of black currants. Judicious is the key word. In most public places in this country, the bartender has a very heavy hand with crème de cassis and

a kir with an excess of syrup can be vile.

It was quite some while before I discovered the origin of the drink. I knew, of course, that a kir was nothing more than a *vin blanc cassis,* which had been around for a long time in Burgundy. But I learned from Samuel Chamberlain, an uncommonly learned gastronome, food writer, and professional etcher, that it was named for a mayor of Dijon, Félix Kir, who was a crew-cut priest and Resistance hero who enjoyed a tremendous affection among his fellow Burgundians. Apparently, he enjoyed a glass of vin blanc cassis or two and the drink was dubbed with his name. *See also* Cassis.

Kirschwasser

Kirschwasser is distilled brandy made from cherries, complete with the pits. Although kirsch (the German word for "cherry") adds a tantalizing, desirable flavor to cheese fondues, it is not really necessary to a good, wholly acceptable dish. You could add another white brandy or Cognac to the fondue, but it would not give the same flavor.

Kiss-Me-Quick

Kiss-me-quick is a steamed pudding made with brown sugar, butter, preserves, flour, and baking powder. The batter is put into a mold and steamed until done. I am familiar with this pudding only through hearsay and cannot testify as to its goodness.

Knedlicky

Knedlicky is the Czech word for dumpling, and the dumplings are made from many things in Czechoslovakia, including liver, marrow, brains, and ham. There are also fruit dumplings that serve as dessert. The word is related to the German *knödel,* which means dumpling, from which the French derived the word *quenelle,* as in *quenelle de poisson,* fish dumpling.

Knives

To those who complain about rusty or stained knives, I have two suggestions.

First, if you can afford it, go out and buy the best grade of stainless steel knives and give your present knives to your least favorite charity. Today, good high-carbon "stainless" or "no stain" steel knives remain just as sharp as the old-fashioned, easily stained carbon blades. If you can't afford replacements, wash and dry carbon steel knives after each use. Never leave soiled knives in a wet sink.

It is especially important that you rinse and dry knives that have been used to slice

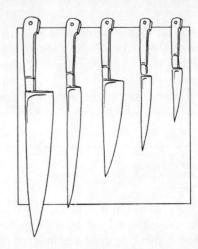

lemons, oranges, tomatoes, and any other acidic foods the moment after using them. Acid quickly discolors and "rusts" the ordinary carbon steel knives. The knives also will transfer their dark properties to the foods in question.

Once new knives are purchased, they should be maintained in first-rate shape, clean and sharp. The most basic professional method for sharpening knives is with a carborundum stone. The most basic of these stones has a rough side and a smooth side.

The knife should be sharpened first on the rough side, then on the smooth side, holding the knife at a twenty-degree angle and pulling the knife first away from you, then toward you. The knife should then be "finished" on a sharpening stone, which "turns the edge," again holding the knife at a twenty-degree angle against the steel.

That's theory. I use a professional electric knife sharpener recommended to me years ago by my fish dealer in Amagansett. There are motor-driven oxide belts, and I can put a keen edge on all my knives within a ten-minute period—all forty-two of them.

Some experts say it wears the blades down, but I live dangerously and have some of the sharpest knives on the eastern end of

Long Island—other than my fish dealer, that is. The sharpener has the trademark Hook-Eye and is manufactured by Ludwig Schiff.

Knob Celery

See Celery root.

Königsberger Klopse

See Capers.

Koo-Chul-Paan

See Korean specialties.

Korean Specialties

There are certain dishes I've had just once that were so good the taste of them lingered in my mind long afterward. Among these are two Korean specialties that were first prepared for me years ago in Seoul. Their names, when transliterated, are sin-sul-lo and koo-chul-paan. They're rather elaborate dishes that are traditionally served for special events.

Koo-chul-paan is an appetizer. The word literally means nine-hole or nine-section dish, which refers to the way it is usually served—in a lacquered octagonal container resembling a wooden candy box with a lid.

When the lid is lifted, there is a center section in which small, round, thin pancakes are stacked. Around the center are eight re-ceptacles that hold various savory, finely shredded foods to be added to each pancake before folding, dipping into a mustard-soy-sauce, and eating. The fillings can vary from table to table but normally include such things as shredded beef, mushrooms, carrots, and cucumbers.

Sin-sul-lo is a soup of many ingredients, served in a deep, cylindrical bowl surrounding a funnel that serves as a chimney. It may be one large pot to serve many or individual pots at each place to serve one guest.

Here again, the ingredients that go into the kettle of broth can vary, but they often include small beef patties, small meat-filled dumplings, bits of sautéed fish cut into small rectangles, cooked baby shrimp, dried black mushrooms, and assorted vegetables—even nuts, such as gingko and walnut meats.

When I dined at the home of Dr. Kim Kyung Won, South Korea's permanent observer at the United Nations, and his wife, Park Akyong, I was delighted to discover that my hosts felt the occasion "special" enough to warrant serving these two wonderful dishes.

Their elegant menu also included kim-chee, a spicy pickled Chinese cabbage redolent with garlic and considered—along with bul-kogi—to be one of Korea's national dishes. Bul-kogi, which we also had, is grilled meat, generally beef, marinated in a soy sauce and spice mixture and grilled over charcoal or broiled.

As we sipped the broth that simmered in the individual pots, Dr. Kim offered a translation of sin-sul-lo. "Sin-sul," he said, means, vaguely, "angel descending." "Lo," he said, means fire. The description is accurate.

I suggested that certain aspects of Korean cooking seemed to indicate that it had been influenced by the Mongols, and Dr. Kim concurred. Bul-kogi is extremely popular in Korea, and it strongly resembles Mongolian grill. And sin-sul-lo seems very much akin to the Mongolian hot pot in which guests cook their own foods in a charcoal-fired simmering liquid as they dine. *See also* Kimchee.

Kosher

Prior to going on a low-salt diet I used ko-sher salt in my kitchen. I preferred the "feel" of it to regular salt. In theory, you would need a slightly greater quantity of the coarser salt because of the density involved. That is one reason that many recipes specify "salt to taste" rather than a specific quantity.

Kreplach

See Dumplings.

Kritharaki

See Orzo.

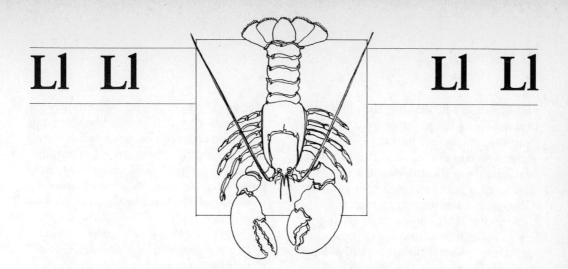

Lady Curzon Soup

Lady Curzon soup was named for an American, Mary Leiter, the Chicago-born daughter of Levi Leiter, a partner of Marshall Field.

In 1895 she married Lord Curzon, Viceroy of India during the period when British power was at its height. Her biography states, "She occupied the most splendid position which any American, man or woman, has ever held in the British Empire, and fulfilled the role with incomparable grace, courage and distinction."

The soup is a green turtle soup flavored with curry plus a touch of sherry. Its origin is unknown and it is not mentioned in the biography.

Lamb

For a city dweller, a slugabed who regards an alarm clock as one of the devil's more bizarre contrivances, it was an adventure. The wake-up call in Durango, Colorado, had come at 3 A.M. and, with a slow gait and eyes at half-mast, I checked the rear of the station wagon for supplies. The fifty-five-pound fresh carcass of lamb was indis-putably there. So was a five-foot, motor-driven spit, more than one hundred pounds of charcoal, and an enormous kettle of shepherd's stew—four kinds of beans with tomatoes, slab bacon, and onion, which had, the night before, simmered long on the back burner of the hotel's kitchen.

And shortly we were off, to a Rocky Mountain lamb roast, the headlights slashing through the pitch black of early morning. The air was dry, almost holy in its purity. And it was cold.

More than an hour later the station wagon came to rest on the banks of a lake named Andrews, eleven thousand feet above sea level. The grill was unloaded and the owner of the ranch, Grant Paulek, a rugged, second-generation American of Lithuanian stock, arrived in a pickup truck with a generator to power the grill and allow the lamb to rotate on its spit.

The charcoal blazed, and a short while later the carcass, glistening with olive oil and seasoned with oregano and salt, was set in motion. With a sudden rush, the mountains, until then invisible in the star-studded blackness of early morning, were set in bold silhouette against a devastatingly blue and cloudless sky. The tallest mountains, one noted, were bordered by irregular mantles of snow. The shepherd's stew was put on slightly away from the coals, so that it barely

243

simmered. Bill Broscovak, the chief cook and master of the grill, removed his shoes and walked barefoot into the lake to submerge a watermelon or two. The cold water was bracing to the ankles and feet; it was also so clear that you could spot an empty Coors beer can on the bottom ten feet away.

A group of sheepmen were getting together for that feast to curse coyotes, extol the virtues of wool (wool, as well as meat for fine feasting, is the blessed yield of sheep), and swap sheep stories, some of which are notable for their cunning lack of sophistication. (Sample: "Did you hear about the ram who committed suicide by butting his head against a brick wall? He overheard Frank Sinatra singing 'There Will Never Be Another Ewe.' ") In any gathering of sheepmen out West, one learns, early on, that the banes of a sheepman's existence are three: coyotes, domestic dogs, generally strays, and plain old-fashioned people otherwise known as rustlers. Today's rustlers generally go about their thievery in pickup trucks, moving vans, and station wagons; in one or two instances they have used helicopters.

In sheep territory in Kentucky, to choose one region, coyotes pose no problem, but stray dogs are a menace. In Colorado, however, coyotes are considered an almost intolerable burden and plague. Mention the word "coyote" and faces flush, nerve ends tighten, speech is embittered; sheepmen become veritable Jobs in sackcloth and ashes.

One of the most interesting and intriguing pieces of information overheard on my trip through Colorado sheep country had to do with sheep culture in France. One sheep grower was telling another about new techniques in the country where they produce the famed pré-salé in Brittany.

"Where sheep production in France is concerned," one man said to the other, "the unions are very strong. And the shepherds are adamant in their demands for weekends off. The demands are so strong, in fact, that there is currently work under way using hormone therapy at the time of breeding, to permit all the ewes in the flock to have their lambs on Thursday and Friday, precisely 148 to 149 days after they are bred."

"That's progress," he added, either admiringly or grudgingly.

A problem in sheep production, a relatively new one, is finding people to tend the animals. These people are called sheepherders or shepherds, depending on the section of the country. In the West, most people speak of sheepherders.

Most young men tend to drift away from the ranches. A sheepman commented: "Tending sheep for most of them is a tedious, boring, and lonely job. But the pay is good."

In years past, many of those who tended the sheep were brought from Europe, including Basques from France and Spain. Some tenders were from Mexico and Greece. More recently, there have been workers from Peru. It is said that most of these sources are drying up.

Though Americans have an all but in-

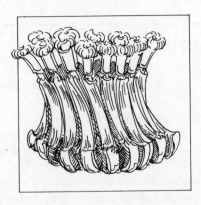

satiable appetite for beef, most epicures hold veal and lamb to be the two most elegant meats. A great irony of the American diet pattern is that the people of regions noted for one food specialty or another are, generally, not all that keen on that particular specialty. Lamb is a case in point.

Most of the sheep grown in America are raised in Texas, Wyoming, California, South Dakota, and Colorado. Most of the "lamb eaters" in the nation are in New York, California, Illinois, Massachusetts, and New Jersey.

New York State consumes 31 percent of all lamb produced in America, more than twice as much as any other state. California, second, consumes 16 percent.

There are basically three kinds of lamb produced in America for the kitchen. First, there is baby lamb or hothouse lamb, produced out of season, principally for the Boston and New York markets.

"This is available," a spokesman for the lamb industry said, "from December through April, and the lambs are generally six to twelve weeks old. The lambs weigh from fifteen to thirty pounds when ready to be put on a spit or roasted in the oven.

"Then there is so-called spring lamb, a label that is to a great degree misleading. You can only market lamb that bears that name from the first Monday in March through the second Monday in October. But you can buy lamb of the same age and quality all year long. Off season—that is, after the October cutoff date—this is called 'genuine' lamb. Genuine lamb is lamb no more than twelve months old.

"Yearling lamb comes next," the spokesman continued. "This is from one to two years old.

"After that, the lamb becomes mutton, a food much treasured by many connoisseurs, particularly in the form of mutton chops." (Unfortunately, mutton is a rare commodity even in New York. The meat is, to some tastes, too strong in flavor. It is the best meat, however, for couscous.)

While lamb producers could never hope, with or without the attrition of coyotes, that the American palate would switch from marbled Porterhouse and T-bone steaks to the likes of lamb racks, ribs, and chops, the demand for lamb in this country is greater than the supply.

Those producers would not want for a market if the demand dwindled to zero. "The industry has been approached on several occasions by buyers from the Arab nations," a sheep grower said. "They'd purchase the entire production for the next ten years."

Back to the lamb roast. At 1 o'clock that afternoon the talk of sheep on the hoof turned to thoughts of lamb on the spit.

For six hours, the fifty-five-pound animal had turned continuously on the spit, and bits of fat burning on the coals had teased the nostrils. And now the basting—with oil and the juice of more than a dozen lemons—was done. For those who waited, it was worth the candle, or the coals. In that gloriously refined Colorado air, one felt the ravening hunger of heaven's hounds. And suddenly chef Broscovak's spitted masterpiece—along with his shepherd's stew, his mélange of salads, and the ice-cold watermelon retrieved from the lake—was no more.

Lamb Pré-Salé

Lamb pré-salé is considered by connoisseurs to be the finest lamb in the world. The name means salty field, and the term is applied to lamb or sheep that graze on meadowlands on the shores of the English Channel or the Atlantic. These lands are washed by the salt tide as it ebbs and flows, and the grass gives a delicate flavor to the meat of the sheep that feast on it. The best known area for pré-salé lamb is near Mont-St.-Michel in France.

If you are served lamb called pré-salé in this country, there's an off chance you are being conned by the management.

Lane Cake

For years I have been trying to find the origin of the name lane cake. The dessert is a southern layer cake, the layers of which are spread with a filling of nuts, coconut, and dried or glazed fruits.

Recently I learned that an explanation of the name is to be found in *Savannah Sampler Cookbook* by Margaret Wayt DeBolt. Mrs. DeBolt credits the cake to Emma Rylander Lane of Clayton, Alabama. She adds, "The cake won a state fair prize in Georgia and is now perhaps the South's favorite Christmas cake."

Langouste

See Spiny lobster.

Laos

Laos is an essential ingredient in Indonesian cookery and it is called for in hundreds of

savory dishes. One of the finest books on Indonesian cookery, *The Indonesian Kitchen* by Copeland Marks and Mintari Soeharjo, notes that laos is a type of gingerroot.

The dried root of the plant is used, which has the diameter of a penny and is sliced thin or sold in powdered form. Known in English as galingale, it is a member of the ginger family.

Indonesian cookbook authors seem to agree that there is no reasonable substitute for laos.

Lard

The best lard is made from leaf-fat, which comes from the pig's abdominal walls. Rendering is done in large, open kettles and, properly prepared, the lard will be clear in color and a bit grainy with a firm texture and a good flavor.

According to a spokesman for Armour & Company, one of the principal producers of lard in the United States, leaf lard is considered one of the purest kinds of lard and is frequently used in professional bakeries for pastries.

Today, the spokesman advised, leaf lard

is rarely found on the mass market. Small quantities are produced for professionals, but you're not apt to find it on supermarket shelves. One reason for its scarcity is that "hogs are not as fat as they used to be."

It does make an excellent piecrust. But almost any solid fat, such as butter, could be used as a substitute. The closest approximation to lard in my opinion would be a solid white shortening, the best-known, of course, being Crisco.

The word *lard* in French means bacon, fatback, or "streak of lean." *Lard gras* or fat lard means fatback. *Lard maigre* means lean pork fat that is salted, smoked, and turned into bacon in America. The word for shortening or lard, as it is known in English, is *saindoux* in French. It is made by rendering pork fat.

A larding needle is so named because you "lard" or thread very lean meat with strips of fat before cooking.

Lavender

Although I am familiar with the scent of lavender, I have never sampled it. To my knowledge, that is. I have an old book titled

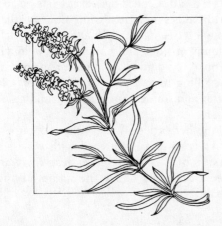

Herbs, Salads and Seasonings by Marcel Boulestin and Jason Hill and the authors declare as follows: "Lavender. Certain hot and fragrant little sweets made of candied lavender seeds are occasionally seen in confectioners' shops, but lavender has such particular merit that it need make no great pretension to be comestible."

However, in Kay Sanecki's *The Complete Book of Herbs,* the author advises that the plant is "perhaps not to be dismissed as . . . associated only with perfume, its former and revived use in relieving nervous headaches and calming hysteria." She adds that one William Turner explains that the name is derived from laver, meaning to wash, and that lavender was used "to wash men's heads 'which had any deceses therein.'"

Leeks

If leeks were fairly obscure on the local scene until recent times, they are ancient history to European cooks. For centuries, their popularity extended from Wales (where they are known as the national vegetable), England and Scotland across the Continent to Persia. They were enjoyed by the early Greeks and Romans. In France, where they are known as *poireaux,* they are among the foundations of both classic and bourgeois cookery.

Despite the French admiration for leeks as a vegetable, they use the word *poireau* as a vituperative term. It means a simpleton, while *faire le poireau* means to keep someone waiting.

Leeks, as most European cooks can testify, are an incredibly versatile vegetable. Although they are a member of the onion family, leeks have a flavor of such delicate

nature that it never dominates a dish. They are the basis for splendid appetizers such as leeks vinaigrette and, Rumanian-style, cold, dressed with olive oil, tomatoes, and olives. I well recall that years ago the chef of the Four Seasons, the late Albert Stockli, served a fine leek and sausage pie said to have been inspired by research into the works of Apicius.

Leeks find their way into a multitude of soups including those made with vegetables and/or meat. Boiled leeks are delectable baked with a cheese or Mornay sauce.

Leeks are an inevitable ingredient in the French *potage bonne femme* and *potage parisienne* (almost identical). One of these was the origin of vichyssoise when it was created in this country by the late Louis Diat, chef of the old Ritz Hotel, after Diat puréed the soup and added cream. A quiche made with leeks and cheese is a celestial delight.

The principal reason that leeks are known as winter vegetables is their hardy nature. They are one of the rare vegetables that can survive the snows and other adverse weather of the cold months. Leeks are planted about five or six inches deep, and it is the buried bottom section of the leek, the part not exposed to the sun, that comes up white or "blanched."

Whether news events loom large or small often depends on the mind's bent. As an unbridled enthusiast where leeks are concerned, one of the most fascinating dispatches (to my mind, that is) came from a small mining community of northeast England. It seems that in Ashington the inhabitants have little to do other than work the mines, repair to the local pubs, and grow leeks. The latter is such a happy diversion that there are annual leek-growing competitions.

The latest winner was a nineteen-year-old plumber's apprentice, Keith Davidson, who tends to the leeks in the miners' houses during the week and tends his own leeks on weekends. As he was awarded his prize, he stated modestly, "I just sat back and watched them grow." His winners measured four to five inches in diameter and were as long as his arm. That would make an awful lot of what the French call pot au feu; the Scots, cock-a-leekie; the Irish, brotchan roy, and the Welsh, cawl.

Lefser

Lefser is a flat, rolled-out cake. In shape and texture it is similar to a white-flour tortilla, though lefser is usually made with a small amount of flour and potatoes. The dough is cooked on a griddle and must remain soft. The filling may consist of a blend of soft butter and sour cream with a sprinkling of sugar.

Another variety, made without potatoes, cooks crisp and is softened with water; a version of it is available in Scandinavian specialty shops under the name Viking Bread.

Lemon Curd

Lemon curd is of English origin and recipes for it rarely appear in American cookbooks. In England it is often served with buttered bread or toast at teatime.

I am also told that it might be used as a cold filling for a baked tart. Some of the British recipes I have run across caution that it does have poor keeping qualities.

One of the few American recipes that I could find refers to the spread as a lemon cheese. To make it, combine the juice and rind of 6 lemons with 2 pounds of granulated sugar. Add ¼ pound of butter and 6 eggs, well beaten. Cook, stirring, over low heat until the sugar dissolves and the mixture barely begins to simmer. Remove from the heat and let cool. Store in tightly closed containers in the refrigerator.

Lemon Grass

Lemon grass, widely used in Southeast Asia, has tall, slender leaves and a firm-textured

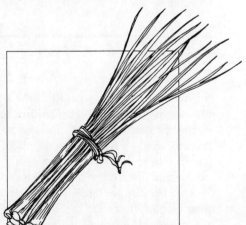

base. When cut it has a lemony taste and aroma and when pressed it yields lemongrass oil. It may be used whole; the base may be cut off and used; it may be peeled and the center finely minced. Available in both powdered form and dried, it is appearing increasingly in Asian markets in this country. Asian cookbooks, mainly those of Indonesia and Thailand, describe its uses. Lemon rind is sometimes recommended as a cooking substitute.

Licorice

Licorice is derived from the root of a plant known as *Glycyrrhiza glabra,* and it is used in the preparation of a black candy (sometimes called licorice stick), tobacco, liqueurs, and some medicines. The British prefer the spelling liquorice.

Limes

Basically there are two kinds of limes that are used by the public in this hemisphere. There are the Persian limes, which are commonly found in supermarkets and grocery stores. Then there are Key limes, which are smaller, a bit more tart, and with a slightly more pronounced flavor. These grow in Florida and throughout the Caribbean. The latter are essential to the preparation of an authentic Key lime pie. The name derives from the Florida Keys.

Limes have a somewhat "exotic" flavor to my taste, although they are quite common. Lemons have a far more neutral flavor.

For example, I would use lime juice in "exotic" dishes such as seviche and in tropical drinks. Generally speaking, I would use lemon juice on such commonplace dishes as freshly broiled fish, broiled chicken, and so on. On the other hand, if I were out of lemons and a citrus juice was essential, I would most certainly resort to limes.

Linguiça

I have dined on linguiça in Portugal and Brazil but I have never prepared it. The basis seems to be coarsely ground pork that is cured and stuffed into sausage casings. One friend, a reliable sausage maker, tells me that the seasonings are cumin, cinnamon, garlic, and hot red pepper. Some recipes call for such ingredients as a touch of sugar, vinegar, paprika, pepper, and marjoram. The seasonings apparently vary from producer to producer.

Litchi

Litchi (the word is also spelled lychee, lichee, and lichi) nuts are a fruit of a Chinese evergreen tree. Originally grown only in Asia,

they are now found in California, Florida, Hawaii, and Jamaica, among other places. Fresh nuts occasionally appear in Chinese groceries in June and July for a brief period. They may be refrigerated for two weeks.

In the finest Chinese restaurants, fresh litchis are served in or out of their shells as desserts. They are good, too, when eaten out of hand and sucked out of the shell when freshly purchased.

Littlenecks

See Clams.

Lobster

Lobsters are, to many palates, one of the most luxurious of foods, ranking somewhere up there with foie gras and caviar. There is an old wives' tale to the effect that when a lobster is split for eating, you should remove and discard the small tough sac near the eyes because the sac is poisonous. I feel quite certain, however, that if you bit into it, you would only find it unpleasant, like biting into a nasty bit of shell. To my mind it is no more poisonous than the lungs of the lobster. I can't imagine any body wanting to swallow either one.

I also remove the long intestinal tract that extends along the upper part of the tail, but this is only a refinement and not a cautionary step.

The green matter in the body of the lobster is the sea creature's liver, frequently referred to in high gastronomic circles as a delicacy. It is sometimes called the tomalley, a name attributed to the Caribs, an American Indian tribe that inhabited northern South America and the Lesser Antilles. The original word is *taumali* or *tumali,* and referred to a lobster sauce.

The liver, or tomalley, exists in lobsters of both sexes. The female lobster is considered preferable to the male because the meat is, generally speaking, more tender.

There is one principal way to determine whether a lobster is male or female. On the underside, centered at the juncture of the tail and main part of the lobster, there are two protrusions similar to the feelers that line both sides of the lobster tail. If the protrusions are limp and soft to the touch, the creature is female. If they are rough, it is a male.

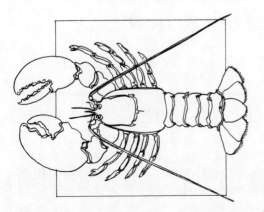

As to the freshness of lobster, if it has not been properly refrigerated and is dead for a day or longer I would discard it. If, on the other hand, I knew lobsters were alive only a few hours before, I would cook them with confidence.

Someone once asked me if I would ever serve culls, or lobsters with only one claw, and the answer is that if I wanted to be fancy and impress a group of guests, I would choose the lobsters with two claws. That, however, is pure snobbery. If I were to choose lobsters to prepare a salad, a soup, and so on, I would definitely buy the less-expensive culls. I can assure you that the main meat from the lobster's body is equally sweet, tender, and abundant in the whole lobster and the one-clawed creature. The difference is purely aesthetic.

Soft-shell lobsters, on the other hand, are one manner of food that I have never sampled and, daresay, never will. I know of one "gourmet," however, long celebrated for the one shining hour in his life when he raised a lobster in his home fish tank with the express thought that he would dine on soft-shell lobster.

The story goes that he and his wife took turns peeking at the tank for the magic moment. And one fine afternoon the lobster creeped out of its shell, at which point they fished the creature out with a net and had it, body and all, as I recall, amandine.

I received a letter from a woman in Oakdale, Maine, who reported that at that very moment she was on her way to her favorite soft-shell lobster restaurant, a place called Steve's, in nearby Waterville.

"If you have never tasted a soft-shell lobster," she observed, "you are living a deprived life. Although these lobsters contain less meat than the hard-shell, each piece is succulent and tender beyond description.

They are smaller, too, weighing only about one and one- quarter pounds each. But they're so rich only a gourmand would eat more than one at a single meal." The soft-shell variety, she added, is seasonal.

I telephoned Steve's Restaurant in Waterville and talked to one of the owners, Alfred Joseph, who told me: "We do, indeed, serve soft-shell lobsters, but they are not available throughout the year.

"There are always a few lobsters that will be shedding in local waters," he said, "but they are starting to harden up now." I asked what the advantage was in eating a soft-shell lobster.

"None," he said, "but that's my opinion. The meat is firmer in the hard-shell. Some people claim the meat is softer and, therefore, better in the soft-shell." At Steve's, the soft-shell lobsters are boiled or steamed. Sometimes, however, they will stuff and bake them.

A historical note about lobster:

In 1885, the *Lewiston* (Maine) *Journal* noted that fishermen were getting splendid prices for their lobster—ten cents a lobster—the public was paying ten to twelve cents a pound, and people were complaining about high prices. *See also* Paquette, Spiny lobster.

Lobster Américaine

There are two great controversies that have enlivened French discussions of gastronomy for generations. One of them concerns the number and kinds of fish to be used in a bouillabaisse and whether a true bouillabaisse can be made anywhere except the southern coast of France. The other concerns the true name for lobster or langouste américaine or armoricaine. The question

arises simply because the French insist it is a genuine French dish and could not be of American origin. Thus, it was conceived somewhere in dim memory that perhaps lobster is a dish from the Armoricain or Brittany coast, which is noted for its lobsters. Waverley Root points out in his scholarly *The Food of France* that the dish is "obviously not Breton, but Provençal, the lobster being cooked in oil and accompanied lavishly with tomatoes—and indeed until the middle of the nineteenth century virtually the same dish was known as homard à la provençale." He surmises the dish might have been created by the chef of a now-defunct restaurant Américain in Paris.

Lobster Sauce

The "lobster sauce" in shrimp with lobster sauce is one that was created to be served or cooked with lobster Cantonese. It consists of minced pork, scallions, beaten egg, and so on. A recipe titled "Shrimp cooked with the sauce used in making lobster Cantonese" would be a bit unwieldy in anybody's book.

Locust Bean

See St. John's bread.

Lomi-Lomi

Salmon, I have been told, does not exist in the Pacific waters a thousand miles from Hawaii and yet lomi-lomi, made with salted king salmon, is one of the national dishes. The origins of the dish date from the time of the trading vessels that anchored in the islands en route from the United States or Europe to the Orient.

The vessels, of course, carried stores of salted foods that would not spoil easily. They traded salt salmon to the Hawaiian natives for fresh fruit. The Hawaiians soaked the salmon, worked it with their fingers (lomi-lomi derives from the way the salmon is prepared with the fingers) to the desired texture, and served it with tomatoes and scallions.

London Broil

London broil is a distinctly American invention, and you will never find it—except in reference to the American dish—in British cookbooks.

It is, of course, a beefsteak, more often than not flank steak, that is quickly broiled. It is served hot, sliced across the grain, as often as not with a béarnaise or a bordelaise sauce, or with a sauce of melted butter and parsley.

Long Island Duck

There are scores of foods on this earth that are irrevocably, reflexively linked to the names of regions and villages. Bresse chickens, Kobe beef, Galway oysters, Maine lobsters, Dublin Bay prawns, the oranges of Seville, the foie gras of Strasbourg, the truffles of Périgord, and so on.

There are three places on this globe that are, more than any others, unfailingly iden-

tified with the cultivation of ducks. They are Peking in China, Rouen in France, and that forked, hundred-or-so-mile stretch of land east of Manhattan called Long Island.

There are numerous families on Long Island whose histories for three-quarters of a century or more have been closely associated with the raising of ducks, but there is none more intimately tied into duck culture than the Corwins.

The Corwins have lived there for more than two hundred years, more than a century before ducks were even introduced into America. They got into the duck business early this century and now, the Crescent Duck Farm, founded by Henry Corwin, is said to be the fourth largest duck farm in the United States. The farm produces three-quarters of a million ducks a year, which are shipped throughout the United States including Hawaii (one of the best markets for ducks) and the Caribbean.

Ironically, the other three leading duck farms are not on Long Island. There is one in Wisconsin, another in Indiana, and a third in Virginia.

In a visit to Lloyd Corwin, the affable fifty-year-old present owner of the farm, I learned that ducks arrived on Long Island in what was, indeed, a circuitous fashion.

As with most century-old legends, it is difficult to separate duck facts from fiction.

Corwin family history has it, nonetheless, that the Long Island duck industry began at least 104 years ago when a British major named Ashley, then stationed in Peking, cultivated a few white native ducks of uncommon size for his private consumption. In 1873, an American clipper ship, based in Stonington, Connecticut, entered the port of Peking and among the passengers was a Yankee trader named James Palmer.

Palmer was introduced to Ashley, and it turned out to be, as far as ducks are concerned, one of those historic meetings, like Lewis and Clarke, Currier and Ives, and Moët and Chandon.

Palmer persuaded Ashley to allow him to return to the States with a small flock of those unusual specimens. He arrived in New York on March 13, 1873, with one drake and three ducks still alive, enough to start a fledgling enterprise on Manhattan.

Thus, the hegira began. The offspring of the original ducks were transferred to Connecticut and shortly thereafter to the tidewater streams of eastern Long Island. Within a very short while there were more than 125 small duck farms on the island.

One of the tidewater streams was known as Meeting House Creek, situated in or near the farming community of Aquebogue, a name derived from an Indian tribe named Occabauk that wintered there. Although the Corwins owned a good deal of property in the region, the men were mostly farmers and carpenters. It was not until 1909 that Henry Corwin started pairing off ducks that would someday become Crescent.

Because of the community's proximity to New York and because of the railroad that passed through the village facilitating shipping, the duck farm even in its then primitive state flourished. Oddly, Lloyd Corwin attributes that success not to the sophisticated tastes of New Yorkers as a whole, but rather to the immigrants who lived in the city.

In those days, he said, the average citizen from Maine to California knew little about ducks and less about how to cook them. But the immigrant population, those who had come from Czechoslovakia, Poland, Hungary, Germany, and so on had an appetite for ducks, an appetite that had naturally developed in their homelands. Ducks were popular in French restaurants, but home-cooked ducks were rarely considered.

The earliest shipments to the city were shipped as what were known as "New York Dressed." That was back in the days before refrigeration, before mechanical pluckers and machines that eviscerated fowl were even dreamed of. Instead, the ducks were plucked by hand, quickly cooled, and packed thirty to a barrel for shipping. All the duck pickers were women and the most skilled of them could pick from 60 to 110 ducks a day.

Today, the Crescent duck farm is equipped with the most modern duck processing equipment. The ducks are waxed, plucked, eviscerated, plastic wrapped, frozen, and shipped throughout the country to reach their destination in a matter of hours.

Lovage

Lovage is a member of the carrot family and has fairly dark green leaves, shaped somewhat like those of the celery plant or Italian parsley. It is, in fact, sometimes referred to as love parsley.

I have rarely used it, but those who ad-

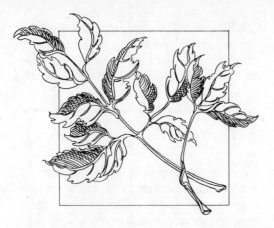

mire it say they use it raw in salads, in soups and stuffings. It is hard to be specific in describing its flavor. Some say it tastes sweet when first sampled and then has a bitter aftertaste; one writer describes the flavor as like "musky lemon-scented celery," and another as like the flavor of yeast.

The stems are candied for angelica.

Love-in-Disguise

Love-in-disguise has been around for two hundred years and is still served on special occasions, especially in Herefordshire, a county in west central England. Love-in-disguise consists of hearts of veal filled with ground meat and bacon stuffing. It is baked for a considerable time, coated with bread crumbs, and further roasted until the exterior is crusty.

Lox

See Smoked salmon.

Lucullus

Lucius Licinius Lucullus is conceivably remembered as the greatest epicure of all times. His name signifies great luxuries and dishes that bear his name are those with rich and splendid ingredients. An omelet Lucullus, for example, contains pure foie gras as an essential ingredient.

Lucullus, who lived from 110 to 56 B.C., was a Roman general celebrated for his victories over Mithradates VI, the king of Pontus. He was immensely wealthy and lived in dazzling style, proffering the elite of his day banquets, each of which cost hundreds of thousands of dollars. His table was invariably graced with the rarest of foods, and legend has it that on one occasion when he dined alone, his servants offered him exceedingly splendid fare, but the courses were modest in number. Outraged, he thundered, "Do you not comprehend that I am Lucullus and Lucullus is dining *chez* Lucullus?"

Ludicrous Recipe

Those who work in food professionally are often asked to deal in hyperboles. What is the best meal you ever ate? What is the worst meal? What is your favorite kind of food? What do you like to cook more than anything? And so on.

Within recent memory I have been asked to name the most ludicrous recipe I have ever read and the award goes to a newspaper. Both the name and region in which it is published are withheld for reasons that will be obvious. The recipe follows without comment.

GELATIN EGGS

2 dozen large eggs
4 packages of flavored gelatin: 1 lime,
  1 lemon, 1 cherry, and 1 orange
  Water

1. Blow out contents of eggs without breaking shells: Prick one end of the egg with a pin and make a slightly larger hole in the other end with an icepick. Holding egg over bowl, blow into the pinprick hole. Yolk and white will be blown out the other hole.

2. Run water through the eggshell and rinse out well. Mix each package of gelatin separately according to package directions, but omitting ¼ cup of water for each flavor.

3. Light a candle and close the pin-sized hole in the eggs by dripping candle wax over it. Stand eggs, wax end down, in egg cartons.

4. Fill eggs with gelatin, one flavor per egg, by using an eyedropper. When all eggs are full, return carton to refrigerator and chill several hours.

5. To remove gelatin egg from shell, carefully crack shell like it was a hard-boiled egg. This part is a little tedious, but produces beautiful results if done slowly and cautiously. Makes 3 eggs for each of 8 servings.

Luganega

Luganega consists of pure ground pork meat plus fat to which is added a minimum of spices other than salt and pepper. In *The Classic Italian Cook Book*, Marcella Hazan states that the finest luganega is made with pork shoulder and grated Parmesan cheese. It is, she writes, "available in long, continuous coils, not separated into lengths."

You can find it in America in good Italian butcher shops and groceries. It does not contain fennel seeds, which you find in many hot and sweet Italian sausages. In local markets, it does usually contain cheese.

Lukewarm

Lukewarm is surely one of the most curious and curious-sounding words in the English language. It means moderately warm or tepid, of course. I had never bothered to trace the origins of the word until, at a recent dinner, one of the guests wondered idly about its etymology.

A quick glance at the *Oxford English Dictionary* indicates that it derives from the Old English *hleow*. Thus informed, another guest suggested that it was related to the word "lee" as in leeward. A glance at that word indicates that it, too, may derive from *hleow*.

Wouldn't it be curious, someone volunteered, if the word lukewarm is in someway related to leeward, meaning the point toward which the wind blows?

Lule Kabob

Lule kabob is of Persian origin. The name, being a transliteration, is spelled in various ways. The dish is made with ground lamb seasoned with onion and cinnamon or other flavorings. It is divided into individual portions, molded into sausage shapes, and arranged on skewers, then grilled, and basted over charcoal.

It is generally served with a rice dish called chello, raw egg yolks, and powdered nonpoisonous sumac.

Lumb Crab

See Crab.

Lyonnaise

Lyons is frequently called—particularly by the chefs who were born there—the capital of French gastronomy. The name has also, since antiquity, been associated with dishes containing identifiable amounts of onion in one form or another. The best-known dish lyonnaise in America is, probably, potatoes lyonnaise.

Other dishes termed lyonnaise and containing a good quantity of onion are made with calf's liver, another with tripe.

Lyons is, of course, famous for many dishes that do not smack of onions and these would include the delicate and famed fish quenelles lyonnaise.

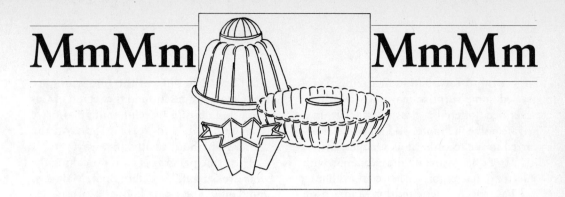

Macaroons

See Almonds.

Macédoine

Macédoine is one of the most interesting names in French menu terminology. It means a mixture of numerous things, generally a combination of cubed fruits, served as a dessert, or a combination of diced vegetables. The name derives from the kingdom of Alexander the Great, Macedonia, which was formed by a combination of many small states.

Mâche

Mâche is relatively unknown in America, where it is called corn salad or field salad. Occasionally it may be purchased in season at greengrocers. Most fanciers in this country grow it from seed. It is generally listed in seed catalogues as corn salad.

A seed expert has told me that there are several varieties of corn salad, and the commonest is *Valerianella olitoria*. There are some varieties with spoon-shaped leaves and some with larger round leaves. He could not describe how to determine, simply by looking, which has a fuller flavor or better texture.

Much of the corn salad in this country is grown in the South during the winter. There is also an Italian and Mediterranean version of corn salad known at *Valerianella eriocarpa*. It is imported from Europe in limited quantities into certain markets.

Madeira

I was once vividly entertained on a visit to Madeira when a wine merchant informed me—to my astonishment—that France is the largest importer of Madeira wine. I expressed some surprise inasmuch as I have never been offered a glass of Madeira in a private home in France, and it has never occurred to me to order it as an apéritif.

"They don't drink it," he explained with a degree of discomfort. "They cook with it."

I have been fascinated by Madeira on several levels for a long time. One of the consummate liaisons of wine and food is Madeira with fresh walnuts, cracked and eaten. *Sauce madère* is the classic sauce for tongue and ham. And Madeira has an amusing history. In the early days of its export, Madeira was shipped around the globe and frequently to very hot climates. It was discovered that the heat had a distinct influence on the flavor of the wine and improved it. With this knowledge in hand, the wine merchants of Madeira then started heating their wines on the island.

Madeira was the most coveted and popular drink of the Americas before the Revolutionary War. It was said to have been to the public of that age what the cocktail is today. The American thirst for Madeira diminished when the vines of the island were knocked out by the same disease, a phylloxera, that wiped out the vineyards of France during the 1870s. It was about this time that the cocktail came into being, and the ubiquitous taste for Madeira was never revived.

If you travel anywhere in Madeira, you are apt to see vineyards that may contribute to the annual harvest. Unlike the well-known vine-producing regions of Europe where the vineyards may be contained over the grounds of great estates or on well-defined plots on hillsides, the vines of Madeira grow in small plots alongside banana groves, vegetable gardens, and sugarcane plantings. The bulk of the fine wines are made from grapes around the region of Camara de Lobos, a fifteen-minute taxi drive from Funchal, and Porto Moniz on the western tip about two hours away.

The principal grapes used in making the wine are Sercial, Verdelho, Boal, Malmsey, and Tinta. The grape known as Terrantez disappeared in about 1873. I can testify that it produced a superior wine. In the company of my friendly wine merchant, I sipped and savored a bottle of Terrantez 1862. It was one of the last bottles left in the world. The oldest wine in my friend's cellar was a Boal 1838.

The labeling of Madeiras varies. The bottles frequently bear the name of the grapes from which the wine is derived. In ancient days, they were named for the places where the wines had traveled to "age" them. Thus, you might have purchased an India or Japan Madeira.

There is a Madeira called Rain Water, and it is of enormously obscure origin. Some say it is an American invention—that an American used a sun treatment on his imported treasures to make them light in color while retaining their finest qualities of flavor. Those are the properties of today's Rain

Water, a name that any merchant could put on a bottle of Madeira.

Sercial achieved a certain notoriety in America many years ago when an Army man on the $64,000 Question identified it as a Madeira. Perhaps the most famous of all Madeiras, however, particularly in England, is Malmsey, chiefly because George, Duke of Clarence, drowned in it, thus the phrase "drowned in a butt of Malmsey wine."

When to drink Madeira is a personal matter, but it is generally considered that Sercial or Verdelho, which are the driest, are the best wines to serve, preferably well-chilled, as an apéritif. Rain Water would also be in that category. Malmsey and Boal are the best dessert or after-dinner wines and should be served at room temperature.

If you are curious to know where America stands in the import picture, it is about eighth after France, Germany, Sweden, Denmark, England, Belgium, and Finland.

Madeira Cake

See Seedcake.

Madeleines

Almost without question, the most memorable association of food and literature is that of madeleines and Marcel Proust. The thought that intrigues, however, is that countless people who are aware of that association have never gotten past page 10 of Proust's *Remembrance of Things Past*. There are others, too, who, aware of the

association, could not describe in precise (or even vague) detail what madeleines are.

In case you wonder, madeleines are small, scallop-shaped butter cakes baked in individual molds. They have a texture that is much like that of a génoise or sponge cake. They are also related historically to Illiers, Proust's childhood hometown, in that a scallop shell worn in the hats of medieval pilgrims who stopped there was the inspiration for the cakes.

Mahimahi

Mahimahi—it is sometimes spelled as two words or hyphenated—is a type of dolphin, though no relation to the mammal usually referred to as a dolphin. In the *Encyclopedia of Fish Cookery*, A.J. McClane states that while mahimahi is "one of the most delicious seafoods," the annual yield is small. In Hawaii, he writes, "mahimahi has become synonymous with island cuisine," although "traditionally there was never much demand for dolphin among island people" and "it was only with the influx of tourism since the 1950s that any market developed."

Mahleb

Mahleb, also spelled mahlab, is a seasoning made from black cherry kernels or pits. It is used in Middle Eastern cookery as a flavoring for cakes and breads and is available in shops that specialize in Middle Eastern foods.

Maître d'Hôtel Butter

Maître d'hôtel butter, a composed butter used as a topping for grilled meats, is simple to prepare.

Take butter at or near room temperature, and add chopped parsley, lemon juice, salt if desired, and freshly ground pepper to taste. If you want, add a dash of Worcestershire sauce. Let this butter chill slightly until it can be rolled or shaped, tube fashion, in wax or parchment paper. Chill until firm and cut into slices before using it as a topping for steaks or whatever. Tightly wrapped, it will keep a week or longer in the refrigerator.

Other composed butters are anchovy butter, made by blending butter at room temperature with anchovy paste, and snail butter, made by adding chopped garlic and shallots (plus thyme and ground rosemary if you wish). You may use this immediately or it may be chilled until ready to use.

Malakoff

In classic French cooking (you will find it in Escoffier), a Malakoff pudding consists of an English custard to which gelatin has been added. This is turned into a mold and layered with ladyfingers, a purée of cooked fruit, such as apples or pears, currants, raisins, almonds, and chopped candied orange peel. When unmolded it is served with a sabayon sauce flavored with kirschwasser. Most French food encyclopedias refer to Malakoff as being the name of a noble Russian family.

Maltaise Sauce

A maltaise sauce is a hollandaise sauce to which the grated rind and juice of blood oranges have been added. Blood oranges are to be found only in limited quantities and for a very brief season in this country. Therefore, most if not all chefs resort to the juice and grated rind of sweet American oranges from California or wherever.

Blood oranges are so named because of their red, juicy pulp. Most of them come from southern Spain or Italy. They are also called maltese oranges in English and *maltaise* in French. That is why the sauce is so named.

To prepare such a sauce you would use about ¼ cup of juice and 1 teaspoon of grated rind to each 2 cups of freshly made hollandaise.

Malted Bread

As anyone conversant with the foods of England knows, malted breads are popular in that country.

In the original edition of Elizabeth David's *English Bread and Yeast Cookery*, published in England, the author says that malt extracts are sometimes used as improvers for breads. The extracts are sold in health food stores, as is malted meal.

The author quotes a member of the National Association of Master Bakers in Britain, who says that he finds malt "the most useful of all bread improvers" and that when used in a dehydrated form in correct, small proportions, the "taste is undetectable in the finished bread."

Mrs. David says that the malt "enhances the bloom on the crust of a loaf." The directions for use, she says, are to be found on the container of malt extract.

Mamaliga

Mamaliga is a dish related to grits, also made with a kind of ground corn.

A well-informed cook wrote to me, "what pasta is to Italians, potatoes to the Irish, mamaliga is to Rumanians. It was the staple food of the nonaffluent masses in Slavic countries. Even in America, good times have not been able to wean the taste of mamaliga from many Rumanian diets.

"I was married into a Rumanian family. When my mother-in-law came to visit our home in the 1950s, she brought with her a five-pound bag of ground corn, garlic, and a pound of brinza, the Rumanian equivalent of feta cheese.

"Taking my largest pot, she boiled water in it, added the ground corn and watched it for twenty-five minutes, stirring vigorously with a wooden spoon. At the right moment, she turned the contents of the pot over a clean dish towel, which she placed on the table. It fell out . . . like a twelve-egg sponge cake."

This "cake" was then sliced in half by pulling a thick thread through the center to produce two layers. The layers were stuffed with the crumbled cheese and hot butter containing chopped garlic. It was served in thick slices with cold sour cream to be added at will.

I made this version of mamaliga and it was delicious. But I received a lot of letters on the subject. One woman wrote:

"Though born in Rumania, I never heard of garlic being used in its preparation. The peasants eat it with onion, which they smash with the fist on a wooden table. It is also eaten with a fried egg on top of the melted cheese and this is called à la Nea Nae, which means 'à la Uncle Nicholas.'

"Incidentally, brinza is the Rumanian word for cheese in general. Brinza de Braila (from the port on the Danube) is the equivalent of feta cheese."

A reader in Fair Lawn, New Jersey, stated that the mention of mamaliga brought a rush of memories. She added that the proper ingredients should include "bright yellow cornmeal, crumbly brinza, melted sweet butter, and no sour cream.

"Sour cream on mamaliga sounds like a Russian imposition," she said, adding, "In our house, leftover cooked cornmeal was packed into an oiled loaf pan and chilled. Next day it was sliced, dipped in beaten egg and crumbs, and then fried. Apparently Rumania's version of hush puppies."

Mango

A mango is one of the finest fruits I know. The commonest variety available in America has a succulent, sweet, golden flesh, a bit exotic in flavor. The flesh surrounds a flat but rounded seed or stone. Most of them have a greenish-yellow skin.

about the size of a small to medium orange, and in exterior appearance slightly suggests the pomegranate. Its juicy, rose-tinted or creamy pulp is sweet and slightly tart." The text adds that it "combines all the good qualities of the pineapple, grape, peach, and strawberry." The tree has been cultivated in the West Indies.

There is also a stuffed pickle preparation called mango, which may be made either with green peppers or green tomatoes. The vegetable is stuffed with salted shredded cabbage, mustard seeds, vinegar, and sugar.

I have been familiar with this preparation since childhood, but I did not know why the filled peppers or tomatoes were referred to as mangoes until I heard from many people, mostly in the Middle West, who said that the word mango commonly refers simply to the sweet green pepper known as a bell pepper. Judging from the letters, the usage is common in Indiana and Ohio, as well as in Pennsylvania Dutch country. One person wrote that green peppers are called mangoes in Iowa, Missouri, Illinois, and Kentucky.

Maple Syrup

See Vermont madness.

Maraschino Cherries

I happen to think that maraschino cherries can be ranked or lumped along with marshmallows, iceberg lettuce, California black olives, and maple syrup as notably unsophisticated foods. How about all-day suckers and lollipops? Maraschino cherries are a traditional garnish for whiskey sours and just as deplorable as that frothy liquid bartenders (and others) frequently add to cocktails to give them a "head."

Curiously, very few people seem to know the origin of the words "maraschino cherries." There is a wild cherry called the marasca. This is used to produce a cordial called maraschino. The maraschino cherry is an ordinary sweet cherry that has been cooked in a red-dyed syrup flavored with imitation maraschino.

Mangosteen

Mangosteen is a delicacy that has been called "the world's choicest fruit." One of the best definitions of it is to be found in Ward's *The Encyclopedia of Food.* "The fruit of a tree native to the East Indies, distinguished by long, oval, leathery leaves and a flower like a single rose. . . . It is generally

Marchpane

See Marzipan.

Margarine

Margarine is a table spread and a cooking fat that was invented in France in the 1860s. Its manufacture includes hydrogenated vegetable oils, emulsifiers, and coloring matter. At first it was referred to as oleomargarine, and sometimes simply as oleo, because it was a derivitive of animal fat, but this is no longer true.

For what it is worth, I recall when it was illegal to add yellow coloring matter to margarine to keep it from being confused with butter. It can be substituted for butter in most recipes, but I prefer the flavor of butter.

Marinade

I am frequently asked if marinades can be used over and over again. If the marinade is kept extremely fresh, I can see no reason why it could not be used a second and perhaps a third time.

When you marinate raw meats, such as pork, beef, or chicken, some blood will naturally seep into the marinade. Therefore, if you use a marinade for chicken, I would use it only for chicken the second time. The same with pork or beef.

I would definitely restrict the number of times a marinade is used because the flavors will thin out after a short while. And if you add chopped scallions, for example, to the marinade the flavor and texture will diminish in two or three days in the refrigerator. You must be judicious.

Ideally, it would be best to marinate almost any given food outside the refrigerator to give the meat or whatever a more pronounced flavor of the marinade, a flavor frequently referred to as "wild or gamy." Prior to refrigeration, particularly in Europe, most marinating was done in a cool place, a cellar or another room, depending on outside temperatures. The recommendation of refrigeration is largely a precaution to ensure against unwanted, possibly injurious, bacterial action. Under guaranteed and certain conditions, marinating may be done in the old-fashioned manner, but conscious care must be taken that temperature and other conditions are such that there could be no question of food spoilage.

One expert who does not believe in marinades is Charles Chevillot, a scion of the family that has owned the Hôtel de la Poste in Burgundy and the proprietor of two estimable restaurants in Manhattan, La Petite Ferme and Les Tournebroches, the latter of which specializes in grilled dishes. When he grills meats or seafood en brochette, he does not marinate the foods even briefly. He coats the foods lightly with a neutral oil simply to prevent them from sticking. Salt and pepper are added at the last moment. He prefers white pepper to black pepper because it is less forceful in flavor. And he serves the grilled foods with béarnaise sauce. "The trouble with a ketchup sauce," he says, "is that it tends to disguise flavors, so much so that you can't taste the natural flavor of the foods."

Marinara Sauce

As nearly as I can determine there is no such thing as a "classic" marinara sauce.

The words *marinara* in Italian and *marinière* in French refer to "marine style" or "sailor style." Marinara sauce does not appear, for example, in Marcella Hazan's two well-established books on Italian cooking. It does not appear in Ada Boni's *Italian Regional Cooking* or in Giuliano Bugialli's *The Fine Art of Italian Cooking*.

There is a recipe for a marinara sauce that contains red wine (no tomatoes), anchovy paste, and garlic in Luigi Carnacina's *Great Italian Cooking*. Another, with tomatoes, onions, and herbs, appears in Ed Giobbi's *Italian Family Cooking*. And there are two recipes (one with tomatoes, the other without) in Luigi Carnacina's *Italian Home Cooking*.

Marlborough Pie

Marlborough pie is supposed to be a Thanksgiving dish, and I am told it is a traditional dessert in Massachusetts. It is an open-face pie with a custard-like filling prepared with applesauce, eggs, butter, lemon juice, and other flavorings.

Marmalade

Legend has it that the word "marmalade" originated with the French word *malade*, which means ill. The story goes that Mary, Queen of Scots, was inordinately fond of an orange preserve that she had dined on in France. She felt a particular craving for this spreadable sweet when she became ill. As a result, it became known to her courtiers as *Marie-malade*.

This is pure nonsense. The fact is that the name derives from the word *marmelo*, the Portuguese name for quince. The original marmalade was made from this fruit. Over the years chefs and cooks have developed numerous marmalades, including lime, grapefruit, peach, and plum.

Marrow

Marrow is to be found in most bones, generally veal or beef, but it is best to use the larger bones, such as the shin bone. You may cook the marrow in several ways. It is always best to have the raw bone split but not broken in half before cooking. You may wrap the bone in cheesecloth and let it simmer in beef broth or you may wrap it in foil and bake it in a moderate oven for about forty-five minutes.

In the good old days of Queen Elizabeth, it was customary to serve the marrow bone on linen napkins. The marrow was extracted with specially made, slender sterling marrow spoons. When removed, the marrow was spread on hot toast.

The most notable current dish with marrow bones is ossobuco, a Milanese specialty of veal knuckle bones cooked in a stew with vegetables.

Marrow is one of the richest of all foods you can swallow, and the high cholesterol content discourages many people from eating it. It is absolutely prohibited for those on cholesterol-restricted diets.

There is also a marrow that is totally different called vegetable marrow, and I have noted the many uses for it in books on British cookery. The best-known varieties of vegetable marrow in this country are zucchini and summer squash.

Marshmallows

The first marshmallows were made from the root of a plant that is known as a marsh mallow (*Althaea officinalis*). I have not a clue as to how you would go about making marshmallows in the unlikely event that you came across a batch of that root. Marshmallows today are made from sugar, water, gelatin, and egg whites, and can be counted among my least favorite foods.

Mary Ann Cakes

One of the most interesting and curiously named pastries bears the name Mary Ann. Mary Ann cakes, as they are sometimes called, come in two sizes: large and small (or miniature). Basically, a Mary Ann is sponge cake that is round like a standard cake, but has a shallow, uniform depression in the center. (Mary Ann pans, essential for creating this shape, can be purchased in fine kitchenware shops across the country.) The reason for the depression is to receive an assortment of garnishes—such as sweetened cut fruits or berries, custard or whipped cream, and, quite often, a combination of such good things.

Marzipan

Marzipan is, in a broad sense, all candies based on almond paste. Almond paste is, by the way, nothing more than blanched almonds that have been ground to a paste with a meat grinder, food processor, or electric blender. There are several ways to go about making marzipan, which is generally tinted and shaped into various figures—small animals, vegetables, and fruits. You can mix almond paste with fondant, or you can (as a tin of almond paste states on its label) put the almond paste into a bowl and add 2 ounces of light corn syrup, 6 ounces of powdered sugar, and ⅔ cup of marshmallow cream or melted marshmallow. Shape and tint as desired.

A more traditional technique is as follows: Put an egg white into the container

of an electric mixer. Beat briefly until it starts to froth. Do not, however, beat too much air into it. Add 1 cup of almond paste, cut into pieces, and beat until well blended. Gradually beat in 1½ cups of powdered sugar. Shape as desired and then tint.

The name marzipan, sometimes referred to in English as marchpane, derives from an Italian word, *marzapane*. The original Italian indicated "a fine box for confections."

To go back even further, I was informed that the name derives from the Latin *Marcus panem* meaning Mark's bread—*i.e.,* the bread of the Feast of St. Mark.

Masa Harina

Masa harina, used in the preparation of tortillas, is dried corn that has been finely ground. It is available in almost all shops that specialize in Latin American foods.

Mascarpone

Mascarpone, a rich and delectable cheese, was originally made in the Lombardy region of Italy, but is now produced all over the country. It is quite soft, and perishable, because it is made with double or heavy fresh cream.

I am told that in the district of Friuli, mascarpone is often blended with mustard, spices, and anchovies. The version I prefer is blended with Gorgonzola.

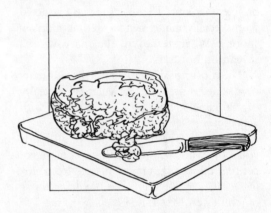

Masséna

One of the greatest egg dishes in the world is an inspired creation known in French as *oeufs Masséna*. It is an indecently rich concoction, made with poached eggs nestled in hot artichoke bottoms and garnished with two sauces, one béarnaise, one made of fresh tomatoes.

Most dictionaries of food attribute the name of this dish to André Masséna, Duke of Rivoli and Prince of Essling, who lived from 1758 to 1817, and fought under Napoleon. Although histories agree that Masséna was "brave, resourceful and indefatigable" and one of the great soldiers of France, the *Encyclopedia Britannica* points out: "In private life [Masséna was] indolent, greedy, rapacious, ill-educated and morose."

Whatever his personal shortcomings, the dish that bears his name is indisputably food for heroes.

Matjes Herring

I have made many inquiries of Scandinavian chefs and other food authorities, but none has been able to supply me with a recipe for matjes herring, which I consider one of the greatest herring preparations.

I cannot explain this and have never been able to re-create matjes herring myself. I have several tins in my refrigerator; the labels say that the ingredients are "skinless and boneless matjes herring fillets, water, sugar, vinegar, salt, and spices."

Matjes means maiden herring; that is, the dish is prepared from young fish that have never spawned.

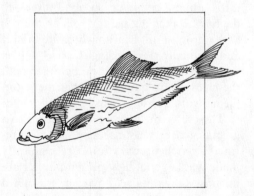

Matzoh

See Moon matzohs.

Mauby

I had never heard of mauby, a root-beer-like beverage found in the Caribbean, but I found a recipe in *The Complete Book of Caribbean Cooking* by Elisabeth Lambert Ortiz. In a preface she says: "So far as I have been able to find out, mauby bark, sometimes mawby, in Spanish *maubi,* is the bark of the algarroba (carob) tree. It can be found in Puerto Rican or tropical markets."

The drink made with the bark is popular as a refreshing soft drink in most of the islands. The recipe consists of cooking mauby bark with water, cinnamon stick, cloves, dried orange peel, and brown sugar.

Maven

In the world of food, maven refers to someone with a passionate appetite for one thing or another.

In *The Joys of Yiddish* Leo Rosten notes that the word rhymes with raven and means "understanding" in Hebrew. His own definition is "an expert; a really knowledgeable person; a good judge of quality; a connoisseur."

Mayeritsa Avgolemono

See Greek Easter.

May Wine

Woodruff, a woodland herb and ground cover, is called *waldmeister* in Germany, the land of May wine. I find the drink too flowery and perfumy for my palate, but this is one man's description of how to make it, taken from David A. Embury's *The Fine Art of Mixing Drinks:*

"Sprinkle a half dozen bunches of *waldmeister* with ½ to ¾ pound of powdered sugar. Place in a glass bowl or glazed crock and add ½ pint cognac and 1 quart Moselle or other white wine. Cover and let stand overnight. Stir and strain. Pour over ice into a punch bowl and add 3 quarts of Moselle and 2 quarts of champagne. Charged water may be substituted for the champagne, if desired."

I am told that in this country there is a similar drink called a May wine punch that consists of white wine, Cognac, and a nice dose of Benedictine liqueur, but I have never sampled it.

Mayonnaise

The origin of mayonnaise is generally attributed by serious sources to the cook or chef of the Duke of Richelieu while the latter was instrumental in securing Port Mahon for France in 1756. Port Mahon is the capital of Minorca, the second largest of Spain's Balearic Islands (the largest is Majorca). If this tale is true, the name might well have been mahonnaise. There is some argument as to the accuracy of this origin. Some say the word "mayonnaise" did not appear prior to the nineteenth century. Others say the name derives from the French word *moyeu,* which was the name sometimes given to the yolk of an egg, which is, of course, the base for making mayonnaise.

Mayonnaise is easily made in the home, and is far superior to the commercial version.

The important thing in making mayonnaise is to ensure that you add your acid in the form of vinegar, lemon juice, and mustard—often a combination of all three—to the bowl containing the egg yolk *before* you add a drop of oil. Beat this mixture briskly and gradually start adding the oil.

If you do not add the acid before the oil, the chances are quite likely that the ingredients will not homogenize properly.

The oil for the mayonnaise depends to a great degree on personal taste. The most refined French preparations are generally made with a good, light peanut oil. For all-purpose mayonnaise, however, I prefer a mayonnaise made with all or part olive oil. In the south of France and in Italy, many recipes for mayonnaise call for light or heavy olive oil, depending on the use. If you are preparing an aïoli, a garlic mayonnaise for cooked salt cod and so on, you would generally use a very heavy olive oil.

There is nothing wrong with making mayonnaise using an electric mixer. In fact, it produces a mayonnaise equally as good as that made with a wire whisk. I prefer the latter because it takes only a few seconds, and with the whisk there is no dismantling the beaters of the mixer and loosening the bowl. In other words, using a whisk saves time and steps.

There is also nothing wrong with making mayonnaise using a food processor. Unless you are careful, however, you may overbeat your egg yolks in the beginning, causing them to overhomogenize. This means the mayonnaise will not thicken properly.

Homemade mayonnaise should be kept only a few days and no longer than a week to guard against spoilage. Commercially prepared mayonnaise has an indefinite storage life if properly refrigerated.

Mead

Mead is basically a blend of honey and water that has been fermented. According to the *Encyclopedia Brittanica,* such alcoholic beverages were common throughout Europe during the Middle Ages. "Mulsum," the encyclopedia continues, "was a form of mead with the addition of wine."

Measuring Cups

Glass and metal measuring cups are designed for different purposes. Glass cups are designed for liquid. You add your water or milk or whatever to the cup, hold it up to the eye and thus determine the exact quantity in the cup.

Metal cups are destined for measuring solids, such as flour, sugar, or salt. You add your solids to the cup, scrape off the top precisely and there you have an exact cup, half a cup, quarter cup, and so on.

And thus it was a bit unsettling recently to receive the following note from a New Jersey woman.

"In order to simplify the assembly of ingredients for a recipe, I recently acquired an assortment of measuring cups.

"For some unknown reason, I decided to test the various glass ones as well as the Lucite and plastic ones for liquid measurements against each other."

She was, she adds, disturbed to discover that each cup of different make held a different amount of water for the same measure.

"I thought," she added, "that a cup is a cup is a cup." Alas, she notes, it isn't true.

This note sent me sauntering back to the kitchen to conduct my own experiments, and sure enough. To choose but one example, I poured 3 cups of water from a standard Pyrex measuring cup into a 4-cup Lucite measure. The 3 cups indicated in the

Pyrex measure "expanded" to almost 3¼ cups in the Lucite measure.

It is shameful, of course, that there is no precise standardization in these measures. But as a word of consolation to readers, 1 tablespoon of liquid more or less will not be all that critical in most recipes. The difference of a tablespoon (of baking powder or salt, for example) could be disastrous in the case of dry ingredients, but as my correspondent pointed out, the various cups to be used for dry or solid ingredients turned out to be uniform from one manufacturer to another.

Meatball

See Albondiga.

Meat Loaf

There are several factors to consider in making a meat loaf. The first is that the meat should contain a certain amount of fat if you want a moist meat loaf. To make an all-beef meat loaf, the best all-round choice is probably chuck. Many professionals think that an ideal meat loaf is made with a combination of beef, veal, and not-too-lean pork. Bread crumbs, used judiciously, give lightness and texture to meat loaf, but if they are used to excess, the meat loaf becomes spongy. If the meat loaf is covered with a layer of fat, such as strips of bacon or salt pork, this will also help the meat loaf to be moist and more tender. It is best to let a meat loaf stand for a brief period after it is removed from the oven—twenty minutes or

longer—before serving.

Among the methods suggested to me for producing a more juicy loaf are:

—Knead some tomato sauce into the meat before baking. But care must be taken to avoid over-kneading or the texture of the meat will be lost.

—No matter what other ingredients are used, and these vary depending on what is on hand, always add a generous helping of applesauce to the mixture.

—Into the beef chuck, grate a bit of onion and a small apple, plus a potato, which keeps the meat fluffy. Instead of bread crumbs add a mashed wet slice of white bread and a tablespoon of salad oil.

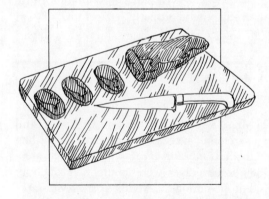

Medallion

The word "medallion" usually refers to a solid round cut of meat, veal, beef, and so on, that is generally sautéed. The word in its original sense means something that resembles a large medal, generally round or oval in shape. I see no reason why it could not be loosely applied to a round patty of meat.

Mehlsuppe

Mehl is German for flour, and mehlsuppe is a soup that is made with flour browned in fat. Milk is stirred in and, finally, sugar and cinnamon. At the end, the soup is enriched and further thickened with egg yolks and may be served with a slice of white bread floating on top.

Melba

See Opera names in food.

Ménagère

Ménagère relates, of course, to matters of the ménage: house and home. The word means housewife, but it also implies thrift and frugality. Dishes labeled ménagère are generally very plain and unpretentious, French country-style

Menudo

Menudo is, in my view, one of the greatest of Mexican dishes. It is a soup made with tripe plus a calf's foot, cooked long with onion, garlic, and chilies (ancho and poblano). It is combined with cooked whole hominy and served piping hot in soup bowls with a sprinkling of oregano.

If you like it spicy, you may add chopped hot green chilies. Other accompaniments may include chopped onion and lime wedges. For what it is worth, the dish is supposed to cure a hangover. In Mexico, it is traditionally served on New Year's morning.

There is also a menudos gitanos, a specialty of Andalusia. To prepare it, the tripe is cooked with onions, carrots, and tomatoes, plus sweet peppers, garlic, paprika, herbs, and spices. To the stew are added chick-peas and sausages, including chorizos and morcilla, or blood sausage. It is sometimes flavored with saffron.

Meringue

Meringues were probably the creation of a Swiss pastry chef who first conceived the notion of beating egg whites with sugar before baking or frosting a cake. He worked in the small town of Meiringen in Switzerland. The name, of course, would derive from that of the town.

A perfect meringue has a snow-white and crisp surface. The reason that beads of car-

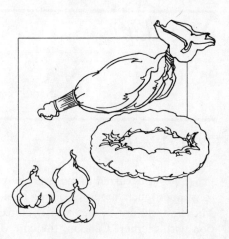

amel sometimes form is because the sugar was added to the egg whites too carelessly and too quickly. In other words, the sugar was not thoroughly incorporated and dissolved in the whites. The undissolved sugar crystals become caramel.

Another problem that sometimes occurs with meringue is that the peaks fall when it is used as a topping for pie.

There may be two reasons: The meringue may not have been beaten long or firmly enough in the beginning. The meringue mixture must be as stiff as it can be before spreading on the pie. A second cause may be baking at too high a temperature.

The temperature must be moderate (200 to 250 degrees), so that the meringue has a chance to cook through before it achieves that nice brown texture on top.

Merles

See Blackbirds.

Mezedaki

See Appetizers.

Michelangelo

It had never occurred to me over the years to wonder much about the dining habits of Michelangelo until I had a brief conversation with Herbert Cahoon, the curator of autograph manuscripts at the Pierpont Morgan Library.

It had been my understanding that Michelangelo had led a fairly ascetic existence. I had read somewhere that his daily fare was generally bread and wine, which he ate and drank in solitude.

But, in fact, there are menus, Mr. Cahoon said, that demonstrate that Michelangelo Buonarroti, to use his full name, may have had considerable interest in what he ate.

"There are two documents," the librarian said, "in the Buonarroti Archives in Florence that show his style of dining to be a bit elevated from what is normally supposed.

"These documents, including three menus, came to my attention in a 1940 issue of the *Art Quarterly* in an article by Charles de Tolnay," Mr. Cahoon said.

The documents were written by Michelangelo when he was fifty-five years old when, for political reasons, he had to make a hasty exit from Florence and travel to Venice, taking with him as many of his possessions as possible.

"The documents show that Michelangelo owned napery, silverware, soup tureens, plates, and other dishes suitable for entertaining," Mr. Cahoon continued. "It was a collection of dinnerware that would have brought culinary distinction to any family of the time outside the nobility."

The menus written by Michelangelo were also illustrated. It is assumed that the drawings were for the enlightenment of a new and not too well educated servant.

In any event, Mr. Cahoon stressed, the menus vary greatly in quality and quantity.

"The first," he pointed out, "consists of only two courses: one of fish (*una aringa*, a herring) and one of pasta (*tortegli* or *tortelli*), and the bread and wine indispensable for even the poorest Tuscan meal. As only two rolls (*pani dua*) and one jug (*bochal*) of wine are indicated, this is probably a menu for one—a modest meal for Michelangelo.

"The second menu has more courses: fish once again and anchovies (*alice*) this time and also the *tortelli,* and it calls for a salad (*una salata*), a vegetable (*spinaci*) and two dry wines, one in a jug and the other in a quarter-liter container (*quartuccio*). This more elaborate menu is evidently planned for two persons, since four rolls and four anchovies are indicated. It may well represent a meal that Michelangelo shared with an important guest.

"The third menu is once again fairly simple and has only two courses: two soups with fennel (*dua minestra di finochio*) and a fish, once again a herring. However, with six rolls and two servings of soup, it is for two persons — probably for a guest of medium importance and perhaps for one of his *garzoni,* or apprentices, who would have an appetite for extra rolls."

Milanese

The word "milanese" means in the style of Milan, and probably comes from the fact that grated Parmesan is part of the dish.

It almost goes without saying that the most famous milanese dish on earth is veal cutlets (or chops or scaloppine) milanese. To prepare the dish you coat pieces of veal with flour, then eggs, and finally bread crumbs. The bread crumbs are blended with grated Parmesan. The meat is cooked in butter and/or oil on both sides. The dish is generally served with spaghetti in marinara

sauce on the side. The proportion of bread crumbs to grated cheese is about five to one. In French kitchens, it is known as milanaise.

Miltz

Because I have never cooked nor eaten miltz, I rely on a Brooklyn gentlemen to describe the intricacies of preparation of this delicacy, which some call Jewish soul food.

"Order a miltz at a kosher butcher (because it isn't carried in stock). Have him cut a pocket in it for stuffing. While the oven is preheating to 325 degrees, wash the spleen throughly (What a mess!), then run water through it to see where all the holes are. Dry it with paper towels, then sew all the holes with needle and thread (just like a surgeon).

"Run water though it again to spot the holes you've missed, then suture some more. When the operation is complete, mix together 4 cups all-purpose flour, ¾ cup matzoh meal, 1 finely chopped medium-size onion, and about ½ cup of coarsely chopped beef and chicken fat. Salt and pepper to taste.

"Stuff the miltz with this mixture and sew some more, closing up the slit and any other holes the stuffing might escape through. Place it in a roasting pan with 1 whole large onion (chopped), 1 whole clove garlic (unchopped), and ½ cup water.

"Roast, covered, for 2 hours, then uncover and keep roasting until it turns a gorgeous dark brown, basting with the pan juices as it goes.

"Serve hot, sliced, preferably with challah —to soak up the delicious gravy—and maybe a little seltzer on the side to wash it down."

Mincemeat

It is a curious fact that the most coveted character of some foods evolved not as a matter of flavor, but as a matter of preservation of food.

The list is long and would include scores of smoked foods, such as ham and sausages, salted foods, such as cod, and such other fish as salmon and sturgeon.

To a lesser, but by a no means less delectable, extent, the list would include food preserved in alcohol, including cherries and the multiple fruits in tutti-frutti.

All this came to mind while I was delving into the origins of mincement.

Mincemeat, according to food histories, came about as a matter of preserving various meats, including such game as venison and rabbit. Alcohol and various spices were added to retard spoilage. Around the middle of the seventeenth century, these meats were made more sophisticated and palatable through the addition of various preserved fruits and spices.

According to Dorothy Gladys Spicer in *From an English Oven*, the ancestor of today's English mince tarts was a gigantic affair, "weighing over a hundredweight and bursting with 'neats' tongues, chicken, eggs, raisins, orange and lemon peel," plus large quantities of such other ingredients as sugar and spices.

There is an entry in Samuel Pepys's diary dated January 6, 1662, noting that he had dined at the home of Sir W. Pen, who celebrated his wedding anniversary with "eighteen mince pies in a dish, the number of years that he had been married." Presumably, he dined on the newer, sophisticated version of mincement. There are probably as many recipes for mincemeat in England and this country as there are for Welsh rabbit or Yorkshire buck.

As indicated in Dorothy Spicer's book, the original mincement concoctions contained neats' tongues. Neat is an old English term for ox.

Many recipes call for the addition of both beef and beef tongue, while others eliminate these "neats" entirely and consist solely of preserved fruits, apples, spices, a bit of brandy, and so forth.

Minestra

Minestra means soup, generally a thick soup. Minestrone is a form of minestra. Italy has countless versions of minestra; most are made with root vegetables, such as potatoes, carrots, and parsnips, and some contain mushrooms and dried beans. One has tomatoes as a principal ingredient. *Minestra torinese* is made with cabbage, leeks, tomatoes, and celery root. I am told that in Malta, minestra refers to a thick soup containing, among other things, pumpkin and turnips.

Mirlitons

See Chayote.

Miroton

A miroton is made with leftover sliced beef. It consists of cooking sliced onions in butter until they are wilted. The onions are sprinkled with flour and beef stock is added. You season it with salt and pepper and a touch of vinegar. With the sliced beef added and after being cooked for about half an hour, it is a little like a thickened onion soup.

The name, according to *Larousse Gastronomique,* suggests an old French nursery rhyme, which had a refrain, "Mironton, mironton, mirontaine."

Mississippi Mud Pie

A Mississippi mud pie, with its nursery-like name, is a quite serious, sinfully rich dessert. It is made with butter, unsweetened chocolate, corn syrup, and sugar. It is baked in a pie shell until the top is a bit crunchy and the filling is set. It is best served warm with a scoop of vanilla ice cream on top.

A Mississippi mud cake is also rich as Croesus. It is made with cocoa powder and chopped pecans, baked with a marshmallow topping, and covered with a cocoa and pecan icing.

Mixed Grill

Number among my other passions an English mixed grill, that inimitable assortment of lamb and sausages and mushrooms and bacon and broiled tomatoes with béarnaise sauce and straw potatoes on the side.

A mixed grill isn't mentioned in Mrs. Beeton's estimable and definitive work on early English cookery, her *Book of Household Management.* A dish of many parts, one can only speculate that the classic mixed grill, as it is now composed, probably began with the simple likes of assorted parts of the lamb—chops and kidney plus liver—grilled and served with a broiled tomato, a most likely combination.

Another chef probably further embellished the dish with the straw potatoes and watercress garnish. Another took note of the harmonious nature of these things with the tarragon-flavored butter sauce and still another contemplated the compatibility and added grilled mushroom caps with bacon.

I do not hold with the theory that all the foods for the mixed feast must be cooked on a grill, nor do I recommend it. The meats, yes. The tomatoes, no. They're best broiled. Straw potatoes, one of the more sublime forms of that vegetable when freshly cooked, are a bit tricky to make, and store-bought shoestring potatoes are most acceptable.

I look on a mixed grill as a highly variable affair. For example, the straw potatoes and even the béarnaise sauce could be omitted, though sooner the former than the latter.

As to the mushrooms and bacon, the ordinary or usual way of serving these is to broil or grill the mushrooms and fry the bacon strips crisp. I find it preferable both from the standpoint of flavor and garnish to wrap the mushrooms in bacon and then to bake and grill. The sausages could be grilled or pan-fried.

If no grill is available, all the grilled foods may be cooked under a home broiler. One word of caution: If a grill is to be used, the grids on the grill must be fairly close together to prevent the pieces of liver and kidneys from slithering through.

Mizutaki

I have for many years admired and dined on chicken mizutaki. In Koh Masuda's *New Japanese English Dictionary,* mizutaki is defined as "chicken boiled plain." In Shizuo Tsuji's *Japanese Cooking, a Simple Art,* the dish is made with chicken and vegetables cooked at the table and served with a ponzu sauce made with a base of lemon juice and soy sauce.

Mocha

The word "mocha" can refer to a coffee flavor alone although more often than not it refers to coffee plus chocolate.

The name originated from the Yemen port of Mocha, now called Al Muklha. The port was at one time a renowned center of the world coffee trade. Mocha is a kind of rich Arabian coffee and the word is used loosely to refer to any kind of very fine coffee.

Mock Turtle Soup

Mock turtle soup is so named because it is an imitation of green turtle soup, one of the finest of dishes. Unfortunately, genuine green turtle soup is rarely made today, for the green turtle is among the endangered species.

Mock turtle soup is made with a calf's head that, when cooked and cut up, has a gelatinous, meaty texture and a flavor that tastes deceptively like turtle meat. The recipe, available in many first-rate cookbooks, is quite complicated to do correctly. It sometimes also contains tongue, ham, and mushrooms and, often, chopped hard-boiled eggs.

A long-simmered soup, it has many spices, including mace, allspice, and cloves. A generous amount of Madeira is ordinarily added before serving.

Molds

For people who have trouble unmolding foods that have either been baked or chilled in molds, here are some suggestions.

For foods baked in molds, it is presumed that the mold in which the food was cooked was generously buttered or oiled, or lined with buttered paper before the food was added. Generally speaking, it is best to let the dish stand briefly, although this is not absolutely essential. Using a small sharp knife, such as a paring knife, carefully and quickly run the knife around the perimeter of the food, holding the knife close to the sides of the mold. Invert a plate over the

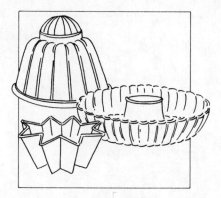

mold, then quickly turn the plate over to its upright position, inverting the mold at the same time. If the food does not immediately loosen itself from the mold, tap the bottom of the mold (now inverted) in several places with the back of a heavy knife.

For cold gelatin molds taken from the refrigerator, it is presumed that the mold was rinsed out with cold water or was lightly oiled to prevent the food from sticking. When the food has set, use a small sharp knife, such as a paring knife, and carefully and quickly run the knife around the perimeter of the food, holding the knife close to the side of the mold. There are two ways to proceed from here. If you are dexterous enough and the dessert is firm enough, you may run the inverted mold under running hot water, turning the mold quickly right side up when you feel the gelatin mixture start to loosen. Wipe off the bottom of the mold, then invert onto a plate as usual. Or, invert the mold onto a plate and cover the mold all over with towels that have been soaked in very hot water and wrung out. Continue adding hot towels until the gelatin mixture loosens. If the mixture does not loosen, try tapping the mold with the back of a heavy knife. That failing, turn the mold

right side up, serve directly from the mold, and pretend it's the thing to do.

Mole Crabs

See Sand crabs.

Mongolian Grill

I have long nourished a keen appetite for a Genghis Khan or Mongolian "barbecue" in which foods are cooked at the table over a curved grill that resembles a rather broad and shallow helmet.

The name is said to derive from the twelfth century when the hordes of the conqueror built fires under their rounded metal headpieces and cooked their lamb, or whatever else was at hand, on top.

The Mongolian grill is made with thinly sliced meat—lamb, beef, chicken, and so on—dipped in or brushed lightly with a soy sauce and ginger mixture. The meat is grilled quickly and dipped into more of the sauce before being eaten. After the meat is cooked,

other items, such as watercress, mushrooms, bean curd, and spinach, are added to the grill. This is a guest participation dish in which those assembled cook their own foods. No silks and satins, for the oil tends to sputter into the air when the foods are cooked.

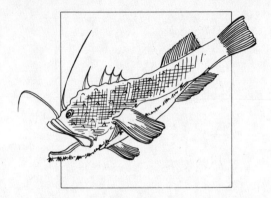

Monkey Bread

My dictionary informs me that monkey bread is the gourd-like fruit of the baobab tree and that this fruit is a favorite of monkeys. The baobab tree is a bombacaceous tree with a thick trunk, a native of Africa. It is mentioned quite prominently in Saint-Exupéry's *The Little Prince*.

Waverley Root, in his book *Food*, states that monkey bread is "so full of starch it can be converted into a meal." There is also a yeast bread filled with currants known as monkey bread.

Monkfish

More and more monkfish are being sold in American markets, particulary on the East Coast. It is by no means a new fish, however, having been prized in European cookery for many generations, particularly around the Mediterranean. In France, it is known as *lotte* or *lotte de mer* and *baudroie,* and is commonly used in bouillabaisse. The other names that it goes by in this country are angler fish, belly fish, and, rarely, goose fish and sea devil. It is an uncommonly ugly fish and until recently was invariably discarded as trash fish.

I use it often in fish soups; it has both a fine flavor and a more meaty texture than many fish. When using it in soups, you will find that it requires a slightly longer cooking time than most of the more common fish.

Moon Matzohs

Moon matzohs, which resemble other matzohs except they contain poppy seeds, derive their name from the German word for poppy, which is *Mohn*. So it's the seeds, not the shape of the matzohs, that are responsible for the name. Technically, I suppose, they should be called mohnsamen matzohs. *Mohnsamen* is the German word for poppy seeds.

Morcilla

Morcilla is the Spanish word for blood sausage, what the French call boudin noir, the Irish drisheen, and the English blood pudding. The morcillas of Spain come with a variety of seasonings, depending on the province where they are made. They all have a base of pork blood, which is combined with an assortment of spices, pork fat, and so on. The mixture is stuffed into sausage casings and cooked, which allows the blood to become firm. There is also a white sausage, or morcilla blanca, made with chopped chicken or with pork innards, plus seasonings. Morcillas are served broiled, grilled, in soups, stews, and so on.

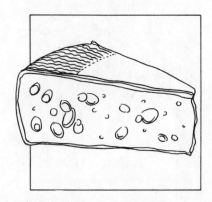

Mornay Sauce

A sauce Mornay is, of course, one of the finest and most basic of sauces in the French repertory. It is a simple béchamel or white sauce to which grated Gruyère and/or Parmesan cheese is added.

A book titled *Classical Recipes of the World and Master Culinary Guide,* written by Henry Smith, attributes the name to a French Protestant, Philippe de Mornay, "known as De Plessis Mornay, born 5th November, 1549." The author does not specify whether the sauce was created by Monsieur Mornay or simply named for him.

A French source, which I consider much more reliable than the Smith book, states that the sauce was created by a cook named Voiron and dedicated to a Monsieur Mornay, a chef of the last century. There is no reference to the origin of the name in *Larousse Gastronomique.*

Mother of Vinegar

Vinegar is the result of acetic fermentation of wine, according to *Larousse Gastronomique.* This fermentation is caused by a fungus known as *mycoderma aceti,* which, when added to wine, is apparent in the form of a thick, gelatin-like skin that occurs on the surface of the wine in a crock, cask, or whatever.

In French, this is known as *mère de vinaigre* and in English, mother of vinegar. The growth of the fungus and transformation of wine into vinegar is best cultivated at temperatures ranging from 59 to 86 degrees Fahrenheit.

The mother, incidentally, can, indeed must, be divided and discarded or transferred to another batch of wine as it expands, otherwise it will fill the crock or cask.

"A good vinegar," *Larousse* continues, "must be clear and transparent, colorless if it is made from white wine, pinkish if it comes from red wine, but always lighter colored than the latter, it must have a frankly acid taste, and an aroma recalling that of the wine from which it comes."

I received numerous letters assailing my erudition.

An associate professor of biology of the College of Saint Rose in Albany, New York, stated, "Your vinegar is, I hope, better than your microbiology: The acetic fermentation of wine is caused, not by a fungus, but rather by a bacterium, one of the genus acetobactes.

"This organism, which oxidizes the alcohol in wine to acetic acid, is ubiquitous and usually available 'free' to anyone who leaves a bottle of wine uncorked for several weeks. Best to cover it with cheesecloth to keep flies out. You may borrow some mother from a friend."

I have one more word about vinegar-making in the home. I cannot vouch for the technique used by a Brooklyn man, nor can I vouch for the quality of his product, but he writes as follows:

"I recently opened a bottle of champagne and found it flat. Rather than throw it away I mixed it with white vinegar in equal parts and added several sprigs of tarragon. The result after two weeks is so great it is worth buying an inexpensive champagne and letting it go flat."

I came across a mother of vinegar several years ago and quite by accident. It started as a film that developed in a bottle of ordinary commercial vinegar purchased in a supermarket. I transferred the batch to an enamel crock with a spigot and commenced adding wine. The mother prospered and I was shortly producing enough homemade vinegar for my own purposes and those of my friends.

And then one summer, during one of my extended absences from home, the mother was neglected and subjected to intense heat. It died.

Mouclade

A mouclade is one version of steamed mussels and it is a specialty of the region near Charente in France where Cognac is produced. Basically it is steamed mussels in a sauce, generally thickened with a little butter and flour (beurre manié) and enriched with egg yolks and heavy cream. There are numerous variations of this. Some recipes call for a little curry power, but most authorities on French cooking state that this is not a basic ingredient. The curry concept was probably an English innovation.

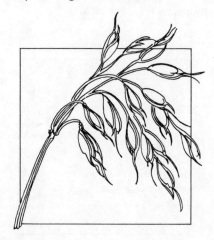

Muesli

Muesli is commonly found on the shelves of supermarkets and grocery stores and consists basically of raw rolled oats with dried fruits and nuts to which fresh fruits, milk, or cream may be added. I was told while still a student at the Swiss hotel school that the mixture was first conceived more than half a century ago by a Swiss doctor, Maximilian Oskar Bircher-Benner, a nutritionist who worked in health resorts. It is sometimes called birchermuesli on European menus.

I had never seen a detailed recipe until a letter arrived from a woman who outlined a recipe she had found in a German health-food cookbook by Lisbeth Ankenbrand, *Die Rohkostküche,* published in 1928.

"One tablespoon oat-flakes (rolled oats) is soaked for 12 hours in three tablespoons of water. In the morning, mix in one tablespoon sweetened condensed milk. Cream or fresh milk can be used instead; in that case, omit the water. Refrigerate.

"A large apple is cleaned and grated. Use the whole apple, skin, pits and core. As you grate the apple, mix it into the oats to keep the muesli nice and white.

"Add the juice of half a lemon and sprinkle with a tablespoon of grated nuts such as hazelnuts or walnuts.

"This portion is for one person. It is important not to use too much oatflakes, as otherwise a thick, solid mush results. There must always be ten to fifteen times as much fruit as flakes."

Muffineer

See Caster.

Mulberries

Although I grew up in the South and there were many mulberry trees in the front and

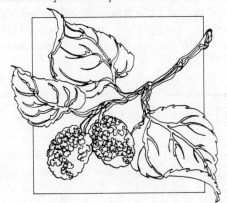

back yards, I never heard of recipes in which the berries were cooked. I ate them raw.

Theodora FitzGibbon, in *The Food of the Western World,* notes that the red mulberry is a native of the United States. "Its long, red berries are delicious in pies and tarts," she writes. "They also make an excellent jelly, a liqueur, and mulberry gin, which is far better than sloe gin."

Mulliatelle

Mulliatelle is a Neapolitan sausage made with the innards of a calf, including the brains, heart, and lungs. It is highly spiced with red peppers and is stuffed into animal casings. It is generally roasted over coals and served on buns.

Mulligatawny Soup

There are probably as many versions of mulligatawny soup scattered throughout the world as there are recipes for chile con carne in America. It is always curried and almost invariably contains a meat broth. Some versions include rice. The name, incidentally, derives from the Tamil, a people who inhabit southern India and Ceylon. There are two words involved, put together as *milagutannir* meaning pepper and water. The implication is that the soup should be quite spicy.

Madhur Jaffrey, in *An Invitation to Indian Cooking,* states that to judge from the Tamil origin of the soup's name, "one might deduce that it originated in the Madras region ... 100 to 300 years ago under the benevolent gaze of British patronage. British in concept but Indian in its ingredients, this hearty soup became very popular with the Anglo-Indians scattered all across India, and there are probably as many recipes for it as there are Anglo-Indian families.''

Muscovy Duck

There are some foods that are not readily available in supermarkets and grocery stores throughout the country, though they have enormous appeal in areas where they can be found. This is increasingly true of something called Muscovy duck.

These ducks arrive at markets in late fall and are available throughout the winter, frequently at local poultry farms. Unlike most domestically raised birds, they should not be cooked until they are well done. They should be cooked to a rare or medium-rare state. Otherwise, the meat tends to become dry.

The choicest part of the Muscovy duck, which has a gamier flavor than regular duckling, is the breast. When the duck is done, transfer it to a carving board and neatly carve away half of its breast. Place the breast half skin side up on the board and cut it slightly on the bias, as for London broil. The thighs may be carved off the bone into thin slices, because the meat of the thighs and legs tends to be just a trifle tough.

A mystery of sorts exists over the origin of the duck's name. According to Dr. Harold E. Nadler, director of the division of animal industry at the New York State Department of Agriculture and Markets, "Originally the duck was known simply as a musk duck, for no reason apparent to me. Somehow, someone apparently presumed musk to be short for Muscovy and started calling it that in error." It has nothing to do, he said, with Moscow. More than by the name, Dr. Nadler is fascinated by the fact that the Muscovy is one of the few ducks that can perch in trees.

Mushroom

A mushroom is a gadget made of wood or metal that looks almost precisely like a perfectly formed mushroom with a very long stem. Its "cap" is smooth and fairly broad. In the old days (before the food processor) you would grind your fish for a fish mousse, put it on a flat sieve, and rub it through the sieve by working the rounded top of the mushroom back and forth. A tedious affair at best.

Mushrooms

Brillat Savarin's notion, included in his *Physiologie du Gout,* that "the discovery of a new dish does more for the happiness of man than the discovery of a star," has given many a gastronome something to ponder over these last hundred years or so. I have a little list, in fact, of things in the world of food that have had far more impact on me than discoveries of stars.

Example: The person who discovered that egg yolks beaten with oil or butter would homogenize and thicken to produce a mayonnaise or hollandaise sauce.

Example: The Frenchman who attempted the impossible, only to discover that with a little ingenuity a miracle of mycology could be performed—the ability to reproduce in a cultivated state the gastronomical blessing called mushroom.

Since the beginning of time, it has been presumed that mushrooms could not be reproduced. The ancients believed that mushrooms were created by thunderbolts, possibly because they flourished after rain. To this day, no one has succeeded in reproducing those wild marvels of the forest, girolles, cèpes, and morels.

The little Pennsylvania community of Kennett Square, together with its environs for fifteen miles around, is known as the mushroom capital of the United States. I went there to explore mushroom consumption and the techniques of modern mushroom growing with Charles Ciarrocchi, president of the American Mushroom Institute. I joined him at lunch at the family-owned Brown Derby Restaurant in the nearby village of Toughkenamon.

Mr. Ciarrocchi is a vice president of Modern Mushroom Farms Inc. With him was the president of the concern, Vincent Leo.

Over an appetizer of piping hot, deep-fried, breaded mushrooms with cocktail sauce, I observed that many of the leaders in the mushroom field happened to be Italian, with such names as Santucci, Pia, Bertrando, Leo, and Ciarrocchi, and I asked why.

"When our fathers and grandfathers came here, most of the labor was Italian," Mr. Ciarrocchi replied. "They were used to hard work in the old country, and producing mushrooms in those days was hard work. Also, in those days a dollar was hard to come by, and once here, they were trapped. When my father came here in 1913, the cost of steerage class on the Naples-New York run was $42. A lot of money!"

Eventually, these immigrants became managers and owners.

"The strides that have been made in the mushroom industry within the past two decades are staggering," Mr. Ciarrocchi went on. "Twenty years ago, for example, my father worked on what is known as the green-thumb method. To grow mushrooms, he relied almost wholly on sight, smell, and feel. Today, of course, we are thoroughly mechanized and air-conditioned, although a lot of the work still has to be done by hand.

"Until air-conditioning came along, the

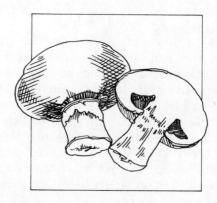

mushroom industry was seasonal. Everything depended on nature, and you could only harvest mushrooms from November to about May."

Acceptance of mushrooms, he said, has worked in a sort of zigzag fashion: "Ten years ago supermarkets, grocery stores, and so on, were reluctant to handle mushrooms in the summer months. It was not that mushrooms were not available in abundance; you simply couldn't buy them in warm weather because they were living by old, established patterns.

A short while ago, Mr. Ciarrocchi said, "the demand for fresh mushrooms fell off dramatically the day after the year-end holidays. Today we ship like crazy 365 days a year."

The reasons for the acceptance and rapid growth of the industry are obvious, the gentlemen agreed. The public is infinitely more sophisticated about food than at any time in history, and mushrooms, as Mr. Ciarrocchi likes to put it, "add a touch of class to everything." I'm inclined to agree.

After lunch, which included mushroom soup—I'm told that most of the restaurants in the area have mushroom dishes on the menu, "otherwise we wouldn't patronize them"—I was escorted on a tour of the Modern Mushroom plant, which is impressively large.

A farm is generally an open-air place with sun, rain, and seasonal changes, but the mushroom-producing plants here are all indoors and are referred to as "farms." And, although the seeds from which the mushrooms are started are natural reproductions, the processors from whom they are bought are known as "seed manufacturers."

Mushrooms are grown in almost total darkness, and it requires five to six weeks from the moment a seed or spore is embedded in compost until it is time to harvest. At Modern Mushroom Farms, mushrooms are grown in sterilized wooden trays eight feet long and four feet wide. The trays are stacked five deep, with a foot or so for space between each.

"Mushrooms," Mr. Ciarrocchi told me, "are without question the purest vegetable on earth."

I asked if the compost was really horse manure, and he said: "Of course. We buy ours at a racing stable. But the manure is sterilized and pasteurized. It is aerated at such a temperature as to kill any form of impurity, anything that could possibly biologically affect the mushroom's growth."

Compared with a stable or a circus, the compost here smells like a somewhat musty eau de cologne. Sterilized, pasteurized peat moss also plays an important role in the compost. Interestingly enough, after the mushroom harvest the peat moss is sold to another concern to be recycled into potting soil for home use.

Modern mushroom-growing is the result of vast amounts of research and involves a great deal of technology. In brief, it involves inpregnating the compost with seeds that develop slowly for two weeks, after which a topsoil is added. Three weeks later, the first mushroom crop is ready for harvesting. A crop is called a "flush." There are five "flushes" to a "season" before the contents of the tray are ready to be discarded or at least sent to the potting soil house for recycling.

Before the harvest, the seedlings are subjected to several mechanically controlled changes of climate through added moisture, warmth, fresh air, and so on. Normal production at the Modern plant is twenty thousand pounds a day.

The mushrooms cannot be harvested mechanically; scores of workers harvest them by hand. Since the growing rooms are dark, the average worker wears a hard hat, banded by an electrically powered miner's lamp. The mushrooms are cut individually by hand, using an expensive, stainless-steel knife that resembles a paring knife.

Mr. Ciarrocchi told me that producers prefer to sell only the natural, freshly harvested mushrooms, such as are found in baskets in grocery stores and supermarkets. These are unwashed but hygienically clean. Sometimes, however, they have traces of mushroom-growing "soil" around the caps and stems. Some people object to this and demand a snow-white product. To achieve this, it is necessry to wash the mushrooms after they are harvested. Mr. Ciarrocchi calls this a "realistic consumer dictate." Once mushrooms are washed, it is necessary to add a Government-approved preservative, such as sodium bisulfate, or the mushrooms quickly turn dark brown. Generally speaking, mushrooms that are packaged, pre-rinsed, in plastic have been treated. Mushrooms sold loose, usually in wooden baskets, have not been treated.

Mushrooms should be refrigerated after purchase to prevent their turning dark. There is no way to state definitely how long they will keep after purchase. If they are in excellent, newly harvested condition, they should keep in the refrigerator, in peak condition, for one and perhaps two days. They will still be good for cooking after five days and even up to a week. The flavor remains even if they are off color.

Although the soil or other material in which mushrooms are cultivated is pure, it is best to rinse the mushrooms in cold water and drain them well before cooking. This will remove the foreign particles that cling to them and will help keep them white. I do not peel mushrooms unless they are old and have an unpleasant color.

Mussels

To a nonathletic type whose sporting blood courses somewhat slowly through his veins, it was a highly unlikely feat on a highly unlikely day. The temperature hovered in the twenties, the sky was overcast and gray, and even the Canadian honkers floating on Plymouth Bay looked desolate and cold. I snuggled more deeply into a quilted ski jacket, wiggled my toes in a pair of borrowed oversize rubber boots, and tried to coordinate fingers to pad as C. Graham Hurlburt maneuvered his Land-Rover bayside, backing his sixteen-foot fiberglass skiff toward the partly frozen bay.

"First time this bay's frozen over in years," he said, which did little to buoy my spirits or warm the air. "But look out yonder." Out yonder, I observed as I descended from the automobile and sank to my ankles

in mud, were vast patches of black, rather large inky islands surrounded by water and ice.

"Everything black there is mussels, millions of them, and that's for lunch." That was a warming thought.

Mr. Hurlburt, who was director of adminstrative services at Harvard University, is convinced that given rope enough and time—and unpolluted water—America or any nation can do much to alleviate world hunger through commercial cultivation of the common, edible blue mussel, the kind that appears on French menus as *moules marinière, moules poulette, moules frites,* and as the basis for Billi Bi, the most delectable of soups.

"Most Americans don't eat mussels," Mr. Hurlburt said. "Only the tiniest percentage of the population knows anything about them. The people who really covet them in this country are Europeans of a first or second generation, people who have traveled a great deal in Europe, or people who frequent European restaurants."

Mr. Hurlburt stated that he had eaten mussels all his life, that he has an adventurous appetite, and practically nothing that wiggles or squirms in Duxbury or Plymouth Bay was beyond his eating.

His intense and highly serious interest in mussel culture came about by good fortune.

"My vice president called me in and asked how I'd like a year's leave to pursue any line of work that interested me, much the same as professors on a sabbatical.

"Living around here all my life, I'd always been fascinated with mussels, how good they taste and how easily they proliferate. I also knew that mussels were grown commercially in Spain, France, and the Netherlands, among other places in Europe, so I decided to take my family, my wife and three of the four children, to investigate the mussel 'farms.' "

In Spain, he noted, they grow one thousand times more pounds of mussel "meat" per acre than we can grow beef in this country. It is possible under the best of circumstances to grow up to 300,000 pounds of mussel meat per acre.

"The astonishing thing to me," he said, "is the nutritional value of the common blue mussel in relation to choice T-bone steaks." He has published a comparison of the two that appears in a Department of Agriculture handbook and it is indeed astonishing. The comparison of three-and-a-half ounces of steak to a comparable amount of mussels found the protein content practically the same. Steak has more than four times more calories than mussels. Beef, the study found, has more than eighteen times more fat than mussels, and mussels have 3.3 grams of carbohydrates. Beef has none. A Department of Agriculture researcher put the cholesterol content of mussels slightly below that of beef.

"The cultivation of mussels is relatively simple. In a natural state, mussels attach themselves to and grow on rocks, on seaweed and themselves. They secrete a liquid that becomes a thread with a 'foot' on the end of it. They attach themselves on any thin solid. Simply put, you can cultivate mussels by using floats with ropes—thousands of them—that hang in the water. The mussels cling to the ropes and a single acre of water can accommodate three to five rafts." In this manner, the gentleman maintains, "in excess of a quarter million pounds of pure meat can be produced annually."

Seafood in this country is diminishing rapidly. "Oysters, clams, scallops, lobsters, they're all becoming scarce. Fishing, if you'll pardon the expression, stinks and most of the fish consumed in America is imported. If mussel cultivation really succeeded here, it would not only be good for mass consumption but would also help unemployment."

Perhaps his dedication to such ideals is inherited. His thirteenth great-grandfather was Elder William Brewster, the preacher on the Mayflower. His family has lived in Duxbury and the environs of Plymouth Bay ever since.

His experiments have caused a good deal of interest in this country and in Canada. Mr. Hurlburt's enthusiasm extends to the kitchen, where his wife, Sarah, spends many hours each year turning out excellent dishes with mussels as a base, things like steamed mussels, marinated mussels with sour cream, mussel stews and chowders, chafing dish mussels with white wine, casseroles, and so on.

Mussels are easy to cook, but they first must be thoroughly cleaned. To do this, put them in a basin of cold water and rub their shells together to eliminate sand and other particles that may cling to the mussels.

You may want to scrub them with steel wool if there is any kind of deposit that clings to the shells. With your fingers, pull off the "whiskers," the sea strands that extend from their hinged shells.

If there is any chance that the mussels contain silt, twist the shells in opposite directions. Those that contain silt will readily open; discard these. *See also* Mouclade.

Must

Must is grape juice that is destined to become wine; it is sometimes referred to simply as new wine. Some authorities maintain that it refers to grape juice, freshly pressed or otherwise, others that it must have been exposed to a degree of fermentation if it is to be must.

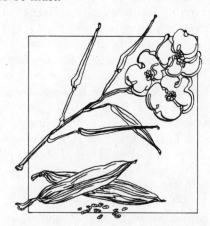

Mustard

Everyone knows that black pepper is the most widely used spice in the United States today. But if you were to hazard a guess as to the second ranking spice, the chances are that you'd be wrong.

It isn't oregano, used with abandon on pizza pies coast to coast. It isn't the bay leaves or thyme that are tossed into a few hundred thousand soups and stews each day of the year. It is mustard, which is to hot dogs and salad dressing what ice cream is to a cone and a pickle is to pastrami.

There are numerous theories as to the origin of the name mustard. The most likely is that the word derives from *mout,* the French word for must, a word much used by wine makers. *Mout,* or must, is the grape juice used as the basis for making wine. It is known as must from the time of its pressing until it ferments and can properly be called wine; the original liquid used in making a paste of mustard seeds to produce the *moutarde* of France was the freshly pressed juice.

Through the centuries, there have been a surprising lot of literary references to mustard, beginning with the Bible: "If ye have faith as a grain of mustard seed, ye shall say unto this mountain, Remove hence, to yonder place; and it shall remove;" and "The kingdom of heaven is like to a grain of mustard seed."

Shakespeare made frequent reference to mustard. In *Henry V, Part II,* Falstaff says, "He's a good wit! hand him, baboon! His wit's as thick as Tewksbury mustard." And, in *The Taming of the Shrew,* "What say you to a piece of beef and mustard?"

The association of roast beef and mustard is recurrent. Anatole France, in *La Révolte des Anges,* noted, "A tale without love is like beef without mustard; an insipid dish."

Boswell, in his *Life of Johnson,* 1791, recorded that "Johnson's conversation was by much too strong for a person accustomed to obsequiousness and flattery; it was mustard in a young child's mouth."

One of the most interesting and curious terms in the American language is "to cut the mustard." It means to accomplish something in an expert manner; to score, to gain respect. In early America, "the proper mustard" meant something genuine and not watered down.

Mustard has been used since antiquity as a healing device for everything from headaches and the common cold to a bad case of the vapors and spider attacks. History has it that as far back as five hundred years before Christ it was considered a proper antidote for the scorpion's bite.

Over the years it has been said to be good for ailments involving the "shoulders, chest, hips, and loins" and mustard oil was recommended for the likes of "rigid sinews and numbness in the loins." As anyone who was a child not too many decades ago must know, mustard plasters applied to the chest would cure coughs and colds overnight (and, one might add, leave you hairless and skinless, once they were removed).

It is purely subjective, but I have my own theories that mustards vary from region to region and that each mustard has a special affinity for certain foods that, in general, are also regional.

Such French mustard as that of Dijon or Meaux, bearing such names as Grey Poupon, Maille, Pikarome, Pommery, and so on, go especially well with such foods à la française as roast leg of lamb, French charcuterie, such as saucisson à l'ail, or garlic sausages, French style, andouillettes (chitterling sausages), boudin noir (blood sausages), and so on.

And it is present in mayonnaise sauces of French origin (most are); half the world's mustards are produced in Dijon.

German mustards such as Düsseldorf are highly compatible with smoked German pork products. Creole mustard, notably Zatarain's brand, made in New Orleans, has no peer as an ingredient for rémoulade sauce (it bears little resemblance to the classic French version) used on shrimp, and for which the Crescent City is named.

The bright yellow mustard, whose color is due to the addition of turmeric, is made in America and most often found in ballparks. It has no challengers when it comes to something to smear on hot dogs. But other than that, it is as unsophisticated and lacking in style as toasted marshmallows.

Mustard plays an important role in Indian cookery, principally in the form of black mustard seeds and in mustard oil. Mustard oil, incidentally, makes a fine dressing for freshly cooked, hot, drained string beans.

In England, one of the most famous personages in mustard lore is a Mrs. Clement of Durham (some say Lancashire). Although mustard paste had been used for many years, this eighteenth-century woman produced a mustard made with a finer powder and a brighter appearance. Starting in 1730, she started to peddle her wares, traveling on a pack horse from house to house. As she became more famous for her "Durham mustard," she accumulated a small fortune. George I is said to have been one of her patrons.

A hundred years later, according to Tom Stobart in his *Herbs, Spices and Flavorings,* at the beginning of the nineteenth century, "a young miller from Norwich, Jeremiah Colman, began to take an interest in mustard and by the middle of the century he had set up a factory." Today, the name Colman is virtually synonymous with English mustard.

The Chinese and the English have a preference for freshly made hot mustard, and it is as ideal as a side condiment for Chinese food as it is for rare roast beef. That mustard can also be used quite respectably in most French recipes that call for mustard. It is, in any case, next choice after Dijon or Düsseldorf. It is simplicity itself to prepare at home.

Blend ⅓ cup powdered mustard, preferably Colman brand, with 2 tablespoons cold water, white wine, milk, or beer, and add a touch of salt. The mustard should stand at least 15 minutes to develop flavor before you use it.

Mustard Fruit

To my mind, the most lucid description of mustard fruit, or *mostarda di frutta,* appears in Elizabeth David's *Italian Food.*

"Perhaps," she writes, "the most remarkable of Italian preserves is the fruit mustard, mostarda di frutta of Cremona. Made of whole fruits, pears, cherries, little oranges, figs, plums, apricots, and slices of melon and pumpkin, preserved in sugar syrup and flavored with mustard oil and garlic, this confection has an absolutely original flavor."

"It is eaten as an accompaniment to cold boiled meat and ham," the writer continues, "and goes marvelously also with tongue, with cold roast pork, and even chicken, turkey, and pheasant."

Mutton

The kindest definition of mutton is, in dictionary terms, the flesh of grown sheep. Proper mutton has an unmistakably perfumed flavor. It is not for all palates, but neither are caviar and snails. Those who dote on it, and I do without apology, have at times what amounts to an actual craving.

A tender, well-grilled mutton chop is among my favorite foods. The fact is that almost all parts of the mutton may be eaten and that includes not only the tenderest parts, including the ribs and loin, but the breast and the shanks. Mutton is used to great advantage in the kitchens of the Middle East. It makes a particularly good and spicy sausage. The problem is that mutton is especially hard to come by in America.

Nam Pla

See Garum.

Napkins

It is one man's opinion that logic at table is the essence and criterion of good manners and, therefore, good taste. Although many people tend to frown on a napkin tucked under the chin, I frequently resort to this in one specific—in Chinese restaurants and in my own home when I dine on a food with a great deal of sauce and when that food is difficult to negotiate into the mouth with chopsticks. I would, of course, tuck a napkin under my chin in only the most casual of circumstances.

I have a thoroughgoing dislike of those bibs provided in certain seafood houses for the service of lobsters. I find them childish.

Natchitoches

See Turnovers.

Navarin

See Blanquette.

Neat's Foot Jelly

"Neat" is a name, once fairly common in England, for an ox. Thus, neat's foot jelly is a jelly or gelatin made from the feet and shinbones of an ox. More often than not, today, one speaks of a calf's foot jelly. A fine gelatin for clear aspics is derived from cooking a calf's or veal's foot with water and seasonings before straining and clarifying.

One also speaks of neat's foot oil, also derived from the ox feet and shinbones. At times, especially in England, one hears of neat's tongue, which is the tongue of an ox.

Negus

Spiced negus is mentioned in both *Dombey and Son* and *Our Mutual Friend,* which led me to a copy of a work titled *The Charles Dickens Cookbook* by Brenda Marshall, in which a recipe for the beverage is offered.

It calls for 1 bottle of port or sherry wine, a wineglass of brandy, 1 lemon, 4 cups of water, about ½ cup of sugar and nutmeg. Warm the combined port and brandy. Slice the lemon into a jug and add sugar and nutmeg. Pour in the warmed wine and add the water when it is boiling. You may decrease the volume of water.

Nesselrode

Since I am inordinately fond of desserts that bear the name Nesselrode, I am happy to pay homage to that little-remembered diplomat and statesman. His full name was Count Karl Robert Nesselrode, and he was a chancellor of the Russian Empire who had quite a hand in international affairs involving Russia and the rest of Europe during the reign of Napoleon. He died in St. Petersburg in 1862.

Thanks to his chef, you will find the name Nesselrode on menus around the world and primarily in association with sweets — custards, puddings, sauces, and the like — containing candied fruits and chestnuts in

syrup and sometimes flavored with a spirit such as rum.

Although the name is also associated with a game consommé, a sturgeon soup, and a cold thrush dish, it is the desserts to which I am partial.

Newberg

Gastronomic lore has it that a gentleman named Ben Wenberg frequented the old Delmonico Restaurant in Manhattan in its heyday and was much respected by the management.

It is said that he created a dish made with seafood and cream and egg yolks, and the dish was called seafood Wenberg on the menu.

Some time later he became involved in an imbroglio with the management, and the dish was thereafter listed as seafood Newberg. There has always been some question as to whether the man's name was spelled Wenburg or Wenberg.

A gentleman, now retired to Lancaster, Pennsylvania, sent me an informative letter on the subject.

"I think," he wrote, "we can assume that Mr. Wenberg was real, and an habitué of Delmonico's, from [an entry in] the book *Delmonico's, A Century of Splendor,* by Lately Thomas; his name here is spelled Wenberg. In the massive book of Delmonico recipes by that restaurant's chef, Charles Ranhofer, *The Epicurean* (late 1890s), a few old menus are given from March 1883, November 1888, and November 1893, whereon terrapin à la Newberg (note spelling) is cited, but nothing with lobster."

My informant, an insatiable seeker after

facts, also informed me that notice of Benjamin Wenberg's death appeared in *The New York Times* of June 15, 1885.

"Louis C. Wenberg, who for two years has boarded at No. 101 Park-place, Brooklyn, died there of consumption last Thursday afternoon, at the age of 39. Benjamin J., his brother, and his senior by 11 years, died at the Hotel Belvidere, in this city, Saturday afternoon after a brief illness. The two brothers were born in Portland, Me., and were the sons of a well-to-do shipmaster. They came to this city when young men, and were for a number of years in business at No. 101 Water-street as shipping merchants. Then they lived in Fifth-avenue, and were prominent club and society men.

"Two years ago Louis withdrew from the firm and his brother carried on the business alone. A year later Louis caught a severe cold, which ripened into consumption.

"When it became known that he would die his landlady, supposing he would like to see a clergyman, asked him what denomination he would prefer.

" 'I don't know,' he said. 'I've never been a religious man. I'll wait and see what Ben professes and I'll profess the same.'

" 'Ben' was sent for, but was ill with pneumonia and could not come. A day or two before Louis died he said to his landlady, 'Ben and I will die about the same time.' Ben was not told of his brother's death and died in ignorance of it. Louis's funeral was to have been held Saturday, but was postponed until today, that the two brothers might be buried together. The body of the elder brother was taken to No. 101 Park-place, Brooklyn, yesterday, and funeral services will be held there this afternoon.

"The interment will be at Greenwood.

Neither of the brothers ever married. Both had a great many friends and both were well-known and prosperous business men."

One final note: The dish in question is spelled "Newberg" throughout the Delmonico work. There is a misprint, however, in the indexing. The terrapin dish that bears that name is spelled Newburg.

Nigella

Nigella, similar to caraway seed, is also referred to as charnuska or black caraway seed. It is small, sharp-edged, and black and is often found on Jewish rye bread and pumpernickel.

Nignon

I can quote chapter and verse about the works and world of Georges Auguste Escoffier, the man who is to the Gallic table what Hoyle is to games. But somehow, in the course of labors in the world of food, I had never heard of Edouard Nignon, another of the titans of French cooking.

I learned of him when Pierre Laverne, the distinguished chef of La Côte Basque in Manhattan, came to wield his knives in my kitchen.

Edouard Nignon did, indeed, have a distinguished career. He worked in many of the most celebrated kitchens of Paris, at the Claridge in London, the Hermitage in Moscow. Toward the end of the First World War, he even served as chef to President Wilson.

Nignon wrote three books, printed apparently in limited editions of two thousand each. They were the *Heptameron des Gourmets, Eloges de la Cuisine Française,* and *Plaisirs de la Table.*

Chef Laverne had in his possession the last two—splendid, serious, dedicated volumes, with hundreds of recipes written with almost poetic precision. They are written with remarkable clarity and with the unmistakable enthusiasm of a man in love with his subject.

Nopales

Nopales or nopalitos, as they are called in Mexico, are the oval or paddle-shaped leaves of the prickly pear cactus. Preparation consists of removing the thorns from the flesh, then cutting the flesh into one-half-inch strips. Cook them in boiling water until tender.

One use is in a cold salad made, say, with tomatoes and onions and dressed with oil and vinegar and a touch of oregano. This salad is sometimes served with pickled jalapeño peppers and cream cheese.

Normande

The Normandy region of France is an area where many of the finest treasures of the French kitchen appear in abundance. Normandy is celebrated for its cream and butter, fish and shellfish, and orchards. Apples are as characteristically Normand as are their by-products, cider and Calvados. Dishes labeled normande generally contain a combination of several of these foods or liquids.

Nouvelle Cuisine

I feel strongly obliged to take issue with any and all of my colleagues—and they are legion—who tend to disparage, damn, and belittle the whole notion of nouvelle cuisine. There are those who moan in their victuals and say it is the worst thing to have happened to the entire culture of good cooking since the invention of the can opener.

Nonsense!

Nouvelle cuisine is the greatest innovation in the world of food since the food processor and, like that machine, it has opened up and broadened horizons in the world of cooking that slightly more than a decade ago were unthinkable. I simply do not understand the naïveté of those supposed professionals who maintain that "traditional" cuisine remains the true and unalterable genius of French (and, therefore, the supreme) cooking.

Let us go back to the origins of traditional French cooking and the beginnings of the nouvelle cuisine revolution in as simple and basic a way as possible.

For more than fifty years, traditional French cooking was pantry-locked, book-bound, and straitjacketed, and all in the name of one man, Auguste Escoffier. Classic, or traditional, French cooking was, thanks to him, a prison whether the kitchen existed in Burgundy, Provence, Paris, or in the so-called French kitchens of Manhattan, Fort Wayne, Indiana, or Singapore. The rules had been codified and set down by that one individual, the priest of grand cuisine. Every well-known chef in the Western world and some few in the East were Escoffier's absolute apostles.

I am not a chef (I classify myself as a cook), but I was trained in the mid-1950s in Switzerland in what was still the heyday of Escoffier's influence. (The great chef had died in 1935.) I was trained at a time when "according to Escoffier" was the not-to-be-questioned "holy writ." To go against his dictates was to face the opprobrium and contempt of your fellow cooks or chefs.

If Escoffier said that *pommes de terre Anna* were created in this or that fashion, then you didn't vary that formula. If this formula for *salade russe* did not include fresh basil, you didn't dare demonstrate an adventurous and inspired genius by adding a leaf or two. If you worked in a professional kitchen, each day you made and used a gallon of hollandaise sauce and tossed it into everything. Each morning you turned bins of potatoes into something called *pommes de terre duchesse*—that is, you made a potato-croquette mixture and piped it out with a "piping bag and star tube" and baked it as a garnish. Or you piped it around broiled meats and browned it.

A relatively large number of foods were cooked *à la minute,* but painstaking hours were consumed in the preparation of other dishes such as a chartreuse of partridge or pheasant in which a host of vegetables were intricately carved and put together in the most elaborate fashion possible to contain your game filling.

On a far less exalted plane, consider the preparation of vegetables, Escoffier style. Such simple things as brussels sprouts or cauliflower were cooked (generally over-cooked) in boiling water until tender. They were then drained and given further cooking in an unconscionable quantity of butter.

I have nothing against an occasional platter (once a winter, perhaps) of a traditional cassoulet with all that pork rind, preserved goose, pork belly, and sausages; nor of a "traditional" sauerkraut with its goose fat, streaky bacon, ham, and sausages.

But these concepts are a far cry from nouvelle cuisine and do not fit in with present concepts of dining in extraordinary style with far lighter, more delicate creations — fresh salmon in sorrel sauce, duck livers with celery root, a simple dish of sole with chives, striped bass wrapped in green lettuce leaves, and a simple grilled lemon chicken, creations of the likes of Paul Bocuse, the Troisgros brothers, Roger Vergé, Alain Chapel, and so on.

I would not exchange my education, which included the entire scope of Escoffier, for all the truffles in Périgord. It is my reasoning that to understand the new cuisine properly, you should know what Escoffier was all about. And in depth. Many of the foundations laid down by him remain rock solid and are essential to the finest nouvelle cuisine — the basic sauces, such as fonds bruns, or light brown sauces; the fumets or basic stocks, and glaces de viande, or meat glazes, or fish or shellfish mousses (that were scarcely possible for home cooks until the introduction of the food processor), and so on.

What nouvelle cuisine has done is to liberate all of us from a monstrous thou-shalt-not way of thinking. If you wish to juxtapose anchovy fillets with your roast goose and orange sauce (I am *not* proposing that seriously), then go ahead and let your guests be the judge. If you wish to add pistachios to your oysters cooked in vinegar (I am not proposing *that* either), that is certainly your prerogative and you are at least master of your own stove.

With the advent of nouvelle cuisine, chefs were allowed to be innovative to the limits of their imagination. I am persuaded that without it, the Western world at large might never have known the likes of those magnificent oils and mustards and vinegars that have now become commonplace in fine food shops around the world.

I do not think we would use so abundantly and prize such things as fresh arugula, raddichio, fresh basil, and fresh coriander leaves. We have learned to adapt our Western kitchens to the good things found in the Orient. We have learned to appreciate fine green salads topped with well-cooked warm meats, such as roast duck and sautéed goose livers, and I am persuaded these are borrowings from Thailand or other points east. We have learned to not overcook fish and vegetables, and I am convinced this is a Japanese influence. French chefs have learned to travel and broaden their scopes and horizons.

The faults of nouvelle cuisine are, of course, many and obvious. But to my mind, the positive aspects far outweigh the negative ones. I have heard of truffles served with a lime ice; of grapes and other fruit served with sauerkraut in a red-wine sauce; ravioli stuffed with snails and peaches. I have even printed a recipe for lobster in a savory sauce flavored with vanilla. (Curiously enough, the flavors are quite harmonious.) And critics, of course, write ad nauseam — not wholly without justification — of the excessive use of kiwi fruit in any and all dishes, main courses included. One also hears that there is too much fiddling with various foods for the sake of artistic arrangement, and that these portions are costly and small.

I could offer you an equal number of attacks on the faults of traditional French cooking. The most primitive and obvious being it was designed for an age in which the "average" man or woman with an adequate purse could dine on ten or more courses during an evening without consideration of the liver or stomach.

In the old days, there was an abhorrent repetition of garnish for various dishes, the fanciest of which was, by far, crescents of puff pastry. Those crescents adorned — world without end — fish, poultry, beef, and so on. They are not at all a bad garnish, except they add unnecessary calories to a meal. And, in their own way, they are, or were, like today's overuse of kiwi fruit.

Mention should be made of the differences in style, preparation, and presentation of dishes today and yesterday. In the old days, say ten to fifteen years ago, whole pieces of food, such as a leg of lamb, a roast chicken, and so on were dispatched to the dining room, where they were carved and arranged on the plate by the waiter or captain. The chefs would scream at the manner in which the food was presented, often complaining that by the time the waiter or captain got the dish in front of the customer, it was cooled and inedible.

Today, most foods, even in luxury restaurants, are sliced and arranged on plates in the kitchens. And what do certain critics complain of? The food is cooled and inedible by the time it is presented at the table.

One of the reasons for the popularity of nouvelle cuisine is that we live in a far less formal and circumscribed age, and the whole style of cooking is based on that concept. We are far more health- and weight-conscious, and our bodies demand a lighter style of cooking. We eat less salt and our intake of fat has decreased.

Nouvelle cuisine most certainly does not ignore butter and cream. But at least the butter sauce is more apt to be a beurre blanc, which is far more delicate than that egg-enriched hollandaise, and the sauce made with cream seems to be used far more sparingly.

And what do I think about the future of cooking in the Western world? It will be increasingly innovative, endless in its possibilities, and productive of great recipes. We have escaped, praise be, from those repetitive banquet dishes like tournedos Rossini and pheasant souvarov. With any kind of luck, I will never again be served a *salade russe* with my poached salmon. Come to think of it, no one has offered me a dish of *salade russe* or *pommes de terre duchesse* in any form in several years.

That's progress.

Nova

See Smoked salmon.

Nuoc Mam

See Garum.

Nursery Desserts

It was about fifteen years ago that I first read an unforgettable essay on the psychology of dining. It appeared in a magazine called *MD,* a publication whose audience is made up mostly of doctors.

The article was titled "Prandial Psychology" and it remains vivid in my mind today. It contained a wealth of trenchant observations, many of them stemming from the thought that "many psychologic aspects of eating are not amendable to reason, probably because they were laid down in the prerational childhood years. . . ."

I am firmly convinced that my craving, my absolute predilection for one certain category of dessert stems directly from the cradle and the years that immediately followed. First in a high chair, then sitting on a stack of *Encyclopedia Britannica* (the telephone book in the town of my childhood was only a quarter-inch thick) to get the mouth and arms in an eating position.

I am not basically a dessert man. At least not in the passionate way of certain friends and acquaintances. I find most European pastries toothsome enough — a well-made *roulade au chocolat;* variations on a génoise; even baked Alaska. But these I can resist. *Crêpes suzette* have a certain appeal, but they do not interrupt my sleep with sweet anticipation.

No, it isn't these confections that make me salivate, that arouse the hound of hunger at the conclusion of a meal. The dessert category that I find totally irresistible is purely and simply nursery desserts, those custards and mousses and glorious, sensual puddings and sauces based on eggs and cream.

When I dine on such ambrosial fare, or even as I regard them, I am reminded of a childhood incident once related to me years and years ago by a neighbor and friend.

This, too, had to do with nursery foods (broadly speaking, nursery foods include things that can be eaten with a fork and/or spoon and for which a knife is not essential; noodles and any kind of spaghetti or pasta dish, creamed vegetables, cream soup).

Anyway, this neighbor told me that in her high-chair days her particular insatiable weakness was mashed potatoes. She simply couldn't get enough, and once on a birthday her mother decided to get her all the mashed potatoes she could possibly desire.

My friend advised me that after the dozenth or so large spoonful had passed her lips and one more bite was obviously unthinkable, she took both her hands, dipped them into the bowl of potatoes, and massaged the remainder of the potatoes into the curls on top of her head.

Nutmeg

I received a letter from a man who said that he had lived in Connecticut for many years and had never seen a nutmeg forest. "Why is it called the Nutmeg State?" he logically asked.

The *Oxford English Dictionary* notes that the name was given to the state on the theory that "wooden nutmegs are there manufactured for exportation."

Another source, a librarian, said that buyers were naïve to speak of "wooden" nutmegs. She stated that nutmegs — the genuine article — were imported to Connecticut from the West Indies and sold by Yankee peddlers along with other wares. "The buyer, perhaps, thought they had to be cracked like a walnut and were not aware that they had to be grated," she added.

Another source, *American Nicknames,* says the name was used "because the early inhabitants had the reputation of being so ingenious and shrewd that they were able to make and sell wooden nutmegs."

Nutmeg Melon

Nutmeg melon is, I am told, another term for a garden variety cantaloupe. In her book *Fresh Food,* Sylvia Rosenthal notes that the cantaloupe is the most popular of the melons. "When fully ripe, it has a rough, netted skin and sweet orange flesh," she writes. "The netting makes it resemble a large nutmeg, and it is sometimes called 'nutmeg melon.'"

Nuts

To store fresh nuts, such as pecans, almonds, and pine nuts after a package has been opened, I transfer the nuts to a plastic container or glass jar and seal the container as tightly as possible and store in the freezer. They will keep indefinitely.

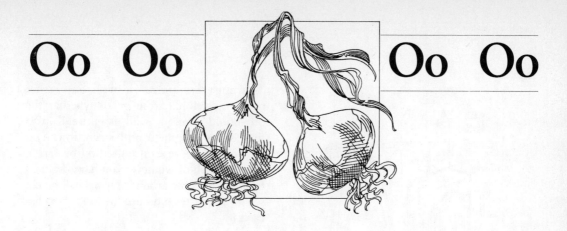

Oo Oo Oo Oo

Oats

Rolled oats are precisely that, oat kernels that have been put through a roller and thereby flattened to make them more palatable. An oat groat (you have to be a born curmudgeon to say that without smiling) or oat kernel resembles any other kernel, including dried corn, when harvested. The old-fashioned method is to roll the oat groats to make one big flake. Quick oats are cut and rolled thinner to hasten cooking time. Instant oats are specially treated to make them instantly edible and hot when boiling water is poured over them in a bowl.

Pinhead oatmeal, according to Quaker Oats archives, are oat groats that have been

broken down into five or six pieces. This is as opposed to quick-cooking oats, which are broken down into two or three pieces. Pinhead oatmeal, I was told, is probably not made commercially in the United States. It is an educated guess that if you have a recipe calling for pinhead oatmeal, quick-cooking oatmeal would suffice. If you crushed the quick-cooking oatmeal in your hands, who knows, you might come out with the pinhead version.

Oils

One of the main problems with cooking oils is their tendency to become rancid after a reasonably short while if they are left in a warm temperature. The custom in my own kitchen is not to refrigerate oils put to frequent use, and these include corn oil (my basic cooking oil and occasional salad oil) and olive oil. I replenish these oils with such regularity that there is little likelihood they will become rancid, so I do not refrigerate them. On the other hand, I use walnut oil and hazelnut oil only occasionally. Both oils become rancid fairly quickly unless they are refrigerated. Olive oil when refrigerated becomes fairly firm, unpourable, and opaque. It then has to be warmed to room temper-

ature to become liquid and is then usable.

As to substituting one oil for another, as a general rule all nonflavored oils, such as corn, peanut, and liquid vegetable oil, are interchangeable. Unless the recipe specifies it, however, you should not substitute an oil with a pronounced flavor—olive oil, for example, or walnut oil.

The flavors of oils are sometimes deceptive and your nose and taste are your best guides. For example, the sesame oil sold in Chinese shops and widely used in Chinese cooking has the pronounced flavor of sesame seeds. Much of the sesame oil sold in health food stores is highly refined and does not smack at all of sesame seeds.

Oil that has been used for deep-frying may be re-used, provided, of course, that the oil has not undergone such changes as burning; that it is not rancid because it has been left standing unused for a considerable length of time, or has a pronounced flavor as a result of food previously cooked in it.

Cooks argue, with reason, that foods fry better in oil that has been used at least once. There are, no doubt, sound chemical facts (unknown to me) as to why foods cooked in oil that has been used for deep-frying obtain a richer, browner color than when they are cooked in fresh.

In any event, the re-use of oil, or whether to use additional fresh oil or whether the oil should be used at all, is entirely up to the cook's judgment and discretion. You can, of course, test once-used oil by frying a small batch of whatever you have destined for a second time around. Fry a small batch, see how it tastes, and use the old oil or discard it.

Oiseaux sans Tête

See Birds.

Okra

See Gumbo.

Oleo

See Margarine.

Omelet

Just why the making of an omelet should daunt the courage of any cook who can turn out a decent scrambled egg might be a mystery, if it weren't for my knowledge of two things that yield to good cookery — proper equipment and self-confidence. Harold Arlen, the composer, once observed in a lyric that "You can't make a nylon pocketbook out of a pig's ear," and a similar association applies to an omelet. You can't turn a proper omelet out of a skillet whose surface is flawed. That is not to say that it is even *necessary* to have an omelet pan to make a perfect omelet. You can use almost any skillet, provided it has a proper cooking surface and is of a proper size in relation to the number of eggs to be used.

Teflon skillets make excellent omelets because of their smooth surfaces. I also own the Rudolph Stanish omelet pan and the French Chef omelet pan and admire them both. They are excellent for omelet making.

If anyone were to ask the "secret" of making a first-rate omelet, I would say to assemble all the ingredients needed for the omelet and have them ready to cook — the eggs broken into a bowl; the other ingredients within easy reach; forks, plates, and pan at the ready, and so on. Cook the omelet as quickly as possible over high heat. Slow cooking produces tough omelets.

Incidentally, I am not of the thought that an omelet pan should never be washed. If it isn't used at reasonable intervals, the oil, butter, or other fat used in making an omelet will become rancid and produce a foul-tasting product. The pan should be washed in warm or hot water with detergent or soap while using a soft sponge or cloth. It should be dried immediately, particularly if it is an iron pan, and preferably over heat to prevent rust from forming.

There is also no absolute reason why an omelet pan could not be put to other uses, provided extreme care is used. The only reason it is not recommended is the off chance that the pan will be scratched in washing. Amateurs have an unfortunate habit at times of removing their dirty work by scrubbing the surfaces of cooking utensils with steel wool or other abrasives. A surface thus marred will more than likely produce an omelet that sticks.

Omelette Norvégienne

Omelette novégienne is the French name for baked Alaska, which is not much in vogue any longer. A baked Alaska, of course, is a brick of hard-frozen ice cream surrounded first by a pastry shell, such as a thin layer of sponge cake, covered with a meringue, and baked at high heat until the meringue is browned and the ice cream still not melted.

The *omelette norvégienne* (it's a joke, son, both Norway and Alaska are said to be lands of ice) has an interesting history. According to *Larousse Gastronomique,* its origin is attributed to an American physicist named Benjamin Thompson whose work in Britain earned him a title. It was supposedly hoisted into fame in 1895 at the Hotel de Paris in Monte Carlo by the hotel's chef, Jean Giroix.

Another theory was recorded in 1866 by a Baron Brisse, who stated that it was the chief cook of the Chinese Mission in Paris who gave the secret of making the dish to the chef of the Grand Hotel.

Onion Storage

See Shallots.

Opera Names in Food

When the Metropolitan Opera celebrated its centennial in 1983, a consultant asked if I could provide him with a brief list of foods that have been named for operas, and opera composers and singers. It was an intriguing assignment and I was able to come up with about twenty-five names, starting with "l'Africaine" by Meyerbeer and ending with "Véronique," a comic opera by Messager. Probably the two most famous names to have foods named after them are Melba and Belle Hélène.

Nellie Melba, of course, was the Australian-born soprano who was christened Helen Porter Mitchell. The most famous food that bears her name is Melba toast, which has an interesting history, according to the biography of *Georges Auguste Escoffier* by Eugene Herbodeau and Paul Thalamas.

It seems that Escoffier often visited his employer, César Ritz, and his wife, Marie, at their home in England while the Ritz Hotel in Paris was in the planning stage. On one occasion Madame Ritz complained that toast was never thin enough for her taste. Escoffier (you'd think he had something better to do) got up and grilled a piece of toast. He split it in half and grilled it again. He dubbed his creation "toast Marie."

Shortly thereafter, Nellie Melba came to stay at London's Savoy Hotel, which César Ritz owned and where Escoffier was executive chef. He noted that the soprano's diet called for toast, so he served her his creation and rechristened it "toast Melba."

As to *pêche Melba*, that is said to have come about because Dame Melba demanded peaches and ice cream so often when she stayed at the Ritz-Carlton in London. One time Escoffier served the peach on ice cream but topped it with a fresh raspberry sauce. It was dubbed *pêche Melba*. Such is the way of legends.

No one knows who created pears Belle Hélène, but there is universal agreement that it was named for the heroine of the Offenbach opera of that name written in 1864. The best-known dish to bear that name is the dessert made with poached pears on a bed of vanilla ice cream, topped with a chocolate sauce and a dollop of whipped cream. Serious food encyclopedias sometimes ignore this dish but go into detail about eggs Belle Hélène. These are eggs mollet (eggs soft-cooked and removed from the shell) or poached eggs, embedded in a chicken croquette mixture, breaded, deep-fried, and served with asparagus tips and a cream of chicken sauce.

It is curious how many egg dishes have

been named for things operatic: eggs Africaine, eggs Bizet, eggs Massenet, and so on. Tournedos, too. Dishes bearing the name Lakmé, Othello, and Halevy are made with tournedos. The most famous tournedos dish of all, however, is tournedos Rossini, the piece of fillet topped with truffle and a Madeira sauce. Tosca is based on roast chicken, Patti on breast of chicken, Verdi on sole, and Aïda on turbot.

It seems to me that the great chefs have lost their romantic touch. I haven't heard a dish named after an opera star or a composer recently.

Aside from opera chocolates, do you know what dishes are called "opera"? There is tournedos of beef opera, in which the meat is sautéed in butter and served on toast or tartlets, garnished with sautéed chicken livers and a Madeira sauce. It is served with buttered asparagus tips. Fried eggs opera are garnished with sautéed chicken livers with a Madeira sauce. This is also served with asparagus tips. *See also* Spaghetti Caruso, Tetrazzini.

Orange Pekoe

In their admirably researched and instructive book, *The Book of Coffee and Tea,* by Joel, David, and Karl Schapira, the authors explain that both orange pekoe and pekoe tea actually fall into the overall category of "black teas." Black teas are divided into two grades: There is the leaf grade and the broken-leaf grade. Before packing, the leaves of the tea plant are sifted. The smaller broken portions of the leaves sift down and obviously these are the broken grades. The larger leaves left at the top are the leaf grades and are the most expensive. Eighty

percent of a typical crop of tea falls into the broken-leaf category.

Orange pekoe tea leaves are "long, thin, well-defined, closely twisted wiry leaves which sometimes contain yellow tip or bud leaf. The liquors are light or pale in color." The tea known as pekoe "consists of small, tightly rolled leaf and some more open leaf. It is not so wiry as orange pekoe but liquors have more color." Souchong, the authors continue, is the largest and coarsest leaf picked and the tea brewed with it is pale.

The name pekoe, incidentally, is of Chinese origin. It derives from two words in the Mandarin dialect, *peh,* meaning white, and *ho,* meaning down.

If orange pekoe tea ever tasted of oranges, it would be because someone added it for a punch or another drink. The word "orange" pertains to the color.

Orgeat

Orgeat is a sweet, nonalcoholic beverage that can be used in numerous drinks, including daiquiris as well as mai tais. It has a pronounced almond flavor and originally, I believe, was made from an emulsion of almonds. I suspect that most of the orgeat sold today is merely almond flavored. I have never used it in food preparation, but there is no reason why it could not be used when an almond flavor would be suitable.

Orloff

Some sources attribute the name Orloff to one Count Grigou Orlov who lived in Russia in the eighteenth century. Others state that the name is simply that of a noble family that held sway in Moscow during the reign of Nicholas the Great from 1825 to 1855. The most famous dish that bears the name Orloff is selle de veau or saddle of veal Orloff. During the days of the tsars in Russia, French—not Russian—was the language used by the aristocrats. Many of the nobles imported French chefs to staff their kitchens. French chefs today are universally and modestly agreed that all of the best dishes that bear Russian names are of French origin.

Orzo

One of the best tasting and most interesting types of pasta is something called orzo, which, curiously enough, is most closely identified with Greek cooking. The word for the pasta in Greek is *kritharaki,* and both it and orzo mean "barley," which refers to the shape of the grain, although orzo, like most pasta, is made from wheat flour. Orzo (or *kritharaki*) also has more or less the same shape and size as pine nuts or long grains of rice.

Oscar of the Waldorf

Contrary to popular belief, Oscar of the Waldorf was neither a chef nor the official manager of the hotel. His full name was Oscar Tschirky, and before joining the Waldorf-Astoria he worked with distinction at the old Hoffman House and Delmonico's Restaurant. At Delmonico's he served Diamond Jim Brady and Lillian Russell. He was well acquainted with the "grand" society of New York throughout his career. He joined the Waldorf on January 1, 1893, the hotel's first employee, when he was twenty-six years old.

In Karl Schriftgiesser's book, *Oscar of the Waldorf,* Oscar wrote, "I've actually never cooked anything more difficult to prepare than a plate of scrambled eggs." Although he was involved in many managerial aspects of the hotel, he states that he was actually, for want of a better word, maître d'hôtel.

Ostrich

Larousse Gastronomique notes that ostrich is forbidden on religious grounds in some homes, but it was much valued by the Romans. One of the earliest cookbooks by the second Apicius (all three gourmands named Apicius in ancient Rome were celebrated for their voracious appetites) offers a special sauce for the cooked bird.

For what it's worth, the encyclopedia adds that "an ostrich, on the average, gives about 60 pounds of meat and 40 pounds of fat."

I have searched my library, in vain, for recipes using ostrich.

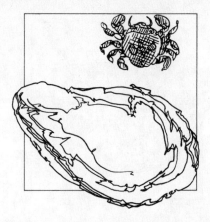

Oyster Crab

Oyster crabs are found in oysters and, on occasion, in mussels. According to A. J. McClane in *The Encyclopedia of Fish Cookery,* the crab "shares the food ingested by its host."

"Unfortunately," the author continues, "all oysters do not harbor these pale pink crustaceans and gathering a sufficient quantity for a meal is akin to looking for pearls—although the crab is more abundant."

They can be eaten either raw, cooked briefly in butter, or deep-fried. One of the best meals I can recall consisted of nothing but deep-fried whitebait (these had been soaked in milk and dipped in flour), plus deep-fried oyster crabs.

If you want to deep-fry them, they should be cooked in the hot fat for only two or three seconds before draining.

Oyster Plant

See Salsify.

Oysters

Despite the elegance of oysters and the connoisseurs' utter delight in dining on oysters on the half shell, it is generally conceded that the man who swallowed the first oyster must have been of fearless spirit, redoubtable self-assurance, or, conceivably, faint from hunger. Jonathan Swift put it succinctly: "He was a bold man that first eat an oyster."

And as John Gay, the poet who lived at the same time as Swift, expressed it:

The man had a sure palate . . . [who]
    on the rocky shore
First broke the vo cozy oyster's pearly
    coat
And risked the living morsel down his
    throat.

In the ages since that first oyster was downed, however, a lust for them has continued unabated. According to the late epicure André Simon, a marshal in Napoleon's army consumed one hundred oysters as a light prelude to breakfast. (I have quoted, too often perhaps, Brillat-Savarin's famed account of the day he invited a guest to eat his fill of oysters on the half shell. After the third dozen, the host could share no more, "After which I let him go on alone, etc., opening them.") In the days of Louis XI of France, according to Mr. Simon, "the learned professors of the Sorbonne ate oysters lest their scholarship should become deficient."

It may well be that, more than any other article of food, the oyster has been written about by serious essayists. In *The Oysters of Locmariaquer,* Eleanor Clark informs that Nero claimed the ability of pinpointing the origin of his oysters by taste. Pliny called oysters "the palm and pleasure of the table," and Montaigne, speaking of the oysters of Bordeaux, exulted that "they are so agreeable, and of so high an order of taste that it is like smelling violets to eat them; moreover, they are so healthy, a valet gobbled up more than a hundred without any disturbance."

Whenever considering oysters, my thoughts turn to one of the finest books that I have encountered about a single food— *The Glorious Oyster,* edited by Hector Bolitho.

One learns from the book, for example, that the oyster is the most tranquil of animals and can be rather eccentric. It tells of an oyster that learned to whistle, another that became a mousetrap, and it explains that in certain lands oysters grow on trees. It is their talent for laziness that makes them, as one expert put it, the most tender and delicate of seafoods.

One of the best places in America to learn about oyster culture is an hour's drive from Manhattan. It is the Long Island Oyster Farm in Northport, an enterprise dedicated to the commercial replenishment of oyster beds on the East Coast to compensate through man-made means for the severe depletion of oysters that has occurred within the past century. There is a small museum there that offers a fascinating account of oyster consumption in this country even before Diamond Jim Brady.

One of the displays there notes that the first oyster "farmers" on Long Island were, of course, Indians, and adds: "When the early settlers arrived in the seventeenth century, they found oysters in natural abundance. Some oysters were as large as a foot long.

"Oysters were an important food for the early settlers, from Colonial days and into the mid-nineteenth century. In 1859, for example, the people of New York City spent more money on oysters than for meat. Some seven million bushels of oysters were consumed each year in those times—about ten bushels per person per year!" Exclamation point, indeed!

Lament regarding over-use of this nation's natural resources is not all that new. An article in *Harper's Weekly,* dated August 18, 1883, states that in 1860, ten million bushels of oysters were annually taken from Chesapeake Bay alone. Twenty-three years later "probably thirty million bushels are withdrawn from the same beds. No natural increase can keep pace with such an exhaustive demand."

Before the First World War, Diamond Jim Brady did his share in depleting America's oyster resources. According to one biographer, his evening meal frequently began with six dozen Lynnhaven oysters, followed by a saddle of mutton, half a dozen venison chops, roast chicken with caper sauce, a game dish, and a twelve-egg soufflé.

The present relative scarcity of oysters is not due, of course, to overconsumption but rather to pollution, diminished coastal places for harvests, and so on. Although the

Long Island Oyster Farm is making heartening strides in cultivating oysters—production has increased tenfold in the past decade—the company's year-round demands at present far outweigh its ability to supply.

I had a nice chat with George Vanderborgh, a vice president of the oyster farm, which was begun by his ancestors more than a hundred years ago.

He told me that thirty years ago Europe was the farm's largest customer and that the *Lusitania* had a large shipment of Long Island oysters aboard when it sank. To breed oysters, they are collected by digging, dredging, or tongs. And when they are bred, it is best to have a "mix"—that is, oysters from different areas—which produces a stronger strain. Within twenty-four hours of dredging, the eggs are fertilized and swimming. After ten days or two weeks, an oyster stops swimming forever and, as Cole Porter once phrased it, becomes "sadder and moister" as he grows and grows. The word "he" is used ill-advisedly in this case. An oyster can change sex throughout its life span.

After the oyster becomes immobile, it is moved only by hand, by tide, by dredge, or some other outside force.

An oyster drinks one hundred gallons of water a day and fattens on the algae it sucks out of the water. According to Mr. Vanderborgh, algae is to oysters what grass is to cattle.

At the farm, once the oysters are six weeks old, they are transferred to the temperature-controlled waters of a nearby lagoon until they grow to be three-quarters of an inch in diameter. Then they are uprooted and planted in bay bottoms such as Northport and Huntington Bay, New Ha-ven, Oyster Bay, Gardiners Bay, until maturity. An oyster, from spawning to table, requires about three years. The best time for oysters is late fall, winter, and early summer.

After purchasing, unopened oysters may be refrigerated in a plastic bag up to three or four days. When ready to use, rinse under cold water to remove any sand and to prevent sand from getting inside the oyster when opening. Place unopened oysters on a bed of crushed or cubed ice for about fifteen minutes. They taste best when well-chilled and the oysters will drink liquid from the melting ice and will be a little plumper and more flavorful.

Oysters Rockefeller

The origin of oysters Rockefeller is generally credited to Antoine's Restaurant in New Orleans. It is said to be the creation of Jules Alciatore, the grandson of the restaurant's founder. He once told an interviewer that he had called the dish, which is made with great quantities of butter, Rockefeller because they are so rich.

Oyster Sauce

The primary ingredients of oyster sauce, used in many Chinese recipes, are shucked oysters, soy sauce, salt, and seasonings, such as garlic, ginger, sugar, and leeks. The sauce is simmered a long time and is generally thickened with cornstarch. Tightly capped, it will keep several days in a cool place. It will keep indefinitely if it is refrigerated.

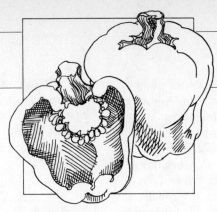

Pp Pp   Pp Pp

Paellita

A paellita is simply a modified version of a paella. A traditional paella is an elaborate affair containing, among other things, such foods as chicken, lobster, clams, mussels, shrimp, sausages, pork, and so on. A paellita, as I have had it in the home of Puerto Rican friends, is tailored to contain, for example, only chicken and shrimp. In principal, the technique for making both dishes is the same.

Paillard of Veal

Paillard of veal, one of my favorite dishes, consists of top-quality veal, pounded until thin and cooked over fairly intense heat, either on a grill (to produce a nice diamond-shape pattern on both sides) or in a fiery hot skillet.

For each serving you should use half a pound of thinly sliced veal steak, not a mere scaloppine. Cook it for only a few seconds on each side and serve it rubbed quickly on both sides with melted butter. Serve with a lemon wedge on the side.

The finest gastronomic encyclopedia that I know (*Dictionnaire de l'Académie des Gastronomes*), speculates that the name originated many decades ago in Paris. One of the town's leading restaurateurs was a M. Paillard. The dish is sometimes spelled with an "e" on the end.

Pain Perdu

See French toast.

Pakora

A pakora is a small snack, served in India, that is deep-fried and has chick-pea flour as a principal ingredient. It may be made of eggplant, fish, or chicken. A chicken pakora contains, in addition to chick-pea flour and ground chicken, spices, such as ginger and cumin, plus chopped onion and garlic. The mixture is blended well, shaped into small patties or lumps, and deep-fried.

Palocleves

In *The Cuisine of Hungary*, the author, George Lang, notes that Janos Gundel created Paloc soup or Palocleves for the author Kalman Mikszath in a private dining room of the Archduke Stephen Hotel in Budapest in 1892. Mr. Lang adds, "Mikszath wrote a book about the Paloc people, inhabitants of northeast Hungary, which became a treasured classic of Hungarian literature."

The recipe Mr. Lang gives is basically a lamb soup with caraway seeds, paprika, and garlic for flavoring. It also contains potatoes and string beans and incorporates sour cream.

Panini

Panini is the plural of *panino,* an overall word for rolls in Italian. *Panini imbotiti,* for example, are the sandwiches you get in cafés—stuffed rolls. And I found a description of *panini di pasqua* in an old regional Italian cookbook. It is a specialty of the Easter season in the Friuli region of northeastern Italy and, the book notes, it is rarely made today. It is a sweet bread made of yellow cornmeal, yeast, sugar, butter, milk, and raisins with a slight flavor of lemon.

Pansotti

Pansotti is a specialty of Liguria and the region that surrounds Genoa. Perhaps the town most closely identified with the specialty is Rapallo. You will find a very good recipe for pansotti in Ada Boni's widely available *Italian Regional Cooking,* one of the best of Italian cookbooks.

Pansotti is a form of dumpling like ravioli. The filling includes spinach, chopped eggs, and grated cheese. It is served with a *salsa di noce,* or walnut sauce, made with ground walnuts, oil, garlic, and ricotta cheese. The word *pansotti* means pot-bellied.

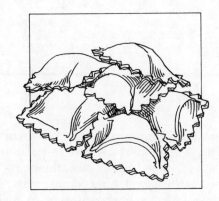

Pantropheon

The Pantropheon, by Alexis Benoît Soyer, is considered one of the great treasures of the world of cookery. Soyer, born in Meaux-en-Brie, France, in 1809, was one of the most famous chefs who ever lived, best known as the chef of the famed Reform Club in London. He transformed the dietary services of the military hospital, invented a military cooking wagon, and wrote many books on cookery.

It was *The Pantropheon* by which he hoped to be remembered. Subtitled "A History of Food and Its Preparation in Ancient Times," the book was published in 1853, a time when he badly needed money. In less than five years the book had sold 200,000 copies. Soyer died in 1858.

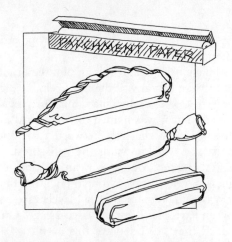

finest version is that made in Florence. It is prepared by cooking coarsely chopped garlic and pepper flakes in olive oil.

Ripe tomatoes are cut into pieces and added. An equal weight of finely diced bread is then added, along with rich chicken or meat broth, salt, pepper, and basil leaves. Cook this for about 15 minutes and then let it stand about 1 or 2 hours. It is a thick soup and is served with additional olive oil and black pepper.

Papillote

In its broadest sense, the word *papillote* means "curl paper." When a person "puts up" her hair by wrapping it around paper curlers, the hair is said to be *en papillote*. In the kitchen it refers to foods that are cooked in paper. Preferably the paper will be of a specially treated kind that will brown but not burn at high heat. The paper is buttered, the food is placed on it, and then enclosed in the paper. The edges of the paper are twisted to seal.

In this country, more often than not, it is fish that is cooked *en papillote* (pompano, red snapper, and so on). In Europe, however, various chops, such as veal or pork, are cooked *en papillote*. That method is not much favored, however, by serious chefs.

Pappa al Pomodoro

According to Giuliano Bugialli's *The Fine Art of Italian Cooking*, pappa al pomodoro is bread soup and the author adds that the

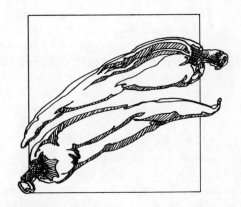

Paprika

It is ruefully true that in many American households paprika is considered nothing more than an element of color to enliven a cheese sauce. And it's no wonder, for the innocuous powder that stores often pass off as paprika has little more character than chalk. In its finer forms, however, paprika is a distinctive and much prized spice. There are three types—sweet, mild, and hot—each with a pronounced flavor. The best is imported from Hungary and, logically enough, is called Hungarian or rose paprika. It is available in the so-called gourmet sections of most high-quality supermarkets and in fine specialty food shops, as well as in Hungarian grocery stores.

Paquette

I had seen the word *paquette* on a menu at the Palace restaurant, and ventured a guess that it derived from the French *paquet de mer,* meaning a heavy sea.

"Not so," said Ruth Spear, author of *Cooking Fish and Shellfish*.

"Paquette is the French name for a female lobster with fully formed eggs, just prior to depositing them. The feeling is that the creature is at its most succulent then, and, accordingly, is regarded as a premium lobster. How one would know one had a paquette until one split it open I do not know. Presumably, at the Palace, the 'ordinary' lobsters were relegated to baser uses, but it seems you'd have to open a huge number to obtain enough to make a dish of them, the odds being what they are. One could lessen the odds by choosing only females to begin with—identified by their soft, hairy, crossed last pair of swimmerets and greater width of tail."

Paris-Brest

A Paris-Brest is one of the finest of French pastries. It consists of a cream-puff (choupaste) mixture that is piped through a pastry tube into the shape of a circle or crown. When this is baked, the circle or crown is slit open and filled with a butter cream containing chopped praline (a hard caramel blend of sugar and almonds). It is often served with whipped cream on top, plus chopped almonds.

I have been unable to pinpoint the origin of the name in any of the most reliable dictionaries or encyclopedias, but always assumed that it was named for the world renowned train that ran between Paris and Brest and was known as the Paris-Brest.

As it turned out, it was an ill-educated guess. Several people wrote to point out that it was actually named for a bicycle race between Paris and Brest many years ago. One added that "to celebrate this event, a Parisian chef concocted the dessert. If you visualize this dessert, you can see that it is in the shape of a bicycle tire."

Parker House Rolls

Before the Second World War, Parker House rolls were probably the choicest and best-known breads in American households. They were produced from a standard dough made with flour, yeast, milk, and a touch of sugar, and originated at the Parker House in Boston.

Their shape is distinctive. After the dough is rolled out, it is formed into circles with

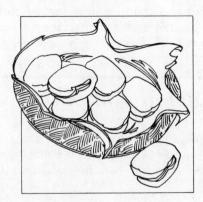

a biscuit cutter. Then a crease is made in the center with a knife and one side of the crease is folded over the other.

When I was a child in Mississippi, they were often referred to as "pocket book" rolls because of their shape after baking.

Parma Ham

Parma ham is a ham — prosciutto — that comes from the province of Parma, the same province that gives Parmesan cheese its name. It is generally conceded among connoisseurs that the finest Parma ham comes from the village of Langhirano, which is south of the city of Parma.

It is said that the air of Langhirano, which is situated in the mountains, is responsible for the exceptional quality of its hams. They are shipped into Langhirano from all over Italy so that they may be given a proper final curing. You can substitute any available prosciutto for Parma ham.

Parmentier

In French gastronomy, almost any dish in which potatoes play a prominent role as a principal ingredient or garnish is called Parmentier. Antoine-Auguste Parmentier is credited with popularizing potatoes in France after a period in which they were generally regarded with scorn and/or suspicion, even as potentially poisonous to the human system. Despite his impact in this respect, remarkably little seems to have been written about him. In the most reliable reference works, his biography is generally contained in a brief paragraph or a sentence or two, and there are conflicting accounts of the year of his death—1813 or 1817—although the later year seems the true one. (He was born in 1737.) Parmentier is identified variously as an "agriculturist writer" and "food expert," "economist," and "agronomist," and as a "military pharmacist." Whatever his occupation, his influence has assured the perpetuity of his name as long as French kitchens and menus exist.

Parsley

If parsley were as scarce as sturgeon eggs and as rare as truffles, it would conceivably be one of the world's most sought-after herbs. Happily, it is almost as abundant as meadow grass, as taken for granted in most kitchens throughout the world as salt and pepper. On any given day, it is tossed, in one form or another, into countless soups and stews and assorted ragouts. Without parsley sprigs what would airline chefs resort to as they garnish those plastic trays?

Although parsley is omnipresent in kitchens, particularly those of the Western world, it is generally regarded as nothing more than a basic flavor, something to be added reflexively to one savory dish or another—a kind of culinary grace note. Actually, there are numerous dishes in the world in which parsley, in one form or another, is used in dominant—or near dominant—fashion.

Chief among these is the famed jambon persillé, a great specialty of Burgundy. This is, of course, ham with parsley, a jellied, molded creation, an appetizer or first course that, when sliced into, presents a red and green mosaic pattern of ham and masses of parsley entrenched in jelly throughout.

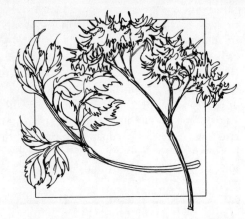

The French kitchen also specializes in what is known as a *persillade* (the French word for parsley is *persil*), a fine, flavorful blend of chopped shallots, bread crumbs, and parsley. This is used in numerous dishes, a last-minute addition to grilled racks of lamb, broiled steak, fish, or chicken and, often, after the persillade is added and grilled briefly, it becomes a bit crusty and delectable.

There are two basic kitchen parsleys available on the market. There are the plain, or flat leaf, and curly leaf varieties. The commonest both in England and the United States is the curly leaf, although it is not necessarily the best. The flat or plain leaf is much more used and admired in the countries around the Mediterranean, particularly Italy. Flat leaf parsley, as a matter of fact, is usually referred to in the United States as Italian parsley.

In Tom Stobart's *Herbs, Spices and Flavorings,* he notes that Neapolitan parsley is a specialty grown in Naples for its stems, which are eaten in the same manner as celery. There is also Hamburg parsley, of which only the root is used for flavoring. Chinese parsley, of course, is not parsley at all but rather the leaf of the coriander plant.

In my own kitchen I use flat leaf and curly leaf parsley interchangeably. Flat leaf parsley may be a trifle more pungent, but I think that taste differences between the two are negligible. However, Italian cooks whom I know are defiant in their insistence that the flat leaf parsley is preferable. I do know that curly leaf parsley is easier to chop in small quantities.

The way to keep parsley fresh is to stick the cut ends in a jar just large enough to hold the bottoms and add cold water to the jar. Cover loosely with a plastic bag and place in the refrigerator. Do not rinse the parsley until you are ready to use it.

Parsley Root

Parsley root is not widely available in American markets, yet it is not all that uncommon either. It does belong to the parsley family and tastes rather like a blend of parsley, which dominates, plus celery or celery root. It is used in soups.

Parsnips

In medieval times, doctors vowed that parsnips possessed properties that could cure toothaches, prevent dysentery, and "keep off adders."

But in modern times, the United States Department of Agriculture has determined that parsnips contain a toxic chemical called psoralens. The report added that peeling the vegetable and cooking it did not reduce the chemical, which is said to cause cancer and mutations in laboratory animals and thus may present some toxicological risk to human beings.

The report did not specify precisely how many parsnips it would require to do bodily harm. I have eaten parsnips all my life, admittedly in limited quantities. My own feelings on the subject are in league with those of a gentleman from Connecticut who wrote, "With so many foibles in life the best motto still seems to be 'everything in moderation' or, 'man should not live by parsnips alone.' "

And I shall continue to eat and enjoy them. Without salt, of course.

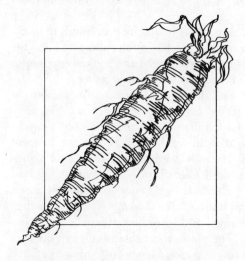

Pasta

America is indeed in the throes of what has been called the "pastarization" of the nation, but this was not always so. As a matter of fact, as history goes, a thoroughgoing appreciation of pasta in this country is a relatively recent thing.

It began with Thomas Jefferson. In an old book I own called *Spaghetti Dinner* by Giuseppe Prezzolini, the author states that Jefferson "was the first man to import Lombardy poplars, Roman architecture, (and)

Tuscan wine into America." He adds that he was the first to import into the country a spaghetti-making machine.

Mr. Prezzolini points out that the Jefferson admiration for pasta could have come about somewhat earlier from dining on Italian food in a restaurant in Richmond near his home. "His expense accounts show," the author notes, "that he had a charge account with one Serefino Formica, or Formicola, an innkeeper of Venetian and Neopolitan origin, who ran a Richmond inn. Serefino had come to America as the maître d'hôtel of (a) Lord Dunmore, and claimed to be a descendant of a Venetian doge. Whatever the merits of that claim, he was certainly a Neopolitan (or part-Neopolitan) and would certainly have prepared spaghetti. And the records do show that Jefferson did eat in his establishment both before and after his trip to France."

Jefferson traveled to Italy in 1787, with a primary intention of buying a rice-husking machine. He also was in pursuit of the mechanical spaghetti-maker. His search for the latter was unsuccessful and he subsequently appealed to a friend, one William Short, who was touring Italy. Short's reply is fascinating:

"I procured at Naples according to your request, the mould for making macaroni . . . it is of smaller diameter than is used in the manufactories of macaroni, but of the diameter that had been sent to gentlemen in other countries. I went to see the macaroni made. The machine for pressing as used at Naples is enormous—much more so than I had expected. The price they told me for fitting up one of these machines with the mortar, etc., was the value of 100 *louis d'or.* . . . The width of the mortar that you desired to know is marked on the mould you will receive . . . it was left with my banker at Naples to be forwarded to you."

A long period ensued, however, between the arrival of Mr. Jefferson's noodle machine and any sort of noteworthy commercial production of pasta in the United States. Some effort at pasta production had begun here in 1848 but it was negligible. Until 1914 almost every strand of pasta eaten in America (and most of it in the beginning was either spaghetti or macaroni) was imported from the pasta makers of Naples. During the First World War, pasta imports were cut off and only then did production in America start on a vast scale.

I still feel that the finest pasta — spaghetti, fettucini, spaghettini, vermicelli, and so on — is imported from Italy. The domestic product is wholly edible, but it does not have the same fine texture and cooking resilience as the imported product. I consider two of the finest Italian brands to be those of S.p.A. Carmine Russo and those of De Cecco. Even when inadvertently overcooked they do not become mushy as most domestic pastas do.

The proper way to cook pasta so that the strands don't stick together is this: Bring a good quantity of water to a boil before adding the pasta. Many experts say that you should use one gallon of water for each pound of pasta. I generally use somewhat less than that.

The important thing, to my mind, is to start agitating the pasta, using a two-pronged fork, the moment the pasta strands or pieces are added. Continue stirring and agitating the strands until they are floating free. If you have a heavy pasta like macaroni, you must also stir carefully on the bottom to prevent them from sticking there. Oil in the water may help, but motion is best.

I continue to agitate the strands until the water has reached a full rolling boil and the strands are softened and cooked enough, so that they do not stick together.

I test the strands often so that I know the precise degree of tenderness or doneness. Many Italian cooks and chefs add a cup or so of cold water to the kettle the moment the strands are properly done; it's a procedure I follow, too.

The added water does not cool the pasta, but it arrests the cooking. The pasta is then drained and served immediately.

There are many things you can do with leftover pasta. Depending on the cut, the quantity, and so on, you may turn it into a salad by blending it with mayonnaise or perhaps a vinaigrette.

I know of one recipe in which the pasta is first marinated with a vinaigrette containing a good deal of finely chopped garlic. It is left to stand in the refrigerator overnight and blended the next day with a little mayonnaise and cooked vegetables, such as peas, chopped celery, and scallions.

You may also add leftover pasta to a variety of soups, from clear broths to vegetable soups—even bean soups. *See also* Orzo, Quadretti, Spaghetti, Strangozzi, Fettuccine.

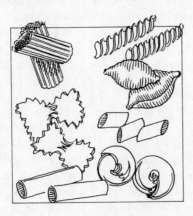

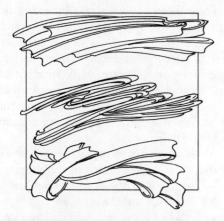

Pasta Asciutta

One of the most lucid explanations I know of *pasta asciutta* (Italian authors generally do not deign to describe anything that is so obviously basic) is that of Jack Denton Scott in his work, *The Complete Book of Pasta*. His explanation is long, but in it he outlines, among others, two categories of pasta. One is *pasta in brodo,* or pasta in broth, which is to say soup. These are the small and odd-shaped pieces of pasta, such as tiny shells, pastina, and so on. *Pasta asciutta,* literally "dry" pasta, refers to all the pastas not specifically designed for broth—spaghetti, vermicelli, rigatoni, lasagne, and so on.

Pasta Etiquette

In the interest of pasta etiquette, it may be time to pause to examine what is right and what is wrong with various techniques for cooking and eating pasta.

For example, is it proper, as Emily Post says, to twirl spaghetti against a spoon? Or, as she also says, with the tips of the fork resting against the curve of the plate? Should bread be served with pasta, another starch? Is it correct to sprinkle cheese on pasta with seafood sauce? When cheese is in order, what is the best cheese? Should strands of long pasta be broken before being tossed into the pot?

The owners of three of the best-known Italian restaurants in Manhattan once convened to feast on pasta and discuss just how and with what it should be eaten. The diners were Adi Giovanetti, proprietor of Il Nido, and his wife, Rosanna, Sirio Maccioni, owner of Le Cirque, and his wife, Egi, and Luigi Nanni, proprietor and chef of both Nanni's and Il Valetto. The elf-like Mr. Nanni cooked, preparing two pastas with sauces, one of which contained Fontina cheese and wild field mushrooms and a *salsa alla militare,* or military sauce, made with tomatoes, fresh basil, and dried hot pepper.

As the meal progressed the discussion became Mount Etna-like in its eruptions. Cheese with seafood pasta? *Never!* Well, maybe. Both Mr. Giovanetti and Mr. Nanni declared vehemently that cheese with seafood would be as much of a sacrilege as pouring ketchup over carpaccio. Mr. Maccioni, however, the most free-thinking of the group, declared that he did not feel strongly about it, that he at times sprinkled a little freshly grated Parmigiano-Reggiano over his shrimp and squid with linguine or his scampi tagliatelle. As far as he is concerned, it is a question of taste.

Mr. Giovanetti and Mr. Nanni conceded that there just might be one exception to their rule: If the base for the dish was butter rather than oil, one might add a touch of cheese to help bind the sauce. But they weren't enthusiastic about it.

As to the use of a fork plus a spoon for eating pasta, all those at the table were adamant. Spoons are for children, amateurs, and people with bad table manners in general.

Egi Maccioni recalled her childhood days of eating pasta. "My grandparents spent hours teaching me how to eat pasta without using a spoon, how to twirl my fork so that not a strand of spaghetti would be hanging down as I lifted that fork to my mouth."

"At home," she added, "if I couldn't master the technique, they'd punish me by taking all the food away."

Is it improper to allow a few strands of pasta to hang down as it is transported to the mouth? "If the pasta is cooked *al dente*," Mr. Nanni said, "you are bound to have a few strands hanging." If the pasta fits that neatly around the fork, Mr. Giovanetti added, it is overcooked.

Mr. Nanni volunteered one exception to the no-spoon argument: "If your sauce is very liquid—a juicy primavera, a clam sauce—you might use a spoon to prevent splattering."

The first bowls of pasta, served with military sauce, were placed before each guest. Mr. Giovanetti forked his way into his bowl and demonstrated that the pasta, perfectly cooked, would not cling wraparound fashion to the fork. He ate with great relish.

It was generally agreed, however, that it is correct to place a spoon at each place setting. "In Italy it is customary to first place the pasta in a bowl or on a plate," Mr. Giovanetti said. "You then spoon the sauce on top and finally cheese, if you use it at all. You use your fork and spoon to toss the pasta with sauce and cheese, and you then eat it with your fork alone."

The suggested techniques for using the fork were: Put the fork into a few strands of spaghetti; let the tines of the fork rest against the curve of the bowl or the curved indentation of the plate, while twirling the fork around and giving it brief quick lifts to prevent too much pasta from accumulating. When one discrete mass of pasta can be lifted, hoist away.

As to whether it is best to serve pasta in a bowl or on a plate, most of those present voted for a bowl. But as for the serving of bread with pasta, there were varying opinions. "I don't believe in it," Mr. Nanni said. "They do that in country homes where there isn't enough money for meat."

"I know that purists say no," Mr. Maccioni said, "but I think you should serve bread. It is always on the table at the restaurant. In the family, one should serve bread to dip in the leftover sauce once the pasta is eaten."

As for whether strands of pasta should be broken before they are tossed into the boiling kettle, the answer from this gathering was absolutely not.

"The reason that notion came about," Mr. Nanni said, "is that in Italy when you go to the market, you buy pasta out of a large drawer in which the strands may be a yard long." The pasta is broken in half to make it more convenient to carry, he said. In this country, however, pasta is relatively short (about eleven inches) and there is no need to break it. If it doesn't fit in your pot, place the ends in first and push down as the water softens it. Tiny strands of pasta, it was agreed, are for children.

What about the best cheese for pasta? The restaurateurs said that their first choice is imported Parmigiano-Reggiano, which must be at least two years old before it is exported. Pecorino goes especially well with certain sauces, Mr. Giovanetti said, and he named three: carbonara, made with pancetta (Italian bacon), eggs, and cheese; matriciana made with onions, bacon, white wine, and tomatoes, and pesto, made with garlic and basil.

(P.S. My own preferred technique for eating pasta? With fork and spoon. I won't be reconstructed.)

"Forget about the argument of forks and spoons," one gentleman wrote. "There's only one way to eat spaghetti, with chopsticks, the original way. Try it. It's a lot easier than you might think. I've been doing it for years after I saw Chinese eating lo mein in a Chinese restaurant."

Pasta Names and Shapes

What many Americans seem unaware of is that the names of most of the various forms of pasta have absolute meanings — some of them descriptive, some humorous, and some pedantic. The very name spaghetti, for example, is derived from the Italian word *spago,* which means simply "string."

Consider the following, some of which will be better known than others: cappelletti (little hats), conchiglie (conch shells), farfalle (butterflies), fettuccine (small ribbons), linguine (small tongues), manicotti (small muff), mostaccioli (small mustache), rigatoni (large grooved), and vermicelli (little worms).

The Italians have one type of macaroni named "clover," so called because when the pasta slides from the box into the water, it makes a decidedly rustling sound, like dried clover falling into the feeding bins for animals.

There is probably not one person in a thousand in this country who knows that the countless sauces destined for pasta cannot, in the classic sense, be used arbitrarily with all pasta regardless of shape, size, color, and texture.

Put otherwise, you cannot serve, indiscriminately, all sauces with any kind of pasta. The rules for which sauce goes with which shape pasta cannot be reduced to a simple, absolute formula.

"Generally speaking," according to Marcella Hazan, "sauces that contain pieces of things — things like chopped meat, peas, ham and so on — go well with a pasta that has a hole (like macaroni), or a shape that catches pieces, spiral shapes, for example, and shells.

"Very thin sauces are destined for pasta like spaghetti or vermicelli. But there is an exception. If the sauce has a base of olive oil and contains clams, scallops, chopped fish or seafood, pasta strands such as spaghetti would be quite suitable. Think of linguine with clam sauce.

"Homemade pastas—freshly made pasta strands—go best with sauces that must be 'absorbed,' which is to say sauces that cling. Like the cream and cheese sauce tossed with fettuccine and known as Alfredo. You would never—or shouldn't—serve packaged spaghetti with that sauce."

"Some pastas," she continued, "tubular pasta or pastas with a hole, such as long strands of perciatelli, are destined to be cooked briefly or at least to let stand briefly covered so that the perfume and flavors of the sauce permeate to a slight degree the 'walls' or 'tubes' of the pasta."

Pastilla

See B'steeya.

Pastis

Pernod and Ricard are a form of anise, better known in the region around Marseilles as pastis. Originally, pastis was developed as a substitute for absinthe, which was banned by law many years ago because it contained wormwood, an ingredient that was, in the words of one book on herbs and spices, "guilty of putting off an evil day to yet a more evil one." Interestingly enough, the word "vermouth" derives from the German world *wermut,* which means wormwood. Needless to say, the vermouths, Pernod, and Ricard on the market today do not contain a trace of wormwood.

I had always presumed that Pernod and Ricard were identical in manufacture. On inquiry, I have learned that they are not.

Pernod is made by a process of distillation and its predominant flavor is star anise. Ricard, I am told, is made by maceration (a long-time soaking) and its predominant flavor is licorice.

When poured undiluted directly from the bottles, Pernod is quite yellow, Ricard a clear brown. When water is added, Pernod turns greenish yellow while Ricard takes on a milky gray look.

Pastrami

See Corned beef.

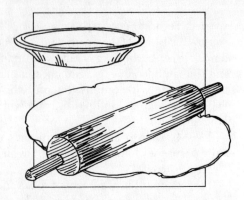

Pastry

The preparation of sweet and savory pie pastries are in many points similar.

Sweet pie pastry is made with flour, a fat such as butter, shortening, salt, sugar, and a liquid, such as water, milk and/or egg, or egg yolk. One tablespoon sugar may be added for a sweet pie or grated lemon or orange rind.

A pâte brisée is one of the best sweet pastry doughs. It is made with butter and/or white shortening, sugar, egg yolk, and very cold water or milk.

The ingredients and utensils for a pâte brisée should, as in all pie preparations, be very cold when combined.

Unlike a regular pie dough for a savory pie, a pâte brisée can withstand considerable handling. It cannot be overkneaded.

A pâte brisée is, preferably, rolled out with a rolling pin. On the other hand, it is basically a cookie dough and could be patted against the bottom and sides of a pie tin to make a crust.

Cracks or splits in the dough as it is rolled out can be patched. Simply cover the crack with a piece of rolled-out dough and roll to seal.

This pastry freezes well.

Regular pie dough for a savory pie is made with flour, a fat, such as shortening or butter, salt, and a liquid, such as water or milk. Solid white Crisco is the best commercial shortening. It is best to have all the ingredients and utensils for the dough very cold. The dough must be handled as briefly as possible.

Ideally, all pastry should be made in cool or cold surroundings. Heat causes the fat in the recipe to "flow." The humidity in a room will have an influence on the amount of liquid used, but it is minimal.

The more shortening or other fat you are able to use while making a manageable pastry, the flakier the crust will be. An excess of shortening will produce a soggy unmanageable pastry.

If a recipe calls for—to choose an arbitrary example—three-fourths to one cup of shortening, it is best to use the larger amount. This will allow more latitude for the quantity of flour that may be used as the pastry is rolled.

You should use a minimum amount of liquid, such as water. The more shortening you use, the less water you will need. If you have added too much water or shortening to a dough, you can possibly correct this by adding more flour, but the crust will not be as tender.

It is not imperative to chill dough before rolling it, but it helps. Chilling and "resting" the dough facilitates handling when it is rolled out. Theoretically, the chilling also tends to retard shrinking once the dough is baked. After the dough is chilled, it should stand for an hour or so before rolling. There is no reason, however, if pressed for time, the dough cannot be prepared and rolled out immediately. If the dough has a high-fat content, it is best to roll it out—particularly in warm weather—on a chilled surface.

It is certainly not essential to use a ruler when instructed to roll out pastry dough to an eighth of an inch thick. You should be reasonably aware, however, of just how thick an eighth of an inch is, and if there is any doubt in your mind you might check a ruler or some measuring tape.

Such an instruction in a recipe is only a random guideline. If your pastry is slightly thicker than that indicated, you will probably not run into trouble. If you roll pastry to much less than an eighth of an inch thickness, you may have trouble fitting it into your pie tin unless you are an expert because the pastry will be too thin.

Leftover scraps of pastry, by the way, may be pressed together into a ball and put to any number of good uses. Add roasted sesame seeds to the dough, roll it out, and cut into rounds. Bake to make benne wafers. Add Cheddar cheese or Parmesan cheese and a little red pepper, roll out, and cut into thin strips. Twist the strips and arrange on baking sheets. Bake to make cocktail cheese straws or use to make small tarts or turnovers.

Patafla

I have seen reference to patafla in only one source book—Elizabeth David's *A Book of Mediterranean Food,* which first appeared about thirty years ago. She describes patafla as a kind of salad served in a sandwich.

It consists of chopped tomatoes, onions, sweet red peppers, pitted black olives, pitted green olives, and gherkins or sour pickles all blended in a bowl.

To this you add olive oil, a sprinkling of paprika, and salt and pepper. Slice a crusty loaf of French bread and pull out the soft inner part. Cut the soft part into small cubes and add it to the vegetable mixture, then stir. Spoon the vegetable mixture into the two halves of bread and combine, sandwich fashion. This is chilled well and then sliced.

The sandwich, Miss David adds, is best made a day in advance.

Pâté

A reasonable index of the degree of sophistication engendered in the American kitchen in the past decade or so is that pâtés and terrines are no longer considered exotic "borrowings" from the French. Almost any expert and discerning cook can vouch for the fact that a pâté is nothing more than a well-made meat loaf. It is simply a bit more rarefied — using, perhaps, truffles and Cognac and other out-of-the-ordinary, often expensive, seasonings.

The French, too, have quite basic terms for their not-too-fancy pâtés. They refer to them as a *gâteau de viande* (meat cake) or a *pain de viande* (meat bread).

One of the accomplishments of the nouvelle cuisine has been to broaden the use and variety of pâtés. Less than a generation ago, most pâtés were based largely on meat —pork or veal—and goose or duck livers. Today, however, one encounters fish pâtés, vegetable pâtés, pâtés made with almost anything that can be cooked in a loaf pan.

Incidentally, there is no difference between a pâté and a terrine.

Originally, a terrine was a ground meat mixture baked in an earthenware utensil. The name derives from the word *terra,* meaning earth. Baked meat creations cooked in such molds are often referred to as terrines. The word *pâté* stems from "paste" and is related to such words as pastry and pasta. It is an educated guess that meat creations baked in pastry were dubbed pâté as a result. Today, pâtés are often cooked in and served from terrines or earthenware molds. And terrines are often covered with pastry before they are baked.

Pâte Brisée

See Pastry.

Paupiettes

See Birds.

Peanut Butter

As a child I was told that the person responsible for peanut butter was George Washington Carver (1864–1943), the agricultural chemist and educator who developed many uses for peanuts. His name is mentioned in Evan Jones's *American Food: The Gastronomic Story,* but there is no mention of his having invented peanut butter. The author notes only that "in 1904 at the World's Fair in St. Louis peanut butter was introduced as a health food."

Two other books, *Eating in America: A History* by Waverley Root and Richard de Rochemont and *Cooks, Gluttons and Gourmets* by Betty Wason, attribute peanut butter to a St. Louis physician who introduced it in 1890. Unfortunately, they do not give the physician's name.

Subsequently, I learned that the inventor was Dr. John Kellogg, medical superintendent of Battle Creek (Michigan) Hospital. One book, *The Shadow of Blooming Grove* by Francis Russell, referred to "the autocratic Doctor J. P. Kellogg, the inventor of peanut butter and corn flakes."

Another book, *Legacy,* by Richard A. Schaefer, offers an anecdote about an assistant of Dr. Kellogg's, who, having been scolded for roasting peanuts in the hospital kitchen, went home and, in anger, smashed one with a hammer. He found to his surprise that it had an agreeable taste and texture, according to the account, and his boss then became interested in the substance and marketed it.

Peanuts

Oddly, while goobers or groundnuts seem as earthly American as corn on the cob, they have never figured largely in the nation's most sophisticated dishes.

Don't mistake me. As much as anybody else, I like peanuts, hot and roasted and preferably cracked by hand and taken from the shell. Peanut butter I can do without. But where serious cooking is concerned, America's peanut dishes are simply not all that urbane. This, as opposed to the cuisines of several other nations.

The Indonesians do marvelous things with peanuts — mostly in sauces for things on skewers and the like. One of the greatest of Szechwan dishes is Kung Pao chicken, a stir-fried dish made with cubed chicken breasts, peanuts, and a hot chili sauce. It was named for Ting Kung Pao, a Chinese official who fled Szechwan as a political refugee a few hundred years ago during the Ching dynasty. I cannot vouch for the fact that the original dish contained peanuts, but at whatever century they were added to the dish it was a marvelous inspiration.

If one had to list America's greatest additions to peanut cookery, peanut brittle would probably lead the list. And there's one thing to be said for peanut soup. It's rich.

Pearl Tea

See Gunpowder tea.

Pease Pudding

Pease pudding is nothing more than a thick purée of split peas, either green or yellow, and is of English and Irish origin.

Quite often the peas were wrapped in a cloth bag and cooked along with various meats, including salt beef and corned or pickled pork. One volume of mine states that the Irish method, once the peas are cooked and turned into a purée, calls for beating in a whole egg to make the dish richer and creamier.

Pecans

Most Americans probably believe that pecans are as universal as grapes, but this is not true. Like corn on the cob, they are probably more American than apple pie. So it is amusing to read an English food dictionary's explanation of pecans: A pecan, this volume informs us, is "a thin-shelled, oblong nut . . . with a rich, nutty flavor, not unlike an extremely good walnut." The pecan tree, is in fact, a North American member of the walnut family and its name comes from the Algonquian *pakan*.

Pecans are said to have first flourished in this country in Oklahoma; from there they were introduced to Texas. Whatever their origin, pecans have a venerable and deserved popularity in many American foods, from the main course, as in poultry stuffing, to desserts, such as pecan pie and pecan ice cream.

There are several techniques for preparing freshly shelled pecan halves. They may be brushed lightly with oil or you may rub

a mixing bowl with oil and toss the nuts in the bowl until lightly coated. When coated, sprinkle lightly with salt.

The nuts may then be roasted slowly in an oven preheated to about 200 degrees. If you intend to roast the nuts, you may skip the oiling and wait until afterward, when they are spread out on a baking sheet. For each cup of nuts add about 1½ tablespoons of oil and stir to coat. Sprinkle lightly with salt and bake, stirring often for a uniform color, 10 to 15 minutes, or until golden brown.

The nuts may also be pan-fried. Drop the oiled nuts in a skillet, using about 2 tablespoons of hot oil for a cup of nuts. Cook, stirring constantly, for 2 to 3 minutes, or until delicately browned.

Or the nuts may be deep-fried. Put them into a frying basket and lower them into the hot oil to cover. Cook for 30 seconds to a minute, or until the nuts are delicately browned. Drain well. Drain further on absorbent toweling.

Pêche Melba

See Opera names in food.

Pelmeni

See Dumplings.

Penuche

Penuche is a creamy candy that belongs in the fudge category. There are many types of penuche, all with a brown sugar, milk or cream, butter, and vanilla base. There is a plain penuche, a coffee penuche, and even one made with chopped preserved ginger rather than nuts.

The name derives from the word *panocha* or *panucha,* a coarse and presumably brown sugar that is produced in Mexico.

Peppercorns

Green, black, and white peppercorns all come from the same vine, although they vary in flavor. The vine, *Piper nigrum,* at first produces underripe berries that have a green color. A certain amount of these are

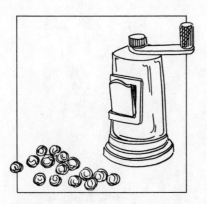

picked and preserved in several ways. They may be pickled in brine or wine vinegar, or they may be frozen or air-dried. These are green peppercorns.

As the berries age for a time on the vine they are harvested and dried. These are black peppercorns, which are said to be the world's most popular spice.

As the berries further mature they turn pink or red. At this point the skin of the berries is easily removed, usually by soaking in water. This leaves a light-colored inner kernel. When this is dried, it produces white peppercorns. Most sources state that white pepper is milder than black pepper, but I don't find this necessarily so.

White pepper is used by chefs in white sauces on the theory that it will not add black specks to the food as black pepper will. White pepper is used a good deal in Chinese cooking because of the flavor. It is a favored ingredient, for example, in hot and sour soup.

It is the pepper that contributes the hot flavor and not, as many people believe, hot chilies or chili oil.

Peppers

The hot pepper problem—which pepper is which—is one of the most confusing you encounter in international cookery. Not only are there so many kinds of peppers, but so many are available only at specific times of the year. And frequently the green-grocer himself can't identify one from another. I find that the long skinny fresh green and red peppers can substitute for any pepper in almost all recipes. These, fortunately, are widely available throughout the year in

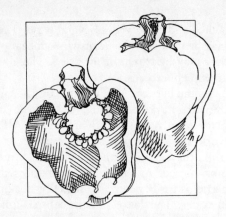

international markets, principally Chinese and Mexican. There is no way to tell whether a pepper is hot or mild by looking at it; often both hot and mild peppers are sold in the same batch. You can tell only by taste.

Sweet peppers, of course, are no problem, whether they are green, red, or yellow. These mild peppers are delicious roasted, and to do this they are usually turned over a gas burner, under the flame of a broiler, or over charcoal until the skin is burned. I prefer to cook them under a hot gas flame, keeping them four inches or so from it. You must turn them so that they are burned evenly. The moment they are cooked I toss them into an ordinary brown paper bag and let them steam until cool. I find that the skin is easily removed if the peppers are held under cold running water. Pat them dry.

I use a fair number of dried chili peppers because of my fondness for Mexican dishes, and to store them I keep them wrapped in plastic in the vegetable bin of the refrigerator. They are free from insect invasion and remain as moist as when they were bought.

In almost every case that I can think of, dried red pepper flakes can be substituted for whole dried hot red peppers. The pepper flakes are made, of course, by grinding the whole dried peppers. Their uses are the same, the major difference being that the pepper flakes would be distributed throughout a dish whereas the whole pepper pod could be removed from the soup or stew during or after the cooking.

Red pepper flakes, or crushed red pepper, seem to vary from producer to producer. Some of the flakes are smaller than others, some contain red pepper seeds and some do not. It is also true that the strength or hotness varies from jar to jar, but the only way to determine this is through use from batch to batch. The hottest I have found are Thai red pepper flakes, which are available in Oriental markets.

I generally keep a bunch of dried hot red peppers gathered together on stems. At times I crush these pods to make flakes and sometimes I use them whole.

Perche-Pierres

Perche-pierres, as it is known in French, is a plant that grows on sea cliffs and has a characteristically salty flavor. It is imported fresh from France and has recently become popular in several luxury restaurants across

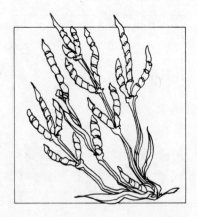

the nation. Perche-pierres is sometimes pickled and sometimes used raw in salads.

In English, it is called samphire, Peter's cress, sea fennel, glasswort, and chicken claws. It can be found in abundance on American shores, and a neighbor of mine in East Hampton said that she had "gathered and pickled the American substitute, which grows in the Accabonac marshes near my house and yours (and in other places nearby, I'm sure)."

Periwinkles

Periwinkles grow in abundance on rocky shores that border the sea. When boiled or steamed with aromatics, such as bay leaf or thyme, they are delicious but tedious to eat.

Authorities differ as to how long to cook the periwinkles. Cooking times vary from a few minutes to two hours or longer. I suspect that thirty minutes would be a happy medium.

The periwinkles, which resemble very small snails, vary in size. The meat is generally extracted from the shell by using a toothpick or even a sewing needle. They are generally served without sauce.

Pernod

See Pastis.

Perry

I am indebted to a woman who wrote: "There are books from the nineteenth century that refer to 'perry,' the pear equivalent of apple cider, and speak in glowing, almost rhapsodic terms. Perry seems to have been as or more popular than cider then. Why did the enthusiasm for perry disappear and is perry to be found at all today? Pear enthusiasts are almost as common as apple freaks, so why can't we go on to the cider equivalent?"

Quite frankly, I had never heard of such a drink, and it sent me thumbing through several dictionaries and encyclopedias.

The *Oxford English Dictionary* states that a perry is not only "a beverage resembling cider, made from the juice of pears expressed and fermented," but also "a pear tree; sometimes distinctively the wild pear tree."

The beverage perry is also described as

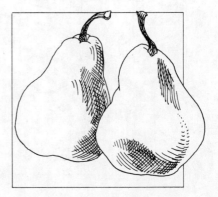

cider made from pears in American dictionaries.

A perry maker who dubs himself "Mr. Apples of High Falls, New York," wrote:

"We make pear cider every fall as the pears ripen in our orchard. It is one of the most successful items on the stand. We can only do it for two or three months, since our pears have a much shorter storage life than apples. I first heard of 'perry' from an English girl who once worked for us picking pears."

Pesto

When I first joined *The New York Times* a quarter of a century ago, pesto was almost unheard of in this country. Fresh basil and pine nuts were also novelties. Today, of course, fresh basil flourishes in gardens across the land and pine nuts have become almost as common as walnuts, although more expensive. The word "pesto" is related to pestle, and there are many Italian cooks who contend that a pesto can only be made properly with a mortar and pestle. I do not necessarily agree.

Judging by the number of inquiries I get about freezing pesto, it must be consumed all winter in many American homes. It does, indeed, freeze well, or can be kept in the refrigerator.

Prepare the pesto and spoon it into freezer containers (glass jars or plastic). Make sure there are no air bubbles. Spoon a little olive oil over the top and seal. The pesto, tightly sealed, will keep for several days or a few weeks in the refrigerator. As you use it, replenish the oil on top to prevent the sauce from coming in contact with air. If you freeze the pesto, leave half an inch of head space on top of the pesto before you cover it.

Peter's Cress

See Perche-pierres.

Pho

One of the great dishes of summer is, curiously enough, a hot soup of Vietnamese origin—elegant, humble, and eminently edible. It is essentially a summer dish in that its goodness is based, as with so many Vietnamese dishes, on fresh raw herbs. The basic herbs that I use are the ones generally available in America—fresh basil and fresh mint along with fresh coriander, usually obtainable throughout the year in Chinese and Spanish markets. Made with rice noodles, the soup is called *pho*. When served with chicken, it is called *pho ga;* with beef it is *pho bo.*

Phyllo Pastry

The wizardry of phyllo-making (phyllo is simply the Greek version of strudel) is in the preparation of a dough that is supple yet has so much holding power it can be rolled, then stretched using the backs of the hands over a broad surface until it has the texture of sheerest silk, a texture so fine even minute print can be read through it. Practiced phyllo-makers can toss and stretch a nine-foot square with dazzling virtuosity in less than a minute.

Commercially made phyllo pastry that is not hand-stretched is sometimes prepared by using a large metal disk that stretches the pastry as it revolves.

Ground rules—the basic ingredients, that is—for making phyllo vary from home to home, baker to baker. One formula consists simply of flour (9 to 10 pounds), salt (¼ pound), and water (about 3 quarts). Some recipes call for eggs, some for oil, or both.

Customarily the phyllo sheets, whether handmade or machine-made, measure about nineteen inches square when ready to be filled. Each sheet, the thickness of onion skin, must be brushed liberally with butter before filling. Sometimes two or more sheets are stacked before folding or rolling into a myriad of shapes. These include large and small triangles, squares, and cigarette and cigar shapes. When baked in the oven, the layers of pastry puff up and the finished pastry is crunchy to the bite.

Both the French and Greeks use the term "leaf" to describe their most delicate pastries. Thus, in French, the name for *pâte feuilletée,* or puff pastry, is derived from *feuille,* meaning leaf. Similarly *phyllo* (pronounced fee-low) is the Greek word for leaf.

Picadillo

There are some dishes in this world that are all but impossible to describe because their contents change from home to home and country to country. I would place picadillo (picadinho in Brazil) in this category, for I have never found two versions closely allied. The only ingredients that seem common to all picadillos are ground meat, tomatoes, and onions. Some versions include eggs and red wine, some raisins and vinegar, and so on. One of the most interesting picadillos I've ever eaten was served in a private house in San Antonio. It had been catered by the chef of the San Antonio Country Club, where the dish, apparently, is a specialty. In the hunting season, it is made with ground venison, but more commonly it is made with beef. The recipe also calls for, among other things, toasted almonds and chopped or sliced jalapeño peppers. The picadillo in Texas is frequently served as a dip with tortilla chips, although it is good served in a bowl like chili.

Pickled Lemons

There are many recipes for pickled lemons and limes. In each you can substitute one for the other. The commonest recipes call for making slits in the fruit without cutting them through. You add salt, which dissolves as it stands. The lemons or limes are left to stand for a considerable period before serving. In India, where pickled lemons and limes—called achar—are served sweet or hot, various spices are added, including cumin, chili pods, mustard seeds, fenugreek, and so on.

Pickled Walnuts

There are a few score meals that, over the years, have been ineradicably etched in my mind. Not the least of these was a breakfast served to me in a small hotel in Torquay, England, shortly after the Second World War. Rations were scarce, but somehow the owner had managed to find kippers and eggs, tomatoes, and the makings of toast. As a consequence I dined on the best broiled herring I ever dined on before or since, creamy scrambled eggs, and grilled tomatoes. Plus buttered toast, dark orange marmalade, and cups of scalding-hot English breakfast tea. The food was devastatingly good, and I was also offered a novelty in the form of pickled walnuts.

Now, I have eaten walnuts all my life. When I was a child, two giant black walnut trees flourished in the backyard and my mother was famous in the region where I grew up for a spectacularly delicious, outrageously rich black walnut cake. Of the young, undeveloped nuts, I recall that if you broke the smooth, shiny green skin, the fingers and hands would be smeared with a brownish stain, which, I was told, could be used as a dye. But unripe walnuts, pickled and destined to be eaten, were something new. And intriguing. They tasted faintly sweet. They had a rough exterior, more or less like that of freshly harvested, unbrushed truffles. And they were pitch black in color. They had a pleasant acid flavor and the trace of several spices.

Years later I learned that pickled walnuts, imported in bottles, are widely available in specialty food shops in this country, the most famous label being that of Crosse and Blackwell.

On a trip to the West Coast, I saw pickled walnuts for sale in several outdoor markets. There were baskets piled high with the plump, well-filled, green, unblemished skins.

For anyone who has access to black walnuts, there is a formula for pickling them in Mrs. Isabella Beeton's famed *Book of Household Management.*

I hasten to state that I have never followed this recipe, but for anyone who is curious, this is my edited version of how Mrs. Beeton recommends going about the process.

PICKLED WALNUTS

Procure 100 young walnuts. Be careful they are not woody. Prick them all over with a fork. Make a strong brine of salt and water (use about 4 pounds of salt to each gallon of water). Add the walnuts and let them remain in a cool place nine days, changing the brine each third day. Drain, pour them onto a dish and let stand in the sun until perfectly black. They should blacken within two or three days. Empty the walnuts into dry jars, but do not quite fill the jars. Bring enough vinegar to a boil to cover the walnuts when it is added. For each quart of vinegar, add 2 ounces of whole black peppercorns, 1 ounce of allspice and an ounce of bruised ginger. Add a few small peeled shallots, if desired. Pour the hot vinegar over the walnuts and add clean weights to each jar to make certain the walnuts are totally immersed with liquid. Let stand in a dry place. They will be ready to eat in one month and will keep in good condition for two to three years.

Pickle Liquid

The liquid in a pickle or olive jar becomes cloudy if you have removed the pickles or olives with your fingers. No matter how well you wash your hands and fingers there will still remain a trace of natural bacteria and even a trace can cause cloudiness in a pickling brine. Always remove pickles or olives with a clean fork, spoon, or knife.

As to using leftover juice from pickle jars, I must say that in my own kitchen I more often than not discard it. I well recall, however, that some years ago Lois Burpee, wife of the president of the well-known seed company, told me that she invariably included a bit of pickle juice in lieu of vinegar in her salads. She said her salads were usually praised and she attributed it to that one ingredient.

I know of no reason on earth why you could not substitute pickle liquid for vinegar in almost all recipes calling for vinegar.

Pickles

See Cornichons.

Pickling Spice

I seriously doubt that there is any economy in preparing your own pickling spice mix. By the time you buy boxes of all the spices, the cost would be exorbitant for most home spice shelves, and some of the spices, such as dried ginger, mace, and cardamom seeds, have only occasional uses.

I can give you a formula, however, that I have used. It calls for 1 teaspoon each of whole coriander seeds, cinnamon stick cracked into small pieces, and crushed black peppercorns, ½ teaspoon each of whole cloves, dried hot red pepper flakes, mustard seeds, crushed dried mace, and dill seed, 2 bruised cardamom seeds, 2 bay leaves broken into small pieces, and a piece of dried ginger chopped into small pieces.

Picnics

"And we meet with champagne and a chicken, at last." Those words were written by Lady Mary Wortley Montagu in England

in 1749. Now I have never read the works of Lady Mary Wortley Montagu. But I like that line and I have my own visions of the lady and her lover sitting in some ant-free, leafy, sun-dappled glade, munching on that cold roast bird between sips of a bottle of well-chilled brut.

That's because I am romantic by nature and I like marvelous trivia and that's what picnics are all about.

Until recently I've had the origin of the name picnic all wrong. I have always presumed that anything casual and trivial where food is concerned is uniquely American. It isn't true. It began with the French.

According to my redoubtable *Dictionnaire Etymologique de la Langue Française,* by O. Bloch and W. von Wartburg, the word *piquenique* came into the language in the late seventeenth century, notably in 1694. It comes from *picorer,* meaning to pick, peck, or scratch around for food, and *nique,* which in the old days meant something with little value, a trifle. Picnic, the work adds, crossed the Channel into England in about 1748.

According to Theodora FitzGibbon's *The Food of the Western World,* picnics were tremendously popular and elaborate affairs in nineteenth-century England. In that age,

a Picnic Society was formed in London, the members of which "supped at the Pantheon in Oxford Street and drew lots as to what part of the meal each should supply."

Of course, there are no set rules as to what qualifies an outdoor meal as a picnic. One food chronicler has recently defined a picnic as "any outing consisting of a sandwich, a blanket, two ants and a six-pack."

I have assisted (as the French say) at such an outing.

A picnic is what the cook and/or participants make it. It is true that almost any cold portable food is suitable for a picnic, plus quite a few dishes that may be grilled, whether it be beside a mountain stream, ocean, or bay, in the midst of a lush and verdant park, or simply at a parking/picnic area on the perimeter of a public highway.

Beside the basic or principal dishes—sandwiches, cold roast chicken, whatever—much thought should be given to incidentals.

There is nothing worse than wanting to bite into a hard-boiled egg, only to discover no one remembered the salt and pepper. Or how do you open that bottle of Montrachet, carefully chilled in that rivulet, when there isn't a corkscrew or a neighbor for miles around? What about kitchen knives to slice the onion or a clam knife to open those littlenecks freshly retrieved from the cold and salty bay nearby?

And what about lemons? Limes? Pickles? Horseradish, anyone? Tabasco? Worcestershire? A careful and thoughtful picnic planner will always produce napkins, be they in two-ply paper or double damask linen; and glasses, be they stemmed plastic or Waterford. Beer can openers, sardine can openers, buckets of ice. Knives, forks, plates, serving pieces, kitchen towels, both cotton and paper, charcoal and charcoal lighter, in addition to the grill to facilitate the proceedings.

And lots of large plastic bags for trash. A post-picnic cleanup is essential.

Pignoli

See Pine nuts.

Pilot Bread

See Hardtack.

Pineapple

Christopher Columbus is often credited with naming pineapples. He referred to them as the "pines of the Indies." For what it's worth, the pineapple is known in France as *ananas*. This derives from an American Indian word for the fruit. It is said that the South American Guarani Indians had a word for it, *nana,* meaning excellent fruit.

Pine Nuts

Pine nuts are, quite simply, the edible seeds of the pine tree. At times, during the "season," they may be purchased in the pine cone from which they derive. They first became commonly known in this country about twenty or so years ago when America discovered pesto sauce.

The most commonly used pine nuts are small, white, and oval in shape and resemble, to a degree, the shape of puffed rice. They are smooth and slightly oily in flavor and go by many names throughout the world.

American Indians and Mexicans refer to them as piñons, pignons, pignolas, Indian nuts, and stone nuts. Italians call them pignoli. I am told that they are also referred to as pinnochio. It is said that in medieval England they were referred to as pynotys. Pine nuts have countless uses. In addition to being an ingredient in pesto they are used in many other sauces, in soups, salads, main courses, and, of course, desserts.

According to a spokesman for the A.L. Bazzini Company, one of the country's largest importers and packers of nuts, pine nuts and Indian nuts are not the same.

"Both pine nuts and Indian nuts are from pine trees, but of different varieties," he said. "The nuts differ in shape, flavor and uses.

"Pine nuts (pignoli) are longer in shape, their flavor is more pronounced and a bit sweeter. Pine nuts also have a higher oil content. They also adhere better when added to things, such as cakes and cookies, when they bake. Pine nuts come from Italy and Spain.

"Indian nuts come from the American West and are harvested once a year. Indian nuts are much scarcer now than they were a few years ago because of the difficulty in finding someone to harvest them."

Pinhead Oatmeal

See Oats.

Pipérade

A pipérade, a specialty of the Basques, consists of cooking together sweet green or red peppers with tomatoes, onions, and garlic. Herbs, such as parsley and basil, may also be added. Eggs are broken into this mixture and cooked until thickened like scrambled eggs. The pipérade may be served from the pan or allowed to set on the bottom and turned out onto a platter.

Piping Hot

I frequently use the term "piping hot" in recipes and, to my mind, it is apt.

According to the *Oxford English Dictionary* the term means "so hot as to make a piping or hissing sound, as a simmering liquid, or a dish freshly cooked; hissing hot; hence generally very hot."

Pirog

There are many excellent dishes that can be attributed to the kitchens of Russia. Some of the best-known, of course, are borscht, blini, beef Stroganoff, and chicken Kiev. But one of my favorites is a baked filled pastry known as a pirog, particularly when it is prepared with an outer crust of brioche and stuffed with fillings ranging from salmon and dill to meat and mushrooms to mushrooms and eggs. Pirogi, for the record, differ from piroshki in that pirogi are of a substantial size, and piroshki, their cousins, are small enough to be consumed in one or two bites.

One of the best explanations of the names, and differences, of the two is to be found in the *Russian Tea Room Cookbook,* by Faith Stewart-Gordon and Nika Hazelton: "The word *pir* in Russian means feast, thus pirog (plural, pirogi) and pirojok (plu-

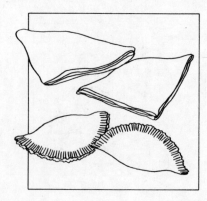

ral, piroshki) are two versions of a versatile pastry with many uses and many kinds of fillings."

Piroshki—best made with a rich, sour-cream pastry—are usually served with soup: a rich clear beef broth, borscht, cabbage, or sauerkraut soup, and so on.

Pistachio

If pistachio is not the most lyrical word in the cook's vocabulary, it is one of the nicest ingredients in the cook's cupboard. For those who wonder about such things, the origin of the word is Persian. It derives from *pistah,* which means simply nut, and was dubbed "pistachio" by the Italians.

Although shelled pistachios have a greenish tinge on the outside and yellow meat within, the green color of pistachio ice cream is an added color, probably a vegetable dye. The same is true of most peppermint stick ice cream; a few drops of red are added to give it the distinctive color.

Pithiviers

Pithiviers is made with two rounds of puff pastry or flaky pastry. One circle of dough is placed on a baking sheet and the center is covered with an almond pastry cream. The other circle is placed on top and the pastry layers are sealed around the edge with beaten egg. The cake is baked and is best served warm.

The name derives from the town of Pithiviers just south of Paris, where the dessert is a great specialty.

Plantain

Plantains are a popular "vegetable" in the Caribbean Islands and Central America, where they are known as plantanos, the accent on the first syllable. They are sometimes referred to as cooking bananas, and they have numerous uses in the kitchen both as a cooked dessert and in baked savory dishes. They can be candied, cooked in syrup, or baked alone or with cheese and meat.

Pletzel

Evelyn Rose's book, *The Complete International Jewish Cookbook,* has a recipe for pletzel, which she refers to as dimple rolls.

The base is challah dough made with yeast, eggs, flour, and a touch of sugar. You take a piece of this dough about the size of an apple, place it on a tray to rise until doubled in bulk, then press your fingers into it to make a dimple. You brush with an egg wash and sprinkle with poppy or sesame seeds before baking until brown.

Pleurotes

Pleurotes are mushrooms that are becoming increasingly available in America; they have long been harvested in France. They come in diverse shapes, most of them varying in length from one to four inches. They are grayish-brown and white in color and have a rough top. They generally come in clusters. They are quite spongy and are excellent if bland in flavor.

Pojarski

Once upon a time, according to legend, there was a small and prosperous town between Moscow and St. Petersburg called Torjok. Travelers changed horses there. And in the town was a tavern. The tavernkeeper was named Pojarski, and if the dishes that bear his name today are an index of his talents, he must have been an extraordinary chef as well as host. The specialties of the house of Pojarski were ground meat dishes, more often than not made of a game or a blend of game and beef. Today in French gastronomy, there is an assortment of dishes called Pojarski, including one with salmon. It is made with ground salmon, shaped like a pork chop, breaded, browned, and served with a brown butter sauce. This is food for the tsars.

Polenta

There are three foods of consummate goodness that may be served either as a main course or a side dish in the Italian kitchen. These are pasta, rice in the form of risotto, and polenta. Of the three, polenta, which is infinite in its variations, is relatively and regrettably little known and appreciated in this country.

In its most basic form, polenta is very much like the cornmeal mush of the American South. Stretching a point a bit, Philadelphia scrapple made with pork and liver and cornmeal could be called a kind of polenta. And polenta is very much akin to mamaliga, a specialty of Rumania.

The cooking of polenta is simplicity itself, but it can't be hurried. The cornmeal must be cooked for a minimum of forty-five minutes (as opposed to American cornmeal mush, which is cooked for ten to fifteen minutes) to as much as two and a half hours.

The excellence, I might say the irresistibility, of polenta is like that of pasta. In itself it is more or less neutral in flavor and depends for its goodness on the sauce or dish that accompanies it. Because of its neutral character, the polenta steps up the flavor of its sauces.

Basically there are four ways in which polenta is served:

Traditionally and family style, it is turned out, once cooked and boiling hot, preferably onto a wooden board. Traditionally the board is made of poplar. The polenta can then be cut with a string. Or it can be spooned and scraped onto a serving dish. A sauce is spooned over and diners dig in with a fork or spoon.

Or a portion of the cooked polenta can be spooned into a baking dish and baked with cheese. The simplest version of this (also admired in French kitchens) is to allow the polenta to cool, cut it into fancy shapes (rounds, crescents, and so on) and arrange the shapes on a baking dish. This is sprinkled with grated Parmesan cheese, melted butter is poured over, and it is baked until golden brown.

Or it can be served piping hot as a side dish like mashed potatoes.

Or the polenta may be left briefly (it becomes soft-firm within a short while) and sliced to serve like bread.

There is one easily avoided pitfall in cooking polenta. In the initial step, the cornmeal is poured into vigorously boiling water. It is imperative that the cornmeal be stirred rapidly into the water, preferably with a wire whisk. Otherwise it will form lumps and you're in trouble.

As a precautionary measure, the producers of cornmeal in America recommend that you bring 3 cups of water to the boil. They suggest that you blend 1 cup of cornmeal with 1 cup of cold water, then stir this into the boiling water.

Experienced practitioners of polenta cookery recommend that it be stirred, once the cornmeal is added, with a stick. I use a 16-inch-long, 1-inch-thick rolling pin for this. A sawed-off handle of a broom would do, or, instead of a stick, you can use a heavy wooden spatula to stir.

The polenta must be stirred at frequent intervals, making certain that the stirring rod covers the bottom of the cooking vessel. A crust will probably form on the bottom of the utensil. The theory is that the longer you cook polenta the better it becomes.

A final word: Polenta at its most traditional should be cooked in an unlined copper pot known as a *paiolo*.

Polonaise

There is nothing mysterious to relate about the name polonaise. It means simply Polish

style. It consists of serving vegetables—principally cauliflower and asparagus—with a garnish of melted butter cooked until foamy and almost brown with chopped hard-boiled egg, bread crumbs, and chopped parsley added.

Pomegranate

The pomegranate is one of the most aptly named of all fruits, for pomegranate translates as "an apple with many seeds." If you ask a dozen experts about the proper way to eat the fruit, you will probably receive as many varied answers.

As far as I am concerned, there is no fastidious way of eating a pomegranate out of the hand. You simply outfit yourself with a set of clean napkins, one tucked into your collar to act as a bib, and use a knife or fingers to cut or break the tough outer skin.

Some people recommend cutting the fruit in half and scooping out the seeds with a spoon, but I find that as foolish as it is precious. To attack a pomegranate properly, you must throw decorum to the wind and cut or break it into pieces. You then simply dig your teeth into the juicy seeded insides

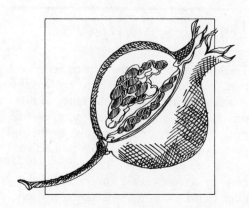

and crunch away. Dribble you will, which is why my appetite for pomegranates is about one per annum.

Pomegranates have certainly been around long enough for someone to have established a tidy technique for attacking them. They are mentioned in Homer and the Bible and are part of the legend of Persephone. Myth has it that this nubile creature was hauled off to Hades by Pluto and was lured into his trap by eating a pomegranate.

Pomegranates seem to thrive in almost all the world's climates. I have seen marvelous pomegranate trees flourishing in the Forbidden City of China. And the uses of pomegranates are many in the world of cookery.

In Mexico, they dine on an uncommonly tasty creation called *chiles en nogada.* This consists of chiles poblanos stuffed with a meat filling known as picadillo. You prepare a sauce of walnuts and sour cream, a touch of sugar and cinnamon, and spoon over the stuffed chilies. On top of this you sprinkle the seeds of one small pomegranate.

There is a traditional Persian soup made of lamb shanks, split peas, beets, spinach, fresh coriander leaves, and rice, plus pomegranate juice. *See also* Grenadine.

Pommes Soufflées

There is one dish in the French repertory that, more than most, seems to fire the imagination and capture the fancy of non-professionals—*pommes soufflées,* or soufflé potatoes, those crisp, hollow, zeppelin-shaped oddities served hot from the kitchen.

It is said that soufflé potatoes came about quite by accident in the kitchen of the Pavillon Henri IV in Saint-Germain-en-Laye,

that splendid small suburb of Paris. The story goes that when the chef got word that a trainload of dignitaries was en route from Paris to the restaurant, he tossed some potatoes into a kettle of hot fat. Moments later, word came that the train was delayed. The chef quickly removed the partly-cooked potatoes and drained them. When the guests finally were assembled, he gave the potatoes a second frying—*voilà! pommes soufflées.*

The oil for the first cooking should be at a relatively low temperature, and high for the second.

Poor Knights of Windsor

See French toast.

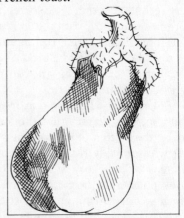

Poor Man's Caviar

Over the years, I have been served a dozen baked or broiled and mashed eggplant dishes that have been referred to as poor man's caviar. The reference is to the eggplant seeds, which in theory resemble tiny grains of caviar. It is possible that the origin of the dish is Greek, known as mel-intzanosalata.

To prepare it, the eggplant is cooked in the skin in a very hot oven, over charcoal, or over a flame until it is collapsed and until the skin takes on a slightly burned or smoky taste. The pulp is chopped and to this are added diced tomatoes, finely chopped onion, lemon juice, olive oil, and chopped parsley.

Variations on the dish have included tahini or sesame paste, chopped anchovies, capers, and even mustard.

Popcorn

I have always said that there is no subject that has not already been treated in depth in a cookbook. And would you believe there is a cookbook dedicated to popcorn. It is called *Cornzapoppin'!* by Barbara Williams. I turned to that for an answer to the question of whether popcorn is made from regular sweet corn, and I quote:

"Many people assume that popcorn is regular sweet corn which has been treated in some way to make it pop. Actually, there are three main varieties of corn—sweet corn, which is the kind you eat as a vegetable for dinner; field corn, which is the kind grown as feed for hogs and cattle; and popcorn, which is the favorite snack food of most Americans. Of the three kinds of corn, popcorn is the only one that bursts into a delicious white morsel when exposed to high heat. Scientists assume that the popping process results from a combination of the hard shell and the internal moisture of the popcorn kernel.

"Most of the world's popcorn is grown in the midwestern part of the United States—principally in Nebraska, Iowa and Indiana, where it can get mighty hot in the summer. Old-timers tell of one particular summer when it got so hot the corn in the fields started popping right off the stalks. The cows and pigs thought it was a snow blizzard and they lay down and froze to death."

Poppy Seeds

A correspondent asked if I could tell her why recipes call for "twice-ground" poppy seeds as fillings for various pastries.

I allowed that it was a bit of foolish and unnecessary terminology, adding that a proper instruction would be poppy seeds ground as finely as possible. I added (another educated guess) that if I wished to grind poppy seeds as finely as possible, I would use my small, handy, multipurpose electric coffee- or spice-grinder, the one that is much used for grinding spices such as quantities of black pepper, coriander seeds, cumin seeds, and so on.

But I was wrong. Marshall Neale, long

associated with the American Spice Trade Association, notes: "Our experience has been that poppy seeds have too high an oil content to grind satisfactorily in gadgets used for the other spices. This is the reason there is a special grinder—a tool often present in Middle European homes where poppy seed fillings are frequently made.

"Also, there is an excellent prepared poppy filling for such baked goods, which is nothing more than ground poppy seeds and honey (the sweetening most often called for in poppy fillings)."

Pork Rind

See Cracklings.

Possum

When I was a child, possum was occasionally cooked in my mother's kitchen. The skinned and cleaned animal was simmered until tender, then drained, rolled in seasoned flour, and roasted until glazed and nicely browned. It was almost invariably served with yams or baked sweet potatoes.

"Treeing a possum" was considered great sport by southern menfolk. A spirited description of this activity is found in *The Savannah Cook Book* by Harriet Ross Colquitt.

When you tree the possum (with the help of lanterns and hounds), you may see "a piece of Spanish moss, which you mistake as your prize, or a bunch of mistletoe may deceive you," the author explains, "but suddenly two bright eyes burn from a silent mass and you know you have him in your reach. A possum will never move and when once you catch his gleaming eye, it is all up with him and in short order he is dropped safely into a crocus sack and headed for home."

The author recommended that if the possum is taken alive, it be pen-fed for two weeks on milk, bread, and persimmons before cooking. By the way, a crocus sack, sometimes called a croker sack, is made of burlap.

Potage Esau

Chefs, like other men, amuse themselves, and the man who gave lentil soup the name that has appeared on French menus for generations must have been pleasantly amused. It is potage Esau (pronounced aze-ah-ue in French). An obvious name, and there is a bit of sophistication in its naïveté.

I dusted off the Old Testament and can now quote chapter and verse.

"Then Jacob gave Esau bread and pottage of lentils; and he did eat and drink, and rose up, and went his way . . ." Genesis, XXV:34.

Potatoes

Perhaps because of the universal liking for potatoes, there has always been a good deal of elaboration in my books and elsewhere about the care and cooking thereof, as well as about the nomenclature of potato dishes.

As a matter of culinary license, potatoes that have been cooked in water are frequently listed on menus as steamed potatoes, if for no better reason than that

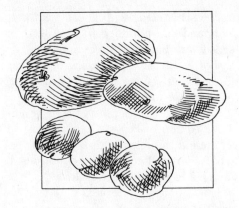

steamed potatoes sounds more stylish than boiled potatoes.

I received an amusing note about this from a gentleman who stayed at a resort hotel on the Belgian coast when he was a child before the Second World War. "We were served boiled (steamed) potatoes *every* day" and each day they were given a different appellation. "The names," he recalled, "were as follows: pommes vapeur, pommes maison, pommes au beurre, pommes persilleés, pommes bouilliés, pommes nature, and pommes anglaise."

Incidentally, it has been determined that the greenish cast found on some potatoes is harmless and that the color is determined by chlorophyll that forms when they are exposed to artificial light. There is no difference in flavor and nutrition between potatoes with a greenish cast and those without it. *See also* French fries, Parmentier, Pommes soufflées.

Pot Cheese

See Cottage cheese.

Potted Foods

Potted foods are quite common in British cookery. I presume, logically I hope, that potted foods are so-called because they were originally and often still are served in small pots or crocks. Potted salmon and other fish are first skinned, boned, and cooked. They are then put in a crock or other container and covered with clarified butter. Perhaps the most famous of Britain's potted foods are shrimp. These, too, are covered with butter and eaten cold with hot toast.

Poulette

A poulette sauce is a delicate cream sauce, enriched with yolks and flavored with lemon juice. It is strongly reminiscent of the sauce for a fricassee of poulet, or chicken. Poulette is the diminutive of poulet.

Pousse-Café

Pousse-café was a drink much admired in fancy bars, but I doubt that there are very many bartenders today who could describe it in detail. It consisted of several liqueurs in rainbow colors that were poured into a very small glass. The important thing in preparing the drink was to understand the specific gravity of each liqueur before adding them. When properly added, the liqueurs did not blend but rather remained in bright layers.

Here is one version, the liqueurs to be added in the precise order in which they are listed. Pour one part of each of the following into a glass the size of a double or triple thimble: grenadine syrup, yellow Chartreuse, crème d'Yvette, white crème de menthe, green Chartreuse, and Cognac.

Poussins

French chefs and many serious home cooks often lament the fact that here they are unable to find the small poussins, or young chickens, that are so widely available in the markets of France. Poussins differ from just any young chickens in that they have reached maturity and developed flavor, yet they generally weigh only about one pound. On rare occasions, one can buy these little chickens in rural areas where poultry farms exist. An excellent substitute for the small bird, however, is the Rock Cornish game hen, which is said to be a cross between a White Rock and a Cornish game bird. The word "game," in the case of these hens, has long since lost its meaning, for the chickens do not smack in the least of a wild bird. Nonetheless, they are a delicacy and are remarkably easy to prepare. One unstuffed bird, roasted or grilled, will serve one. When filled with a meat stuffing, one bird will suffice for two servings.

Powdered Goose

Once, a while back, an entry in the diaries of Samuel Pepys, dated January 1, 1667, was pointed out to me. In it he wrote, "Home to dinner, where the best powdered goose that ever I eat . . ." was served. I was fascinated and puzzled and conjectured that what he had in mind was, perhaps, potted

goose. This is made with goose meat that is chopped and pounded to a paste then blended with butter and seasonings.

I shortly learned that I was wrong. I was informed by a gentleman from Glen Head, New York, as follows:

"According to the glossary in the eleven-volume edition of Pepys' Diary, published over the past fourteen years by the University of California Press, the word 'powdered' as applied to meats means 'salted.'

"This definition is borne out by the *Oxford Dictionary*, which defines 'powdered' in its earlier meanings as: 'Preserved; cured; corned.' *Webster's New International Dictionary* (Second Edition), which qualified the definition as now being Scottish or Dialect English, says that 'powdered' means: 'Spiced; seasoned; also, pickled; preserved; corned.'

"Pepys, incidentally, did not wait until New Year's Day of 1667 for eating powdered meat. His entry for January 4, 1663 says: 'And so home to dinner to a good piece of powdered beef, but a little too salt.' "

Salted goose, incidentally, is a staple of traditional French cookery in which it is known as confit d'oie. It is often added to cassoulets.

Prawns

The use of the words "prawn" and "shrimp" on American menus seems to have been a puzzlement to native restaurant goers for more years than I can count.

In *The Encyclopedia of Fish Cookery*, A.J. McClane states that "prawns differ from shrimp in having more slender abdomens and longer legs but the names are used synonymously in commercial trade."

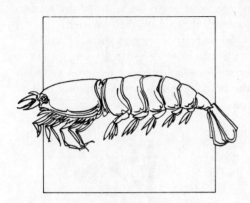

It is my considered opinion that in America, prawns, when mentioned on a menu, simply refer, correctly or not, to large shrimp that are cooked in olive oil with finely chopped garlic and served sprinkled with chopped fresh parsley.

Preserved Eggs

See Hundred-year eggs.

Preserved Goose

See Confit d'oie.

Prickly Pears

Prickly pears, also known as the Indian pear, the India fig, the Barbary fig, and the tuna fig, are the spiny fig of the cactus plant. Removing the prickly skin of the fruit can be a chore, but not so much as to deter those who enjoy the sweet succulent flesh inside.

First, make one long lengthwise cut down the side of the pear. Proceed then as for an avocado, removing the skin in long slices. It is usually eaten raw as a dessert.

For what it's worth, the Israeli word for prickly pear is *sabra*, a name that is applied to native-born Israelis because, "like the prickly pear, they are tough on the outside and soft and pleasant on the inside."

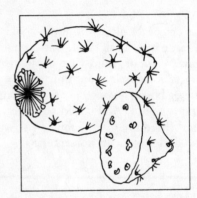

Princess Margaret

See Cordon bleu.

Prosciutto

See Parma ham.

Provençale

Dishes named provençale generally contain or are served with a sauce made with tomatoes and garlic. The name means, of course, in the style of Provence.

The kinds of foods that may be cooked provençale style are seemingly endless and include scallops, snails, blowfish (chicken of the sea), and so on. The foods are generally cooked in oil—olive oil, primarily—before the sauce is added.

Ptcha

Ptcha is one of the glories of Jewish cooking. I have made it with calf's feet, water, onions, bay leaves, a lot of garlic, vinegar, and lemon juice. You cook it about four hours and remove the bones, leaving only the meat and gelatinous liquid. Add sliced hard-boiled eggs and sliced onion and chill. Dust with paprika and serve with horseradish.

Pullman Loaf

The name Pullman, usually capitalized as the trademark for railroad parlor and sleeping cars invented in the nineteenth century by George M. Pullman, may have been given to the loaf because bread of this type was common on dining cars. It is a square loaf frequently used for sandwiches and usually baked in a lidded or covered pan so it will retain its shape.

Pumpernickel

Pumpernickel is a type of rye bread. The color derives from the rye flour or rye meal used in its preparation; indeed, the flour or meal is sometimes referred to as pumpernickel flour. There are gradations in color

of rye flours, and the color of the finished loaf will depend on the one used.

Some recipes for pumpernickel call for a small quantity of molasses and this, too, contributes color to the dough. Originally, the bread was made in Westphalia in Germany.

Pumpkin

The best pumpkins to be used for cooking are the small ones, three to four pounds and about the size of a good-sized cantaloupe. Large pumpkins are full of fibers.

When ready to cook, cut around and discard the stem. Cut the pumpkin into eighths. Scoop away and discard the seeds and fibers from the pumpkin pieces. Place the unpeeled pumpkin pieces in the top of a steamer large enough to hold them. Cover and steam over boiling water for about fifteen minutes, or until the pumpkin flesh is tender.

Remove the pumpkin and let it cool. When cool enough to handle, scrape the flesh from the outer peel. Discard the peel. Blend the flesh, using a food processor or blender, or put it through a ricer.

Pytt i Panna

Pytt i panna, which means small things (pytt) cooked in a frying pan (i panna), is a simple but excellent Swedish dish. Cook chopped onions until golden brown and remove; brown diced cooked potatoes in the same skillet and an equal portion of diced leftover meat, such as beef or veal. Blend the ingredients and serve garnished with chopped sour pickles and, if desired, fried eggs.

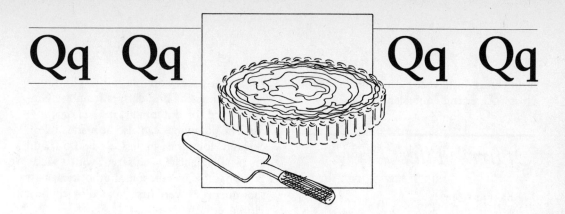

Quadretti

Quadretti are tiny squares of pasta, and they are sold on supermarket shelves in this country as egg noodle "flakes." It is possible that they are also imported as quadretti, but I have never found them. One of the best soups I have had in Rome combined quadretti and chicken livers in a rich chicken broth.

Quagliette di Vitello

See Birds.

Quahogs

See Clams.

Quaking Custard

A quaking custard is made with milk, eggs, and sugar and cooked until thickened. Softened gelatin is added and whipped cream and beaten egg whites are folded in when the mixture cools. The mixture is then poured into a mold and chilled until firm. When the custard is turned out of the mold, it will "quake" if shaken. It is very much like a Bavarian cream dessert.

Quark

Quark is a white German cheese prepared, up to a point, like cottage cheese, for which semisolid milk is drained to separate the curd (the cottage cheese) from the whey. Quark is made with both the whey and the curd. The whey proteins add nutritional value. Cottage cheese includes a lactic culture that is not present in quark, so there is

351

a difference in flavor. Farmer cheese is the closest American equivalent.

Quarry Tiles

See Baking stones.

Quatre-Épices

There is reputedly a tree of African origin whose fruit has an odor that resembles a blend of four spices, or quatre-épices. There is also a blend of spices sold under this name and available in so-called gourmet shops. The blend includes ground white pepper, grated nutmeg, powdered cloves, and dried ginger.

Quenelle

The best known and most fashionable quenelle is that made with fish of one sort or

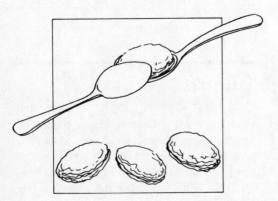

another—pike, sole, salmon. The name means dumpling and derives from the German word for dumplings, *knödel* or *knoedel*. The dumplings can also be made of veal, chicken, foie gras, giblets, and so on, and are usually poached and served with a sauce. For what it is worth, some authorities insist that quenelles were first created by chefs in Florence, Italy.

Pierre Franey tells me that any American pike—Great Northern, pickerel, walleye—can be used to prepare quenelles. Great Northern is what is used in France, he says.

Quetsche

Quetsche is the name of a large oval blue plum, the best known of which is harvested in Alsace-Lorraine. Its finest uses are as an ingredient in pies or tarts and in a white eau-de-vie or spirit.

Quiche

Quiche comes from the Alsatian-German word *kuche,* meaning a kind of cake. Originally, before quiches soared in popularity over the last fifteen years or so, it was a simple custard pie made with cheese, bacon, eggs, and cream, the top dotted with butter and baked. Today, of course, the repertoire of quiche dishes or "inventions" is seemingly limitless. Quiches are made with almost anything edible that comes from the garden, including zucchini and tomatoes. Most of these new creations are a far cry from Lorraine, or Alsace, for that matter.

Rabbit

When it comes to the absolute enjoyment of certain foods, it is not a mere figure of speech to say that there is more than a gulf of difference in taste. In one case—rabbit—it is the entire Atlantic Ocean.

For centuries, rabbit and hare have been a coveted, much treasured part of the diet of epicures and civilized bon vivants throughout Europe. It would be hard to conceive of the French kitchen without its *civets de lapin* and its *pâtés de lièvre*. The Italian *cucina* would be a far poorer place but for the likes of its *cogniglio alla cacciatora* or *pappardelle con la lepre*. Deprive a Spanish chef of his *conejo en pepitoría* or a Greek gastronome of his *lagos stin salmi* and they're apt to man the kitchen barricades.

Despite the sometime American preoccupation with nutrition, it has not penetrated the public consciousness that rabbit is one of the most nutritionally perfect of meats. It has one-third fewer calories than a boneless sirloin of beef, more protein than chicken or beef, and a potassium content of 1,379 milligrams per pound. That's high.

The uses of rabbit are legion. There is no chicken preparation that could not be put to good use with rabbit as a substitute. It is equally versatile as a substitute for pork, beef, or veal. I had occasion to talk with Glenn Van Bramer, director of the Richmond Market Gardening Center of Pleasant Valley, New York. The center is a nonprofit organization that would encourage family-style, small-scale suburban agriculture.

He said the best rabbits for home raising include New Zealand white, Flemish giant, and the California breed. He explained the differences between rabbits and hares:

"Most people think that hares are wild, which isn't true. The Belgian hare is great for breeding in captivity. The difference is that the young of a rabbit are born furless, eyes closed, and helpless. A hare is born with fur on, eyes open, and ready to run."

Such phrases as "breeds like a rabbit" and the notion that rabbits are always in heat are not based entirely on fact. "The basis for this," Mr. Van Bramer said, "is that female rabbits are always fertile. They can literally kindle a litter and rebreed on the day following. In addition to which the gestation period is only thirty-one days, which is a little hard for mom."

In breeding rabbits, he continued, there is not, as with most animals, a cycle or season that has to be followed.

Rabbits are ready to eat when they are

about eight weeks old. At that age they are just right for frying or sautéing. When they are twelve to fourteen weeks old, they are good for roasting. Older than that, up to a year, they are good for stews, ragouts, and the like.

Mr. Van Bramer ascribes the American squeamishness toward eating rabbit to what he calls the Easter Bunny syndrome. "The American public can't stand eating anything they might have given a name to or something they've fondled as a pet."

He adds that this extends even to those who grow and eat rabbits once they have reached maturity. He says that many friends of his who grow rabbits will kill a batch of them and put them in the freezer before cooking.

"The freezing, they feel," Mr. Van Bramer said, "puts a certain distance between them and the rabbit and when, a few weeks after freezing, they pick out a rabbit to defrost for cooking, they don't remember which it was."

Mr. Van Bramer has a considerable library on rabbit cookery, rabbit culture, and rabbit lore. One book, *The Rabbit Fancier,* by C. N. Bement, is dated 1855. In it there are recipes for boiled rabbit smothered with onion sauce, roast curried rabbit, and stewed rabbit. A section on French ways of cooking rabbit includes a rabbit marinade, a gibelotte or stew of rabbit, rabbit pâtés, and a civet of rabbit.

The largest producer of rabbits for the nation's kitchen is the Pel-freez Company in Rogers, Arkansas. It sells more than two million pounds of ready-to-cook rabbit each year. There are several smaller rabbit-producing companies on the West Coast.

I spoke with Paul Dubell, the owner of Pel-freez and a native Californian. He said his family had been in the rabbit business since 1911, when his father opened a small enterprise in Los Angeles. I asked him who, in his opinion, were the people who were buying his product.

"Mostly ethnic groups," he said, including immigrants and children and grandchildren of immigrants, people who came to this country from such places as Italy, Spain, France, Germany, and so on, and that most of them live in the northern and eastern part of the country.

Mr. Dubell said that his market is expanding each year—some 20 to 30 percent annually. "The more people travel in Europe and sample rabbit or hare on menus, the more they are aware of its goodness and potential," he said, adding that a good many people discover rabbit in the military. His concern sells several hundred thousand pounds of rabbit each year to the Army and Navy.

His merchandising plans include encouraging chefs of what he terms "white cloth" restaurants to put rabbit on menus; this, in turn, educates the public to a different meat for home menus. Most Americans, he said, have never been exposed to the dish in any form.

Yet, next to chicken, rabbit is one of the least expensive meats. If the demand were increased, industry spokesmen say, the cost would decline enormously.

Raclette

When I recall my first encounters with the good things of the Swiss table, my mind fairly aches and reels with nostalgia and pleasure.

I remember my first sampling of deep-fried fresh perch and truite au bleu, the perch and the trout taken from the then crystal-clear waters of Lac Leman (or, as the English would have it, Lake Geneva). There were platters of fine-textured and slightly salted, wind-dried beef from the Grisons and my first taste of a kirsch-perfumed genuine fondue made with a full-bodied, nutty-flavored Gruyère cheese. At the same time I discovered another cheese dish that had, perhaps, an even greater impact on my gastronomic sensibilities and the dish was called raclette.

It was in my student days then and, when cold weather came on, it was my pleasure and persuasion to visit what is called in the French-speaking canton of Valais, a carnotzet, of which there were several. A carnotzet originally was the sampling room of a cellar, situated in front of the wine storage area. Gradually it came to be a place where one sampled both wine and cheese dishes as well. A typical carnotzet has steps leading down into a room, generally quite small, with walls sketched with Swiss scenes— mountains, ski slopes, ski lifts, chalets, Saint Bernard dogs, wine casks, and Swiss cheese in numerous shapes.

There were three sorts of dishes served in the carnotzets I visited: the Grisons beef (called viande sechée in French, bündnerfleish in German), served as the preface to the others; fondues; and the raclette, which I consider the most interesting and certainly the most festive of cold-weather foods.

The name raclette stems from the French word *racler,* which means to scrape. The name is applied to the cheese dish because of the traditional technique for serving it. Originally half a wheel of a cheese known as bagnes, or raclette cheese, was placed before a blazing wood fire and, as the surface of the cheese melted, it was scraped onto a small plate to be eaten along with small boiled potatoes in the skin, small sour pickles, known as cornichons, and small pickled cocktail onions. Plus a loaf of crusty bread, a glass of dry white Swiss wine or, perhaps, a glass of kirschwasser. And a pepper mill on the side to give the dish added zest.

This outdoor technique, which still exists in some areas in Switzerland, was modified for the carnotzets. The wood fire was replaced by a perpendicular charcoal brazier with the cheese placed in an upright position close to the heat to melt it. It was served with the traditional accompaniments on small plates. It almost goes without saying that one scraping would scarcely make a meal and thus during the course of an hour numerous plates would stack up before the customer. The customer would be charged according to the number of plates.

The possibility of serving raclette in the home has materialized in America within very recent memory. A short while ago, bagnes or raclette cheese was all but unheard of here. I was delighted during the course of a visit in the home of Heidi Hagman (at the time she was called "the barefoot caterer of California"), who is Mary Martin's granddaughter, to be served a genuine raclette party at her hands. Her hands, that is to say, preparing and scraping the cheese for the guests.

Not only was the cheese available to her in half wheels, but she had at her disposal an electric machine for melting the cheese. Both the cheese and that machine are widely available in the New York area. The machine consists of a solid base plus a swinging arm containing an infrared lamp for heating the surface of the cheese. Half a wheel or a quarter of a wheel of raclette cheese is placed between clamps to hold it securely. The heating arm is swung directly over and parallel to the surface of the cheese, which it heats to bubbling. The arm is swung away and the cheese is scraped onto small hot plates.

Later I was introduced to a much simplified, much less costly and admirable raclette "oven" imported from Switzerland and widely available here. It consists of a round enameled cover that houses a round electric heating coil. There are four small pans designed to be filled with squares of cheese and situated for heating directly under the hot coil. Four pans will serve for a party of two. It is best (in the interest of uninterrupted dining) to have eight pans for a party of four so that you can eat and heat simultaneously.

I was fascinated to learn from the chef at the Swiss Embassy in Washington that these small electric cookers are now used at the embassy when they serve raclette.

In that raclette is a specialty of the Valais region of Switzerland, the best wine to serve with it is a white wine of the same region. That is a Fendant. On the other hand, any very good, light dry white wine would be excellent. If you wish to give a bit of a kick to the party, you might also serve a few small glasses of kirschwasser at room tem-perature. Beer would also not be amiss. The traditional dessert for the dish is assorted cut fruits and berries tossed with sugar and chilled, or, perhaps, a fruit tart.

Radicchio

Radicchio is becoming increasingly available and, therefore, increasingly popular. A form of wild chicory, it is most commonly associated with Italy's Veneto region, where one version is referred to as red treviso, Treviso being the name of a town north of Venice. I find radicchio to be one of the finest of salad ingredients. Shaped somewhat like a small cabbage but with tender red leaves and white stalks and veins, it adds a delicately bitter taste to a salad. Its texture is a bit firmer than that of Boston lettuce.

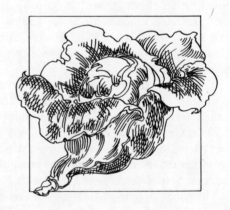

Raie au Beurre Noire

See Skate.

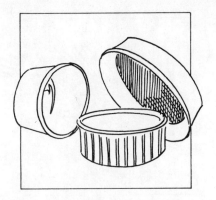

Ramequin

A ramequin means two things. It is often applied to small tarts or tartlets, generally with a custard or cheese filling. A small, baked, open-face cheese pie is called a ramequin au fromage. The name is also applied to small individual baking dishes, usually in terra-cotta.

Ramos Gin Fizz

For a recipe for Ramos gin fizz, I turned to *The New Orleans Restaurant Cookbook* in which Deirdre Stanforth writes that "this delightful drink was invented by Henry C. Ramos, who came to New Orleans in 1888." He operated a saloon on the same site as the Roosevelt Hotel (now the Fairmont). To prepare a Ramos, combine in the bottom of a cocktail shaker 2 tablespoons of powdered sugar, the juice of ½ lemon and ½ lime, 1 teaspoon of orange flower water, an egg white, 1½ ounces of gin, and 2 tablespoons of heavy cream. Add a good

quantity of crushed ice and shake for 2 to 3 minutes. Strain into an 8-ounce glass and add 1½ ounces of club soda or seltzer.

Ramp

Almost annually there are new accounts of ramp, which grows wild in many parts of America. In all probability it is most closely associated with North Carolina, for that state has an annual convention of the "North Carolina Friends of the Ramp."

The ramp is said to have its ardent fanciers and its equally vociferous opponents, who declare it to be an "abominable cross of onion and garlic with the worst features of both."

The vegetable is eaten both raw and cooked. Some uses for it, when chopped, are in meat loaves and scrambled eggs. Ramp is eaten raw in the South with barbecues and fried ham. The ramp is most often referred to as a wild leek. It does resemble a scallion.

One authority declares that the name derives from "ransom," a common name for

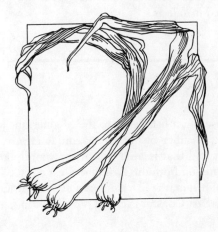

an unrelated plant, the European bell-flower known as *Campanula rapunculus.*

However, I received a letter from a Connecticut woman who refutes that.

"Ramp," she wrote, "is a wild, northern European leek known in England as 'ramson.'

"It is *rams* in Danish, Swedish, and German, with related names in Gaelic, Lithuanian, and Bavarian.

"I have," she added, "ramp transplanted from the Georgia mountains growing in our woodlands here in Connecticut. It is said to be superb as a substitute for onions in any recipe for French onion soup."

Rampions

I've never eaten rampions, a vegetable mentioned in the fairy tale "Rapunzel." In *Herbs, Spices and Flavorings*, the late Tom Stobart noted that the plant is quite rare today except in France and Switzerland. He said that it produces a white, radish-like root about a foot long and half an inch thick and that the roots and the leaves may be used in salads.

Rascasse

Rascasse, a fish native to the Mediterranean, is a member of the Scorpaenidae family. I am told that related fish of that family are found on both the East and West coasts. In California, the fish is known as sculpin. On the East Coast it is called red scorpion fish.

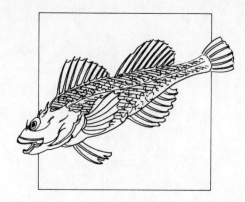

Although I have not seen either of these at my fish sources, if you can find them they ought to make a good substitute for rascasse in bouillabaisse.

Rasher

Rasher means "a single slice," and is most frequently applied to bacon. It is also used to indicate a single slice of ham. The *Oxford Dictionary of English Etymology* discounts the notion that rasher derives from something "rashly or hastily roasted." It states that the origin is unknown.

Rassolnik

Rassolnik is an excellent Russian soup made with veal or beef kidneys, beef broth, and vegetables. Among numerous variations are those with pearl barley, with pickled cucumbers, or with spinach.

I have also been informed that *rassol* is the Russian word for brine or pickle, and rassolnik is soup made from brined or pickled cucumbers (ogurtsy) and their brine or pickle. Moscow rassolnik includes beef or veal kidneys, but there is also beef rassolnik, chicken giblet rassolnik, and many kinds of vegetarian rassolnik. As with most transliterations, the name is spelled variously—rossolnick, rassolnick, and so on.

Ratafia

Ratafia is a little used word today, but apparently it has enjoyed a vogue in one place or another in one century or another in the Western world. It is probably of French origin and in France it is a liqueur generally used as a cordial. In the American South, principally in Louisiana, ratafia was made of numerous bases, including orange rind, brandy, and sugar.

Ratafia biscuits are, for some unknown reason, small macaroons, which enjoyed their greatest popularity during the Victorian age. They are strongly flavored with almond, generally almond extract.

The following was found in Patrick Forbes's admirably researched and well-written *Champagne, the Wine, the Land and the People.*

"Ratafia," the author explains, "is the thick sweet, peach-colored aperitif of the Champagne district. . . . It is extremely and deceptively strong . . . people who drink it for the first time are often disconcerted halfway through their second glass by the joyful effect it is having on them. Its manufacture is comparatively simple: a few moments after the juice has been pressed out of champagne grapes, brandy (ideally Cognac) is added to it; the brandy kills the wine-yeasts and stops the juice from fermenting. The mixture is then put in a cask and later bottled. It is usually ready for sale a year after being made . . . it is a highly suitable drink to have before a meal at which champagne is to be drunk exclusively. It should be served in small balloon-shaped glasses. Half a cantaloupe melon with a little ratafia in the center is delectable, infinitely preferable to half a cantaloupe with port in the center.

"The origin of the word 'ratafia' is curious. It is derived from two Latin words, *rata fiat,* which formed part of the following formula used to validate legal transactions in the Middle Ages: *De quibus est res, ut rata fiat, publicum fecimus instrumentum* (We have executed a public document concerning the matters with which the transaction deals, so that it may be confirmed). Once these words had been spoken by both parties in front of a notary, the deal was 'ratified;' custom then required the signatories to drink to the occasion from a bottle provided by the notary, a little ceremony which came to be known as the 'ratafia'." *See also* Edinburgh fog.

Rat Cheese

Almost every traditional recipe for Welsh rabbit specifies "unprocessed American cheese at least one year old." This is the yellow cheese once called rat cheese in America. Unprocessed American cheese is rarely found labeled as such in supermarkets and grocery stores today, but you can use a good grade of yellow Cheddar.

Rattlesnake

I have learned over the years that there are some wholly edible foods in this world that many people would classify as "unmentionable." This would include snake. I have many times enjoyed the snake dishes in a few of the snake specialty restaurants of Hong Kong. In Texas, the eating of rattlesnakes is not at all uncommon.

There is a recipe for fried rattlesnake in *The Wide Wide World of Texas Cooking* by Morton G. Clark. It is called Vibora de Cascabel:

"A snake of 3 to 4 feet has the best quality meat. To prepare: Cut off the snake's head and let the body drain. Skin as though removing a glove. Slit the snake up the middle. Discard the entrails. Rinse under cold water and pat dry. Cut the body crosswise into 1- to 2-inch lengths. Dredge in lightly salted cornmeal. Let stand a few minutes for the coating to set. Fry in hot lard."

Ravioli

See Dumplings.

Razor Clams

I have rarely eaten razor clams and prefer to borrow from A. J. McClane's book *The Encyclopedia of Fish Cookery*. He says the clams are found on both coasts. True to the name, they are shaped like an old-fashioned straight razor with a long, thin, narrow shell. They are too chewy to be eaten on the

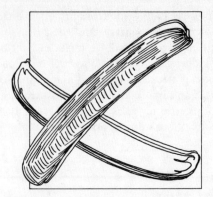

half shell except when very small.

The razors are slightly different in shape on the East and West coasts. Eastern razors are best when steamed; the western variety is most often fried. Both can be chopped and turned into fritters.

Rebecca Pudding

Rebecca pudding is a very old American dessert, whose recipe appears in the first and many subsequent editions of *The Boston Cooking School Cook Book* by Fannie Merritt Farmer.

It is essentially a blancmange, that is, a molded pudding made with milk, cornstarch, and sugar, with egg whites beaten stiff and folded in. It is generally served with a sauce made with eggs and sugar, plus wine or brandy.

Recipe Grammar

I am in receipt of a highly amusing criticism of my use of the English language.

"Your direction for chopping onions," a

woman from Cranford, New Jersey, writes, "is written in a way that causes me to think you have inadvertently confused an adverb with an adjective.

"The instruction I refer to is: 'Slice onions thinly.' This brings to my mind the picture of a very thin housewife, standing sideways so as to be even thinner, slicing her onions in a thin manner.

"I am also disturbed when you instruct the cook to chop the onions finely, as it brings to mind a person in formal dress, chopping with white gloves on, so as to be fine enough for your recipe."

I intend to steer clear of the fray, but am pleased to print the rebuttal of another grammarian of Whitestone, Queens, who gets into the battle as follows:

"Your critic is herself confused. I write in your defense as to the correct grammatical structure of your 'slice onions thinly.'

"In your sentence 'slice' is a transitive verb followed by the direct object 'onions' and the adverb 'thinly' describes the manner of slicing the onions. The same applies to 'chop onions finely.' "

Back to the first correspondent:

Your grammarian's rebuttal, she stated, "is not a rebuttal at all as she misses my point; the verb 'slice' cannot be modified by the adverb 'thinly,' as it is not the manner of slicing that is being modified, but the onion.

"Surely, she does not brew her coffee strongly, pound her veal flatly, beat her egg whites stiffly, or fill her salt shaker fully. Why then does she slice her onions thinly?"

And this from Lancaster, Pennsylvania:

"In the matter of 'slice thin' versus 'slice thinly' I find myself unable to remain silently and keep coolly. In my opinion, the word 'thin' is needed as an adjective describing the condition resulting from the action of slicing.

"However, the overcorrect folk who always get things wrong because they don't know when to stop will probably continue not only to slice their onions thinly, but also lay them flatly, fry them brownly, keep them warmly, and serve them hotly. The rest of us will try to steer clearly of such grammatical constructions."

Red Beans and Rice

Red beans and rice is a specialty of Louisiana. The most authentic recipes call for cooking the soaked red kidney beans with ham hocks, chopped onion, green pepper, celery, bay leaf, garlic, and salt and pepper to taste. When the beans are done, add fried country sausage and serve over rice with chopped parsley.

Red-Eye Gravy

Red-eye gravy, to those unaccustomed to the nobler things in life, requires first a good, well-cured country ham. Smithfield and genuine Virginia hams are ideal for this.

Take a slice of uncooked ham with most or much of the fat left on. Fry the ham in its own fat until nicely browned on both sides. When it is cooked, transfer the ham to a warm platter and add boiling black coffee to the skillet, scraping to dissolve the brown particles that cling to the bottom and sides.

That is red-eye gravy, which you pour over the ham and serve.

Red Scorpion Fish

See Rascasse.

Reducing Sauces

The eye of a trained chef or cook will know within a spoonful or so the moment a sauce is properly reduced. Otherwise, if you want to be really exact, it will be necessary to pour the sauce into a measuring cup. In most cases, if you miss the cooking-down time by a quarter of a cup or so, it isn't going to spoil the desired results.

In *The Saucier's Apprentice,* Raymond Sokolov suggests using a wooden chopstick to measure before and after a sauce is reduced.

Refried Beans

The best explanation I have found for the term "refried beans" is in Diana Kennedy's fine book on Mexican cooking, *The Cuisines of Mexico.* "Several people," she says in the book, "have asked me why, when the beans are fried, they are called refried. Nobody I asked in Mexico seemed to know until quite suddenly it dawned on me. The Mexicans have a habit of qualifying a word to emphasize the meaning by adding the prefix re-. Thus *refrito* means well fried, which they certainly are, since they are fried until they are almost dry."

Another explanation came to me from a New Yorker who wrote: "Traditionally my grandmother would make a pot of fresh pinto beans, mash them and then fry them in oil. When they came to a point where they resembled a runny porridge, she took them off the fire and left them to cool.

"These beans were usually refrigerated, then, to last the week. It was only when they were to be served that they were refried until they were dark and dry.

"While the beans can be eaten after the first frying—they have a clean, fresh taste—it is not the same dish at all. The dry, nutty flavor and texture come from the refrying."

Refrigeration

There is some controversy about whether to refrigerate foods when they are hot or to let them come to room temperature first. Some cooks say that quick refrigeration causes moisture to condense on the surface and that this can cause souring. A chemist, to whom I have mentioned this, says that it is thoroughly safe to store foods in the refrigerator while they are still hot.

Generally speaking, I let food reach room temperature before refrigerating because of a longtime habit. It is also true that if you store hot foods in the refrigerator, it is going to warm up the inside of the cooler.

Rennet

Rennet is a cheese-making agent that is derived from rennin. Rennin is an enzyme that occurs in the inner linings of the stomachs of calves and other ruminants. There is also a vegetable rennet. Rennet converts milk into curds and whey.

Rennet tablets are sold under the trade

name Junket in supermarkets. On the box is a formula for making nonfat cheese.

Restaurant Prices

Not long ago I was invited to dine in one of Manhattan's fancier restaurants. Four of us were at the table; our host was a well-off man about town, which proved a good thing: When the bill arrived, it was about $300 before tips. That tab, of course, could have been equaled or exceeded in a score of similarly luxurious dining spots in this city.

The lunch, it must be said, was excellent. I had sautéed foie gras as an appetizer, roast pheasant with figs for a main course, a selection of sherbets for dessert, and coffee. We had a round of drinks and consumed two bottles of wine, a Mâcon-Lugny (one of the best and least expensive white wines from France) priced at $20 and a California cabernet sauvignon at $30.

Later that afternoon, back at my home on Eastern Long Island with my host, I was looking through the bookshelves in my reference room and my eye fell on a 1934 restaurant guide titled *Dining in New York* by Rian James. I handed my friend the volume, observing that only six of the three hundred restaurants listed are still in existence.

Thumbing through the pages he found the entry for Sardi's, where the cost of a complete lunch was recorded as 65 cents, and dinner as $1.35. A footnote added that "drinks are reasonably priced, but good." The book also informed us that the food at Sardi's was Italian-American and that there, "you will find Miriam Hopkins rubbing shoulders with Greta Garbo, Maurice Chevalier, Rudy Vallee, the Astaires" and so on. Curious, I pulled out another book,

Dining Out in New York, written by G. Selmer Fougner and published in 1939. Mr. Fougner was considered by many to be the finest local wine and food critic in those years. He wrote a column titled "Along the Wine Trail" for *The New York Sun.*

Although very few restaurants in his book survive today, one that is still very much alive and maintains its prestige is the "21" Club. I handed this volume to my friend, and he read, "The patronage is select and many are those who visit the place merely to get a look at the celebrities ever present, either in the ground-floor room in front of the bar or upstairs."

From Mr. Fougner's "specialities culled at random," my friend read of a boned squab stuffed with wild rice, foie gras and truffles and served with a Madeira wine sauce. The à la carte cost was $2.25. A main-course lobster dish cooked with port wine was priced at $1.75. The cost of an excellent bottle of Burgundy, a Nuits-St.-Georges, was $3.50.

To be fair, these prices are close to half a century old. What about something more recent, my friend asked. I searched my files and discovered my original review, dated March 28, 1961, of Lutèce, a restaurant that was and remains one of the grand dining spots of Manhattan.

Under the headline, "Lutèce Both Elegant and Expensive," the review began: "Lutèce was the original name of Paris. It also is the name of a recently opened restaurant in Manhattan that is at once impressively elegant and conspicuously expensive."

These were some of the prices that set off such alarms: soup, $2.25; first course, $4; main courses, $8.25; desserts, $2.75. Wines, I had noted, ranged from about $8.50 for a 1958 Meursault to $14 for a 1957 Chambertin. And I had added: "A recent dinner for two included two aperitifs, two first courses, salad with cheese, a bottle of 1957 Chassagne-Montrachet and two demitasses. The cost was $52.30."

Still, my friend observed, those are prices from the Dark Ages—more than twenty years ago. How about the 1970s?

I opened a copy of *The New York Times Guide to Dining Out in New York* dated 1976, and found the write-up of one of my all-time favorite luxury restaurants in the city, La Caravelle. The restaurant, the guide noted, was "relatively democratic in its treatment of the anonymous, but well-stuffed wallet." Such a wallet could purchase a full-course lunch for $13.75 and a full-course evening meal for about $20.75.

With that I descended the ladder from the top shelves of my library with the feeling that I had attained some historical wisdom. If twenty years from today a restaurant critic or sociologist of sorts should chance to read this, perhaps he or she will regard with wonder the small cost—a mere $300 plus tips—for a party of four to have lunch at a luxury restaurant in Manhattan.

Reuben Sandwich

My wish to learn the origins of the Reuben sandwich provided me with an abundance of letters, most of them pinpointing 1956 as the year the sandwich gained national prominence. I have traced the history to the sponsors of the National Sandwich Contest held that year. The following treatise, from the National Kraut Packers Association, includes the original winning recipe:

"The Reuben sandwich, submitted by a waitress, Miss Fern Snider of Omaha, Nebraska, took first place honors in the 1956 National Sandwich Contest. Since that year, the sandwich has steadily grown to its now acclaimed popularity. Today, practically every restaurant, club and diner in the country features a version of the Reuben.

"The idea originated with one of Miss Snider's employers, the Schimmel family, who has operated the Blackstone Hotel in Omaha for years. During 1920–1935, Bernard Schimmel's father belonged to a weekly poker group. Fixing their own sandwiches became the most enjoyed weekly 'feast' on these poker nights. One player, a wholesale grocer named Reuben Kay, devised the combination of kraut, corned beef and Swiss on rye. Thus, in honor of its 'founder,' the Reuben was named.

"Bernard Schimmel, a retired European-trained chef, says the secret of the Reuben is in its bread. It should be fresh pumpernickel, preferably the sour-dough kind. The sauerkraut should be crisp, chilled and well drained. At the Blackstone, he explains, only the best ingredients are selected—that is, rich homemade Russian dressing, Emmenthaler Swiss cheese and kosher-styled corned beef sliced very thin.

"Assembling the Reuben is an 'art,' too. Schimmel puts corned beef on one slice of pumpernickel, Swiss cheese on the other. Next, he tops one side of the sandwich with a thick layer of kraut mixed with dressing. Then he either butters and quickly grills it, or serves it cold without the butter. If grilled, he believes the sandwich should be hot on the outside, cold on the inside."

Although I am persuaded that the above is the true origin of the Reuben sandwich that I have indulged in on many occasions and the sandwich I had in mind when I pondered its origins, I am also in possession of a letter from Patricia R. Taylor of Manhattan who claims that her father, the late

Arnold Reuben, was the originator of ALL Reuben sandwiches. Arnold Reuben was, of course, the proprietor for many years of the now-defunct and well-remembered Reuben restaurant on Fifty-ninth Street.

I feel obliged in all fairness to reprint portions of Mrs. Taylor's letter:

"I am prompted to write after reading of your search for the original Reuben sandwich. Your search is over, here I am, the daughter of the horse's mouth.

"My father . . . for over forty odd years made his restaurant an institution in New York. To quote Damon Runyon, 'Reuben has always been famous for his sandwiches, which are regular productions, not just slabs of bread with things between them. For years it has been Arnold's custom to apply to these masterpieces of the sandwich architect's skill the names of persons of more or less notoriety in our fair city.'

"I would like to share with you the story of the first Reuben's Special and what went into it.

"The year was 1914. Late one evening a leading lady of Charlie Chaplin's came into the restaurant and said, 'Reuben, make me a sandwich, make it a combination, I'm so hungry I could eat a brick.' He took a loaf of rye bread, cut two slices on the bias and stacked one piece with sliced Virginia ham, roast turkey, and imported Swiss cheese, topped off with coleslaw and lots of Reuben's special Russian dressing and the second slice of bread. (The bias cut bread made his sandwiches a sandwich and a half.)

"He served it to the lady who said, 'Gee, Reuben, this is the best sandwich I ever ate, you ought to call it an Annette Seelos Special.' To which he replied, 'Like hell I will, I'll call it a Reuben's Special.' "

Let me compromise and say that Arnold Reuben, the sandwich genius, produced a forerunner of what is now served coast to coast as the Reuben sandwich named by coincidence for Reuben Kay, the wholesale grocer in Omaha.

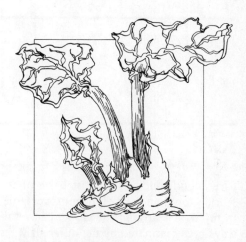

Rhubarb

I was curious to know why the word "rhubarb" is used to describe a noisy conflict, so I turned to the *Morris Dictionary of Word and Phrase Origins*. "Rhubarb, meaning a heated argument, often between professional athletes in the course of a game, comes from the language of the theater, TV and movies." In the early days of films, when a crowd was supposed to be muttering in a surly mood, the director would have them say "rhubarb" over and over again.

Ribollita

Ribollita means twice-cooked (actually, twice-boiled), and is a kind of minestrone. It was served to me, well chilled, on a scorching hot day at the distinguished Sabatini restaurant in Milan. One rarely thinks of bean soup as something to serve cold, but this one is delicious.

Ricard

See Pastis.

Rice

Rice is both one of the most basic of the world's foods and one of the most versatile. In my travels around the globe, I have always been fascinated by the different ways it is cooked. In Japan, recipes commonly call for washing the rice an hour before it is to be cooked and then letting it drain in the open air. In China, it is sometimes rinsed in several changes of water and cooked for an hour and a half. In the American South, recipes for Creole rice often call for cooking it in a vast amount of water before draining and buttering. In my kitchen, except for special so-called foreign meals, the rice is rarely washed, but it is cooked in one and one-half times its volume of liquid for exactly seventeen minutes.

There are differences in taste between long-grain and short-grain rice, but they are subtle enough in most instances as to be inconsequential. In Western kitchens, long-grain rice is usually preferred when you want to serve rice as a separate dish. When cooked, long-grain rice (and the name means specifically that—the grains are longer than in short- or medium-grain rice)

tends to be fluffier and lighter than short-grain. Thus it is often recommended for rice salads and so on. Short- and medium-grain rice cooks to a moister state and is preferred for custards, rice puddings, and dishes that are destined to be unmolded. The grains stick together. Short-grain rice is often used by Chinese and Japanese cooks because of this characteristic. It is easier to handle with chopsticks. *See also* Basmati, Brown rice, Carolina rice, Risotto, Wild rice.

Ricer

A good many years ago, almost every kitchen in this country had what is called a food ricer or potato ricer. Then came the food mill and finally the food processor.

A food ricer is a cylindrical basket with perforated holes. It has a flat metal disk or plunger operated by a lever. The cooked potatoes, carrots, or whatever are placed into the basket, and the disk is placed over it and pushed down with a lever, forcing the food through the perforations.

By some stretch of the inventor's imagination the food, as it emerged from the holes, had the look of rice.

Rice Vinegar

Rice vinegar is an excellent vinegar most commonly used in the preparation of Japanese dishes such as the cold rice for sushi and the salads known as sunomo. The vinegar, almost colorless but sometimes with a pale yellowish cast, is made from sake mash. Sake, of course, is the traditional rice wine of Japan, and the mash is the soft pulp that remains after the clear beverage has been drawn off.

The preparation of rice vinegar does not vary to any greater degree than that of making other vinegars, such as those of berries, particularly those that produce red and white wines made from grapes. Rice vinegar is wholly adaptable to almost any salad dressing that calls for vinegar.

Ricotta Cheese

See Cottage cheese.

Rijsttafel

It took a lady from Indonesia to persuade me that the famed rijsttafel of her country is one of those rare and sought-after devices for entertaining: a complete menu with dishes that are elaborately good, but most of which can be prepared a comfortable length of time before guests arrive. A menu that is not a race against time and that will, as they say in the best manuals, allow one to appear cool, calm, coherent, and collected.

Now I have dined on rijsttafels before, both in Amsterdam and Bali. But until I made the acquaintance of Melita Soeharjo I had not realized the easy scope, logic, and cultural details of such a feast.

In Indonesia, Mrs. Soeharjo said, the weather can be passionately hot. Unlike the foods of many other cultures—French, Italian, and so on—a vast number of those of the Indonesian kitchen are delectable served hot, lukewarm, or at room temperature. There are no cream and butter sauces. Various spices, including hot chilies, are accented. The foods, in short, are marvelously compatible with a hot climate and especially suited to summer dining.

"A rijsttafel," Mrs. Soeharjo said, "is what the Dutch came to call the traditional Indonesian buffet, our slaametan or buffet dinner."

In the word *rijsttafel*, which literally translates as rice table, both the "t's" are pronounced and the initial "r" is rolled. Thus, it comes out like "rrrriced-tahful."

The foods that made up that Indonesian meal in Mrs. Soeharjo's home were very much to the point. The admirable grated coconut patties had been cooked an hour in advance. The succulent spicy shrimp in coconut cream had been made a short while later and rested in a warm place. The rice rolls—for the rice table—had been made the day before and were now steaming, without need of attention, in a cooker.

An irresistible cold salad of shredded greens with vinegar and ginger dressing was mellowing to advantage in the refrigerator. A spicy peanut sauce and another dip or sauce made of hot chilies were table-ready. And two satays, or Indonesian brochettes, were seasoned and skewered and waiting as a charcoal grill was fired. The omnipresent *krupuk*—deep-fried shrimp wafers—were precooked, and the chilled mangoes were sliced and cut, native style.

At that rijsttafel in Mrs. Soeharjo's home, there were only six or seven ingredients, including herbs and spices, that would not be familiar to the average cook in a Western home and all are available at specialty food shops. These are laos, a root known in English (equally obscurely) as galingale; salam, a kind of bay or laurel leaf, which differs in flavor from its Western counterpart; tamarind, a sour-sweet seed enveloped in a soft flesh, which must be soaked before using; kencur, a ginger-like plant; shrimp paste, a powerfully (and to some, unpleasantly) perfumed paste of dried shrimp, quite familiar to Chinese chefs; krupuk, dried shrimp or fish wafers that expand notably when deep fried; fish sauce and kecap manis, a sweet, aromatic soy sauce.

Rillettes

Rillettes, a dish that is exceedingly palatable and exceedingly rich in calories, are usually made of pork pieces cooked for a long time over low heat in melted lard or rendered pork fat that is seasoned with herbs, such as bay leaf and thyme. When the pork is cooked until it is almost falling apart, it is pounded and blended with the cooking fat.

Rillettes are generally served cold. Rillons, also referred to at times as rillauds and rillots, are cooked in the same manner, but when the pork is ready it is drained and served hot or cold.

The name derives from the French word *rille*, meaning a thin layer of lard. Rillettes may be made from any meat, including rabbit, goose, and sardines. The city best known for rillettes in France is Tours.

Rinsing Food

If I am more or less confident of the origin or source of my foods, I do not feel it incumbent on me to rinse the foods, provided they are as fresh as I would hope them to be. For example, if I buy a freshly dressed chicken from my local poultry farm or a piece of freshly filleted fish from the local fish market, I do not bother to rinse the pieces before cooking.

If there is any slight off odor detected in foods that I might have purchased at a supermarket meat counter, I would probably rinse the item in the hope that it would, as it often does, eradicate the smell. I also do this at times with foods that have been held a day or so in my refrigerator. I almost invariably rinse fresh fruits in cold water since they may have been sprayed at the source before harvesting.

Pursuant to this I received a letter from a food specialist with the Cooperative Extension Service at Oklahoma State University in Stillwater, Oklahoma.

"Poultry should always be washed before cooking," she informed me. "It is frequently contaminated with salmonella. Statistics from the Public Health Service show 25,000 people a year are reported to be ill with salmonella infections, most of which are caused by food.

"Because symptoms are flu-like (vomiting, diarrhea, general malaise and headache), many people do not realize that they have food poisoning. The 25,000 cases are probably only 10 percent of the actual incidents that occur. There is concern for children under four and people over sixty-five salmonella can cause severe illness and in extreme cases it can be fatal."

Risotto

I admit to a certain passion for Italian cooking and rank it next to the French and Chinese as one of the great cuisines of the world. I must confess—and it is a confession—that I have never been all that keen on risotto and especially as it is cooked in, of all places, Italy. Risotto, an affectionate and diminutive term for *riso*, or rice, meaning little rice, is one of the dishes most closely identified with Milan, and there are many ways to cook it. Basically, however, it is rice cooked in a broth, frequently with saffron, and it is always served with grated cheese. It is served, like spaghetti, as a first course. My objection to most of the risottos I've eaten in authentic Italian kitchens is a quality that a risotto-doting Italian most admires. That is the *al dente* nature of the rice. The rice must be cooked in the broth to a creamy state and yet the kernels of rice must retain an inner "bite." On a trip to Milan, I dined for the first time on what I consider the perfect risotto. It was *al dente,* the rice retained an inner texture, but it did not have the raw interior—like biting into

tiny chalk pellets—that I had previously been exposed to. From all standpoints, this was sublime.

Rizzard Haddies

Rizzard haddies is a fish dish made with haddock. I was told once by a Scottish cook that one must use a haddock of considerable size because the smallest version will become dry when cooked. Simply take the cleaned, skinned fish and flour it lightly. Cook it over charcoal or other fire until done, pour melted butter over it, and serve.

Robalo

See Snook.

Rocket

See Arugula.

Rock Salt

Rock salt is wholly edible, but according to a spokesman for the Diamond Salt Company in St. Clair, Michigan, it is not as pure chemically as table salt. "I personally," he stated, "rarely use it, for table salt is esthetically superior, and 99 percent pure salt. Rock salt does contain a slight amount of calcium sulfate, a natural mineral that is not considered deleterious."

He added that there is one primary use for rock salt in cooking that he personally recommends. That is for cooking a standing rib roast packed in salt before baking. "The salt," he stated, "cakes around the roast and the results are fantastic."

Rock salt is also used as a stable base for oysters when they are to be baked.

Rødgrød

The classic pudding known in Danish as rødgrød is made with the juice of red currants and fresh raspberries. The seeds and skin of the berries are eliminated and the juice is heated and thickened with cornstarch or arrowroot. The syrup is flavored with a little lemon juice and sugar and is allowed to set. It is normally served with a touch of heavy cream, which may or may not be whipped.

Rolling Boil

A rolling boil, often called for in jelly recipes and for cooking pasta, is a point of boiling that cannot be stirred down with a spoon or other utensil. Lesser boilings will subside when a spoon or other utensil is stirred in the container.

Root Beer

The basic flavorings of root beer are various roots and herbs including sassafras, wild cherry, sarsaparilla, wintergreen, and ginger.

Root beer is not a favorite of mine, and I haven't drunk it in a number of years. As far as the remembered taste is concerned, I can only vouch for the flavor of sarsaparilla root, which I well recall from drinking sassafras tea in my childhood. It seemed to be the predominant flavor of root beer.

Root beer is sweet and carbonated, and I am told that years ago when made at home it was prepared by using commercially made, packaged flavors and extract. These were combined with sugar and yeast and let stand until fermentation occurred.

I was sent a formula for making root beer at home: To make 5 gallons combine one 3-ounce bottle of root beer extract, 4 pounds sugar, 4¾ gallons lukewarm water and add ½ teaspoon dried yeast dissolved in 1 cup lukewarm water for 5 minutes. Stir well and bottle immediately. Place the bottles on their sides in a warm place for about a week, or until bubbly. Then store in a cool place. Remove the caps slowly."

Rorer

People who think that cooking schools in America are a twentieth-century innovation are about a century behind the times. Shortly after the Civil War there were three well-known cooking schools in this country. They were the Boston Cooking School, the New York Cooking School, and the Philadelphia Cooking School.

The Boston is by far the best remembered, largely because of *The Fannie Farmer Boston Cooking-School Cookbook*. But of the three, the Philadelphia was by far the most interesting, because of the dazzling and eccentric woman who founded and administered it, Sarah Tyson Rorer.

Until she was thirty years old, and the mother of three children, she had never cooked a serious meal in her life. After she took up cooking as a career, however, she became known as the high priestess and queen of the nation's kitchens.

She felt that cooking was the "cleanest, easiest and nicest work that could befall a housekeeper."

She put on cooking demonstrations across the land and, to prove her point, invariably appeared in an Indian silk dress with "dainty sleevelets" and with a lace fichu over her shoulders. She would cook a six-course meal in less than an hour, with never a spot to mar her costume. Men, as well as women, flocked to her lectures and demonstrations. Her audiences were of such size they were described as "Paderewskian."

Mrs. Rorer was a food columnist and at one point her readership is said to have numbered in the millions. She was even celebrated in song on Broadway. When Jerome Kern and P. G. Wodehouse wrote *Sitting Pretty*, which opened at the Fulton Theater in 1924, part of the score was a lengthy song, "Mr. and Mrs. Rorer," which included the lines, "She kept her husband well supplied / With ev'ry appetizing dish / That any hungry man would wish."

Mrs. Rorer, known to her friends as Sallie, was born Sarah Tyson Heston in Bucks County, Pennsylvania, on October 15, 1849.

Her chief biographer, Emma S. Weigley (*Sara Tyson Rorer: The Nation's Instructress in Dietetics & Cookery*) states, that very little is known about Mrs. Rorer's early years. She was married at twenty-one to a passive, unambitious man named William

Albert Rorer, a clerk whose chief asset, aside from a decent family inheritance, seems to have been fine penmanship. Mrs. Rorer gave birth to three children, one of whom died young. She became listless and depressed and suffered an undiagnosed illness, described as largely imaginary. She had little appetite and a "bad stomach." Her interests were limited and, outside of her family, nonexistent. A maid took care of the house.

She had been married eight years when a cousin persuaded her to attend cooking lessons given by a Miss Devereux at the Philadelphia New Century Club. She went for want of something better to do. She was captivated and considered the lessons an almost religious experience. She learned the fine points of making sauces and stocks and breads. She quickly became the teacher's favorite and soon was conducting classes at the club. She studied all the books on cookery she could lay her hands on. *Mrs. Beeton's Book of Household Management* became her bible.

Her Philadelphia Cooking School opened in October 1883 and her students, it was noted, "came almost exclusively from families of wealth, refinement and fashion." Three years later *Mrs. Rorer's Philadelphia Cook Book* appeared.

Mrs. Rorer appeared in large lecture halls, addressing the members of the audience but with an aside here and there to a kitchen helper. Occasionally, says her biographer, a snide remark would be heard about Mrs. Rorer's fine dress, while the "toting and dirty work was done by the assistant who wore calico!"

The cooking expert had her pet peeves. She claimed to loathe fried foods, waste (she once informed a garbage man that she and her family ate all the garbage, meaning leftovers), any food made with pork, and desserts. And bad cooking in general. Bad cooking, she held, was the reason for the "crowded conditions in our insane asylums, almshouses, prisons and hospitals" and crime. She loved taking potshots at Boston (no doubt because of that city's cooking school). Boston, she said, "'is a great place for nervous prostration which is the result, not of brain exertion, as many Boston people claim, but of bean eating."

She looked with disdain on vinegar ("If salt and vinegar will eat away copper, what will it do to the lining of the stomach?") and mustard ("added to salads, mustard reacts in the stomach the same way as a mustard plaster affected the outside of the body").

She proselytized for two things in particular—the chafing dish and fresh green salads. She said that salads should be eaten 365 days a year, that salad purifies the blood and clears the complexion. Someone asked if she ate ham. She replied, "No product of the hog is fit to eat. Do I eat ham? Certainly not. I have no time to eat anything which takes five hours to digest." And of brandy: "Don't ever embrace the fallacy that brandy makes mince pie more digestible. Never. It preserves the mince in your stomach exactly as it preserves in a bottle."

Mrs. Rorer's wit was audacious.

American men, she said, don't make decent waiters for they are "better adapted to piano moving, and have a deep-rooted habit of plate smashing that makes them dangerous in a small room." Mrs. Weigley quotes her as having said fish was not brain food, for no fisherman of her acquaintance was overly brilliant. And, "The question of choosing evening refreshment is not which is more wholesome, but which is more deadly."

An English physician once described white bread as the "staff of death"; that became one of Mrs. Rorer's favorite phrases.

During her demonstrations Mrs. Rorer would offer a lengthy diatribe against eating one thing or another, all the while preparing that very dish.

She would say, "Under protest I shall make for you some new desserts which I hope none of you will think of imitating. Remember, desserts are both unhealthy and unnecessary as articles of food." And, "Desserts of any sort have very little value as food, so my subject today may be classified as a somewhat dubious one." And with that she would delight her audience with a charlotte russe with chocolate sauce, murmuring, "All these things look so good but they are so deadly." Or she would say that any fried foods would hasten you to the grave, all the while preparing a splendid platter of fried chicken.

One summer—in 1882—Mrs. Rorer spent ninety days abroad, exploring the markets of France and Germany and visiting cooking schools in England and elsewhere. On her return, she was fairly exuberant about French cooking and markets but she regarded German cooking with great disdain. Writing in *The Philadelphia Inquirer*, she said:

"It is said that suicides are very prevalent among Germans, and one fully believes this after even one month's stay in Germany on real German food. In fact, I marvel that they live at all on such food as the majority eat."

She said food was served too often and that the portions were gross. She mentioned, in particular, an evening meal that included "rye bread sandwiches with cheese and another glass of beer. Why would not one think death a joy after a month of such fare?"

Although Mrs. Rorer occupied an enviable position in the annals of American gastronomy, the last years of her life were pathetic. She was estranged from her husband and lived with her oldest son, Billy, whom she pampered. Mrs. Rorer lost a great deal of money in a restaurant that failed. It was called the Rorer Restaurant in New York. The restaurant was still listed in the New York telephone directory as late as 1925.

She became involved in an enterprise that involved packaging "Mrs. Rorer's Own Special Blend of Coffee," which also failed. In the 1930s, in her mid-eighties, she was ill and destitute. A fund was started in her behalf, but only $2,385 was collected. She died of pneumonia on December 27, 1937. She is buried in Colebrook, Pennsylvania.

Rose Hips

Rose hips are the red-orange fruit or berries that appear in late summer after the petals have dropped from the rose bushes. It is actually the roundish base to which the petals are attached. Most rose hips are gathered from wild rose bushes and are said to contain a sizable amount of vitamin C.

To prepare them, select the unblemished hips, rinse and dry thoroughly, and cut away the tops and tails with a knife or scissors. Split open and discard the seeds. For making tea, the hips are crushed and used or dried and crushed before using.

Rose Water

Rose water is a clear nonalcoholic liquid widely used in the cookery of the Middle East and Far East. Its customary use is in desserts. I have two bottles on my pantry shelf, one imported from India, the other from France. The French bottle lists as the ingredient distilled water; the bottle from India states that rose water is not only used in the kitchen but in religious rituals.

Although rose water is available in specialty food shops and many drugstores, I have received several letters explaining how to make it at home.

Andrée Abramoff of Andrée's Mediterranean Cooking School in Manhattan wrote to say, "There is indeed no substitute for this pure, unadulterated distilled essence, which is simply the condensation of distilled rose petals (or orange blossom petals for orange flower water).

"My grandmother used to make both these essences in Egypt each spring, usually about the time of Passover. The steaming pot she used was actually a kind of still which she called an alambic, using the French word for alembic. It resembled a clam steamer with a spiral spout on top.

This was called a serpentin, also after the French.

"My grandmother would place the flower petals, which she purchased by the bushel, in the perforated container of the steamer and add water to the bottom part. The steam in the upper portion of the still would form droplets that would drip down into the spiral spigot under which she had placed her bottles.

"Her whole house smelled like a perfume factory when she did this, and she used her precious waters for everything from appetizers to desserts to a cure for baby colic."

Rosé Wine

Although it may be true that rosé wines are acceptable with fish, red meat, and game, to serve them at random shows about equal amounts of insecurity and lack of imagination. It's like using black-and-white film exclusively because that's what you're accustomed to. Quite honestly, I find that rosé wines are on the dull side, best served well chilled at picnics, barbecues, and other outdoor summer occasions.

Rosina

See Funeral pie.

Rossel Borscht

Rossel borscht, according to Florence Aaron, my favorite food expert on such matters, is generally made only during the Passover season, although there is no reason it could not be made anytime.

To make it, she added, cut beets into large cubes and put them into a crock with water to cover. Let stand a week to ten days in a place that is not too warm. It should start to ferment. Strain the liquid and to each quart of rossel water add 6 freshly grated peeled beets.

Cook ten to fifteen minutes until the beets are tender. Beat three eggs with a little water and add them gradually, stirring rapidly off heat. Return to the heat and bring just to the boil, stirring, but do not boil or the eggs will curdle. Serve it hot or cold with sour cream.

She added that she believed rossel meant fermented.

Not so, says Harold Schwartz, professor of history at Kent State University. "I have known the term rossel borscht all my life but never gave the matter any thought, because I am an experienced eater, not a cook.

"However, your speculation that rossel means fermented is erroneous. Uriel Weinreich's *Modern English-Yiddish/Yiddish-English Dictionary* defines rossel as 'brine' or 'broth.'

"On page 40 in the English-Yiddish part,

broth is defined as either 'rossel' or 'yoich' while brine is defined as 'leeag.' I guess that the nuance between 'rossel' and 'yoich' is very subtle if they both translate as 'broth.' In my family, 'yoich' was the broth that resulted from preparing gefilte fish."

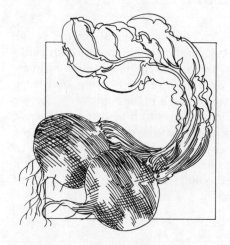

Roux

In traditional French cooking, a roux is simply butter cooked with flour, generally without browning. There are certain chefs who contend that a roux should be cooked for several minutes to get rid of any trace of a raw taste in the flour. Generally speaking, however, this is a tedious refinement.

A brown roux is a staple of Cajun and other Louisiana cookery. In those kitchens, it is usually made with oil or bacon fat, the flour added and stirred for a long period until the flour takes on a brown-amber color. This is the basis for many soups, stews, and other dishes.

Rum

It is largely a matter of taste whether you use light or dark rum in a recipe. It would seem logical that you would use dark rum, which has a richer and more potent flavor, if you wanted a pronounced rum flavor. Light rum would be preferable if you wanted to give a more subtle taste to the dish. If I wanted to flavor a baba au rhum, I would probably use the dark rum, prefering a stronger flavor. If I wanted to flavor fresh berries with a touch of rum, I would probably choose the lighter rum.

Rumbledethumps

Rumbledethumps is a Scottish specialty but the origin of the name eludes me. A friend of mine, a good cook and native of Edinburgh, informs me that basically the dish consists of cooking equal amounts of potatoes and cabbage in separate kettles until tender. The vegetables are then "mashed together" with butter and seasoned with a generous amount of black pepper. Chopped onions cooked in butter are sometimes added to it. Cheese, he states, would make a nice addition, but he does not believe it is standard.

A gentleman from Victoria, British Columbia, sent a far more precise recipe that he found in Sheila MacNiven Cameron's book, *The Highlander's Cookbook*. Following is the recipe:

RUMBLEDETHUMPS
"Combine equal quantities of hot cooked

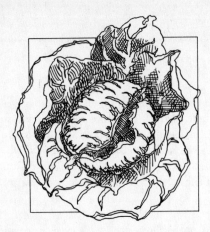

Cheddar cheese, and place in a hot oven for about 10 minutes, or until the cheese melts and browns lightly. Allow 4 cups for 4 persons."

Russian Dressing

I rather doubt that you will find a recipe for Russian dressing in any Russian cookbook, and it seems quite definitely of American origin. To the best of my knowledge you won't find it in the French repertory of cooking under sauce Russe or otherwise. It is my belief that the original recipe for the dressing contained caviar, in addition to mayonnaise, chili sauce, horseradish, and grated onion, and that that is the source of the name.

cabbage and cooked, cut up, hot potatoes. Add 2 tablespoons of chopped chives or 1 small onion that has been chopped and sautéed briefly in 1 tablespoon of butter. Add salt and pepper to taste, and a lump of butter, and mix all well together. Turn into a greased casserole, sprinkle with grated

Sabayon

See Zabaglione.

Safflower Oil

The safflower plant is an herb of the same family as the thistle and the daisy. The reddish-orange flowers are used in vegetable dyes, and oil is produced from the seeds. Producers of the oil emphasize that is is relatively high in polyunsaturated fat.

I am told that safflower oil has been used for many years in India. Safflower is sometimes referred to as Mexican saffron and is used as a saffron substitute.

Saffron

Stem saffron or whole saffron is the stigmas of the saffron crocus, collected and dried. The saffron "threads" can be put through a mill to produce a ground or powdered version.

In theory, whole and powdered saffron are interchangeable. I prefer the stem variety in the belief that the ground variety is easier

for unscrupulous producers to adulterate.

Most saffron comes from Spain and it is necessary to gather it by hand. It is estimated that nearly seventy-five thousand stamen must be harvested to produce one pound of the herb. Saffron has many uses in cookery, including as a flavoring in cakes. The herb imparts a particularly fine flavor to various fish soups, including bouillabaisse.

If saffron has been tightly closed and stored in a relatively cool, dark place, it will keep indefinitely. Some of its strength might dissipate, but I doubt it.

I have received numerous inquiries over the years as to whether the stamens of ordinary, garden-variety crocuses in this country could be used to make saffron, the most expensive spice in the world.

The most lucid comment I have ever read on the subject came from Paul A. Cox, a doctoral candidate in biology at Harvard University's Biological Laboratories: "Stamens, of course, are the male organs of a flower; they produce pollen which can fertilize other flowers and can also afflict sufferers of hay fever.

"The saffron of commerce comes from the stigmas of *Crocus sativus*. Stigmas are part of the female organs of flowers and are the surface upon which pollen grains germinate prior to fertilization of the ovules. The stigmas are dried and allowed to fer-

ment slightly. It is unlikely that a home gardener could produce very much saffron without a good deal of space or ingenuity since each saffron flower produces only three stigmas; more than twelve thousand stigmas are required to produce a single ounce of saffron. This is one of the reasons why saffron is one of the most expensive spices in the world."

Saganaki

Most recipes for saganaki, the Greek cheese dish, call for either kasseri or kefalotiri cheese, which are available in the finest cheese specialty shops and shops that specialize in Middle Eastern and Greek foods. The cheese is generally cut into slices about half an inch thick. Some recipes recommend that the slices be coated lightly in flour and then fried on both sides in butter or olive oil. They are then served with a squeeze of lemon juice and, perhaps, a sprinkling of oregano. The cheese should always be served on very hot plates. Some recipes state that it may be placed on a dish and broiled, but this is not nearly as tasty.

Steve Johnides, who owns and is a cook at the Old Stove Pub in East Hampton, Long Island, prepares his saganaki as follows:

Heat the oven to 500 degrees. For each serving, cut ¼ pound slab of kasseri cheese into 3 rectangles about ¾ inch thick. Arrange these pieces close together in an individual heatproof ramekin or serving dish. Pour about ¼ cup of olive oil over the cheese and sprinkle with 2 tablespoons of lemon juice. Bake for 9 to 10 minutes, or until cheese is melted and bubbling hot. Serve with heated pita or whole wheat bread. Serves 1.

Sailor's Duff

Black pudding is a more refined, if less interesting, name for a dessert called sailor's duff. It is a steamed pudding, probably of English origin, made with molasses, egg, flour, baking soda, and water. It is served with a cream sauce. Spinoffs of this recipe are ginger duff, in which ginger is added, and plum duff, to which raisins and/or currants are added before steaming.

St. John's Bread

St. John's bread, also known as a locust bean, has a long pod and seeds that have a sweet pulp. Some people say it came to be known as St. John's bread because, according to legend, it was the locust bean that sustained John the Baptist when he dwelled in the desert, although the Bible states that he fed on locusts and honey.

Although I have never used locust beans in cooking, I know that they are used in the preparation of certain candies and cakes.

Salad

In that America is doubtless the most dedicated salad-eating nation in the world (and has contrived the greatest number and some of the most imaginative salads on earth), it is small wonder that salads seem much on the mind of native gastronomes.

I received a letter from a woman who raises the question of when to serve salad. "At home, we always had salad along with the main course as a vegetable, but usually we ate it after the main course. I think that must be something the way the English serve a savory.

"Then when I was grown up, I started eating in restaurants, and some time along the way, the salad came early. I think it was called 'California style' back in the thirties.

"My own preference is still for salad as we had it at home. I don't know if that is nostalgia or if it is sound gastronomically. Sometimes in a restaurant I try to defend at least part of my salad for later in the meal, but mostly I just go along with the way things are."

I have heard many theories over the years as to how salads jumped from third or fourth course to first course a few decades ago. Some say it came about with the craze for slimming practices during the so-called golden age of Hollywood.

This theory has it that a large salad, substantial enough for a complete meal, was served at the beginning of a meal in order to dull the appetite for anything that followed. Another theory holds that California mothers started serving salads at the beginning of meals to encourage children to eat their needed amount of greens.

To my mind there is no absolute, hidebound "classic" moment during which a salad should be served in the course of a meal. It is highly subjective.

In my own home a simple salad made with such things as Boston lettuce, romaine, watercress, endive, and perhaps arugula (anything but iceberg lettuce) is almost invariably served during the course of an evening meal. It is almost always served as a third or fourth course, depending on the menu, which might include a soup or a fish course, plus a main course. The salad would be served with cheese and followed by dessert.

A clergyman from Altoona, Pennsylvania, wrote as follows concerning "the delicate question of the position of salad on the menu. In the day of my pious and impressionable youth, some Roman maestro of the culinary art indicated his preference as after the soup and before the pasta and main course. The reasoning being that if the salad were served with the main course, its vinegar-based dressing would be hostile to the appreciation of the accompanying wine."

Another gentleman goes on at some length about the appropriateness of serving salad after the main course: "For your edification and, I am sure, interest, it is gastronomically proper to eat a salad after the main course, assuming that the main course is a protein or mixture thereof. Proteins require a generous amount of hydrochloric acid in your stomach in order to be properly digested. When you eat carbohydrate-rich foods such as vegetables, your stomach does not secrete much hydrochloric acid, because it is not needed for the digestion of carbohydrates. If you first fill your stomach with predominantly carbohydrate foods (as you do when you start your meal with a large, raw vegetable salad, as 'experts' tell you to do) and then finish your meal with a protein food, the protein will remain largely undigested because of an insufficient amount of hydrochloric acid in the stomach. Therefore, it is best to eat protein foods first, on an empty stomach, when the hydrochloric acid secretion will be generous; then continue with carbohydrate foods."

I have spent many an hour in the company of my peers listening to rather lengthy and tiresome discourses on the demerits of serving salad during the course of a meal where wines, particularly fine wines, are served.

The argument, logic, or whatever you choose to call it is that anything with vinegar in it—a salad dressing, for instance—is anathema to wines because it will, in turn, convert the wine into vinegar once the two are joined in the stomach. Some of these epicures will concede—reluctantly—that a salad dressing made with a touch of lemon would be acceptable.

I find the argument precious and almost invariably serve salad with cheese, bread, and wine at every serious dinner.

Salad Bars

I have heard salad bars categorized and attacked as unsophisticated, inane, and sophomoric. I think they're enormous fun, which reminds me of that classic put-down the French chefs use. If one of their number has a tendency to put too many ingredients into a dish, one more pinch of this, one more touch of that, they refer to him as a *vrai pharmacien*, or real pharmacist.

When it comes to salad bars, I delight in my expertise, pharmacy-style. A touch of Gorgonzola salad dressing on my special

blend of romaine and chicory; a bit of anchovy and a sprinkling of grated Parmesan on the spinach and mushrooms; cottage cheese on the side; and bacon bits and toasted croutons over all.

I will even add a dab of Russian dressing if it is well made, garnish the whole with raw onion rings and sliced green peppers and a few radishes, and a short while later I am ready for seconds. I have been known to take a bite or two of three-bean salad. But there is one traditional item on the standard bar that I will not indulge in. The multiflavored gelatin salad.

It should be noted that three of the salad dressings found at a salad bar may include French, Italian, and Russian, all misnomers.

Frenchmen who seriously care about their stomachs are puzzled at what Americans blithely choose to call French dressing—some of it resembles milky pink axle grease. A Frenchman's basic *sauce salade* is nothing more than a good grade of oil and vinegar, judiciously blended and seasoned with salt and pepper.

A respectable Roman would scoff at what we label Italian dressing, the dominant perfume of which is garlic and oregano. And the only thing Russian about Russian dressing is rarely used in this day and age—that is pure caviar pearls, used in the original recipe and thus the reason for the name.

Salad Bowl

One would be curious to know who started the idiotic notice that salad bowls should not be washed. That idea was quite prevalent in my childhood about half a century

ago. It is only logical to wash a salad bowl and dry it thoroughly after each use. Otherwise, the oil gets into the wood and becomes accumulatively rancid.

If a wooden salad bowl has a rancid smell from the continuous use of oil, you should try scrubbing it often with any of several things and, perhaps, try them all at intervals. Scrub with lemon and coarse salt, rubbing thoroughly and for a prolonged period inside the bowl. Rinse well and let stand in the open air (one trusts it is a good solid wood and will not warp). Or use a strong scouring powder. At some point you might try soaking the inside of the bowl with a strong hot vinegar solution, letting it stand overnight. Then rinse and scrub once more and let stand in the open air. You may have to soak the bowl several times, drying well after each soaking. If after a reasonable period the odor has not dissipated sufficiently, you might use the bowl as a planter.

Salade Olivier

Salade Olivier is made by combining cooked breast of chicken with sliced cooked potatoes, thinly sliced dill pickles, and mayonnaise. It is served in a pyramid and garnished with tomato, egg wedges, and olives.

In the late Alexandra Kropotkin's book, *The Best of Russian Cooking,* the author states that this salad was "invented and served for the first time at the Winter Palace to Tsar Nicholas II by his French chef, Monsieur Olivier. Unlike his royal employer, the chef escaped from Russia after the revolution and prospered as the proprietor of a Berlin restaurant."

Salad Greens

It sometimes seems to me that the kitchen customs of many Americans are even more fascinating than their food preferences. Over the years, I have written numerous times about whether greens for the salad bowl should be torn with the fingers or cut with a knife. I have delved into this matter not so much as a matter of personal interest, but because I am so often queried about it, as though the total success or failure of a meal lay perilously in the balance on this point.

To restate a position, I almost invariably cut salad greens with a knife. I find it more expeditious and tearing the leaves can cause bruising. In my opinion, the result is equally as appealing to the eye. I would find the whole thing grandly unimportant, caring far more about the seasoning in the bowl than whether the green morsels contained therein have more of an angularity (cut) or roundness (broken) to them. But some still take pen in hand and will not let the argument lie. Basically, the counteroffensive has nothing to do with aesthetics, which I had thought was the point, but rather it has to do with chemistry.

To quote from one of the missives: "I know that cutting lettuce with a metal blade, though quicker, starts an oxidation process that causes the cut edge to darken in a short time. As a gourmet cook, I know that for best results each salad leaf should be lightly coated with oil or dressing. This is virtually impossible to do when lettuce has been cut."

I hasten to add that in my own kitchen these days I rarely use anything but stainless steel knives that are impermeable to rust. And the cut edges of lettuce leaves, provided the cutting blade is of stainless steel, will not darken.

And then there was a letter about drying lettuce. "A friend of mine may be a little confused. She read in one of your columns that you spin-dry lettuce. She says that she does this, too. She rinses the lettuce, puts it in a pillowcase and adds this to a clothes dryer. She dries it on low speed. Is she kidding?"

I answered that I most certainly think so, and I most certainly do not intend to test her lettuce-drying technique. I use a commonly available Swiss import called a Rotor, made by the Stockli Company.

There is also the Moulinex, a very good salad dryer imported from France. Basically, the gadget consists of an inner basket into which rinsed lettuce leaves are put. The inner basket spins around (mine by pulling on a string) and this extracts the excess moisture from the leaves. That is what I mean by "spin dry."

However, I have heard from more than a score of people who wrote to assure me that America's washing machine manufacturers are a godsend for those who entertain on a large scale.

"When preparing salad greens for twenty or more people," one woman advised, "I wash the lettuce, put it into a pillowslip or pillowcase, tie the top together tightly with a rubber band, put the pillowcase with its lettuce load into the washing machine and turn the machine on for the gentle spin cycle." Within moments, she continues, you will have dried, uncrushed lettuce for your party.

A pillowcase, as it turns out, is the most popular container for the lettuce. Other readers, however, use a large bath or Turkish towel, or two bath towels that have been sewn together. One uses a large mesh-type onion bag because her region is famous for its onions.

And Alice Knopf, the wife of the publisher, notes that she also washes spinach "on the gentle wool cycle" of her washer.

Salamander

The primary use for a salamander, which is attached to a professional range, is to give a nice brown glaze to foods that have been baked. To choose a most basic example, let us say you have baked a macaroni and cheese casserole until it is bubbling and hot throughout. And yet it is only lightly golden on top. If you run the casserole under a preheated salamander, it will become nicely browned (watch it carefully so that it doesn't burn) in seconds under the unit.

I would never consider broiling a chop or a steak under the salamander. In the first place, it is messy and the salamander unit, top and bottom, is a nuisance to take apart and clean. I prefer to "broil" meats in a skillet or a ridged grill that fits on a stove burner, or on an electric or charcoal-fired grill.

I would use the salamander to broil certain foods that are not likely to drip fat as they cook. A whole fish or fish fillets, placed in a pan and dotted with butter, sprinkled with bread crumbs and so on.

I also use the unit to roast peppers and to make toast. It may be a personal idiosyncrasy, but I prefer toast made under a broiler to that made in an electric toaster. The best toast, however, is made in the oven.

The name salamander derives from that of the legendary lizard-like animal that could live in fire.

Sally Lunn

I have heard two versions of the origin of the Sally Lunn. The first is that the bread originated in Bath, England. It was sold on the streets of the town by a young woman named Sally Lunn. She sold her recipe to a baker who retained her name.

I have also read that the name is that of George Washington's Virginia cook, who specialized in the yeast bread that bears her name. I am inclined to think that the more likely origin was Bath.

Salmagundi

One of the most interesting and curious words in the English language having to do with food is salmagundi. It is a word of uncertain origin, but most authorities think it stems from the French *salmagondis,* described in *Larousse Gastronomique* as a reheated ragout of meats, including chicken.

According to the *Wise Encyclopedia of Cookery,* the French version "stems from a very special salmis . . . first concocted by an eighteenth-century chef named Gondis or Gonde." It is supposed, Wise continues, to have been "a combination of game and chicken with fillets of anchovies, in a sauce of eggs, shallots, garlic, fines herbes and white wine."

"For a hearty salad course, a salmagundi may be made by taking half-inch cubes of chicken, lamb or veal combined with smaller quantities of diced carrot, boiled potato, eggplant, peas and beans and marinating the mixture in oil with vinegar or lemon juice, grated onion, salt, pepper and a touch of tarragon vinegar. Drain well, toss with fresh mayonnaise and serve with hearts of lettuce or crisp watercress. Anchovy fillets may be added effectively, in keeping with the original formula."

There is a club named Salmagundi in New York, whose members are said to be "unqualified critics of food."

There is something about the word "salmagundi" that has an unmistakable appeal for savants with a leaning toward gourmandism.

A further explanation of the word's etymology came from a New York writer. That linkage of salmis and Gondis or Gonde, is "very plausible, very neat. In fact, so unusually neat that it aroused my never-quite-dozing skepticism, sending me running to check *The Wise Encyclopedia of Cookery* against one of my favorite French source books, a fifty-year-old relic that belonged to my father, entitled, *Dictionnaire Synoptique d'Etymologie Française.*

"Salmis, says the *Dictionnaire,* is of unknown origin, but (and I translate) 'one is tempted to see in it a contraction of a type salgamicius, from Latin *salgama,* things preserved or pickled in brine. Salmigondis is without doubt the word salmis amplified by Latin *conditus,* improved or seasoned.'

"*Webster's Second International* gives a similar explanation, inviting us to compare the parts of salmigondis with the Italian *salame* (salted meat) and the Italian and Latin *condire* (*Webster* gives this verb's meaning as 'to pickle' but it can mean 'to season, preserve or pickle' in both Italian and Latin).

"Poor Gondi, or Gonde. How soon his meteoric career has flickered and died. May he rest in peace!"

Jay Jacobs, the food writer, rushed to another source.

"A discussion of the term salmagundi impelled me to consult the indispensable *Book of the Table,* first published in 1877 and ghost-written for the London restaurateur Auguste Kettner by Eneas Sweetland Dallas, a leading literary critic of the time and an indefatigable philologist. In an essay too exhaustive to be gone into in detail here, Mr. Dallas convincingly establishes that as an English word 'salmagundi' long antedates the eighteenth century (and the possibly nonexistent French chef Gondis, or Gonde, credited by the *Wise Encyclopedia* with the authorship of 'a very special salmis').

"As to the term's 'uncertain origin,' Dallas brings a wealth of scholarly evidence to bear on his argument, which, stated simply, is that the syllables 'sal' and 'ma' mean 'sauce' and 'bird,' respectively, and that 'magundi,' like the 'mawmene' of early English cookery treatises, is 'a fowl frayed—what we still call pulled chicken.'"

And, finally, the cookbook author Paula Wolfert (*Cous Cous and Other Good Food from Morocco*) wrote, "There exists in Jamaican cuisine a dish called Solomon Gundy (note the spelling), which consists of a paste of red herring, garlic and Jamaican spices used as a relish or dip and I suspect there is a connection between the two dishes."

Salmon

In gastronomic lore, there's an imaginary land called Cockaigne where "the houses are built of sugar and cake, the streets are paved with pastry," and "the shops supply their wares for free." Birds fall out of the sky, spit-roasted and oven-ready, and fish spring out of rivers and streams into the nets of fishermen. It is said that in the earliest days when white men arrived on this continent, the rivers of New England and New York were so filled with salmon it seemed like Cockaigne. So much so that after the Declaration of Independence was signed it became a New England custom—principally around Boston and in the Connecticut area—to serve steamed salmon with green peas and new potatoes as the holiday meal, with strawberry shortcake for dessert.

Salmon, it would seem, has always been a prized fish. There is said to be an etching of one on a cave wall in southern France that dates back more than twelve thousand years. To Pliny is attributed the observation that in southwestern Gaul "the river salmon is preferred to all the fish that swim in the sea."

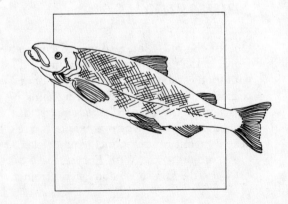

Perhaps for genuine salmon fanciers, the ultimate time to have lived was in an era described by Sir Walter Scott, who lived from 1771 to 1832.

"Salmon," he wrote, was in that age "caught in such plenty . . . instead of being accounted a delicacy, it was generally supplied to feed the servants, who are said sometimes to have [protested] that they should not be required to eat a food so luscious and surfeiting . . . above five times a week."

Remember the legend of Jonah and the whale? There is a painting in the Smithsonian Institution, executed by an American Indian of the Northwest a century or so ago. So awed was the artist by the salmon that it shows Jonah in the stomach of an enormous salmon.

According to John von Glahn of the Fishery Council, and my favorite authority on such matters, the vast majority of the fresh salmon consumed on the East Coast arrives from the Pacific by air freight. Predominant is the king salmon.

Nearly 850,000 pounds are sold each year. Some 58,000 pounds of silver salmon satisfy the appetites of gastronomes. Another 23,000 pounds of Atlantic salmon arrive by truck from Canadian waters. In addition to which 1,137,000 pounds of frozen salmon are directed to those who smoke fish commercially, supermarkets and fish markets, and for canning purposes. *See also* Smoked salmon.

Salsify

Salsify is often referred to in this country as oyster plant, and it is an excellent winter vegetable. It is a root plant, white in color and shaped somewhat like a carrot. The

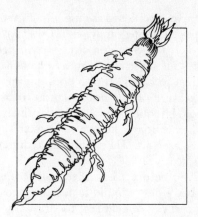

most basic preparation for salsify is to scrape them, cook them briefly in water, and then sauté them in butter.

There are many ways in which they may be cooked and served, including in a cream sauce. The reason they are known as oyster plant is that to some palates they have a vague oyster-like flavor.

Salt

I have not used salt for several years, because of hypertension, and many people ask if I ever put a saltshaker on the table to permit guests to help themselves. The answer is yes, on occasion. If a saltshaker and pepper mill are not placed on the table before guests sit down to dine, it is more often than not through negligence.

If a guest at my table wants salt, I will happily supply a saltshaker with apologies, and I certainly feel no slight if a guest wishes to add salt to the food off my stove. There is one thing I cannot abide in that area, however. It is those people who in Chinese restaurants douse their food with soy sauce, frequently before they sample it.

I never questioned the use of salt in many recipes, including candy, until I was advised to go on a low-sodium diet. In retrospect it makes no sense to me to add salt in any amount to candy. It also does nothing for the texture and is not essential to bread dough. I frequently make bread, principally the French loaves known as baguettes, and never use salt. The results are eminently satisfactory.

Even before I banished salt from my kitchen I never found it necessary to salt down slices of eggplant to draw out the water. It does work, of course. Enough moisture emerges so that it can be drained. It is also true of cucumber slices. I can assure you that this step can be omitted and that the end result will be as tasty as you desire. *See also* Kosher salt, Rock salt.

Salt Cod

Freshly caught cod is the foundation for one of the great preserved fish of all times, salt cod. Salt cod is highly prized in Europe, particularly by the inhabitants of the Mediterranean countries. It goes by the name of

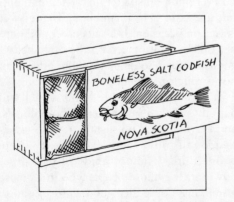

bacalao in Spain and *baccalà* in Italy. The French term is *morue*. There is a mousse of salt cod in the south of France known as brandade de morue, which is a staple at my New Year's Eve festivities.

Salt-Rising Bread

Salt-rising bread is one of those regional American dishes for which some people have a passion and which inspire in others something short of aversion. The bread is made by a natural fermentation, and for a period it is a bit malodorous. The finished product is a bit tangy with a flavor that is at times described as "cheese-like."

Unfortunately I have never known of a commercial source for salt-rising bread north of the Mason-Dixon Line, nor, for that matter, since my childhood in the South.

Samp

Samp is a coarse hominy made from kernels of dried corn. Although many of today's residents on the eastern end of Long Island may not know it, it is as typical of the region—if not more so—than clam pies. Many tales are told by long-time residents of the area, including the legend that whaling vessels plying the bay waters offshore, even in the thickest fog or darkest night, could tell from the sound of samp-pounding how close in-shore they were.

The name is derived from the Narragansett word *nasaump,* meaning corn mush. The difference between samp and hominy is that the former is made from whole hulled kernels, while hominy has had the germ removed.

Samphire

See Perche-pierres.

Sand Crabs

I had never heard of cooking sand crabs, also known as mole crabs, until I came across a publication that explained that the crabs are used in preparing an Ecuadorean soup called *barquito*. Here are two recipes offered in *Sea Secrets,* a monthly publication of the International Oceanographic Foundation in Miami.

For making barquito, "one begins by catching one to two pounds of live mole crabs, rinsing them in fresh water until clear of sand, and cooking them until they are tender. The crabs are mashed and strained. Two or three red onions, chopped and fried in oil and butter, are mixed with the strained

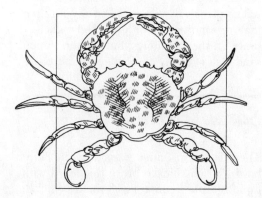

crab broth, some water, and minced coriander. Then add thin noodles, rice, cut-up potatoes, or toasted wheat flour.

In another recipe, fifteen or twenty well-rinsed crabs are dropped into four cups of boiling water, along with one chopped tomato, two stalks of celery with leaves, one sliced carrot, one medium onion, chopped lemon rind, salt and pepper. "Cook these ingredients until tender, adding one can of garbanzo beans (drained) in the last five minutes. The crabs may be removed before serving, if desired. The most difficult part of the recipes is catching the little crabs, as they burrow rapidly into the sand for survival."

And then came a letter from a Manhattan gentleman.

"I recall," he wrote, "eating them several times in Spain in 1938, in Cambrils, a fishing town on the coast, south of Tarragona. I had never seen them eaten before or since.

"When I was first served these tiny crabs on a bed of rice, the friendly fisherman explained to me that these were *los cangrejos que andan atras* (crabs that walked backward). They were valued primarily for the flavor they imparted to the rice, as there was nothing to eat in them.

"Those were hungry days in Spain and those rice dishes were gourmet feasts. I recall that they were accompanied by fried smelts caught during the night. Thanks for the memories."

Sandwiches

England's greatest contribution to gastronomy has nothing to do with Brussels sprouts, toad-in-the-hole, bubble and squeak, or roast beef and Yorkshire pud-

ding. It is purely and simply the sandwich, that portable edible whose consumption in America alone must total in the billions in the course of a year.

The legend of the origin of the name is almost as familiar as that of George Washington, the cherry tree, and his moral incapacity to tell a lie.

Almost any schoolboy can tell you that the sandwich was named for John Montagu, the fourth Earl of Sandwich, who, in his desire not to leave the gambling table, requested his manservant to bring him meat between bread to assuage his hunger.

What that schoolboy will not be able to tell you is that the fourth Earl of Sandwich was far better known in his day as a scoundrel, a rogue, and a scandalous blackguard, a reputation well recorded in my favorite source book, the eleventh edition of the *Encyclopedia Britannica*.

Montagu held his posts in his day. He was at one time or another postmaster general of the British Isles, secretary of state, and the first lord of the Admiralty.

"For corruption and incapacity," the encyclopedia reveals, "Sandwich's administration is unique in the history of the British Navy." Under his direction, the book adds, "offices were bought, stores were stolen, and, worst of all, ships, unseaworthy and inadequately equipped, were sent to fight battles of their country."

Not a line in praise of the father of the BLT; the Monte Cristo; the Reuben; pan bania; the club; mozzarella en carrozza; the croque monsieur and the croque madame, and those tall-stacked and inspired creations of the Stage Deli. No heroes? No submarines? Without him the residents of New England might well have been spared something I have only heard of by reputation, sandwiches made with baked beans!

There is no end, of course, to what sandwiches can be and are made of, and connoisseurs of the open, single-, double-, or triple-deckers have strong opinions about how they should be made. Should they be buttered or does mayonnaise suffice? I personally plump for no butter with lots of mayonnaise, preferably homemade and, depending on the filling, one slice smeared with mustard. A hamburger would be an exception to that rule in my kitchen. I like a hamburger on a lighly toasted, buttered bun and, occasionally, an English muffin. No mayonnaise, no mustard, but a slice of onion and lots of ketchup with the bottle left on the table, diner fashion.

Some people don't trim the crusts of sandwiches made with sandwich bread. I demur. Don't serve me an untrimmed sandwich, please. I will stand in my kitchen making sandwiches for hours and munch at times on the trimmings, but an untrimmed sandwich is to my eyes vulgar and crude.

Sarah Bernhardt

There is a consommé named Sarah Bernhardt, a rich chicken broth thickened with tapioca and containing small chicken dumplings, truffles, poached marrow, and asparagus tips. There is also a stuffed-egg dish named Sarah Bernhardt in which the filling contains the yolks, chopped chicken, and bread crumbs; these are covered with a truffle sauce and baked until piping hot.

The Sarah Bernhardt cookie was named for Bernhardt during a visit to Denmark in 1893. The recipe was brought to this country by a Danish pastry maker named Jesperson. The cookie is actually a macaroon with a filling of cream and chocolate and coated with chocolate.

Sardines

There are certain facts and legends about food that stick in my mind like scorched sauce in a kettle. One of them has to do with sardines.

Twenty or more years ago, I was told of a society of sardine fanciers in France whose communal interest was in the aging of sardines in cans. I have been told that sardines, like wine in bottles, do age well. The members of that group, I was informed, met once a year to make a ritual of turning over an entire pantry full of tins in order to redis-

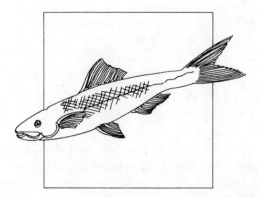

tribute the oil in which the sardines were packed. That was so the sardines would age more evenly.

After the turning process, the ladies and gentlemen of the society sat down and dined on their vintage fish with crusty loaves of French bread. It is the kind of story that stimulates my imagination.

Do they use a squeeze of lemon to bring out flavor? Would that be gastronomic heresy? How long, do you suppose, has the society been in existence, and how old is the oldest tin in the pantry? Who first conceived the idea that the sardines would improve when left standing? Does the texture of a sardine, say one that is from a fifty-year-old lot, improve as well as the flavor?

The whole idea is a bit of a burden to me, for I recall thinking that I would much like to taste one of those aged sardines. And now I am angry that I didn't stash a tin or two away for a present-day sampling. I could sit here with a vintage sardine and see how it stacks up with one out of a can just purchased at the local supermarket.

Satays

No food preparation, to my knowledge, is better suited to warm weather and the summer season than the one known in Indonesia as satays. For those unfamiliar with them, they might best be described as less-than-elaborate shish kebabs with a curried flavor. When I say less than elaborate, I mean that the meats, while threaded on skewers, are not alternated with layers of mushrooms, green peppers, onions, and the like.

I have been hooked on the concept of satays since I first visited Bali and its environs a good many years ago. They are easy to prepare and are particularly good when cooked over charcoal. Often, satays are served with a sauce made of ground peanuts or peanut butter, one of the noblest and most tempting uses for that product. The sauce is spicy and often a trifle sweet.

Satays can be made of almost any sort of meat, poultry, or seafood (such as shrimp). Ideally, I prefer to dine on an assortment of them prepared on separate skewers—for example, one of chicken, one of beef, one of lamb, and so on.

To be altogether pure in the preparation of satays, one should use several exotic spices and herbs, such as lemon grass, shrimp paste, and leaves, such as those called salam and lime. These are rare, though available, in this country. With a few modifications, however, enormously tempting satays can be turned out using herbs and spices from the pantry shelf— cumin, coriander, turmeric, etc.

The one sauce that can be found with relatively small effort is called *ketjap manis* and is available in many shops that specialize in Asian foods. It adds a good deal to the marinades of certain satays. If it is not to be found, one may substitute a dark soy sauce, blended with an equal volume of sugar, a touch of water, and a couple of crushed garlic cloves.

Sauce

Basically a sauce and a gravy are the same thing. A sauce is, to my ears, simply a more sophisticated and better sounding word than gravy.

To stretch a very fine point, it seems to me that a gravy would probably contain

flour as a thickener and would not be as refined as a sauce. But I have received comments from those who disagree: "There *is* a difference to us of Italian origin who have had the ecstatic pleasure of smelling Mom or Grandma's gravy slowly simmering for hours on a Sunday morning. (You know, Sundays and Thursdays were traditional pasta days; not Wednesdays.)

"Gravy, as we learned, was that sauce that had been highly elevated in taste by sautéing of the braciole, and subsequently, meatballs. (Some Italian families sometimes added sausages or pork chops for a slightly different-tasting gravy.)

"Thus, without meat we knew it as tomato sauce and with meats, gravy. Yes, there is a difference despite the fancy marketing of the various brands of 'sauces.' Come to my house sometime and take in the wondrous aroma of real gravy!"

Sauce Bâtarde

There is an interesting sauce in French cookery known as sauce bâtarde, which, if you will excuse the expression, means bastard sauce. It achieved that name, not in the slurring or demeaning sense where taste is concerned, but because the liquid used in making the sauce is not a stock or broth but plain water.

Sauerkraut

Like most things in cooking, whether to wash sauerkraut is a question of individual taste. Some people enjoy mildly flavored sauerkraut. Some like it pungent with its original brine. I like it in almost any preparation, but personally I believe in compromises. Frankly, I prefer unwashed sauerkraut. On the other hand, in my own kitchen, I empty the sauerkraut into a sieve and press to extract as much of the original brine as possible. Within reason, of course. I then put it into a kettle and add about equal portions of chicken broth and dry white or semi-dry white wine, a little chopped garlic, and several peppercorns. A juniper berry or two, or caraway seeds, are not at all amiss. Incidentally, if you want to experiment, substitute a bit of dry or semisweet sherry for part of your cooking liquid. It adds an interesting flavor.

Unfortunately, my present intake of sauerkraut is exceedingly limited because of the salt content.

Saumur

A saumur in French cookery is purely and simply a brine that is used for pickling meats. It can be used over and over if it is kept refrigerated or in a cold place.

Sausages

See Andouillettes, Boudins blancs, Frankfurter, Garlic sausage, Linguiça, Luganega, Morcilla, Zampone.

Sautéing

See Frying.

Savarin

A savarin is a sweetened yeast bread made with an ample quantity of eggs. The recipe is related to that of the baba as in baba au rhum. One source book, *Dictionnaire de l'Académie des Gastronomes*, notes that the sweet cake or bread was created by "the brothers Julien" in 1845 and that it was dedicated to Brillat-Savarin. The cake or bread is often doused with a sweet syrup, plus rum or kirsch, and is served for dessert. It might also be served with afternoon tea.

Savories

The savories of the British Isles, a curious and fascinating category of food, have always intrigued me, particularly because of their original placement on a menu.

As the name implies, savories are foods that are piquant and pungent to the taste, distinctly lacking in sweetness. The names of the dishes are often amusing, names such as angels on horseback, devils on horseback, Scotch woodcock, and Welsh rabbit.

But piquant and pungent though they may be, savories were never considered as openers to a meal. To the contrary, they were, during Victorian times, almost invariably served as a separate course at the very end of the meal after the sweet course or dessert. The explanation was that these dishes would clear the palate and, where the male at the table was concerned, prepare it for the port wine.

Today, I am told, savories (and they appear as such in the best and most modern British books on food) are more likely to be served at lunchtime or at a leisurely brunch. They are also offered as quick snacks and sometimes at high teas.

Scallions

See Green onions.

Scalloped

Scalloped dishes are generally those made with a cream base such as scalloped oysters, scalloped potatoes, scalloped clams, and so on. At times, the cream base consists of a thickened sauce, sometimes pure cream. Many scalloped dishes are made with bread crumbs or cracker crumbs. The dishes, after they are assembled—frequently in layers—and dotted with butter, are baked until bubbling hot and golden brown. The term "scalloped" presumably came about because such foods were served in scallop shells.

Scallops

Scallops are, conceivably, my favorite bivalve, with an incredible versatility where preparation is concerned. Recently at lunch I asked a very young neighbor as he speared his fork into a large platter of broiled scallops what it was that he admired so much about the bay scallops. With scarely a pause he answered, "No bones." Now that is putting it simplistically.

It is curious that so many people who willingly eat raw oysters and clams are sometimes dubious about eating raw scallops, which are delicious. Almost any kind of fish or shellfish can be used in the making of seviche, which is a blend of raw fish marinated in lime or lemon juice with seasonings. Scallops are excellent in a seviche. It goes without saying, of course, that the fish or shellfish must come from unpolluted waters.

I went scalloping in Monkauk Lake one time with Lex McClosky, a tall, blond, handsome Bonacker with a fine toothpaste grin. He lifted a freshly harvested bay scallop from a yard-long dredge, opened it with his pen knife, and threw the top shell over the side. He discarded the gooey dark mass that surrounded the scallop's coveted white muscle and popped that morsel into his

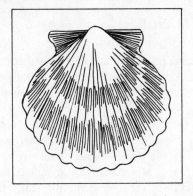

mouth. No lemon juice, no salt, no nothing.

"Sweet," he averred and added, "I like scallops, but I can't afford to eat 'em that often."

Mr. McClosky—twenty-eight years old—was pursuing the profession that he has followed almost all his life, scalloping all winter, fishing all summer.

"When I was a kid," he said, "I scalloped with an old man named Harvey Fields. He paid me $10 a day. I went on my own when I was fourteen."

"How on earth could you afford a boat?" a passenger asked.

"Well, it wasn't much of a boat."

The scallop season in Bonacker waters (the name derives from the people who live around Accabonac Lake in East Hampton, but is has come to be applied to people who have lived on the eastern tip of Long Island for several generations, as well as to places there that are landmarks) lasts from about the middle of September to the end of March.

"During the first two weeks of the season when the weather's good and the whole lake is loaded with scallops, I take my wife along," the fisherman continued. "With two people in a boat you can legally take twenty bushels of scallops in state waters; but when

you're alone, you're only allowed ten."

Mr. McClosky's workday, summer and winter, is from before dawn to after dusk. In the winter, clad in double and triple-weather gear, he gets into his boat just before sunup and, short minutes later, his boat arrives in the middle of Montauk Lake.

"The only time I miss," he said, "is when the harbor's frozen or when it's too rough or too cold. The wind's the worst that can happen to you. It *really* takes the fun out of it when it's under 20 degrees."

The scalloping procedure is backbreaking, but it is relatively simple. Mr. McClosky's eighteen-foot boat (scallop boats hereabouts are called sharpies) has six dredges, metal frames with seine-like, interlinking metal rings or woven line.

Either four or six of the dredges are thrown over the side into the six-foot-deep waters for each haul. The front dredges are primarily for clearing away sea grass and "sputnik" grass. A visitor asked how the latter achieved such a recently coined name.

"These waters don't always have that kind of grass," he said. "It showed up in the lake at about the same time the Russians put up their first sky launch so everybody called it sputnik grass."

The skipper hauled up the second dredges, and mingled with a few dozen scallops were strands of sea grass, empty shells, and rocks. The scallops in the shell were quickly sorted and tossed into a half-bushel basket.

Scallops, the gentleman explained, have an eighteen-month life span. Like an oyster, when a scallop is spawned it is so minute it is not visible to the naked eye. A full-grown scallop is possessed of a "growth" ring that occurs at the end of the first cycle of its life.

The ring, which occurs halfway up the

scallop shell, is curved and parallel to the upper perimeter of the scallop. The scallop at its maturity measures about two and a quarter inches in width, and the scallop must have either the growth ring or that measurement to be taken legally.

At the end of the day the young man had harvested slightly more than five bushels of scallops, which he considers not a bad haul for an average season.

At the end of each day's harvest the scallops in the shell are taken to local shucking sheds, where professional openers, generally women, wield their knives to extract a pure white muscle.

It is an act that goes so fast as to resemble prestidigitation. A knife is quickly, almost surgically, entered into the shell and whisked around the white muscle, which is reserved. All the other parts, including the roe, are jettisoned.

Which explains why, generally speaking, Americans cannot get the prized arc-shaped coral that is part and parcel of scores of scallops dishes served in other countries.

Out of curiosity, I purchased six or so scallops, unopened in the shell, from my local fish market. I opened the scallops and reserved the roe and cooked it briefly with the muscles.

The roe from scallops near my home is smaller than that found in European waters. It is not particularly appealing to the eye, having a rather insipid beige color and a too-soft texture. In short, I found it had little going for it. *See also* Coquilles St.-Jacques.

Schav

See Sorrel.

Schiacciata

Schiacciata is a pizza-like dish made with pizza dough baked with a coating of salt and olive oil. No tomatoes, no mushrooms, no anchovies.

The most tempting schiacciata recipe I have comes from a New Yorker whose recipe for the dish "comes from my grandmother's hometown, Ragusa, Sicily. The bread dough is stretched until nearly transparent, covered with a mixture of olive oil, parsley, and basil, then folded into a rectangle. This is then covered with tomato sauce and caciocavallo cheese, folded again and baked. With a really elastic dough, the result is delicious, flaky bread, a family favorite, and by the way, much better than pizza."

Scofa

I have never sampled scofa bread and have never heard of scofa meal sold in America. But Elizabeth David, in her book *English Bread and Yeast Cookery,* states that bread mixes, with the chemical raising agents already mixed in, are available to the general public and these include scofa meal, either brown or white, "which makes quite an attractive, coarse and rough scone-type loaf."

Scrapple

Scrapple is, to my mind, one of the greatest regional American specialties. The name derives from the word "scrap" and relates to scraps or odd parts of the pig from which it is made. Scrapple is of Pennsylvania Dutch origin; it was first made by the early German settlers in that state. It consists of chopped or minced pieces of pork liver, pork hearts, pork skin, and so on, which are blended with cornmeal. The finest commercial scrapple I have ever sampled is made by the Jones Dairy Farm of Wisconsin. It has no artificial ingredients and I find it the equal of homemade scrapple. It is sold frozen in one-pound packages.

When I prepare scrapple in my own kitchen, I flour the slices before cooking, but this new product, when sliced, is fine and crisp without flouring. *See also* Goette.

Scrod

A man arrives in Boston on a first visit. All his life he has hungered for Boston scrod. He goes to a restaurant, glances at the menu, and tells the waitress, "I'd like an order of Boston scrod, please."

"Sorry, sir, I just sold the last order."

He leaves the restaurant and goes to a fish house across the street, looks at the menu there, and tells the waitress, "I'd like an order of Boston scrod, please."

"Sorry, sir, we're out of Boston scrod."

He departs, goes to the curb and hails a cab. "Is there any place in Boston," he asks the driver, "where a man can get scrod?"

The driver stares at him a moment and says, "Mister, I been driving a hack in this town for thirty years but you're the first person I ever heard ask for it in the pluperfect past tense."

The name scrod, according to the New England Fish Exchange, is applied to the small sizes of four fish, notably cod, haddock, cusk, and pollock. The name scrod is generally applied to fish weighing from one

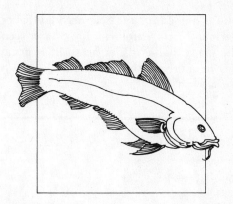

to one and one-half pounds (the exceptions are young cusk and pollock, which may weigh up to three or four pounds).

These are all members of the cod family. The listing of fish also details small scrod—including the above four fish plus hake, which is also a member of the cod family—and specifies that these fish that weigh less than one and one-half pounds "shall be called trash and not to be taken as scrod."

Sculpin

See Rascasse.

Scungilli

See Conch.

Scuppernong

As a Southerner I am altogether familiar with the sweet, pungent, "grapey" taste of Scuppernong. It is a variety of muscadine and is named for the Scuppernong River basin in North Carolina. I have never seen the grape marketed nor heard of it being grown in the North. It is used in the South for a relish.

Sea Biscuit

See Hardtack.

Sea Fennel

See Perche-pierres.

Sea Robin

Sea robin is not widely available in American fish markets; you'll have to depend on a friend. If you know a weekend sailor or fisherman and he hooks something that grunts when it is hoisted on deck, have him bring it home.

It is easy to fillet a sea robin, according to my colleague Pierre Franey. He says, "Cut

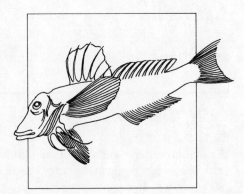

right behind the head to the center bone of the sea robin. Do not cut through that center bone, however. Instead, when you reach that bone, turn the boning knife so it is almost parallel to the bone. Run the knife in the direction of the tail all along the bone's length. This removes one fillet. Turn the fish over and remove the other fillet in the same manner."

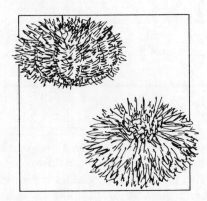

Sea Urchins

I have been tremendously fond of sea urchins since first trying them years ago in Marseilles. The most basic method of serving them is to clip away those prickly spines on the outside. Use a pair of shears to cut a hole in the top and serve the delicate roe on the half shell, raw, chilled, with lemon juice. The Japanese serve them on top of rice as sushi and they are a costly delicacy.

In the Caribbean, I have often had the roe of the sea urchin removed from the shell and cooked and served in a spicy casserole. I have never cooked sea urchins, probably because I have never had them in large supply in my kitchen.

Larousse Gastronomique mentions sea urchins that are lightly boiled and eaten "like an egg." It adds that the roe is sometimes rubbed through a sieve and blended with a béchamel sauce.

Seedcake

In England a seedcake is based on what is known as a Madeira cake. The Madeira cake is a rather plain cake made with sugar, butter, flour, and eggs and halfway through the baking the top is decorated with a little candied citron or orange peel. The name arises because it is or was customarily served with a glass of Madeira. The cake becomes a seedcake if a small amount of caraway seed is used in lieu of the candied fruit peel.

In America, a seedcake is a derivative of a simple poundcake in which caraway seeds and candied citron or orange peel have been mixed before baking.

Self-Rising Flour

See Flour.

Seltzer

Pure seltzer water is a natural gaseous water with a substantial natural mineral content. Carbonated water, also called seltzer water, is produced by using a seltzer bottle containing a CO_2 cartridge or other means to introduce carbon dioxide into "plain" water, that is to say tap water. Club soda generally contains other elements. One of the most popular brands, one that I carry on my shelf, states that it is made with "carbonated water, sodium bicarbonate, sodium citrate and artificial flavoring consisting of specifically blended mineral salts."

The name seltzer is of German origin. It derives from the waters of the Nieder Selters, a district near Wiesbaden, West Germany, which is or was famous for its natural sparkling waters.

Semolina

See Flour.

Senate Bean Soup

I have often pondered what there is about Senate bean soup that has made it the subject of so much controversy as to its origin and formula. I had innocently assumed that the controversy was of relatively recent origin, say the past twenty years or so.

An acquaintance, involved in research of a wholly different nature, recently glanced through the Sunday magazine section of *The New York Times* dated January 23, 1938, and uncovered an article entitled "Cookery of a Nation Centers in the Capitol." On that date the "maestro of the skillets" in the Senate kitchen was a chef named George Dietrich. And bean soup had appeared, according to the article, on the menus of *both* the House and Senate "for more than fifteen years."

The recipes for both the House and Senate versions are virtually the same except that the House chef "simmers the soup four hours and adds a bit of pork." The Senate chef cooks his soup a shorter time.

The best bean for the soup is said to be "a pea bean from California."

"Other ingredients are a ham hock and chopped onion," the article continued. "The beans are soaked overnight and then boiled gently with a piece of ham and bone. A large onion, chopped fine, is braised in a little butter and added to the soup. The beans are lightly bruised to cloud the soup a little, and salt and pepper are added to taste."

Nowhere is there mention of mashed potatoes, which, some current authorities insist, are the chief difference between Senate bean soup and any other white bean soup.

One chef theorizes, and, in all probability, rightly so, that at one random meal—no inspiration aforethought—the chef in the Senate made a mistake one day and ladled into the soup a considerable helping of the mashed potatoes that were warming on an adjacent burner.

Senegalese Soup

For years I have believed that the name for Senegalese soup, a curried cream-of-chicken soup, derives from Senegal, formerly part of French West Africa. Then I received a highly informative letter from a Jersey City gentleman who said he had always assumed that the soup came from Sri Lanka, as Ceylon is now known. "There are several Sanskrit names, including Lanka, for that country, and one of these is Sinhala or Singhala," he said. "Curry is scarcely to be connected with Senegal." People "always reach for the more familiar term when taking over foreign sounds," he added.

Serve Immediately

There is an understandable hang-up in many American cooks' minds, and, with an apology, food writers and editors are as responsible for this longstanding misconception as anyone. Perhaps more so. The vast majority of recipes for hot dishes specify in no uncertain terms, "SERVE IMMEDIATELY." Well, it's time for a qualified retraction and confession: You really don't have to serve that fine roast goose and a gaggle of other dishes the moment they emerge from the oven. Relax. Have a glass of white wine. Go in, sit down, and make your guests feel at home. And, while you are at it, make yourself at home. Those well-planned victuals you cooked in advance are not going to be contaminated or otherwise desecrated while you sit with your guests and enjoy yourself. With a little bit of prestidigitation during the last fifteen minutes before you sit down at the table and pick up the fish fork, that dinner is going to taste every bit as good as if you had stewed and fussed and followed the dictate to "SERVE IMMEDIATELY."

I once printed a recipe for stuffed shad and the directions required removing the fish from the oven after baking and then making a cream sauce with the pan drippings. The total time for preparing the sauce was fifteen or twenty minutes.

I had an inquiry from a perplexed cook who asked how on earth such a dish could be kept warm with such a time lapse.

The reply would apply to almost any dish that must remain warm for twenty minutes or longer after it is removed from the oven. Of course, there are some dishes that should stand twenty minutes once cooked, including roast lamb and roast beef, so that the juices will be redistributed after roasting.

In the case of the stuffed shad, however, the answer is to remove the fish to a warm but not overly hot place and cover it fairly loosely with a sheet of aluminum foil. If covered too closely, the food tends to steam through retained heat and this is not desirable.

As the dish stands, the plates on which it is to be served should be heated thoroughly. When the sauce is finished, it should be boiling hot or thereabouts. When the dish is served on very hot plates and the piping hot sauce spooned over, you will give the impression of serving a very hot main course.

Serving

When you are passing a food, a casserole for example, to allow guests to serve themselves when seated at table, you offer the food from the left because it is more logical. Most people are right-handed and, therefore, it is easier for them to manage the service—the fork in the left hand, the spoon in the right. Service from the right side is clumsy and awkward. This argument is based on the rule that the majority—in this case, right-handed people—wins. On the other hand, you pour wine from the right side. That is because the wine glass is placed on the right side of the place setting, and it would be awkward to pour the wine from the left. Similarly, you remove dishes by reaching over the right shoulder of each guest. Custom follows logic.

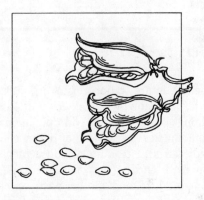

Sesame Seeds

Sesame seeds come in various colors including white or cream, which are the commonest. They may also be red, brown, or black. To the best of my knowledge, the flavors and oil content are identical. You may produce sesame oil from any color, and it will be almost tasteless and colorless. As far as I know, the use of one or the other seed is simply for color. I know that black sesame seeds are often used to coat the outside of buns before baking.

Seviche

Seviche derives from the Spanish word *cebollo*, which means onion. On some menus, seviche is spelled cebiche. If I am not mistaken, chopped onion was a dominant ingredient in any preparation of the raw fish and lime juice dish.

Today, of course, seviche, like chili con carne, comes in limitless variations and flavors and some of the versions do not contain onion at all.

Sfogliatelle

Sfogliatelle are Italian turnovers that are made, preferably, with flaky or puff pastry, although a short pastry will do. The usual filling is made with a blend of ricotta cheese, candied fruit, egg, vanilla, and a pinch of cinnamon. The pastry is cut into circles, the filling is added, and another pastry circle is placed on top and sealed all around. These are then baked until done.

The word *foglia* means "leaf," and, as with other Italian words, when you put an "s" in front of it, it means deleafing.

Shad

I am frequently asked to name my favorite food and that is a bottomless exercise in futility. I *can* cite my favorite poem about food, however, without hesitation. The author is unknown to me, but I came by the lyrics through the late and marvelously urbane Lucius Beebe.

Oh, the spring is in his bones
(And the shad has bones to spare)
As he steers himself and moans
For the warm bright Delaware . . .
Don't wish him any less bones
He'd be too good if he had
But cry it in tempest tones,
The fish of fish is shad!
Brown and white to the heart's delight
The broiled and beautiful shad.

The availability of shad in this country usually begins early in February in the rivers around Florida. The fish travels up the Altamaha and Ogeechee rivers in Georgia, through the waters of the Carolinas, then

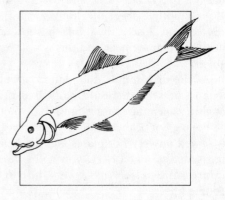

the Chesapeake and the Delaware and, eventually, it is found in some unpolluted sections of the Hudson (shad will neither swim nor spawn in polluted waters for lack of oxygen). The season ends in Connecticut near the end of May.

Legend has it that a hundred years ago shad was considered, in America at least, "trash fish." Particularly in the South, where it was abundant, it was never eaten by the white aristocracy. It was food for slaves and at times was used as fertilizer. That conception, or misconception, about the delicate nature of the fish and the roe in particular is gone forever.

Shallots

A genuine shallot is either round or elongated, with an onion-like interior (it is a member of the onion family) and with a thin skin that is reddish brown or sometimes a gray-blue color.

In Louisiana, green onions or scallions are often referred to as shallots. When French settlers entered that region they undoubtedly resorted to green onions as a substitute for the shallots of their homeland and so referred to them as shallots.

The important thing about storage of shallots is to keep them in a fairly airy, cool, and well-ventilated space. In my own kitchen, such things as shallots, onions, and garlic are kept in a drawer with a metal bottom above which rests a mesh rack. The rack allows air to come in contact with the bottoms of the vegetables. It may help, of course, to buy shallots in modest quantities. Over a very long period they are likely to spoil, no matter how much air circulates around them.

Shark

I have often been asked whether shark is edible. The answer is quite definitely yes, and one of the best seafood dishes I've every sampled was a platter of mako shark prepared teriyaki-style and cooked over a charcoal fire by my friend Shizuo Tsuji, the distinguished head of the Tsuji Hotel School in Osaka, Japan.

He happened to be a visitor in my home when a neighbor and fisherman brought in a mako steak from a shark he had caught off Montauk, Long Island. Shizuo proceeded to cut the fish into cubes before marinating it in a blend of soy sauce, mirin (a sweet sake), garlic, ginger, and so on.

Unfortunately, much of the shark that is caught in American waters is improperly handled and it spoils easily. When mishandled, shark flesh has a distinct smell and taste of ammonia. Ideally, when it is caught it must be packed in ice as quickly as possible and treated as highly perishable.

One of the best-known methods for preparing fresh shark meat is to salt and smoke it. According to the old Artemus Ward *Encyclopedia of Food,* "dried, salted flesh [of shark] is sold in Folkestone, England, as 'Folkestone beef.'"

For centuries, of course, the Chinese have prized the fins of sharks for shark's fin soup, considered one of the great banquet dishes of the Chinese table.

Shchi

The broadest description of shchi (pronounced SHCHEE) is cabbage soup. There is a good deal of latitude in its various preparations, however. There are, in fact, as many recipes for the dish as there are for clam chowder in this country. In its commonest form it is made with cabbage, shredded or coarsely chopped, plus other winter root vegetables, such as carrots, celery root, turnips, potatoes, and so on. These are cooked in a broth, generally pork or beef. To the basic mixture are added or substituted such things as tomatoes, dried mushrooms, dill, parsley, sauerkraut, and sausages. Among the many kinds of shchi, there is *shchi soldataki,* or soldier's shchi, in which all sauerkraut is used in lieu of cabbage.

Maria Robbins, a neighbor and cookbook author who was born in the town of Poltava in the Ukraine ("the breadbasket of Russia"), says that to her mind shchi is a more common "everyday" Russian dish than borscht, which is, of course, to most Western minds the national soup of the Soviet Union.

"Shchi is seasonal and doesn't have to be made with sauerkraut," she said. "Sometimes it is made with sorrel, sometimes with cabbage or sauerkraut, and it is served with or without potatoes and sour cream."

She-Crab Soup

She-crab soup, a specialty of Charleston and of Savannah, Georgia, is one of the most talked-about soups in American regional cooking.

It is one of the simplest of soups to make because its base is merely a white sauce of butter, a little flour, and milk. The sauce is thinned and enriched with heavy cream and flavored with onion juice, mace, Worces-

tershire sauce, and dry sherry. In theory the soup should be made with the flesh and eggs of the female crab (obviously, the male does not yield eggs).

Some books state that if you are unable to obtain the female meat and eggs, you may resort to the male flesh and add a few crumbled, hard-boiled egg yolks to the bottom of each soup bowl as a substitute for the real McCoy.

Sherbet

The name sherbet has an interesting etymology. It comes to us from the French word *sorbet,* and I had long presumed that the dessert was of French origin. Actually, according to the most reliable food encyclopedias, the French word derives from the Italian *sorbetto;* the Italian comes from the Turkish *charbet,* which means a sort of beverage, and sherbets came from an Arab confectioner.

Sherbets are very much a part of nouvelle cuisine and their character has been vastly expanded. They are quite often prepared not only with berries and fruits from strawberries to passion fruit and kiwi fruits, but with herbs and spices as well. I have dined with pleasure on sherbets and ices made with cinnamon and rosemary. *See also* Ices.

Shiitake

A few years ago it would have taken a mycologist to positively identify the wild mushrooms that now confront shoppers in virtually every specialty food store and vegetable market. In truth, of course, a few years ago only a mycologist would have cared. That was before wild mushrooms had been "discovered" by many American cooks, who have now had ample opportunity to sample the culinary riches of morels, enokitake (or enoki) mushrooms, chanterelles, porcini, cèpes, pleurotes, Black Forest mushrooms, and, predominantly, shiitake mushrooms.

The shiitake—the name is pronounced she-TAH-keh—is a large, dark, wide-capped mushroom that, when cooked, has a full-bodied taste that many people have likened to that of steak. Shiitakes have a variety of uses; they can be broiled, grilled, or sautéed, blended in sauces, or served with spaghetti. And they have far more character than the cultivated white mushrooms usually found in supermarkets. A sure signal that shiitakes have "arrived" on the culinary scene can be found in scanning the menus of the finer restaurants in New York, where they turn up under several names, including oak mushrooms and porcini, the latter being the fabled wild Italian mushrooms that have a similar taste.

Shiitakes traditionally come from Japan and Korea, but recently several shiitake "farms" have been started in Vermont, Maine, and Washington State, and at Arvonia, Virginia, about forty miles west of Richmond. There, on fifty-four acres, more than 100,000 pounds of shiitakes are grown a year; over the next five years annual production is expected to increase tenfold, which should bring prices down.

The farm, with its odd, symmetrically spaced beauty, is like a forest of tall, slender oak trees that has been dedicated to logging. Masses of logs five or six feet long have been stacked in one or two neat patterns. Some resemble an elaborate assembly for a game of tick-tack-toe; others are stacked ends up, like rifles. On closer inspection you discover that thousands of newly sprouted mushrooms are protruding from the logs.

The manager of the mushroom enterprise, which is owned by the Elix Corporation, is Woen Eung Sik, a forty-five-year-old Korean whose jet-black hair is slightly graying in places. "These mushrooms," he explained, "are identical to the dried black Chinese mushrooms with which many American cooks are so familiar. Curiously, all those black mushrooms are imported into China from both Korea and Japan."

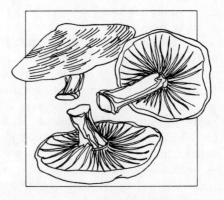

"Many people believe that there is only one mushroom that can be cultivated, and that is the plain white mushroom which is so widely found in this country," said Mr. Woen, who grew mushrooms in his homeland before he came to America in 1980. "But growing these oak mushrooms is really quite simple, though you do need the spores, or seeds, which we develop ourselves from the original seeds we brought over a few years ago from Korea."

Before planting, the spores are cultivated in glass jars under controlled temperatures in a fairly elaborate blend with sawdust, honey, and wheat. After the logs are stacked, small holes are drilled in the bark, filled with a small amount of the preparation, and enclosed with porous plastic cylinders.

Mr. Woen said the site was chosen because its moderate temperatures and humidity approximate the conditions in which mushrooms are grown in Korea. The farm needs a steady supply of water, so a sprinkling system has been installed.

The smallest shiitakes that are shipped to market are three to four inches in diameter, Mr. Woen said, and the largest eight to ten inches.

He said most of the mushrooms were cultivated on oak trees, which is why they are sometimes referred to as oak mushrooms, though they may be cultivated on cherry, hickory, or maple trees.

According to Mr. Woen, the finest shiitakes are those with a tortoise-shell pattern, predominantly brown on top and with shallow white fissures like those of a slightly cracked frosting. I have found that, if refrigerated in a tightly sealed carton or plastic bag, shiitakes will keep for days; the producers maintain that they will last for weeks given the proper treatment.

Shortening

Shortening is very much an American term, and it refers to any fat, such as butter, lard, vegetable fats, both solids and oils, and so on that are used in baking. The source of the name is difficult to pinpoint, but an English dictionary states that it derives from the fact that the "fat" or shortening contains no liquid and, therefore, gives a flaky, crisp "short" texture to baked goods—a theory that I believe should be discounted. Strawberry shortcakes, shortening bread, and so on derive from the name. Part of the confusion arises from the fact that some products are labeled "shortening" or "vegetable shortening," leading the novice to assume that shortening is a specific kind of fat. Any recipe that calls for "butter and shortening" is redundant, although the shortening in that case undoubtedly indicates Crisco, which is probably the most widely used shortening.

I was sent an interesting explanation of the term.

"I am the wife of a potter, and when a potter says his clay is 'short,' he means it's too dry! This ancient craft has preserved an ancient use of the word. Isn't that lovely?"

Shrimp

To devein or not to devein shrimps is a question that seems to be moot in the minds of a multitude of home cooks.

When I was a child, we had shrimp feasts in which the shrimp were boiled and drained and spread out on newspapers. Everyone sat around peeling their own shrimp, eating as they went along, simply dipping the shrimp in a sauce of melted butter with lemon juice, Tabasco, and Worcestershire sauces. No one bothered to devein the shrimp.

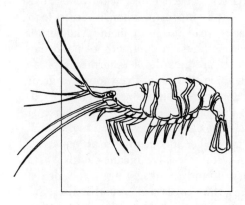

On the other hand, it is a lot more refined to devein the shrimp and on rare occasions the vein can be gritty. You can do this by using a small knife to remove the intestinal tract, or you may rinse the shrimp under running cold water after they are shelled and cut lengthwise down the back. If rinsed, they should be drained well and perhaps patted dry before using.

If shrimp have an iodine flavor, it means that the water from which they were harvested had an iodine taste and has nothing to do with freshness. A spokesman for the Fishery Council in New York recently told me that brown shrimp are more likely to smack of iodine than white or pink ones, which, incidentally, are more costly than the brown.

But there are times when shrimp, after a day or two in the refrigerator, develop a slightly off odor, although they are still edible. It was Virginia Lee's technique to rub the shrimp with baking soda and let them stand for a brief while. The shrimp were then rinsed thoroughly in cold water to remove every trace of soda. They then smelled totally clean and had no taste of soda.

Leaving the tail ends of shrimp intact when they are to be cooked is simply a culinary conceit. In some dishes there is a certain appeal to the sight of the shrimp's tail.

The tail of the shrimp could logically be used in "casual" soups, in casseroles with thin tomato sauces, such as Greek shrimp with feta cheese, and in salads dressed with thin oils and vinegar dressings. Logically, the tail should not be left on if the sauce is thick and sticky, or in salads dressed with mayonnaise. *See also* Prawns.

Shrimp Wiggle

I have heard of shrimp wiggle, but it is nothing in which I would take national pride. I will make the recipe as concise as possible.

Blend 4 tablespoons each of butter and flour in a saucepan. Add 2 cups of milk and stir until well blended, thickened, and smooth. Season with salt, pepper, and celery salt and a little juice squeezed from grated onion. Add 2 cups of cooked, peeled, deveined shrimp. Heat and serve.

As to why the dish is called shrimp wiggle, who knows? As Edmund Wilson once wrote in an essay on an Agatha Christie novel, "Who cares who killed Roger Ackroyd?"

Shrub

There are many versions of shrubs. A basic, nonalcoholic shrub is made by combining the juice of fruit or berries with sugar to taste. This is simmered briefly, stirring. You then add about 3 tablespoons of white wine vinegar for each cup of juice and chill, and serve over ice.

A shrub with alcohol is made by blending light or dark rum with the rind of lemon or orange. This is allowed to stand for two days or longer. For a lemon shrub you would then add 1 cup of lemon juice for each quart of rum that is used, about 2 cups of sugar simmered briefly with 4 cups of water. The mixture is then bottled for a month or so before serving. It is served over ice. The word "shrub," incidentally, derives from the Arabic word *shurb,* meaning a drink.

Sidecar

A sidecar is made like a daiquiri with an orange-flavored liqueur, such as triple sec or Cointreau, plus lemon juice and brandy. According to David Embury's book, *The Fine Art of Mixing Drinks,* the sidecar was invented by an acquaintance of the author at a bar in Paris during the First World War. It was named after the sidecar of a motor-

cycle in which the officer was transported to and from the bistro where the drink was created and christened.

Sifting

See Flour.

Sight and Food

I am, relatively speaking, a newcomer to eyeglasses, a need I first acknowledged in horror one morning when I had to lean closer to read the print in the Manhattan telephone book (telephone books and dictionaries are great levelers in this respect). Well, since that time, I've thought a great deal about the relationship of sight to food. And I've concluded with good reason, I think, that sight is almost equal to the smell and taste when it comes to the art of eating.

How often I have recalled with warm pleasure (and thanksgiving) a few dozen dishes that took on special emotional meaning because of their physical wonder. I recall an *omble chevalier,* a marvelous European fish, in a superb white wine sauce enriched with hollandaise I once enjoyed at the Baumanière at Les-Baux-de-Provence in France several years ago. Despite its magnificence in taste, it was a glory to behold because of one small, cardinal red crayfish strategically placed in one arc of the oval platter. I remember the lambs turning on spits before an open grate in an ancient château in Switzerland, an incredible prelude to an actual feast. I recall the first croquembouche, that stunning pyramid of cream puffs, I ever saw and the first bowl of *oeufs à la neige*. This visual thing is the reason for the simplest tomato rose, for sprigs of parsley, and for all the candied flowers on earth.

One of the most poignant things I ever read was contained in a letter of André Simon, the celebrated English wine and food expert. Ninety-four years old and having lost his sight, he wrote to Eleanor Lowenstein of New York's Corner Book Shop:

"Although I do my best to be brave and duly grateful for having lived to ninety-four, practically without pain or an ache, I must confess that I am not at all happy. I knew last year that I would never be able to read again, but I did not know what I know now; that I would lose—as I have now lost—interest in food since I cannot see what is on the plate before me. . ."

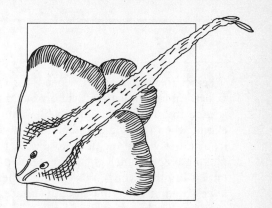

Silver Tip Roast

A silver tip roast is from the top sirloin. If you cut a top-sirloin roast down the center, my butcher says, you will find that half the meat has a "silver" coating—a thin membrane. This, he says, is the better half, with less waste and no gristle.

Sin-Sul-Lo

See Korean specialties.

Skate

There are scores, if not hundreds, of fish swimming around in American waters that are all but unknown on the American table, often because fishermen toss them back into the sea. But some are startlingly good and can be purchased in season in fish markets. One of the greatest and tastiest fish known to man is skate, known in France as *raie*. *Raie au beurre noir,* or skate with black butter sauce, is a supreme invention.

Skate, found on sandy bottoms along the New England and mid-Atlantic coasts, has a keeping quality that seems to be unique. It is best when eaten three days old.

The edible portions of the fish are the pointed wings that extend from the body. These should be cut off, holding a knife parallel to the backbone. There is a tough cartilage centered on each wing, and you may "fillet" the meat from the cartilage. You should cut away the skin before cooking.

To make *raie au beurre noir* you simmer the wings, either whole or as fillets, and serve with butter cooked slightly beyond the browning stage until it starts to burn. You add a dash of vinegar and some capers and pour it over your drained fish.

I have seen recipes for skate, also known as cownose ray, in which cubes of it are skewered onto picks, and broiled or baked with mustard or cut into cubes and served in a curry sauce.

Skillets

Whether to wash a skillet depends on the skillet. An iron skillet, particularly one that is used frequently, should not be washed except when it becomes essential. Such an iron skillet would include those used for making crêpes, omelets, and sautéing potatoes. In other words, those dishes where a well-used or cured but smooth surface is necessary for best results.

As skillets are used—and the more the better—they develop a natural surface coating that prevents sticking. These skillets should be cleaned with salt and paper toweling. Simply sprinkle the bottom and sides after each use with salt, preferably coarse salt, such as kosher salt, and rub briskly with dry paper toweling.

If no particles have stuck to the bottom after using, it is not even necessary to use salt. If the skillet has been subjected to foods that cling relentlessly to the bottom, it may be necessary to use an abrasive such as a plastic or steel wool scrubber. At any time water is used to clean an iron skillet the surface of the skillet must be wiped dry immediately or it will rust.

Incidentally, there are those who contend that foods cooked in iron pots, saucepans, or whatever, actually absorb small quantities of iron, which is good for you.

I have a friend, a fine Persian cook, who tosses a nail in one dish called fosenjohn (duck and meatballs in a walnut sauce), not for the iron content but because the iron gives dark coloration to the stew.

Let me go on record as stating that I am not encouraging the addition of nails and so on to stews. But a black iron skillet and a black iron kettle for cooking greens are a part of my background.

To season a skillet, add a hefty quantity of cooking or salad oil. Place it on the stove and heat the oil almost, but not quite, to the smoking point. Turn off the heat and let the skillet stand until the oil is cool. Pour out the oil and the skillet, when cleaned, is ready for use.

Once seasoned, it is best to simply wipe the skillet well with paper toweling or a clean cloth once food is cooked in it. If, on the other hand, food is stuck to the bottom or sides of the skillet you will have to clean it as noted above.

If you have a problem with pots that have collected burned foods and other stains, here's a solution from a Connecticut woman.

"When you have a cabinet full of baking sheets, pans, and casseroles so grimy or burned it seems nothing will clean them," she wrote, "here is my solution: I place the utensils, other than those that have wooden, plastic, or other easily damaged materials, in my self-cleaning oven. I turn the oven to self-clean and let them stand for the time recommended to clean the oven. They come out like brand new."

Skimming Soups

Some time ago I received a letter from a Southbury, Connecticut, woman who wrote to state that she always skimmed the surface of her soups as they simmered because she had always been taught to do so by her mother.

I am curious, she stated, as to whether in this case some of the nutrients of the soup are removed.

"I have been cooking for forty years and have only just begun to question my mother's directions." Perhaps, she added, the skimming is contrary to modern ideas of nutrition.

I was intrigued by the letter for more reasons than one, for the inquiry brought to mind other voices, to borrow a phrase from Truman Capote.

Quite directly, my answer is as follows:

The scum or film that forms on the surface of soups as they cook is frequently referred to as "impurities" or "foreign matter," while the truth is that this scum is, except under what might be considered highly peculiar circumstances, not in the least injurious. The scum is removed, purely and simply, for very good and sound cosmetic reasons. When the film is removed, the soup simply looks more palatable and, therefore, more appetizing. Also, when skimming off the scum, you remove a good deal of unwanted fat.

This brought to mind the memory of a lecture given by a professor of mine at a hotel school in Switzerland.

He observed that a perfectly conceived consommé would be crystal clear in body and surface. This clarity would be achieved, he noted, by taking the long-simmered rich broth, skimming the surface with patience, then blending the broth with raw meat and egg white. This would be brought slowly to the boil and the whole would be strained through muslin.

"On the other hand," he advised, "many customers may look askance at this jewel of a consommé, for they will recall with affection mother's beef or chicken broth, which always had a little fat floating on top."

In that case, he advised, if the customer sends back his consommé, add a small dash of any neutral-flavored oil and send it back piping hot. "He will be mollified."

Skoal

One of the commonest drinking toasts is "skoal," and the word derives from the word for drinking cup, which is *skaal* in Norwegian and Danish and *skal* in Swedish. Both words also mean bowl. The use of the word *skoal* as a toast dates from the days of the Vikings.

Skunk Cabbage

I have never eaten skunk cabbage. In fact, until an inquiry from a friend sent me to several reference books, I was not even certain that it was edible. Some dictionaries identify skunk cabbage as a broad-leafed, foul-smelling plant of modest height that grows in moist ground.

However, in *The Wise Encyclopedia of Cookery,* skunk cabbage is said to be good eating "when the thick, almost white leaf stalks are boiled and the water is changed two or three times." "Cooked tender, seasoned with butter, pepper and salt," the encyclopedia says, "all the offensiveness disappears with the boiling. In cream or other sauce, or cold in salad form, the skunk cabbage is delicious."

Slumgullion

Slumgullion is a weak and watery stew and the term is used contemptuously to refer to cheap, badly prepared food.

Ruth Kershner's *Irish Cooking* has a slumgullion recipe calling for browned ground lamb or beef cooked with chopped onions, cubed potatoes, chopped carrots, water, salt, pepper, and Worcestershire sauce. It is cooked for an hour and served over mashed potatoes.

Smoked Salmon

"You," David Sklar said, "are the 4,742d person to ask me that question."

I hastened to explain that after twenty-five years I still felt like a newcomer to the New York scene, and if at this late date I still didn't know the difference between lox and "nova," it should be excused on the ground of obviously arrested development.

Mr. Sklar is one of the owners of the Nova Scotia Food Products Corporation in Brooklyn. He is a man with gentle manners, an easy smile, and a patient air. He is considered by many to be perhaps the leading authority on smoked fish in this area.

"A long time ago," he began, "back in the early 1920s, universal refrigeration was a rarity. The only salmon shipped to New York back in those days came from Alaska in barrels, and salt was used as a preservative. It was very heavily salted, in fact, and

to make it edible it was necessary to remove most of the salt. To do this the salmon had to be soaked for a long time in cold running water." That was the original lox.

"Back in those days," the gentleman continued, "we took it one step further. We smoked the lox briefly." But mark it well, good reader, lox today is no longer smoked. It is simply soaked to the desired degree and sold over the counter. "We stopped smoking lox at approximately the end of the Second World War," Mr. Sklar noted. The word "lox" derives from the Scandinavian word for salmon, which is *lax,* and the German, which is *lachs.*

And then he elaborated on Nova Scotia salmon, which is also spoken of as "nova," or simply "smoked salmon." "Smoked salmon has been a European tradition for many, many years, and in this country it is—relatively—a recent thing," Mr. Sklar pointed out. "There are still vast areas in America where it is largely unknown."

When the smoked salmon or Nova Scotia salmon industry had its origins in the United States, the salmon used for it was shipped from Nova Scotia. Eventually the market grew until it became necessary to seek other sources of supply. Now the name "nova" is applied to genuine smoked salmon (as opposed to lox) no matter where the fish itself is shipped from.

There are great differences in the quality, flavor, and texture of salmon from source to source. It is generally agreed that the finest salmon is "Eastern" or "Atlantic" salmon from the East Coast. The salmon used to prepare lox comes only from western waters. Smoked salmon, or "nova," may come from eastern or western waters, and while the fish from the western sources may be eminently edible, it is not in the same class with the eastern variety. It is this differential, incidentally, that would account for the great variance in prices between a pound of "nova" at one outlet and another pound at another.

Smothered Foods

I dote on the so-called classic foods that are indigenous to one region or another of the United States—oysters Rockefeller, scrapple, Creole and Cajun cooking, soul food, barbecued chicken and ribs, chili con carne, clam chowders, the cioppino of California, and so on. I am reminded of one dish that was very much a part of my Mississippi childhood, one that was dubbed smothered chicken. I suppose it could be regarded as soul food, basic, easy to prepare; in my books, it belongs in the "comfort" category, a food that gives solace to the spirit when you dine on it.

In its most basic form, it consists of cooking a chicken that has been split down the back and opened up as for broiling, the breast unsplit and left intact. You cook it breast-side down in a black iron skillet (this is essential) with a plate on top. The plate is weighted down and it is this that con-

tributes the name smothered. The chicken is turned over and continues to cook in a flour-thickened gravy until it is exceptionally tender, the meat almost falling from the bones.

The word "smothered" also applies to vegetables, such as onions, that may be cooked in a tightly covered skillet or various cuts of meat that are tough and need long, closely covered cooking. The word applies to foods that are covered rather abundantly with other foods: calf's liver, for example, that is smothered or thickly spread with onions. *See also* Etoufée.

Snails

If I had to name the single "best" convenience food imported from France, it would be the snails that come packaged in tins. The reason is that snails, long considered a great delicacy, require hours, if not days, of tedious preparation; they must be washed several times, "purged" in a blend of salt, vinegar, and flour, cooked, and so on.

Curiously, packagers rarely include the proper instructions for cooking the snails in a court bouillon once they are removed from the can and drained. This gives a "fresh" taste to the snails and makes them more tender.

Although most people use canned snails, there is an interesting explanation of how to prepare live snails in Elizabeth David's book *French Provincial Cooking*. The instructions are attributed to a Mrs. Millet-Robinet's *Maison Rustique des Dames,* a book that was extremely popular in the mid-nineteenth century and that, judging from the manner of its arrangement and content, may well have had some influence on Mrs.

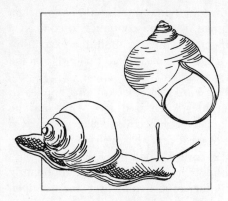

Beeton, the British cooking authority. Here is the recipe:

"The first essential is to leave the snails to starve for at least one month, enclosed in some kind of vessel, left in a cool but not damp place. There are cases of accidents having occurred when this precaution has not been taken: the snails, having fed on noxious plants, have caused food poisoning. At the end of this time, the snails are thrown into a caldron filled with boiling water (to which some add wood ash) and they are cooked for 20 minutes. This done, they are taken from their shells; the little intestine is removed; they are washed in several waters; they are put again into fresh water, salted and boiled for a few minutes, and then they are drained."

As for snail shells, I rinse them in a basin of warm water containing a detergent to rid them of their initial crumbs, butter, and so on. I then place them in a kettle or saucepan with water to cover and a capful of ammonia. I bring them to the boil for a few seconds and drain. They are then given a second go-around with warm water with detergent. Drain and add hot water and then a final draining, this time opening-side down.

Snapper Soup

See Turtle.

Snickerdoodle

I have tasted a recipe for snickerdoodle that came from Tennessee. Essentially it is a short (which is to say rich) cookie that is flavored with cinnamon. I do not know the origin of the name, but it has been proposed that it is of German origin and derived from the word *schnecken*, i.e., sticky buns.

Snook

Snook, also called robalo, occurs in the United States waters only in southern Florida.

According to *The Encyclopedia of Fish Cookery,* by A. J. McClane, the skinned fillets of snook are sold as "red snapper" in Florida that it would take a keen eye and palate to tell the difference. He states that the Pacific counterpart of the fish is the black snook to be found from Baja California southward to northern Peru.

Snow Almonds

Snow almonds were served to me once in the home of Neset Eren when her husband was Turkey's deputy ambassador at the United Nations. The recipe appears in her book, *The Art of Turkish Cooking,* and it is delectable. The almonds should be shelled but the dark skin left on. Place the almonds in a plastic container with a lid. Add cold water to cover and place in the refrigerator. Let stand for four days.

On the day before serving them, rub off and discard the skins and return them to the container. Add cold water and cover once more. Let stand until serving time.

When Mrs. Eren served the almonds, she filled a six-inch-high glass serving bowl with water to within two inches of the rim. The bowl was then placed in the freezer until the water was solidly frozen. At serving time the almonds were drained thoroughly and poured on top of the ice.

Soapstone

A soapstone griddle should be cured the way an iron skillet is. If the stone is not new, you should scrub it well and dry it thoroughly. In any event, heat the stone over low heat and apply vegetable shortening to the top surface. Let the stone remain over very low heat for an hour, rubbing it lightly with a bit more shortening. Let it cool and

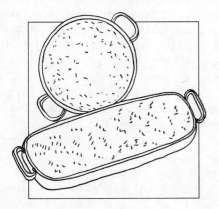

wipe off the fat, which will come off easily.

Store the stone until ready for use. If it is properly treated, pancakes, to choose one dish, may be cooked on the stone without further greasing.

Soda Fountain

Did you know that all-American institution, the soda fountain, was originated by a Frenchman?

According to the *Wise Encyclopedia of Cookery,* drugstores in America originally went by the name of apothecary shops. An apothecary was a man licensed to sell drugs.

In 1825 a Frenchman named Elias Magloire Durand opened a drugstore in Philadelphia. Durand had been a pharmacist in Napoleon's army and for one reason or another had been exiled. Philadelphia during those years had a growing French colony and was said to have been the nation's chief center for pharmaceutical drugs. It was only natural that Durand gravitated there.

Carbonated water was relatively new at the time. It had first come into commercial production during the closing years of the eighteenth century.

Durand was familiar with the product when he arrived in America. When he came to Philadelphia, he worked first in apothecary shops throughout the city and eventually conceived the profitable and far-reaching notion that a shop that specialized in medical supplies might do very well if it sold cigars and sparkling water as well. He sent to France for equipment and supplies and opened his own establishment close by Independence Hall.

It must have been fairly impressive, if accounts about it are correct: It had a glass front, mirrors, and a marble counter at which he instituted his soda "fountain." It is said that the first mating of carbonated water and ice cream occurred at that counter.

Durand was socially prominent in the City of Brotherly Love and was a friend of the Marquis de Lafayette. In short order, his pharmacy became well known as a social center.

Sofrito

Sofrito is a fairly thick liquid seasoning that occurs quite often in Caribbean recipes, particularly those of Puerto Rico. It is added to many kinds of stews, soups, and so on. Basically it is a sauce composed of salt pork, which is rendered from fat. To this is added chopped green peppers, garlic, onions, and ham, which are cooked until the vegetables are tender. Achiote seeds are added to give color. Chopped tomatoes, cilantro or fresh coriander leaves, oregano, salt, and pepper are then added. This sauce is cooked until reasonably thick. It is then bottled or otherwise reserved to be used as needed, according to some Caribbean cookbooks.

Bottled sofrito is available commercially where Puerto Rican products are sold and in the specialty food sections of many supermarkets.

I subsequently learned in a letter from a New Yorker that "sofrito is not cooked for storing; it is sautéed as needed." She adds that the ham or salt pork is cooked at the last minute and that achiote seeds are never used whole but are heated in oil until the coloring and flavoring are acquired; the seeds are then discarded.

She offered a basic recipe for Puerto Rican sofrito: cut up green peppers, garlic, onions, and coriander leaves and put them into an electric blender. Add a little oregano, salt, and pepper. Add small amounts of oil and vinegar to retard spoilage. Blend to a fairly thick paste. Cut up ham or salt pork, and cook this, mixed with two or more tablespoons of sofrito, or as much as any given recipe calls for.

Sole

It is purely a matter of personal taste, but the greatest single fish for cooking is possibly the sole that swims in the English Channel or, as the French would call the body of water, *La Manche*. That sole has a sweetness of flavor and tenderness of texture rarely if ever matched in any other fish. A long time ago I heard a brief history of a futile effort to spawn that sole in American waters and I believe every word of it. It is said that during the first half of this century an interested group backed with government enthusiasm had hundreds of live English sole brought to these shores. Upon arrival they were properly tagged and introduced to the East Coast's briny deep. Well, less than a week later, faster than the old *Queens* could ply the Atlantic, they were found off the coast of Land's End, tags and all, back in their own home waters.

There is no fish whose name has a vaguer meaning than "sole." On the East Coast of America, various fish from Atlantic waters, such as yellowtail flounder, grey sole, lemon sole, plus winter and summer flounder (fluke), are legally sold as fillet of sole. On the West Coast, the Pacific yields lemon sole, rex sole, and rock sole. Sole in Amer-

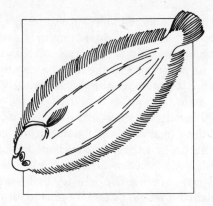

ican recipes usually means any flatfish from Atlantic or Pacific waters. In New York, most of the fish sold as "fillet of sole" is a flatfish more accurately known as yellowtail flounder.

Sopa Seca

Sopa seca, or dry soup, seems to be a contradiction in terms.

In her book *The Complete Book of Mexican Cooking*, Elisabeth Lambert Ortiz says, "No one quite knows why these dishes are called dry soups in Mexico." She postulates that the term came about with the arrival of the Spanish in the territory. Prior to that, the Aztecs served "wet" soup, meaning soups with a preponderance of liquid.

The Spanish came in and added pasta, such as vermicelli and rice, to these soups. At this point there was some confusion as to where these "less wet" foods fitted into a meal. Thus they were called dry soups to distinguish them from their more liquid counterparts.

Dry soups, the cookbook author noted, are often "served as a separate course in the way the Italians serve fettuccine or risotto."

So-called dry soups may be thickened with tortillas, among other things, and I have enjoyed these soups served as a luncheon dish.

Sorghum

Sorghum is a grass that is cane-like in appearance. It is used to prepare a syrup generally known as sorghum molasses. This syrup is very thick and sweet and has its own characteristic—to my taste, heavy—flavor. I have rarely if ever seen sorghum molasses in supermarkets outside the South.

Sorrel

Oddly enough, with one notable exception, sorrel has never enjoyed the reputation in this country that it has in Europe. The exception is schav, a soup whose principal ingredient is sorrel and a dish most commonly appreciated, and associated with Russian and Polish Jews or those of Russian and Polish descent. The name of the soup derives from *szczaw*, the Polish word for the herb.

Next to schav, the most famous soup in the world containing sorrel is the French *potage Germiny*, also made with chicken broth and shredded sorrel, plus eggs as a thickener. It is one of the absolute marvels of soupdom and can be eaten hot or cold.

Sorrel leaves, which are rounded and sometimes slightly pointed, resemble the leaves of young mustard or turnip greens and have a distinctly sour or acid taste. This acidity offers a welcome counterpoint to foods noted for their fat content, eel, for example, which is splendid in a green sauce cooked with sorrel, among other flavorings.

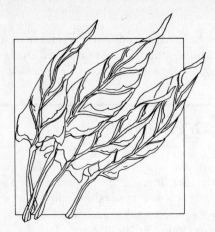

The name sorrel had its origins in a Teutonic word meaning sour and it is said to have been known to the inhabitants of ancient Egypt. Its vulgar English name is sour grass, probably because it grows like weeds.

Sots-l'y-Laisse

Sots-l'y-laisse is a highly uncommon dish, a ragout, recipes for which are found only in French cookery books of a few generations ago. The sots-l'y-laisse were the "oysters," the two tender meaty morsels that are found at the after-end of the chicken's backbone, one on the left side, one on the right. Some connoisseurs declare them to be the best part of the bird and the name, translated, means "only fools leave it."

A charming note about the delicacy came from Hamilton, New York:

"In my childhood those two ovals of meat were referred to by my father, usually as he carved the holiday turkey, as 'the oysters' and the choicest morsels on the bird.

"But once long ago, as a bride, I caused a minor flap at my in-laws' Thanksgiving board, by speaking of the 'oysters.'

"It was unacceptable; such meat by any name did not exist. My mother-in-law was the daughter of a poultry-raiser. That was all the proof needed. She raised her sons to believe ladies ate white meat, the gentlemen the dark.

"Man carved the beast, woman cleaned off the carcass for salad, sandwiches, etc. Therefore, all these years I have happily made my sandwich of those nonexistent oysters, savoring the delicacy that I once watched my father carefully reserve for his own special pleasure. How nice to know that in France they have a name and a recipe!"

Soufflé

The name soufflé is, of course, as French as the dish itself. Soufflé in French has to do with things like breath and wind and puff, and that is what happens when you add beaten egg whites to a cream sauce thickened with yolks.

The last-minute preparation required for a soufflé creates a problem for many home cooks but several things can be done be-

forehand to expedite the final assembly.

The basic sauce—a simple white sauce to which yolks have been added, or a custard base also made with yolks—may be prepared hours in advance and kept in the refrigerator. Have the whites ready, with the beater placed beside them, and they can be beaten and folded into the sauce in seconds.

With these details taken care of, your main concern is baking time. Soufflés are not as delicate as people think and the baking time is not as critical as is widely believed. I prefer a soufflé with a very soft center.

The baking time may range from twenty to thirty minutes, depending on the volume of the dish. Consult your recipe for the baking time recommended. If the soufflé must remain in the oven for five or ten minutes longer it may miss perfection but it will still be edible.

Soul Food

Soul food started, of course, among the slaves of the old South: Blacks had to subsist on the meager, less fancy rations of the garden and the stable, which included various hardy greens, such as collard, turnip and mustard, and the lesser parts of the pig—pigs' feet, ham hocks, which are often brined and smoked, and chitterlings, the lower intestine of the pig.

The principal ingredients for soul food fall into four main categories: cornmeal, dried beans, the aforementioned greens, and the odd parts of the pig. Chicken, of course, also plays a large part in soul-food cookery, but it is a universal ingredient in all southern cooking. One of the staple dishes of the soul food table is coleslaw, which is a borrowing

from the table of the white masters.

Few people are aware that the ingredients used in soul food are very much a part of the cooking of certain areas of France, notably Alsace and the Languedoc region. Some of the parallels between soul food and French cooking are quite remarkable. The classic cassoulet of Toulouse and Carcassonne is quite similar to the traditional black-eyed pea preparation of the soul-food kitchen.

A cassoulet is made with dried peas cooked with a weighty amount of salt pork with rind, plus garlic sausage and goose fat and often with a little additional fat of one sort or another added at the end for flavor. It is cooked for a long time.

The black-eyed pea dish is made with the dried peas plus ham hocks with fat and rind, which are cooked for a long time. At the end the ham hocks are cut into pieces and served with the beans.

Two other common regional dishes of France, which are comparable to the soul food of this country, are breaded pigs' feet and andouilles and andouillettes, which are nothing more than zesty sausages whose basic component is chitterlings.

Soup

I have an abiding and unabashed passion for soups. They remain one of the few foods for which I develop a true craving when the winds of winter chill the bones. Give me a bowl of hot soup made with beans or bones, fish or fowl, meat or game, and I find it time to cry comfort and peace on earth where the appetite is concerned.

I have, equally, an unabashed passion for literary references to food, and it amuses me

to think that this most praiseworthy—and, in the minds of many food authorities, most ancient—of foods has been so little celebrated, sung about, lauded, and lyricized by poets over the years.

Search your most valued and hallowed volumes, dictionaries, and encyclopedias with famous quotations, and very few lines will be related to that most nourishing and bracing of liquids with its myriads of possible flavors and textures. The most famous and oft-quoted of all is, of course, contained in a bit of versifying by Lewis Carroll in *Alice's Adventures in Wonderland,* which says, "Soup of the evening, beautiful soup."

Personally, when it comes to soup, I feel more at home with my ninth volume of the *Oxford English Dictionary,* which contains numerous references to soup, most of them obscure to the general public. There is an eighty-year-old reference to "soup-plate bonnets and round-brimmed hats," a number of legal mentions, for the reason that a legal brief was once referred to as a "soup," and a thought with which I disagree: "A light soup is better than a thick one, which clogs the appetite."

Although America is noted for a number of soups of estimable nature—among them the various clam chowders, vichyssoise

(created by Louis Diat in New York while chef of the Ritz-Carlton dining rooms), Philadelphia pepper pot, she-crab, and terrapin—it has always been my feeling that some of the finest hot soups are "borrowings" from European kitchens.

I am addicted to certain soups of French inspiration such as *soupes de poissons,* or fish soups, particularly when they are served with a lusty garlic mayonnaise, a *sauce rouille,* plus croutons, or hearty onion soup with a cheese topping. Other soups to which I am partial include the goulash soups of Hungary and the hearty bean soups from Latin countries.

Sourdough Starter

Sourdough starter, a blend of liquid and flour, is the basis for making sourdough bread. There are two ways to prepare a starter: You can combine flour and water and let it stand until the natural yeast from the air takes over and makes the blend ferment, or you can start with a blend of yeast, flour, and water, which will ferment at room temperature. You then keep adding flour and liquid as necessary to perpetuate it.

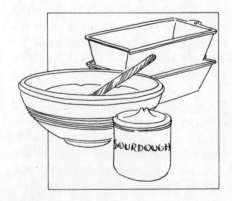

I have known people who contend that their starter is fifty or more years old, passed down from one generation to the other. As far as I can determine, a starter in theory could last forever, provided it is properly added to and properly stored. (To store, pack loosely in a plastic or glass container to allow the starter to breathe. Refrigerate and stir down often and keep adding to it.)

Sour Grass

See Sorrel.

Sour Salt

Sour salt is not salt at all, according to Howard Hillman in his highly informative book, *Kitchen Science.*

"Sour salt," he says, "is citric acid, not sodium chloride. This white, tart, crystalline compound, which looks like salt, is used as a substitute by some salt-watchers because it adds needed zest to saltless foods and its salt-like appearance makes it psychologically satisfying."

He adds that the individual could just as easily substitute another acidic flavoring agent, such as vinegar, "with much more interesting gustatory results." Certain recipes call for sour salt, including borscht.

Sour Sop

I have never sampled sour sop, but it is defined in *Cook's Ingredients* by Philip Dowell and Adrian Bailey as a custard apple, "a term covering a group of fruits" of a tropical nature; "the flesh of the sour sop is white and more acid than the others in the group." Waverley Root, in his book *Food,* refers to sour sop as "alias the corossol, alias the prickly custard which has, depending on whom you read, (a) a biting wild taste, (b) a taste which much resembles that of the black currant, (c) a flavor of perfumed cream, or which (d) unripe tastes like turnips."

Soused Foods

See Escabeche.

Soy Sauce

In Chinatown and in groceries where Oriental foods are sold, there are some bottled soy sauces labeled "thin," which is the same as "light," and "black," which is the same as "dark." You can determine the difference by holding the top of the bottle of soy up to the light and holding the bottle at an angle. The "dark" soy sauce will have a greater viscosity. It is somewhat thicker and more opaque than the "light." Dark soy gives both color and depth of flavor to foods.

A more comprehensive answer was received from a lecturer in home economics: "Light soy sauce," she elaborated, "is saltier than dark. It is made from soy bean extract, salt wheat and yeast. Some of these have sugar added, but good ones don't. Dark soy sauce, also called thick, black, or heavy, always has molasses and caramel and soy extract, salt, wheat, and yeast.

"Therefore, now that ingredients must be

listed on the label, the key word is molasses and/or caramel. This you will recognize as dark soy sauce, as light soy will never have these ingredients. Also, if the bottle is tipped to one side, the dark soy clings to the glass longer and, therefore, the glass clears more slowly. Light soy sauce clears instantly."

Some soy sauces are lower in sodium than others, but the amount is still substantial. So-called low-sodium soy sauces, low only in a relative sense, are available in health food stores, but I am not inclined to use them. *See also* Kecap.

Spaetzle

Spaetzle are, in a phrase, rather casual egg dumplings, probably of German origin but popular in Austria and Switzerland. I say "casual" because they are made from a simple batter that is pushed through a sieve with large holes into boiling salted water. The dumplings are done when they rise to the surface of the water. They are then drained and sautéed quickly in butter. There are machines for the home designed for making spaetzle, but a colander works just as well.

Spaghetti

The messages on the backs of cereal boxes are part of the culture and literature of childhood. Having outgrown that age a few years back, one can't recall giving serious thought to package drollery except to note what chemicals the manufacturer now uses to flavor and preserve.

Recently, however, my attention was ar-

rested by the side panel on a package of Agnesi spaghetti, one of the finest brands of imported pasta available in this country.

The notation that caught the eye was the instruction for "A New Method for Cooking Spaghetti." The instructions are as follows:

Bring 5 quarts of water to the boil in a large kettle and add salt to taste. This will be sufficient for 1 pound of spaghetti.

Add the spaghetti and stir well until strands of spaghetti float free. When the water returns to the boil, cook the spaghetti for 2 minutes and immediately remove the kettle from the heat. Cover with a clean cloth and then add the lid. Let the spaghetti stand for approximately 9 minutes. Do not uncover the kettle during this period. Drain the spaghetti and serve with a sauce.

I tried this method, and the reactions of those who tasted it were generally favorable. The spaghetti was left to stand exactly 9 minutes after the pot was covered. To one guest, who prefers his spaghetti *al dente,* my offering seemed a trifle overcooked.

Of course, it is logical to ask what the advantages of using such a method would be. For a professional Italian chef or an experienced spaghetti cooker there are probably no advantages. To many home cooks,

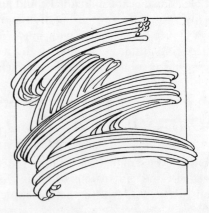

however—the numerous people who find the cooking of spaghetti tedious and tricky—it is a great simplification. By using the method it is not necessary to lift slippery strands of the pasta from the boiling water to test for doneness.

Should you consider using this method, adjust the standing time of the spaghetti according to your own taste. If left to stand 8 minutes instead of 9, you will come out with firmer strands.

Accordingly, the packages note that if cooking a pasta that is thicker than spaghetti, it should be boiled for 3 minutes instead of 2.

Spaghetti alla Chitarra

Spaghetti alla chitarra is known in English as "guitar-string spaghetti." This is a long, thin pasta that is cut on a wooden board by wire cutters that resemble a guitar, although the resemblance may be in the mind's eye. It is sometimes rolled into nest-like vermicelli clusters. I do not know of a source for spaghetti alla chitarra in the United States.

Spaghetti all'Amatriciana

Ada Boni, whose book I often mention as among the best books on pasta cookery, states that spaghetti all'Amatriciana takes its name from the little town of Amatrice in the Sabine Hills. It is "frequently known, erroneously," she explains, "as spaghetti alla matriciana—the sound of the phrase when spoken (is) exactly the same."

Spaghetti alla Puttanesca

One of the most amusing names in the Italian cooking repertory is spaghetti alla puttanesca, or spaghetti whore's style. My friend Ed Giobbi, the artist and cookbook author, avers that the name originated with the ladies of the night in Naples. It is said that the scent of the ingredients—tomatoes, garlic, anchovies, and olives—would tempt passers-by.

Spaghetti Carbonara

The origin of the name of spaghetti carbonara is difficult if not impossible to pinpoint, but I can tell you an amusing story about the origin of the dish itself. It was told to me by Ed Giobbi, the artist and cookbook author, who, in turn, heard the tale from his art dealer in Rome.

"During the war, a young, homesick, Italian-American came to Rome and visited a restaurant there. He ached to have spaghetti made exactly as he had it at home back in America with slivers of prosciutto and so on. His command of the Italian language was poor. When he told the waiter that he wanted spaghetti made just like his mother made it with fresh eggs, the waiter mistook him to say egg tossed with the pasta. He consulted with the chef and the result was spaghetti carbonara."

But I have received, as well, the following account:

"The legend I grew up on was that the dish was created by Garibaldi's troops during the war for Italy's unification in the

1850s, the Risorgimento. Lacking other means for cooking, the soldiers prepared their spaghetti over a charcoal fire, hence the name carbonara."

And also this explanation of the legend:

"According to my great-grandmother, who is ninety-two years young and an authority on most things Italian, linguine alla carbonara refers to both a secret society that at one time tried to overthrow the Italian government and to men who work with coal. Following is Mama Josefina's version. Serves four to six.

"Twelve slices bacon cut into the size of a fingernail, fry until crisp, pour off all grease as it cooks. Four eggs beaten. One cup fresh grated Parmesan cheese. Good big handful chopped Italian parsley. Lots of milled black pepper.

"Mix eggs, cheese and parsley in a big bowl. Throw in the pepper, beat well so all is well blended together and creamy. Add a tablespoon of the crisp bacon and mix again. Place the bowl on back of the stove so it warms, but doesn't get too hot to cook the eggs.

"Now cook the linguine al dente. Do not drain. Fork the pasta directly from pot to warm bowl with the egg sauce, shake off water before you add each forkful to bowl. Pasta must be *very hot* so eggs slightly get set as you toss it. Serve the crisp bacon on top of each serving. Accompany with good Italian bread.

"Break off chunks of bread. Mama says it's a sin to cut the bread with a knife."

Spaghetti Caruso

One of the most curious omissions in books about American cooking is the dish called spaghetti Caruso named, of course, for the great Italian tenor who achieved fame at the turn of the century.

There is a recipe in James Beard's *American Cookery* in which he specifies that spaghetti Caruso has a tomato-meat sauce topped with a few chicken livers that have been sautéed in butter.

That is the version that I have always presumed to be the true and original, but I received a note about a different version:

"The late chef and cookbook author, Louis P. De Gouy, who was European by birth and training but American by adoption, claims to have concocted this recipe." He referred me to De Gouy's *The Gold Cook Book*. Sure enough, there is a recipe for "Spaghetti alla Caruso" without chicken livers, and in parentheses it states, "Original recipe as prepared by this writer."

Then another note from a Bryn Mawr correspondent quoted from a thirty-three-year-old cookbook written by Lillian Bueno McCue and Carol Truax. The book is titled *The 60 Minute Chef* and the recipes are preceded by a running narrative in which the authors comment on the various ingredients and origins of one dish or another.

Carol Truax, she continues, apparently knew Caruso when she was a child. The book notes in the first chapter that she was "brought up on celebrities and good food.

"She grew up in the old house of her father the judge at 12 East Sixty-fifth Street, just off Fifth Avenue," the book continues.

The judge entertained often with dinners and they were attended with a good deal of anticipation, according to the book, which states:

"The guests were beginning to arrive, and silk hats were mounting the brownstone steps. Under the hats would be Elihu Root and Enrico Caruso, Lyman Spalding and

Ambassador James Gerard." The account of spaghetti Caruso begins as follows:

" 'When you feel hungry,' scrawled Enrico Caruso on the picture he gave Carol, 'a dish of spaghetti is all right, what?'

" 'Yes, my dear Mr. Caruso,' scribbled John Brown, Metropolitan Opera comptroller, on his half of the picture, 'but when I feel hungry, I haven't time to wind the damn stuff around my fork.' "

But such evenings were most fun, the account continues, in the kitchen, "when Mr. Caruso clapped on the high chef's cap and created an enormous platter of his own very special spaghetti, with chicken livers."

But *did* Caruso really don a chef's apron and prepare that dish that he allegedly created or had created for him?

I have been made aware of a passage from a book by Iles Brody, *On the Tip of My Tongue,* which says, "Spaghetti with meat sauce, or with meatballs, can be delicious. So can spaghetti Caruso, designating the addition of chicken livers and mushrooms which, by the way, Caruso never liked. He ate his spaghetti plain, with butter and cheese only, and was addicted to large cuts of meats, such as baron of lamb."

In an amusing book on pasta printed thirty years ago, titled *Spaghetti Dinner,* Giuseppe Prezzolini writes about the dining habits of Enrico Caruso.

Caruso was from Naples and naturally was addicted to his daily dish of spaghetti. Like many Italian men, he was proud of his reputation as a cook.

"At the Hotel York, Caruso went into the kitchen to supervise personally the preparation of spaghetti for some friends. He made a sauce with tomatoes, basil, parsley, red pepper and olive oil in which garlic had been fried. He gold dusted the macaroni with Parmesan cheese and decorated it with coins of zucchini squash that had been fried."

Whether it included chicken livers, we'll never know.

Spaghetti Museum

When it comes to the great art museums of the world I am a self-confessed fool and Philistine. It is not that I cannot admire the works of a Titian, Rembrandt, Pollock, de Kooning, and Motherwell, it is simply that in most international edifices that house an embarrassment of riches I feel claustrophobic, a sense of panic.

There is in the small town of Pontedassio not far from the Ligurian Sea a museum that is difficult to pinpoint on maps and one that goes largely unnoticed on tourist itineraries. It is a modest museum concerned with its own kind of art, and it is precisely within my perhaps rarefied range of comprehension and style.

It is called the Museo Storico degli Spaghetti or the Historical Museum of Spaghetti, and it is most unusual.

If you are on a gastronomic tour of Italy, it is probably best to conceive of its location in terms of Genoa. It is approximately a two-hour drive from that seacoast town, fabled for, among other things, that inimitable, richly perfumed basil sauce known as pesto Genovese. From Genoa you drive to Imperia and thence five or six miles to Pontedassio and the museum.

Let me hasten to add at this point that the museum is open to the public by appointment only, and you should never attempt to visit without advance notice. Write or telephone Vincenzo Agnesi, Via Schiva

1, Imperia, 18100. The telephone number is 21-651.

Although some of the most precious volumes relating to pasta are kept under lock and key at the museum, the scope of the material available to public eye ranges from the serious to the absurd and comic.

There are, of course, working models of pasta-making machines that date from the primitive to some activated by the most modern technology. There is an ancient grinding device once turned by hand or manpower and later by machine, now found throughout Italy, in which filled pastas, such as tortelloni, tortellini, and ravioli can be rolled, stuffed, and twisted, so many hundred per minute.

Among the many writings about pasta there is an article by F. T. Marinetti that calls spaghetti, "the absurd gastronomical religion of the Italians."

There are cookbooks published during the Second World War, detailing recipes for making pasta-meal from corn, used when wheat was scarce.

The walls are hung with numerous enchanting sketches and paintings of various people eating pasta: A dominant figure is Pulcinella, the Neapolitan clown with his beaked nose, black half mask and white pantaloons, always with a plate of spaghetti; a marvelous oil by G. B. Torriglia, titled "To Make One's Mouth Water," showing a monk greedily shoveling pasta toward his mouth; and scores of watercolors and prints that show Neapolitans feasting on pasta, lowering the pasta strands into their up-turned mouths and using the unadorned fingers as the eating device. The latter were said to be the favorite souvenirs of foreigners who visited Naples during the late eighteenth and early nineteenth centuries.

As noted, a good deal of the lore about pasta and pasta-making is not immediately apparent to the casual visitor to the museum. There are, however, stashed away in drawers and otherwise filed, scores of documents, books, handwritten manuscripts, and so on that pertain to pasta either directly or tangentially.

Tangentially, for example, I have before me a copy of material relating to Gioacchino Rossini (1792-1868), celebrated as a composer and to a lesser extent as a gastronome and dedicated pasta-eater.

In 1824, we learn, Rossini went to live in Paris. For years it was the constant preoccupation of Paris society to have him condescend to come to a party. If he would consent to sit at the piano, it was an agreeable event; should he also agree to toss the pasta with the sauce and cheese, it was considered the ultimate complement.

Rossini's earnings from his music were notoriously small. But bankers, hoping to have him as a guest, vied with one another to offer him shares in gilt-edged investments they could obtain sub rosa.

Rossini, it is said, preferred a gift of food to all honors, political and ceremonial. One journal of his day, *Spirito Folleto,* in 1865, carried a cartoon of him seated at table with the caption, "Ah, those crazy citizens of Pesaro. They're planning to put up a statue of me. If only they'd send me a couple of mortadella instead."

Rossini was married to a woman known for her miserly nature. Once when Alexandre Dumas came to dine on macaroni, the portion served the writer was so pitifully small that Rossini offered to share his portion saying, "*Quod superest date pauperibus,*" or one is obliged to share with the poor. . . . A grand gesture for a man whose appetite for macaroni was said to be insatiable.

Mrs. Rossini also kept the keys to the musician's cellar, and bottles were doled out with such caution that when the Prussians invaded Passy, they discovered an incredible assortment—great Chambertins, Château d'Yquem, champagnes, Madeira, and so on—and drank them all.

Incidentally, a letter is also extant that he wrote from Paris to a friend, in which he signed himself ruefully, "Rossini without macaroni."

There are in the museum several amusing puppet shows of various origin. One of them instructs the viewer that "In Peking seven hundred years ago, Marco Polo saw that even the Chinese also ate pasta."

One of the documents available to visitors to the museum undermines or at least disputes the long-held theory that Marco Polo discovered pasta in China and thereafter introduced it to Italy on his return from the East.

It states:

"Oddly the most widely accepted legend is the most dubious of the lot. According to this legend it was Marco Polo who, on his journey through China, saw spaghetti being made there and brought it back to Venice, where it speedily gained favor and became Italy's national dish.

"This tale with an infinite number of colorful variations has so well established its place in spaghetti lore that it usually appears unquestioned in the most scholarly cookbooks and compendiums of culinary history. The trouble is it is just not true.

"Marco Polo came back from his journey through Asia in 1292. But already by the year 1279 the food was well enough known in Italy to be mentioned in a historical document. The notary Ugolino Scarpa, in his deed of Feb. 4, 1279, giving a list of what the soldier Ponzio Bastone was leaving to

his heirs, quotes a *'bariscella plena de macaronis,'* that is a small basket full of macaroni. (State Archives of Genoa, II register, page 51). This is the most ancient and authenticated news about macaroni."

Spatchcock

The *Oxford English Dictionary* defines spatchcock as "a fowl, split open and grilled after being killed, plucked and dressed in a summary fashion." References are also made to "a hen just killed from the roost, or yard, and immediately skinned, split and broiled." *Webster's New International Dictionary*, Second Edition, says that when used as a verb the word means "to prepare (a fowl, etc.) for eating as, or as if, a spatchcock."

In common American cookbook parlance, I believe that it would relate to the word "butterfly" or "butterflied," as in a boned leg of lamb. It's a pity the word is so little used in this country. I would much prefer advising one to "spatchcock a leg of lamb" than to "butterfly" it.

Speculaas

Speculaas are butter cookies that, I am told, are generally eaten in Belgium on St. Nicholas Eve, which is December 5. They are made with brown sugar and with baking powder as a leavening agent. The spices include cinnamon, nutmeg, and cloves and they may be garnished with almonds and candied orange or lemon peel before baking.

Spice Parisienne

Spice parisienne is used generally for making certain pâtés and terrines. Quantities of the ingredients vary, but they include such spices as thyme, bay leaf, coriander, mace, and so on.

It hasn't been available in the United States for some time, and a spokesman for Maison Glass told me why:

"We carried spice parisienne for many years, but it is no longer imported because the French producer refused to label the ingredients on the packages. Chef's secret, or something. The Food and Drug Administration insisted that the ingredients be listed and that's where it stands."

The American Spice Trade Association sent its recipe for Parisienne spice blend, as follows, with indications for its use:

PARISIENNE SPICE BLEND

Measure 3 tablespoons ground white pepper, 5 tablespoons ground cloves, 3 teaspoons ground nutmeg and 3 teaspoons ground ginger into small jar with a tight-fitting lid. Shake to blend thoroughly. Add

according to taste in stews, wine and raisin sauce, sweet yellow vegetables, such as carrots or sweet potatoes or to bean-and-bacon soup. A quarter teaspoon is about right for 3 cups pea soup. Delicious over sautéed mushrooms. When it is to be sprinkled over a broiled meat, mix the spice blend with the necessary salt so that it can be distributed evenly.

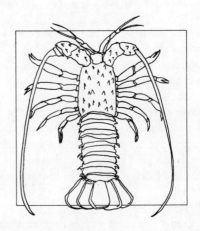

Spiny Lobster

The spiny lobster, which is commonly found in salt water all over the Caribbean, Florida, and the Bahamas, is the same as the *langouste* of France, the *aragosta* of Italy, and the *langosta* of Spain. It is sometimes referred to in the English-speaking world as a crayfish.

The spiny lobster has a large tail like the typical Maine or Long Island lobster; it has five pairs of legs but no claws. Though the flavor is good, it lacks the fine texture of the Maine or Long Island lobster. The crayfish, smaller and with a lobster-like shape, is found primarily in fresh water.

Spirits

There are spirits that, when added to foods, impart a definite geographical flavor. Two are the curiously appealing, anise-flavored drinks, Pernod and Ricard. Add a dash of one to a fish soup or stew and you are dining in Marseilles or another port in Provence. Another such spirit is Calvados. Add it to your *tripe à la mode* and you are whisked away to Normandy.

Pernod also makes a fine and unusual addition to a cream sauce, such as an English custard. Then again, so do the sweet liqueurs, such as Grand Marnier or the tangerine-flavored drink called mandarine. Such flavored sauces are delectable on tarts or on sweetened berries in season. Similarly, the famed white eaux de vies, such as framboise and kirsch, are used mostly in the preparation of cold, uncooked sauces. They are not at all amiss in custard sauces, however, added at the last minute for flavor, and they are good when added to an ice cream base before freezing.

Spit-Roasting

See Barbecue.

Split Peas

Split peas are simply sweet green peas that are dried and split by machine. I am told by a spokesman for the Graham Company, producers of Redbow dried beans, peas, lentils, and so on, that most of them sold commercially are grown in the Northwest, principally in Oregon and Washington. There is also, he adds, a yellow pea that is dried and split in similar fashion. The green and yellow dried split peas are blended.

Spotted Dick

Spotted Dick is a suet pastry filled with raisins and sultanas, sugar and spices. The pastry is then either boiled or steamed in a cloth or basin.

Sprat

See Brisling.

Squab

A squab is a cultivated pigeon too young to fly but old enough to make an elegant meal. The Chinese as well as the French are well

aware that such a bird is one of the finest of esculents.

And I find squab more toothsome than most winged creatures. It has a texture that is uncommonly agreeable and I am addicted to the flavor, which is more game-like than any other bird raised in capitivity.

It is one of the most versatile of birds, whether it is cooked in the oven or on top of the stove. I also find squab appealing whether it is served hot or cold. To my mind, there is nothing better suited to a picnic basket than roast squab with rosemary, served cold or lukewarm.

Squid

Browsing through the international sections of a number of cookbooks, I noted that almost every one of them lists recipes for squid. That interested me because Americans seem to have a very small appetite for squid, a delicacy that I would place in the highest category of good things to eat from the sea.

Squid are often referred to as voracious predators because they enthusiastically consume large and small fish as well as other

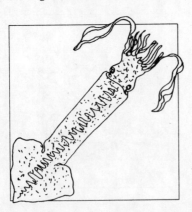

squid. I feel equally voracious when faced with a platter of cold squid salad, neatly dressed with oil and lemon; or stuffed squid in almost any fashion—filled with a delicate mousse of shrimp, for instance; or a well-made fish soup to which the pieces of squid add both flavor and an admirable texture.

Perhaps it is the squid's appearance that makes many Americans hesitate to eat it: Squid are, indeed, among the ugly ducklings of the deep (they navigate from near the surface to nearly a mile below) and range in size from about one inch to sixty feet long.

To name a few national or regional squid dishes, one could not ignore the classic version of Spain, which is known as *calamares en su tinto*. This is one of the most curious of Spanish dishes, curious because the name means "squid in its own ink." Squid have a small, fragile sac that contains a liquid of almost Stygian blackness.

The Greeks have a word for squid, of course, and it is *kalamaria*. In Japan, where squid is prized for, among other things, sushi and sashimi, it is known as *yika*. In Italy, it is *calamari* and in France, it goes by many names, but principally *calmar*. In Provence, it is called *tantonnet* and *claougeous*. My absolute favorite name for squid, however, is the Basque word *txipirones*.

There is a false notion that squid requires long cooking to tenderize it. The actual cooking time is quite brief, depending on the uses to which it is put. I know of one Chinese dish in which it is cooked only thirty seconds in boiling water; for salads, the squid pieces should simmer in a court bouillon or cooking liquid for about one minute.

It may be that the cleaning of squid creates a negative feeling in the minds of many home cooks. The fact is that squid, despite its forbidding aspect in the natural state, is not all that difficult to clean. Simply remove the head and all the interior material, then remove and discard the beak and pull or rub off the outer skin, a quick operation all in all. The tentacles are eminently edible.

Squid is very much a seasonal food. It is obtainable in markets from about the last two weeks in March throughout the summer, when it becomes abundant. It is frequently found frozen. *See also* Fisherman's joke.

Stamp and Go

Stamp and go is a well-known dish of Jamaican origin. It is nothing more than codfish cakes made with dried salt codfish that has been soaked until tender and drained.

It is blended with flour, baking powder, salt, milk, butter, and onions, plus chopped hot green or red pepper. It is deep-fried and served hot. The hot pepper gives it a pleasant spiciness.

Star Anise

See Anise.

Steak au Poivre

Steak au poivre, in the historical sense, is a comparatively new dish. It does not appear, for example, in the works of Escoffier, who died in 1935.

But an old friend sent me a recipe he had discovered in a book that I have had in my library for nearly twenty years, *Bull Cook and Authentic Historical Recipes and Practices,* by George Leonard Herter and Berthe E. Herter, an old compilation of food facts and recipes, many of questionable authenticity. It is an interesting and much-quoted book, however.

The recipe is for beefsteak Leopold. My friend proposes that if the recipe is authentic, perhaps it is the original one for steak au poivre. It says:

"Leopold I was born a Prince in 1790 in Saxe-Coburg, Bavaria, Germany. He was a great eater and made a great study of recipes. He become King of Belgium and was well liked by the Belgians. His first wife died in childbirth. He not only had a taste for good food but an eye for beautiful women. His second wife was Louise Marie of Orleans, a real beauty and daughter of King Louis Philippe of France.

"Leopold and his wife both were experts on cooking; but Leopold himself was the one who created the recipe. Like all really great recipes, it is a simple one.

"Now take your beefsteak, whatever kind that you desire, and lay it onto a plate. Salt it on both sides to taste. Now take your peppermill and grind a thin coating of pepper berries over one side of the steak. Take your fingertips and press the pieces of the pepper berries into the meat as much as possible. Turn the steak over and do the same for the other side. Now broil the steak as described under broiling steak elsewhere in this book. Remove the steak when done as you desire it and quickly take a heaping spoonful of butter and spread it over the entire steak. The butter blends with the herb flavors of the pepper berries and gives the steak the best flavor you have ever tasted in a steak. It does something for beef that you just would not believe possible.

"Beefsteak Leopold is available at many fine restaurants in New York and goes under the name of Steak Poivre. At Maxim's in Paris, France, it is called Steak Albert. At Maxim's they use white pepper instead of whole ground pepper. They pour one ounce of hot brandy over the steak before serving it. It is very good, too, but I prefer holding to the original recipe to the letter."

Steak Tartare

I have long been fascinated by the use of the word tartar, or tartare, in cookery. This has been since my first sampling in childhood of a tartar sauce, and later when I ate steak tartare. A Tartar (or Tatar) is, as any schoolchild should know, a member of the Mongolian hordes who, under Genghis Khan, overran parts of Asia and central Europe in the thirteenth century. I assumed the two were related, and it was confirmed by a Bridgeport, Connecticut, gentleman:

"Tartars were fierce Mongolian horsemen who invaded much of Eastern Europe in the twelfth and thirteenth centuries. The Tartars, who lived on horseback, had a way of tenderizing their meat by placing it under the saddle and riding on it before consuming it raw, probably dressed with tartar sauce, which was originally mare's milk, allowed to stand for a few days and seasoned with native spices."

Incidentally the word is spelled tartar in many English dictionaries and *tartare* in most French ones (although there are listings in the *American Heritage Dictionary* and in *Webster's New World Dictionary* for steak tartare). When spelled without the "e," the accent is on the first syllable; with the "e," it is on the second.

Steamers

See Clams.

Stilton

It is a question that will seem in the minds of many about as moot as how many angels can dance on the head of a pin. But I've spent a good deal of time pondering the best and most efficient technique for serving Stilton cheese. Do you scoop it with a scoop or with a spoon and leave a standing rim, or slice and cut the cheese with a knife, serving the rim as well?

One time in London I visited Paxton and Whitfield, the cheese shop across the street from that other endless source of good things for the table, Fortnum and Mason. I ordered a small baby Stilton from the shop, and, when it arrived, the package contained a highly enlightening four-page brochure published by the cheese maker. It offered the method of cutting and serving Stilton cheese as recommended by the Stilton Cheese Makers Association. (The brochure also pointed out that the name Stilton is registered worldwide by the Stilton cheese maker, and only the genuine article may bear the name.)

The cheese is produced around the town of Melton Mowbray and was first mentioned in the early 1800s. The name of the originator is unknown, but early records indicate it was sold at the Bell Inn, Stilton, in Huntingdonshire to the coach and carriage traffic.

"The landlord," the brochure states, obtained his cheese-making supplies "from the wife's sister who was married to a farmer

named Paulet near Melton Mowbray. She had learned to make the cheese from their mother who was housekeeper to a Lady Baumont at Quenby Hall.''

Quite wisely, to my mind, the cheese makers recommend a knife rather than a scoop or spoon. If a scoop or spoon is used, the shell of the cheese dries out. In using the recommended knife technique, the cheese is cut into wedges similar to cutting a pie, slicing down an inch or so, left and right, to indicate the size of the wedge. The knife is then inserted beneath these cuts and sliced across so the wedge may be lifted up and served.

The association states firmly that port wine should never be poured into the cheese. This is a silly conceit, a detriment to the wine and the cheese itself. Instead, the wine should be served to be sipped in tandem as the cheese is eaten. Beer also makes an excellent accompaniment to Stilton cheese.

A crusty loaf is recommended for the cheese. I have personally never understood the use of water biscuits, English or otherwise, with any cheese and have always been puzzled that anyone with supposedly good taste would serve these biscuits, so basically unsophisticated, with any fine cheese.

Stirring

There is a kitchen "rule of thumb" as to when to use a wooden spoon or a wire whisk to stir sauces.

A wooden spoon is generally used to stir sauces that contain ingredients such as tomato pieces, vegetables, and so on. The spoon can reach to the bottom of a saucepan for stirring to prevent the sauces and ingredients from sticking on the bottom. A wire whisk is generally used for smooth sauces in which the wires of the whisk can flow freely without having the center of the whisk clogged with the bulky ingredients, which could be difficult to shake off. A wire whisk's greatest use is in the preparation of cream sauces and mayonnaise.

One of the saddest cooking experiences I've ever been witness to occurred on the sun deck of a beach house a few doors down from my own home.

I had been invited one splendid summer day to indulge in the provencal-style feast known as an aïoli, an elaborate combination of foods including cooked salt cod, chickpeas, hard-boiled eggs, and various vegetables including artichokes, cauliflower, carrots, tomatoes, and so on. The cornerstone of the feast is, in addition to the cod, a kind of mayonnaise heavily spiked with raw garlic.

The lady of the house, a marvelous cook, was a Frenchwoman whose family came from Provence. She had been taught to cook by a grandmother.

The lady, our friend, had spent the better part of that Sunday making mayonnaise. Almost the entire morning. Not that the quantity of mayonnaise she was to serve was all that vast. She simply decided to make mayonnaise "like Grandma used to make," which is to say with a wooden spoon. No fancy modern devices, thank you. No wire whisk, no electric beater, nothing that smacks of a gadget.

Grandma made her mayonnaise with a wooden spoon, and what's good enough for Grandma in Provence is certainly good enough for the eastern shore of Long Island.

Well, when you make mayonnaise with a wooden spoon, here's how you go about it. You add an egg yolk or yolks to a wooden bowl along with seasonings like salt and pepper and mustard and a little vinegar and then you start stirring with that wooden spoon while gradually adding a good grade of olive oil, preferably from Provence. And you stir. And stir. And stir. And stir. "And always stirring in the same direction," she cautioned. "Grandma said so." With any kind of luck the mayonnaise starts to thicken and you're home safe.

Well, madame stirred and stirred and stirred and eventually the sauce started to thicken just before she got what might be called mayonnaise elbow.

Anyway, she got the sauce ready along about noon, with guests arriving at one, and she had this enormous German shepherd, a huge animal that answered to the name of Graf. And Graf was, as German shepherds tend to be, hungry, so he jumped up on the rail and dived into that bowl and with two enthusiastic licks the vessel was so clean you'd have thought the party was over.

That is an incident that is apt to haunt someone who is addicted to sauce making with wire whisks. Especially that notion about "always stirring in one direction."

It came to mind recently when a letter arrived from Carmel, New York.

"Please settle a question for me and my husband," the woman wrote. "I was taught by my Hungarian mother (a cook of some renown) to stir all things, but especially batter, clockwise in order to incorporate air into the batter and not 'beat it down.' I am teaching my two sons, aged eight and eleven, to cook (their wives will bless me someday, I hope). I have trained them thusly. My husband is an avid chef—but not a baker—and he insists (intelligent engineer of electronics, that he is) that it makes no difference. Could you please arbitrate and we will abide by your decision."

It is, once more, only an educated guess, but I am willing to share your husband's opinion. I can't see that it could possibly make one iota of difference as long as you don't stop beating. If you interrupt the rhythm of beating, a sauce might be encouraged to "curdle" or separate.

Then a letter arrived from Jane Sarnoff, co-author of *The Monster Riddle Calendar* and *The Monster Riddle Book*, stating that the idea of single-direction stirring is solidly based on a long-held superstition.

"In my research," she wrote, "I found it a widespread belief that foods should be stirred only clockwise. The superstition is ancient, dating back to days of sun worship. It was thought an insult to the sun (and thus unlucky) to do anything against the direction of the sun. To bring luck to any movement, including stirring cake batter, it had to be done with the sun—the direction we now call clockwise."

Stock

See Broth.

Stovies

Stovies is a simple potato dish popular in Scotland. The potatoes are generally sliced and cooked in a minimum amount of water with butter added. They are cooked covered until tender, shaking the skillet until tender and browned. Sometimes onion is added. And sometimes it is sprinkled with a little oatmeal shortly before the cooking time is over. Stovies, according to some sources, is delicious when served hot with ice-cold buttermilk.

Strangozzi

Strangozzi, which seem related to Spoleto, are ribbon noodles made with flour and water and without eggs. The "paste" is rolled out and cut into very thin strips. The most typical sauce, Italians say, consists of tomatoes, basil, parsley, salt, and pepper and a little garlic cooked in olive oil. The sauce is tossed with the noodles and the dish is served with freshly grated Parmesan.

Stroganoff

I have noted before that there have been through the ages many people of distinction, men and women who loomed large in their lifetime, whose fame would have disappeared with their last breath if some good chef had not seen fit to honor them while they were alive and quick and cutting a figure in the world. Among these can be counted the Count Paul Stroganoff, a member of the court of Tsar Alexander III and the Imperial Academy of Arts in St. Petersburg. He lived at the end of the last century, dined well, lived the good life, and that is about the sum and substance of what is remembered about him. In any event, his name is legend because of various dishes made with beef, veal, pork, or game, always enriched with sour cream and frequently seasoned with a touch of mustard.

Sturgeon

See Albany beef.

Sugar

See Brown sugar, Caster, Demerara sugar.

Sugar Pie

Sugar pie, or tart, is one of the most basic of Canadian desserts, and I have been told there are dozens of variations. The filling may be all sugar or it may contain part sugar and part maple syrup. The recipe with which I am familiar is made with 1 cup each of water, white sugar, and brown sugar, which are cooked together for 5 minutes or longer.

You add about 2 cups or slightly less of heavy cream and let it simmer about 10 minutes longer. Blend ½ cup each of flour and butter and stir in the cream syrup, using a wire whisk. Let cool, pour the filling into an unbaked pie shell, and bake in a 350-degree oven for about ½ hour.

This pie is served at room temperature, often with a scoop of vanilla ice cream on top.

Sunchoke

See Jerusalem artichoke.

Sundae

Every now and then there's a food legend that smacks of whole cloth. A sample: the ice cream sundae. A news account of some years back informs me that the sundae originated in the town of Ithaca, New York.

It seems that years ago, when Ithaca was not much more than a hamlet, there was a small pharmacy that boasted a soda fountain that was not well patronized during the weekdays, the reason being that it was situated directly across from a hotel bar that flourished.

The bar was closed on Sundays and the drinking class repaired to the drugstore to cool their throats with ice cream sodas. One particularly sensitive individual complained to the management that he could not stomach his weekly ice cream soda because the fizzing in the carbonated water contributed to the pounding in his already bursting head. He ordered his ice cream with syrup only.

In no time at all, according to this legend, the "dry" version of the ice cream soda caught on and was called "The Sunday Special."

The story has it that the spelling was later changed to sundae because it was held to be irreverent to name a dish after the Sabbath.

Sun-Dried Tomatoes

Sun-dried tomatoes are a luxury that can be found in most fine-food specialty shops and their uses are legion. Most of them come from northern Italy, primarily from the region of Emilia-Romagna. It is said that the northern tomatoes of that nation are sweeter than those of the south. The tomatoes are split in half by hand and the seeds are removed. The seeds, if left inside, contribute a bit of acidity and bitterness and for that reason are eliminated.

The production of the tomatoes is far more elaborate than simply putting them in cans and processing them in a water bath. The finest grades of these tomatoes are layered on grates under cane "pergola" and they are not dried in direct contact with the sun. They are given proper ventilation and kept slightly moist during their "drying" period by an occasional spray of water.

When dried, the tomatoes are put in vats along with herbs and olive oil and left to ferment for a few weeks, perhaps as many as six. They are then drained of oil, the herbs are cast aside, and they are repacked with virgin olive oil.

One of the great admirers of sun-dried

tomatoes is Ed Giobbi, the artist and cookbook author. Appalled at the cost of the imported version, he turned to his home-style electric fruit and vegetable drier and applied that technique to drying his own. His home-prepared tomatoes, he admits, are not as dry as those from abroad.

Sushi

To the uninitiated palate, sushi—raw fish served on rice—is one of the gastronomic curiosities of the world. Some people, even those who dote on raw oysters and clams, find the thought of eating raw fish in any form bizarre.

To those who enjoy sushi, however, it is one of the natural gastronomic wonders, in or out of its native Japan, and to call sushi an appetizer—as many people do—is not to understand the nature of the dish. Of course, it may be served in small portions at the beginning of a meal, but to dig into the subject like a native you must sit at a sushi bar pointing with glee and uncontrollable gluttony at the scores of pieces of fish and seafood on view behind the glass of an immaculately polished display case.

In Japan, there is a good deal of interesting folklore surrounding the dish. Legend has it beginning two thousand years ago near Tokyo with an emperor who dined on fish that was just beginning to ferment. Tokyo to this day is considered the sushi capital of the world (although the finest sushi house I've ever stumbled on anywhere is the Fukki-zushi in the Minami district in Osaka).

For want of written records, it is impossible to determine the exact date when sushi was created, but the greatest likelihood, according to food authorities in Japan, is that it probably started in China in a different form. It is theorized that, originally, raw fish was packed between layers of rice and left until the fish started to take on a slightly fermented, sour taste. Then it was eaten with a new-found relish. This technique was probably imported to Japan, where eventually the present custom of serving nothing but the freshest of fish on a hand-shaped pad of vinegar-flavored rice came into being. There are said to be still in existence in Japan a few rare places where fish is lightly fermented between rice layers as in the original manner.

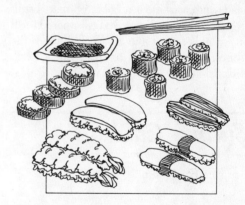

The kinds of fish and shellfish that can be eaten raw as sushi are practically endless. It is true that tuna, one of the favorite fish used for sushi, is seasonal, but any very fresh and edible ocean fish or shellfish can be used. Sea bass, striped bass, and fresh mackerel are all excellent. Salmon roe, sometimes called red caviar and available in jars twelve months a year, is delicious as a topping for seaweed-wrapped sushi rice. Thinly sliced raw clams, even the large chowder clams sliced razor thin along the meaty section, are delectable. Sea urchins, that delicacy so prized in Mediterranean regions, offer an incredibly good roe best eaten raw. The important thing is that each morsel to be served should of the freshest quality and sliced bite-size before using.

Incidentally, although sushi is made with rice, it is a great vehicle for maintaining a stable weight and is enormously gratifying to the appetite.

Svid

I have heard of but never sampled svid, a traditional dish of Iceland. I am told it is made with a whole head of lamb that is split in two and, brains removed, simmered until the meat is tender and almost falling off the bones. It is served hot or cold, and the traditional accompaniment is mashed turnips.

Swamp Cabbage

See Hearts of palm.

Swan

A swan is "a fine bird to watch on the water or in flight, but a poor one to eat" according to André Simon, considered one of England's great epicures of the last half century. In his *Concise Encyclopedia of Gastronomy,* he adds that cygnets used to be served on festive occasions in England.

"At the banquet given by the Bishop of Durham for King Richard II, in 1387, fifty swans graced the board. On Christmas Day, 1512, five swans were provided for the Duke of Northumberland's table; on the following New Year's Day, four more, and on Twelfth Day of the same year, another four swans."

Sweat

The word "sweat," in cooking references, such as "sweat the onions," is a translation of a commonly used culinary term in France. The French is *suer les oignons*. It means adding the onions to a saucepan, generally using butter or oil, and cooking the onions without browning them.

The onions are generally cooked, covered, over very low heat. The reason for this is obviously a question of taste. Onions that have been cooked until they are dry or browned have a different taste than those that have been cooked in the gentler fashion.

I find the translation of the phrase a bit pretentious and don't recall ever having used it in a recipe. "Cook the onions over low heat in a tightly covered saucepan without letting them brown" sounds better to my American ears than "sweat the onions."

Sweetbreads

There is no more reason why sweetbreads are the basis for some of the most elegant dishes in the world than there is in why people climb mountains or take to the air in ascension balloons. Sweetbread dishes are simply a natural thread in the fabric of fine dining and have been for centuries. Sweetbreads, the tender thymus glands of calves, often serve interchangeably between first courses and main dishes.

People frequently ask why sweetbreads must be soaked and weighted. The answer is that they, like fresh fish bones and heads, are likely to contain a certain amount of residual blood, which will turn dark on cooking (blood also clouds broths, such as fish broth). The soaking aids in getting rid of much of this. Sweetbreads are weighted down after cooking because it gives them a firmer, more appetizing texture. If they are not weighted, they have a spongy texture that may be acceptable, but it is not preferable.

Some dictionaries say the name is a description of the dish when it is cooked since the person who coined the name considered the meat to be an exceedingly good, breadlike edible. I tend to concur with the *Oxford English Dictionary,* however, which states that "the reason for the name is not obvious."

Sweet Cumin

See Anise.

Sweetmeat

A sweetmeat is not a specific dish but refers, rather, to almost any dainty food, such as candy, which is made with sugar or another sweetening agent.

As far as I know, there is nothing regional about the word, which strikes me as being a little antique.

I have been informed by a good number of Southerners, principally Virginians, that a sweetmeat was made from the rind of watermelon.

Sweet Potatoes

See Yams.

Swizzle Sticks

Swizzle sticks are for invalids and other people whose stomachs cannot support the gaseous bubbles in champagne. They destroy in a second that which took years and endless care to produce.

Syllabub

The word "syllabub" is of uncertain origin; it has an Early Modern English antecedent, solybubbe. It is, like zabaglione, a beaten dessert made with wine, but the Italian dish is more elaborate. Of the many versions of syllabub, the most common consists of a simple syrup or sugar beaten with milk, cream, and fortified wine, such as sherry. Some recipes call for bourbon, others for Cognac or rum.

Tt Tt  Tt Tt

Tabbouleh

See Bulgur.

Tahini

Tahini is a thick paste made of sesame seeds, and it is widely used in Eastern and Middle Eastern dishes, particularly those of Greek, Turkish, and Chinese origin.

If you can't find tahini in your community, the chances are you won't find sesame seeds either. And to continue on a negative note, I seriously doubt that you could, using ordinary household equipment, prepare a paste thick and smooth enough to be the equivalent of the commercially prepared tahini.

Food processors and electric blenders would only partly crack and crush sesame seeds, which are exceedingly small.

In an emergency, it is possible to substitute finely ground peanut butter diluted, perhaps, with a little water.

While I am on the subject, I have seen numerous recipes that refer to tahini as sesame oil; it isn't. Sesame oil is quite thin, like most salad oils; sesame paste is quite thick.

Tamales

The earliest reference to tamales in the *Oxford English Dictionary* is dated 1856. The quotation I prefer, in *The Boston Journal* in 1884, noted that "a queer article of food known as 'tamales' is sold in the streets of San Francisco at night by picturesquely clad Spaniards."

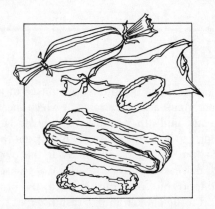

Tamarind

Tamarind is a highly acid, somewhat sweet fruit that is actually a bean that grows on trees. It is available in various forms in the

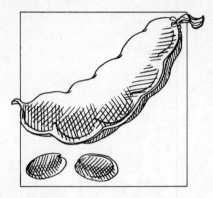

United States—fresh pods, packaged with seeds for preparing a paste at home, and as a ready-made paste in bottles. To make a tamarind paste, take lump tamarind purchased in Indian stores and soak in a little very hot water to cover for several hours. Work the mixture with the fingers, pushing the pulp through a sieve and discarding the seeds. Recipes using tamarind can be found in almost any Indian or Middle Eastern cookbook. *See also* Worcestershire sauce.

Tandoor

A tandoor is a traditional oven used in Indian homes and restaurants in which meats, breads, and other foods are cooked. Tandoori chicken, for example, is chicken that has been skewered and cooked in this oven.

For years it has been traditional to use a red food color on meats, chicken, and other food to be cooked in this fashion, and this gives the food an appealing reddish cast. The kind of food color varied. Originally it was probably saffron. I asked my friend, Jati Hoon, an owner of Gaylord's Restaurant in Manhattan, about the color they use, and

he told me that it is a pure food dye called Egg Color, distributed by Captain Post Horse Radish and Pickle Company of Manhattan. A spokesman for that firm stated that the color is not sold commercially to the general public.

I then telephoned another Indian friend, Madhur Jaffrey, and she said that she had formerly used a red food dye to bake chicken, Indian style, in her home oven but no longer. Too difficult to find. She tried paprika and it wasn't satisfactory.

"The principal reason for the color was eye appeal, anyway," she said. She added that on her most recent trip to her homeland she discovered that many restaurants are not using any kind of dye for tandoor-cooked foods.

A favorite commercial *tandoori* spice mixture is Monorema's *Tandoori*. The directions for use are on the bottle and I quote:

" 'For a marinade: For every 2 pounds of meat, combine 2½ tablespoons tandoori powder, 2 tablespoons oil, 1 tablespoon lemon juice, and 1 tablespoon water (or 2 tablespoons yogurt). Use marinade for steaks, chops, roasts, etc.'

" 'For tandoori chicken, rub tandoori

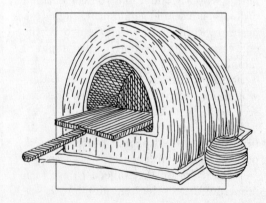

marinade well into a 2½- to 3-pound broiler. Marinate for 45 minutes. Place whole or kebab-size pieces of chicken on skewer. Broil or barbecue until done. Serve with saffron rice. (Makes 4 servings)."

Tangerine

I am told that the tangerine is native to China and Laos. That is undoubtedly why the fruit is also referred to as mandarin orange. The name tangerine, however, means the orange of Tangier, the Moroccan city.

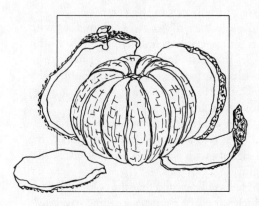

Tapas

Tapas are "small foods," resembling appetizers, that come in a thousand varieties and are served in tascas, or small bars, that are gathering places for Spaniards who like to sip sherry or beer and exchange gossip. Tapas may range from fresh sardines or squid in olive oil and vinegar to snails in a sauce to chorizo (Spanish sausages), dried ham, and cold Spanish omelet, which is made with sliced potatoes, onions, and eggs and is totally different from the omelet with a Creole sauce that is called a Spanish omelet in America.

Tapenade

See Capers.

Tapioca

Tapioca is derived from the cassava or manioc plant, which thrives in the tropics. The roots of the plant are roasted and dried and sifted to produce three grades of tapioca: fine, medium, and pearl. The tapioca is quite starchy and when blended with a liquid becomes opaque. It is used in puddings, soups, and desserts. The cassava or manioc plant also yields *farinha de manioca*, which is widely used in Brazil to sprinkle over that famous national dish, feijoada.

Tarator

Tarator is a Yugoslav soup made with yogurt, finely minced garlic, cucumbers, walnuts, olive oil, and chopped mint. In Greek kitchens, I am told, the soup bears the name taratouri and there is a similar soup in Turkey called cacik. I am also told it originated in Bulgaria but became popular throughout the Balkans.

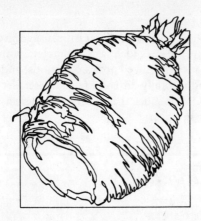

Taro Root

Taro root is a food enjoyed by many peoples in the Pacific. It is best known in Hawaii, where it is turned into a paste-like staple called poi.

It is, for most nonislanders at least, a bland, characterless supplement to the diet. In Tahiti it is referred to as *dasheen* and in the Maori language as *eddo*. Taro root is also found in Chinese cuisine, where it is braised, steamed, and stir-fried. You will rarely find recipes for it in cookbooks.

Tarte Tatin

Tarte Tatin is also referred to in French as *tarte des demoiselles Tatin,* or "the tart of two unmarried women named Tatin." In her book *French Regional Cooking,* Anne Willan writes that the pie comes from the Loire Valley and was named "after two impoverished gentlewomen from Lamotte-Beuvron in Sologne, who were forced to earn their living by baking their father's favorite apple pie with caramel topping."

Taste

One of the most intriguing news items to cross my desk came from United Press International and had a Davis, California, dateline.

It said that, like Pavlov's puppies, the public appetite responds to, and likes, what it is accustomed to, even things that are quite impure by the highest standards. Howard G. Schutz, a psychologist and associate professor of consumer services at the University of California, has determined that the typical American prefers tinned tomato juice to fresh or bottled, because over the years he has become accustomed to the taste of the tin from the can.

People "learn" to associate quality with certain experiences and sometimes without logic. I find humor as well as grim truth in his observation that the general public prefers potato chips that are slightly stale to those that are freshly cooked.

"The characteristic flavor of slightly rancid oil is one which the consumer has come to identify with a potato chip that tastes 'just right.' "

He has also noted that the color of butter, which varies, of course, according to a cow's diet as well as the season of the year, must be standardized with color added by the industry or people won't buy. When the fruit gelatin people tried to shift to true fruit flavors and away from the artificial flavors, product acceptance fell off.

He also observes that people who are hung up on organic foods buy only brown eggs because they consider plain old white eggs less wholesome. But the average consumer prefers white eggs, thinking them better and more nutritious. In truth, he adds, there is no difference in taste *or* nutritional quality.

I could add a lot of things to the good scientist's sad list. People who dote on bull shots—that combination of beef broth with vodka, lemon juice, and seasonings—infinitely prefer a canned consommé with its beef extract taste rather than a pure broth. And consider the gimlet, one of the nation's more popular cocktails. Make it with pure lime juice and sugar and people start a rumor you're a lousy bartender. You never heard of bottled lime juice, huh? Right here on the label it says concentrated lime juice, sugar, water, artificial colors, preserved with less than 320 p.p.m. sulphur dioxide. What are you, some sort of fresh fruit kook?

Another item for the list: Approximately twenty years ago while I was pursuing what might be termed the epicurean habits of people who live in Palm Beach, Florida, I was fascinated to learn that the residents— seasonal or otherwise—were given to drinking champagne on the rocks. To my mind, ice, like swizzle sticks, eliminates the bubbles in that most wondrous of beverages—bubbles that had required some cellar master a good number of months, if not years, to instill.

It was equally impressive to hear a grande dame, wearing ropes of gold, fingers burdened with precious stones, explain that food is not discussed in polite society. I have pondered that remark for a good number of years and often wondered if there was a scientific name for people who have an absolute indifference to food and food flavors.

I have a letter from a man in Lancaster, Pennsylvania, who writes: "We have the words color-blind and tone-deaf. Did you know there is actually a medical term 'taste blind'? It describes aptly those people who are poor at tasting things. The fine technical term for this condition is ageusia (ah-jue-see-yuh), implying the absence or impairment of the sense of taste." The word derives from the Greek *ageusic*.

And yet I think that some people, and I suspect a great number of people, are born with the gustatory equivalent of perfect pitch. Whether they develop that ultimate sense of taste and smell (where taste is concerned, smell is irrevocably interbound) is another matter. The pursuit and sharpening of taste involve continuous and reflexive familiarization with and analysis of myriad flavors and odors.

I have an acquaintance in the wine field who told me quite seriously that he believes in reincarnation and that in his past life he was a canine (a basset hound, he hoped) for as a child he sniffed everything, flowers, herbs, grass, the leaves of plants, other animals, and so on simply for the pure joy of smelling.

I boastfully claim a kindred nature, and if I were placed in a closed room of filtered air, I could conjure up dozens of the smells of my childhood. The scent of newly mown hay, the warm, musty smell of freshly baled cotton (I grew up in the Mississippi Delta), and more than these the commingling of flavors in my mother's kitchen—onions and celery and green peppers sautéed in butter.

I have total recall of the first time I smelled or dined on tarragon. It was in Paris in a restaurant on the Ile St. Louis called Le Bossu. It no longer exists, but I supped on the most elegant scrambled eggs (or so I thought then) known to the gods, and there were chopped fresh tarragon leaves to perfume them. It was a time of ultimate bliss.

I also know, incidentally, that the palate can be wildly confused and with no damage done, except, perhaps, to one's ego. One way to do this involves a game that, if you care to play, can net you five to one (an arbitrary ratio) if you can find a taker or two who boasts about his unerring palate.

It is a blindfold test involving, let us say, seven or more strong spirits such as Scotch, vodka, bourbon, rye, Cognac, rum, and gin. The beverages are listed on a scorecard, and as samples are poured at random the blindfolded subject is asked to rate one at a time.

Characteristically, the subject is able to identify the first and possibly the second sample. After that he is *more* than apt to confuse a majority of the remaining alcohols, mistaking rum for Cognac, rye for bourbon, bourbon for rum, even Cognac for vodka, and so on.

Having participated in this charade with a few of the grander gurus of food and drink, I can vouch for the fact that a score of 50 percent is excellent. A score of 70 percent is phenomenal and, in my experience at least, a score of 100 percent is unknown.

Oddly enough, there is one drink that is more often identified correctly than any of the others. That is gin, probably because of the distinct nature of the juniper flavor.

There are numerous other ways to modify taste, and one of the most dramatic, in my experience, came in the form of a harmless pill brought to my kitchen by a young researcher who works in flavors.

The substance in the pill was derived from a natural growing plant commonly called miracle fruit. The plant is bookishly called *Sysepalum dulcificum*. The plant derives from tropical areas in West Africa, and is now also grown in the United States.

The miracle fruit derived from the plant resembled a light purple aspirin tablet with the same texture. It was held in the mouth until it dissolved, and immediately after I

was encouraged to suck on half a lemon. It was for all the world like a saccharine-sweet undiscovered fruit. A Scotch and soda taken shortly thereafter was all but undrinkable, and a glass of wine was too sweet to be recognizable as wine. The taste modification endured for approximately twenty minutes.

Although miracle fruit is little known to the general public, it is widely known and discussed in laboratory circles that deal in food and flavor analysis.

People who have dined on artichokes, if they have probing and sensitive taste buds, know that they alter the flavor of such a basic item as water. Artichokes alter the taste in such a way that water taken immediately afterward takes on a distinctly sweet flavor.

Similarly, to a more or less degree, they alter the flavor of wine, which is why I know certain purists (yours truly not included) who will not serve and flatly eschew artichokes in any and all forms during the course of so-called gourmet meals where fine wines are to be poured. Similarly, they avoid salads tossed with vinegar.

It is a personal thing, but during the course of a meal in which my colleagues eschew artichokes and salad with vinegar, they wind up their festivities bathed in clouds of cigar smoke. And, as I have noted at other times, if there is anything that can cripple, deaden, or anesthetize my personal sensibilities, it is cigar fumes. Given my choice, I would prefer an artichoke served as a salad and bathed in vinegar.

Although I make modest claims for an ability to detect subtle seasonings and so on, I admit to justifiable confusion where the cuisines of three countries or regions are concerned. These are India, Mexico, and Indonesia. And I hunger for them all.

The spur for the confusion is obvious; it

is the highly complex mixture of spices that go into many of the best dishes of each area. I have before me an Indian recipe that I greatly admire for tandoori chicken, the delicious "barbecued" item in which chicken—on home territory at least—is bathed in a multitude of spices, then baked in a fiery hot underground clay oven.

In addition to onion, garlic, ginger, lemon juice, and yogurt, the recipe calls for a blend of spices including coriander, cumin, turmeric, mace, nutmeg, cloves, cinnamon, cayenne pepper, cardamom seeds, and cumin seeds.

Similarly, many of the dishes of Mexico and Indonesia employ a highly complex mélange of seasonings, and to analyze such foods the best one can do is hazard, one hopes, an educated guess. Oddly enough, and here is a personal reaction, Chinese cookery, like the French and Italian, responds quite easily to basic analysis. The flavorings or seasonings are far more subtle (which is to say limited) and yield their identity more readily.

Someone recently sent me a copy of a reference work called *Principles of Sensory Evaluation of Food* by Amerine, Pangborn and Roessler of the University of California. It is by no means the jauntiest reading in the world (it is, in fact, a textbook for "food majors" in college), but there is one chapter that should be of interest to the general public.

I learned to my total fascination that Aristotle first proposed that man has five primary senses—sight, hearing, touch, smell, and taste. In this more enlightened age, we know that there are other such important sensations as heat, cold, pain, hunger, thirst, fatigue, and equilibrium. Even sex.

The authors also note that the sound of foods is important in eating, including the "snap, crackle and pop" of certain cereals, the crunchiness of celery and carrots, and the sizzling of steaks.

Some of the facts put forth in the book are, to my mind, amusing, if open to question. One is the strange proposition that if blanched almonds are eaten with smoked finnan haddie, the fishy flavor will be diminished in the eater's mind because of the distinction of all that crunching and munching.

Tatties an' Herrin'

Tatties is a Scotch word for potatoes. I learned on a visit to Scotland that tatties an' herrin' is made with new potatoes parboiled or steamed until half done, then covered with fillets of fresh-caught herring, covered with a cloth and steamed until the potatoes are thoroughly tender without being overcooked.

Tea

One of the first essays on food I ever wrote—it was more than a quarter of a century ago—dealt with tea, a beverage of which to this day I am passionately fond. That epic included what remains as one of my favorite "recipes" for preparing beverages. The origin of the formula was attributed to a French missionary who, a couple of hundred years ago, recommended that "tea leaves be allowed to steep no longer than is necessary to chant the Miserere psalm in a leisurely fashion."

A reminiscence of that tea-making ceremony came to mind during a brief stay at the Peninsula Hotel in Hong Kong, surely one of the ten greatest and most delectable hostelries on earth. In my room there was included the hotel's magazine published, if memory serves, on a monthly basis. It included a fascinating article on tea by Robin Moyer, who is credited as a "freelance photojournalist who works in the United States and Asia."

In it, the author recounted what must be the oldest legend in the world pertinent to the origins of tea. I have long been familiar with the legend but rarely have I read it so neatly expressed.

"Somewhere," the author wrote, "deep in the misty mountains . . . Ta Mo, the Bodhidharma, fifth reincarnation of Buddha, faced a stone wall and meditated. Spring mists became summer rains and the flower-covered hillsides turned green. Bamboo forests swayed like oceans in the soft warm breezes. And Autumn came with crisp air and the leaves colored and fell, soundless to the earth. Winter came, its light snows dusting the wall and Ta Mo's coarse cloak. Still he meditated. Unblinking. Unsleeping. Unsearching. And the cycle of seasons began again. And again. The years passed but the Bodhidharma remained. Finally his attention wavered and his chin dropped, his eyes closed to gentle sleep.

"When Ta Mo woke, perhaps a day or a month, perhaps a year later, he was so angry with himself for failing in his task of meditation that he sliced off both his eyelids with a sharp knife and cast them to the ground. Immediately upon hitting the rich soil of Szechwan the saintly eyelids sprouted roots and grew into what we know as the tea bush, symbol of wakefulness."

Whatever the origins of tea, one of the most interesting things about it is the enormous variety to be sampled: the sternly elegant and pure breakfast teas, generally a blend of Ceylon and India teas; the smoke-flavored teas like lapsang souchong; and the exotic romantic teas like jasmine. In view of the wide selection of tastes, the thought occurred over a pot of steaming hot breakfast tea, that tea drinking can be more of an adventure than almost any nonalcoholic beverage, and better suited to a larger variety of foods.

There are foods, for example, that are totally incompatible with coffee in any form—light roast, dark roast, or whatever. Two obvious examples that come to mind are two of my favorite breakfast dishes, finnan haddie and broiled kippered herring. The flavor of coffee with or without cream is totally at odds with either dish, whereas tea is wholly complementary. Not all teas are, however. In that both kippers and finnan haddie are smoked, they would not be complemented with a smoke-flavored tea such as lapsang souchong.

Too much, as they say, of a muchness.

See also Earl Grey tea, English breakfast tea, Green tea, Gunpowder tea, Iced tea, Orange pekoe.

Tea Eggs

The Chinese appetizer known as tea eggs is prepared by cooking eggs until firm. The shells are then crushed all over. The eggs, with their shells still on, are then returned to a saucepan and cooked with a strong tea solution for an hour or so, then left to stand in the tea for half an hour longer. The eggs when shelled have an interesting brown mottled pattern on their surface.

To my mind, tea eggs are prepared mostly as an amusing food that appeals to the eye. They do taste vaguely of tea but tend to be tough.

Tea Towel

I have had numerous responses to the question of the origin of the term "tea towel." A Manhattan gentleman stated, "The late Sri Singh Suryanarayan, tea taster-buyer, said that in the early 1700s tea tasters found that Irish linen was most effective for drying tea tasters' cups and removing all traces of tannic acid"; thus the term.

And one correspondent quoted his seventy-eight-year-old father, who is English: "The proper word is tea cloth. Only the middle classes would have referred to it as a tea towel.

"The main reason for having a tea towel," he added, "was for wiping dry the tea things. A special cloth would have been set aside to separate it from the rest of the drying cloths that would be hanging around the pantry. A proper tea towel would have been made of linen and would generally have had a red border with the words 'tea cloth' woven into it so it would be distinguishable from the rest."

Tempura

I have frequently observed that all the world's cuisines can be categorized according to their most characteristic cooking medium: Chinese cooking is based on oil, French on butter, and Japanese on water. It has long been a source of fascination—puzzlement even—that where the Japanese kitchen is concerned, there is one outstand-

ing exception to that thought: tempura. Whereas dishes such as muzutaki or mizudaki made with chicken or fish cooked in water with vegetables, or shabu shabu with liquids, seem so much part of a pattern, tempura, consisting of a variety of food, all deep-fried in oil, has always seemed a welcome intruder. Enormously appealing but nonetheless foreign. On a visit to Osaka I discovered why.

"It is well documented," my friend Shizuo Tauji told me, "that tempura was brought into Japan by Portuguese priests who came to this country by way of Nagasaki in the sixteenth century." Mr. Tauji is the distinguished head of the Ecole Technique Hôtelier, the largest hotel school in Japan. He is a scholar and an author (his books include *The Life of Escoffier* and annual travel guides to the restaurants of Europe for the Japanese public).

The word "tempura," or tenpura as it is sometimes spelled, is derived from a Portuguese word, *tempero*, that has to do with cooking. Tempura's original form in Japan was probably similar to what the French call beignets and the English call fritters. The most important ingredient in tempura—indeed, the essential ingredient—is batter-fried shrimp, with other foods such as batter-fried vegetables used only as a complement to the meal.

Mr. Tauji, who ranks as one of the nation's best-known gastronomes, is in the process of assembling a history of French cooking since its inception. He interrupted his labors long enough to let me come into his school's hotel kitchen to learn various facets of the art of Japanese cooking, including, of course, the preparation of tempura. I had as my instructor a jovial gentleman named Kaneyoshi Goto, a superb technician who demonstrated techniques that transcended the usual batter-fried shrimp, vegetables, and fish. His repertory for tempura includes multi-colored and appetizing tidbits, such as shrimp sheathed in crushed almonds, fish fillets coated with broken noodles and deep-fried to resemble porcupines, bite-sized deep-fried, miniature hard-shell crabs, deep-fried gingko nuts stuffed with shrimp paste, and deep-fried shrimp toast.

Tenderloin Trout

See Catfish.

Teriyaki

Teriyaki is one of those Japanese dishes with an almost universal appeal. Basically it consists of beef in a marinating sauce of soy sauce and mirin (a kind of sake that is slightly sweet), ginger, and sugar. It is usually cooked over charcoal. *Teri* means shiny; *yaki* means baked or broiled.

Terrine

See Pâté.

Tetrazzini

Although the proper name Tetrazzini is Italian in origin, the dish known as chicken Tetrazzini is about as American as Waldorf salad. It is not to be found in any of the standard European reference works and its origin is unknown. It was undoubtedly named for Luisa Tetrazzini, the Italian coloratura soprano who lived from 1874 to 1940. As to whether it was created especially for her is a matter of question.

James Beard in his *American Cookery* speculates that it was "probably created in San Francisco, where she loved to sing and eat."

There are several dishes called Tetrazzini—one with chicken, one with turkey, and another with seafood—but they are basically the same. Cooked meats combined with pasta, such as spaghetti or macaroni, in a cream sauce with grated cheese. Sometimes mushrooms and almonds are included.

Thousand Island Dressing

A hide-bound, "classic" recipe for Thousand Island dressing would be a rare thing to find and very few recipes for it in the best reference works are the same. You would be safe in calling a dressing Thousand Island if you combined mayonnaise with chili sauce or ketchup, a bit of chopped onion and/or chives, chopped egg, and chopped olives. But you would also be safe if you elaborated on this and added capers and chopped olives and chopped green pepper and parsley.

The much-used *Wise Encyclopedia* offers four recipes for Thousand Island dressing. The first two are conventional. The third calls for mayonnaise with "1 tablespoon each of finely chopped green maraschino cherries, red maraschino cherries, candied ginger, candied pineapple and pistachio nuts." That reference work adds, "It is especially good for fruit salads."

The fourth recipe is for another wild creation that calls for, in addition to the multicolored maraschino disasters, candied apricot, chopped raisins, and chopped angelica. Then, glory be, you fold in a cup of whipped cream colored with a little grenadine. That, too, we are informed, is "especially good for fruit salads."

Enough!

One explanation of the origin of the name Thousand Island came from a New Jersey woman:

"When I was a little girl," she writes, "in 1925 or so, and spending the summer, as usual, with my grandmother at her little resort hotel on Lake Michigan, an incident occurred which was told and retold for years by Grammy.

"A distinguished man and his wife, with French accents, came into the parlor from the dining room, having just eaten our cook's plain but well-cooked American dinner. He complimented my grandmother on the dinner, especially the salad. As Grammy told the story, she thanked him and went into a detailed explanation about all the cooking, as the gentleman nodded appreciatively. Something in his manner led Grammy to ask if he knew anything about cooking. He answered yes, that he was head chef at the Drake Hotel in Chicago!

"Grammy recovered from her mortification enough to have quite a lengthy conversation with him, during which he told her that he and his wife had had a trip through the Thousand Islands some years before. On his return, he had concocted a new salad dressing. His wife, noticing all the lumps, had said, 'It looks like a Thousand Island,' so they named it that.

"I believe the chef was Belgian and had a name that sounded like Reum."

Thousand-Year Eggs

See Hundred-year eggs.

Tian

A specialty of Provence, tian is somewhat like a vegetable pie made without a pastry crust. The vegetables—onions, zucchini, tomatoes, spinach, and Swiss chard—are sliced or chopped and cooked with garlic in olive oil. If sliced, the vegetables are layered in a flat dish, sprinkled with bread crumbs and chopped thyme and/or grated cheese, and baked.

The name tian, I'm told, comes from the sizable earthenware pot in which the dish was originally cooked. I discovered it when Roger Vergé, owner-chef of Moulin de Mougins, the restaurant in the hills above Cannes, prepared it at my home (curiously, it is rarely served in restaurants).

Tiffin

The word "tiffin" is Anglo-Indian in origin, from tiffing, which is drinking or eating, and it means lunch in British usage.

Tilltugg

See Appetizers.

Timbale

Chapters could be written exploring the various connotations and meanings of timbale. In its original and purest sense, a timbale was a small, round, generally metal container about the size of a custard cup. The first timbale was used for drinking. Gradually it has come to mean foods cooked in round, sometimes decorative molds. At times the term applies to foods cooked in a pastry-lined mold. As the term's meaning has broadened, it has come to mean foods piled high and served in bowls.

Tin

In my own vocabulary, the words "tin" and "can" are used interchangeably. I am of the opinion that the British more often than not use the word tin as applied to metal containers for tuna, sardines, potted meats, soups, and so on, while Americans generally prefer can.

There might be an edge of snobbism in an American using the word tin, but somehow to my ears (tin at that) it sounds a touch more elegant.

I also have this amusing anecdote:

"A Britisher some years ago, while visiting this country, was traveling in a club car on a train that passed through countless miles of tall stands of corn growing in fields on both sides of the track.

"He turned to a fellow traveler, an American, and said, 'My good man, what on earth do you do with such an incredible abundance of corn?'

"The American turned to him and said, 'We eat what we can and what we can't we can.'

"The Britisher considered this a real hip-slapper and guffawed at some length.

"A few weeks later he was sitting in his private club in London regaling his companions with his visit to the United States.

"We were traveling through Kansas by train and I saw the most astonishing sight, mile after endless mile of tall corn growing on either side of the track. I turned to the chap sitting next to me and said, 'Tell me, young fellow, what on earth do you do with all that corn?'

"He glanced me straight in the eye and said, 'Well, sir, we eat what we can and what we can't we put up in tins.'"

Incidentally, anyone who thinks that

America, often called "the home of the tin can," was the point of origin for that boon to mankind is an ocean wide of the mark. The tin can was invented in France by a Frenchman named Nicolas Appert, a confectioner and chef. I have a passion for trivia and happen to know that the 228th anniversary of his birth was October 23, 1980.

In 1809 the chef was awarded twelve thousand francs by Napoleon Bonaparte. Appert, so it is said, knew that his method worked, but he did not know why. In his lifetime he canned about fifty types of foods. The *Encyclopedia Brittanica* has observed that "the method of preserving foods in tins is probably defensible as the greatest of all inventions in historic times."

Tisane

Tisane means any dried herb that is steeped or brewed like tea. It is served hot and is said to have medicinal qualities. You can make a tisane of almost any dried herb— mint, rosemary, lemon verbena, sage, and so on.

The infusion may be made from dried whole leaves or flowers or from powdered leaves or flowers. The word derives from the Latin word *ptisana,* meaning barley water. The drink is said to be centuries old and was known to the early Greeks.

Toad-in-the-Hole

Toad-in-the-hole is one of those serio-comic names that the British find pleasure in coining for various dishes. It is a variation on the traditional Yorkshire pudding and is often served as a dish at noon or for supper. To prepare it, you cook small link sausages until done and pour the fat into a baking dish. You add the sausages and pour a Yorkshire pudding batter over all. When the batter is baked and golden brown, the sausages are the "toads-in-the-hole." The dish is sometimes referred to as a toad, and a recipe might state, "Do not open the oven door while the toad is baking."

Toast

The best of all possible toast is made in the oven. This takes a bit more time and effort, however, than making it in a toaster. To bake toast, preheat the oven to 400 degrees and trim off the crusts of the bread slices. Butter one side of each slice and arrange the slices, buttered side up, on a baking sheet. Place in the oven and bake for 5 minutes or so, or until the slices are golden brown on one side. Turn and continue baking until golden brown all over.

Tofu

Tofu is made from soybeans, which are widely sold in this country in health food stores and many supermarkets. There are said to be seven kinds of tofu in Japan, varying according to taste, texture, etc.

Tofu can be made in the home; the technique involves soaking soybeans, cooking them in a certain amount of water, pressing them in a sack, combining the resulting "milk" plus the pressings, and allowing the mixture to "curd."

The best book on tofu making I know is

The Book of Tofu, by William Shurtleff and Akiko Aoyagi. Published in paperback, it contains not only detailed instructions but also five hundred recipes.

Tomalley

See Lobster.

Tomatillos

See Green tomatoes.

Tomatoes

It's simple to peel a tomato. Drop it into boiling water and let it stand approximately twelve seconds, no longer. Use a paring knife and simply pull away the peel. If you're going to peel many tomatoes, you may let them stand in the water a bit longer than twelve seconds because the large mass will reduce the temperature of the water and it will take longer for the heat to penetrate the skin.

Incidentally, it may make your peeling easier if you cut away the core before adding the tomato to the pot or kettle. Some people cut a shallow cross in the other end of the tomato.

It's also equally easy to seed tomatoes. Cut the tomatoes crosswise in half. Pick up one half, holding it in the palm of one hand over a basin or other utensil. Squeeze the tomato gently; take care not to bruise the outer shell. As you squeeze, give it a small twist with your fingers. Continue squeezing and twisting in this fashion until the seeds and the loose pulp containing them are extracted. If any seeds remain, you may remove them, using a small spoon, such as an after-dinner coffee spoon.

It is my own opinion that seeds should be removed from tomatoes (those to be broiled or stuffed, for example) more for aesthetic reasons than because of taste.

But I have friends who are excellent cooks who declare that seeds do contribute a certain bitterness to sauces. *See also* Canned tomatoes, Sun-dried tomatoes.

Tomato Paste

See Canned tomatoes.

Topinambour

See Jerusalem artichoke.

Toque Blanche

There is a fairly elaborate explanation of the origins of this white hat worn by chefs in Norman Krohn's book, *Menu Mystique*, which says the cap was patterned after a black hat worn by priests in Byzantine monasteries during the Middle Ages.

Mr. Krohn says many cooks, who took refuge from their tyrannical masters in the monasteries, distinguished themselves from the monks by changing the color of the cap from black to white. He recounts another version in which thousands of years ago a king of Assyria wore a tall white cap. He allowed his private cook to wear a cap of similar design as "material proof of his trust." Most kings, it seemed, feared being poisoned.

produce a standard tortilla when made between the palms.

Flour tortillas, on the other hand, are made with flour and water and rolled out with a rolling pin. Thus, these can be made of any reasonable dimension and are generally larger than the cornmeal tortillas.

Tortillas

In my travels through New Mexico and Arizona and elsewhere, I have noted to my amusement that flour tortillas are almost invariably larger than those made with cornmeal. I have discussed this with experts in Mexican cooking and the explanation seems to go along these lines:

Traditionally, tortillas are made with a blend of cornmeal and water. When the two are blended to make a dough, small quantities of the dough, enough to be handled between the palms of the hands, are patted back and forth to make the round tortilla.

When some enterprising manufacturer decided to make a tortilla press for amateur cooks, he fashioned the disks, which press the dough, of the same diameter as would

Tourtière

Tourtière is a national dish of Canada. It is made with ground pork and the essential seasoning is savory, which is widely available but little used in United States kitchens. Helen Gougeon, who is perhaps Canada's best known cooking authority and the author of several cookbooks, states that the tourtière is a traditional dish served at réveillons, the meal served after midnight mass on Christmas Eve.

Trail

Trail is short for entrail. The dish is not for the squeamish, but it is delectable.

I have sampled it, chiefly made with woodcock though snipe may be used, as it is served in France and Switzerland. You roast the bird, open it, and scrape the innards into a skillet or chafing dish. You add Cognac and, perhaps, a little brown sauce and stir. The bird is served on toast with the sauce.

I have never sampled a similar dish made with an uncleaned fish, such as red mullet, but I am told that it is prepared the same way.

Treacle

Treacle is a British term for a special kind of molasses. There are three kinds of treacle. Dark molasses is referred to as black treacle in England. There is also a medium-colored molasses and this, I am told, is the one that is generally referred to simply as treacle.

There is a third type that would be the equivalent of what is sold as golden syrup in America. In England, treacle is used in preparing not only puddings but pies as well.

Tree Ears

Living in an age when so many foods that are desirable in taste and texture are damned as fattening or otherwise unhealthy, it is a comfort to discover one that is considered not only a pleasure to eat but salutary as well.

The happy news came from a scientist at the University of Minnesota who reported that he had found evidence that black tree fungus, an ingredient widely used in Chinese cooking, may be one reason why people in China have far less heart disease than Americans and other Westerners.

If you are reasonably well-versed in Chinese cookery, you will know that the tree fungus is more often than not listed as tree ears or tree ear mushrooms. If you have ever eaten those staples of a Chinese menu, hot and sour soup and moo-shu-ro, you have undoubtedly sampled tree ears, whether you knew it or not.

The Chinese word for tree ears is *mo-er,* which rhymes with purr. In the Cantonese dialect it is also known as *wan-yee.* The most important medical property ascribed to the fungus is that it may slow the tendency of the blood to clot.

The scientist Dr. Dale E. Hammerschmidt of the university's medical school was conducting an experiment on the clotting properties of human blood when the discovery came about. The blood of one man participating in the experiment failed to clot normally. It was found that he had recently finished a meal with a dish of Sichuan hot bean curd as the main course. Further tests showed that a principal ingredient of that dish had been the tree ears.

Dr. Hammerschmidt, writing in *The New England Journal of Medicine,* said tree ears had for many years been regarded as a health food that enhanced man's potency and longevity.

"Coronary artery disease in China in general and in the southern provinces in particular is uncommon," he said. "It is interesting to speculate that chronic consumption of mo-er, often with scallions and garlic, may contribute to this observed low incidence of atherosclerotic disease and thus explain the reputation of this fungus as a longevity tonic."

Dr. Hammerschmidt said the responsible substance in tree ears remains to be identified, but he noted that seven batches had been tested and all had been found to inhibit clotting in varying degrees.

Tree ears are available in abundance in Oriental groceries and supermarkets throughout America. They are sold in dry form and a handful of the fungus goes a long way in stretching a dish. Three or four tablespoons of small dried tree ears will expand to about one cup when soaked in water. I stress the word "small" because the fungi come in two sizes, small and large. The various names for the tree fungus include, in addition to tree ears, wood ears and cloud ears. The larger versions are generally known as cloud ears.

Large or small, tree ears have a sort of brownish-gray cast. When purchased dry, they have a withered, tightly closed, gnarled look. After soaking they are both soft and slightly crisp or resilient when bitten into, but, truth to tell, the flavor of tree ears is rather bland, and it is the crunchy texture that is one of their more admirable qualities.

It is a curious fact that tree ears and tiger

lily stems are almost always used in tandem in Chinese dishes. Perhaps it is because the textures and flavors are so complementary.

When I found myself the recipient of several batches of tree ears, the obvious suddenly occurred: Why not substitute these tasty, well-textured morsels in a classic French-style dish? Would they serve in dishes that call for the likes of expensive dried mushrooms, such as morels and chanterelles? The results of my experiment were altogether elegant and more than worthwhile, although the tree ears do lack some of the depth of flavor of morels. *See also* Fungus.

Trifolati

Trifolati means truffles, but, curiously enough, truffles are rarely if ever used in dishes that bear the name.

On one occasion when Marcella Hazan cooked in my home, her morning roster included a savory sautéed onion sauce made with white wine and funghi trifolati. Funghi, of course, means mushrooms. Trifolati does not mean, as I was once inclined to think, clover, as in trefoil.

"Trifolati is a cooking base," she explained. "It means the combination of olive oil, garlic, and parsley in a dish. Some people add anchovy to their funghi trifolati. I don't." In Italy, the mushroom is the much cherished, relatively rare, and expensive field mushroom known as porcini (*Boletus edulis*). Mrs. Hazan has contrived a fine adaptation of the dish using a small proportion of dried porcini soaked, then cooked with fresh cultivated mushrooms. Blended together, the mushrooms take on a fine porcini-like flavor.

"This can be served as a vegetable dish if the mushrooms are sliced," she said. "It can serve as a pasta sauce if the mushrooms are chopped."

She added that she didn't know why it was called trifolati, but that it might be because it is as delicious as truffles.

Tripe

I find myself smiling whenever I open my venerable *Wise Encyclopedia of Cookery*. It is chockablock with good recipes and fascinating information about the origins of certain dishes and foods. As evidence, here is the Wise explanation of tripe, which I have quoted many times:

"Tripe, like certain alluring vices, is enjoyed by society's two extremes, the topmost and the lowermost strata, while the multitudinous middle classes of the world look upon it with genteel disdain and noses tilted. Patricians relished tripe in Babylon's gardens, plebeians have always welcomed it as something good and cheap, and always the peasant cook has taught the prince how to eat it."

There is no indication as to the authorship of this trenchant observation. But it sounds remarkably like the late Lucius Beebe.

Tripe, it is true, is one of those foods that is adored or abhorred—or ignored.

Because of the puritanical and generally middle-class nature of American cooking, tripe somehow sounds terribly un-American, like an old vice one should never adopt. Oddly enough, tripe is a principal ingredient in one of America's best-known regional dishes, the Philadelphia Pepper Pot.

There are numerous kinds of tripe available in France, each with its own texture depending on what part of the animal's stomach is used. In the United States, only honeycomb tripe is generally used because of some government regulations (what they are I've never discovered). When the French cook tripe in the style of Lyons, the kind of tripe used is *gras double,* or double-fat tripe.

Triple Sec

The name triple sec originated years ago when certain distillers decided to put orange curaçao through three distillations, according to Sam Aaron, president of Sherry-Lehmann Inc. This, they claim, gives a more subtle, drier flavor. The best triple sec is Cointreau, formerly labeled Cointreau Triple Sec. Some years ago they decided that the name was redundant so they dropped the words "triple sec" from the label.

Trou du Milieu

See Coup du milieu.

Truffles

White truffles are mostly of Italian origin, appearing for a brief harvest that generally starts in late October or November. They are one of the more curious if not to say glorious treasures of gastronomy and scarcer than the celebrated black truffles of Périgord. Curious because they have an intense odor that to some noses resembles garlic. Because of this pungent, acrid smell, some people find them offensive. Some have called the odor indecent, decadent, and even "reeking of death." I had my first whiff of white truffles several years ago while seated one Christmas dinner in Passeto's Restaurant in Rome. Quite truthfully, I thought I was in the presence of something unfortunate. The odor came from my left. Then it came from my right. At that moment I realized that the guilty thing was a brownish white object that the waiter was grating onto a dish of creamy fettuccine. Shortly, I made the mistake of sampling white truffles on fettuccine. I say "unfortunate" because from that moment I became hopelessly addicted to the flavor. And the cost of white truffles, like caviar, ascends every year and it is, like that of caviar, almost out of sight.

In any event, I had the good fortune of meeting the truffle king of Italy some years ago, a gentleman named Urbani. He had dispatched to me in New York a few white truffles that must have cost something like the Kohinoor diamond. Cherish them as I may, I could not see myself sitting down all alone to a feast of white truffles. I would wait. I would create a special occasion, perhaps with black tie and champagne and very special guests, a few who would know what white truffles were all about.

Well, the obvious happened. I stored them in rice (a traditional method of storing white truffles; they perfume the rice) in a plastic container and put them in the refrigerator. I drove to New York and the cleaning woman came.

"Lord help us," she told me later. "I never knew things could stink so. I threw those things in the East Hampton dump."

Unused black truffles should be transferred to a small jar with a tight-fitting lid. Cover the truffle with Cognac or a fortified wine, such as Madeira or sherry. Close the jar tightly and refrigerate. I have kept truffles for months by using this technique. And, incidentally, the liquid can also be used later for cooking dishes to which the taste of truffles would be an asset.

Many people think they can substitute mushrooms for truffles, but it just isn't so. Truffles, both white and black, have a bouquet and texture almost wholly different from mushrooms either fresh or dried, wild or cultivated.

You can, of course, use mushrooms in place of truffles, but the differences would be quite apparent to anyone familiar with truffles. The only thing in common between truffles and mushrooms is that they are both fungi. Let me add that in most cases of recipes that call for truffles you could simply omit them.

Truite au Bleu

To prepare *truite au bleu* in the classic sense, you must start off with live trout.

First, you start with a basin of boiling

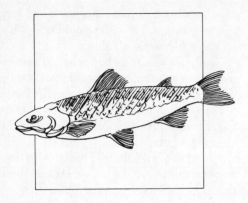

water to which vinegar and salt have been added. When it boils, and only then, you kill your trout quickly by striking it a blow on the head.

You eviscerate the trout as rapidly as possible and drop it into the boiling water. The immediate nerve action of the trout as it lands in the water will cause it to curl. The trout is cooked as briefly as necessary and drained. It is then served with melted butter and lemon or with hollandaise sauce.

I do know that at times some chefs who do not have access to living trout will "cheat" by tying the tail of the trout to the mouth. They cook the trout and serve it as indicated.

If you cannot find freshly caught trout, whether still alive or not, it is best not to attempt this dish. The vinegar gives the blue color to the trout and that is why it is called truite au bleu.

Try Out

The term "try out" fat is old-fashioned, although it is still in common usage in some regions of this country. It simply means to cook salt pork—and the technique is has-

tened if the salt pork is cut into small cubes—until it is rendered of its fat. This is a common technique for such regional dishes as chowders. Both the liquid fat and the rendered solids may be used in preparing the soup.

Tulipes

One of the most delicate, elegant, and yet easily made of French pastries is something known in the pastry chef's kitchen as *tulipes*. They are fragile, brittle, wafer-thin "cups" into which a multitude of good things go. The fillings may consist of one or more scoops of sherbet or ice cream, either a single flavor or several; a fine layer of irresistible pastry cream topped with fresh fruits or berries and perhaps a dusting of confectioners' sugar, and so on.

Although *tulipes* have been around for a good many years, they have become much more evident in restaurant dining rooms since the introduction of nouvelle cuisine.

These pastry cups are not at all difficult to make in the home kitchen. One simply blends butter and sugar in a bowl and beats

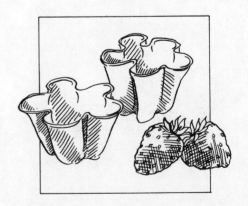

in flour. Then beaten egg whites are folded in and the batter is smeared, a little at a time, into rounds on a flat baking surface. The rounds are baked briefly (less than four minutes), removed with a spatula, and, while they are still hot, fitted into a cup or other mold and pressed down so they have fluted, ruffled edges. When the cups are cool, they become delectably crispy. The preparation, overall, may be a bit time consuming (an oven can hold only so many baking pans at a time), but it is certainly worth the effort.

Turkey

Almost all holiday symbols are directly traceable to their origins. The Easter egg is attributable to pagan rites of spring and the season of rebirth; the custom of a Yuletide goose is almost certainly an offspring of that celebrated feast in Dickens's *A Christmas Carol*. No one knows precisely, however, when the turkey became the national bird for the Thanksgiving table. It is presumed that the serving of a roasted tom turkey, a gobbler, came into popularity at about the beginning of the nineteenth century. As pointed out in a marvelously researched work on the Thanksgiving bird, *The Wild Turkey* by A. W. Schorger, "There is a widespread belief that from the first Thanksgiving in New England in 1621 this celebration became an annual affair and that turkey was always served." Not so, says the author. In the beginning, Thanksgiving was celebrated only on an irregular basis. The time of celebration was proclaimed by the heads of individual colonies or states. Thanksgiving first became a national holiday through a proclamation of President

Lincoln, and it was celebrated on the fourth Thursday of November 1864. Since that time each successive President has followed his example. (Curiously, some southern states had objected to the proclamation on the ground that "it was a relic of Puritanic bigotry.")

Perhaps the first official association of the holiday and turkey was made by Alexander Hamilton, the statesman and first Secretary of the Treasury from 1789 to 1795. "No citizen of the United States," he opined, "should refrain from turkey on Thanksgiving Day."

On the other hand, the author of *The Wild Turkey* points out, one valid document of the period declared that "even the wealthiest inhabitant of Hampshire, Massachusetts, did not have a tame turkey for Thanksgiving until after the Revolution."

By the first quarter of the nineteenth century, however, turkey had become a solid part of the holiday custom. A visiting Englishman named Stuart visited Boston during Thanksgiving in 1828 and wrote in his book, *Three Years in North America*, published in 1833, "The annual Thanksgiving Day in the state of Massachusetts was held while we remained in Boston. We were advised to see the market on the evening previously. It was handsomely lighted, and was filled with provisions of all kind; but the quantities of turkeys in relation to other kinds of food seemed to us most extraordinary, until we were told that on Thanksgiving Days persons of every condition have a roasted turkey at dinner . . . and the turkeys were sold quickly at from three to five and six shillings sterling."

Mr. Schorger adds that according to one reliable source, "Andrew Jackson's Thanksgiving proclamation of November 29, 1835, reads in part: 'We thank Thee for the bountiful supply of wildlife with which Thou hast blessed our land; for the turkeys that gobble in our forests.' "

Whatever the historical associations may be, the custom of serving turkey is a happy one, for turkeys are, in truth, easy to cook and one fine, fat fowl serves many. And the subsequent uses of a not-too-lean leftover carcass are a joy to consider—turkey carcass soup, turkey casseroles, turkey salads, and, best of all perhaps, a cold turkey sandwich on well-textured bread with fresh mayonnaise.

Speaking of turkey: In his remarkable and much quoted work, *The Physiology of Taste,* Jean Brillat-Savarin states that in his opinion turkey is "one of the most delightful presents which the New World has made to the Old."

"When the vine tenders and the plowmen of our countryside want to treat themselves to a party on a long winter night," the author asks, "what do you see roasting over the bright kitchen fire where the table is laid? A turkey.

"When the practical mechanic or the artisan brings a few of his friends together to celebrate some relaxation all the sweeter for being so rare, what is the traditional main dish of the dinner he offers? A turkey stuffed with sausages or with Lyons chestnuts."

But then he asks, "In our most renowned gastronomical circles, in those exclusive gatherings where politics must yield place to dissertations on the sense of taste, what do the guests wait for? What is it that they want? What is served up in the place of honor? A truffled turkey."

There are two dishes in the French repertory that could be referred to as a truffled turkey. One consists of a fine fat fowl that is stuffed with suet, foie gras, and chopped truffles. Sliced truffles are then inserted under the skin of the turkey and it is wrapped in buttered paper and cooked on a spit before an open fire.

A far more subtle, delicate, and elegant dish is *dindonneau en demi-deuil,* which translates—in jest, of course—as turkey in half-mourning.

In this preparation slices of truffles are inserted under the skin of the turkey. The turkey is stuffed with a *farce fine,* a finely puréed stuffing. This is one of the purest of stuffings, mousse-like in texture and with a zephyr-like, intangible subtlety in flavor. The turkey is then poached in a broth, and when sliced it is served with the truffle-scented stuffing plus a silken sauce suprême made with the richly perfumed liquid in which the turkey was poached plus heavy cream.

Equally as elegant as a truffled turkey is a sublime creation called a galantine (the word is believed to derive from gallant when used in the sense of elegant).

This is a cold "loaf," a kind of pâté that when sliced into has a colorful mosaic pattern consisting of bits of ham, pistachio nuts, and more truffles. It is made by boning a turkey, filling the skin with the ham and pistachio preparation, then rolling and stuffing the turkey in cheesecloth. The "loaf" is simmered until set and tender and allowed to cool. Ideally it is coated with aspic before serving.

Turnovers

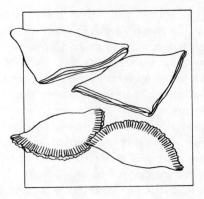

Turnovers, which are festive and are almost infinite in their variety, also pinpoint to a degree the migrant influences in America. Just consider their backgrounds: There are Cornish pasties, which indicate the early presence of Welsh miners in Michigan, the Mexican-influenced empanadas and empanaditas of the West and Southwest, and the curiously named hot-ta-meat pies of Louisiana that indicate a borrowing from the Spanish.

Even spring rolls—the more refined version of egg rolls, which can most certainly be classified as turnovers—can be found almost anywhere in the nation where Chinese chefs have settled.

Where their American history is concerned, I find the Cornish pasties most interesting, not because of their flavor especially but because of the uses to which they have been put in this country. The concept was brought here in the late 1700s and early 1800s with the influx of miners from Wales who came to the Upper Peninsula of Michigan to dig for copper and iron.

Basically, pasties are a half-moon-shaped not-too-rich pastry filled with meat, mostly beef, plus diced vegetables, including onion, potatoes, turnips, and sometimes carrots and with a minimum of seasonings.

The fillings and flavorings varied from household to household and oftentimes within a single household. According to Theodora FitzGibbon in her *Food of the Western World,* before the pasties were cooked, a small pastry initial was pasted in one corner to earmark it for each individual. The proper way to eat the pasty was to hold it in the hand and eat it from the uppermost point down to the initial. That way, an uneaten portion could still be identified by the rightful owner.

Once the pasties were established in this country, it did not take long for the non-Welsh of the region to take to them with relish and to add a distinctly American touch. Today if you dine on them at a lunch counter, they are apt to be served with tomato ketchup, plus slivers of dill pickle.

Empanadas, far more savory than Cornish pasties, reflect the more adventurous palates of the Spaniards and Latin Americans. The term "empanada" comes from the Spanish word *pan,* meaning bread. Their piquancy derives from a variety of flavors that may include hot fresh or dried peppers, olives, and capers. Empanaditas, of course, are nothing more than diminutive versions of the empanada.

One of the most interesting of all turnovers is a pastry-filled fried food that I dined on in a town in Louisiana called Natchitoches (the name is pronounced NACKY-tosh). These spicy turnovers were once referred to as hot-ta-meat pies, but now they're simply called Natchitoches meat pies. The most famous in town are served at a small restaurant called Lasyones. I am certain that these pies are very much related to empanadas and came about through the influence of Spanish settlers in the state. They are decidedly un-French.

Basically speaking, turnovers are cooked in one of two ways: deep-fried or baked. A good many recipes for turnovers of whatever nature call for baking powder, but I feel that it is not essential and imparts a slightly unpleasant acidic taste.

Turtle

The genuine, authentic snapper soup is made with the meat of a snapping turtle (which is one of the few turtles not on the list of endangered species) and laced with sherry. There are, however, some recipes that call for long-simmered veal and chopped hard-boiled eggs to substitute for the McCoy. I would vouchsafe that most of the so-called snapper soup served in America does contain veal with occasionally a few bits of snapping turtle thrown in. I once had snapper soup that contained chopped, hard-boiled turtle eggs. It is the only time I have sampled them. I feel quite certain that turtle eggs are probably quite nutritious.

I have an amusing book titled *Unmentionable Cuisine,* by Calvin W. Schwabe,

and in it the author offers a formula for skewered turtle meat from Maritius. "Marinate 1-inch cubes of turtle meat in lemon juice, salt, crushed garlic and a little oil," it says. "Alternate on skewers with pieces of turtle liver and grill over charcoal. Serve with boiled turtle eggs, a hot chutney sauce, and rice."

First you catch your turtle.

Further on turtle eggs, there is an interesting essay on cooking them in *The Savannah Cook Book,* written by Harriet Ross Colquitt:

"They should be cooked about 20 minutes in unsalted water—and opinion differs widely as to the most recherché method of disposing of them after they have been correctly cooked," it says.

"One camp holds that anyone who knows what is what simply pinches a little hole in the very elusive shell, inserts a little Worcestershire sauce and salt into the opening, and bolts the whole thing, much as if it were a bitter dose which should be disposed of as quickly as possible, and about which the less said the better.

"Others hold that the whites of the eggs, which never get firm, no matter how long you cook them, were never meant for eating purposes anyhow, and that the correct form is to open the egg, take out the yellow, season it to taste and eat it like a gentleman.

"You can pay your money and take your choice."

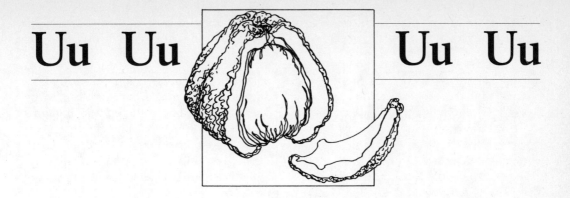

Uccelletti

Uccelletti is the term used by Italians to describe small edible birds, including thrushes, larks, and the edible blackbird. The birds are usually roasted in a hot oven or grilled over an open fire. They are commonly served with polenta. The name is also applied to beef or veal "birds," meat slices that are filled and rolled, and then sautéed and braised or cooked over hot coals.

Ugli Fruit

Ugli fruit, as the name misspelled implies, has an unattractive exterior and resembles a badly bruised grapefruit. It has a very thick skin and is said to be a blend of grapefruit and tangerine. It has an excellent flavor, very sweet and juicy, which resembles a blend of bitter orange and/or tangerine and grapefruit juice. It is primarily from Jamaica but is now grown commercially in Florida.

Uni

Uni is the Japanese word for sea urchin eggs or roe. It is one of the most delectable and luxurious toppings for sushi.

Usquebaugh

Usquebaugh, also spelled usquabae, is an Irish and Scottish word for whiskey. It is derived from the Gaelic words uisce beathadh, meaning water of life.

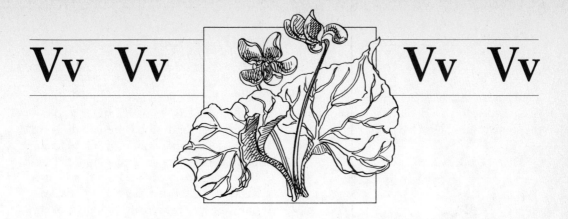
Vanilla Bean

Vanilla beans are derived from a tropical climbing plant that belongs to the orchid family. I am told by a chemist that the pods are aged for about six months until they start to ferment.

Fully grown vanilla beans come in sizes that vary only slightly. If a recipe specifies a "2-inch vanilla bean," then the recipe is poorly edited. It should read "a 2-inch length of vanilla bean."

Offhand, I would say that most of the vanilla beans that are sold (and they are available in most shops that deal in fine herbs and spices) vary in length from about six to eight inches.

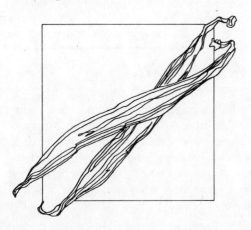

One vanilla bean can be reused honorably a number of times, as often, in fact, as it still maintains a reasonable aroma and continues to impart flavor. Some recipes call for splitting vanilla beans before adding them to milk and so on before cooking. When split, the tiny, dark center beans are released into the liquid and those contain flavor also.

After a vanilla bean has been used—to prepare ice cream or a custard, for example—the bean should be washed well in cold water. It is then best stored in a container of sugar, which serves a double purpose. It prevents the bean from drying out and also flavors the sugar. The flavored sugar may then be used for any desserts that benefit from a vanilla flavor.

In my own kitchen I use pure vanilla extract or, more rarely, whole vanilla beans. The standard for pure vanilla extract, according to the American Spice Trade Association, is 13.50 ounces of vanilla beans for a gallon of alcohol. You would, of course, obtain a stronger flavor if you used more beans for each gallon of alcohol.

You should take care to buy pure vanilla extract rather than an extract made from vanillin, a synthetic product; if it is pure it will state this on the bottle.

Powdered vanilla is nothing more than a

vanilla bean that has been processed into a fine powder. It is available in some shops in the United States, but I have never tried it.

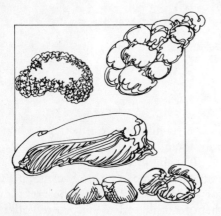

Variety Meats

There was a time in this country when almost all the "specialty" cuts of meat—innards if you will—found such poor favor they were scarcely more expensive than soupbones. As public taste has become more sophisticated, sweetbreads, veal kidneys, calf's liver, and the like have become equally elevated in price. One notable exception is chicken livers, which still can be bought for a relatively modest sum.

Vark

The shiny silvery sheet covering many Indian dishes is real silver foil, called vark. In *Classic Indian Cooking,* Julie Sahni says it is made from silver that has been beaten to the consistency of cotton candy and then pressed to form a sheet. "Its sole purpose," she says, "is to adorn sweetmeats, kabobs, and special pilafs. Moguls used it to decorate their elaborate food presentations, to keep the food at par with their splendiferous courts. Today vark is used on special occasions, such as wedding buffets and religious festivals." It is tasteless and odorless. It may be purchased in Indian grocery stores.

Veal Oskar

There are many versions of veal Oskar. The veal chop is sometimes topped with crawfish and sometimes crab meat. It almost invariably has asparagus spears as another garnish. And generally speaking, the sauce is a béarnaise.

The dish, according to legend, was named for King Oskar of Sweden. He is said to have had a fine eye for the young ladies of his country and would often take them, secretly, to midnight suppers in one small hideaway or another in Stockholm. He was said to have had a special liking for veal, crawfish, and asparagus. The chef of one restaurant had the inspiration to combine all these in one dish and the result was veal à la Oskar.

Veal Piccata

In Italian gastronomy *piccato* means "larded." In Europe, far more than in America, various cuts of meat and game are larded, which means inserting slivers of fat such as pork fat with a larding needle to make very lean meat more juicy and give it a richer flavor.

Presumably the first veal piccata was made with pieces of scaloppine or other cuts that had been so "needled." These days veal piccata is usually made by coating pieces of scaloppine with flour, cooking on both sides in oil until browned, pouring off the fat, and cooking briefly with white wine, veal broth, and butter.

Vegetable Marrow

See Marrow.

Vegetable Stock

Like most stocks made of meat, broths from cooked vegetables are fairly perishable. If you are going to keep them in the refrigerator for an extended period, you should remove them every three or four days, bring them to the boil, cool them once more, and return to the refrigerator. Otherwise, it is best to freeze them and defrost them as necessary.

Velouté

The word "velouté" means velvet or velvet-like, and in the world of food it pertains to sauces or soups with a velvet-like quality. That is to say, they are smooth rather than lumpy or grainy. The simplest velouté is a basic sauce made with butter, flour, milk, and seasonings.

Vermont Madness

One of the most intriguing press releases I've ever received came from a monthly magazine called *Country Journal* published in Brattleboro, Vermont. The release is titled, "Maple Syrup, Doughnuts and Dill Pickles Recommended by Vermonters" and begins:

"It may not sound enticing, but the combination of maple syrup, doughnuts and dill pickles is such a popular dish in New England that it's become a tradition."

Writing about it in *Country Journal*, Noel Perrin, author and Dartmouth College professor who makes maple syrup in Vermont, compares the dish to sweet and sour pork served in a Chinese restaurant. But he warns that anyone on a diet, in fact anyone who is not something of a glutton, should not read his account:

" 'The ingredients are simple: a dozen plain raised doughnuts (two dozen if there are more than four people), a large jar of dill pickles and a quart, or more, of maple syrup.

" 'Merely boil the syrup down by a third so that it has the consistency of a sugar glaze. Meanwhile, quarter the dill pickles and put them in a dish in the middle of the table, next to the doughnuts. While the syrup is warm, pour some in the bottom of a soup dish for each person. Everybody takes a doughnut, dips it in his or her syrup and begins to gorge. At least twice per doughnut, stop and eat a bite of pickle.

" 'With this constant resharpening of the palate, it is possible to eat an astonishingly large number of doughnuts,' Mr. Perrin says. He suggests concluding the feast with a cup of coffee and then going to bed."

Sorry, I'm not sleepy. The thought of what those Vermonters eat keeps me awake nights.

Vermouth

It amuses me that so many people have an ample supply of dry vermouth in their wine and spirits cabinet while they suffer a shortage of dry white wine. That is my supposition, at least, from the frequency with which I am asked whether one can substitute dry white vermouth for white Burgundy, Loire Valley, Rhine wine, and so on. And the answer, of course, is almost always yes. The only exception would be in the preparation of a great, classic dish au vin blanc. In that case, I would certainly buy a very good white wine.

There is obviously a difference in using the aperitif known as dry vermouth and using a white wine. A dry white vermouth is designed to stimulate the appetite and is composed of, among other things, white wine, plus a bit of sugar, herbs and plants, and, at times, the bark of trees. When cooking with it, or substituting it for white wine, one will naturally produce a sauce that is a touch sweeter and more aromatic.

Véronique

Véronique is a name applied to various entrées that contain seedless grapes as an ingredient, such as sole Véronique. I had always assumed it was named after an opera of that name by the French composer André Messager.

But a note arrived from a professor of history at Brooklyn College. He contends that the late chef Louis Diat would have disputed this.

Diat's version, the professor wrote, was that the dish was first created in the kitchen of a colleague, Emile Malley, chef of the Carlton Hotel in London. Malley, the story goes, had dreamed up the notion of preparing a traditional fish in white wine sauce to which would be added the seedless white grapes. The chef was called away from the kitchen for a few minutes and turned the preparation of the dish over to a young underchef. On the chef's return he found the young man in a state of great excitement and Malley then asked the cause for his jubilation.

As it turned out, the young man had only a moment before learned that he was the father of a baby girl who would be christened Véronique. Malley then immortalized the child's name in French menus and in French kitchens by calling the dish sole Véronique.

Vesiga

One of the classic—but optional—ingredients for a coulibiac of salmon is called vesiga. It is a ropelike, gelatinous substance, actually the spinal marrow of sturgeon. The vesiga, after cleaning, must be simmered for several hours until tender. It is then chopped and looks like chopped aspic. It has a very mild, bland flavor, and its principal contribution to the dish is its slightly tender but chewy texture.

Vichy

One of the most amusing stories I know about the names of food concerns Vichy. It is, of course, the famous spa that, during the Nazi occupation of France in the Second World War, acquired so bad a reputation that some hotels in this country changed the name Vichyssoise on their menus to De Gaulloise.

In any event, the most famous dish that bears the name is carrots Vichy. They are, I am told, a frequent part of the Vichy diet and there they are made with the famed local mineral water. Actually the dish consists of thin carrot rounds cooked until glazed with sugar, a little water, and butter.

Vichyssoise

There are probably few foods and especially soups in this country that have been written about at greater length than vichyssoise. The reason is that it is one of the few "French" dishes to have been created in America.

It is common knowledge that Louis Diat, while chef of the Ritz Hotel in New York, concocted a peasant soup of his childhood, a hot potage made with leeks and potatoes. He puréed it, added heavy cream, topped it

with chives, and served it cold. The date of this invention is generally given as 1910. But according to an old edition of *Vanity Fair*, the soup was presented at the opening of the hotel's roof garden. That event took place in June 1917.

Viking Bread

See Lefser.

Vinaigrette

Vinaigrette is a classic sauce in French cookery, the name of which is often misused or loosely used even by professionals.

Many cooks refer to a vinaigrette sauce as a simple blend of three parts oil to one part vinegar plus salt and pepper. Actually, that sauce is known in classic French kitchens as a *sauce salade*.

A true vinaigrette is more elaborate: that basic sauce, plus chopped onion and fines herbes, such as chopped parsley, chervil, and

chives. You may also add chopped cornichons (sour gherkins) and chopped capers.

Technically, a sauce made with oil and
lemon should not be called a vinaigrette.
And as far as I know there is no word to
refer specifically to an oil and lemon dressing. Someone has suggested citronette, but
that sounds like a mosquito repellent. I feel
quite certain that most French chefs would
refer to an oil and lemon sauce as a vinaigrette, knowing that they were using the
term loosely.

There is also a vinaigrette made in a
fashion that resembles a mayonnaise. Begin
with a very small amount of egg yolk, ½
teaspoon or perhaps a fraction less. Add 1
teaspoon mustard and 1 tablespoon vinegar
or lemon juice. Start beating with a wire
whisk while adding 3 tablespoons of the oil
of your choice. Add salt to taste, if desired,
and freshly ground pepper.

Unlike a true mayonnaise, the result is a
thin sauce, on the white side, and it coats
the greens more evenly than a true vinaigrette. A bit of heavy cream or sour cream
can be added to make the whiteness even
stronger.

Vindaloo

Jati Hoon of Gaylord's Restaurant in Manhattan tells me that vindaloo is a dish from
Goa and, therefore, has a Portuguese-Indian
heritage. *Vinho d'alho* in Portuguese, he
adds, means wine and garlic. Hence vindaloo means meat that has been seasoned
or marinated in wine or vinegar with garlic
and other spices.

Vinegar

The food specialty shops of America have
been, within recent years, inundated with
vinegars of various flavors, some with fruits
and berries like raspberries and plums, others with herbs and spices, such as rosemary,
oregano, garlic, and thyme.

It is my contention that if any of these
vinegars are properly made (and if they bear
a decent label and come from a reputable
specialty shop, it is presumed that they are
proper), they may be used interchangeably
in salad dressings, in deglazing various
dishes, such as calf's liver lyonnaise or
whatever. Each vinegar will contribute a
light and delicate flavor of the fruit, berry,
herb, or spice with which it is scented.

A taste in vinegars, as in honeys, is to
some degree subjective. Pierre Franey rarely
uses anything but a well-known brand of
red-wine vinegar imported from France
(Dessaux Fils) for salads. On my no-salt
diet, I happen to enjoy salad dressings made
with a malt vinegar (HP brand) imported
from England. *See also* Mother of vinegar,
Rice vinegar.

Vine Leaves

Most recipes for stuffed vine or grape leaves recommend using the bottled leaves. But if you have access to fresh grape leaves you can use these, according to an excellent book called *The Regional Cuisines of Greece* by the recipe club of St. Paul's Greek Orthodox Church in Hempstead, Long Island.

In the section on the preparation of grape leaves, it advises selecting tender young leaves from the ends of the vines—you may use the leaves of grape vines that grow wild. Trim off and discard the stems, wash the leaves thoroughly in cold water, and bring a large quantity of water to a boil. Add the leaves and let simmer about 5 minutes. Remove, drain well, and rinse in cold water.

If you wish to freeze the leaves, place them dull side down in stacks of about 30 leaves each, which is sufficient for 1 pound of ground meat.

Arrange each stack on a square of plastic wrap and roll the leaves and plastic wrap into cigar-shaped bundles, squeezing out excess water as you roll. Place in plastic bags and freeze. To hasten thawing, place the rolls in warm water.

Violets

I have enjoyed violets—pronounced vee-oh-LAY—in Marseilles but have not seen them elsewhere. They are not mentioned in my source books, but a French encyclopedia on sea creatures calls them mollusks, according to a Long Island correspondent. He says that the violet is common to the Mediterranean coast, where it is also known as a vioulet or bijus. He says it has a pouchlike body enveloped in a thick, leathery tunic and an orange-yellow interior, with the name deriving from the color of its shell.

Vorspeise

See Appetizers.

Waffles

Many of the dishes that appear in *The Times* reflect a nostalgia of our childhoods—mine in the American South, Pierre's in French Burgundy. Waffles are no exception. I recall in vivid detail the electric waffle irons that were plugged in—sometimes in the dining room, sometimes in the kitchen—in the mornings of my early youth and watching that pale batter as it was poured on the grill, emerging minutes later crisp and golden brown to be served with any of a number of homemade jams and jellies along with country sausage or home-cured ham. (Even as a child I had a loathing for maple syrup, one of my few food prejudices.)

Pierre, with equal fervor, remembers his grandmother standing over a wood stove as she manipulated a thick black waffle iron to which she had added a lumpy beige batter. The iron was placed directly on the intense heat and, when the waffles were properly cooked, they were devoured with jam, powdered sugar, and butter. "Too much was never enough," says Pierre.

Things have indeed changed radically in waffle-iron manufacturing since those days. Today's machines are streamlined, built for rapid cooking, easy cleaning, and convenient storage.

In Pierre's boyhood, his grandmother greased her waffle irons with fatback to prevent sticking. In today's models, that greasing is unnecessary in many appliances, which have nonstick surfaces.

One of the pleasures of waffle-making is, and always has been, the limitless flavors with which the waffles may be made and served: a blend of flours (such as whole-wheat and regular flour), cornmeal, various cheeses, nuts (such as pecans or hazelnuts), and so on. One of my favorite nonbreakfast waffle treats involves a topping of creamed chicken, or other creamed foods, to make an admirable luncheon or supper dish.

Waldmeister

See May wine.

Walnut Oil

Walnut oil is considered by many dedicated cooks, particularly professionals, to be one of the great salad oils. That is its primary use. It is obviously the oil of pressed walnut meats, just as olive oil is derived from olives, peanut oil from peanuts. It has a distinctly nutty flavor and is quite agreeable. Use it sparingly and, if you desire, in combination with an oil with a less pronounced flavor, peanut oil for example. It must be added that some cans of walnut oil do not seem to have the keeping qualities of, say, olive oil. Taste the oil before you use it. If it is rancid, discard it. On the other hand, do not mistake the unusual flavor of the oil for a spoiled taste.

Wash-Boiler Clambake

Blessed are those who live by the sea for theirs is the kingdom of shellfish and sea-weed, the two principal ingredients of an old-fashioned clambake. Clambakes in East Hampton come in two sizes: the large traditional back-breaking affair with pits to dig and rocks to fire and sand to sweep, and the more recently evolved wash-boiler clambake for smaller gatherings. The latter, of course, may lack the color of the original,

but I can state emphatically that the results are more or less equal. And there is one vast and important difference. The marvelous, old-fashioned clambake demands six hundred pounds of seaweed. With the wash-boiler type you can settle for a child's portion—twenty-four pounds. Bonackers—the natives who were born on the eastern tip of Long Island (and specifically in the vicinity of Accabonac)—have their own method for testing the doneness of a wash-boiler clambake, which is cooked on top of the stove. They put a raw potato in the center of the top layer of seaweed. When the potato is tender without being mushy, it is time to feast.

Wassail

The name wassail comes from the Old Icelandic *ves heill* and Old English *wes hal*, which loosely translated became "Keep in good health" or "Wish you good fortune."

When you drink to the good health of friends at Christmas the beverage, or wassail, usually is a liquor of some sort, often a spiced ale. A wassail bowl may be the bowl or cup that holds this liquid or it may refer to the drink itself. If the salutation "wassail" is used when you lift your bowl, cup, or glass, the reply should be "drink-hail."

Wat

I have dined on wat in Ethiopia, where wats in one form or another are probably the national dish. Basically, the word *wat* means a stew. It may be made with meat, poultry, fish, or vegetables. These stews are generally elaborately spicy, not only from hot ground peppers, but from other spices, such as cardamom, allspice, fenugreek, and so on. The wat is generally served over hard-boiled eggs.

Water

I am frequently asked whether water that is used for boiling foods, such as pasta or potatoes, must be cold to start with. Many people prefer, in the interest of time, to start with hot tap water. I almost invariably draw water to be boiled from the cold tap. The theory is that you have a better chance of getting fresh water—that is, water that has not been stored in a hot-water tank in the basement or wherever. Water that has been stored for a considerable period inevitably takes on a particular taste.

The water from both my taps is used so often that I suspect the results for cooking would be more or less equal. Nonetheless, out of habit, I will continue to draw water out of my cold-water tap before bringing it to a boil for pasta, potatoes, or eggs.

Water Bagel

See Bagel.

Water Bath

See Bain-marie.

Water Chestnut Powder

Water chestnut powder, which is white and finely textured, is commonly found in groceries and supermarkets that deal in Chinese merchandise. It is available in quantity in the Chinese markets of metropolitan areas. In a pinch, you could substitute cornstarch for water chestnut powder, but the McCoy would be preferable.

Watercress

Superficially there isn't much to distinguish Oviedo from any other small town in the central sector of Florida. It's a sleepy village with lots of Spanish moss and palmetto, and most people in nearby Orlando have never heard of it.

In fact, there are probably a lot of people in the town itself who do not know that Oviedo is what might be called the watercress capital of the world.

Watercress is—with its deep green color and roughly heart-shaped leaves—one of the most eye-appealing greens known to man, and its peppery flavor gives a desirable fillip to salad bowls.

Watercress is by no means typically American. It is grown all over the world including China, France, Italy, Switzerland, Cuba, and England. Britain, in fact, may be the nation that prizes it most highly. There are approximately thirty watercress producers in America—Ohio, California, Tennessee, Texas, Colorado, and so on; more than twice that number thrive in Britain.

When I arrived at the B & W watercress farm in Oviedo—the full name is B & W Quality Growers Inc.—the management was intrigued to know how I'd ever heard of the enterprise. I admitted in truth it was almost by accident. I'd stumbled over a box of watercress in my local grocery store a few days earlier and, as a watercress fancier of long standing, I noted the name and address of the shipper on the box.

The B & W farm has two owners, Don Weaver, fifty-four, and Richard Burgoon, forty-seven. ("My wife's family," Mr. Burgoon explained, "started the business here about a hundred years ago.") Today, the firm distributes its product, generally by refrigerator truck, sometimes by air, from Texas to Canada and throughout the East Coast. New York City consumes almost 50 percent of its output.

Watercress, as the name implies, depends on water—lots of it—for its sustenance. The 225-acre B & W farm is divided into enormous, rectangular sunken tracts or beds—each about a sixth of an acre. These are constantly moistened by artesian well water that gushes onto the beds at the rate of twenty gallons a minute. Only the roots of the greens are covered with water. The sprigs are airborne.

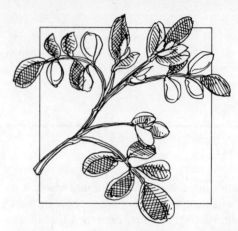

No one has ever devised a method to harvest watercress mechanically, and thus it is all done by hand. There are workers in the field who have been at their occupation for twenty-five or more years.

Each cutter has his own equipment, principally a hand-honed eight-inch butcher knife, which is used for the harvest. The cutters, in hip boots, bend to their task, grabbing a good-sized bundle of watercress in one hand, slashing it off at the stem with the other. The bundles are either tied with string or bound with rubber bands and deposited in wire baskets that are later carted to the packing warehouse.

I have always been impressed with the cleanliness of most of the bunches of watercress that have come my way, and one of the things I have long wondered about is whether the processors of watercress recommended washing their product in the home before using. The answer is "Yes."

"It isn't a question of impurities," Mr. Burgoon explained. "The fields are pure and the water is pure, but there are times when you may get a random piece of string or wood inside a bunch. So, why not wash it?"

After the watercress is gathered and bundled, it is carted to the packing house, where the bundles are chilled immediately in cold water and run on an "endless" conveyor belt until it's time to box them. The boxes are iced and eventually relayed to refrigerator trucks for the journey to wherever. Watercress gathered on Tuesday, to choose a random day, is delivered to New York grocery stores on Thursday morning.

"We'd like to convert to packing watercress in plastic bags, and it's a tough decision," Mr. Burgoon said. "The American public is used to recipes that call for one 'bunch' of watercress and they'd be confused, in the beginning at least, if it came loose in plastic bags. A bag of cress would simply be a loose bunch.

"But then we remind ourselves of the story of the man who first thought of packaging spinach in plastic bags. You know what happened. He went broke because the public couldn't adjust to it immediately. Today, of course, it's different. Nobody—well, almost nobody—buys spinach in bulk."

Weisswurst

See Boudins blancs.

Welsh Rabbit

There is something curiously appealing about that dish that is known variously as Welsh rabbit or Welsh rarebit. It is made, of course, with butter and beer, grated sharp yellow cheese, and seasonings such as dry mustard and Worcestershire sauce. Since childhood I have pondered the name and I now subscribe to the story that a Welshman went hunting and returned home empty-handed. His wife concocted a dish with melted cheese and dubbed it "rabbit." Thus, Welsh rabbit, not rarebit.

White Chocolate

See Chocolate.

White Pepper

See Peppercorns.

White Sauce

I almost invariably add cold liquid to the butter and flour roux when making a white sauce. This way, it takes exactly the same length of time to bring the liquid to the boil as it would if you heated the milk separately. And you dirty only one saucepan.

In classic cooking it is recommended, but not essential, that a basic white sauce simmer for a minimum of ten minutes. There is a reason for this: The long cooking time, according to the books, rids the sauce of its raw taste of flour. However, I do not usually simmer white sauce for an extended period. Often, other ingredients, such as cheese and seasonings, are added before serving and the difference in flavor when it is cooked longer is so slight as to be negligible.

White Truffles

See Truffles.

Wild Chicory

See Barbe de capucin, Radicchio.

Wild Leek

See Ramp.

Wild Rice

If I had to name the single cereal that is the most sophisticated in the world, it would doubtless be an American Indian contribution, one that goes by the name wild rice. This product, as the late Waverley Root notes in his excellent book titled *Food*, "is not rice, but it was so called by the early explorers who found American Indians liv-

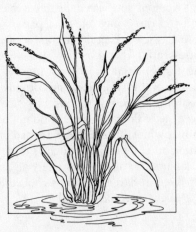

ing on it in the Great Lakes region because, like rice, it grows from the water . . . looking very much like rice in a paddy. French explorers preferred to call it 'crazy oats.' "

There is something about the texture and flavor of wild rice that elevates it to a special state in the sphere of gastronomy. And it is undeniably a luxury item in that to this day most of the wild rice sold commercially must be harvested by hand.

In their book, *Foods the Indians Gave Us,* Wilma and R. Vernon Hays note that in the early days, "the Chippewas in the Lake Superior area were fortunate to have the largest natural fields. . . . Only recently has 'wild' rice been planted successfully in places where it had never grown before.

"The slender stems of wild rice often grow twice as tall as a man. The grain forms in delicate plumes at the top.

"Men and women still harvest wild rice in the birch-bark canoes that the Chippewas make so well. The man may pole the canoe through the dense rice field while the woman unties the bundles and whacks them with a stick to beat off the grain. Most of the rice falls into the canoe, but some falls into the water and seeds the field for another season."

Wilted Lettuce

Wilted lettuce is a salad on which many of us dined as children. I do not believe it is a regional creation, but I found a recipe in *The New England Yankee Cook Book* by Imogene Wolcott.

It calls for 3 shredded bunches of garden lettuce. You cook 4 slices of lean bacon until crisp and remove from the skillet, reserving the fat. Crumble the bacon and set it aside.

Add ¼ cup of vinegar, salt and pepper to the fat, simmer, and pour over the lettuce.

Add a sliced hard-boiled egg and toss. Sprinkle with the bacon bits and serve.

Wine

The following are the most frequently asked questions about wine, a subject that intimidates many people.

What are the "best" wines in the world?

The judging of wine is a highly subjective thing and it is a matter of personal taste. The best wine is the wine that gives you the greatest pleasure. It is generally conceded, however, that the wines of Burgundy and Bordeaux are the finest wines produced the world over, and even the greatest wine enthusiasts will disagree over which is the greater, Burgundy or Bordeaux. The wines of Bordeaux are longer-lasting than those of Burgundy. Bordeaux have a high tannin content, which accounts for their long life, and it is this quality that makes the wines seem, to some palates, a trifle "harsh," particularly if the wine is drunk too young. Burgundies, to many palates, have a rounder, softer, fruitier quality.

Can American wines compare with those of Europe's vineyards?

Indeed, they can and do. Although America has yet to produce a wine in the same league as the greatest wines of Burgundy and Bordeaux, the best table wines of California are equal or superior to some of the most popular table wines of Europe, and I feel that anyone who drinks imported wines to the exclusion of all domestic products is guilty of acute snobbism. In my own home, for ordinary purposes over the course of a year, I use fairly impressive quantities of California wines for both cooking and drinking.

Should red wines ever be chilled?

On occasion. The perfect temperature for a fine, vintage red wine is 60 to 65 degrees, which may be considerably less than room temperature. Thus, even fine red wines may benefit from a short—very short—stay in the refrigerator. No more than fifteen minutes. Young, ordinary red wines, such as Beaujolais or the common red wines of Italy, should be served at a temperature of about 55 degrees and, thus, need a bit longer chilling. They should never be served cold, however.

Dry white wines and rosés are best at a temperature of 45 to 50 degrees. The temperature of champagne and sweet dessert wines such as Sauternes is a question of personal taste. Most experts recommend that they be chilled only to a temperature of 40 to 45 degrees. I prefer them somewhat colder than that. Peasant taste.

Is it all right to chill white wine and champagne bottles in the freezer?

Yes, but take care that they do not remain in the freezer for such an extended period that they freeze or the bottles burst. Chilling wines in the freezer is recommended only in an emergency. And a preferable method for quick chilling is to place the bottle or bottles in a wine bucket or other deep container and surround the bottles with ice. A handful of coarse salt scattered over the ice also helps.

What is the best technique for opening a bottle of wine?

Stand the bottle firmly on a flat surface. Run a sharp knife around the lead foil that covers the top of the bottle. Run the knife neatly around the foil about one-half inch from the top. Remove that portion of the foil. Using a clean napkin, moistened with a little water if desired, wipe off the top of the cork.

Insert the tip of the corkscrew in dead center of the cork and carefully pull out the cork. Should the cork break while it is being extracted, reinsert the corkscrew into the cork once more but at an angle. If a cork becomes a crumbly mess and falls into the wine, strain the wine through a piece of clean cheesecloth that has been wrung out in cold water.

When the cork has been removed, wipe off the lip of the bottle once more with the clean napkin. That done, the host or hostess pours a small amount of the wine into his or her glass and samples it. This is done for two reasons. That sample would probably extract any bit of cork that had fallen into the wine. The sample would also be a guide as to whether the wine is spoiled.

Are wine cradles "proper"?

Wine cradles are designed for old wines that have a deposit. In theory, the very old wine is carefully placed in the cradle before it is brought to the table. Again in theory, the cradle helps eliminate "jostling" the wine and stirring up the deposit. There is one more functional reason for using a wine cradle and that is in a restaurant where there might be danger that a waiter might accidentally knock over the bottle. For young wines, free of deposit, however, a wine cradle is totally nonessential.

Are the size and shape of wineglasses important?

The most basic requirement is that the glasses have a stem and be of pure clear crystal. Although I have an assortment of wineglasses including Bordeaux, Burgundy, and champagne, I use on most occasions what I consider an all-purpose glass. It is bowl-shaped and has a capacity of approximately two cups. It is actually a glass for the red wines of Burgundy, but I use it for Bordeaux, champagne, red and white wines of whatever nationality. Generally speaking, glasses for the red wines of Burgundy have a larger capacity than Bordeaux, while glasses for red Bordeaux have a larger capacity than those for white wines.

Champagne glasses come in numerous shapes including saucer, flute, and tulip. The preferred shape is the tulip. Because the rim of the tulip glass shapes inward, the bubbles have less exposure to the air and the effervescence is retained.

Who makes the finest wineglasses?

Baccarat. They are wildly expensive and delicate, but the shapes of the glasses are incomparable.

What is the proper amount of wine to pour into a glass?

Most guides tell you to fill a glass no more than one-third to one-half full. This is misleading, however, inasmuch as there is a wide divergence in the size of wineglasses. A preferable measure, I feel, is one-half cup of wine no matter whether the glass is a larger one for Burgundies or a smaller one for Bordeaux. More than this is a vulgar excess. An exception is a champagne glass. It may be filled on festive occasions to three-quarters or more of its capacity.

How do you store wineglasses?

It is one man's opinion that glasses should be stored stem-side down. When stored upside down (the rim on the shelf), the bowls of the glasses often take on an odor, no matter how slight, from the rim's close contact with the wood. This odor is distracting, whether you subsequently serve wine or water in the glasses. If the bowls become dusty after no use, I simply put them in the dishwasher—all or a few at a time.

Should a bottle of wine be wrapped in a napkin before pouring?

Not unless you are ashamed of what you are pouring.

Is it strictly true that white wines should be drunk with "white" meats and red wines with "dark" meats?

The people who coined that notion should be lumped with the people who decreed that salad bowls shouldn't be washed. They then should be stripped summarily of their medals and discharged. Dry white wines almost invariably should be drunk with fish, but otherwise there is vast variance in what "should" be served with what. While there are no strict rules, a good red Bordeaux or red Burgundy or red California wine will go excellently with most chicken dishes. But full-bodied dry white wines are wholly acceptable with these dishes if that is your preference. Although red Burgundies are quite compatible with roast turkey, a red Bordeaux or red California wine seems preferable. For cold sliced turkey, however, a dry white wine goes best. On the other hand, by all means serve a full-bodied dry white wine with your roast turkey if you so choose. Red Burgundies and a full-bodied California red wine go best with game and geese. Sweet wines such as imported Sauternes should, generally speaking, be served with dessert. But never mistake a genuine Sauternes (the name always bears an "s" at the end) from France with a California Sauterne. The latter is watery and generally nonsweet. The traditional wine for oysters on the half shell is Chablis. Almost all cheeses marry well with full-bodied red wines. Italian red wines go splendidly with dishes containing tomato sauces. But perhaps the greatest marriage of food and wine is fresh foie gras and a fine Sauternes.

Similarly with choosing wines for cooking, generally speaking red wines are used in sauce making for "red" meats such as beef or dark-fleshed game. Beef bourguignonne is a case in point. On the other hand, both red and white wines can contribute agreeably to sauces for white-fleshed foods such as poultry, and the less robust kinds of game such as rabbit.

It comes as something of a cultural shock to some cooks to discover quite respectable fish dishes in which the fish is cooked au vin rouge—salmon or carp Chambord poached in red wine, a matelote of eel poached similarly, and so on. It has been stated often that you do not have to use rare vintages to produce excellent wine sauces. The best theory is that any wine you choose to serve at table would be suitable for the sauce to be made in the kitchen. On the other hand, if you are out to produce a dazzling dish with truffles, foie gras, and other luxuries, the finer the wine you use, the finer your sauce will be.

What can I substitute for wine in cooking?

Substitutes for wine will depend on the wine that is called for. In French cooking, for example, you may substitute chicken or veal broth in recipes that call for dry white wine. The result will not give you an exact duplicate of flavors, but it will be acceptable.

Mirin is one of the principal wines called for in Japanese cooking. Shao-hsing, another rice wine, is used primarily in Chinese cooking. A dry or fairly sweet sherry may be substituted for the Japanese and Chinese rice wines.

Why are wines cooked down before a dish is completed?

I have an indelible memory of the pretender in the kitchen, a rank but unhumble amateur among the pots and pans, who decided that all his spaghetti sauce needed to give it zip was one more cup of red wine added just before serving. It was inedible.

Dry red or white wines have a natural, built-in acidity and this must be dissipated by cooking down before the dish becomes appetizing.

If you prepare a dish with wine only to discover the moment before serving that the sauce is too thick, in the name of St. Vincent, the patron saint of wines, don't add a glass of red wine, white wine, or champagne. You will destroy the dish. Rather, add a bit of broth—chicken or beef, for example—to produce the right consistency. Bring to the boil and serve immediately.

In a similar vein there are those who will ceremoniously serve their sauerkraut piping hot on a platter, then add a split of champagne to the center to bubble over the dish. To each his own novelty. *See also* Champagne sauce, Cooking wine, Decanting, Fortified wine, May wine, Rosé wine.

Wok

The best woks are made of heavy gauge steel and they do rust when exposed to water. If rust has accumulated, I would certainly recommend re-seasoning the wok. First off you

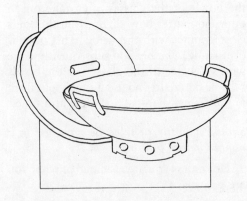

should scrub it well, using a scouring cleanser and a wire brush or a heavy scouring pad with lots of elbow grease. Make certain that all the rusty surface is clean. Wash and dry it, preferably over a low flame. Add oil almost to fill the wok and heat it almost to the smoking point. Let it stand overnight. Pour off the fat and wipe it dry without washing. Ideally, until the wok is well seasoned (with a built-in coating that comes with use) you should not wash it. Instead, add coarse salt, such as kosher salt, and scrub it clean with paper towels.

Won Tons

See Dumplings.

Wooden Equipment

Wooden cooking utensils and cutting boards must be kept immaculately clean because they can harbor harmful bacteria.

First, let me state my position on butcher blocks and cutting boards. I do have a professional-style butcher block in my kitchen that is one-foot deep. For cutting I have two white, dense, rectangular plastic boards that, unlike wood, do not splinter. They measure about sixteen by twenty inches overall. I prefer these to wood, because they are not as apt to harbor bacteria. They are nonporous and do not dull knives any more than a wooden board would.

To my mind it is important that both the chopping block and the cutting boards be washed and/or scrubbed after each and every use. As to the cutting boards, I remove them from the work surface and wash them

well with a sponge, detergent, and hot water. On the chopping block I generally use a scrub brush with a scouring powder to begin with, followed by further cleansing with a sponge, detergent, and hot water. I end by rubbing with a clean sponge and more hot water.

If you do use a wooden pastry or cutting board, I would simply transfer it to the kitchen sink and scrub it after each use with a sponge and hot soapy water. If necessary, I would give it a good scrubbing. But take care that you dry it thoroughly after each use; otherwise the board may warp.

As for wooden utensils, I have very few that will not fit into my dishwasher.

Woodruff

See May wine.

Worcestershire Sauce

There are certain names in the world of wine and food that are inextricably linked. These pairings include Moët and Chandon, Fortnum and Mason, Cross and Blackwell. Another pairing indelibly inscribed on the gastronomic roster is Lea and Perrins, makers of the original Worcestershire sauce, "the original and genuine, from the recipe of a nobleman in the county," as it reads on the label. The county in question, of course, is Worcestershire, England. The label does not reveal the name of the nobleman nor to this day will the producers of the sauce reveal it.

Just how this sauce came about is an amusing and tangled history of secrets and intrigues, alleged deceptions, family jealousies, British officialdom, and two continents. It is a supposedly true account that would have done justice to the talents of Somerset Maugham.

The saga of the sauce dates back to the first years of the 1800s, when the governor general of Bengal returned from his post to his native England. He had in his possession a formula for a sauce that had been created in India, one that he had relished at his table and offered his guests.

At that time, there were two chemists in the English Midlands named John Lea and William Perrins, partners in a then novel enterprise, a "chain" of chemist shops. Their association had begun in the 1820s. Their main office was in the town of Worcester in the shire, or county, of the same name.

The governor general took the recipe to Mr. Lea and Mr. Perrins with a request that they try to reproduce it as closely as possible. The story goes that the chemists produced a concoction that was to their noses and tastes unpalatable. They stored it in the cellar and forgot it.

Months, perhaps years, later they sampled it once more and found it not only acceptable but haunting in its flavor. Within a short while they were bottling the stuff, and it is a matter of genuine historical record that, without any kind of advertising as it is known today, in a few short years the Worcestershire sauce of Mr. Lea and Mr. Perrins was known and coveted in kitchens throughout the world. The governor general's family, not invited to join in the production and marketing, was quite naturally out of sorts and adamantly refused to allow the family name to be used in its sale.

Some historians of Worcestershire sauce put forth the fanciful theory that its origins lie in the days of ancient Rome. It is amply recorded that the early Romans were addicted to a sauce called garum, made with the visceral parts of fish. These parts were well salted and allowed to bake in the sun to develop a character that must have been assertive, to say the least. To this base was added a liquid and this, too, was aged before straining and serving.

The theory of these chroniclers is that later Romans followed the spice routes, and the garum formula was elaborated on in Indian kitchens, altered and handed down from generation to generation until it came into the possession of the English official.

The incredible haste with which the fame of Worcestershire sauce spread is generally credited to the fact that the manufacturers loaded cases of the sauce on all the ocean liners that plied in and out of English waters. The stewards of the ocean-going liners were "encouraged" with a few shillings here, a few pounds there, to offer the sauce to the passengers. The passengers frequently purchased samples to take with them wherever they embarked (it is said to have been a fine foil for some of the food then available in certain Pacific outposts).

I once traveled to Fair Lawn, New Jersey,

where Lea & Perrins is manufactured, to speak to Ransom Duncan, the great-great-grandson of the original American importer.

Mr. Duncan, a tall, angular, amiable man, greeted me before an antique display case in the lobby of the building where the sauce is aged and bottled. The case, which had been built for the Exposition of the Industry of All Nations in New York in 1853 and was used again for the centennial exposition in Philadelphia in 1876, housed a few score of the earliest bottles of Lea & Perrins available in this country. Some of the labels are an amusing commentary on table and eating patterns in this country.

One label read, "Butlers in best families . . . tell you that soups, fish, meats, gravy, game, salads and many other dishes are given an appetizing relish if flavored with Lea & Perrins sauce." Another, "Club men and all good livers appreciate the appetizing relish given to Oyster cocktails, Welsh rarebits, Lobster Newburgh [sic] and all dishes flavored with this sauce."

Ransom Duncan told me that his family has been in this country since the American Revolution.

"My great-great-grandfather, John Duncan, had a small business in Manhattan principally importing liquors and wine from Europe, and preserves, jams, and jellies from England," he continued. "His firm was known simply as John Duncan and Sons. He learned of this odd sauce that was said to be famous in England in the 1830s and he ordered a small shipment. The imports gained tremendously in a very few years and there were salesmen peddling it all over the country. They traveled by train as far south as Texas. Demand became such that he opened a processing plant using the exact English formula and using English imports."

Since my own childhood, I have marveled in reading the bottle's labels, for to my very young mind it was a study in exotic things and faraway places: tamarinds, anchovies, shallots, garlic, molasses, soy, and so on. Superior to "snap, crackle, and pop" in every way.

Mr. Duncan told me that to this day the product duplicates as much as possible the original. There are some modifications due to government restrictions and regulations. He himself scours the Mediterranean for the anchovies best suited to the sauce. Most of them come from Spain and the northern coasts of Italy and Sicily.

One of the thorniest ingredients in making the sauce from year to year is the tamarind, most of which comes from India, although, said Mr. Duncan, "if desperate, we buy it from the West Indies."

Tamarind (much used in Indian cookery) is a brownish red bean that grows on tall trees. It adds a certain sweetness, a touch of tartness, plus color to foods and liquids in which it is used. The crop varies from season to season and region to region, and the imports must be carefully screened to eliminate destructive insects.

Mr. Duncan also mused over the fact that ingredients have changed with world changes. "We use tons of hot chilies and these vary around the world. The old-fashioned, scorching-hot chilies are more difficult to come by. We used to buy only the small, hand-picked, wild variety, but no one does that kind of labor anymore. The cultivated peppers are larger, but they also have less taste."

Peppercorns used in the sauce come from Zanzibar, China, Mombasa, and other places around the globe. "Today we must be more painstaking than ever against buying products with impurities," said Mr. Duncan. Speaking of impurities, he noted that the best molasses—the bulk of it from Barbados—is the least pure. It is the impurities that give it color.

Around the curing vats there was a pleasant smell resembling that of fruitcake. "Cloves," Mr. Duncan observed.

The principal ingredients used in the aging process are, in addition to tamarind and anchovies, unpeeled heads of garlic and unpeeled red-skinned onions. The onions are one of the few domestic ingredients in Lea & Perrins Worcestershire sauce. They come from the Finger Lakes region of New York State.

Worcestershire sauce, like champagne, has become, for better or for worse (and most connoisseurs think for worse), a generic term. There is no doubt that the original sauce, prepared and first labeled Worcestershire sauce by Mr. Lea and Mr. Perrins, is the finest known brand.

"Nobody," James Lund, president of the American company, told me later, "nobody in his right mind would ever start producing our product today if it hadn't already been invented." And there are few who would dispute him. The aging process, whether in wines or foods, is a costly proposition. No one was willing to say precisely how long the base for the sauce must lie in the thirty-five giant wooden vats used for the aging process (the vats hold a total of six thousand gallons), but it is reckoned a minimum of two years. Originally, the product was aged in four thousand barrels purchased years ago from a bourbon distillery, but the larger fir vats are more economical.

Incidentally, most Americans pronounce it "woo-stuh" whereas British friends claim that that "woo" should not rhyme with "true" but that the double "o" should be more like that in "took."

Wow Wow Sauce

See Bubble and squeak.

Yakitori

Barbecue seems synonymous in many American minds with grilled foods of any sort; thus the false assumption that grilled dishes are of Yankee origin. Nothing, obviously, is further from the truth. It takes little enough reason to know that grilled foods must have come about shortly after man began to use fire and many thousand years before Charles Lamb wrote his famed dissertation on roast pig.

Having made frequent excursions to yakitori restaurants in Japan, I reflected that yakitori, which must go back a few hundred years, must be a relatively advanced and sophisticated example of cooking grilled foods. Actually, yakitori is a combination of two Japanese words, *yaki*, meaning grilled, and *tori*, meaning birds. The most usual bird used for yakitori is chicken, which is, more often than not, cut into boneless cubes and arranged on skewers before grilling. The pieces include not only the flesh but the hearts, livers, gizzards, and so on. The skewered portions are brushed when grilling with a fairly sweet sauce composed generally of sake, mirin, soy sauce, and honey among other things. The sauce is known as yakitori-notare.

Yams

I know that sweet potatoes and yams are often considered the same, particularly in the South. Botanically, I am told, they are absolutely not the same, although they are quite similar in both looks and flavor. Waverley Root, in his book *Food*, devotes four pages to pointing out the differences. "What is a yam?" he asks. "First of all, definitely not a sweet potato." Although, he concedes, the two resemble each other, they are botanically wholly different. The sweet potato is of the genus *Ipomoea*, the morning glory family; the yam is of the genus *Discorea*.

Dudley Sanders, a former commercial vegetable grower in Gleason, Tennessee, who specializes in sweet potatoes, offers a definition: "The Department of Agriculture designates sweet potatoes as dry flesh and moist flesh according to the feel sensation experienced in the mouth during the eating of cooked or baked sweet potatoes. These terms do not refer to the moisture content of the potato." Yam, he adds, is, purely and simply, the name applied inaccurately, no doubt by those who sell sweet potatoes, in referring to the brick-red, moist-fleshed type of sweet potatoes.

487

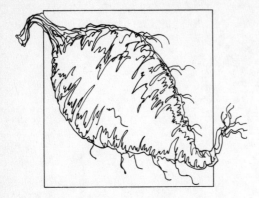

According to Charles Brader, director of the food and vegetable division of the Department of Agriculture, true yams are rarely if ever grown commercially in this country. We import them in limited quantities and they are sold only through specialty purveyors.

A spokesman for the United Fresh Fruit and Vegetable Association has a different view:

"Botanically, all sweet potatoes and yams sold in the United States today are basically sweet potatoes. One variety is copper skinned and a deep orange color inside. They are moist, sweet and juicy and this variety is marketed as 'yams,' when in effect, they are botanically a variety of the sweet potato.

"The other variety is tan in color on the outside and light, creamy yellow on the inside. This variety is very dry, as compared to the moist variety which is usually purchased in preference.

"The true yam is not grown in the continental United States, but may be found in tropical areas to a limited extent. The yam (*Dioscorea batatas*) is sometimes called the Chinese yam, or Chinese potato.

"The roots are used as sweet potatoes, but are not palatable to most tastes and they have not become popular in areas where sweet potatoes grow well. The sweet potato (*Ipomoea batatas*) is produced in warm parts of the United States.

"Many consumers confuse sweet potatoes and yams since one variety of sweet potato is actually advertised and sold in this country as yams."

Yeast

Each standard envelope of yeast weighs a quarter of an ounce, slightly less than one tablespoon.

The standard yeast cake (compressed yeast) weighs three fifths of an ounce. To substitute granular yeast for a yeast cake, use one package of granular yeast for each yeast cake.

I am told by a spokesman for this country's largest producer of granular yeast that the shelf life is about one year if stored in a cool dry place, and that using outdated yeast is not recommended. I was fascinated to learn that the use of "dry" yeast (as opposed to cakes of compressed yeast) goes back forty years.

Yogurt

There is an Indian cookbook that refers to yogurt as "immortal nectar." In India, the author says, hair is washed in it, demons are exorcised by it, gods are bathed in it, and ceremonies are sanctified with it. Although Americans may not yet have reached the state in which yogurt is thus glorified, we may be well on our way. The younger generation in this country may accept yogurt as a fact of life or a run-of-the-mill staple much the same as butter, eggs, and milk, but they do not realize that until the 1960s, yogurt was a relative curiosity, something to be consumed by eccentrics and food faddists. As recently as 1954, the consumption of yogurt in this country was less than two ounces per person a year. Today it is more like three pounds per person per year.

The word "yogurt"—and all its variations (yaourt, yoghurt, yoghurd, yogourt)—strikes my eyes and ears as one of the most curious in the language. The *Oxford English Dictionary* points out that it is derived from a Turkish word bearing a similar sound. It lists several uses of the word plus their dates, including "1625 Purchas Pilgrims II. Neither doe they (sc. the Turks) eate much Milke, except it bee made sower, which they call Yoghurd."

Where the kitchen is concerned, I find yogurt to be one of the most unusual foods to work with. I personally do not like the texture of basic yogurt. I find it too drearily and too unrelievedly sour. In its raw state I prefer it blended with vegetables and chilies and cumin to be served with curries.

I also prefer yogurt when it is converted into "cheese." This is easily if not hastily done. Simply line a sieve or colander with cheesecloth that has been wrung out in cold water. Pour the yogurt into it and bring up the corners of the cloth, which should be tied with string. Then suspend the cheesecloth bag over a bowl and let it hang in a cool place, preferably the refrigerator, for any given length of time. The longer it hangs, the firmer the yogurt becomes. I generally let it hang overnight, at which point it takes on the texture of a tender cottage cheese.

If you sweeten the yogurt before letting it drain, it becomes quite spreadable and makes a fine filling for a graham cracker-crust pie with berries on top.

Pierre Franey and I also find that yogurt cheese produces a better yogurt ice cream than does plain yogurt.

There are numerous ways to prepare frozen yogurt or yogurt ice cream. The most basic is to combine plain yogurt with frozen berries or fruit and sugar to taste before freezing. I find this basically dull and distasteful.

Yogurt, because of its watery nature, needs a stabilizer to give it a smooth texture when frozen. This can be achieved by using gelatin and, if you want a smoother texture, heavy cream or evaporated milk.

The best frozen yogurt ice cream that can be made in the home is, I believe, made by adding yogurt "cheese" to a basic ice cream mixture made with eggs and milk and very little heavy cream. The yogurt gives an appealing tangy taste to the ice cream. This ice cream is best, incidentally, when eaten immediately after freezing. If it is left to stand in the freezer, ice particles tend to form.

Yogurt, as any Indian cook can tell you, is a great ingredient for tenderizing meats. You can marinate a leg of lamb or chicken or whatever in yogurt and the results, when grilled or broiled or baked, are excellent. Meats thus prepared are delectable when turned into a curry.

No one knows precisely when and where yogurt was discovered, but its existence no doubt came about by accident. It first gained international prominence as a medical novelty in the early 1900s when Ilya Metchnikov, a Russian bacteriologist, observed that the life span of Bulgarians, whose diet included the consumption of large quantities of soured milk, was eighty-seven years and beyond.

Today, yogurt has become a Western commodity. It bears many names, including *laban* in the Middle East, *hangop* in the Netherlands, and *mezzoradu* in Switzerland and Sicily. Some forms of yogurt develop an alcoholic content in the course of their fermentation. These include the Russian koumiss and kefir of the Caucasus. For what it's worth, the word *laban* and the word "Lebanon" both derive from the Arab word that translates as milk.

Yucca

There is a fascinating Panamanian appetizer called carimañolas, a very special shallow-fried turnover made with the Caribbean and Latin-American vegetable known as yucca. The vegetable is, incidentally, widely available at Spanish-speaking markets. The yucca, a root vegetable, is peeled and cored and cooked until tender like potatoes. It is then mashed and shaped into a turnover with a fine filling of ground pork seasoned with oregano and garlic. Crisp outside, tender within.

Yufka

Yufka is the Turkish word for the "see-through" pastry known in Greek as phyllo pastry.

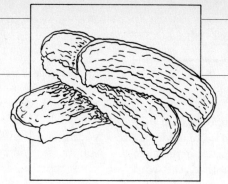
Zabaglione

One of the finest and most popular desserts in the Italian repertory is one of the last of the desserts in any dictionary. It is zabaglione, also spelled zabaione, and on French menus, sabayon. I have it on the authority of one more erudite that the word really means "an Illyrian drink," Illyria being an ancient Adriatic coastal region.

The original Italian zabaglione consisted of egg yolks beaten over heat with sugar until they thickened. You continue beating while adding Marsala wine, which is sweet. In time this becomes as thick as a well-made

custard. It is served in warmed crystal glasses.

In theory the word "sabayon" or "zabaglione" usually refers to a dessert. By extension it can mean a sabayon preparation, which is to say a thickened, custard-like mixture, sweet or not, prepared by beating egg yolks over heat with the addition of a liquid. That liquid might be a fortified sweet wine, such as Marsala, but it also might be a dry white wine.

Zakuska

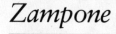

See Appetizers.

Zampone

Zampone is a North Italian sausage and frequently has the identical pork filling as cotechino. A cotechino is sausage-shaped whereas the filling for zampone is stuffed inside the skin of pigs' trotters. A zampone is more often than not much larger than a cotechino and, therefore, requires a longer cooking time.

Zest

Zest is simply another term for rind. It may be grated or not. The word quite obviously means something that gives zest in flavor to one food or beverage or another. The word is applied to the skin of oranges or lemons.

Zeste in French means "peel," as in the peel of lemons, oranges, tangerines, and so on, and I believe the English usage is a borrowing of the last two or three decades. I heard "zeste de citron, zeste d'orange" and so on in France long before I heard it in this country.

The word *ziste* also appears in *Larousse Gastronomique*, which defines it as the "white pith found in oranges and lemons just under the colored peel" and "has a rather bitter taste."

Zoo Sandwich

Curiously, something called a zoo sandwich does exist. A brief search through volumes that deal with American cooking terms and histories revealed nothing. By accident I found it in *Joy of Cooking* by Irma S. Rombauer and Marion Rombauer Becker. The sandwich is, the authors explain, "for very young children's parties." It consists of simply using fancy cookie-cutters to cut out sandwiches made of bread and filled with not-too-spicy fillings. The sandwiches are cut into the shapes of animals.

Zwieback

Because I savor the learning of word origins with almost the same relish commonly reserved for smoked salmon, cold herring, or caviar, I was intrigued with a conversation shared with Narcissa Chamberlain, widow of the distinguished food authority, architect, and etcher Samuel Chamberlain.

During the course of the evening she remarked that biscuit and zwieback had more in common than the mere fact that each was a kind of bread. Both names, basically, mean "twice-baked."

Biscuit springs from the French *bis* meaning twice and *cuire* meaning to cook. The name is related, of course, to the Italian word *biscotto*. The original is the medieval Latin *biscotus,* meaning twice-cooked.

Zwieback comes from an Old High German combination *zwie* meaning twice and *backen* meaning to bake.

Acknowledgments

Over the years I have spent many hours poring over books related to food and culling information from them for my own edification and the enlightenment of my readers. The most widely used and comprehensive of these books are the following, for which I am indebted to the authors.

Ali-Bab. *Gastronomie Pratique*. Paris: Etudes Culinaire, 1907.

American Egg Board. *Eggcyclopedia*. 1981.

American Heritage Dictionary of the English Language. Boston: Houghton-Mifflin, 1969.

Androuet, Pierre. *The Complete Encyclopedia of French Cheese*. New York: Harper's Magazine Press, 1973.

L'Art Culinaire Français. Paris: Flammarion, 1950.

Baxter, Ena. *Scottish Cookbook*. Edinburgh and London: Johnston and Baker, 1974.

Beard, James. *American Cookery*. Boston: Little, Brown, 1972.

Beeton, Isabella. *Mrs. Beeton's Book of Household Management*. London: Jonathan Cape, 1968.

Bloch, Oscar and Von Wartburg, W. *Dictionnaire Etymologique de la Langue Française*. Paris: Presses Universitaires de France, 1968.

Bolitho, Hector. *The Glorious Oyster*. New York: Horizon Press, 1960.

Boni, Ada. *Italian Regional Cooking*. New York: Bonanza Books, 1969.

Booth, Letha. *The Williamsburg Cookbook*. Williamsburg, Virginia: Colonial Williamsburg Foundation, 1971.

Boulestin, X. Marcel and Hill, Jason. *Herbs, Salads and Seasonings*. London: William Heinemann Ltd., 1930.

Boyd, Lizzie. *British Cookery*. London: Overlook Press, 1979.

Brillat-Savarin, Jean Anthelme. *The Physiology of Taste*. New York: Heritage Press, 1949.

Brown, Helen Evans. *The West Coast Cook Book*. Boston: Little, Brown, 1952.

Bugialli, Guiliano. *The Fine Art of Italian Cooking*. New York: Quadrangle, 1977.

Carnacina, Luigi. *Italian Home Cooking*. New York: Doubleday, 1972.

Casas, Penelope. *The Foods and Wines of Spain*. New York: Alfred A. Knopf, 1982.

Chang, K. C. *Food in Chinese Culture*. New Haven: Yale University Press, 1977.

Chu, Grace Zia. *Madam Chu's Cooking School*. New York: Simon and Schuster, 1975.

Clark, Eleanor. *The Oysters of Locmariaquer*. New York: Pantheon Books, 1959.

Clark, Morton G. *The Wide Wide World of Texas Chili*. New York: Funk & Wagnalls, 1970.

Colquitt, Harriet Ross. *The Savannah Cook Book*. Charleston, South Carolina: Colonial Publishers, 1933.

David, Elizabeth. *English Bread and Yeast Cookery*. New York: Viking Press, 1977.

————. *French Provincial Cooking*. New York: Harper & Row, 1960.

————. *Italian Food*. New York: Alfred A. Knopf, 1958.

Davidson, Alan. *North Atlantic Seafood*. New York: Viking Press, 1979.

DeBolt, Margaret Wayt. *Savannah Sampler Cookbook*. Norfolk: Donning Co., 1978.

Dictionnaire de l'Académie des Gastronomes. Paris: Aux Editions Prisma, 1962.

Dowell, Philip and Bailey, Adrian. *Cook's Ingredients*. New York: William Morrow, 1980.

Embury, David A. *The Fine Art of Mixing Drinks*. New York: Doubleday, 1948.

Encyclopedia Britannica, 11th edition. New York: Cambridge University Press, 1910.

Eren, Neset. *The Art of Turkish Cooking*. New York: Doubleday, 1969.

Escoffier, Auguste. *Le Guide Culinaire*. New York: Mayflower Books, 1921.

Evans, Ivor H. *Brewer's Dictionary of Phrase and Fable*. New York: Harper & Row, 1959.

Farmer, Fannie Merritt. *Boston Cooking School Cook Book*. Boston: Little, Brown, 1930.

FitzGibbon, Theodora. *The Food of the Western World*. New York: Quadrangle, 1976.

————. *Irish Traditional Food*. New York: St. Martin's Press, 1983.

Forbes, Patrick. *Champagne, the Wine, the Land and the People*. London: Victor Gollancz, 1977.

Grigson, Jane. *Jane Grigson's Vegetable Book*. New York: Atheneum, 1979.

————. *The Art of Charcuterie*. New York: Alfred A. Knopf, 1968.

Hays, Wilma and R. Vernon. *Foods the Indians Gave Us*. New York: Ives Washburn, Inc., 1973.

Hazan, Marcella. *The Classic Italian Cook Book*. New York: Alfred A. Knopf, 1976.

————. *More Classic Italian Cooking*. New York: Alfred A. Knopf, 1978.

Herbodeau, Eugene and Thalamas, Paul. *Georges Auguste Escoffier*. London: Practical Press, 1955.

Herter, George Leonard and Berthe E. *Bull Cook and Authentic Recipes and Practices*. Waseca, Minnesota: Herter's, 1960.

Hillman, Howard. *Kitchen Science*. Boston: Houghton Mifflin, 1981.

Jaffrey, Madhur. *An Invitation to Indian Cooking*. New York: Alfred A. Knopf, 1973.

Jones, Evan. *American Food: The Gastronomic Story*. New York: Vintage Books, 1981.

————. *The World of Cheese*. New York: Alfred A. Knopf, 1976.

Kennedy, Diana. *The Cuisines of Mexico*. New York: Harper & Row, 1972.

Kimball, Marie and Garrett, Richard. *Thomas Jefferson's Cook Book*. Richmond, Virginia: Garrett & Massie, 1949.

Kropotkin, Alexandra. *The Best of Russian Cooking*. New York: Charles Scribner, 1964.

Lang, George. *The Cuisine of Hungary*. New York: Atheneum, 1971.

Mariani, John F. *The Dictionary of American Food and Drink*. New York: Ticknor & Fields, 1983.

Marks, Copeland and Soeharjo, Mintari. *The Indonesian Kitchen*. New York: Atheneum, 1981.

Marquis, Vivienne and Haskell, Patricia. *The Cheese Book*. New York: Simon & Schuster, 1964.

Marshall, Brenda. *The Charles Dickens Cookbook*. Toronto: Personal Library, 1980.

Masuda, Koh. *New Japanese English Dictionary*. Tokyo: Kenkyusha Press.

McClane, A.J. *The Encyclopedia of Fish Cookery*. New York: Holt, Rinehart & Winston, 1977.

Mitchell, Jan. *Luchow's German Cook Book*. New York: Doubleday, 1952.

Montagne, Prosper. *Larousse Gastronomique*. New York: Crown, 1961.

Morris, William and Mary. *Morris Dictionary of Word and Phrase Origin*. New York: Harper & Row, 1962.

Neithammer, Carolyn. *American Indian Food and Lore*. New York: Collier Books, 1974.

Ortiz, Elisabeth Lambert. *The Complete Book of Caribbean Cooking*. New York: M. Evans & Co., 1973.

———. *The Complete Book of Mexican Cooking*. New York: M. Evans, 1965.

Oxford English Dictionary. London: Clarendon Press, 1933.

Peck, Paula. *The Art of Good Cooking*. New York: Simon & Schuster, 1966.

Pratt, James Norwood. *The Tea Lover's Treasury*. San Francisco: 101 Productions, 1982.

Prezzolini, Giuseppe. *Spaghetti Dinner*. New York: Abelard-Schuman, 1955.

Prudhomme, Paul. *Chef Paul Prudhomme's Louisiana Kitchen*. New York: William Morrow, 1984.

Quennell, Nancy. *The Epicure's Anthology*. London: Golden Cockerel Press, undated.

Romagnoli, Margaret and G. Franco. *The New Italian Cooking*. Boston: Little, Brown, 1980.

Rombauer, Irma S. and Becker, Marion Rombauer. *Joy of Cooking*. Indianapolis: Bobbs-Merrill, 1931.

Root, Waverley. *The Food of France*. New York: Alfred A. Knopf, 1958.

———. *Food*. New York: Simon & Schuster, 1980.

———. *The Food of Italy*. New York: Atheneum, 1971.

Rose, Evelyn. *The Complete International Jewish Cookbook*. New York: St. Martin's Press, 1976.

Rosenthal, Sylvia. *Fresh Food*. Tree Communications/E.P. Dutton, 1978.

Rosten, Leo. *The Joys of Yiddish*. New York: Pocket Books, 1968.

Sahni, Julie. *Classic Indian Cooking*. New York: William Morrow, 1980.

St. Paul's Greek Orthodox Church. *The Regional Cuisines of Greece*. New York: Doubleday, 1981.

St. Stephen's Episcopal Church. *Bayou Cuisine*. Indianola, Mississippi, 1970.

Sanecki, Kay N. *The Complete Book of Herbs*. New York: Macmillan, 1974.

Saulnier, Louis. *Le Répertoire de la Cuisine*. Woodbury, New York: Barron's Educational Series, 1976.

Schapira, Joel, David, and Karl. *The Book of Coffee and Tea*. New York: St. Martin's Press, 1975.

Schoonmaker, Frank. *Encyclopedia of Wine*. New York: Hastings House, 1964.

Schorger, A. W. *The Wild Turkey*. Norman, Oklahoma: University of Oklahoma Press, 1966.

Schriftgiesser, Karl. *Oscar of the Waldorf.* New York: E. P. Dutton, 1943.

Schwabe, Calvin W. *Unmentionable Cuisine.* Charlottesville, Virginia: University Press of Virginia, 1979.

Scott, Jack Denton. *The Complete Book of Pasta.* New York: William Morrow, 1968.

Settlement Cookbook, The. New York: Simon & Schuster, 1965.

Shurtleff, William and Aoyagi, Akiko. *The Book of Tofu.* Berkeley, California: Ten Speed Press, 1975.

Simon, André. *Concise Encyclopedia of Gastronomy.* New York: Harcourt, Brace and Co., 1952.

Smith, Henry. *Classical Recipes of the World.* London: Practical Press, Ltd., 1954.

Smith, Leona Woodring. *The Forgotten Art of Flower Cookery.* New York: Harper & Row, 1973.

Smith, Page and Daniel, Charles. *The Chicken Book.* Boston: Little, Brown, 1975.

Sokolov, Raymond. *The Saucier's Apprentice.* New York: Alfred A. Knopf, 1976.

Soyer, A. *The Pantropheon.* London: Simpkin, Marshall & Co., 1853.

Spear, Ruth A. *Cooking Fish and Shellfish.* New York: Doubleday, 1980.

Spicer, Dorothy Gladys. *From an English Oven.* New York: The Women's Press, 1948.

Stanforth, Deirdre. *The New Orleans Restaurant Cookbook.* New York: Doubleday, 1976.

Stein, Gerald M. *Caviar! Caviar! Caviar!* New York: Lyle Stuart, 1982.

Stewart-Gordon, Faith and Hazelton, Nika. *Russian Tea Room Cookbook.* New York: Richard Marek, 1981.

Stobart, Tom. *The Cook's Encyclopedia.* New York: Harper & Row, 1981.

————. *Herbs, Spices and Flavorings.* New York: McGraw-Hill, 1970.

Tolbert, Frank X. *A Bowl of Red.* New York: Doubleday, 1972.

Tsuji, Shizuo. *Japanese Cooking, A Simple Art.* Tokyo: Kodansha, 1980.

Villas, James. *American Taste.* New York: Arbor House, 1982.

Ward, Artemus. *Encyclopedia of Food.* London: Peter Smith, 1941.

Warner, William W. *Beautiful Swimmers: Watermen, Crabs and the Chesapeake Bay.* New York: Penguin Books, 1977.

Webster's New International Dictionary.

Webster's New World Dictionary.

Wildman, Frederick S. Jr. *A Wine Tour of France.* New York: William Morrow, 1973.

Williams, Barbara. *Cornzapoppin!* New York: Holt, Rinehart and Winston, 1976.

Wise Encyclopedia of Cookery. New York: William H. Wise Co., 1948.

Wolcott, Imogene. *The New England Yankee Cook Book.* New York: Coward-McCann, 1939.

Wolfert, Paula. *Cous Cous and Other Good Food from Morocco.* New York: Harper & Row, 1973.

Wood, Morrison. *More Recipes With a Jug of Wine.* New York: Farrar, Straus and Giroux, 1956.